GOVERNMENT OF SOCIALIST CHINA

John Yin, Ph.D.
Professor of Political Science
Laurentian University

UNIVERSITY
PRESS OF
AMERICA

LANHAM • NEW YORK • LONDON

All University Press of America books are produced on acid-free
paper which exceeds the minimum standards set by the National
Historical Publications and Records Commission.

Preface

    This work results from several years' effort. It went through five drafts one of which was virtually rewritten. In order to keep abreast of the kaleidoscopic change in that country, we constantly revised the text in the light of what was unfolding there. Upon perusing it, one is expected to have a bird's-eye view of the People's Republic. Since ours is purported to be an introduction only, those who desire to delve into given areas would have to use bibliographical tools or trade journals to get the specialized titles on them. This publication is no substitute for many fine outputs dealing with particular topics of China.

    No book, needless to state, is agreeable to everyone. In political studies, the margin of concurrence is razor-thin. Some opinions of ours will no doubt meet with criticism or even stricture. Perhaps this is the way writings should be, and we certainly do not take ill of it, being fully aware that dialectic is the locomotive of scholarship. It takes man toward a universal truth, although it never lands him on it. With an open mind, we are expecting judgment from the readers' tribunal.

John Yin

Sudbury, Ontario

Table of Contents

Preface

Table of Contents

Chapter I   The Land and People

The land   1
    River systems   2
    Physical geography   5
Population
    General characterization   7
    The growth of population   8
    To halt the line   11
Ethnic composition   13
Minority regions   18
Traditional thought patterns   27
    Confucius — moralist   28
    Han Fei Zi — legalist   29
    Yang Zhu — individualist   30
    Lao Zi — naturalist   31
    Mo Ti — pragmatist   32

Chapter II   A Short History

Exhaustion of the mandate   35
The 1911 coup   36
Yuan Shikai and restoration   40
Warlords   42
Sun-Yat-sen at the south pole   45
The Northern Expedition   47
A miserable republic   52
The National Government at war   58

Chapter III   The Communist Party

Its foundation   63
First United Front   65
Second United Front   68
Statutory principles
    Historical materialism   71
    Class struggle and contradiction   71
    No worship of party leaders   73
    Major policies   74
    Democratic centralism   74
Membership   75

Organizational matters
National Congress 81
Central Committee (CC) 84
Politburo 88
Standing Committee 90
General Secretary 92
Central Advisory Commission 93
Party discipline and disciplinary bodies 95
Local organizations 97
Primary party organizations 98

Chapter IV   Power Struggle

Introduction
Escalation of the Kremlin rift 101
Struggle among the Jiangxi Soviets
A. Chen Shaoyu 104
B. Zhang Guotao 105
C. Tan Pingshan 106
D. Unknown mavericks 107
Zhenfeng and its aftereffect 108
Regional challenge 110
Military challenge 111
The party-apparatus challenge 113
Armed coup 117
The Gang of Four 121
Hua Guofeng and Deng Xiaoping 124

Chapter V   The State: Principles and Policies

Introduction 129
Sovereignty 134
Nature of the state
Socialist 136
Unitary 137
Ideological behests 138
Direct and indirect democracy 140
General policy
Four modernizations 141
Taiwan annexation 141
Civil rights 143
Rotation of office 144
Separation of state from party 144
Economy and ownership patterns 145
Social control 148
Foreign and military affairs 150

TABLE OF CONTENTS

Chapter VI   The State: Institutions

National People's Congress   153
Standing Committee   160
President of the CPR   165
State Council   168
Local government
    Division   173
    Organization   174
    Election   178

Chapter VII   The Army

Gun, the Almighty!   181
Responsibility of the armed forces
    a) Win the civil war   187
    b) Pacification   188
    c) Mobilization   189
    d) Frontier work   189
    e) Politicizing and revolutionizing   190
    f) Production   190
    g) Deterrent   191
    h) Forward defense   192
    i) Foreign aid   193
    j) Taiwan liberation   193
The command structure   194
Strength   199
Nuclear buildup   204

Chapter VIII Diplomacy

Constitutional basis   209
The United States   212
The Soviet Union   221
Asia   232
Other countries   242

Chapter IX   Agriculture

The peasants and land reform   251
Collectivization   255
    A. Mutual-aid team
        1. Temporary type   256
        2. Permanent type   257
    B. Agricultural producers' co-op (APC)
        3. Elemental type   257
        4. Advanced type   258
The commune
    1. The decision   258
    2. The operation   261
    3. The failure   264
Modification   266
Current problems   274

Chapter X   Industry

Rehabilitation............................ 285
Modernization, Russian style.............. 289
Restoration and setback.................. 293
Modernization, Chinese style.............. 297
Pragmatic orientation 303
Finance 308
Transport................................ 312
Energy.................................. 315
Daqing.................................. 320

Chapter XI   Foreign Trade

Leaning on the Russian trade.............. 323
Period of transition, 1961-1970 327
The US trade............................ 333
Import and the balance situation............ 338
Export 344
What steps are taken to promote trade? 349
The rugged trade route 356

Chapter XII Education

An overview............................. 363
Pre-secondary system
    Literacy campaign...................... 366
    Nursery 370
    Primary school........................ 371
High school 373
Post-secondary system................... 376
Science and art.......................... 383
Spiritual culture 390

Chapter XIII Health and Human Services

Introduction 399
Medical cadres 401
Collective health services................ 403
Unemployment
    1) Urban............................. 407
    2) Rural 409
    3) Reasons for unemployment 410
Job creation............................. 411
Small business 416
Wages 419
A pretty messy market 424
Retirement, housing, care for the handicapped 428
Infanticide and sterilization................ 430

Chapter XIV Civil Law

      Outlook on law 435
      Underdeveloped civil law 439
      Law on domestic relations
          Marriage............................. 444
          Divorce.............................. 449
      Law on Joint Ventures 451
      Lawyers 454

Chapter XV Criminal Law

      Bases of criminal justice
          The righting of past wrongs 463
          Counterrevolutionary criminality 465
          Ex post facto law...................... 467
          Presumption of innocence 468
          Judicial independence 470
          Mass line 472
          Equality before the law 474
      Crime and punishment 476
      The court 483
      The procurator 490
      The prison 496

Bibliography 499

Index 531

CHAPTER I
The Land and People

The land

To get to know of a country, the logical point to start is the geographical locus. The farthest limits of the Chinese People's Republic (CPR) are as follows.[1]

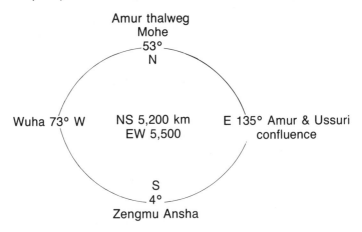

Amur thalweg
Mohe
53°
N

Wuha 73° W   NS 5,200 km   E 135° Amur & Ussuri
              EW 5,500   confluence

S
4°
Zengmu Ansha

Washington and Beijing are close to the same Latitude, as are such cities as Los Angeles and Nanjing, and Houston and Shanghai. Taking 7% of the world's land surface and 46% of Asia, China has 9,600,000 sq km, smaller than Canada by 355,709, but bigger than the US by 237,000.[2] She is the third largest country of the world, trailing behind, of course, the Soviet Union with its 22,402,000 sq km. On the north she neighbors Mongolia, the Russian Federal Republic (6,803 km) and North Korea. On the south, she is adjacent to Vietnam, Laos, Sikkim, Burma, India, Hong Kong, Bhutan and Nepal; on her western border are Afghanistan (72 km), Pakistan and the Kazakhstan, Kirgiz and Tajik Republics of the USSR (2,000 km). Across the East China Sea (Donghai) she looks out to Japan. The land boundary is 22,000 km,[3] and the coastline stretches 18,000 km from the mouth of the Yalu in the north to Beilun (abutting Vietnam) in the south.[4] Of the 24 temporal zones, 6 intersect the country. When the easternmost township of Lienqin (Jalinda) of Heilongjiang province

[1] *Zhong guo di tu ji*, text by Lin Chong and maps by Huang Jiushun, Hong Kong: Xin yu chu ban gong si, 1980, p. 34; the name Bawei Ansha along with Zengma Ansha is mentioned in *Zhong guo shou ce*, Hong Kong: Da gong bao, 1981, p. 1.

[2] Vadim Medish, *The Soviet Union*, Englewood Cliffs, New Jersey: Prentice-Hall, 1981, p. 2 (table); *Xin hua ci dian*, Beijing: Shang wu yin shu guan, 1980, pp. 1221, 1229.

[3] *Zhong guo shou ce*, p. 1; *Renmin ribao*, June 17, 1981, p. 1.

[4] *Renmin ribao*, June 17, 1981, p. 1; *Beijing Review*, January 10, 1983, p. 27 (table).

is at 12 midnight, it is 6 p.m., the previous day at the westernmost edge of Xinjiang Autonomous Region.

Perhaps the best way of depicting the size of the CPR for the people of the Western Hemisphere is to superimpose it on North America. It would show that Lienqin lies in the neighborhood of James Bay, while Hainan coincides with Jamaica. The western tip of Xinjiang is off the shore of California and the confluence of the Ussuri and Amur touches Cape Breton Island. For Europeans, a similar exercise of ours would indicate the CPR covering the Mediterranian from end to end, with Lienqin in the vicinity of Moscow and Hainan near Khartoum in the Sudan.[5]

China has many fine but by no means excellent harbors on her rocky coast in the north and a few mediocre ones on the sandy beaches in the south.[6] There are 26 outstanding harbors, among them the five best are Fuzhou, Ningbo, Shanghai, Xiamen and Guangzhou. These were forced to open by the British gunboats in the Nanjing Treaty of August 29, 1842. The next nine best were also forced to open to the great powers in the 1860's.[7] Along China's seashore fringe more than 5,000 islands of which the two giants are Taiwan (35,786 sq km) and Hainan (34,380 sq km); none of the remainder has more than 6,400 sq km. The strewn pattern of the islands varies greatly. Over 2,900 of them flank Zhejiang, Fujian and Guangdong provinces, mostly the second-named. What may be called Free China's Jinmen and Mazu are within the sight of Xiamen and Fuzhou of Fujian respectively. Skirting the CPR in the east and south are four seas: Bohai, Huanghai, Donghai, Nanhai. The first is a mare clausum embraced by Liaodong and Shandong peninsulas, and the other three are virtually covering the continental shelf.[8]

The country forms a self-protective domain. On the land frontier are either deserts (Gobi) or high mountain ranges (Pamirs, Kunlun) or deep ravines (Hengduan).[9] Along this arch are two apertures to Korea and to Vietnam. The relations between the two and China through history alternate between suzerainty and outright dependence, more of the former than the latter. On the oceanside, the CPR is dangerously facing Japan, which was her harasser and aggressor from 1374 to 1945.

River systems

Of these there are four: a) the internal system which features water oozing into deserts or streaming into isolated lakes, b) the Arctic

[5] Thomas R. Tregear, *China, a geographical survey*, New York: St. Martin's Press, 1971, pp. 80, 85, 88 and 94.

[6] R.R.C. de Crespigny, *China, the land and its people*, New York: Halsted Press, 1980, p. 2, col. 2.

[7] Michael Roskin, *Countries and concepts, an introduction to comparative politics*, Englewood Cliffs, New Jersey: Prentice-Hall, 1982, p. 288.

[8] *Zhong guo bai ke nian jian*, Beijing: Zhong guo bai ke quan shu chu ban she, 1980, p. 39, col. 1.

[9] George B. Cressey, *Land of the 530 million, a geography of China*, New York: McGraw-Hill, 1955, p. 43, cols. 1-2.

system which has only one rivulet in northwest Xinjiang. With a drainage area of 5,900 sq km inside China, she flows into the Soviet Union where she develops into the Ob. In the southwest there is the c) Indian-ocean system containing Nujiang, Yarlung Zangbu Jiang and Indojiang.[10] The most elaborate is the d) Pacific system to be discussed below. The CPR has 48 major rivers (longer than 170 km), of which 10 form boundaries with foreign states or run through them to the sea.[11] The length of the rivers totals upwards of 400,000 km.[12]

The Pacific system consists of four subsystems each associated with a main trunk. Beginning from the north, the Amur drains 890,000 sq km inside China; running between Heilongjiang province and the USSR's Far East and Birobidjon Autonomous Regions, it freezes 140-160 days a year, with a navigable period from late April to mid-November. Amur has three tributaries: Mudanjiang, Sungari, Ussuri. The first two drain northeastern Manchuria and the third divides the CPR from the USSR. The Yalu and Liao, although not connected with the Amur, also pass the same part of the Chinese territory.

Rushing through north China's nine provinces is the Huanghe (5,464 km), draining an area of 750,443 sq km. The Yellow River, to use a translated name, derives her appellation from the muddy color owing to a very high sediment level. Picked up in the loess land of the upper course, the sediment is carried downstream as the water moves swiftly. When it slows down on the plains, the element settles and fills up the river bed. Along nearly all her course, there are embankments on both sides. This makes her stand above the ground. Dikes must be constantly heightened and repaired. As recently as September 1981, when the upstream bed could not hold the rising volume of water due to an unusually steady rain, the State Council issued an order to the local authorities to "pile up the embankments" to prevent a mishap.[13] For these piling ups, various governments spent the lion's share of their budgets. Once the banks are broken, several millions of hectares of wheatland would be inundated and countless lives taken. In a few times in history, moreover, Huanghe changed her course, with all the disasters this entailed.[14] Men had once contributed to the tragedy. During the summer of 1946, the communist rebels, hard pressed by the pacification troops, deliberately blew up the dikes to stop the pursuit and make good their escapes. It inflicted enormous casualties on the civilians as well as on those troops.

Huanghe forms an arch, known as Hehao (river loop) north of Shanxi and Shaanxi provinces. It is here that she behaves tamely

[10] *Zhong guo di tu ji*, p. 37.

[11] *Zhong guo shou ce*, pp. 14-16.

[12] *Renmin ribao*, June 17, 1981, p. 1.

[13] *Guangming ribao*, September 13, 1981, p. 1.

[14] Yifu Tuan, *China*, London: Longman, 1980, pp. 17-19.

and proves to be somewhat useful, but not fantastically so as claimed for her in many a book, because there are just too few irrigations there to make use of the water. The capricious and angry Huanghe earns her the sobriquet of "the sorrow of China." Belonging to this artery are eight tributaries crisscrossing the immense northern plains. They all are normal rivers, that is, ones which have created no disasters.[15]

The Yangzi, the world's third longest river (after the Nile and Amazon) originates in Tibet and journeys eastward through nine provinces to Shanghai which perches at the estuary on the Pacific. The drainage area is 1,807,199 sq km. Due to irregular precipitation in this part of the country, deluges are common (monotonous is the right word). Every year there is at least an overflow somewhere along the 6,300 km course, which visits severe hardship on life and property. In 1980 her central stretch inundated five provinces; the damage is said to be the worst in "several tens of years."[16] In 1981, it was her upstretch in Sichuan province that brought a devastation headlined in the press as the "worst in years."[17] Again in 1982 the whole watercourse overflew. July 1983, once more, witnessed the full-course flooding. The Yangzi is not much better than the Huanghe. She is also the sorrow of China.

This river accounts for 65 percent of China's inland navigation system.[18] The Chinese maintained that in the 50's there was a steady growth of the freight traffic on her. Then set in a 16-years' stagnation. However, from 1977 to 1982 the total cargo volume doubled.[19] The potential of Yangzi lies in the fact that her annual waterflow is 1,000,000 million cubic meters. This is 21 times that of the Huanghe.[20] Crossing the Yangzi are six railway lines: Chengdu-Kunming, Beijing-Guangzhou, Beijing-Shanghai, Chongqing-Guiyang, Chengdu-Chongqing, Ziaozuo-Zhicheng. They join the waterway to the country's land transport nexus.[21] Yangzi has 14 principal and 700-odd minor tributaries. These tributaries are more than 70,000 km. A gigantic project is said to be underway to divert the water to the north via the Grand Canal.[22] No details are given on this plan, however.

The southernmost subsystem is the Zhujiang network which embraces three branches in Guangxi, Guangdong and Guizhou, totaling 2,129 km draining 425,000 sq km. On them boat traffic is fairly brisk, providing livelihood for tens of thousands.[23]

[15] R.R.C. de Crespigny, op. cit., pp. 77-79.

[16] Renmin ribao, December 27, 1980, p. 1.

[17] Ibid., July 19, 20, 1981 both on p. 1; Sudbury Star, July 21, 1981, p. 38.

[18] Beijing Review, March 7, 1983, p. 21, col. 1.

[19] Ibid., col. 2.

[20] Ibid., p. 24, col. 1.

[21] Ibid., p. 21, col. 1.

[22] Ibid., April 18, 1983, pp. 8-9.

[23] Chiao-min Hsieh, "Physical geography," China, a handbook, edited by Yuan-li Wu, New York: Praeger, 1973, pp. 29-43 at 29, 30, 31.

Lakes are scattered all over the country, covering 80,000 sq km. Two thousand eight hundred of them have an area of more than 1 sq km each, with 12 lakes having upwards of 1,000 sq km each.[24] Forest covers 12.7 percent of the whole of China.[25] Higher types of plants count more than 32,000, among which seed plants number 24,600. There are 1,170 kinds of birds, and 400 plus species of animals. China has abundant minerals said to be more than 140, including coal, asbestos, molybdenum, manganese, aluminum, wolfram, mercury, nickel, zinc, lead, gold, tin and antimony. However, another source says that there are 134 categories of minerals, namely, 6 energy minerals (coal, petroleum, gas, etc.), 5 ferrous metals, 20 non-ferrous metals, 28 rare or rare-earth metals and 75 nonmetal minerals.[26] This source also reveals that coal deposits amount to 642.7 billion tons, iron ore deposits, 44.31 billion tons.

Physical geography

The country is in the shape of a dish tilting southeast-ward. Towering in the north and west are four plateaus:[27]

name	provinces/regions	altitude	sq km
Neimenggu	Neimenggu, n/Gansu	2,750-3,050	2,000,000
	Hebei, n/Ningxia		
	Heilongjiang		
Qingzang	Tibet, Qinghai, w/	4,000 plus	2,200,000
	Yunnan, w/Sichuan		
Huangtu	Shanxi, Shaanxi, s/	1,000-2,000	866,000
	Gansu, n/Ningxia		
Yungui	Guizhou, ne/Yunnan	1,000-2,900	1,740,000
	Hunan, sw/Sichuan		
	Hubei, Guangxi		

There are 157 mountain chains and 8 outstanding peaks, the lowest being Moganshan (724 meters) in Zhejiang province and the highest Chumolungma (8,848 meters) on the border of China and Nepal. From 1980, the Chinese government opened some peaks to foreign mountain climbers "on the fee-paying basis."[28] Chumolungma is one of them.[29]

The northwest is marked by a great desert draining many mountain ranges. The Caidam basin (2,750 meters) is bounded by the arms of Kunlun (3,050 meters). There are the Zungarian and Tarim basins at about a fourth of the Caidam elevation. To the east the basins

[24] *Zhong guo bai ke nian jian*, p. 40, col. 2.

[25] *Ibid.*, p. 41, col. 1 provides this and the following data on plants, birds, animals and minerals.

[26] *Beijing Review*, January 10, 1983, p. 27.

[27] *Zhong guo shou ce*, pp. 4, 5; *Zhong guo di tu ji*, p. 37.

[28] *Zhong guo bai ke nian jian*, p. 602.

[29] *Ibid.*

narrow and then open out again into the Menggu plateau. The desert wasteland is unfit for the sedentary argiculture of the Han, but it provides support for the nomadic Menggu and Turks. The southwest is featured by many corrugations running eastward and then toward the south. This part of the country is replete with steep hillsides, narrow river valleys and small delta levels. The broken terrain isolates the population settlements. It perpetuates the existence of minorities and numerous linguistic groups among the Han. Extemely difficult are communications; this gives rise to communal autarky, with each tiny clustering of villages developing its own self-sufficient economy. The only vital article which not every place can produce is salt. Owing to its scarcity, the salt business was lucrative. The father of Jiang Jieshi was in that business. It is interesting to note too that one of the effective ways for the National Government and the various warlords to dislodge the Reds from Jiangxi in the autumn of 1934 was the salt blockade imposed on their base (see also Chapter III).[30]

More than ninety percent of the CPR is rugged and six percent is a kilometer and a half above the sea. The topographical distribution is as follows.[31]

mountains	33 percent
plateaus	26
basins	19
plains	12
hills	10

The 12 (some references mention 10) percent level land is found in 9 great plains with a combined area of close to one million sq km.[32] The nine are Dongbei (Manchuria), Huabei (north), lower Yangzi, Yinchuan, Weihe, Hehao, Hangjiahu, Zhujiang delta and Chengdu.[33] The first-named three constitute nine tenths of the total. Thus, 88-89 percent of that country restricts or completely excludes human endeavors.[34] The sheer landmass of China has inflated her greatness. There is just too great a demand on such a limited usable area. The per capita acreage reaches a starvation proportion. And an already limited acreage is continuously diminishing as the population mounts with the passage of years. According to a Chinese source, in 1949 the per capita tillable land was 2.71 acres, but in 1978, it became 1.56 (more of this in Chapter X).[35]

[30] Franz Michael and George Taylor, *The Far East in the modern world*, 2nd ed., New York: Holt, Rinehart and Winston, 1964, p. 417.

[31] *Beijing Review*, January 10, 1983, p. 27.

[32] *Zhong guo shou ce*, p. 2.

[33] *Ibid.*, pp. 3-4.

[34] *China's birth rate, death rate and population growth, another perspective*, Committee on International Relations, US House of Representatives, Washington: Government Printing Office, 1977, pp. 8-10.

[35] *Zhong guo bai ke nian jian*, p. 626 (table).

Population
General characterization

The CPR has taken three censuses in 1953, 1964 and 1982. The last was carried out swiftly in 10 days (July 1-10) under a joint decree of the Central Committee of the Communist Party and the State Council. However the spadework went on from early 1981; more than five million census takers were coached. Beijing media praises the result of the census as of "high standard."[36] Although a more detailed coverage still waits to be developed, the broad categories are made available.

The population reached 1,031,882,551 as of the zero hour of July 1, 1982.[37] In the 29 provinces, municipalities and autonomous regions on the continent, it numbered 1,008,175,288, a figure not including Jinmen, Mazu and other islets of the Fujian coast. Allegedly only 28,001 persons had to be estimated because census takers could not get to them due to extraordinary difficulty in communication. The residents of Taiwan, Jinmen and Mazu were derived from the Taiwan sources: 18,270,749 in all. Nor did the communists travel to Hong Kong and Macao to count the noses. In this case, the records of the officials there were taken for granted. The Chinese there were 5,378,627. What is more, the overseas Chinese were uncounted. One category, i.e., the armed forces, is, however, separately enumerated. Their number was 4,238,210. Let's look at the attributes of the Chinese as revealed by the census.

a) In regard to increase, the 18 years from July 1, 1963 to the same date of 1982 saw the addition of 313,593,529, a growth of 45.1 percent. The average annual growth is 17,429,863, a 2.1 percent increase. In the light of this revelation, the regime laid down a plan whereby the next 18 years will have an increase of only 190,000,000 which is 0.95 percent a year; the Chinese have confessed, however, that it is hard to achieve.[38]

b) The census records 519,433,369 males and 488,741,919 females: 51.5 percent against 48.5. And the proportion of both sexes is 106.3 to 100.

c) Educational count yields the following statistics. Among the more than one billion people there were:

4,414,495	university graduates
1,602,474	current university students and the ones not finishing the courses
66,478,028	senior high graduates and those not graduated
178,277,140	junior high graduates and those as above
355,160,310	primary graders and those as above

---

36 *Gongren ribao*, October 28, 1982, p. 1; *Beijing Review*, November 8, 1982, p. 20.

37 Data below are derived from the census report, in *Beijing Review*, November 8, 1982, pp. 20-21; and January 3, 1983, p. 25.

38 *Beijing Review*, February 14, 1983, p. 21, col. 3.

For the sake of comparison, in every 100,000 population there were
in 1964:   but in 1982:
  415 university educated   500
  1,319 senior high students   6,622
  4,680 junior high students   17,758
  28,330 primary graders   35,377

Illiterate and semi-literate (those who are 12 years of age and who
cannot read or can read only a few words) numbered 235,830,002.
As against the 1964 census, this category came down from 38.1
percent to 23.5.

d) The number of births in 1981 was 20,689,704 and deaths
6,290,103; these represent 20.91 and 6.36 per thousand respectively.
The natural increase of 14,399,601 is 14.55 per thousand.

e) The urbanites (excluding rural population of the 24 counties
annexed to Beijing, Tianjin and Shanghai) were 206,588,582. Of these
144,679,340 were in 266 cities and 61,909,242 in 2,664 towns.
Compared with the 1964 census, the urbanites are up by 79,485,541
or 62.5 percent. The ratio of these to the total population is up from
18.4 percent in 1964 to 20.6 in 1982.

f) In re age structure, the published census does not disclose any
information, but Qian Xinzhong, Minister in charge of State Family
Planning Commission, revealed that half of the population is under
21.[39] This contrasts with the corresponding soviet figure of 36.7
percent.[40] The CPR has a much younger people than her northern
neighbor.

The growth of population

During early history, the size of the Chinese kept pretty constant.
Not until the mid-18th century did it commence to enlarge and did
so rapidly. This situation coincided with the decay of state authority.
The ruling apparatus, besides being unable to stave off foreign
encroachment, failed to feed the increasing mouths.[41] The upsurge
pattern is as follows:

slow pace   quick pace
A.D.   thousand 1110 46,673b   A.D.   thousand
2   59,500a 1200 45,000a   1644 100,000c 1964 685,457h
156   56,490b 1290 58,840b   1741 143,400a 1965 725,380e
609   46,020b 1292 63,600a   1775 313,000a 1975 919,700e
742-755 51,000a 1393 60,500a   1849 430,000a 1978 958,090f
900   53,000a 1500 60,000a   1949 548,770d 1979 970,920e
1080   33,300b 1651 60,000a   1953 595,550d 1981 996,220e
                                       1957 656,630d 1982 1,031,882g

Sources:
a) Lucian Pye, *China*, p. 100.
b) *Zhong guo bai ke nian jian*, p. 625.
c) Michael and Taylor, *op. cit.*, p. 19.
d) *Zhong guo shou ce*, p. 18.
e) *Beijing Review*, March 28, 1983, p. 19.
f) *Zhong guo bai kian jian*, p. 626 (table).
g) *Beijing Review*, November 29, 1982, p. 13, col. 1.
h) *Ibid.*, November 8, 1982, p. 20, col. 2.

[39] *Ibid.*, February 14, 1983, p. 21, còl. 1.

[40] *World almanac*, 1982, p. 586, col. 2.

[41] Thomas R. Tregear, *op. cit.*, pp. 205-208.

Although the general direction is obvious, there are drawbacks (sad enough) at times, particularly before 1651. Frequent periods of warfare and natural calamities destroyed lives by the millions. The size of the population, as the above table shows, came down from 59 million in 2 A.D. to 56 million in 156, further dropping to 46 million in 609. A more drastic dip was from 53 million in 900 to 33 million in 1080. Other studies tell that the population reached 100 million by 1200, but nose-dived to 65 million in 1368 toward the end of the Yuan dynasty.[42] Afterwards it shot up to 150 million by 1600. But famine reduced them to 100 million around 1680. Then the size expanded to 430 million by 1800, but a 15-year drama of starvation, banditry and large-scale rebellions left only 380 million. Again it climbed up rapidly. The rising curve is that from 1741 to 1848 the size tripled, and from 1849 to 1949, another 118,770 thousand were added, and from 1949 to 1982 the addition was 460,000 thousand.[43] The increase in the 32 years of the People's Republic was 3.6 times the 128,000 thousand increase in the 109 years between 1840 and 1949.[44]

How to account for this phenomenon? Running down the explanations, first there is the deepest-ingrained tradition which dates allegedly from Mengzi, the great disciple of Confucius, that a woman's failure to produce male offspring is the worst of all impieties.[45] Second, there is the popular fetishizing of "more children more happiness" and of "branching out of the family tree."[46] In particular, the rural folks have held steadfast onto the saying that "a roomful of kids means good luck," and that boys are superior to girls since they keep the family name alive.[47] Third comes what may be called the social-security argument, that is, one had better bring up children today in order to have someone to rely on in the declining years.[48] Fourth, it is asseverated that population multiplication stems from "social stability and improvement of living standards and public health which boosted the birthrate and considerably reduced the mortality rate."[49] Fifth, the growth is also attributable to the "once prevalent one-sided and mistaken understanding of the question of population." For two decades many felt that a big population is a law of socialist development and that the "more hands we have, the easier we get things done."[50] Sixth, the much vaunted regime of job

---

[42] These data are in *Americana*, international ed., 1978, vol. 6, p. 496, col. 1.

[43] *Beijing Review*, March 28, 1983, p. 17, col. 2.

[44] *Ibid.*, p. 17.

[45] *Ibid.*, February 14, 1983, p. 24, col. 2.

[46] *Ibid.*, November 1, 1982, p. 3, col. 1.

[47] *Ibid.*, March 28, 1983, p. 19, col. 1.

[48] *Ibid.*, November 1, 1982, p. 3, col. 1.

[49] *Ibid.*, March 28, 1983, p. 18, col. 1.

[50] *Ibid.*

responsibility in rural construction has led people to hold that the larger the family, particularly the male members, the more the output.[51] Although the Chinese authorities refute the relation of the said regime and population, there is an undeniable truth in it. Seventh, finally, an explanation is offered for the sudden outburst of population in the mid-17th century by the improvement of farming technique and the introduction of sweet potatoes,[52] and then there was the import of aphrodisiacs from the Roman Empire which stimulated the Chinese male and female to produce.[53] Undoubtedly, each of the seven reasons has contributed a bit to the population avalanche.

Turn to the pattern of distribution, the 1982 census calculates the density of population to be 104 to the sq km.[54] But the figure can convey no more than a general idea. It is really misleading. China, in fact, is overcrowded in the south and east, but thinly populated in the northwest and southwest. With fast industrialization in the 20th century, urbanization went apace. Many big and middle cities have expanded quickly. This happened even before the advent of the modernization-happy communists in 1949. In rural China, most are settled in the arable regions. These are located in the northern plains, the Sichuan plateau, the river valleys in the south center, and deltas along the coast. Comparing specific locales, one finds that the density of north China is half of the lower Yangzi areas.[55] A closer examination of the picture reveals that the seven most and seven least populous provinces and regions have the following number to the sq km:[56]

Jiangsu	605	Tibet	1.5
Shandong	496	Qinghai	5.0
Henan	445	Xinjiang	8.0
Zhejiang	388	Neimenggu	16.0
Anhui	382	Ningxia	64.0
Guangdong	282	Heilongjiang	71.0
Hubei	265	Yunnan	83.0

All the right seven are on the parameter of the country and mostly are inhabited by minorities. China, true to say, has plenty of room to shift her enormous population around within her homeland. She does not need to send them to Russia's Far East, for example. The *Xiafang* has moved millions of youth to all but the last of the seven least populated provinces, Yunnan.

[51] *Ibid.*, col. 3.

[52] Lucian Pye, *op. cit.*, p. 81.

[53] *Ibid.*, p. 101.

[54] *Beijing Review*, January 10, 1983, p. 27.

[55] *Americana*, vol. 6, p. 495 mentions that the delta has three times population per sq km as the north. The 1982 census suggests that that estimation needs to be updated.

[56] Calculated from data provided in *Beijing Review*, January 3, 1983, p. 25.

To halt the line

The growth, although partly reflecting an achievement of the regime in providing medical care for the common people, is not an unmixed blessing, because the modernization plan is thereby hampered. It has been candidly declared that the absolute gain on the industrial and agricultural fronts is offset by the added mouths to feed and backs to cover.[57] Writing in *Beijing Review,* two publicists emphasized that the speedy increase of the Chinese gives rise to problems in employment, education, housing and transport. The livelihood of men, they concluded, cannot be bettered on account of this situation. It is assessed by another author that each of the next 18 years will witness 20 million people reaching the marriage age (and 13 million get married). This means that about 13 million babies are to be born annually.[58] The total Chinese, given this proliferation, would become 1,300 (one author mentions 1,500) million in 2000 A.D.[59]

There is an extremely interesting revelation by Minister Qian Xinzhong that 2,200 yuan are needed to support a child until he is 16, and that presently China's fixed assets are 110,000 million.[60] Consequently, these assets are only adequate for 50,000,000 people. With the current population of one billion plus, for every 100 Chinese, 95 are then too many, this the Minister tries to convey.

The Beijing court is determined to keep the population in 2000 A.D. to 1,200 million, instead of allowing it to reach 1,300 million, the limit of the natural growth.[61] This interdiction would save the state 220,000 million yuan. Since the 1970's, it is averred, thanks to family planning, the natural growth plummeted from 26 per thousand in 1970 to 10.7 per thousand in 1980.[62] The result is that as many as 68 million fewer babies were born in the decade covered. This diminution is said to have played a positive part in enhancing the well-being of the working people.[63] However, the rate is again up, because in 1981 it became 14.55.[64]

In an attempt to control the rate, the communist regime has resorted to a number of steps (see also Chapter XIII). A couple who wish to have a second child must apply for a permit from the government, and the grant of it is guided by a) if the first-born is a non-hereditary disabled and cannot become a normal member of the labor force,

[57] *Ibid.,* February 14, 1983, p. 21, col. 3.

[58] *Ibid.,* col. 1.

[59] *Ibid.,* col. 2; March 28, 1983, p. 18, col. 1. The number of 1,500 million is in *ibid.,* November 29, 1982, p. 13, col. 1.

[60] *Ibid.,* February 14, 1983, p. 21.

[61] *Ibid.,* March 28, 1983, p. 18, col. 2.

[62] *Ibid.,* p. 17, col. 1.

[63] *Ibid.,* February 14, 1983, p. 22, col. 1.

[64] *Ibid.,* col. 2.

b) if, in reorganized families, one spouse has a child by his or her first marriage and the other is married for the first time, and c) in case of those who had not borne children for years but were pregnant after adopting other's children. But "under no circumstances is the birth of a third child allowed."

Different kinds of pressure are brought to bear on parents and administrators in the campaign to control birth. Awards and honors are handed out to one-child families, especially if the child happens to be a girl, and economic sanctions are meted out to those who are so stubborn as to give birth to unauthorized births.[65] It is the only child who is accorded preferential treatment in social welfare benefits, medical service, enrollment in kindergarten and employment.[66] On top of that, a peasant is given the chance to sign additional contracts, that is, to receive more land, if he fulfils the one-child pledge.[67] This involves the double-contract scheme. In accordance with such an arrangement, a peasant initials twin agreements, one on grain (or some other things) and one on a baby. The latter is restricted to one and one only. It is a legal commitment, a breach of which, although constituting no criminal offense, entails severe financial handicap (regarding fines, see Chapter XIII). This is all the more cruel in a system of austerity and material privation like the CPR. The pressure technique applied to parents was also applied to the bureaucrats in charge of family planning. It is that whoever does a sloppy job is berated, his bonus "blocked" and promotion denied, while the one who performs a satisfactory work will be advanced in position.[68]

A frenzied effort is exerted on persuading people to get married late and to defer child-bearing. The work is done by peer groups or work collectives.[69] We find it very strange that the 1981 marriage law (see Chapter XIV) reduces, instead of increases, the legal wedding age by five to eight years in comparison with the minimum set up by various local communities when the family planning program was first initiated.[70] This law has obviously boosted the number of young people producing babies. Little wonder the net gain of population is up from 10.7 per thousand in 1980 to 14.55 in 1981. The lowering of the marriage age, as stated in Chapter XIV, resulted from the general demand of Chinese parents who just want to see their children marry sooner rather than later.

There has been set in motion a massive propaganda campaign for marriage consultation. It is drummed out in every conceivable way and it goes on even in the tiniest of villages. Each January is

[65] Ibid., p. 23, col. 2; March 28, 1983, p. 19, col. 1.

[66] Ibid., November 1, 1982, p. 3, col. 3; February 14, 1983, p. 23, col. 3.

[67] Ibid., February 14, 1983, p. 26, col. 1.

[68] Ibid.

[69] Ibid., March 28, 1983, p. 18, col. 2.

[70] Ibid., November 29, 1982, p. 13, col. 1.

earmarked as family planning month.[71] Ideological education is carried out at the grass-roots level to wean all parents from the obsession with more offspring more luck and boys better than girls. Instead, stress is placed on fewer but healthier births conducive to the country's economy and social improvement. The administration has furnished contraceptives, safe operation and maternity care, and sterilization on a massive scale (10 million in Sichuan and 600,000 in Shanghai) for those who have given birth to two children.[72] Addressing the 6th NPC on June 6, 1983, Premier Zhao Ziyang has urged, among other things, sterilization as an urgent task facing the nation in the effort to curb the population.[73] For a number of years now, the regime advocated the setting up of five guarantees of food, clothing, fuel, schooling and burial expenses for childless and infirm old persons; some localities organize homes for the aged, and others develop pensions for retired peasants. These measures purport to relieve the one-child parents of their anxiety.[74] As a result of the above steps, it is claimed that "over 100 million couples of child-bearing age have adopted birth-control measures."[75] It is further alleged that sixty percent of the newborns are first births, higher than the 58 percent envisaged in the Sixth Five-Year Plan and the rate of first births has surpassed 90 percent in Shanghai, Beijing and Tianjin.[76] Although the Han race grows fast enough, the minorities have undergone a prodigous multiplication, and this we shall see in the next section.

Ethnic composition

We begin our discussion by explaining the name of China. As a statehood, it derives from the dynasty Chin (Qin in pinyin) which for the first time united that country after armed conquest of six other rival states in a space of 34 years (255-221 B.C.). This ruling house, however, is the shortest-lived of all China's ruling houses, lasting from 221 to 207 B.C. Foreigners thought it fitting and proper to call the new system Chin. The Chinese as an ethnic group, however, is known as Han, a word coming from the longest dynasty by that name which lasts from 207 B.C. to 222 A.D. Han signifies national identity. Beginning with this house, the Chinese proceeded to extend their dominion north- and west-ward into areas inhabited by the non-Han who used different languages or in most instances, different vernaculars of the Chinese. To the east, China came into contact with Japan whose cultural missions and merchants traveled by the droves

[71] *Ibid.*, February 14, 1983, p. 23.

[72] *Ibid.*, col. 2.

[73] *Renmin ribao*, June 24, 1983, p. 2, col. 3.

[74] *Beijing Review*, February 14, 1983, p. 23, col. 3.

[75] *Ibid.*, March 28, 1983, p. 18, col. 2.

[76] *Ibid.*

to the Capital city Changan in Shaanxi province. The Chinese also had trade relations with the Roman Empire through Central Asia.[77] Businessmen arrived from India, southwest Asia and the Middle East as well.[78] It was in the same Han dynasty that Confucianism was canonized as state ideology.[79]

The Han are the overwhelming majority of the inhabitants of the country. The 1982 census put it at 936,703,824, making up 93.3 percent of the total; this leaves the minorities as 6.7 percent, and their absolute number is 67,233,254.[80] Compared with the 1964 census, the Han increased by 285,407,456 or 43.8 percent but the minorities increased by 27,309,518 or 68.4 percent. As to the number of minority races, Chinese sources are seldom in agreement, ranging from 54, 55 to 58 and even more.[81] Those with a population of more than one million increased from 10 in the 1964 census to 15 in the 1982 one.[82] The following table compares the size of the Han and the most numerous minorities in a space of 30 years.[83]

1953 ('000)	1982		% increase
547,280	936,703	Han	71
6,610	13,378	Zhuang	102
3,640	5,957	Uygur	63
3,560	7,219	Hui	102
3,250	5,453	Yi	67
2,770	3,870	Zang (Tibet)	39
2,510	5,030	Miao	100
1,460	4,299	Manzhou	194
1,120	3,411	Menggu	204

By the 1982 census, besides the 15 minorities having more than one million, 13 consist of between 100,000 and one million, 18 between 10,000 and 100,000 and 8 between 10,000 and 1,549. The five least numerous minorities on the list of 54 are:[84]

Orogen	in Neimenggu, Heilongjiang	4,132
Tatar	Xinjiang	4,127
Russian	Xinjiang	2,935
Loba	Tibet	2,065
Gaoshan	Fujian (ca 400,000 in Taiwan)	1,549

[77] Lucian Pye, op. cit., p. 38.

[78] World almanac, 1980, p. 721.

[79] Lucian Pye, loc. cit.

[80] Beijing Review, November 8, 1982, p. 20, col. 2.

[81] Zhong guo di tu ji, pp. 34, 35 mentions 54; Beijing Review, May 16, 1983, p. 9, col. 1 and November 8, 1982, p. 20, col. 2 mention 55; Zhong guo shou ce, pp. 155-158 refers to 58; and more than 58 is mentioned in Beijing Review, May 23, 1983, p. 20, col. 2.

[82] Beijing Review, November 8, 1982, p. 20, col. 2.

[83] The 1953 figures are in Europa, 1979, vol. 2, p. 117; and the 1982 figures in Beijing Review, May 23, 1983, p. 19, col. 1.

[84] Beijing Review, May 23, 1983, p. 20, col. 1.

Not on the list, but appearing elsewhere is the 800-member Heze in Heilongjiang.[85] The Beijing oligarchy established an autonomous unit for nearly all the minorities (the most notable exception are the Manzhou). Overwhelming Han are in the 21 provinces and three municipalities directly administered by the central government. Similarly most minorities are in the five autonomous regions, but as the next section shows the Han constitute a majority in three of the five and the minorities are a sprinkling, sometimes in compact form, in the Han realm. In order to accommodate them, the communists set up 58 autonomous counties in the provinces, a sort of enclave of the minorities.[86] However, there are no autonomous prefectures in the provinces, all the 30 such prefectures being under the jurisdiction of the autonomous regions. In the latter there are only 14 autonomous counties: 8 in Uygur and 6 in Guangxi Zhuang Autonomous Regions. There are 178 counties which do not have the adjective autonomous in the five regions. We do not know if the Han are sufficiently numerous and compact in a region they can enjoy some autonomy by organizing an autonomous county.

In the majority of cases, the ethnic components are such that most inhabitants in an autonomous area are Han, but the areas still bear the eponymies of the minorities. For example, statistics show that the Tujia and Miaozu Autonomous County of Hunan province has a population of 1,826,000, of whom the two races Tujia and Miaozu are only 39,000 and 35,000 respectively.[87] Another example, the Ruyuan Yaozu Autonomous County of Guangdong province has such a small number of 9,300 composing the minority among its more than 100,000 residents.[88]

The CPR's nationality policy is governed by a number of provisions in the Constitution. A whole section of it (Articles 112-122) is devoted to the regional structure, with a bill of rights and obligations of the minorities placed in one article (4). In matters of organization, a region is like a province with a few minor modifications. There is the people's congress, the standing committee of this body and the government, i.e., administration. The first is vested with the right to elect the latter two. Their functions and authorities are to be exercised within the ambit of the Chapter III, Section V of the Constitution which regulates the provinces and their subdivisions (this assimilates regions to provinces). Unlike a province, however, the government of a region, or autonomous prefecture or autonomous county, must be headed by a native son or daughter (Article 114). This rule is scrupulously observed, even before the present constitution came into force (the 1978 Constitution did not lay down such a requirement), for the good reason that the government head is not a powerful figure there, but

[85] *Ibid.*, September 27, 1982, p. 6, col. 3.

[86] *Zhong guo bai ke nian jian*, pp. 60-61; *Beijing Review*, May 23, p. 20.

[87] *Zhong guo shou ce*, p. 164.

[88] *Ibid.*, p. 166.

the party secretary is. This individual is always a Han (see next section).

The chairmanship and vice-chairmanship of the standing committee of the people's congress of an autonomous region (or a sub-area) shall include a citizen or citizens of the nationality or nationalities exercising regional autonomy there (Article 113, paragraph 2). The Constitution in Article 99, paragraph 2 speaks of the budgetary power of provincial people's congress, but it is silent on the financial or taxation autonomy of a province. On the contrary, such autonomy is expressly provided for the region in Article 117. Mention is also made of specific regulations enacted by a region in keeping with the political, economic and cultural characteristics of the nationalities there. These regulations, if issued by the autonomous region, are made subject to the approval of the NPC Standing Committee; but if they are made by the sub-regional jurisdiction, they are subject to the sanction of the standing committee of the regional people's congress; they are, however, required to register with the NPC Standing Committee "just for the record of it" (Article 116). Organs of self-government in an autonomous unit, according to Article 120, can form local public security forces in the light of the demonstrated needs, but this move must obtain the approbation of the State Council. As of mid-1983, no region has such a security arrangement.

The minorities have the right to use their written and spoken languages during transactions of official business. But the State Council is empowered by Article 19, paragraph 5 to promote the *putonghua* (official common language) throughout the land. On December 21, 1982, fifteen departments of the State Council advocated the use of this official language as a compulsory means of communication in the organizations under their jurisdiction; minorities are certainly handicapped by this discrimination.[89] Also regions are entitled to state financial and technical aid. Perhaps for the sake of emphasis, this point is mentioned twice, once in Article 4, paragraph 2, and again in Article 122. It is mandated in Article 4, paragraph 3 that whenever there is a minority living compact in a place, an autonomous unit be established for them. To all this array of rights are set the corresponding duties not to seek secession from the People's Republic. This obligation is, perhaps again for the sake of emphasis, talked of thrice in the Constitution (Preamble, paragraphs 1 and 3 of Article 4). It is, finally, specifically mentioned that the nationalites ought to observe the Constitution (Preamble).

The Chinese autocracy has verbosely praised the amicable relations between the Han and the minorities. Very loudly they call upon them to cooperate in carrying through the four modernizations. Premier Zhao Ziyang, in a keynote speech to the 6th NPC on June 6, 1983, appealed to the minorities to make concerted efforts to build

---

[89] *Zhonghua renmin gongheguo guowuyuan gongbao*, March 5, 1983, pp. 43-45.

an industrialized economy in China.[90] The fact, however, is that integration of the minorities into the mainstream of the Han is never seriously attempted; and frictions erupted frequently in the frontier mixed areas and this in spite of the few ethnic leaders willing to collaborate with the Chinese generals.[91] Further, the regions are serving as suppliers of raw resources, and their economies are geared to the needs of the Han provinces. Hardly anything is done to diversify their production to satisfy the daily wants of the population there, the gibberish communist propaganda notwithstanding. Particularly disheartening the native peoples are a) that they are, for the most part, not a majority in their region, being outnumbered by the Han, b) that authority is in the hands of the Han, and c) that only a token presence of minority leaders in central organs, subsidiary at that. Leaving the first two points to the next section, we note here that the most important policy body, the Standing Committee of the CC has no representatives of the regions. Below we tabulate the racial components of the various bodies of the party and state (following the 12th Congress of the CCP and the 6th NPC):

Party (a)	Han	minority	minority /total
Central Committee			
a) full members (210)	196	14	6.1
b) alternates (138)	122	16	11.6
Central Advisory Commission (172)	167	5	2.9
chairman and vice-chairmen (5)	5	0	
Central Commission for Discipline Inspection (132)	124	8	2.9
Secretariat (8)	8	0	
Politburo (25) (one died in June 1983)	23	2	
Standing Committee (6)	6	0	6.0
Secretariat (9)	9	0	
Military Commission	4	0	8.0
Chairman and vice-chairmen (5)	5	0	
State			
6th NPC (2,978) (b) (55 races)	2,575	403	13.5
6th CPPCC (2,086) (c)	1,998	88	4.0
State Council (55) (d)	55	0	

Sources:
(a) The Twelfth National Congress of the CPC (September 1982), 1st ed., Beijing: Foreign Languages Press, 1982, pp. 145-157.

(b) Renmin ribao, May 11, 1983, pp. 2-3; Beijing Review, May 30, 1983, p. 5, col. 2.

(c) Renmin ribao, May 8, 1983, p. 2.

(d) Beijing Review, May 10, 1982, p. 4. Fifty-five posts were taken by 49 individuals, one Hanized Hui, Yang Jinren, is counted as Han.

[90] Renmin ribao, June 24, 1983, p. 4, col. 3.

[91] Globe and mail, June 14, 1983, p. 4, col. 1.

The above quantification tells that the voice of the minorities at the national level is feeble. But in percentage, they are doing not too badly. Beijing is never small-minded, particularly in such innocuous agencies as the NPC and the alternate members of the CC. Two other interesting points may be noted here. A) In the State Council there is set up a Commission of Nationalities Affairs headed by Hanized Yang Jingren,[92] who also heads the party's United Front Department. He has quite a propaganda job in his hands. B) Only 16 of the fifty-odd nationalities are represented in the several party bodies.

Of the 210 members of the CC there is one each from Yi, Chaoxian, Miao, two each from Hui, Zhuang, Menggu, Zang and three from Uygur; the 138 alternate members have among them one each of Bouyei, Dai, Bai, Miao, Yao, Manzhou, Zhuang, Li, Kazak, Tujia, two Zang and three Hui. Among the 172 members of the Central Advisory Committee there is one each of Yao, Manzhou, Li, Menggu and Zang. Entering the 124-member Central Commission for Discipline Inspection are one Chaoxian, one Hui, one Manzhou, one Zhuang, two Menggu and two Uygur. And sitting in the 25-member Politburo are Wei Guoqing, a Zhuang and Ulanhu, a Menggu. The latter individual aged 76 was elected on June 18, 1983 as the vice-president of the Chinese State by the 6th NPC.[93] It is impossible to describe all the minorities, but we find it necessary to have a closer look at the five principal ones.

Minority regions

The Manzhou provided the last ruling house, the Qing, continuing from 1644 to 1911 (technically 1912). Their base is in today's northeast China. Originally the Manzhou were a small Tungal tribe that hailed from the Changbeishan at the Korean border. Their leaders call the men under their command Manzhou.[94] This race has its own language cognate to the Arabic, which becomes all but extinct. Little wonder the People's Broadcasting System of the CPR uses all but the Manzhou language.[95] In 1982, the government commissioned a group of 20 to study, or rather salvage, it. In 1880, Manchuria was thrown open by an edict of Empress Cixi to her Han subjects who did not take too long to overwhelm the natives.[96] According to the 1953 census Manzhou numbered 1,460,000; in 1964 and 1982 this rose to 2,700,000 and 4,299,159 respectively. They were scattered all over

[92] Beijing Review, May 10, 1982, p. 4, col. 1.

[93] Globe and mail, June 20, 1983, p. 9, col. 1.

[94] Michael and Taylor, op. cit., p. 61.

[95] Zhong guo shou ce, p. 450.

[96] China paper, physical geography and people, Washington: Naval Intelligence Division, 1944, vol. 1, pp. 39, 62, 63, 102.

Liaoning, Heilongjiang, Jilin, Hebei and Neimenggu.[97] Is it because of the lack of heavy concentration that there is no autonomous community of whatever name ordained for them? Or, is it because of the Han's revenge against a minority who misruled them for two and a half centuries and who brought shame to China at the end? We may note, too, that the ten nationality colleges (supposedly instituted for the diverse minorities, but the majority of students and teachers are Han) are located in all minority areas except Manchuria,[98] and that there is no Manzhou newspaper although all the major minorities each have theirs.[99] Some evidence shows the Manzhou's presence in a few nominal policy organs of the party and state. To be specific, they have one alternate member in the CC, one each in the Central Advisory Committee and Central Commission for Discipline Inspection. To the 6th NPC they sent 37 deputies coming from different parts of the country, among them eleven are women.[100]

The Russian Menggu live in what is in the CPR called Waimenggu and the Chinese ones in Neimenggu.[101] The latter was formed into an Autonomous Region as early as May 1, 1947.[102] It is older by four months than the CPR itself. The size of the Chinese Menggu grew from 1,460,000 in 1953 to 1,920,000 in 1964.[103] The 1982 census put it at 3,411,657.[104] This is their total in China, not just the ones residing in the region under consideration. Outside the region, they are found in Xinjiang, Liaoning, Jilin, Heilongjiang, Qinghai, Hebei, Gansu and Yunnan. How many Menggu are settled in Neimenggu? The total residents, says the 1982 census, are 19,274,279.[105] Suppose all the Menggu (3,411,657) live in the region (of course, this is not the case), they would have to be outnumbered by 15,862,627. Thus the ratio comes to be five to one. This is quite a minority in a region set aside for them to exercise autonomy in.

The region has 15 colleges attended by 15,674 of whom Menggu are only 3,900; 84 middle vocational schools, by 32,274; 3,484 conventional high schools, by 1,528,200; and 27,796 grade schools, by 29,340,000.[106]

Menggu are represented by two full and one candidate members

[97] *Zhong guo shou ce*, p. 156; *Zhong guo bai ke nian jian*, p. 668.

[98] *Zhong guo shou ce*, p. 174.

[99] *Zhong guo jian kuang, xin wen, guang bo he chu ban*, Beijing: Wai wen chu ban she, 1982, p. 2.

[100] *Renmin ribao*, May 11, 1983, pp. 2-3.

[101] *Xin hua ci dian*, p. 579, col. 2; Wang Tunglin, *Zhong guo min zu shi*, 2nd ed., Beiping: Wen hua xue she, 1934, pp. 613-614.

[102] *Zhong guo shou ce*, p. 162. However, *World almanac*, 1969, p. 504, col. 1 mentions May 12, 1947.

[103] *Zhong guo shou ce*, p. 162.

[104] *Beijing Review*, May 23, 1983, p. 19.

[105] *Ibid.*, January 3, 1983, p. 25.

[106] *Zhong guo bai ke nian jian*, p. 72, col. 1.

in the CC, one in the Central Advisory Committee, two in the Central Committee for Discipline Inspection and one in the Politburo. The region sent 64 to the 6th NPC, of whom thirteen are female.[107] In ethnic composition, among the 64 Han are 40, followed by 19 Menggu, and one each of Orogen, Ewenki, Manzhou, Daur and Hui. In the NPC there are 12 Menggu from outside the region. In the region, the dominant figure, namely, the first secretary of the party is a Han, as are the second secretary (only one such secretary), four of the five secretaries and one of the three deputy secretaries. Although the chairman of the regional government, as required by Article 114 of the Constitution, is a native, but two of the three vice-chairmen are Han; the chairman of the CPPCC is a Han and the ten vice-chairmanships are evenly divided between the two races. A Menggu chairs the standing committee of the regional NPC; and among the eleven vice-chairmen six are Han and five Menggu. It is a Han who takes the presidency of the high court and another the chief procuratorate.

Presently in the region there are eight leagues (equivalent to prefecture), four towns directly under the league control and three towns directly under the regional jurisdiction; twenty-two counties (n.b. without the adjective autonomous), fifty-three qi (equivalent to county), and three autonomous qi (equivalent to autonomous county).[108] We suppose since there are so many Han in the region, they may have formed their own counties enjoying autonomy within the reputedly autonomous region.

Neimenggu underwent considerable change of boundary during early years of the People's Republic intended perhaps to dilute the native contents. In 1950, the region consisted of northern Chahaer and parts of Liaoning and Heilongjiang. Suiyuan province was added to it in June 1954, as was the eastern part of Rehe the following year.[109] The Menggu embrace Lamaism which differs from the Tibetan kind primarily because celibacy is not their cup of tea, so to say, and the spiritual hegemon is called Khutukhtu, instead of Dalai Lama.[110] Nearly all are not practicing Lamaists. Falling under an ultra-modern ideology (communism), the Menggu, for the most part, still live a nomadic fashion of life.

Regarding the Zang (Tibetans), a little noticed fact is that theirs is a generic term. It contains several tribes, such as the Khamba, Monba and Loba. There are charges of prejudices and even persecution by the majorities. However, they all hold at arm's length the minority yet dominant Han in the region. The 1982 census gives

[107] These data are derived from *Renmin shou ce*, Beijing: Renmin ribao chu ban she, 1979, pp. 1089-1090; *Renmin ribao*, May 11, 1983, pp. 2-3; May 16, 1983, p. 1; April 28, p. 1; *Zhong guo bai ke nian jian*, pp. 71-72.

[108] *Zhong guo bai ke nian jian*, p. 60; *Zhong guo shou ce*, p. 19.

[109] *World almanac*, 1969, p. 504, col. 1.

[110] Michael and Taylor, *op. cit.*, p. 354.

the total Zang of China as 3,870,068,[111] up from 2,500,000 in 1964,[112] and 2,770,000 in 1953. The lessening of 270,000 between 1953 and 1964 may well be explained by the exodus of the Zang to India and Nepal beginning in October 1959. The 1982 census reveals the total population of the region to be 1,892,393.[113] Of these, Zang are 1,780,000.[114] This leaves 110,393 Han in Tibet. Both Zang and the Han are concentrated in Lhasa where they numbered, according to a Western estimate, 120,000 and 70,000 respectively.[115] Most, if not all, Han are garrison troops. The above figures show that more than two million Zang are outside the region, taking up residence in the neighboring Sichuan, Qinghai, Gansu and Yunnan provinces.[116] With reference to the total Zang in China, two Western and one Tibetan sources give much higher estimates than the Chinese census (3,870,068). The 1984 World almanac, p. 487, col. 1 writes of 5,700,000 and John Fraser gives a round figure of 6,000,000.[117] And significantly Dalai Lama came out with the latter number.[118] To this spiritual leader, the Chinese communists, owe, as it were, 2,129,932 Tibetans.

Among the five regions, Tibet is the youngest, dating from September 9, 1965.[119] In size, it is one eighth of the CPR, carved into five prefectures, one city (Lhasa) and 71 counties.[120] The region has four colleges, one being called College of Agriculture and Shepherding in Linzhi.[121] The total matriculation of the four is 1,500. Middle vocational schools number 22 attended by 5,000; conventional high schools are 55 enrolling 20,000; and the 2,266 grade schools have 250,000 pupils.[122]

Among the minorities, the Tibetans have the highest sense of identity, with their unique language, theocratic regime and conservative tradition. For these reasons, the communists are perforce to deal with the region in a somewhat different manner. During their conquest of the whole of China in 1949-1950, they shot their way into all parts of it, except this "roof of the world." With it

[111] Beijing Review, May 23, 1983, p. 19.

[112] Zhong guo shou ce, p. 156.

[113] Beijing Review, January 3, 1983, p. 25.

[114] Ibid., May 21, 1983, p. 4.

[115] John Fraser, The Chinese, portrait of a people, Toronto: Collins, 1980, p. 117.

[116] Beijing Review, May 23, 1983, p. 19.

[117] John Fraser, loc. cit.

[118] The Champaign-Urbana News, June 30, 1981, p. B-6.

[119] Zhong guo shou ce, p. 162.

[120] Ibid., p. 60; Zhong guo bai ke nian jian, p. 61.

[121] Zhong guo bai ke nian jian, p. 554.

[122] Ibid., p. 115, col. 1.

they elected to make a *modus vivendi*. Very possibly, the Reds felt, since Tibet was a de facto protectorate of India, it would be highly dangerous to grab it by their habitual recourse to arms. Hence, from April 29 to May 21, 1951, representatives of Tibet and Beijing negotiated a protocol to manumit that region.[123] The document signed on May 23 bound the communists to respect the position of Dalai Lama and the Zang's autonomy in religious and economic affairs.[124] As events were soon to prove, Beijing was not to honour its words. In the autumn of 1959, the Chinese oppressive policy there reached the unbearable point. The PLA evicted, as it were, Dalai Lama and hundreds of thousands of his people from their land. Interestingly enough, on May 20, 1983, the Beijing autocrats even celebrated the 32nd anniversary of what they claim to be the "complete liberation of Tibet."[125] More of this below.

Tibet, as well as other regions, is just like a province in the Han area, without semblance of homerule. Great havoc was played by the Red Guards there and Zang leaders were butchered by the thousands, a crime now fashionably charged to the Gang of Four.[126] Gradually, Beijing has made some efforts to "buy off" the native hierarchs. One or two of them are treated particularly well. Ngapoi Ngawang Jigme is appointed as chairman of the standing committee of the regional NPC and given the concurrent vice-chairmanship of the NPC Standing Committee at Beijing.[127] It is even claimed that there is a retired Living Buddha in China, a certain Dongga Luosangchilie. He is said to be an assistant professor at the Central Institute of Nationality Studies and at the same time to be directing the Institute on Tibet.[128] There is even said to be a "woman Living Buddha" by the name of Sanding Doje Tagno who is a deputy to the NPC (*Beijing review,* August 8, 1983, p. 27) An array of propaganda tracts appeared recently in *Beijing Review* painting the region as a true paradise on earth.[129] Perchance enticed by this olive branch, the exiled Dalai Lama dispatched in late 1982 a 3-man delegation to Beijing supplicating the masters to accord his theocracy the same treatment as is offered by them to Taiwan, namely the nine points of autonomy. The most important point is the economic and military self-rule. Going further however than the Taiwan deal, qua 10th point perhaps, the Dalai Lama asked for a pan-Zang domain embracing parts of Sichuan, Qinghai, Gansu, Yunnan, and wherever the Tibetans

123 *Ibid.,* p. 638, col. 1.

124 Bill Brugger, *Contemporary China,* New York: Barnes & Noble, 1977, p. 74.

125 *Renmin ribao,* May 21, 1983, p. 4.

126 *Zhong guo bai ke nian jian,* p. 115, col. 2.

127 *Beijing Review,* November 22, 1982, p. 14; *Renmin ribao,* May 16, 1983, p. 1.

128 *Beijing Review,* October 4, 1982, p. 22, col. 2.

129 *Ibid.,* October 4, 1982, pp. 22-23; November 22, 1982, pp. 14-18; December 6, 1982, pp. 21-24; December 20, 1982, pp. 36-38.

live.[130] What a forgetful and simplistic man! and what a pipe-dreamer! Tibetans are represented by two full and two alternate members in the CC and one in the Central Advisory Committee; to the 6th NPC the region sent 19 deputies of whom five are female; among the 19 are 15 Zang, one Loba, one Monba and two Han.[131] One of these two is Yin Fatang, the boss of Tibet (party's first secretary there). In the NPC, there are, in addition, 17 Zang from other provinces and regions, and this makes the number of Zang in that august body 32. In the regional regime, the first secretary, as just said, is a Han, as are two of the five secretaries and the only deputy secretary. On the government side, the chairman and four of the five vice-chairmen are Zang, as are the chairman and eight of the ten vice-chairmen of the Standing Committee of the regional NPC. Further the Zang are doing very well in the regional CPPCC whose chairman and eleven of its twelve vice-chairmen are Zang. However, the president of the high court and the chief procurator are both Han.

This discussion of the Tibetan region is incomplete without mentioning a disappearing tribe. Besides Loba who are numbering only 2,065 and Monba only 6,246 according to the 1982 census, there are also the Khamba.[132] This is the most numerous tribe of the three, but alas, it has no representation in whatever organ, government or party and at whatever level, regional or national. This people is not even mentioned on the racial manifest in various media. The Khamba, it will be remembered, are hostile to the Chinese domination in Tibet. Located in the eastern part of the region, the tribesmen are engaged in a persistent struggle, in the form of guerilla warfare, with the Chinese garrison. At times they had to withdraw to Nepal or Burma to seek temporary sanctuary. In March 1959 they penetrated to the outskirts of Lhasa and posed a threat to the PLA stationed in the city. The Chinese general urged the Dalai Lama to order them to retreat. But he refused to comply. The denouement is the flight of the Dalai Lama and the countless thousands of Zang from Tibet.[133] An ethnic unit like the Khamba, in the Chinese eye, is traitorous to their fatherland and have hardly the right to be represented, even the right to exist.

The Uygur (also spelled Uighur) reside mainly in Xinjiang, given an autonomous-region status by a decree of the Chinese Communist Party on October 1, 1955.[134] The region is exactly one sixth of the CPR. The 1953, 1964 and 1982 censuses record the Uygur to be

---

[130] *Beijing Review*, November 15, 1982, pp. 3-4.

[131] The personnel makeup is derived from the following sources: *Renmin ribao*, May 11, 1983, p. 2-3; May 16, 1983, p. 1; *Zhong guo bai ke nian jian*, p. 114; *Renmin shou ce*, p. 1093; *Zhong guo shou ce*, p. 91.

[132] Figure in *Beijing Review*, May 23, 1983, p. 20, col. 1.

[133] Harold Hinton, *An introduction to Chinese politics*, 2nd ed., New York: Holt, Rinehart and Winston, 1978, pp. 198-199, 274; Michael and Taylor, *op. cit.*, p. 512.

[134] *Zhong guo shou ce*, p. 162; Michael and Taylor, *op cit.*, p. 66.

3,640,000, 4,000,000 and 5,957,112 respectively.[135] There are, strange enough, a number of Uygur in Hunan province,[136] which is two thousand km away and is intervened by three provinces. The total residents of Xinjiang is 13,081,681 according to the 1982 census.[137] Of this, the Han are about 5,720,000 and Uygur 6,110,000.[138] Thus in the region bearing their name, the Uygur constitute less than one half of the residents. The Han keep pouring in thankful to the *Xiafang*. Each year sees several hundred thousands arrive from the provinces. They are all virile individuals. The intent of the Beijing policy is only too obvious. Before long the Han will certainly outnumber the Uygur. Besides the two giant races, Xinjiang has Kazak (close to one million), Dongxiang (quarter of a million), Kirgiz (about 100,000), Daur (about 94,000), Xibe (about 83,000), Tajik (26,503), Uzbek (12,453), Tatar (4,127) and Russian folks (2,935).[139] A Western source mentions 520,000 Hui.[140] All the preceding races, except the Hui, have brethren across the border in the USSR. From time to time, the Russians fomented in the mixed area revolts against the Chinese and they supply them with arms. Hinting at this situation, a Chinese official in Xinjiang said in 1983 to a Western reporter that the Soviets "like to interfere in the internal affairs of other countries."[141] Border crossings and barterings between these brethren were prohibited until the recent thaw of the Sino-Soviet tension following the demise of Leonid Brezhnev and the cooling off of the Beijing-Washinton diplomacy, although this injunction did not prevent the propaganda broadcastings of both China and the Soviet Union "to woo families who have members on each side of the border."[142]

Xinjiang, as big as the combined area of England, France, Germany and Italy,[143] is divided into seven prefectures, five autonomous prefectures, three cities directly under the regional government and five towns under the prefectures, 74 counties and six autonomous counties.[144] The Uygur are represented by three full members in the CC and two members in the Central Commission for Discipline

[135] The 1964 figure is in *Zhong guo shou ce*, p. 162, and the 1982 figure in *Beijing Review*, May 23, 1983, p. 19, col. 1. The 1953 figure, cited by us previously, in *Europa*, 1979, vol. 2, p. 117.

[136] *Beijing Review*, May 23, 1983, p. 19, col. 1.

[137] *Ibid.*, January 3, 1983, p. 25.

[138] *Zhong guo bai ke nian jian*, p. 84, col. 1 gives the 1979 figures for Han and Uygur as 5,200,000 and 5,640,000 respectively. We update the figures to 1982 by taking into account the increase rate as shown in the first table in the section on ethnic composition. *Globe and mail*, June 16, 1983, p. 4, col. 1 writes of 60 percent of the 13 million are non-Han.

[139] *Beijing Review*, May 23, 1983, pp. 19-20.

[140] *Globe and mail*, June 16, 1983, p. 4, col. 1.

[141] *Ibid.*, June 6, 1983, p. 9, col. 3.

[142] *Ibid.*, June 14, 1983, p. 4. col. 2.

[143] *Ibid.*, col. 1.

[144] *Zhong guo bai ke nian jian*, p. 61.

Inspection.[145] To the 6th NPC, Xinjiang region sent 57 deputies of whom 13 are women.[146] Among the 57 are 22 Han, 22 Uygur, five Kazaks, two Hui, and one each of Kirgiz, Xibe, Uzbek, Tajik, and Russian. In the NPC at Beijing, there are two Uygur from outside Xinjiang and this makes a total of 24 Uygur in that body. As for the region itself, the party's first and second secretaries (only one such secretary) are Han, as are four of the five secretaries and the only two deputy secretaries.[147] Come to the government side, the chairman and two of the six vice-chairmen are Uygur (three of the six are Han and one is a Kazak); the standing committee of the regional NPC is chaired by a Uygur, and among the 13 vice-chairmen are five Han and five Uygur, one each of Kirgiz, Hui and Kazak. In the regional CPPCC the chairman is a Uygur, as are three of the 12 vice-chairmen (the remainder are four Han, one each of Salar, Hui, Kirgiz, Uzbek and Kazak). Although the president of the high court is a Uygur, the chief procurator is a Han. Xinjiang has 10 colleges attended by 11,393 (minority students are only 5,125); 90 middle vocational schools, by 38,993; 1,985 conventional high schools, by 794,000 (minority students 295,000); and 4,111 grade schools, by 2,007,000.[148]

Officially coming into being on October 25, 1958,[149] Ningxia Autonomous Region is made up of two prefectures, one autonomous prefecture, one city directly administered by the region, 33 counties and five autonomous counties.[150] The residents of the region number 3,895,578, according to the 1982 census,[151] of this the Hui make up 1,120,000.[152] The Hui in China total 7,219,352.[153] Thus only one of every six or seven Hui lives in their region. They are widely scattered in the two regions of Xinjiang and Neimenggu and 12 other provinces.[154] The Han in Ningxia are more than two and a half million, outnumbering the Hui by two to one. This being the case, among the 17 deputies sent by the region to the 6th NPC, no less than seven are Han (actually they are under-represented); there are nine Hui and one Naxi.[155] In China as a whole, though, the Hui are represented

[145] The Twelfth National Congress of the CPC (September 1982), pp. 145-157.

[146] Renmin ribao, May 11, 1983, p. 2-3.

[147] The personnel makeup is derived from Zhong guo bai ke nian jian, p. 84; Renmin shou ce, p. 1091; Zhong guo shou ce, p. 94; Renmin ribao, May 16, 1983, p. 1.

[148] Zhong guo bai ke nian jian, p. 84.

[149] Zhong guo shou ce, p. 162.

[150] Zhong guo bai ke nian jian, p. 60.

[151] Beijing Review, January 3, 1983, p. 25.

[152] Zhong guo bai ke nian jian, p. 81, col. 1.

[153] Beijing Review, May 23, 1983, p. 19.

[154] Ibid.

[155] Renmin ribao, May 11, 1983, p. 3.

by a total of 52 in that body (NPC), of whom 13 are women. Among the full members of the CC are two Hui and among the alternate members of the same body are three Hui. In addition, one Hui sits in the Central Commission for Discipline Inspection.[156] In the regional apparatus, the first secretary of the party is a Han, as is one of the two secretaries; all three deputy secretaries are Han. On the government side, the chairman and five of the eight vice-chairmen are Hui (three are Han).[157] The regional NPC's standing committee has one Hui as its chairman and three Hui as its vice-chairmen (five Han vice-chairmen). And both the president of the high court and chief procurator are Han.

The region has five colleges, attended by 3,239; 20 middle vocational schools, by 6,295; 560 conventional high schools, by 238,000; and 5,129 grade schools, by 5,930,000.[158]

The last of the minority regions in our study is Guangxi Zhuang which was officially inaugurated on March 5, 1958.[159] In it are four cities directly under the region and two directly under the prefectures, eight prefectures, 72 counties and eight autonomous counties.[160] In 1982, there were 36,420,960 residents in Guangxi,[161] but there were only 13,378,162 Zhuang there and in Yunnan, Guangdong and Guizhou.[162] Thus the Han must be at least twice as many as the native Zhuang (in 1979 Zhuang in the region numbered 11,604,400 but no similar figure is revealed by the 1982 census).[163] In spite of this imbalanced situation, the communists still think it logical to set up Guangxi as an autonomous region named after the minority.

The region sent 86 deputies to the 6th NPC. Among them are 42 Zhuang, two Miao, two Yao, one Dong, one Jing, one Mulao, one Maonan and 36 Han. The Han are thus grossly under-represented from that region.[164] In the NPC at Beijing, there are 48 Zhuang, six hailing from outside Guangxi. At the party center, Zhuang have two full and one alternate members in the CC, one member in the Central Advisory Committee and one in the Politburo.[165] On the regional level, the first and second secretary (there is only one such secretary) and all the seven secretaries are Han. While the chairman of the regional

156 The Twelfth National Congress of the CPC (September 1982), pp. 145-157.

157 The personnel makeup is derived from Renmin ribao, May 16, 1983, p. 1; Renmin shou ce, p. 1090; Zhong guo bai ke nian jian, p. 81; Zhong guo shou ce, pp. 90-91.

158 Zhong guo bai ke nian jian, p. 81-82.

159 Zhong quo shou ce, p. 162.

160 Ibid., p. 20; Zhong guo bai ke nian jian, p. 106.

161 Beijing Review, January 3, 1983, p. 25.

162 Ibid., May 23, 1983, p. 19.

163 Zhong guo bai ke nian jian, p. 106.

164 Renmin ribao, May 11, 1983, p. 3.

165 The Twelfth National Congress of the CPC (September 1982), pp. 145-157.

government is a Zhuang, three of the five vice-chairmen are Han.
In the regional NPC's standing committee sits a Zhuang as chairman,
and there are three Zhuang, one Dong and six Han as vice-chairmen.
Heading the regional CPPCC is a Zhuang; among the eleven vice-
chairmen there are only three Zuang, but eight Han.[166] Finally the
president of the high court and the chief procurator are both Han.
Culturally Guangxi is the most advanced of all the five regions. It has
17 colleges enrolling 21,229; 156 middle vocational schools, 483,000;
2,395 conventional high schools, 1,801,500; and 13,239 grade
schools, 5,030,200.[167]

By way of concluding this section, the former regime of Nanjing
exercised a sort of the old-fashioned suzerainty over the remote
territories. In general, Ningxia and Tibet were loosely allied with it. Their
actual relation with the National Government was a matter of peaceful
co-existence. More accurately, they did not raise independent flags
in defiance of the central authority, as did Guangxi on two occasions.
In return, Nanjing tolerated their complete autonomy. The rulers and
the minorities' lifestyle there were never ordered around by Jiang
Jieshi. The status of Xinjiang was murky; following the invasion of
China by Japan in 1937, the opportunistic governor, Sheng Shicai,
gradually brought his fiefdom under the lordship of Stalin until he saw
the USSR's imminent defeat by Nazi Germany. Suddenly he veered
aroung toward Nanjing. Soon he was replaced, however. From 1931
to 1945 Neimenggu came under the sway of Japan. The Nationalist
regime nominally administered Neimenggu and Tibet through the
Mengzang Commission. Apropos of Guangxi, it was at no time
subordinate to that regime. This situation, however, was thankful to
the warlords there rather than the assertion of minority right of the
Zhuang. On the surface, the autonomy setup in the CPR resembles
the pre-1949 system in that the ethnic aggregates maintain some
identity, but Beijing's heavy hand contrasts sharply with Nanjing's
laissez-fairism toward them.

Traditional thought patterns

There is the universal view that the Chinese society and state are
dominated by the philosophy of Confucius. He undoubtedly has
influenced the mind of his countrymen, but if we attribute to him the
only strand of thought, it would be wrong. There are many other
doctrines and teachings equally powerful, and in this author's opinion,
much more powerful and enduring in China. One can even argue that
Confucianism receives only lip service of both the rulers and the ruled
through history. The preachings and theories competitive to
Confucianism maintain their vitality and definitely molded the Chinese
demeanor.

---

[166] *Renmin ribao*, May 16, 1983, p. 1.

[167] *Zhong guo bai ke nian jian*, p. 108, col. 2.

Confucius (551-479 B.C.) — moralist

He flourished in a period of anarchy and convulsion, a period which he labeled "Autumn-Spring" (722-481 B.C.). This was the declining period of the Zhou dynasty when the central government lost its authority. This and the immediately following period up to the year 222 B.C. which is known as one of Warring States was replete with chaos and bloodshed. The principalities and dukedoms fought each other ferociously. No sooner had they entered into an alignment than they broke it up only to ally again. In response to such a Hobbesian state of nature, each intellectual propounded his position on how best to restore order. The free climate produced the now famous "hundred schools of thought." Everyone "hawked" his idea in the marketplace. Among them five had the most "buyers."

By far the best known, but not the most successful scholar is Confucius. At the uppermost of his heart is the restitution of peace (he-ping). He traveled far and wide, intending to persuade the lords of the numerous states to cease combating each other. However, he did not set his foot in the soil of Qin, the most warlike state; perhaps he thought that the trip was not only futile but also risky.

Confucius is every inch an elitist. He often made derogatory remarks of the uneducated poor (xiaoren). For example, he said, they are prone to revolt and defiance of superior authority, have no sense of shame, are ruthless, take sides,[168] dislike low-quality meals and clothes, and do not want to work.[169] On the other hand, he flattered profusely the junzi who, he said, have both intellectual and moral virtues, do not slander others, are righteous, impartial and incorruptible and above all, stay away from sex.[170] Junzi should not make friends with xiaoren. If he wants them to do something, Confucius stated, he needs only give the command, but by no means tells them why.

Akin to the denunciation of war is the emphasis on moderation. In fact, one of his Four Books is entitled by that word. He called on people to avoid extremism because, he averred, everying in the universe is nothing but a harmony of two opposite ends.[171] This holding is, however, contradicted by his admonition that one must not surrender one's position. Once you have made up your mind, stick to it unswervingly, he taught. Everybody should identify with a principle from which he must not deviate for one moment. Should the principle be deviable, it is not a principle at all. Confucius operated on this stand himself. His uncompromising is evidenced by the fact that when he reviewed and edited historical records, folk poetry and rites, he weeded out pitilessly what did not suit his liking.

---

[168] Confucius, "Lun yu," *Si shu du bing*, Taibei: Zheng wen chu ban she, 1967, p. 61.

[169] *Idem*, "Da xue," *Ibid.*, P. 7.

[170] *Idem*, "Zhong yun," *Ibid.*, p. 33.

[171] *Ibid.*, p. 18.

Confucius wrote a tract on an ideal commonwealth which represents the highest human development.[172] It depicts a blissful land. In many key points, e.g., freedom from crime, it adumbrates Lenin's *State and Revolution*. The text was inscribed on a plaque hung on the entrance of the United Nation's mansion in New York. When the CPR won admission to that body, it ordered an immediate removal of the plaque because Confucius, up to that time (1971), had been regarded by the communists as a heinous defender of the exploitative class, and henceforth he is one of the many historical personae non-gratae.

Confucius' teachings on social relations focus on ren (kind), yi (righteous), li (courteous) and xin (faithful).[173] He indefatigably preached these as much as on peace. We are of the opinion that the reason why he placed stress on them is because he found that they are very weak in the Chinese character. Otherwise, why should he take so much pain in stressing these virtues?

Han Fei Zi (280?-233 B.C.) — legalist

Not a contemporary of Confucius, this man was the father of the legalistic school generally considered to be opposing the Confucian moral system.[174] His thought was elaborated and put into effect by Lord Shang Yang, the executive of the state Qin. Objecting to Confucius' obsession with the perfection of personality as the basis of a consummate regime, Lord Shang placed stress on the regulation of conduct as it affects the public order.[175] It is impractical, he felt, to expect everybody to be morally impeccable and it is equally unrealistic to teach everybody to comport himself well. Law and order is grounded on man's fear of physical coercion.[176] Lord Shang laid down rigorous rules of conduct of a legal nature and imposed penalty for the breach of them. Law is above the emperor and ministers as well as the common people. "He had, it turned out, offended the emperor's son, so when the latter succeeded his father, he quickly put Lord Shang to death" by dismembering.[177] The rule of law, although receiving scanty attention by Confucius, was practiced throughout the ages of China. There is no dynasty which did not issue a large number of edicts and rescripts and had them neatly codified.

---

172 *Idem*, "Da tong pian," partial text can be found in Robert Elegant, *The Centre of the World, Communism and the Mind of China*, London: Methuen, 1963, p. 152.

173 *Confucius*, "Lun yu," pp. 111, 146, 159.

174 *The Complete Works of Han Fei Tzu, a Classic of Chinese Legalism*, translated from the Chinese by W.K. Liao, London: Arthur Probsthain, 1939, 2 vols., vol. 1, pp. 15-25.

175 Yang Kung-sun, *The Book of Lord Shang, a Classic of the Chinese School of Law*, translated from the Chinese with introd. and notes by J.L. Duyvendak, London: Arthur Probsthain, 1928, pp. 1-7.

176 Donald Paragon, "Some firsthand observations on China's legal system," *Judicature*, no. 10, 1980, pp. 477-484 at 478, col. 2.

177 Lucian W. Pye, *op. cit.*, p. 37. Alfred Forke, *Geschichte der mitteralterichen chinesischen Philosophie*, 2nd ed., Hamburg: Cram, de Gruyter & Co., 1964, pp. 74-80.

This demonstrates how important a role was played by legalism as the technique of governance.[178] Moral principles as a basis of relations between the subjects and the superiors and the relations between subjects themselves took a secondary place.

It cannot be proved, of course, that were it not for the Confucian moralizing, crime would have been in rampancy in China. The stark fact, however, is that the Chinese society is charcteristic of friction, perhaps more so than other societies. The annals of China record countless wars and uprisings claiming tens of millions of lives. No doubt the Confucian counsel of moderation, humaneness and personal virtue is unheeded. What has kept the statehood from falling apart and from lapsing into total anarchism, we suppose, is the flaming sword of the law.[179] The Chinese need to be deterred by the stern hand of justice. We call the reader's attention to the truth that all China's educational devices are bent toward socializing the people, instilling them with good sense and teaching them to respect the law, to avoid extremism, to be kindly to one's neighbors. High character is considered to be the object of schooling and parental inculcation. The result of all this concerted and costly effort is disappointing. Does not China have her share of the world's armed conflicts (more than others), lawlessness, crimes, deceptions in business, betrayals of associates and tribal vendettas? These are taking place in a society reputedly basked in the Confucian sun! Legalism, we hold, has exercised a generally unappreciated role in keeping order in China and Confucianism is honored by its breaching rather than by its practicing.

Yang Zhu (400-360 B.C.) — individualist

Both Confucianism and legalism are grounded on the collectivist philosophy. They recognize the need for the summum bonum and call for sacrifice, if need be, of one's self for the society.[180] Confucius assumes that when proper relation requires it, one has to bear some inconveniences. That is why selfishness is bitterly attacked by him. In fact, he equates it to wickedness. If man is motivated only by his personal concern, the wider community would come to grief. Confucius and his follower, Mengzi, accused the contemporary rulers of pursuing their own objective, regardless of the consequences. These philosophers are, however, opposed by Yang Zhu.[181] He declared that men should seek personal gratification. In doing so, they cannot at the same time take others' interest into consideration. One of his widest quoted sayings is: "I'd rather not tear off one hair

[178] Wade Baskin, ed., *Classics in Chinese Philosophy*, New York: Philosophical Library, 1972, p. 225.

[179] William Theodore de Bary, ed., *Basic writings of Mo Tzu, Hsün Tzu and Han Fei Tzu*, New York: Columbia University Press, 1967, p. 9; Donald Paragon, "A note on China's legal tradition," *Judicature*, no. 10, May 1980, p. 478, col. 2.

[180] Kung-chuan Hsiao, *A History of Chinese Political Thought*, translated by F.W. Mote, Princeton, New Jersey: Princeton University Press, 1979, pp. 42, 47, 48.

[181] *Encyclopedia Americana*, 1980 ed., vol. 29, p. 646, col. 2.

of mine to benefit mankind." Yang Zhu's individualism is truly rugged. It is on this score that he was rebuked by Confucian scholars. He left behind no writings as did other controversialists of the time. One may well surmise that even if he produced something, it would have been suppressed, so distasteful were his ideas to the moralists. Whatever is known about his views is through quotations and imputations of his denigrators.[182] On account of an incomplete knowledge of him, we are, after all, not sure whether he thought of human beings as selfish by nature, or whether he advocated that men should be egoistic.[183]

Has Yang Zhu's strand of thinking played any part in molding the Chinese mind? This author would like to answer yes. There is much evidence that Chinese politics and society are shot through by selfishness. Witness the widespread nepotism and corruption in that country. Confucian intellectuals keep on sermonizing public morals and on condemning the pursuit of sordid end exactly because the Chinese have little of the former but are doing too much of the latter. We do not argue that everyone in the government is a nepotist. Some incorruptible mandarins are indeed recorded in history. These, we would say, are exception to the general rule. Their rarity makes them recordable in the first place.

Lao Zi (b. 604 B.C.) — naturalist

The putative founder of Daoism was for the most part, mystic. There is an uncertainty surrounding the man's identity and even about his very existence. Born Li Er, he lived as a recluse and once worked in the library at the court of Zhou. Upon meeting Confucius in the year 517 B.C., he scolded him for his ambition and pride. The oldest text of Daoism, the *Dao de jing* is attributed to Lao Zi. While passing through the mountain gate on his way to an unknown world to retire there, he relayed his ideas to the guard. The man jotted them down and they became the just mentioned text.[184] He advocated natural law, or the way things are moving in their primordial manner. The focal point is that man must live in tune with the Dao. In doing so, he has to do away with any formalism which Lao Zi believed runs counter to the law. Great emphasis is placed on passivity.[185] A complete accord with nature requires subjection to it. In other words, it calls for the elimination of human effort. To practice Dao, one must never engage in laboring which would give rise to friction. Lao Zi said inaction is at the core of the universe. Living harmoniously with heaven and earth, we must note, is also suggested by Confucius, but the

182 Heinrich Hackman, *Chinesischen Philosophie*, Munchen: Verlag Ernst Reinhardt, 1927, pp. 190-191.

183 "Yang Tchou," *La grande encyclopédie, inventaire raisonné des sciences, des lettres et des arts*, Paris: H. Lamirault et cie, 1886-1902, vol. 31, p. 1265.

184 Kung-chuan Hsiao, *op. cit.*, pp. 37, 42-44, 48, 50.

185 Wing-tsit Chan, comp., *A Source Book in Chinese Philosophy*, Princeton, New Jersey: Princeton University Press, 1963, pp. 136-176.

advocacy of actlessness is in direct collision with his social value.[186] Daoism later degenerated into a) escapism, and b) a legend of reward and punishment after life.[187] The former provided a refuge for the learned and disdainful individuals in periods of tumult. Certainly, it is not in keeping with the Confucian virtue of positive and proper relations with fellow creatures. Civil responsibility is replaced by the later Daoists with a naturalistic self-identity. They would be quite congenial to Jean Jacques Rousseau's savage nobles, as civilization and government that goes with it tend to debase the probity of man. The Confucian ideal of constructive order is never threatened by such isolationists. However, they are not without impact on Chinese society. By retaining the view on the tribulation after life, religious Daoism is widespread and strikes deep roots in the masses.[188] They found the arid Confucianism unable to satisfy their inner yearnings. Although one cannot say the idea behind the tribulation is totally contrary to the teachings of Confucius who, we shall remember, held agnosticism, the position on reward or punishment according to one's deeds during lifetime is definitely out of joint with that sage's basic secularism.[189] Daoism also gave birth to clandestine societies which impose discipline on or exact loyalty from the members. In history, these societies rose many times to challenge the establishment. It is to be noted that Confucianism relates the individuals directly to the state, whereas these societies come to stand in between them. They are, in modern language, intermediate groupings.

Mo Ti (5th-4th century B.C.) — pragmatist

Confucius set up very complicated rites for each and every occasion ranging from the proclamation of an adolescent into adulthood upon the attainment of the 20th birthday to obsequies. All steps, however trivial, are minutely controlled and nothing is left to chance. A thorough observance of the li (translated as rites or ceremonies) would surely make life unbearable. Over against such regimentation, Mo Ti propounded the view of simplicity and pragmatism.[190] What was needed, held he, was not the meticulous regulations of human affairs, but a few functional guidelines. It was enough, for example, to use one coffin of flimsy wood which is not thicker than three inches, to intern the dead and the dirge should be of short notes. The practice of Mo Ti's time was to have double sarcophagi, one inside another, made of the best wood, and to play an elaborate wailing music.

The Confucian li, a time-wasting process of doing things, was

---

[186] *Ibid.*, pp. 140-141, 344, 358.

[187] "Lao Tsey," *Bol'shaya sovetskaya entsiklopediya*, 2nd ed., Moskva: Gosudarstvennoe nauchnoe izdatel'stvo "bol'shaya sovetskaya entsiklopediya," vol. 24 (1953), p. 288.

[188] Ed. Chavanues, "Lao Tse," *La grande encyclopédie*, vol. 21, pp. 938-940.

[189] K. Satchidananda Murty, *Far Eastern Philosophies*, Prasaranga: University of Mysore, 1976, pp. 5, 6, 27-28.

[190] Gungphsing Wang, *The Chinese Mind*, New York: John Day, 1946, pp. 74-84.

followed by none other than the affluent and the highly situated. As far as the masses were concerned, it was a nuisance and a financial burden. For them, the procedures in such matters as the betrothal, the birth of a child, the coming of age and the offer of a sacrifice to the ancestors, were cut to the bare bone or abandoned completely due to lack of leisure and means. This is in keeping with Mo Ti's advisement of frugality and diligence. Unnecessary spending must be eschewed. Even the rich, he maintained, should not squander their money.[191] Man ought to do useful labor and should never be idle or indulge in extravagancy. In China, by far the greatest number of the population are practicing Mo Ti's teachings of utilitarianism, not Confucius' formalism. The latter became increasingly vulnerable following the downfall of the imperial order and the inauguration of the republic when Confucius was made a target of attack. It was declared to be out of touch with modern reality. The de-Confucianization gathers momentum as time rolls on. In the CPR, it surges to the fore periodically in its early years, during the Cultural Revolution and after Lin Biao's death (the pi-Lin, pi-Kung move). More recently, however, scholars are allowed openly to oppose or defend the sage. The regime has seen it fit to take a disinterested stand toward this by-and-large Platonic exercise.[192]

---

[191] Marcel Hertseus, *Sagesse éternelle de la Chine, pensées et préceptes*, Paris: Centurion, 1968, pp. 170-174.

[192] "Reassessment of Confucius," *Beijing Review,* May 30, 1983, pp. 18-21; Kuang Yaming, "Appraisal of Confucius: why? and how?" pp. 22-24.

CHAPTER II
A Short History

Exhaustion of the mandate

To say, as many do, that China has been in the process of evolution through the ages is not a revealing idea, for each succeeding government has undertaken some reform. More important, however, is the tempo of change. The last ruling house, the Qing, underwent a great deal of alteration, more than any of the preceding nine houses (two foreign), counting from Qin. Beginning in 1849, the Manzhou dynasty started its nose dive to the final crash in 1911. The six decades before the latter year signify the decadence of the imperial order,[1] while the four decades after it mark the flunk of the republican test. In a comparative sense, less changes occur in the former period (1849-1911) than the latter (1911-1949).[2] This chapter seeks to analyze the latter, a transition to the *Zhong guo renmin gong he guo* (Chinese People's Republic).

We begin by noting an observation made by some Western scholars that consequent on the erosion of the Confucian dispensation, Cathay was rapidly disintegrating.[3] This view supposes the sustaining or legitimating myth of that dispensation, but in reality, it only begs the question. Confucianism, as we have argued, was given an unwarranted halo in China. The buttress of the Chinese body politic is not Confucianism but a) the downright inertia of the mandarins at the court and b) the draconian method of rule. After a new conqueror broke up the resistance and ruled with an iron hand, he could ensure his own tenure, and the tenure of his progenies for a long period of time. Next to Qin, the shortest dynasty is Sui (589-617 A.D.). Longer than Sui is the sway of the Mongols (1278-1368). All six other houses endured hundreds of years each. The Chinese may have been easy to control, but faint-hearted emperors cannot fair well. Allen S. Whiting made a perspicacious remark on the political style of Jiang Jieshi (1888-1975) which we think characterizes all other rulers. "Had the regime (Guomindang) been harsh enough, it might have survived the communist challenge."[4] The American scholar spoke of the "halfway measures" taken by Jiang Jieshi in dealing with the Reds. He explicates: "We must not ignore the fact that some of the failures to institute thoroughly ruthless and successful repression lay in the opposition within the Guomindang circles to an uncompromising acceptance of authoritarianism." A democratic government, the

---

[1] Li-ung Bing, *Outlines of the Chinese history*, Shanghai: The Commerical Press, 1914, pp. 530-628.

[2] Percy Horace Kent, *The Passing of the Manchus*, London: Edward Arnold, 1912, pp. 274-302.

[3] Lucien W. Pye, *China*, Boston: Little, Brown, 1972, p. 128; John A. Harrison, *China After 1800*, 1st ed., New York: Harcourt, Brace & World, 1967, p. 107.

[4] Allen S. Whiting, "China", *Modern Political System: Asia*, edited by Robert E. Ward and Roy C. Macridis, Englewood Cliffs, New Jersey: Prentice-Hall, 1963, pp. 117-214 at 136, col. 2. All these quotations are drawn from the same source.

statement may well imply, can dig its own grave. On the contrary, a terroristic regime is in a position to secure a firm hand and keep on governing. This kind of regime is dictated by the Chinese national attributes, attributes which according to some commentators also appear in the Russians.[5] The Manzhou originated in today's northeast corner of China. Their armed conquest of her was little short of a Blitzkrieg.[6] It took them only 18 months (February 1644 - August 1645) to mop up the Ming remnants, although Formosa held on until 1683. Then the Chinese, that is, the ethnic Han, became quiet for two hundred and sixty-seven years. The first challengers to Qing were not the Chinese, but the English. The defeat in the three years of Opium War (1839-1842) was the beginning of the end.[7] Thenceforth an array of setbacks at the external front combined with a number of internal rebellions to desiccate the heavenly mandate. Be it noted too that the insurrections were not from the Han, but the outlying areas, the Nians and Moslems in southwest and west China. Even the Taipings (1850-1864) were from the Zhuang in Guangxi. The typical Chinese were behaving sheepishly toward the Manzhou until 1911.

The 1911 coup

The Guomindang employed the word "revolution" to describe the removal of the Manzhou from power. This usage is as inapposite as the word "liberation" utilized by the communists to label their ouster of the GMD in 1949. Actually, there was not much shooting and pitched battle on October 9-11, 1911 between the defenders and opponents of the Qing.[8] What happened was that the Court, panic-stricken and unwilling to resort to mass terror as it could, turned to one of the Han generals (already retired), Yuan Shikai, for a negotiated settlement. This man, taking advantage of the desperation of the Court, decided to exact harsh terms in return for his services. It reminds one of General Charles de Gaulle when he was called upon by an equally panic-stricken President René Côte on June 9, 1958 to save the French republicanism. Yuan dictated that "he be given military power" to handle the crisis.[9] Qing's New Army, for which Yuan Shikai had been mainly instrumental in bringing about, was too much for the rebels. They were defeated at a crucial point. On December 27, 1911, the new army took the cities of Hankou and Hanyang (now Wuhan) from the revolutionaries. If Yuan was to be faithful as Zeng Guofan, another Han who helped the Court to squelch the Taipings, the Qing dynasty may well have been saved, but Yuan had quite an

⁵ Hedrick Smith, *The Russians*, Quadrangle/The New York Times Book Co., 1976, p. 188.

⁶ Kenneth Scott Latourette, *The Chinese, their History and Culture*, 2nd ed., New York: Macmillan, 1934, vol. 1, pp. 327-329.

⁷ S. Wells Williams, *A History of China*, New York: Charles Scribner's, 1897, pp. 218 ff.

⁸ Edward Thomas Williams, *A Short History of China*, New York: Harper, 1928, pp. 472ff.

⁹ John A. Harrison, *op. cit.*, p. 98.

ax to grind.[10] He sounded out the opinion of both sides, just to see which was willing to go further in the bargain.[11] Having been assured by the rebels of the presidency in the contemplated republic, he sided with them. The regent, the young dowager and the six-year old emperor were abandoned by him.[12]

In the last three moons of imperial China there were two governments: the Court in Beijing and the headquarters of the rebels in Hankou which moved to Nanjing on December 4, 1911. The dyarchy was coming to a close on December 19-20 with a deal reached in the foreign district of Shanghai. The child-emperor, Henry Pu Yi, retired on February 12, 1912 and Yuan Shikai became the president of the Republic (succeeding Sun Yat-sen). In the imperial abdication it is enunciated that "the universal desire (for a republic) is clearly expressed by the will of the Heaven, and it is not for us to oppose the disapproval of the people merely for the sake of the principles and power of a single House."[13] This terse rescript finished up a mandate of 267 years.

There is little doubt that Yuan Shikai was the central figure (even midwife) at the birth of the republic and in its infancy as well.[14] However, Sun Yat-sen was also important, if not as a political power but as a revolutionary symbol. He was born on November 12, 1866 (his widow Song Qingling died on May 29, 1981), near Guangdong in the district of Xiangshan later rechristened Zhongshan after his well-known name. He received an occidental education but read little and knew still less about politics. His writings and speeches were to become a bible for the Guomindang later on. In fact, they are an admixture of undigested democratic precepts of the West and lots of Chinese tradition. The apt description for it is an ideological chop suey. While a student in China, this author had to take bows before Sun's image every Monday morning in a ceremony called Zongli Memorials. Zongli is the official title which Sun assumed as chieftain of the Guomindang.[15] All students in China must read his books. Frankly, we remember only a few of his teachings, one being that people should eat hog's blood which he asserted is the best part of the beast.

Sun was of a humble stock. He enrolled in a private school until age 12 when he was taken to Hawaii by his brother. This deprived him of a chance to learn more about China. In Hawaii, the young Sun entered an English missionary school. Because Chinese education

---

[10] Jerome Chen, *Yuan Shikai*, 2nd ed., Stanford: Stanford University Press, 1972, pp. 90ff.

[11] R. Verbrugge, *Yuan Che-k'ai, sa vie, son temps*, Paris: Librairie orientaliste Paul Geuthner, 1934, pp. 85ff.

[12] Emelin Waltz, *Far Eastern History*, Boston: Christopher Pub. House, 1950, pp. 291ff.

[13] John A. Harrison, *op. cit.*, p. 100.

[14] John B. Powell, *My Twenty-five Years in China*, New York: Macmillan, 1945, pp. 28-34.

[15] Roger Pelissier, *The Awakening of China, 1793-1949*, 1st American ed., New York: G.P. Putnam's, 1967, pp. 239-248.

was part of the curriculum there, he also acquired some knowledge about his native land, but now in a new environment. Sun became Westernized and was converted into a Christian. On a visit back to Xiangshan at the age of 17, he and another friend set out to vandalize the village temple. For this they were chased out by an angry mob. Repairing to Hong Kong, he completed medical studies there with an M.D. He practiced briefly in Macao but his license was revoked because of failing to establish residence there. Unable to pursue his calling, he turned his attention to revolution. Later Sun dated his effort to topple the Manzhou from the humiliating defeat of China in the war with France in 1884. He appealed to Li Hongzhang, one of the few Han governors-general, with a memorandum for some sort of political reform, but Li refused it. Dejected, he began working in earnest for the overthrow of the regime and in November 1895, organized a secret society in Honolulu after the Sino-Japanese war.[16] This society consisted of like-minded students and took the name Xing Zhong Hui (revive China club). Next year it prepared an uprising in Guangdong and an attack on the government buildings. The attempt failed, with a loss of many comrades of Sun's. He had to flee and became a fugitive from then on. The Court hung a price on his head. Traveling abroad, Sun was very successful in enlisting the support of his compatriots.[17]

He circulated among the Chinese communities in Japan, the US and England. At a meeting in Tokyo in 1905, a new body called Tong Meng Hui (combined league club) was organized, comprising mainly of the members of Xing Zhong Hui plus a sprinkling of others. Over three hundred joined it, with Sun elected as its chairman. The leadership of Sun was based on his personality, his sincerity and energy. Wherever he went, he contacted young people and secret society leaders. They were assigned such tasks as readying putsches, gathering men and munitions, or simply promoting the idea of revolution. Particularly remarkable was his ability in raising funds for his operation.[18] He both collected and administered it. Donations came in mainly from Chinese merchants who gave their life savings. To convince them of his right cause, Sun expounded republicanism and democracy after the Qing was removed.

In August 1905, Sun enunciated his program in Tokyo when the Tong Meng Hui was being organized.[19] It contained the so-called three popular principles: Min zu (national independence), Min chuan (rights of the citizens), Min sheng (public welfare). The last is sometimes rendered incorrectly as socialism. Also in the program were such

[16] Renmin ribao, September 18, 1981, p. 5, col. 1.

[17] Bodo Wiethoff, Introduction to Chinese History from Ancient Times to 1912, London: Thomas & Hudson, 1975, pp. 111, 114.

[18] Manahendra Nath Roy, Revolution and Counterrevolution in China, Calcutta: Renaissance Publishers, 1946, pp. 251-258.

[19] Renmin ribao, September 18, 1981, p. 5, col. 3.

planks as universal peace, nationalization of land, good relation with Japan and the seeking of the support of great powers.[20] The immediate aim, however, was the destruction of the Manzhou regime. Xing Zhong Hui and Tong Meng Hui each staged a number of armed assaults on the yamens in the district or provincial cities. These attempts, ten in all, were put down by the Qing. One action was planned to take place in 1900 on the island of Taiwan with the backing of the Japanese adventurers. It did not take place however when the promised shipment of weapons did not arrive due to a change of government in Tokyo. Other revolts were launched from Indo-China at the connivance of the French. The crucial move was, however, the infiltration of the garrison troops, the aforesaid New Army, of central China. The Tong Meng Hui, wanting to take advantage of the Sichuan unrest in protest of nationalization of railways there, schemed a coup in the Yangzi valley on October 10. But, on October 9, owing to mishandling of materials, there was a premature explosion in their hideout. Lest they should be ferreted out and hanged, the Tong Meng Hui members decided to act in the open. Hence the revolution.[21]

The initiative was, however, taken out of their hands the next day (October 10) by the Wuchang regiment which went on mutiny. Other places were also seized soon afterwards by these troops. In the absence of available Tong Meng Hui members, they conferred the leadership on their reluctant brigadier Li Yuanhong (later president of China). Immediately Beijing summoned Yuan Shikai for help. Sun Yat-sen was in Denver, Colorado on October 10. He left at once for China when the news of revolution reached him and arrived on December 23, 1911. Forthwith, the Tong Meng Hui elected him President of the Republic.[22]

Having been given full military power by the Court, Yuan directed his forces against the rebels. Not only did he bar them from moving north, but he also defeated them in the central Yangzi area and recaptured Wuhan. Yet he did not wish to annihilate the revolutionaries. He negotiated first with Li Yuanhong and then with Sun Yat-sen. The willingness of the revolutionaries to talk peace was not only because of their military inferiority but also because they were not in agreement on the type of government to be set up. No matter which view, they all wanted to be included in a regime likely organized by Yuan Shikai. On February 9, 1912, an agreement, originally worked out in Shanghai, was initialed. By this Sun was to resign the presidency in favor of Yuan. In return, the latter was to bring about the dethronement of Pu Yi. The dethronement took place on February 12, and the resignation the next day. On February 15, Yuan was

[20] Manahendra Nath Roy, *Revolution und konterrevolution in China,* Berlin: Soziologische Verlagsanstalt, 1930, pp. 39, 83.

[21] Adolf S. Waley, *The Remaking of China,* New York: E.P. Putnam, 1914, pp. 10, 31.

[22] Hellmut Wilhelm, *China Geschichte,* Peiping: Editions Henri, 1942, pp. 182-191.

elected by the interim parliament as the new president.[23]

Yuan Shikai and restoration

Upon assuming office, Yuan decreed that the Du Juns (governors-general) of the provinces carry on as before, and this vital decision shunted the country off to a strange tangent of warlordism, a situation which most scholars assert lasted until 1927 when Jiang Jieshi "united" the nation, but it truly lingered on until 1937 when Japan's attack drove the Chinese together. Still the unity was illusive. Between 1937 and 1945, there was the Nationalist China, there was the Communist China and there was the Japanese China. Deferring this story to later pages, let's discuss now the Yuan Shikai regime. It really succeeded the Manzhou Court, not Sun Yat-sen, and it bore the sorry legacy of both domestic and external impotence. Ever since the Taiping period, the central authority yielded much financial power to the sub-national level which had the far-reaching right to levy the Li jing. This supposedly temporary device to finance the pacification of the Taipings, was not repealed after they were put down.[24] Li jing was at its inception an excise but in some provinces it assumed the form of a poll tax, a very profitable revenue to the authorities. What became so dangerous to the national government was that the money so collected needed not be remitted to it as originally conceived. After President Yuan formally sanctioned the "fiefs" of the Dun Juns, they came to defend their domain with money and men and denied any obligation to Beijing.[25] The Chinese Republic thus commenced its career with an empty stomach and clay feet.

In order to keep the system going and, more important, to feed the army, Yuan was impelled to approach foreigners for loans. Fortunately for him, the Western countries and Japan felt that they found the man China needed to keep her from sinking into chaos which would be deleterious to their treaty rights. A powerful leadership and a solvent economy, it was hoped, would guarantee the continuation of the new state. Foreigners, therefore, were inclined to come to the aid of President Yuan, and after sixteen months of negotiation, he was able to borrow from a six-power (later five following the withdrawal of US bankers as urged by President Woodrow Wilson) consortium, a sum of 25 million pounds, called Reorganization Loans. However, the deal was struck against the warning of the Chinese parliament. On May 5, 1913, the parliament led by the Guomindang, to which the 1905 Tong Meng Hui was converted on August 24, 1912,[26] refused to approve Yuan's borrowings, but this was to no avail. He avowed to

[23] Guangming ribao, October 26, 1981, p. 4; S.L. Tikhvinskii, Istoriya kitaya i sovremennost, Moskva: Izd-vo "nauka," 1976, pp. 177-180.

[24] Tang Lean-li, The Inner History of the Chinese Revolution, London: George Routledge, 1970, p. 132.

[25] George Taylor, The Struggle for North China, New York: Institute of Pacific Relations, 1940, pp. 11, 12.

[26] Xin hua ci dian, Beijing: Shang wu yin shu guan, 1980, p. 1090, col. 2.

safeguard the well-being of the four hundred million Chinese.[27] The banking consortium headquartered in Hong Kong insisted on the validity of the deal.[28] After getting the wherewithal, Yuan was elected president for a five-year term on October 15, 1913. The M.P.'s, however, did not desist from criticizing him. The following month Yuan moved to dissolve the Guomindang under the subterfuge of its involvement in a sedition. Its members were dispersed and the parliament was left without a quorum, but Yuan had no problem in replenishing it. Quickly a conference was called by him to write a new organic law, known as Constitutional Pact, to be promulgated on May 1, 1914. The conference was attended by many people handpicked by Yuan and the law it enacted was to displace the constitution which was drafted by the now defunct parliament and which envisaged a weak president with a responsible cabinet.[29] The new document provided a presidential system. Yuan had himself chosen president for life. It was a prelude to monarchism. "Despite Yuan's modest protest, a national convention met in Beijing on November 1, 1915 and by unanimous ballot, all the 1,834 members petitioned Yuan to take the throne."[30] The next month saw Yuan burn midnight oil in preparing his heavenly mandate by way of issuing more orders, creating peerage, laying out rites and searching for a dynastic title. From 1911 to the end of 1915, foreign powers shifted their support from the revolutionaries to Yuan, but republicanism not monarchism found strong favor with the broad masses of the country. On January 1, 1916, he was to formally proclaim a Hong Xian dynasty for him and his family.[31]

During 1915, Yuan had already become a target of public opprobrium in connection with his dealing with the Nipponese. Taking advantage of the preoccupation of the great powers with the war in Europe, they prepared in January, 1915 the famous 21 Demands for Yuan's initials. If all of them were acceded to, China would have become a colony of Japan. During the discussion consequent on the transmittal of the Demands, the only means Yuan had was to divulge them to the world in the hope of arousing the indignation of the great powers. It is believed that considerable pressure was brought by England on Japan, her ally at that time.[32] As a result, Tokyo consented to modify some of its conditions and to defer temporarily the fifth batch of the Demands which was the severest of them all. In view of China's

[27] John A. Harrison, op. cit., p. 103.

[28] Elizabeth Seeger, The Pageant of Chinese History, 3rd ed., New York: Longmans, Green, 1947, p. 367.

[29] Franz Schurmann and Orville Schell, Republican China, New York: Vintage Books, 1967, pp. 20-22. The second author is sometimes spelled Orvill Schelle.

[30] John A. Harrison, op. cit., p. 104.

[31] Kenneth Scott Latourette, The Chinese, Their History and Culture, 2nd Ed., New York: Macmillan, 1941, vol. 1, pp. 425-430.

[32] Yun J. Li. The Ageless Chinese, a History, 2nd ed., New York: Charles Scribner's, 1978, pp. 419-426.

weakness and the real threat of Tokyo's military power, the exchanges of notes on May 9, 1915 between China and Japan were probably as good as could be anticipated. Yet the friends of republicanism lost no time to turn all this into grits of their mill. Yuan's own finance minister, a celebrated historian, Liang Qichao resigned from his post. As soon as he reached the foreign district of Shanghai, he launched a scathing attack on the emperor-to-be.

A number of Guomindang leaders met in the Philippines upon the call of Hu Hanmin, to determine their plan of action. They sent members to the provinces in the south on an anti-Yuan crusade. Li Liejun was dispatched to Yunnan. From Japan, Cai O made his way to the same province. On December 25, Tang Jiyao, Cai O and other Yunnan generals declared that province independent and formed a Nation-Protection Army (hu guo jun). Leading a division of armed soldiers, Cai O moved to Sichuan. Two other divisions advanced against Hunan and Guangxi provinces. On March 15, Lu Yongting and fellow-officers of Guangxi did the same. Faced by this situation, Yuan called upon General Xu Shichang, Duan Qirui and Feng Guozhang for succor. However, Feng urged him to abandon the ambition, Xu wanted him to make a compromise with the Yunnan group, and Duan did not wish to do anything to assist the desperate Yuan. Finding himself deserted on all sides, he postponed the ceremony of investure and on December 22, formally decreed the end of the Hong Xian plan. In distress he died on June 16, 1916.[33]

Warlords

In the thirteen years (1912-1926), China had more than 300 political parties, 45 cabinets, 19 prime ministers, 10 presidents, 7 constitutions, and 5 parliaments.[34] What a democratic show! From November 1, 1924 to April 14, 1926, Duan Qirui held the title of interim chief executive. During May 1926 - April 1927 that country had no president, but only a cabinet. This labyrinth of affairs has been narrated in hundreds of books. In a text of ours, a cursory survey would suffice.

With the demise of Yuan there broke completely the flimsy linkage between Beijing and the provinces. The office of the Chef d'état was occupied by military men lacking effective control on the resources of even Hebei province wherein the nation's capital was situated. The parliament, set up soon after the 1911 coup and made up of civilians and members of Tong Meng Hui, wielded no power. It had no say, for example, in the formation of the cabinet. The provincial heads, now called Dudus, sought at once to exact from the masses what they needed to arm themselves. They behaved like feudal lords, having sovereign domain and bureaucracy as well as the strongest asset: Troops.[35] The task of keeping their realms led them to make

[33] Levy Roger, La Chine, Paris: Presses Universitaires de France, 1964, pp. 34-36.

[34] Zhong yang ribao, October 16, 1982, p. 1.

[35] Henry McAleavy, The Modern History of China, New York: Praeger, 1967, pp. 201-216.

alignments only to break up at the slightest suspicion. The ploy of the warriors now waxed into a subtle check-and-balance between them, sometimes taking the form of the north versus the south. Intra-regional combat also erupted from time to time. However, the control of Beijing became the biggest of all the prizes. Once the city fell into one's lap, he could attract foreign loans in the name of a "central government" of China. Also accruing to him was the lucre of the customs revenue which was the second best service (the first being post-office) throughout the country thanks to the English who acquired that right by an agreement signed with the Manzhou dynasty on July 25, 1854.[36] No wonder the warlords were always after Beijing either by intrigue or by straight conquest. However, geographically, it was out of reach of the southern soldiers.[37]

The vice-president, Li Yuanhong, was a friend of parliamentarism. Upon Yuan's death, he became president and Duan Qirui was named prime minister by him. Duan was Yuan's follower, but deserted him during the monarchical move. As the draft constitution envisaged a titular president, actual authority went to the prime minister. This setup was designed to avoid the conflict between the president and the parliament, a conflict which characterized the Yuan regime. There developed a fresh strife, however, over the appointment of provincial rulers, the aforesaid Dudus. The M.P.'s wanted them elected, but the military men liked to see them named by the central government. Alas! the Dudus were neither elected nor named. They appointed themselves.[38]

Down south, military hierarchs were well entrenched in such provinces as Yunnan, Guizhou, Guangxi, Guangdong, Sichuan and Hunan. Each had his territorial integrity and each amassed wealth from taxation. Among them, strange enough, there was not much fighting. All these provinces were not to be controlled by a central authority until the advent of the communists in 1949. Even the lethal threat of Japan was not enough to awake the warlords. In 1916 two alliances developed among them, the Zhili and Anfu. The first had Feng Guozhang as the principal figure and the second came under Duan Qirui. Although both were Yuan Shikai's lieutenants, they ran into armed collision after his death. Yet they shared the same abhorrence of parties and parliamentary democracy. The enmity between parliament and the military came into the open in early 1917 over the declaration of war against Germany. There was a general agreement on it but the declaration by the prime minister without parliamentary approval brought up a call for his resignation. President Li Yuanhong sided with the parliament. During this conflict, the

36 Franz H. Michael and George E. Taylor, *The Far East in the Modern World*, rev. ed., New York: Holt, Rinehart and Winston, 1964, p. 136.

37 Paul Linebarger, Djang Chu and Adath W. Burks, *Far Eastern Governments and Politics*, Toronto: Van Nostrand, 1954, pp. 132-144.

38 C.P. Fitzgerald, *The Birth of Communist China*, New York: Praeger, 1966, p. 43, 50-53.

soldiers of the provinces formed a common front. A conference of these soldiers from the north and central regions were held in Xuzhou (Jiangsu province). It resolved to oppose the parliament. Consequently, Duan Qirui was dismissed.[39] This action against Duan went too far. It irked some governors. They held a meeting in Tianjin and decided to set up a counter-government. A preparation was meanwhile made for an armed march on Beijing. At this juncture, the president asked help from general Zhang Xun. After taking control of the city, he moved to impose a rule of his own. The parliament was forthwith dissolved by him. Being a monarchist, Zhang Xun brought back the abdicated emperor Henry Pu Yi in an attempt to restore the Manzhou dynasty. Zhang's action was undeniably anachronistic. It met stout resistance not only of the parliamentarians but the provinces. A league of warlords thereupon launched an expedition to drive out Zhang and to resuscitate the republic. Beijing was retaken and the warlords suspended the functioning of the parliamentary leaders. Feng Guozhang, the vice-president, now replaced Li Yuanhong as president and Duan Qirui was reinstalled as prime minister. Such a coalition was not to endure. In 1918 the followers of Duan who formed the so-called Anfu Club chased their opponents out of Beijing and put on the president's chair a man of their own, General Xu Shichang.[40]

The Anfu leadership in Beijing survived many a machination until 1920. In that year two generals who had built up mighty regional bases rose to challenge it. One was Zhang Zuolin of Manchuria and the other Cao Kun of central China. The two joined forces to expel the Duan Qirui coterie from Beijing, but the winners came to fight each other. An erstwhile lieutenant of Cao Kun, Wu Peifu, became a key man in the capital. Wu had meanwhile to retreat when he was deserted in the war with Zhang Zuolin by one of his own officers, Feng Yuxiang.[41] For a time, the conflict in north China focused on the trio: Zhang Zuolin in the northeast, Wu Peifu in the Yangzi valley, Feng Yuxiang in the northwest. They all had foreign support. Zhang was paid by the Japanese, as Feng by the Russian and Wu by the English, American and French governments. None of them was liked by the masses. As of mid-1924, the Balkanization of China was as follows:[42]

Beijing area . . . . Cao Kun, Wu Peifu
Manchuria . . . . Zhang Zuolin
Shanxi . . . . Yan Xieshan
Zhejiang . . . . Lu Yongxiang
Fujian . . . . Zhou Yinren
East Guangdong . . . . Chen Junming

[39] R.R.C. de Crespigny, China in this Century, New York: St. Martin's Press, 1975, pp. 25-28.

[40] A. Lozovskii, Revoliutsiya i kontrrevoliutsiya v Kitae, Moskva: Moskovskii rabochii, 1927, pp. 46-52.

[41] Georges Dubarbier, La Chine du XXⁿ siècle des Mandchous à Mao, Paris: Payot, 1965, pp. 39-43.

[42] O. Edmund Clubb, 20th Century China, 2nd ed., New York: Columbia University Press, 1972, p. 126.

Guangdong........................Sun's revolutionaries
Guangxi............Lu Yongting, Shen Hongying, Li Zongren
Hunan.....................................Zhao Hengti
Yunnan, Guizhou............................Tang Jiyao
Sichuan.....Yang sheng, Liu Zunhou, Liu Xiang, Li Zhengshan
Gangsu....................................Lu Hongdao
Xinjiang..................................Yang Zengxin
Tibet.................................13th Dalai Lama
Menggu.....................................Khutukhtu

Wu Peifu gave support to the Beijing regime because it was run by his friends and because he dreamt of uniting all China. Zhang Zuolin dreamt the same way and the two became deadly enemies in 1922.

Wu had beaten Zhang near Beijing and Zhang was ready to retaliate. Battle was joined in 1924. Feng Yuxiang, who served under Wu, betrayed him by seizing Beijing and became the master there. Caught between the forces of Zhang and Feng, Wu had to evacuate by sea from Tianjin. The victors, Zhang and Feng, appointed their man as president. While Wu was busy with regrouping his troops in the Yangzi valley, they quarreled. Zhang withdrew to Shenyang and declaring his renewed friendship with Wu, began a campaign to drive out Feng from Beijing.[43]

Having obtained assistance from Russia in the manner of military advisors and equipment, Feng decided to retire for the time being. He took a trip to Moscow. His successors, Zhang Zhijiang and Lu Zhongling, later had to get out of the Beijing-Tianjin area and shift to Neimenggu. Duan Qirui returned to Beijing as chief executive by the toleration of Zhang Zuolin and soon Feng Yuxiang. Duan wielded no power, having compromised himself with his patrons. On April 20, 1926, he quit politics to study Buddhism.[44] The warlords, in altercation among themselves, did not see the danger rising in the south, the national revolutionaries.[45] If they saw, they would have buried their hatchet and pooled together their forces, 500,000 strong, to destroy the Guomindang army numbering less than one fifth of theirs.[46] To this southern front we now turn.

Sun Yat-sen at the south pole

Sun yielded the presidency to Yuan Shikai on February 12, 1912. It was generally understood that only the latter man possessed the power to dispose of the Manzhou. The presidential office was in effect lent to Sun before that time. After he withdrew from active politics, he acquired a government grant, immersing himself in a study and

[43] Wolfram Eberbard, A History of China, 2nd ed., Berkeley: University of California Press, 1960, p. 609.

[44] O. Edmund Clubb, op. cit., p. 134.

[45] Lucien Bodard, La Chine de Tseu Hi à Mao, Paris: Hallmard, 1968, pp. 131-144.

[46] O. Edmund Clubb, op. cit., p. 133.

research of China's industrialization, railway construction and modernization of port facilities. Not competent in these matters, he produced several pamphlets on this or that project; they are as ambitious as naive. As related in the preceding chapter, the parliament in Beijing was dominated by Guomindang people. In 1914, Yuan Shikai outlawed their activity. At once Song Jiaoren reorganized them under the official title of Guomindang. To nip the trouble in the bud, Yuan had Song assassinated.[47] Yuan's own death in 1916 breathed some measure of life in parliamentarism. Gradually the Guomindang M.P.'s formed a solid opposition to whomever the warlords placed on the presidential chair. This parliament-versus-president in Beijing did not last long. An overwhelming majority of such M.P.'s came from the south, as did Sun Yat-sen himself, and the dominance of the warlords in the north aroused in them a sense of southness. This regional identity, plus the anti-north feeling of the military rulers of southern provinces engendered an atmosphere of unity. Both rulers and M.P.'s there saw the vital necessity of an alignment. Thus a Guangzhou regime articulating a strong force rapidly took shape and the revolutionary symbol of Sun Yat-sen was found extremely helpful.[48]

Having been once exiled to Japan by Yuan Shikai, Sun Yat-sen shuttled, as it were, between Japan and the city of Shanghai for several years working at first for the ouster of Yuan and, after his demise, the reinvigoration of his own machinery. In 1917, as said before, the warlords disbanded the parliament in Beijing and this act was denounced by the leaders of the south. Sun came to Guangzhou in July that year with the intent of establishing there the headquarters of a revolutionary regime. The following month he convened a rump parliament made up of southern M.P.'s and some northerners. They set up in September the Military Government of China, headed by Sun with the title Generalissimo. Tang Jiyao of Yunnan was made one of Sun's two deputies, the other being Lu Yongting who was the strongman of Guangxi and subsequently Guangdong. Both individuals rendered no more than superficial obeisance to Sun. In January 1918, the Guangzhou parliament repudiated Beijing and officially declared itself the Government of China. The country thus was, by and large, polarized. Each claimed, as it were, the heavenly mandate. At that time, all foreign nations which had maintained diplomatic relation with China, recognized Beijing, not Guangzhou. Soon, however, Russia was to recognize both (see below).

Lu Yongting was not to stand below Sun. In reality, the latter's preeminence in the Military Government was more apparent than real. Without troops of his own, Sun was definitely inferior to the provincial governors. Yet he was said to behave like an autocrat and irritated many. In May 1918, the Government underwent a reorganization. Sun was outmaneuvered, being replaced as Generalissimo by a collective

[47] Lin Yi, *A Short History of China, 1840-1919*, Beijing: Foreign Languages Press, 1963, pp. 90-97.

[48] G. Efimov, *Ocherki po novoi i noveishei istorii kitae*, 2nd ed., Moskva: Izd-vo polit. lit-ry, 1951, pp. 245-257.

of seven Directors-General. Among them Sun was only one, not even primus inter pares. Tang Shaoyi and Wu Tingfang, his wholehearted supporters, were also included. The other four were army commanders: Tang Jiyao, Lu Yongting, Zeng Zhongxuan, Chen Junming. Zeng was named chairman. After the inauguration of this body, Sun left for Japan, but soon came back. The warlords with whom Sun was aligning became increasingly worried about the erosion of their own financial power as Sun's machinery seized the salt monopoly for itself. They drove him out of Guangdong in December 1919.[49] However, Sun's friend Chen Junming quickly captured Guangdong in a fight and asked him to return from Shanghai. He did, and was elected president of the "republic." Yet his effort to organize a regime in Guangzhou was doomed to failure because he still could not command the loyalty of the Guangdong armies, even though those of other provinces backed him up. Before long he ran into difficulty with Chen Junming over his demand that Chen's military formations be placed under civilian authority.[50] Sun's heavy taxation also alienated Guangzhou business circles. Not unexpectedly, Sun was driven out of Guangdong once more in June 1922. Fortunately for him, a war broke out between Guangdong on the one side and Guangxi and Yunnan on the other, which ended in the driving out of Chen from Guangdong. Now the victorious Yunnan and Guangxi generals wired Sun to come back. He did in 1923. From then on, Sun abandoned the title of president and re-capped himself as commander-in-chief. Thanks to the Yunnan troops, he came to dominate Guangdong. The actual administration, however, was operated by a loyal and capable police chief, Wu Techeng. Beginning in 1923, Sun proceeded to build up soldiery of his own and to retool the party organization with the help of the Russians.

The Northern Expedition

A little ahead of the warlords, Sun solicited the assistance of foreign powers (in his case, Japan). This he began as early as 1913 while an exile in that country.[51] The following year, in his campaign to oust Yuan Shikai he sought desperately the aid from that quarter. In two letters, one addressing Prime Minister Okuma and another the head of the political bureau of the Japanese foreign ministry, he offered far-reaching concessions at the expense of China's sovereignty. Although the concessions were nothing more than a promissory note, made contingent on the Guomindang's coming to power, it intimates how far Sun was willing to go in order to win out in the civil strife. There was to be all sorts of cooperation between Japan and China.

[49] Heng Sheng Zhu Ren, *Chen Junming pan guo shi*, Shamen: Xinming yin shua suo, 1924, *passim*.

[50] *Bei fa jian shi*, Taibei: Guo fang bu shi zheng ju, 1967, vol. 1, p. 27.

[51] Marium B. Janse, *The Japanese and Sun Yat-sen*, Cambridge: Harvard University Press, 1954, cited in Michael and Taylor, *op. cit.*, p. 224.

The former country was to be given financial and military advantage over other foreign states in China. Sun's readiness to use economic enticement to get outside succor was revealed in similar negotiations with other countries as well. Nothing, however, came out of all this, because Sun was not seen as a man able to take power. It is understandable that he was disappointed with the Western democracies and with the Japanese. In 1922, however, an unsolicited regime extended a hand to him: Soviet Russia. This new support, plus southern warlords inviting him to Gungzhou to be the president of China, brought a gleam of hope for his national revolution.

Lenin dispatched Adolf Ioffe to Beijing in 1922 to obtain some rights and privileges from a harassed government.[52] Ioffe demanded, on behalf of Lenin, the permission of stationing of Russian troops in Urga until Manchuria was cleared up of the anti-Soviet Japanese and White Guard units, the grant to Russia of more rights in the Chinese Eastern Railway and the recognition by Beijing of all Soviet interests in China.[53] Beijing refused. Immediately Lenin sent Ioffe to see Sun Yat-sen who he thought was reasonable enough to cooperate.

Although having a few nice words for socialism in his writings, Sun was no lover of communism which he frankly and repeatedly said did not suit China. However, in a time of need, he welcomed the Soviet emissary. In July 1922, Ioffe and Sun had a rendezvous in Shanghai and another in Guangzhou.[54] The Russian confided his government's goodwill toward Sun. The leadership of the peasants' and workers' state was said to be ready coming to his help in the buildup of a unified, democratic and progressive system. The followers of Sun were "flattered" as representatives of the masses. With Moscow's enthusiastic aid, believed they, the national interests of China would be furthered and imperialists evicted. A joint communique of Sun and Ioffe (January 26, 1923) embodied these aspirations, promising that Soviet advisors and materiel would be coming to Guangzhou to help strengthen the Guomindang and its armed forces. Meanwhile, a team was sent by Sun to Russia. It was led by no less a figure than Jiang Jieshi who was to get acquainted with the proletarian regime, the "friend in need" of the Guangzhou Republic. A nucleus of Soviet formation, technically speaking Comintern agents, led by Michael Borodin and Vasily Blucher (known as General Galen by the Chinese) arrived at Guangzhou. They put themselves at the disposal of the national revolutionaries.[55] From now, Sun mouthed the Russian communists' slogans of "down with the imperialists," "land to the peasants," and "nationalization of big enterprises" (Russia's NEP left small enterprises private). However, he stopped short of "class war." This did not interest him.

[52] Jiang Yunzheng, *Baoloting yu wu han zheng chuan*, Taibei: Zhong guo xue shu zhu zuo wei yuan hui, 1963, pp. 1-23.

[53] John A. Harrison, *op. cit.*, p. 128.

[54] Xu Langxuan, *Zhong guo jin dai shi*, Taibei: Zheng zhong shu ju, 1974, pp. 128-131.

[55] John A. Harrison, *op. cit.*, p. 219.

Borodin and company set out to develop the Guangzhou regime into a disciplined and efficient force able to do revolutionary battle against the northern warlords and to administer the provinces once snatched from them. For this purpose, the famous Huangpu Academy was instituted.[56] Its cadres were to shoulder the military and civilian responsibility. No less important to the southerners was the arms assistance which kept flowing into Guangzhou harbor from the Soviet Far East. Without this, the Guangzhou troops, only one fifth of those of the warlords, could not carry on an offensive for any length of time. When all this was taking place in the southern city, the military leaders up in the north were fully aware of it. They themselves invited Sun to Beijing for a negotiated solution of the unification problem. It was hoped that some *modus vivendi* might be reached to avert a bloody showdown. On his part, Sun was very impatient with the tempo things were moving in Guangzhou. In the meantime, he needed medical treatment which was only available at the foreign, that is, the hated imperialists' hospitals, in Beijing. While there he died of cancer on March 12, 1925. With his departing from the scene, the attempted compromise did not materialize.[57]

Borodin accompanied Sun to the north incognito. There he met Feng Yuxiang, trying to enlist his backing of the expedition to be launched from Guangzhou. It is reported that Feng, better known as Christian General, talked of humanism but not revolutionary violence to the Russian, but Borodin succeeded finally in changing his mind. Feng showed his great admiration for the Soviet state. Later he accepted an invitation to visit it, as we mentioned before.[58]

Sun's death left the revolutionary camp in disarray. The split in it, already latent while he was still alive, now surfaced. Besides the communists who were told by the Comintern to ally with the Guomindang, there were three groupings each standing for a different outlook and policy. On the Guomindang left was the Wang Jingwei coterie. They were pro-Soviet.[59] Wang had nothing but contempt for other factions in the Guomindang, priding himself as the rightful heir of the just-deceased Sun. Years later during the Sino-Japanese war he headed a puppet regime in Nanjing.

At the center stood a less ideological team headed by Jiang Jieshi. It had broad appeal to the rank and file of the party and was greatly advantaged by being able to control the majority of the cadres of the above-said Academy. The right wing comprised such notables as Hu Hanmin. It was their purpose to unite China on an anti-communist program discussed at West Hill of Beijing on November 18-20, 1925. This wing goes down in history as the West Hill Clique.[60] Hu Hanmin

[56] Xie Qijia, Jian Bin, *Zhong guo ge ming jian guo shi*, Taibei: Hua xin wen hua ji ye zhong xin, 1977, pp. 39ff.

[57] Bei Hua, comp., *Zhong guo ge ming shi*, Shanghai: Guangming shu ju, 1925, pp. 191-192.

[58] John A. Harrison, *op. cit.*, p. 108.

[59] N.I. Konchits, *Kitaiskie dnevniki 1925-1926 gg.*, Moskva: Izd-vo polit. lit-ry, 1969, p. 5.

[60] *Xin hua ci dian*, p. 900, col. 1.

and other supporters of his were put under arrest by Jiang Jieshi. He later withdrew from politics, lived in Hong Kong and died there in 1937. During the immediate post-Sun uncertainty, Jiang Jieshi took the decisive step of assuming the military command. He was resolved that the goal of unification set by Sun was to be achieved sooner rather than later. Suspect of the left-wingers, he authorized the raids of their quarters on March 20, 1926.[61] All Soviet advisors were detained. In the meantime, Wang Jingwei who thought that the army led by Jiang ought to be subordinate to civilian control, resigned in protest from the government. Soon he rejoined it after a rapprochement with Jiang Jieshi. In April 1926, the latter decided that the Russian alignment was to continue.[62] He had the Soviet advisors released and together with them was actively planning for the expedition.

The northern campaign started out from Guangzhou on July 9, 1926, with eight corps totalling about 100,000 men.[63] They were more confident than the Soviets who had counseled against it in light of the half a million enemy troops posed toward them. However, Jiang Jieshi believed that the national revolution must broaden its base in order to gain an upper hand over the rivals. He was also heartened by the cooperation of Feng Yuxiang who was in control of Henan and Shaanxi.[64] Two corps spearheaded north and aimed at Wuhan. They took it in October 1926. Another corps led by Jiang Jieshi himself moved northeast. According to the plan, they were to take Shanghai in December. Although Jiang had the larger of the two columns, the enemy was stronger. It was not until March 1927 that his forces reached Shanghai.

The headquarters of the Guangzhou government moved to Wuhan in January 1927. The Soviets were with this column and it was they who actually developed the operation strategy. Now the Wuhan regime, deeming itself the government of China, called a meeting of the Central Executive Committee of the Guomindang and wired Jiang Jieshi to attend. This he refused because he considered his as the main force and therefore he was invested with the legitimacy to represent the national revolution. Upon his decline, the Wuhan leadership issued an order to relieve him of his chairmanship of the party.[65] He was even demoted by Wuhan on February 7 from Generalissimo to the commander of the First Army Corps. Now "Commander" Jiang and Feng (commander of the Second Army Corps) were instructed by Wuhan to head for Beijing. All the decrees of Wuhan were ignored by Jiang Jieshi who, instead, called for a party

[61] A.I. Kartunova i V.K. Bliukher v Kitae, Moskva: Izd-vo polit. lit-ry, 1970, p. 44.

[62] Bei fa zhan shi, vol. 1, pp. 29-30.

[63] M.F. Iur'ev, "Severnyi pokhod, 1926-1927," Bol'shaya sovetskaya entsiklopediya, Moskva: Gosudarstvennoe nauchnoe izdatel'stvo "bol'shaya sovetskaya entsiklopediya," 1949-1958, vol. 28 (1955), p. 136.

[64] A.I. Cherepanov, Severnyi pokhod natsional'no-revoliutsionnoi armii Kitaya, zapiski voennogo sovetnika, Moskva: Izd-vo polit. lit-ry, 1968, p. 10.

[65] Ibid.

congress in Nanjing which had been taken by his troops on March 24, 1927.[66] The Wuhan Guomindang was honeycombed with communists and there were leftist leaders like Sun Fo and Song Qingling, son and widow of Sun Yat-sen respectively. Displaying profound anticommunism and detestation of the Guomindang deviators in Wuhan, Jiang Jieshi embarked on a purge of the communists in the area under his control. At this time (1927) there were three governments at: Beijing, Wuhan and Nanjing. The Soviet Union had relations with them all. To Jiang's troops in Shanghai, it shipped arms from Vladivostok. When these troops were approaching that Chinese city in April, the Soviet supplies were seized by the communist-dominated trade unions.[67] Upon their refusal to hand them over to him, Jiang ordered his men to search and seize them. In the process, a clash erupted and casualties were sustained on both sides. Later the communists made a great noise and charged Jiang with the so-called Shanghai massacre.

Although communist-infiltrated, the Wuhan regime was far from being communistic.[68] The principal leaders were, on the contrary, afraid of the Reds' takeover. Their worry was not a fancied one. Stalin ordered, in late May 1927, his agents in Wuhan to stage a coup and to place communists in power. Borodin felt the order was not feasible. M.N. Roy (whose works we cited), a Comintern man from India and operating in Wuhan, had seen the order. He suspected that Borodin was dragging his feet.[69] Meanwhile, this Russian revealed Stalin's instruction to Eugene Chen, foreign minister of the Wuhan government but unable to speak Chinese because he was born in Trinidad. He immediately sensed Russia's tricks. The Wuhan leadership was shaken to its foundation by the publication of the Moscow behest. As a result, Wang Jingwei expelled all the Soviet advisors.[70] The entire episode now turned to be Jiang Jieshi's propaganda ammunition, because he already declared war on the leftists and cleansed his area of them. Perhaps more importantly, the just described event shows how close the Wuhan and Nanjing politicians were in their views on the issue of alliance with the communists and on Stalin's wish to make China a Soviet Union satellite. There still remained the problem of unification of China after the setback of the leftist force in Wuhan, in Nanjing and in Beijing. It was exactly at this time (April 1927) that the government in the last-named city ordered the arrest of communists and the search of the Soviet consulate.[71]

[66] John A. Harrison, op. cit., p. 138.

[67] A.A. Martinov, "Kitaya, istoricheskii ocherk," Bol'shaya sovetakaya entsiklopediya, 3rd ed., vol. 12 (1973), cols., 627-630.

[68] P. Mifa, "Kitai, istoricheskii ocherk," Ibid., 1st ed., vol. 22 (1936), cols. 599-617.

[69] V. Rait, "Borodin, Gruzenberg Mikhail Markovich," Ibid., 1st ed., vol. 7 (1927), col. 182.

[70] Chen' Bo-da, Chan Kai-shi, vrag kitaiskogo narod, per. s kitaisk., Moskva: Izd-vo inos. lit-ry, 1950, p. 15.

[71] "Borodin, Gruzenberg Mikhail Markovich," Bol'shaya sovetskaya entsiklopediya, 3rd ed., vol. 3 (1970), cols. 1720-1721.

To isolate Wuhan, Jiang struck an alliance with Wu Peifu in May 1927. Wuhan had two strong corps, the fourth and the eighth. Besides, it controlled the Hanyang arsenal. More significant yet, it had an ally in Feng Yuxiang. This man held the balance between Wuhan and Nanjing. Jiang was approaching him, while the communists did likewise.[72] The Reds stated to him that the crisis was serious for him and that in return for the support derived from the Soviets, he must take an anti-Jiang stand. If he did not, the communists would fail. Despite this plea, Feng sided with Jiang, because the latter gave him a more concrete price: War Minister in the Nanjing government. This situation led to the dissolution of the Wuhan regime whose leader, Wang Jingwei, had already been discredited by the Comintern conspiracy. The last leg of the northern march was to drive Zhang Zuolin out of Beijing. As the revolutionary forces moved north, Zhang abandoned the city for his stronghold, Manchuria, but the Japanese military leaders barred the said forces from going further when they reached Shandong. Meanwhile, they blew up Zhang Zuolin's train and killed him. Manchuria, in the mind of the Nipponese, was to be theirs.[73] On the surface, China was rid of the warlords, but there was to be no unification.

A miserable republic

Only externally did Cathay have a central government from 1927 to the end of the Sino-Japanese war in 1945. The government established in Nanjing by Jiang Jieshi rapidly acquired diplomatic recognition by major Western powers. Yet, the country was badly split. With the disappearance of the warlords who dominated in the north and east during 1916-1927, there set in a new type of feudal division. The Nanjing regime was tolerated rather than obeyed as a superpower. Being a nominal government of China, the regime found itself in an extremely unenviable situation. For one thing, it could not gain full and enthusiastic support of the provinces not under its authority. For another, it was manhandled by the Japanese who made its life miserable, one not worth living. Had the Nanjing authority traversed a more placid era, it could have survived. Even during these turbulent years, that is, prior to the all-out assault by Nippon in 1937, it had made by no means negligible progress in construction and economic development.[74] The ultimate failure of Guomindang cannot by any stretch of imagination be attributed to the fantastic communism, as supposed by scholars of sinistral proclivity.

China could be regarded, at the most, as a confederation. The government in Nanjing enjoyed some advantage, for it not only had the foreign recognition, but, more importantly, broader domain. Directly

72 Victor A. Yakhonotoff, The Chinese Soviets, New York: Coward-McCann, 1934, pp. 74ff.

73 M.S. Kapitsa, KNR: tri desyatileya, tri politiki, Moskva: Izd-vo polit. lit-ry, 1979, p. 6.

74 Chao-chu Wu, The nationalist program for China, New Haven: Yale University Press, 1929, pp. 34ff.

under Jiang were four provinces (Zhejiang, Jiangsu, Anhui, Jiangxi) on the lower Yangzi, which is the most desirable part of the entire country. Jiang Jieshi's rivals had one province each, with the exception of the northeast where Zhang Xueliang ruled three provinces. In the true sense of the word, the provinces were medieval fiefs.[75] In the Northern Expedition, the military leaders of several southwest provinces sent no troops to join it. When Jiang's forces marched out of Guangzhou, these leaders shouted out to him a sort of moral support. Jiang, on his part, found it cheap or expedient to honor them by nominally appointing them Commanders-in-Chief of such and such army corps of the *Guomin ge ming jun* (National Revolutionary army), or governors of such and such provinces of the Chinese Republic. These titles were attractive and prestigeous and the warlords undoubtedly loved them. Amidst the martial excitement, Jiang thought exclusively of the warlords before him, but forgot those behind. To the north and northwest, his troops never went. There the situation remained what it was before 1927, as did the situation in the southwest. China was the same old divided nation.[76] The Nanjing regime was left to handle foreign affairs, but the provinces had undisputed autonomy. A few matters were made uniform throughout the country, with the tolerance of the provinces. For example, the governor was renamed chairman of provincial government, no more Dudu or Tujun. Under this government there were four bureaucratic commissions. Identity also prevailed in the educational system, judicial structure and local functionaries. Beyond these matters in which the warlords took no interest (because they were rather dull), the central power could not go. Some provinces, Sichuan for one, even issued their own currency and levied numerous categories of tax, remitting no single penny to Nanjing. Jiang Jieshi and the provincial bosses had in essence initialed a pact of non-interference.

In almost every year, Nanjing experienced some trouble with the provinces. The year 1929 saw a revolt by Li Zongren in Guangxi, and a second one by Tang Shengzhi in Hunan. Feng Yuxiang joined forces with Yan Xishan in a rebellion during 1931. The Guangdong generals declared their independence in the meantime. Two years later, the Nineteenth Route Army raised their flag of independence in Fukian. In 1935, before Japan's final and full invasion of China the leaders of Guangdong and Guangxi once more openly defied Nanjing. All this served very well to dramatize the weakness of the National Government of China. More fatal, however, was the Japanese threat which, without an iota of doubt, was encouraged by the internal cleavage.

The warlord Zhang Zuolin of Manchuria, as mentioned above, was killed by the Japanese in 1928. Although they financed him for all his activities, he was too fickle for them to trust. In fact, Japan had

---

[75] Michael and Taylor, *op. cit.*, p. 405; John A. Harrison, *op. cit.*, p. 157.

[76] P. Mifa, "Kitai, burzhuazno-pomeshchichie politicheskie partii i militaristicheskie kliki v kitae posle 1927," *Bol'shaya sovetskaya entsiklopediya*, 1st ed., vol. 22 (1936), cols. 703-709.

already earmarked Manchuria as hers and from there she was to swallow the whole of China.[77] This scheme is evidenced by the Japanese army's blocking in Shandong province of the Chinese troops from moving north. Manchuria was seized by Japan following an engineered incident of September 18, 1931 in Shenyang. The Nipponese easily expelled the hordes of Zhang Xueliang who had three years before succeeded, à la feudalism, his father as the ruler there. Almost at once a scheme was hatched by the Japanese to detach from China proper five provinces south of the Great Wall.[78] Gone was Rehe province in 1933. Hebei province came next in 1935. Eastern Neimeng and Chahaer were made "autonomous regions" under Japanese influence. The local warlords, behaving with contumely toward Nanjing, showed only white feathers in front of the Japanese arms. Out of revenge against the killing of his father, but not for the affection of Jiang Jieshi, Zhang Xueliang in 1928 terminated his domain's independence and declared his submission to the National Government in Nanjing.[79] He knew too well that the days of his domain were numbered. He would perhaps like to see that it was Jiang Jieshi, not he, who lost it. The other bosses in north China, likewise, could defy Jiang arrogantly, but were meek in their encounter with Japan.

Finding themselves helpless in the face of Japan, they had to accept Nanjing as their spokesman. "To negotiate with the Nipponese is such a frustrating and annoying affair! Let Nanjing have it," they must have said to themselves. On its side, Tokyo would not recognize the provincial powers as able to represent the Chinese Republic. All treaties between Japan and China were signed by the plenipotentiaries of Nanjing.[80] Tokyo, after all, wanted to have a legitimate entity, the Central Government, to carry out the responsibility of international agreements. In all probability, the provincial leaders felt that all was lost and that it was pointless to deny the "National" government the right to stand out on their behalf in an apparently hopeless situation. There is hardly on their part a sense of patriotism or obedience to Jiang Jieshi.

The most minatory and, as events were to prove, the deadliest foe of the Nanjing regime was the communist force.[81] In the next two chapters, we shall study it in more detail, but here we must relate that regime's difficulty with it at the early stage. The resources of Nanjing, very limited at any rate, had to be budgeted for the defense

[77] B.K. Pashkov, R.V. Vatkin i A.A. Martynov, "Dunbei, istoricheskii ocherk," Bol'shaya sovetskaya entsiklopediya, 2nd ed., vol. 15 (1952), pp. 292-295 at 294; "Chzhan Tszo-lin," Ibid., 2nd ed., vol. 47 (1952), p. 349, col. 1.

[78] Jean Escarra, China Then and Now, Beijing: Henri Vetch, 1940, pp. 221-227.

[79] "Chzhan Sui'elyan," Bol'shaya sovetskaya entsiklopediya, 2nd ed., vol. 44 (1957), p. 348, col. 1; also same title, 3rd ed., vol. 29 (1978), col. 532.

[80] L.A. Lyall, China, London: Ernest Benn, 1934, pp. 229ff.

[81] Stuart Gelder, The Chinese Communists, London: Victor Gollancz, 1946, pp. xi-xiii.

ᴀ from Japan which was to come sooner or later, but before that happened, it thought it essential to excise the communist tumor. To do this, Jiang, in league with provincial leaders, made a series of armed campaigns. The communists took full advantage of these leaders' lack of cooperation in the matter by operating on the borderlines.[82] There was no hot pursuit of them by the troops of one province for fear of violating the territorial sovereignty of another. The communists found it easy therefore to escape and to build up their nest. However, when their forces became strong, they concentrated here and there, first in Jiangxi and then in Hunan. In the former province, a Soviet regime was organized as early as 1929. At the height of their power, they controlled 15 million people in 50 counties. Of these, 30 in Jiangxi and 20 in Hunan.[83] On November 7, 1931 (the anniversary of the Bolshevik Revolution) the first Congress of Soviets was called at Ruijin which was made the capital of the Chinese Soviet Republic. The Congress enacted a constitution and instituted a government. From a safe distance and with full irresponsibility, it even declared war on Japan.[84]

Headed by Mao Zedong, the Jiangxi Soviet had all the trappings of a state. It was a replica of the USSR. There was the fiction of the dictatorship of the proletariat which the constitution proclaims. Besides armed forces, the regime had a judiciary, a chain of administrative command, a post system and last but not least, a mint and a machine to collect revenues.[85] In order to equalize the land possession, an agricultural reform granted land to poor peasantry. There was no outright confiscation. Also not implemented was such typical deal of the communists as collectivization of farming. There seems to be no question that some segment of the populace felt obliged to the Reds for the improvement of their lot. After all, there was no bloody struggle between the classes, another typical deal of theirs. Against this moderation, however, was the gloomy necessity of military service. Recruitment was vital if the Soviet government wished to stave off the combined onslaught of Jiang and warlords.[86] Nearly all the able-bodied were conscripted at the most critical time, that is, just before the Long March.[87] Needless to state, casualties were horribly high now that the defenders were smaller in size and

[82] Lawrence K. Rosinger, China's Wartime Politics, Princeton, New Jersey: Princeton University Press, 1944, pp. 36-44.

[83] Peter Tang and Joan Maloney, Communist China: the Domestic Scene, 1949-1967, South Orange, New Jersey: Seton Hall University Press, 1967, p. 57.

[84] Hu Pu-yu, A Brief History of Sino-Japanese War, 1937-1945, Taibei: Zhang wu chu ban gong si, 1974, pp. 295-311.

[85] N.B. Zubkov, "Pervaya postoyannaya konstitutsiya kitaiskoi respubliki," Kitaya, obshchestvo i gosudarstvo, sbornik statei, Moskva: Izd-vo "nauka," 1973, pp. 241-260.

[86] K.S. Karol, La Chine de Mao, l'autre komminisme, Paris: Robert Laffont, 1966, pp. 97-103.

[87] Myao chu-khuan i V.P. Iliushechkin, "Severno-zapadnyi pokhod," Bol'shaya sovetskaya entsiklopediya, 2nd ed., vol. 38 (1955), pp. 340-341; A.S. Timov, "Serveno-zapadnyi pokhod," Ibid., 3rd ed., vol. 23 (1976), col. 413.

used inferior arms. Each family must have had at least a couple of persons killed in battle. Noteworthy too, was the onus of tax levy on the inhabitants. No doubt the communists "had alienated an important segment of the population" under them.[88] The Jiangxi Soviet was and indeed had to be a garrison state simon pure.

Beginning as early as December 1930, Jiang Jieshi and company staged formal assaults against it.[89] It was thought sanguinely that it would take them about six months to do the job. The enterprise was not that easy, however. In the first campaign, two of the twelve divisions of General He Yingqin were wiped out by the Reds. The second launched in February 1931 faired no better. The government troops resorted to the tactics of conventional warfare and their numerical superiority was totally offset by the surprise tactics of the Reds forming themselves into small details. The third campaign was commanded personally by Jiang Jieshi headquartered at Nanchang, a strategical city of Jiangxi province and famed during the Northern Expedition. It began on July 9, 1931, and the troop strength increased to 300,000. The defenders who engaged a few pitched confrontations at the initial phase of the war, switched to hit at the flank and rear of Jiang and succeeded in annihilating two divisions. When the Manchuria incident erupted in early fall of 1931, the Jiangxi operation was perforce suspended. The public came to think that during the national crisis, the priority of government should be shifted. Bowing to the general demand, Jiang called a temporary halt in Jiangxi. As a matter of fact, he pulled all his forces away from there and concerned himself with the foreign enemy.

Through 1932, the Reds continued to expand. Jiang Jieshi was aware that they posed an equal, if not greater, threat to China than the Japanese. He would resume at the first opportunity their suppression. Not waiting for the easing of the tension in the north, he started the fourth campaign in April 1933.[90] Put in charge of it was one of his favorite generals, Chen Cheng. A horde of 250,000 troops, plus local units half that size, were mustered. The Nineteenth Route Army, which distinguished itself in the fight with the Japanese in January 1932 in Shanghai, was ordered to take the field by Nanjing.[91] Like the preceding three times, this one also met with disaster. Outwitted by guerilla method of combat, Chen Cheng lost three divisions. At once Jiang Jieshi dismissed him. After four defeats, Nanjing began to review the entire situation. In desperation, it turned to German militarists for help. Consequently, the fifth and final drive (September 1933) was to be quite different and effective. It proved just too much for the Reds.[92]

[88] O. Edmund Clubb, *op. cit.*, p. 200.

[89] K.S. Karol, *China, the Other Communism*, translated from the French by Tom Baistow, New York: Hill and Wang, 1967, pp. 78, 87.

[90] G.V. Efimov, "Kitai, istoricheskii ocherk s kontsa 18 v. do 1937," *Bol'shaya sovetskaya entsiklopediya*, 2nd ed., vol. 21 (1953), pp. 198-233 at 231.

[91] *Xin hua ci dian*, p. 760, col. 1.

[92] Tibor Mende, *The Chinese Revolution*, London: Thames and Hudson, 1961, pp. 101, 109, 110.

Jiang Jieshi hired the famed strategist Hans von Seeckt as his
advisor in 1933. His was to reassess the operational plan in Jiangxi.
Assisted by General Georg Wetzell, he developed a new scheme to
counter the Reds' action of retreat, regrouping, long march and short
halt, surprise assault and nocturnal storming. The scheme called for
laying out of rings of stockades to control each and every road leading
to the rebeldom. Commercial traffic was severed completely. Some
of the blockhouses were manned by militia, thus freeing the regulars
to do "search and destroy" missions. This disposition had a telling
effect. It denied the communists the vital supplies, the "vitalest" of
which was salt, so essential for the vegetable diet in this area (a point
mentioned in Chapter I, section on geography). As the government
forces zeroed in, more rings were erected. By tightening them up,
an increasing number of Reds were trapped and killed duck-like. The
mobile tactic of the defenders was finally overcome. Seeing the future
forlorn, the Soviets decided to call it quits. In October 1934 they broke
through the weakest ring on the southern front.[93] There began the
Long March which was blown out of all proportion in the communist
literature in regard to its hardship and heroic fighting on the way to
Yanan.

After the Reds established themselves in northern Shaanxi in
October 1935, the effort of the government had also to be shifted
thereto. This time the troops actually engaging them were those of
Zhang Xueliang and Yang Hucheng. The second man's formation,
the northwest army, played only a minor role in the war, however.
Zhang Xueliang's quarter of a million soldiers had been stationed in
Xian (Shaanxi province) following their exodus from Manchuria in
September 1931.[94] The battles were fierce and losses alarmingly
heavy. The northeast army, cut off from their homeland, were very
sensible to the communist slogan of uniting against the Japanese.
The latter, but nobody else, were the true enemy of the Manchurian
troops and of all Chinese, according to the propaganda of the Reds.[95]
Why, it asked, should the Chinese brethren kill each other, not the
Japanese? What prevented the Chinese from marching shoulder-to-
shoulder to confront the foreign enemy? Gradually Zhang Xueliang's
men showed signs of ignoring their officers' orders. When Jiang Jieshi
flew to Xian on December 12, 1936 to inspect the battle front, he was
arrested by Zhang Xueliang who acted on behalf of his army and that
of Yang Hucheng. Their demand was cessation of the war with the
Reds. This event helped to dramatize the communists' call for civil
peace and resistance to the Japanese. It mobilized public opinion
to pressure the government to stop the anti-communist drive. An
interesting epiphenomenon of the arrest was that Jiang Jieshi's

[93] Hu Pu-yu, Abrégé de l'histoire des forces armées revolutionnaires nationales chinoises, décidé à la memoire
du président Chiang Kai-chek, compilé par Hu Pu-yu, traduction de Hoo Che-shy, Taibei: Li Ming Cultural
Enterprise Co., 1976, pp. 101-109.

[94] A.M. Grigor'ev, "Sovety v Kitae," Bol'shaya sovetskaya entsiklopediya, 3rd ed., vol. 24 (1976), cols. 126-128.

[95] A.A. Martynov, "Kitai, istoricheskii ocherk c 1917," Ibid., cols. 628-630.

enemies came to like him. They did not want to see him killed. Else, no one in China could provide the leadership in a war with Japan.

All the warlords entreated Zhang Xueliang to save his life, and the communists, represented by Zhou Enlai who went to Xian from Yanan, asked for his release, for a price of course. After a feverish negotiation in a fortnight Jiang was freed on Christmas Day. Was there a secret deal? Although no document has been found to prove the existence of one, the hard fact is that there was no longer a bandit-subdual drive after December 1936. The communists indeed got a precious respite. Given ten years' prison term, kidnapper Zhang Xueliang was removed as the second-in-command of the Chinese armed forces, a title which was conferred upon him in 1928 following his submission of Manchuria under the central government in Nanjing. He is now in Taiwan. It is safe to say that if the communists ever succeed in conquering that island, Zhang would be executed by the nationalists, as was the aforesaid Yang Hucheng. This man was shot in Chongqing in 1949 upon the approaching of the communist forces. The story of the anti-Japanese united front and of the Long March will be taken up in the next chapter. Let us say a few words, however, about the Japanese invasion in 1937 as it affected the fate of the nationalist regime and singularly boosted the Reds in their bid for power.

The National Government at war

All Chinese, the communists included, knew well that China was in no position to fight Japan. Leaders of Nanjing must have asked themselves that since it took them five years in five campaigns to eject the Reds from a few rebeldoms in Central Yangzi, how much chance do they have in getting the Japanese out of China? Yet the cry for resisting the Japanese was so shrill and universal in Cathay that a counsel of "wait and see" would savor of high treason. Although the provincial leaders and Nanjing had nothing in common, they all hated Japan. From the various quarters, the loudest voice in demanding Nanjing to stand and fight came from the communists.[96] The rebeldom in Jiangxi, as related above, declared war on Japan in 1931 (as a matter of fact, several times). Not having to take up the responsibility as a national authority, the communists could afford to be demagogic. Their drumming up of the shibboleth of resisting Nippon could not fail to embarrass Jiang Jieshi and company who they said "had dragged their feet" for so long. The shouting and yelling from Yanan begot a great deal of popularity for the communists, often portrayed as sterling patriots. In mastery of the art of deceit, they were hellbent to embroil Nanjing in a war in which it surely would be defeated. The strategy of the communists was to rock the whole boat in the hope of *possible* survival of themselves. What a gamble!

96 William L. Tung, The Political Institutions of Modern China, The Hague: Martinus Nijhoff, 1964, pp. 201ff.

More for the sake of allaying the suspicion of Nanjing than in the interest of true cooperation, the Reds proclaimed their support of the war with Japan by: a) disavowal of their intention to overthrow the existing regime, b) implementation of Sun Yat-sen's three popular principles, c) acceptance of Nanjing as the lawful government of China, d) abandonment of the Soviet republic in favor of the name "special border government of Shaan-Gan-Ning" (later adding Ji-Cha-Jing), e) designation of their forces as the Eighth Route Army under the Supreme Command of the central government, f) desisting from land confiscation. By this set of commitments, a United Front was riveted with Nanjing.[97] The communists were now receiving financial and war supplies from Nanjing, and they had fought the Japanese with some ardor, but not much success from the inception of the undeclared Sino-Japanese war in July 1937 to the end of 1938. During the first 15 months, the invaders with superior equipment, such as tanks and planes of which the Chinese had none, executed a lightning strike. The battle began in the north, but the Japanese were not to localize it. Shanghai was subjected to attack on August 14, 1937 and fell on November 29, and the defense of Nanjing collapsed on December 13. The riflemen of China were not a match for the mechanized enemy. After the first (and only) line of defense was broken, the fighting quickly spread to the upper stretch of the Yangzi. Wuhan fell on December 24, 1938 following relentless air and naval bombardment. Down south, another front was opened by the Japanese. As to be expected, their advance met with no difficulty and Guangzhou was taken on October 24, 1938. Thenceforth, the war came to a standstill until the eve of the V-J Day when a final assault of the Japanese using almost exclusively the puppet government troops nearly captured Chongqing. The Japanese needed time to consolidate their gains now that their line of action was thinly extended.[98]

The principal burden of the war was borne by the troops of the government and those of the warlords, while the communists did some hit-and-runs.[99] The result was heavy casualties on Jiang Jieshi's army, but the Reds suffered marginally. Right here commenced the tipping of balance of power to the advantage of the communists. There is, too, the fact that the territorial base where they operated was fast broadened. The Japanese occupation, it is most important to point out, was not a good job. Although lines and dots were in their hands, the enormous hinterland did not witness one single Nipponese. The Reds, having a superb skill and ruthless technique, made infiltration easily; and they were successful in organizing the villagers. Before long, the central government in Chongqing whereto it moved in 1937

---

[97] Dick Wilson, A Quarter of Mankind, London: Weidenfeld and Nicolson, 1966, pp. 40-42.

[98] A.A. Martynov, "Natsional'no-osvoboditel'naya voina kitaiskogo naroda protiv yaponskikh zakhvatchikov 1937-1945," Bol'shaya sovetskaya entsiklopediya, 3rd ed., cols. 1079-1083.

[99] L. Carrington Goodrich, "China, History of the Republic," Britannica, 1973, vol. 5, pp. 589-595 at 594, col. 2.

began to envision the danger posed by the communists. They now seized the opportunity to expand their power base in order to challenge the government, a government to which they had since 1938 refused even the nominal loyalty.[100] In north China, the Reds' control was indisputable. It was there that they set up two dominions comprising three provinces each: Shaanxi-Gansu-Ningxia, Shanxi-Chahaer-Hebei. Pretty soon they grabbed Shandong, Henan and northern Jiangsu. Down south, the communists controlled the left bank of the Yangzi and established many enclaves there. They defied the government's orders and fought its forces which tried to dislodge them. By 1945, the Reds had an area of a couple of million sq km, and an army of half a million. Their administration was set up in fifteen "liberated" areas in nineteen provinces. One hundred million people lived under the communists. That was 25 percent of the total population of China at that time.[101]

When the atomic bombs were dropped in Hiroshima on August 6, 1945 and in Nagasaki three days later, the Soviet Union by the terms of the Yalta Accord entered the war.[102] Her troops poured into Manchuria, inflicted casualties of 80,000 and captured 600,000 of the Guandong Army of Japan.[103] The Russians turned all arms they seized (except planes) from it to the Chinese communists,[104] who rushed to Manchuria from north China through a much shorter route than the nationalist units who had to be flown in from the Yunnan-Burma border. These units were denied entry by the Soviets who, however, evacuated territory to their Chinese comrades. The race for Manchuria, beginning in November 1945, ended in an easy victory for the Reds.[105] By December 1947 the rich and industrialized northeast came on their scoreboard. In order to avoid full civil war, the US tried to be a go-between. President Truman sent George Marshall to Chongqing whose task was to effectuate a compromise between the two rival governments.[106] Marshall arrived on December 5, 1945 and left on December 10, 1947.[107] During his sojourn, he was instrumental in effecting many ceasefire agreements only to be broken. Numerous historians, playing it safe as it were, blamed both sides. We are however convinced that the Reds were the culprits of

[100] C. Martin Wilbur, "China, History of; the Republic Period," New Encyclopedia Britannica, 15th ed., vol. 4 (1976), pp. 366-378 at 373-374.

[101] D.J. Waller, The Government and Politics of Communist China, London: Hutchinson University Library, 1970, p. 38.

[102] N.V. Eronin, "Man'zhurskaya operatsiya, 1945" Bol'shaya sovetskaya entsiklopediya, 3rd ed., vol. 15 (1974), cols. 1026-1031.

[103] Michael and Taylor, op. cit. p. 361.

[104] Ibid., p. 363.

[105] John A. Harrison, op. cit., p. 187.

[106] E.F. Kovalev, "Kitai, istoricheskii ocherk 1945-1953," Bol'shaya sovetskaya entsiklopediya, 2nd ed., vol. 21 (1953), pp. 238-247 at 239.

[107] Albert Feuerwerker, "China," Encyclopedia Americana, International ed., 1978, vol. 6, pp. 541-545 at 544.

the breach. Can communists anywhere in the world cooperate with others? Has a coalition regime with their participation ever been durable? The Americans tend to think that others are like them in the willingness to reconcile. The communists are just another political party similar to, say, the GOP or the Democratic Party in their country. During the Marshall mission, the National Government was forced to make concessions. For example, at the critical struggle with the Reds, Jiang Jieshi was ordered by Washington to stop military recruitment and to go on demobilization.

The concept of balance of strength seems to obsess the policy-elite of the US. Enjoying the tremendous advantage of being the opposition force, or "party out of power," the communists were viewed with a great deal of sympathy. If the Nationalists were too strong, it was feared, the Reds would not have much chance and this would violate democratic rule, or upset the balance. The fact, however, is that Truman and company had over-estimated the might of Jiang Jieshi, or better yet, underestimated Mao Zedong whom they (or many of them) even considered not as a communist but a land reformer. The American public were given an erroneous picture of the reality inside China. The battle victory of the Reds were loudly shouted as showing their popularity. It is easy (cheap is a more suitable word) to ask: If the communists are disliked, how can they win? In truth, there occurred within the Reds' areas many uprisings, but none within the government domains. Viewing the swift conquest by the communists as evidence of their gaining the hearts of the millions, the American newsmen applied their traditional journalism to an alien milieu and displayed a pathetic ignorance of it. The words "corruption," "incompetent," and the like bristled in the US media to describe the leaders of the national government, but the words "brute," "tyranny" and the like never appeared to depict the Reds. The "democratic" communists did not permit a reporter to enter their territory unless he sent out approved dispatches. The US press did not mention this simple fact.

President Truman and General Marshall in pressing for a peaceful solution supposed that the communists were unaware of their own trump card. After the Soviet entry into Manchuria, the Reds knew only too well that the final victory was theirs, not the government's. In the occupied zones, they channeled all the resources to the military. Unlike the government, they had none of the expenses in maintaining a huge bureaucracy, universities, embassies abroad and a thousand and one other things, which a regime worth calling a national authority, must undertake. Furthermore, the people in the government regions were tired of eight years' struggle with Japan. They had suffered long enough. The morale was bound to fall and the democratic rights, which the US Government forced Jiang Jieshi to respect, served admirably to help the communist agitators to perturb the peace and order. The Reds, few students seem to realize and still fewer openly concede, were placed in power by the American press and US officials.

CHAPTER III
The Communist Party

Its foundation

The humiliation suffered by China at the hands of the imperialists, particularly the Japanese, gave rise to a sense of commiseration amongst the intellectuals. They came to express a general yearning for rejuvenation of the country. Else, China would be destroyed as a nation. The 21 Demands of the Japanese drove home the need for a review of China's past and for a mapping of her future. In September 1915, a mouthpiece of theirs, *Xin qing nian,* appeared.[1] It urged Westernization with the twin conceptions of democracy and science. The two were literally written in block letters. The intellectuals mentioned them as Mr. De and Mr. Sci. On the other side of their mind is the disdain of Confucianism. To varying degrees, all agreed that it was outmoded and deleterious. If China were ever to enter the still fresh (20th) century and survive it, the traditional bondage must be shattered. In this condemnatory chorus, no one asked what was the tradition or what was Confucian tradition. Although not in so many words, the modernizers were screaming: Confucianism was a sorrow of China.[2] The weakness of the nation was dumped on Confucius's lap. On this problem, we maintained in Chapter I that he only taught his countrymen how they *should* behave, but did not describe how they had behaved. The Chinese society was downright un-Confucian. The reformers were, in truth, so impressed by the might of the imperialists that they found Confucius an apt outlet for their frustration. If there were a grain of veracity in their complaint, it was the great Sage's valuation of conservatism which led to the inertia of the Chinese in treading the beaten path; this thwarted the kind of renovation accountable for Japan's rebirth as a great nation within a couple of generations of the Perry Mission of 1853. It is *non sequitur* to relate Cathay's ill to what Confucius had preached. The aforesaid *Xin qing nian,* edited by Chen Duxiu the harbinger of communism, gave vent to the pent-up anger of the Chinese.[3] It advocated change along the occidental line. This train of thought picked up momentum and culminated in the May Fourth outburst of 1919. The event erupted on that day when the victorious powers at Versailles refused to hand back the German rights in Shandong to China, an ally of theirs in the just-ended war.[4] Instead, they were transferred to Japan. The widespread chagrin in China moved the elite to search for ways and means of salvation.

---

[1] *Xin hua ci dian,* Beijing: Shang wu jin shu guan, 1980, p. 936, col. 1.

[2] L.I. Duman, "Konfutsianstvo," *Bol'shaya sovetskaya entsiklopediya,* Moskva: Izdatel'stvo "sovetskaya entsiklopediya," 3rd ed., vol. 13 (1973), col. 249-251, "Konfutskii," cols. 251-252. "Konfutsii," 2nd ed., vol. 22 (1953), p. 497.

[3] "Chen' Du-siu," *Ibid.,* 3rd ed., vol. 29 (1978), col. 784.

[4] V.P. Iliushechkin, "Chetvertogo maya dvizhenie,," *ibid.,* 3rd ed., vol. 29 (1978), col. 351.

The immediate impact of the Bolshevik revolution of October 1917 on China was nil. It was little understood by the warlords, obsessed as they were with their internecine rivalry. Before long, however, the situation started to change. The translations of Marx and Lenin gradually appeared in bookstores and the Russian crisis gained increasing attention. One of the most remarkable events was the revelation in July 1919 of a manifesto drawn up by Leo Karakhan, deputy commissar of foreign affairs of the Soviet Republic. It promises the recession to China, with no compensation whatsoever, of the Chinese Eastern Railway and of Russian mining rights in Manchuria.[5] The Chinese took this to heart. They saw a warm friendship which no other country had tendered. China, it was held, was for the first time treated as an equal by any nation. It is not hard for us to envision the elation of the Chinese and the good will the Soviet state created among them. In fact, the feeling of thanks was so high that when the manifesto was published inside Russia in which the pledge was deleted, the Chinese elected not to take notice of it. They continued to call the Bolsheviks their friends in need. Having been a victim of the imperialists for three-score and ten years, they understandably appreciated the comradely hand from the north. By 1919, the Chinese soil was fertile for the communist seeds to nourish.

Small groups of Marxists had in fact come into existence before the advent of the Soviets. However, these Marxists were not organized. They were Platonists of sorts. Further, they scattered far and wide in the country, clustering in some metropolises like Beijing, Guangzhou, Changsha and Shanghai. Direly needed then was a nuclear body able to coordinate and politicize the isolated groups. Soon this emerged, due to the Russians. The October revolution was viewed by the Bolsheviks as a prelude to global upheaval, but such a vision was dampened by the allied intervention in the Soviet civil war (1918-1920). In the eyes of Lenin and company, the prospect of spreading the revolution to Europe was marginal, but turning toward the orient they spotted China where things looked pretty propitious. As early as June 1918, the Soviet leadership sent a message to China saying that "the Russia of the Soviets and her Red Armies . . . are marching toward the East. We are marching to free the people from the yoke of the military."[6] Having thus both conditioned and enheartened the Chinese, the Comintern founded by Lenin on March 2, 1919 dispatched the first agent, Grigori Voitingskii to Beijing.[7] He arrived on January 11, 1920. Losing no time, he got in touch with professors Chen Duxiu and Li Dazhao of Beijing University.[8] With

[5] Franz H. Michael and George E. Taylor, *The Far East in the Modern World*, rev. ed., New York: Holt, Rinehard and Winston, 1964, p. 343.

[6] R.T. Pollard, *China's Foreign Relations 1917-1931*, New York: Macmillan, 1933, p. 135.

[7] "Voitingskii (psevd., nast. fam. Zarkhin), Grigorii Naumovich," *Bol'shaya sovetskaya entsiklopediya*, 3rd ed., vol. 5 (1971), col. 862.

[8] A.A. Martynov, "Kommunisticheskaya partiya kitaya," *Ibid.*, 2nd ed., vol. 22 (1953), pp. 200-205 at 200, col. 1; "Li Da-chzhao," *ibid.*, 3rd ed., vol. 14 (1973), col. 1284-1285.

the help of the visiting Russian, they came to organize the CCP. There is a controversy surrounding the date of what has been designated the first congress of the communist party.[9] There is also disagreement on the attendants. Most sources point to twelve Chinese and two foreigners. Just who were the latter two was not certain because there were 3 foreigners: Maring (pseudonym of a Dutchman named Sneevliet), Voitingskii, and Nikoruskii. Chen Duxiu was unable to participate due to his work in Guangzhou as education commissioner of a warlord's government there. Li Dazhao was also absent.[10] He sent Zhang Guotao (died in Toronto in 1979) to represent him and the entire Beijing group. Some of the twelve later became disenchanted and turned against communism. Two bade farewell to politics altogether. Mao Zedong, who was hired in the library of Beijing University and came back to his native Hunan province late in 1919 after taking part in the May Fourth excitement, went to Shanghai to represent the communists of that province. The congress took place on July 1 (most authors mention this day) 1921 at a girls' school within the foreign settlement. Although they did not discuss such things as the materialist view of history or the contemporary state of affairs in China, they named Chen Duxiu secretary. When notified of the decision on July 5, he left Guangzhou for Shanghai to take over the post. In the next few years he and Maring assisted Zhang Guotao in instituting the secretariat of the Chinese Labor Union and in fomenting the railmen's and seamen's strikes of north China.

First United Front

The Soviets were highly hopeful of the rapid spread of, and mass reception to, communism in China. They were, however, to be disappointed. Toward the end of 1922, the converts were slightly more than one hundred. Clearly proletarian revolution was not to happen quickly there, and the main stream in China at that time and for years to come had to be the movement spearheaded by Sun Yat-sen.[11] His revolution was, however, of a different kind because he openly declared communism unfit for China based as it is on the psychology of hatred. As he saw it, history is an annal of cooperation, not conflict, of social forces. The Soviets were thus in a quandary. If they gave support to Sun and company, they would have to turn their back on the communists who would then have no hope of gaining control of the masses. The Gordian knot was cut by the ingenious United Front. According to this, the CCP and the Guomindang were to marry expediently.[12] Both partners' interests were believed to be served,

[9] Shao Weizheng, "The first National Congress of the Communist Party of China, a verification of the date of convocation and the number of participants," *Social science in China*, 1 (1980), 108-129.

[10] "Li Da-chzhao," *Bol'shaya sovetskaya entsiklopediya*, 2nd ed., vol. 25 (1954), pp. 112-113; also 1st ed., vol. 36 (1938), cols. 805-806.

[11] "Sun' Yat-sen," *Bol'shaya sovetskaya enstiklopediya*, 2nd ed., vol. 4 (1956), pp. 292-294; G. Kara-Murza, "Sun' Yat-sen," 1st ed., vol. 53 (1946), cols. 214-218.

[12] A.A. Martynov, "Kitai, istoricheskii ocherk s 1917," *ibid.*, 3rd ed., vol. 24 (1976), col. 625.

as was the interest of Russia.[13] Lenin would like to see the imperialists driven out and the warlords toppled, particularly those warlords who were entrenched in Beijing, because they were the ones who had said "nyet" to his demand for privilege and rights in China. Query: If the Beijing government which Russia recognized decided to sign treaties with her, granting her all she wanted (see section on Northern Expedition, Chapter II), would Lenin have taken the course as he did in organizing a counter-force?

The United Front technique cost the nationalists dearly. It legitimated the communists' infiltration while affording them a wonderful start.[14] Adolf Ioffe and Sun Yat-sen initialed a Shanghai communique on January 26, 1923 which laid the foundation of the GMD-CCP alignment. Judging with the wisdom of hindsight, we may argue Sun must have been pressed to subscribe to it, for he knew that it is the CCP which was the beneficiary if for no other reason than that the CCP was the junior and negligible partner. The party was indeed weak in popular appeal and small in size. The situation seems to repeat itself in 1946-1947 when the US tried to bring together the CCP and GMD to form a coalition government, the latter was superior in strength and territorial possession. Although we suspected the pressure on Sun, there was some willingness on his part as foreign help to his cause was most welcome and his dislike of the northern warlords was greater than his loathing of the communists. He did not oppose an alliance, albeit temporarily, with them.

The United Front was unprecedented in political history.[15] It envisioned the members of one party (CCP) to enter another (GMD) as individuals but maintain its own organization outside it. This arrangement gave the colonizer (CCP) the opportunity to a) propagate its germinal doctrines in the colonizee (GMD) and b) operate in the mass bodies set up by the latter. Both overtly and covertly the communists acted to reach the public and influence them through channels which otherwise were closed to them.[16] As things turned out, the CCP took good advantage of the Front. During the Northern Expedition, for example, the Reds carried out en route a bloody class struggle to eliminate the land owners and the country "bullies." The latter incidentally were rural gentlemen who rendered the thankless service in the villages, in the absence of government authority, such as the settling of disputes among the often quarrelsome neighbors (un-Confucian behavior, by the way), the discharging of the minimum responsibility in collecting tax, organizing local defense, providing facilities like communications, schools and charities. They were the

[13] "Borodin, Gruzenberg Mikhail Markovich," *Bol'shaya sovetskaya entsiklopediya*, 3rd ed., vol. 3 (1970), cols. 1720-1721; "Bliukher Vasilii Konstantinovich," cols. 1290-1291.

[14] "Ioffe, Adol'f Abramovich," *ibid.*, 1st ed., vol. 29 (1935), col. 128. His name is deleted from the 2nd ed., but reappears in the 3rd ed., vol. 10 (1972), cols. 1156-1157.

[15] V.I. Elizarov, "Kommunisticheskaya partiya Kitaya," *Bol'shaya sovetskaya entsiklopediya*, 3rd ed., vol. 12 (1973), cols. 1604-1607.

[16] A.A. Martynov, "Kommunisticheskaya partiya Kitiya," *ibid.*, 2nd ed., vol. 22 (1953), pp. 200-205.

kind of people the communists declared as their mortal enemy. Apart from doing the above, the CCP penetrated the GMD structure from top to bottom. Mao Zedong himself was appointed to that party's Central Executive Committee, its highest authority.[17] Jiang Jieshi's Huangpu Academy was honeycombed with the Reds. Zhou Enlai worked there as a political commissar.[18] Among the cadets were those who later distinguished themselves in the communist hierarchy. The ill-started Lin Biao was one of them.[19]

The Guangzhou regime was organizationally weak. It did not have much popular base. The Russian advisors led by Borodin came to restructure the GMD in the Bolshevik image. Democratic centralism was used as the guiding principle (see Statutory Principles below). It is nothing more than an euphemism of party dictatorship, premised as it was on the monopoly of decision at the apex. The CCP was a carbon copy of the Russian original, and it was much more intolerant of dissent than the GMD. When the two parties were formed in the same spirit of exclusiveness, how can they cooperate? The CCP's primary interest in forming an alliance with the GMD was to get rid of it at the first opportunity and to secure an undivided sway.[20] Lenin's outlawing of rival factions, written into the Party Statutes by the Tenth Party Congress in 1921, came to govern the conduct of all communists the world over. This rule augured ill for the GMD-CCP combination, but the situation was more complicated with the death of Lenin in 1924 and that of Sun Yat-sen the following year. Had the two leaders lived a few more years, would the circumstances in China be different? Although it is hazardous to speculate on the matter, one may well argue that the policy laid down by Sun would not have been continued by his successor for long. Neither Sun nor Jiang Jieshi trusted the communists. Can Lenin's China policy be carried on by his successor? In the long run, no. That policy, we shall remember, was based on the assumption of multiclass revolution which was of course not a proletarian one. So long as that assumption remained unchallenged, the GMD-CCP alliance might well have abided. However, it was challenged.

The multiclass slogan was not widely shared in Russia. Trotsky, for one, never mouthed it. During Lenin's time, he, Trotsky, may well have found it impolitical to repudiate it. After his death, however, he no longer had this worry. He now urged Stalin to stop supporting the Front, because he felt that the force centered on Jiang Jieshi was outright bourgeois and that it acted contrary to the best interest of the working class. In Trotsky's mind, only the CCP was that class's

[17] "Mao Tsze-dun," *Bol'shaya sovetskaya entsiklopediya*, 2nd ed., vol. 26 (1954), pp. 244-248; same, 3rd ed., vol. 15 (1974), cols. 1041-1042. The third is written by V.I. Elizarov.

[18] "Chzhou En'lai," *ibid.*, 2nd ed., vol. 47 (1957), pp. 352-353; the same, 3rd ed., vol. 29 (1978), col. 538.

[19] "Lin Biao," *ibid.*, 2nd ed., vol. 25 (1954), pp. 117-118; same, 3rd ed., vol. 14 (1973), col. 1417.

[20] Khu Tsyao-mu, *Tridtsat' let kommunisticheskoi partii Kitiya*, perevod s kitaiskogo, Moskva: Izd-vo polit. lit-ry, 1952, pp. 7-19.

spokesman while the joint revolution served only to strengthen the GMD. When the Northern Expedition was under way, Trotsky wanted the communists to organize the masses, dispossess the exploiters and proceed from joint to proletarian revolution. In opposition to him, Stalin cleaved to the United Front line and talked only of the success of the national revolution to be attained by the effort of several classes. These classes, he reasoned, were stronger than the warlords. However, as in such other matters like industry and agriculture, Stalin came around to embrace Trotsky's stand after he, Trotsky, was evicted from the CPSU. July 1927 saw Stalin instruct the communists to seize power in Wuhan. In effect, he declared the end of the Front and the multiclass revolution. There was to be an one-class revolution instead.[21]

Consequent upon the removal of the Comintern agents, the alignment of the GMD and CCP collapsed. Thenceforth, the communists fled to Jiangxi. There they instituted a Soviet regime. Some of the cadets of Huangpu became its military cadres. On August 1, 1927, they mutinied in Nanchang during the Northern Expedition, a day claimed to be the Army Day of the CPR.[22]

Second United Front

In point of time, the second front was separated from the first by eleven years (1927-1937). Needless to state, the circumstances of the two differed vastly. In the second front there was a new kind of CCP, armed to its teeth and with a territorial domain. While the previous union was leveled at the warlords, the new one was to repel the Japanese invaders from China by the military forces of both parties. After abandoning Jiangxi and several satellite bases in central Yangzi, the Reds headed westward. The Long March was a much more leisurely trip than is painted by the communists. The chasing troops were small and nonchalant. Neither they nor the Reds had modern transport, all going by foot. In front of the communists the armies of the warlords were poorly equipped. Most noteworthy of all, there was no coordination of the commands of Jiang Jieshi and warlords. There was strong evidence of reluctance on the part of the warlords to let Jiang's forces enter their "fiefs", even though they could not themselves keep off the communists. The latter, therefore, met only token resistance. However, the westward escape held little prospect for them. Unlike Jiangxi which was a developed province, the back part of China was barren and its population sparse. There the CCP would have little hope. The only possibility was the fleeing to the Soviet Union via Neimeng, if their new base, Shaanxi, were to be liquidated like Jiangxi. However, a new development was to take place toward the end of the Long March.

The year 1935 marked the alteration of Kremlin diplomacy from one

[21] Li Wei-han, *The struggle for proletarian leadership in the period of the new democratic revolution in China*, Beijing: Foreign Languages Press, 1962, pp. 21ff.

[22] Jacques Guillermaz, *Histoire du parti communist chinois* (1921-1949), Paris: Payot, 1968, pp. 152-156.

of isolation and denouncing the imperialists to one of beseeching them to stop the fascists. Russia joined the League of Nations and moved on to champion a global united front. It called for a) the communists of every country to quit attacking on the bourgeois regimes, and to give them support, and b) an anti-Nazi coalescence of all peace-lovers. In tune with this move, the Chinese communists, who had clamored for "death to Jiang Jieshi," decided to perform a volte-face. Now they said he should not die, but instead should take the country to war with Japan. The Reds exhibited their patriotism by declaring war on that country no less than three times.[23] All these were, of course, empty gestures. No one took them seriously. The official slogan of the CCP was: "United anti-Japanese National Front" led by Jiang Jieshi. This phrase was obviously handed down from Moscow, because its Chinese translation sounded incredibly awkward. The word "national" was rendered as racial (ming zu) by the Reds and it made the slogan ring even weird. Yet there was the fact that a national crisis was brewing at the time, since Japan was feverishly detaching five northern provinces from China and this gave the communist propaganda a measure of plausibility. In December 1935, students in Beijing yelled for standing pat against Japan. Their voice was echoed from one corner of the country to another. The Nanjing regime was pathetically placed on the defensive. It could not but act in response to the national indignation and anxiety.

While still on the run (August 1935), but temporarily halting on the Sichuan-Xikang border which is a vast grassland, the CCP formally wired the United Front idea to GMD. It was both opportune and tactical. At that time, a split had just developed within the CCP. In the Maoergai conference, Zhang Guotao refuted vigorously the hegemony of Mao. This dispute undoubtedly weakened the party.[24] Mao was determined to consolidate its strength by raising the slogan of unity. On its part, Nanjing dismissed the Front proposal as having no merits. Then followed the Xian kidnap already narrated. Jiang Jieshi paid a price for his life: stop fighting the Reds and begin to work for the resistance to Japan. In return, the communists offered the pledge that they would rename (not more than that) their territory from Soviet Republic to Shaan-Gan-Ning border administration under the authority of Nanjing. This proved to be an outright deceit. The Front provided such measures as the organizing of the New Fourth (Red) Army of 10,000 men under Ye Ting.[25] The communists now refrained from criticizing Jiang Jieshi. As the grand initiator of the United Front idea, Russia was gladdened by what happened inside China. She gave generous armed supplies to Nanjing. A great portion

[23] First declaration in November 1931, second declaration in March 1935 (Michael and Taylor, op cit., p. 419), and third declaration in August 1935 (Lucian W. Pye, China, Boston: Little, Brown, 1972, p. 163).

[24] Dieter Heinzig, Die Anfänge für der Kommunistischen Partei Chinas in Lichte der Memoiren Chang Kuo-t'aos, Hamburg: Institut for Asienkunde, 1970, passim (38 pp).

[25] King Ta-kei, From destruction of CCP to birth of Mao-Lin party, Taibei: Asian People's anti-Communist League, 1969, pp. 4-18.

of them went to the Chinese Reds, however. The Front, as it turned out, was short-lived. Having helped to kindle the war with Japan, the communists knew only too well that it would exhaust the national regime. The war in fact afforded them the needed breathing space. It gave them an excellent chance to store up strength, enlarge territory or just watch the mutual weakening of the government and Japanese forces in the abattoir.[26] In a nutshell, the Reds had nothing to lose, but a big country to gain. As we stated, this was a gamble of the Reds. At that time who knew that Japan would be involved in a war with the West, and who knew that China would not be swallowed up as Manchuria?

The First United Front afforded the CCP an opportunity to enter the GMD's armed formation and get control of some units.[27] It was these units which rebelled and became the kernel of the forces in Jiangxi. Although the Central Government liberated the territory in October 1934, it failed to achieve the most crucial objective: destroying of the enemy. Being a professional soldier, Jiang Jieshi was obviously aware of the false triumph of his. The Second United Front was a tactic designed to drag the Central Government into water, thereby saving the Reds. In a Sino-Japanese war, the CCP figured, it was that government which had to bear the burden of the fight and that it would be crushed. Mao Zedong must have the scenario of the Japanese occupation of cities and communication lines, of the Red Army's infiltration and seizing of areas outside these, or forcing out the local officials of the Central authority, and of staging attacks on forces still loyal to the latter. All these had indeed come to pass.[28] In retrospect, the first exchange of shots between the Japanese and the Chinese soldiers (those of the warlord Song Zheyuan) at the Marco Polo bridge west of Beijing on July 7, 1937 sounded the death knell for the Republic of China. The total success of the Reds depended on sheer luck. Had there been no first United Front, would they have had the chance to build up their military cadres? Had there been no second United Front, would they have had the possibility of establishing and steadily widening their territorial sovereignty?[29]

The CCP, we would venture to argue, is an historical unnecessity. Its reason for existence lies in the way it is structured. Just as Lenin used his party machinery to turn Russia upside down, so Mao Zedong used his to turn China that way. Let's look at the remarkable organization of the Reds, but first we propose to examine, all too briefly to be sure, the principles and policy positions the organization

---

[26] Hu Chiao-mu, *Thirty years of the Communist Party*, Beijing: Foreign Languages Press, 1959, pp. 61-77. Russian translation in footnote 20 above.

[27] Myao Chu-khuan, *Kratkaya istoriya Kommunisticheskoi Partii Kitaya*, Moskva: Izo-vo polit. lit-ry, 1958, pp. 7-26.

[28] Howard L. Boorman, *Mao Tse-tung the lacquered image*, Bombay: Manaktalas, 1965, p. 35.

[29] Jürgen Domes, *Vertagte Revolution, die Politik der Kuomintang in China 1923-1937*, Berlin: Walter Gruyter, 1969, pp. 616ff.

is intended to carry out or adhere to (see also Chapter V for some of the principles and policy positions).

Statutory principles

The Chinese communists translate *xian fa* into constitution, but we prefer the word Statute, because in the first place, the CPSU utilize this word (although illogically in the plural form) to name its basic charter and, in the second place, we think it is better to differentiate the party constitution from the state constitution by calling the former statute. The CCP had five Statutes after its advent to power. They appeared in 1956, 1969, 1973, 1977 and 1982. During the same stretch of time, there were four Constitutions coming out in 1954, 1975, 1978 and 1982. Regarding the contents, the last Statute resembles the first Statute, just as the last Constitution resembles the first Constitution (see Chapter V). In the instant section, an attempt is made to summarize the doctrinal matters as proclaimed in the Statute.

Historical materialism

Against the soviet usage of having two instruments of Program and Statutes, the Chinese opt for one Statute but prelude it with a long discourse called "general program." The opening sentence of the latter is a laconic statement of Marxist philosophy. Dialectical and historical materialism, it alleges, elucidates the path of mankind toward a classless society. By means of revolutionary violence of the working people, the world is traversing from capitalism via socialism to communism. The goal of socialism: "from each according to his ability and to each according to his work," will give way to that of communism: "from each according to his ability and to which according to his needs." Because of their articulate policy of reliance on the capitalists for the modernization drive, the Reds consider it prudent to refrain from the heretofore bragging about socialism. Now they write only that "*fundamentally* speaking socialist system is superior to capitalist system." The statute sees the former system as capable of cleansing man of the mentality formed under the latter. This averment is, however, compromised by the warning of the erosive impact of the "decadent bourgeois ideas" still existing in the CPR. Apparently, after thirty-four years' hullabaloo in building up socialism, the Chinese Reds have not yet purified their society. Tacitly the statute concedes that the cathartic power of Marxism-Leninism and Mao Zedong Thought does not work satisfactorily.

Class struggle and contradiction

The Preamble of the Constitution in a 52-word paragraph prescribes the continuation of class struggle and this, in spite of the acknowledgment that the exploiting class has been eliminated. The Statute repeats this anomalous position within, however, a theoretical perspective of contradiction. The theme of contradication, as is known to all, is one of Mao Zedong's pet ideas and is regarded by the Chinese communists as a fantastic contribution to the ideological treasury. The Statute devotes a 127-word paragraph to the theme. There are five interesting points in it. First, class struggle does not end with the annihilation of the exploiting class. In order to avoid the fallacy of shadow-boxing, the Preamble of the Constitution creates a new class out of "those forces and elements, both at home and abroad, which are hostile to China's socialist system and try to undermine it." Not reproducing this statement, the Statute simply refers to this enemy "class". Both documents thus have introduced a different definition of the opposition class. It no longer consists of the bourgeois or land proprietors, but a mixed bunch of undesirables "growing out of domestic circumstances and foreign influences." Specifically they include, according to one Chinese commentator, law-breakers, profiteers, dissenters and counterrevolutionaries. (The soviets do not consider these in their country as a class). It is against this "class" that the workers of the CPR are to wage combat. The Chinese ideologues, although not the Constitution or Statute, have already redefined proletariat as not based on the relation to the means of production, but on embracing the proletarian cause and joining the revolutionary ranks. Any individual, whatever his station in society, his wealth or his occupation, can be a proletarian.

Second, aside from the contradiction in the traditional acceptation, that is, one between classes, the Statute brings in an entirely different species of contradiction, one between the rising material and cultural expectation of the masses and the shortage of means to satisfy it. Mao Zedong's 1957 treatise on contradiction, it will be recalled, does not touch such a type. The Statute even says that it has now become the principal contradiction in China. Clearly this is an addition to or a revision of Mao Zedong Thought.

Third, the Statute asserts that class struggle can at times be sharpened, a conception directly taken from the *Communist manifesto*. But neither the Chinese nor Marx and Engels explain how this situation can happen. Would the new "class" in China pose a threat someday to the existence of the regime? we may be wondering.

Fourth, the said contradiction between people's expectation and its fulfilment, which undoubtedly purports to be a theoretical justification of the current leaders' stress on practical work or de-emphasis of ideology, is alleged to provide the key to the dissolution of other contradictions. It is expressly said that if this "principal" contradiction is gone, other contradictions would disappear. We think this is a dubious hypothesis because the satisfaction of public's wants can hardly be a basis for the solution, for example, of the contradictions in the relation between the CPR and the USSR, or between her and the West.

Fifth, the Statute cites Mao Zedong's dictum of strict distinction and correct handling of the two different types of contradictions between the enemy and ourselves and those among the people. What

is a correct or an incorrect handling is, however, not spel
by Mao Zedong or the Statute. Indeed he himself is now
having committed grave errors by treating contradiction
people as one between "the enemy and ourselves." T
of Mao Zedong's theorem of contradiction into the St
pertinent to note here, shows the strength of the Maoists in the CCP.
The draft Constitution, which appeared on April 21, 1982, and finally
approved by the 5th session of the 5th NPC on December 4, 1982,
does not contain the just cited dictum, but it entered the Statute
promulgated on September 6. There is little doubt that the Maoists
had in the interval put up some struggle to wrest from the pragmatists
some concession to Mao Zedong's teachings.

No worship of party leaders

The trauma from the deification of Mao Zedong is responsible for
the putting in the Statute one of the most striking provisions, one
denouncing personal dictatorship. The document does not have a
comparable article as Rule 27 of the CPSU Statutes which runs that
"the *highest* principle of party leadership is collectivity of leadership
which is an *absolute* requisite for the normal functioning of party
organization." A mild version in the CCP Statute is the provision in
Article 10, cl. 10 that the "party committees at all levels function on
the principle of combining collective leadership with individual
responsibility based on division of labour." But the CCP Statute also

avows: "The party . . . does not allow any member to be divorced
from the masses or place himself above them" (Preamble). In respect
of Mao Zedong's role in history, the document simply states he is
the chief representative of the communists, implying that he is not
the sole builder of the party and state (*ibid.*). This is the only place,
we must note, where his personal name is mentioned in the entire
text of the Statute, aside, of course, from the expression of Mao
Zedong Thought. The latter now stands alongside, but not hooks up
with, Marxism-Leninism. This troika appears four times: twice in the
Preamble, once each in Article 3, cl. 1 and Article 32, cl. 2. An
interesting comparison is that the 1977 Statute having only one fourth
of the length of the 1982 successor refers to Mao Zedong twice (in
the general program), and Marxism Leninsim-Mao Zedong Thought
four times: twice in general program, once each in Article 2, cl. 1,
and Article 19, cl. 1.
    The degradation of Mao Zedong is hinted at in the policy stand of
the Statute. Witness such provisions: the party forbids all forms of
personality cult (Article 10, cl. 5), "no party member, whatever his
position, is allowed to make decisions on major issues on his own,"
"no leader is allowed to decide matters arbitrarily on his own or to
place himself above the party organization" (Article 16, par. 3), and
"there shall be no privileged party member irrespective of his
position" (Article 8). There had already been denunciation of the
arrogance and caprice of Mao Zedong in mid-1981 by the sixth

GOVERNMENT OF SOCIALIST CHINA

plenum of the 11th CC.[30] In order to prevent the development of a
monocracy, the Statute puts the hierarchs under the "supervision
by the party and the people." However, it is thought to be equally
important to warn against the recurrence of the abuse of eminent
figures by the masses (mob is the right word) in the name of
"supervision" as happened during the Cultural Revolution. Article
10, cl. 6 therefore orders the party members to "uphold the prestige
of all leaders" who represent the interests of the CCP and of the
people.

Major policies

Five grandstand plays which the Beijing aristocrats have promoted
during the past several years and which found their way into the
Constitution appear also in the Statute. First are the Four
Modernizations aimed at industry, agriculture, defense and
science/technology. Second is the United Front. Slated to be
embraced are such disparates as workers, peasants, intellectuals,
democratic parties, compatriots of Taiwan, Hong Kong and Macao,
and Chinese nationals residing abroad. What ideas or ideals can unite
them? We believe Marxism-Leninism and Mao Zedong Thought
cannot. Nor can proletarian dictatorship. It must be a true democracy.
Third, there are the five principles of diplomacy, i.e., sovereignty and
territorial integrity, non-aggression, non-interference, equality and
mutual benefit, and peaceful co-existence. Fourth, there is the
quadripartite guideline of (1) people's democratic dictatorship, (2)
socialist road, (3) leadership of the CCP and (4) Marxism-Leninism
and Mao Zedong Thought. Fifth, serving as an underpinning for all
the above are the three essentials: (a) a high degree of ideological
and political unity which calls for "finding truth through practice,"
seeking "truth from facts" and "starting from reality in all matters"
(all these are dicta of Deng Xiaoping), (b) "wholehearted service to
the people," and (c) democratic centralism. The Communists,
Chinese or others, have made a great point of the last (democratic
centralism); and the CCP Statute goes to great lengths about it. Let
us discuss it presently.

Democratic centralism

In accordance with Article 10, there are five planks in it: (1)
subordination of individual members to party organizations, (2)
obedience of minority to majority (this is mentioned in both Articles
10 and 16), (3) submission of lower to higher bodies, (4) election of
all leading bodies "except the representative organs dispatched by
them to the leading party members' groups in non-party
organizations", (5) filing of reports by lower to higher bodies. The
objective of the party is a combination of the "highest degree of
centralism" with the "highest degree of democracy." However

[30] "Guan yu jian guo yi lai dang de ruo gan li shi wen ti de jue yi" (A resolution on several historical points
since the founding of the CPR), *Renmin ribao*, July 1, 1981, pp. 1-5 at 2, col. 2.

various provisions of the Statute vacillate from one end to the other, with centralism emphasized in some while democracy in others. Apparently, the party cannot make up its mind. On major policies affecting the nation as a whole, says Article 15, par. 1, only the Central Committee is within its right to take decisions. Any lower organization, it is insisted, must firmly implement the orders of a higher organization although it may make suggestions or request modifications of the orders (par. 2). Further, the Preamble, after stating full play given to democracy, calls for high centralism and strong discipline so as to ensure the "unity of action throughout the ranks" of the CCP.

On the side of democracy, the Statute is equally, if not more, emphatic. All cardinal questions (except the ones affecting the CPR in its entirety) are to be decided by a party committee after democratic debates (Article 10, cl. 5). A higher body must pay constant attention to the stands of a lower one, and to those of the rank-and-file members (cl. 4). No organization or individual may in any way compel voters to choose or refrain from choosing any candidate in a party election (cl. 11). While deliberating a problem, the authority at any level should normally solicit the views of the constituency (Article 14). Within an organization, the opinion of the majority shall prevail, but if there is no majority or if the opinion is evenly divided, the matter shall be put off for further discussion and investigation (Article 16). If still no agreement emerges, the issue would go to the next higher body for an ultimate ruling.

Although all the previous Statutes contained the planks of democratic centralism, they did not succeed in curbing Mao Zedong's authoritarianism. The present hierarchy of the party seems to be sincere in their attempt to democratize the system. What the Statute writes can no doubt improve the intra-party communication and facilitate the flow of information. Some input may be coming from the ordinary members and officials. From now on abuses of power are likely to meet with criticism and rectification. However, more meaningful democratization is the abandonment of the monopoly of political control. A closed regime like the CPR cannot go far toward popular government merely by some minor adjustment in the decision-making machine of the party.

Membership

Any Chinese worker, peasant, armyman, intellectual or any other revolutionary who reaches the age of 18 and is willing to accept the party program and Statute, to work actively in a party organization, carry out decisions of the party and pay membership dues may apply for membership of the CCP (Article 1). In respect of the five kinds of people, all but the last are easy to identify, but who, in the world, is a revolutionary not to be classed as any one of the preceding four? We would also like to point out that although an applicant may indicate his willingness to work in a party organization, working in it does not constitute a prerequisite for membership, because the overwhelming party members of 39 million are employed in non-party bodies. The CPSU Statutes (Article 1), in comparison, states explicitly that one has to be working in a party organization before he files an application for entry into the party. This stipulation carries over the tradition of the pre-1917 situation when conspiracy requires the membership within the party body. After becoming the ruling party, the soviets never bother to revise the wording of the stipulation.

A new member is admitted by a party branch on an individual basis (Article 5, par. 2). By implication, mass intake is prohibited. An aspirant first sends in an application endorsed by two full members whose qualifications are unstated. Against this the CPSU Statutes (Rules 4 (a)) requires three such members and lays down the conditions that they must have a party standing of not less than five years and have known the applicants from working with them, professionally and socially, for not less than one year. Rule 4 (a) note 2 disqualifies a member or alternate member of the CC of CPSU from recommending anyone (if they do, they would influence decisions of party branches);[31] and note 1 says that in the case of a member of the Leninist Young Communist League seeking membership, the recommendation of that body is counted as one of the three recommendations. All these are absent from the CCP Statute.

The application goes to the general meeting of the branch for action, and thence goes to the next higher party organization. Although the Statute does not identify this organization, it is to be understood as the standing committee (Article 27). When the application is approved, the aspirant starts one year's probation (Article 7, par. 1), and in the meantime he takes a vow before the party flag: "It is my will to join the Communist Party of China, uphold the party's program, observe the provisions of the party Statute, fulfill a party member's duties, carry out the party's decisions, strictly observe party discipline, guard party secrets [also state secrets, see below], be loyal to the party, work hard, fight for communism throughout my life, be ready at all times to sacrifice my all for the party and the people, and never betray the party."

When the probation is over, the party branch is to "promptly" discuss whether he should be advanced to full membership. If he has conscientiously done his duties he will be so advanced. However, if the branch thinks that more observation and education of him is needed, the probation may be prolonged for another year. If he still behaves poorly during the second probation, he would be declared unfit. All the above decisions are to be made by the branch in its general meeting, subject to the review by the next higher party organization (Article 7, par. 3). In exceptional cases, the Central Committee of the party or the party committee of a province, an autonomous region or a municipality directly administered by the central government is within its right to admit members directly (Article 5, par. 6). This happened on May 29, 1981 when Song Qingling, vice-

31 Ronald Hill and Peter Frank, *The Soviet Communist Party*, London: George Allen & Unwin, 1981, p. 21.

chairman of the CPR, was on her deathbed, and the Central Committee resolved to grant her membership of the party. Such direct intake, by comparison, is only implied in Rule 12 of the CPSU Statutes. Yuri Gagarin, it will be recalled, was handed the party card according to this provision immediately after his return from the space flight of 1 hour and 48 minutes on April 12, 1961. The single application of new member, as practiced in China, is in sharp contrast to the double application of the CPSU. According to the CPSU Statutes, Rule 15, the application of full membership follows an "identical processes as the application for candidacy" including the filing of application, the endorsement by three members, the approval by the party branch and a higher body of the party.[32] To acquire a party card in the CPR is much easier than in the Soviet Union, judging by the statutory provisions of the two parties.

Every party member irrespective of his office must be assigned to a branch, cell or other specific unit of the CCP and engage in regular activities of the party organization. He ought to accept supervision by the masses inside and outside the CCP. This requirement is purported to prevent anyone from becoming a privileged member (Article 8), a practice which must have been fairly common. There are four ways to terminate membership. a) Advised withdrawal applies to those who "lack revolutionary zeal, fail to fulfill the duties of a party member, no longer qualify for membership and resist correction" (Article 9, par. 2). b) Voluntary withdrawal (par. 1) seems to be open to all, but there is the proviso that the fact must be made public after a discussion by the general meeting of the branch. One is, very likely, afraid of getting out due to this embarrassing situation. c) Presumed withdrawal happens when one fails to attend regular functions, pay dues or do assigned job for six successive months with no proper reason (par. 3). d) Coerced withdrawal is an outright expulsion (Article 39). More of this anon. We find it pertinent to state that the CPSU Statutes in Rules 8 and 9 respectively provide for c) and d), but not the other two types of withdrawal. In the Russian party, membership is not resignable and a member may not even be talked into quitting.

What are members' duties and rights? Against CPSU's ten duties and five rights (Rules 2 and 3), the CCP lays down eight in each category, seeking to strike a balance. Both Russian and Chinese parties place duties before rights and thus reverse the order in the USSR Constitution (Articles 39-69) and the CPR Constitution (Articles 32-56).

Duties (Article 3)
1. Study Marxism-Leninism and Mao Zedong Thought
2. Be the first to suffer & the last to enjoy

Rights (Article 4)
1. Attend meetings, & read party documents
2. Participate in disucssion during meeting and in newspapers

---

[32] *Ibid.*, p. 23. This double application is never mentioned in other textbooks.

3. Observe discipline, keep state and party secrets
4. Uphold solidarity and oppose factionalism
5. Be honest with party, for good and against bad men
6. Maintain close ties with the masses
7. Play an exemplary role, stick to communist ethics
8. Fight heroically for the motherland.

3. Make suggestions and proposals about party work
4. Offer criticism, demand dismissal or replacement of bad cadres
5. Vote, elect and stand for election
6. Appeal disagreeable decisions to higher organizations
7. Defend one's case during disciplinary hearings
8. File complaints or requests to higher bodies, up to the CC.

There are also other supplemental rules of behavior. In order to dispel the impression that the party forms itself into a special group in the society, the Statute in Article 2, par. 2 calls for "oneness" of the members with the masses. This is followed by the statement in the next paragraph that "members of the CCP are at all times ordinary working people." In no way, that is to say, do they differ from the general public. However, as holds true with all communist countries, party cards do carry considerable advantage in careers, material allotments and psychological satisfactions which are not enjoyed by the run-of-the-mill citizens. It is indeed conceded in Article 2, par. 3 that members "are allowed personal benefits and job functions and powers." In the meantime, members are advised "not to seek personal gains or privileges." This amounts to stating that one joins the party not for selfish ends, but he is to be rewarded. The membership benefits, it is stated, are distributed according to "relevant regulations and policies" (ibid.). Such provision, neither seen in the CPSU Statutes nor in the previous CCP Statutes, intends to outlaw the under-the-counter deals. From now on everything done in the manner of quid pro quo should be within the limits as prescribed by legislations or decrees. It remains, however, to be seen whether such a rule can be enforced.

Ganbu (cadres) are called apparatchik in the CPSU. They are office workers. On account of their pivotal position, the Statute has to devote a whole chapter (VI) to their appointment, responsibility, evaluation and conduct. In the past several years the governing clique talked profusely of ganbu's rejuvenation (lowering their average age), professionalization and revolutionization. This policy is now embodied in Article 34, par. 1, as is the policy of training and promoting women ganbu as well as ganbu of both sexes in the minority nationalities. The latter aims at reversing the predominant profile of party cadres: male and Han race.

There are set down a number of qualifications required of ganbu. Not only must he possess the traits provided in Article 3 for each and every party member, but he must have such extra virtues as "firm grasp of the theories of Marxism-Leninism," earnest study and execution of the "line, principles and policies of the party," fervent dedication to the revolutionary cause, democratic workstyle, disavowal of abuses of power, uniting and working with comrades, and seeking no selfish objectives (Article 35). As if to rectify the past practice of cadres isolating themselves from the rest of society, Article 36 enjoins them to cooperate with non-party cadres, respect them and "learn open-mindedly from their strong points." Further, party organizations are called on to search for capable non-party citizens to fill leading posts. Care should be taken to ensure that non-party officials wield authority commensurate with their roles. The policy of rejuvenation is responsible for the demand in Article 37, par. 1 that "leading cadres at all levels, whether elected through democratic procedure or appointed by a leading body, are not entitled to a life long tenure and they can be transferred from or relieved of their posts." As to how is this to be realized, it is only stated that "old members and members of ill health will be retired according to the regulations of the state" (par. 2). Query: Why the Statute sets no terms of office for the VIP's of the CCP comparable to the two-term rule for the president and vice-president of the CPR (Constitution, Article 79, par. 3), premier, vice-premiers and state councillors (Article 87, par. 2), Chief Procurator (Article 130, par. 2), president of the Supreme Court (Article 124, par. 2), the chairman and vice-chairmen of the Standing Committee of the National People's Congress (Article 66, par. 2)?

Hu Yaobang, General Secretary of the CCP, made a very candid report to the 12th Congress on September 1, 1982. He deplored the low morale and unlawful activity of party members. No doubt, due to this situation an unprecedented Chapter VII (Articles 38-42) on discipline is created in the Statute. Members are advised to operate within the ambit of legislations (Article 38, par. 1). Any deviant is subject to criticism and chastizement in the spirit of learning from the past to improve the future and of "diagnosing the ill to save the man" (par. 2). There are five penalties: a) warning, b) grave warning, c) removal from party post and asking for his dismissal from non-party job by the competent authorities, d) probation, e) expulsion (Article 39, par. 4). The punitive probation, to be differentiated from entry probation, is not to exceed two years. If within that period he does not amend his ways, his party card would be taken away. A decision to sanction a member is advised to be reached with prudence. "It is strictly forbidden," states Article 39, par. 4, "to take any measure against a member that contravenes the party Statute or the laws of the state, or retaliates against or frames up comrades." All inflictions must be endorsed by a general meeting of the party branch. If the case is a complicated one, or involves an expulsion, it must be reviewed by the party commission for discipline inspection at or above the county level. However, under extraordinary circumstances, such a commission or a party committee has the power to directly impose a penalty upon a party member without sending report to higher bodies.

The above rules apply to ordinary members, but the removal of a member or an alternate member of the Central Committee or a local committee at any level from party post, or his placement on probation, or outright expulsion cannot be done except by two-thirds in the party committee to which he belongs. In comparison, Rule 11, par. 4 of the CPSU Statutes says that the party congress can remove CC members, but in the interval between two congresses, it is done by a plenary meeting of the CC by two-thirds of the membership. Below the Chinese CC, any dismissal is subject to approval by a higher party committee. A member or an alternate member of the CC, it is specifically laid down in Article 40, par. 3, who "seriously breaks criminal law" is to be dismissed from the party by the Politburo. The member of a local party committee who does the same is to be expelled by the standing committee of the party committee at the corresponding level. Due to this special treatment, the party hierarchs are put outside the mass control. If the leaders band together and exonerate each other, no amount of public uproar is able to dislodge them. Truly only VIP's can topple VIP's. The Gang of Four were ousted by a colleague of theirs, Hua Guofeng, on October 6, 1976, and he, in turn, was sacked as party chairman by Deng Xiaoping on June 30, 1981 and expelled from the Politburo on September 12, 1982.

To promote legality and protect the members, Article 41 provides for the notifying the disciplined man of the charge against him and for his appeal of the charge. Such an appeal must not be denied. All the regulations just described are copied from the CPSU Statutes except that the CCP can punish not only individuals but also organizations. It is written in Article 42, par. 2 that if the latter infringe disciplinary code in a grave manner and fail to rectify the mistakes, the next higher party committee can restructure or dissolve them altogether. That committee reports the action to the party committee further above for approval and then formally announces and executes the order (see also Article 39, par. 2). Such institutional discipline undoubtedly is intended to destroy the power base of rival leaders. It happens after each shakeup, big or small. With the downfall of a patron not only goes his official family but also goes the "homestead." The Statute now legalizes such practice.

The CCP enrolled 39,000,000 as reported during the 12th Congress in September 1982.[33] Although large in absolute number, the party still has the smallest percentage of the population of all communist countries. Its 3.8 percent compares with 6.5 percent for the CPSU (Chinese mainland population 1,008,233,924, as of "the zero hour July 1, 1982").[34] Actually the size of membership of the CCP does

[33] *Globe and Mail,* September 6, 1982, p. 9, col. 1.

[34] "The 1982 census results," *Beijing review,* November 8, 1982, p. 20, col. 1. The total is 1,031,882,551 including Taiwan's 18,270,749 and Hong Kong's and Macao's 5,378,624.

not mean too much, because citizens of China are ordered by the Constitution to cling to the dictatorship of the proletariat (which is another expression of democratic dictatorship). The difference between a member and a non-member is that one has a party ID and the other does not have it.

The CCP literature says nothing about the number of the purged, in contrast to the 60,000 a year of the CPSU. The Chinese probably consider this both state and party secret, and therefore, it is not revealable (Constitution, Article 53; Statute, Article 3). After the 12th Congress there has been a renewal of party cards which undoubtedly will drop many undesirables, particularly those who entered during the Cultural Revolution. Against the Russian Party Statutes (Rule 71), the CCP Statute does not mention the rate of membership dues although such dues are referred to in Article 1, and Article 9, par. 4. One may infer that most of the party expenses are borne by the state budget. Another point to be made here is that in the CCP if a person fails to pay dues for six months, his membership would be terminated, but in the CPSU this period is only three months.

Organizational matters

National Congress

Article 10, cl. 3 of the Statute designates this as the highest authority of the party. Beginning in 1921, it has met in: (Source: *Beijing review,* September 6, 1982, pp. 20-24)

			number deputies	days	representing
1921	July 23-31	1st	12	9	50 plus
1922	July 16-23	2nd	12	8	195
1923	June 12-20	3rd	30-odd	9	420
1925	Jan. 11-22	4th	20	12	995
1927	April 27-May 9	5th	80	13	57,900
1928	June 18-July 11	6th	84	24	40,000
1945	April 23-June 11	7th	547	50	1,210,000
1956	Sept. 15-27	8th	1,026	11	10,730,000
1969	April 1-24	9th	1,512	15	22,000,000
1973	Aug. 24-28	10th	1,249	5	28,000,000
1977	Aug. 12-28	11th	1,510	18	35,000,000
1982	Sept. 1-11	12th	1,600	12	39,000,000

All of the congresses were assembled irregularly. During 1956-1969, an interval of 14 years, only one congress took place, which is the same interval between the 18th and 19th Congresses of the CPSU (1939-1952). However, commencing in 1969, there were more congresses than required by the Statute. That is, there were four, not two. Such aperiodical pattern is envisaged by Article 18. This stipulation gives a five-year term, with the proviso that the congress may be advanced "if the Central Committee deems it necessary, or if more than one-third of the organizations at the provincial level have so requested." This one-third concession is not in the previous Statutes. Obviously it is designed to democratize the party by protecting the minority rights. Except under special circumstances the congress may not be postponed. There is no mention of extraordinary congress, as is in the CPSU Statues (Rule 30, par. 1).

From 1956 to 1982, all but the last congress were deferred, because all these years were "special." And from 1946 to 1955, the congress was never convened. Of all the post-1956 congresses only the 8th congress met twice (in 1956 and 1958); and this is unlawful because quinquennium is called for by the Statute. After rubber-stamping the resolutions tabled by the CC, a congress adjourns and never returns. A body of more than one thousand and several hundred can scarcely be expected to be more than a rally. It is assembled to applaud the hierarchs, but nothing more.

In accordance with Article 19, the congress has six functions: (1) to hear and examine reports of the CC and (2) those of the Central Advisory Commission and the Central Commission for Discipline Inspection, (3) to discuss and decide major questions concerning the party, (4) to revise the party Statute, (5) elect the CC and (6) the three bodies just mentioned. There is no record showing that the congress has ever vetoed the reports, or even amended them. The personages, supposedly picked by the congress, are in fact named by the top echelon. The panel is handed down for ritual approbation.

An individual of some stature, be he a steel-mill executive, or an engineer of a large construction, or the first secretary of a provincial party committee, let alone a Hu Yaobang, a Zhao Ziyang or a Deng Xiaoping, may be given a seat in the congress. However, we must emphasize that before getting the seat, he would have long distinguished himself in his work.[35] In truth, to be a congressman does not add a whit to his stature. Nobody prides himself on a congressmanship. The title itself does not exist in the first place. According to Article 9 of the 1977 Statute, he is elected through secret ballot by democratic consultation. The membership should be apportioned among the old, the middle-aged and the young. This novelty harks back to the Cultural Revolution. In that year (1977), the CCP oligarchs had not yet conceded to the calamity of the Revolution; and the Statute drawn up then still retained some of its legacies. The Chinese did not define what age is old, what is young and what lies in between. The 1982 Statute deletes this age-group requirement and the aforesaid democratic consultation. However, the latter is kept in Article 28, par. 1 of the Election Law (Article 25, cl. 4) of the CPR (n.b. not the party election). To the National Congress of the party are elected deputies from the provincial and regional congresses, and from the congresses of Beijing, Shanghai and Tianjin. Secret ballot is provided for in Article 11, par. 1. At a given level, the list of candidates is submitted to the party organization and voters for

[35] Franz Schurmann, *Ideology and organization in communist China,* Berkeley: University of California Press, 1968, pp. 85-89.

deliberation. A preliminary selection may take place to produce a list of names for the formal election. However, the preliminary can be dispensed with, but if so, the number of candidates must be larger than the number of the persons to be chosen. By Article 18, par. 2, the size of the National Congress and the procedure of their election are determined by the CC.

The method of democratic consultation in the old Statute was calculated to accommodate the power strife of the party bosses, each seeking to have his followers picked as congressmen. Since the congress was made up of representatives from the provinces, regions, the three largest cities, and army constituencies, the bosses had to exert their influence there. The consultation involved much logrolling and maneuvering. One indication of this process is the postponement of the Ninth Congress from 1962 to 1969, during which time Lin Biao went all-out to build a mighty bloc. That Congress passed a Statute and named him successor to Mao Zedong after he died.

A congress fulfills the role of a high sounding board and is able to legitimate some unusual steps the hierarchs have taken. Each of the last six congresses (1945, '56, '69, '73, '77, '82) writes a Statute. The last congress, most important of all, approves a drastic reform, abandoning revolutionary quixotism in favor of pragmatism. It goes without stating that the leaders can short-circuit the formality of convening a congress even when a terribly important decision is being made, e.g., to oust the Gang of Four.[36]

The civil and military contingents of the congress varied according to the political weather-vane of the time. Eighty-one and nineteen percent of the 8th Congress delegates were civilian and military respectively. This can be explained by the smallest number of powerful commanders at the provincial level in those days. The balance came to change as more and more such commanders entered national politics. During the Cultural Revolution, no single provincial governor (chairman of provincial revolutionary committee) was a civilian. It is largely, if not exclusively, due to armed intervention in the power combat of 1967 that peace of sorts was restituted. By 1969, there emerged a different landscape of politics in China. It was dotted by warlords. Headed by Lin Biao, the military took 45 percent of the 9th Congress delegates. The civilians were a heterogeneous batch of administrative, party, scientific, ideological, industrial or economic personnel. It was a foregone conclusion that the comrades-in-arms were to carry on their shoulders, as it were, Lin Biao to the forefront of politics.

Following the perdition of Lin Biao, the military beat a quick retreat. They made up 32 percent of the 10th Congress and 29 percent of the 11th, with the corresponding civilian percentage to be 68 and 71 respectively in the two congresses.[37] In the 12th Congress, the military

---

[36] Lucian W. Pye, *The spirit of Chinese politics*, Cambridge: MIT press, 1968, pp. 13, 16.

[37] James Townsend, *Politics in China*, pp. 294-295.

complement was 30 percent. For the sake of comparison, the CPSU's 25th Congress selected 30 generals and marshals in the 426-man CC. This is only 7.2 percent.[38]

Central Committee (CC)

Closer to the heart of the policy elite is this body. Article 19, cl. 5 orders the Central Committee to be elected by the congress. This, however, should not be interpreted literally. In reality, instead of being chosen by the congress, the CC chooses the congress itself. It is a much smaller group and meets more often. Following each new congress there is a new CC, albeit its members are overwhelmingly holdovers. The size of the post-1949 CC's is like this:

	full	candidate
8th (1956)	97	96 a
9th (1969)	170	109 b
10th (1973)	195	124 c
11th (1977)	201	132 d
12th (1982)	210	138 e

a) James Townsend, *Politics in China*, p. 264.
b) *Ibid.*
c) Sam C. Sarkesian and James H. Buck, *Contemporary politics*, Sherman Oaks, California: Alfred Pub. co., 1979, p. 207, col. 2.
d) *Keesing's*, December 16, 1977, p. 645, col. 2.
e) *Globe and Mail*, September 11, 1982, p. 15, cols. 1-2 at 1.

The percentage of full members in the congress is fractional: 15 percent of the 10th Congress, 13 of the 11th, and 12 of the 12th. Members are elected by a congress during its first and only convocation. Preeminent and long-standing members are the Yanan cadres, Long Marchers or even Jiangxi soviets aged sixty and above. The published figures of CC members can be correct only for a very short time, because death and power strife quickly take their tolls. The moment the CC list appears in *Renmin ribao,* a few are already gone. This explains why there are so many candidate members. It is written in Article 20, par. 1 that they are made full members only if the incumbent full members vacate their posts, and they are taken in accordance with the votes they received in the congress.

During wartime, the high casualties necessitated a large number of replacements, but in peace, the need for so many standbys can only be accounted for by the victimization of political infighting. CC members must have a party standing of at least five years. The number of full members and candidates is determined by the National Congress. The latter body has the power to elect the CC members, but it cannot remove them.[39] Article 40, par. 3 provides that any decision to repel a member or candidate of the CC from the party post, to place such a person on probation, or to dismiss him from the party is taken by a two-thirds vote at a plenary meeting of the

[38] Donald D. Barry and Carol Barner-Barry, *Contemporary soviet politics*, Englewood Cliffs, New Jersey: Prentice-Hall, 1978, p. 295.

[39] Lucian W. Pye, *The authority crisis in Chinese politics*, Chicago: University of Chicago Press, 1967, p. 13.

...y with awe because its voice is law, nay, supreme law.
...officially taken there and all propaganda revolves around
...CC decision.[43] For students or jurisprudence, it is of utmost
...know that in the CPR one may be prosecuted and convicted
...ot only by citing articles of the penal code but by invoking
...tements of the CC.[44]

...ering several hundreds (candidates have the right to discuss,
...ght to vote), the CC is still too large to be effective, although
...it is useful as an underwriter of the leaders' stand. It has
...own that Mao Zedong, fearing that the 1957 Great Leap might
...edoed by the Politburo, decided to convene the CC which,
...xpected, adopted it without demur.[45] This event reminds us
...a Khrushchev's appeal in the same year (1957) to the CC about
...litburo resolution to fire him. Like Mao, he succeeded. The
...se CC, meeting so rarely, is unable to tackle issues of an
...ng nature. To fulfill this need, a smaller body, the Politburo was
...ed.[46]

...olitburo

...athletic terminology, the Politburo men are heavyweights in the
...te arena.[47] They are appointed by the CC according to Article 21,
...r. 1 of the Statute. Just as the congressmen and CC members,
...e Politburo men are either full members or candidates. Unlike them,
...owever, these two categories are not stipulated in that document.
...is rather a matter of custom. Because the Politburo is the "true
...ocus of authority and power,"[48] its size is kept manageable so as
...o enable it to function well.[49] In the last five CC's, the Politburo had,
...t the time of election, the following size.

total numbers	incl. candidates	in	CC
20	6	1956	CC
21	4	1969	8th
21	4	1973	9th
23	3	1977	10th
28	3	1982	11th
			12th

[43] Neil C. Burton, *China since Mao*, New York: Monthly review press. This source also supplies the information in the next paragraph. 1981 pp. 15ff.

[44] Donald Paragon, "The administration of justice and law in the new China," *New York State bar journal*, November 1977, no. 7, pp. 577-584 at 581, col. 2.

[45] David F. Roth and Frank L. Wilson, *The comparative study of politics*, 2nd ed., Englewood Cliffs, New Jersey: Prentice-Hall, 1980, p. 235.

[46] Richard Baum, *Prelude to revolution: Mao, the party and the peasant question 1962-1966*, New York: Columbia University press, 1967, p. 64.

[47] Robert C. North, *The Chinese communist Politburo and its operational code, a feasibility study*, Stanford: Stanford University, 1967 (typescript), sheets 20-21.

[48] Sam C. Sakesian and James H. Buck, *op. cit.*, p. 203.

[49] Wolfgang Bartke, "Analyse der Politbürofunktionäre des 11. ZK der KPCR, nach dem Stand von August 1979", *China aktuell*, 8 (1979), Juliheft, s. 836-847.

CC. Moreover, a full member or a candidate who violates criminal law shall be expelled from the CCP by the Politburo as stated above. This provision is written, no doubt, in the light of the alleged crimes of the Gang of Four.

What are the authorities of the CC? First, it is empowered to convene the National Congress on its own initiative, or at the instance of one-third of the provincial-level organizations (a point already made by us) and second, CC determines the size of the Congress and the procedure of selecting members to it. Article 20, par. 1, it is interesting to note, gives the congress the right to determine the size of the CC. Each body thus determines the membership of the other. In fact, neither has a say on this matter. It is the Standing Committee of the Politburo which transmits a panel of names to both bodies for rubber-stamping. Third, the personnel in the just-mentioned Standing Committee, Politburo, Secretariat (Article 21, par. 1), and Military Commission (par. 5) are chosen by the CC. Fourth, the latter through a two-thirds vote can discipline its own members or candidates by removing them from party office, placing them on probation, or expelling them (Article 40, par. 2). Fifth, when the National Congress is not in session, the CC directs the entire work of the party. Sixth, the CC represents the latter in its external relations (Article 20, par. 3). Seventh, Article 5, par. 1 declares the CC to be the only body which "has the power to make decisions on major policies" affecting the nation. Eighth, the CC can admit a new party member directly, by sidetracking the regular procedure (Article 5, par. 6). Ninth, it is stated in Article 4, cls. 7 and 8 that the CC may consider opinions of individual members which are found contrary to the decisions of a party organization, and review any request, appeal and complaint of members. Tenth and last, it can entrust the Central Advisory Commission with any task whatsoever (Article 22, par. 3). Reading the CCP Statute alongside the CPSU Statutes, one is struck by the silence of the former on matters of party finance, whereas the latter's Rule 34 says the funds of the party are distributed by the decision of the CC and Rules 71 and 72 lay down the rate of membership dues in a minute manner.

The CC is required to hold a plenum at least once a year (Article 20, par. 2). This is in contrast with the Soviet party's two-plenum a year formula (CPSU Statutes, Rule 37). Quite strictly the Russians have observed such rule after the 20th Congress in February 1956. How about the CCP? Its plenum is anything but predictable in spite of the statutory provisions.

8th CC		Important decisions
1st plenum	Sept. 24-30, 1956	
2nd	Dec. 5-10	
3rd	Sept. 24-Oct. 5, 1957	walk on two-leg decision
4th	May 10-15, 1958	
5th	May 28-29	

6th	Nov. 15-20	
7th	April 1-10, 1959	
8th	Aug. 2-6	Mao-Peng Lushan argument
9th	Jan. 1-14	
10th	Sept. 11-16, 1962	
11th	Aug. 1-12, 1966	16 points on Cultural Rev.
12th	Oct. 13-21	Liu Shaoqi criticized

9th CC

1st plenum	April 24-26, 1969	open to non-members
2nd	Aug. 23-Sept. 6, 1970	Chen Boda dismissed

10th CC

1st plenum	Aug. 28-Sept. 5, 1973	Deng Xiaoping named General Chief of Staff (*Encyclopedia of China today* New York: Harper & Row, 1979, p. 113, col. 1)
2nd	Jan. 8-10, 1975	
3rd	July 16-21, 1977	Hua Guofeng named CC Chairman

11th CC

1st plenum	Aug. 15-26, 1977	Four modernizations approved
2nd	Aug. 18-22, 1978	Gang of Four denounced
3rd	Dec. 18-22	
4th	May 5-8, 1979	abolition of four freedoms.*
5th	Feb. 23-29, 1980	Wang Dongxing, Ji Denggui, Wu De, Chen Xilian dismissed. But Chen came back in 1981, and Wang in Sept. 1982.
6th	June 27-29, 1981	Mao officially criticized by a CC resolution. [*Renmin ribao*,
7th	Aug. 7, 1982	July 1, 1981, p. 3, col. 1]

12th CC

1st plenum	Sept. 12-13, 1982	Deng Xiaoping named Chairman of Military Committion, CCP Statute passed, Central Advisory Commission, Central Commission for Discipline
2nd	Oct. 11-12, 1983	Inspection and CC elected.

While the 8th CC held, on the average, one plenum per annum, the other CC's were not so diligent. The CC members are also congressmen, but they carry considerably more weight than the regulars. In the congress one may spot a few manual workers who have established some work-records (mostly alleged). However, in

---

the CC there are no such indivi⟨ high military elite, officials of natio⟨ first secretaries of provincial part⟨ writers, engineers and the like, or th⟨ ideologues. It is to be noted that sch⟨ candidates but never full members. ⟨ the CC has been tremendous. Factio⟨ in the downfall of many. The 11th Cong⟨ members and 132 candidates on Augu⟨ members and 81 candidates were new.⟨ were the Gang of Four.

The 12th Congress came up with 348 full⟨ of whom 211 or more than 60 percent en⟨ time. Two thirds of the 211 are below 60 ye⟨ being 38.[41] The declared policy of the CC is t⟨ generally more youthful and better educated⟨ the 348, only "a dozen or so (are) proletarian⟨ older generation over the age of 70 who, well-ex⟨ enjoy high prestige at home and abroad and ar⟨ work of the whole party and nation."[42] The ove⟨ of the CC joined the revolution during the war with ⟨ the war of "liberation" (1946-1949) and after 19⟨

An appreciable number of the CC members are⟨ accomplished professionals" in the various econom⟨ Some are "outstanding" representatives in culture a⟨ fields and leading party, government and army cadres.⟨ or 17 percent are career and technical personnel as o⟨ percent on the 11th CC. The election of the CC by the⟨ alleged to give "full play to democracy." The delegate⟨ ballots without making any marks on the list of candid⟨ agreed with all of them. Should they hold different opinions⟨ candidates, they put a sign beside their names. However, if⟨ to choose others, they write their names on the ballots. Thi⟨ is not mentioned in Article 11 of the Statute. According to Ar⟨ an election procedure is still to be developed and approved⟨ CC. No doubt the write-in will be provided for by it.

As related above, the Statute pronounces the congress a⟨ highest body, and during its recess, the CC exercises all its ri⟨ Now that the congress lies dormant for all but a few days in the s⟨ of five years, the CC enjoys the proxy authority with no interrupt⟨ during that long interval. While the congress does not do much mo⟨ than endorse a very lengthy declaration, the CC is a powerhouse⟨ It sets political tone, e.g., modernizations, or seeking truth from fact,⟨ to be reverberated throughout the nation. The CC is looked up by⟨

[40] *Keesing's*, December 16, 1977, p. 28722, col. 1.

[41] *Beijing review*, September 20, 1982, p. 4, col. 3.

[42] *Ibid.*, col. 2.

CC. Moreover, a full member or a candidate who violates criminal law shall be expelled from the CCP by the Politburo as stated above. This provision is written, no doubt, in the light of the alleged crimes of the Gang of Four. What are the authorities of the CC? First, it is empowered to convene the National Congress on its own initiative, or at the instance of one-third of the provincial-level organizations (a point already made by us) and second, CC determines the size of the Congress and the procedure of selecting members to it. Article 20, par. 1, it is interesting to note, gives the congress the right to determine the size of the CC. Each body thus determines the membership of the other. In fact, neither has a say on this matter. It is the Standing Committee of the Politburo which transmits a panel of names to both bodies for rubber-stamping. Third, the personnel in the just-mentioned Standing Committee, Politburo, Secretariat (Article 21, par. 1), and Military Commission (par. 5) are chosen by the CC. Fourth, the latter through a two-thirds vote can discipline its own members or candidates by removing them from party office, placing them on probation, or expelling them (Article 40, par. 2). Fifth, when the National Congress is not in session, the CC directs the entire work of the party. Sixth, the CC represents the latter in its external relations (Article 20, par. 3). Seventh, Article 5, par. 1 declares the CC to be the only body which "has the power to make decisions on major policies" affecting the nation. Eighth, the CC can admit a new party member directly, by sidetracking the regular procedure (Article 5, par. 6). Ninth, it is stated in Article 4, cls. 7 and 8 that the CC may consider opinions of individual members which are found contrary to the decisions of a party organization, and review any request, appeal and complaint of members. Tenth and last, it can entrust the Central Advisory Commission with any task whatsoever (Article 22, par. 3). Reading the CCP Statute alongside the CPSU Statutes, one is struck by the silence of the former on matters of party finance, whereas the latter's Rule 34 says the funds of the party are distributed by the decision of the CC and Rules 71 and 72 lay down the rate of membership dues in a minute manner.

The CC is required to hold a plenum at least once a year (Article 20, par. 2). This is in contrast with the Soviet party's two-plenum a year formula (CPSU Statutes, Rule 37). Quite strictly the Russians have observed such rule after the 20th Congress in February 1956. How about the CCP? Its plenum is anything but predictable in spite of the statutory provisions.

8th CC   Important decisions

1st plenum   Sept. 24-30, 1956
2nd   Dec. 5-10
3rd   Sept. 24-Oct. 5, 1957   walk on two-leg decision
4th   May 10-15, 1958
5th   May 28-29

6th	Nov. 15-20	
7th	April 1-10, 1959	
8th	Aug. 2-6	Mao-Peng Lushan argument
9th	Jan. 1-14	
10th	Sept. 11-16, 1962	
11th	Aug. 1-12, 1966	16 points on Cultural Rev.
12th	Oct. 13-21	Liu Shaoqi criticized

9th CC

1st plenum	April 24-26, 1969	open to non-members
2nd	Aug. 23-Sept. 6, 1970	Chen Boda dismissed

10th CC

1st plenum	Aug. 28-Sept. 5, 1973	Deng Xiaoping named General Chief of Staff (*Encyclopedia of China today* New York: Harper & Row, 1979, p. 113, col. 1)
2nd	Jan. 8-10, 1975	
3rd	July 16-21, 1977	Hua Guofeng named CC Chairman

11th CC

1st plenum	Aug. 15-26, 1977	Four modernizations approved
2nd	Aug. 18-22, 1978	Gang of Four denounced
3rd	Dec. 18-22	
4th	May 5-8, 1979	abolition of four freedoms.*
5th	Feb. 23-29, 1980	Wang Dongxing, Ji Denggui, Wu De, Chen Xilian dismissed. But Chen came back in 1981, and Wang in Sept. 1982.
6th	June 27-29, 1981	Mao officially criticized by a
7th	Aug. 7, 1982	CC resolution. [*Renmin ribao, July 1, 1981, p. 3, col. 1]

12th CC

1st plenum	Sept. 12-13, 1982	Deng Xiaoping named Chairman of Military Committion, CCP Statute passed, Central Advisory Commission, Central Commission for Discipline
2nd	Oct. 11-12, 1983	Inspection and CC elected.

While the 8th CC held, on the average, one plenum per annum, the other CC's were not so diligent. The CC members are also congressmen, but they carry considerably more weight than the regulars. In the congress one may spot a few manual workers who have established some work-records (mostly alleged). However, in the CC there are no such individuals. All of its members are either high military elite, officials of national stature, governors of provinces, first secretaries of provincial party committees, eminent scholars, writers, engineers and the like, or the most vocal but scarcely learned ideologues. It is to be noted that scholars and ideologues are always candidates but never full members. In recent years, the turnover in the CC has been tremendous. Factional collapse invariably ended in the downfall of many. The 11th Congress voted into office 201 full members and 132 candidates on August 13, 1977. Of these, 82 full members and 81 candidates were new.[40] The most famous victims were the Gang of Four.

The 12th Congress came up with 348 full members and candidates, of whom 211 or more than 60 percent entered the CC for the first time. Two thirds of the 211 are below 60 years of age, the youngest being 38.[41] The declared policy of the CC is to make the party cadres generally more youthful and better educated (Article 34, par. 1). Of the 348, only "a dozen or so (are) proletarian revolutionaries of the older generation over the age of 70 who, well-experienced in struggle, enjoy high prestige at home and abroad and are presiding over the work of the whole party and nation."[42] The overwhelming majority of the CC joined the revolution during the war with Japan (1937-1945), the war of "liberation" (1946-1949) and after 1949.

An appreciable number of the CC members are said to be "well-accomplished professionals" in the various economic departments. Some are "outstanding" representatives in culture and educational fields and leading party, government and army cadres. Fifty-nine men or 17 percent are career and technical personnel as opposed to 2.7 percent on the 11th CC. The election of the CC by the congress is alleged to give "full play to democracy." The delegates cast their ballots without making any marks on the list of candidates if they agreed with all of them. Should they hold different opinions on certain candidates, they put a sign beside their names. However, if they want to choose others, they write their names on the ballots. This write-in is not mentioned in Article 11 of the Statute. According to Article 18, an election procedure is still to be developed and approved by the CC. No doubt the write-in will be provided for by it.

As related above, the Statute pronounces the congress as the highest body, and during its recess, the CC exercises all its rights. Now that the congress lies dormant for all but a few days in the span of five years, the CC enjoys the proxy authority with no interruption during that long interval. While the congress does not do much more than endorse a very lengthy declaration, the CC is a powerhouse. It sets political tone, e.g., modernizations, or seeking truth from fact, to be reverberated throughout the nation. The CC is looked up by

[40] *Keesing's*, December 16, 1977, p. 28722, col. 1.

[41] *Beijing review*, September 20, 1982, p. 4, col. 3.

[42] *Ibid.*, col. 2.

the citizenry with awe because its voice is law, nay, supreme law. All policy is officially taken there and all propaganda revolves around this or that CC decision.[43] For students or jurisprudence, it is of utmost interest to know that in the CPR one may be prosecuted and convicted by court not only by citing articles of the penal code but by invoking policy statements of the CC.[44]

Numbering several hundreds (candidates have the right to discuss, but no right to vote), the CC is still too large to be effective, although at times it is useful as an underwriter of the leaders' stand. It has been known that Mao Zedong, fearing that the 1957 Great Leap might be torpedoed by the Politburo, decided to convene the CC which, as he expected, adopted it without demur.[45] This event reminds us of Nikita Khrushchev's appeal in the same year (1957) to the CC about the Politburo resolution to fire him. Like Mao, he succeeded. The Chinese CC, meeting so rarely, is unable to tackle issues of an ongoing nature. To fulfill this need, a smaller body, the Politburo was created.[46]

Politburo

In athletic terminology, the Politburo men are heavyweights in the state arena.[47] They are appointed by the CC according to Article 21, par. 1 of the Statute. Just as the congressmen and CC members, the Politburo men are either full members or candidates. Unlike them, however, these two categories are not stipulated in that document. It is rather a matter of custom. Because the Politburo is the "true focus of authority and power,"[48] its size is kept manageable so as to enable it to function well.[49] In the last five CC's, the Politburo had, at the time of election, the following size.

total numbers	incl. candidates	in	CC
20	6	1956	8th
21	4	1969	9th
21	4	1973	10th
23	3	1977	11th
28	3	1982	12th

[43] Neil C. Burton, *China since Mao*, New York: Monthly review press. This source also supplies the information in the next paragraph. 1981 pp. 15ff.

[44] Donald Paragon, "The administration of justice and law in the new China," *New York State bar journal*, November 1977, no. 7, pp. 577-584 at 581, col. 2.

[45] David F. Roth and Frank L. Wilson, *The comparative study of politics*, 2nd ed., Englewood Cliffs, New Jersey: Prentice-Hall, 1980, p. 235.

[46] Richard Baum, *Prelude to revolution: Mao, the party and the peasant question 1962-1966*, New York: Columbia University press, 1967, p. 64.

[47] Robert C. North, *The Chinese communist Politburo and its operational code, a feasibility study*, Stanford: Stanford University, 1967 (typescript), sheets 20-21.

[48] Sam C. Sakesian and James H. Buck, *op. cit.*, p. 203.

[49] Wolfgang Bartke, "Analyse der Politbürofunktionäire des 11. ZK der KPCR, nach dem Stand von August 1979", *China aktuell*, 8 (1979), Juliheft, s. 836-847.

One cannot but be impressed by the stable size through the years, the more so if he recognizes the fact that the parent body (CC) steadily enlarged itself in the same stretch of time (1956-1982) from 97 to 210 full members. This is more than a 100 percent increase. During the Cultural Revolution, some Politburo sessions were open to non-members as CC plenums were when Mao Zedong needed them to help him carry the day.[50]

Power is located in the Politburo, so naturally the struggle for it rages there too. At such dizzy heights a person's prestige is matched only by the risks he takes. Once losing out there, he has no place to go except jail or worse. On October 6, 1976, a coup saw the departure of four Politburo persons to the detention house and from there to prison on January 25, 1981. Two of them were slated to be shot on January 24, 1983, but were reprieved on January 25, 1983 by the CPR's Supreme Court.[51] The Politburo has the following individuals. (Those with asterisks are newcomers)

11 military	14 civilian
7 generals	
Li Tesheng	Chen Yun
Ulanhu	Deng Xiaoping
Wang Zhen	Deng Yingchao (f)
Wei Guoqing	Feng Yi
*Yang Dezhi	Hu Qiaomu
Yu Qiuli	Hu Yaobang
Zhang Tingfa (died, June 10, 1983)	*Liao Chengzhi
	Ni Zhifu
4 marshals	Peng Zhen
Li Xiannian	*Song Renqiong
Nie Rongzheng	*Wan Li
Xu Xiangqian	*Xi Zhongxun
Ye Jianying	*Yang Shangkun
	Zhao Ziyang

Dropped from the old Politburo were three military figures: Xu Shiyou, Geng Biao, Liu Bocheng, as were three (!) civilians: Peng Zhong, Hua Guofeng, Sey Fudin. As compared with the 11 civilians of the old Politburo, there are now 14, and compared to the 12 military hierarchs there are now 11. There are three candidates: Yao Yilin, Qin Jiwei, and Chen Muhua (f). They are arranged according to the votes they received at the 1st plenum of the 12th CC held on September 12 and 13, 1982 immediately following the adjournment of the 12th Congress.[52] Whether the vacancies of the Politburo are to be filled by the candidates according to the ballots they received is not stated in the Statute, although this method of replenishing the CC is expressly written in Article 20, par. 1. The Politburo convenes

[50] David F. Roth and Frank L. Wilson, *loc. cit.*, also in 1st ed., p. 239.

[51] Time, February 7, 1983, p. 32; *Beijing review*, February 7, 1983, p. 7.

[52] *Beijing review*, September 20, 1982, p. 6, col. 1.

the CC plenum (par. 2). When the CC is not in session, the Politburo and its Standing Committee carry on its functions (Article 21, par. 2). Differing from all previous Statutes, the present one in Article 40, par. 3 grants to the Politburo the right to expel from the party full members or candidates of the CC, if they are found "seriously" in breach of criminal law. Minor offenses, by implication, cannot be grounds for dismissal. It is to be noted here that the CC can also expel its members.

We must argue that the classification of civilian and military complements in the Politburo holds true only for the post-1949 situation. All the Politburo men and the Politburo woman (Deng Yingchao, widow of Zhou Enlai) bore arms during their insurgency. Deng Xiaoping, for one, was said to be within rifle's shot from J. Carter in the Tianjin area in 1946 when the former was leading a unit of the Red Army and the latter was serving in the US Marines sent there to help the National Government forces. They talked about it during Deng's visit to the White House on January 31, 1979. The average age of the 25 individuals in the Politburo is 75. When the CCP scored the final "touchdown" in 1949, the mean age of the Politburo men was 40. In the twenty odd years leading to the victory, they were busy with activities in diverse rebelling areas. Every communist was a soldier then.[53] Even if he had to engage in the administration of a village, that was his "avocation." Dragooning men into the Red Army was the principal concern of a communist, a concern of life and death. In an attack by the government troops, he had to take the field at the head of a squadron or two. One cannot find a civilian as such among the CCP's high priests. On this point, an American author stated well that the line between soldiers and civilian personnel was blurred during the communists' rise to power.[54]

Standing Committee

The title Central Committee is, strictly speaking, not correct because it is still a peripheral organization. If, however, the word "central" has to be retained to name it, the Politburo must be a "centralest" body. Nevertheless, the concentration process goes a step further. At its innermost is the Standing Committee. The Statute in Article 21, par. 1 authorizes the CC to select the Politburo and this Committee. "When the CC is not in session, the Politburo and its Standing Committee exercise the functions and powers of the CC" (par. 2) This provision erases the boundary between the two bodies since both are empowered to discharge the responsibility of the parental CC. There is no stipulation in the Statute that when the Politburo is not in session, the Standing Committee exercises its powers.[55] Nor is there a stipulation that the Politburo elects the

[53] Ilpyong J. Kim, *The politics of Chinese communism*, Berkeley: University of California press, 1973, pp. 47-48.

[54] Lucian W. Pye, *China, an introduction*, Boston: Little, Brown, 1972, p. 165.

[55] Charles Neuhauser, "The Chinese party in the 1960's: prelude to Cultural Revolution," *China in ferment, perspectives on the Cultural Revolution*, edited by Richard Baum, Englewood Cliffs, New Jersey: Prentice-Hall, 1971, pp. 31-34.

Standing Committee. Such an election would imply the subordination of the latter to the former. Taking the statutory provision as it is, we get the impression that the two bodies are co-equal. In actuality, the Standing Committee is superior, because its members have the most seniority and its size is smaller:

5 in 1969
9 in 1973
5 in 1977
5 in 1980
7 in 1981
6 in 1982

It can be viewed as both the permanent body of the Politburo and its nucleus.

The Standing Committee, it is interesting to compare, has no Soviet counterpart. In the CPSU Politburo, the men whom Secretary-General Yuri Andropov consults most often may well be regarded as that party's standing committee. The Chinese Standing Committee is obviously designed to achieve an effective control of the party machinery. The Politburo does not meet on a daily basis, but as the title implies, the Standing Committee does. It is a continuously functioning body for the disposal of ongoing problems and it does this in the name of the Politburo. Since matters at this height are enshrouded in secret, there is no way of knowing exactly how it operates.[56] It is rather trite to say that since the Committee consists of the "almighty" men of China, it is really the ruling clique.

In the same way as a democracy's cabinet, the size of the Committee and the kind of office-holders who may enter it are not fixed by law. However, the 1982 Statute has specified that it must have the following members: a) General Secretary (Article 21, par. 1) b) Chairman of Military Commission (par. 5), c) First Secretary of the Central Commission for Discipline Inspection (Article 43, par. 3), d) Chairman of the Central Advisory Commission (Article 22, par. 2). At the first plenum of the 12th CC held on September 12-13, 1982, the Standing Committee was comprised of Deng Xiaoping who held the dual positions of b) and d), Chen Yun who took the position of c), Hu Yaobang in the position of a), and three other individuals: Ye Jianying, Li Xiannian, Zhao Ziyang. These three can be called committeemen without portfolio. All of the previous Standing Committees were odd-numbered organizations, but the current one is an even-numbered body. Perhaps it will be odd-numbered after Deng Xiaoping dies, when the two seats he now occupies are filled by two men. Would the present even number (6) pose a deadlock? We surmise that Deng Xiaoping is entitled to two votes by virtue of the two constituencies he stands for.

The Beijing regime is a veritable gerontocracy. Witness the ages: Zhao Ziyang 64, Hu Yaobang 68, Chen Yun 78, Li Xiannian 78, Deng

[56] James Townsend, *Political participation in communist China*, Berkeley: University of California press, 1968, pp. 54, 164.

Xiaoping 79, Ye Jianying 86. The average age is 75.5. For the sake
of comparison, the CPSU Politburo as of May 30, 1983 had an odd-
numbered composition (eleven), and they were Yu. Andropov
(Secretary General) aged 69, K. Chernenko 73, M.S. Gorbachev 53,
V.V. Grishin 69, D.A. Kunanev 71, G.V. Romanov 60, V.V.
Shcherbitskii 65, N.A. Tikhonov 78, G. Aliev 64, D.F. Ustinov 75, and
A. Pel'she 84 (died May 29, 1983). Their average age is 69.1. The
Chinese leadership is older by six and half years.

General Secretary

At the 12th Congress, the leadership did away with the CC
Chairman and brought the General Secretary to the fore. This is in
line with the CPSU system. Very possibly such a move is purported
to head off any future buildup of personal dictatorship. The previous
name, chairman, seems to be more in keeping with the traditional
Chinese way of thinking because the term secretary (shuji) connotes
a subsidiary role, while chairman (zhuxi) conveys a commanding post.
Mao Zedong assumed the two zhuxi (party zhuxi and state zhuxi) from
1954 to 1959. From 1959 until 1968, on the two chairs sat two men,
Mao Zedong the party zhuxi and Liu Shaoqi the state zhuxi. When
the latter man was declared to be a traitor, the state zhuxi was left
vacant. In September 1976, Hua Guofeng took over Mao Zedong's
party zhuxi upon his death. From then until the fall of 1980, the party
zhuxi was concurrently the premier. Here is a fusion of the·supreme
political and administrative authority. The resolution of the Politiburo
to have Zhao Ziyang replace Hua Guofeng as premier in September
1980 resulted from a general agreement that the party zhuxi is already
a formidable office and that by adding the premiership to it the holder
would be a potential threat to others. Political power, according to
the contemporary leadership, should be shared but not concentrated.
In fact, Hua Guofeng after being forced to relinquish the premiership
became a titular boss of the party. In all but name, Deng Xiaoping
was the party hegemon. It was not, however, until after June 1981
that the 11th CC at its 6th plenum decided to have Deng's protégé,
Hu Yaobang, take over the party zhuxi from Hua Guofeng. The latter
was demoted to the seventh and the last seat in the 7-man Standing
Committee.[57]

The Secretariat of the party was minutely regulated in the 1956
Statute but was dropped altogether from the 1969 and 1973 statutes.[58]
The Cultural-revolution turmoil, we will recall, was levelled at
revisionism allegedly led by the state zhuxi Liu Shaoqi and the
General Secretary Deng Xiaoping. When the campaign was called
off in early 1969, the victors, still full of hatred for the pair, were
determined that the two offices must go too. The dislike of the men
thus sublimed into the dislike of the offices they once held. How

[57] Renmin robao, June 30, 1981, p. 1.

[58] Andrian Hsia, The Chinese cultural revolution, translated by Harold Oun, New York: McGraw-Hill, 1972,
pp. 213ff.

puerile the Chinese communists are! From 1968 to 1982, there was no state zhuxi, but party secretary reappeared in February 1980 after its disappearance in 1968.

Presently the secretariat has the following full members:[59] Chen Pixian, Deng Liqun, Gu Mu, Hu Qili, Wan Li, Xi Zhongxun, Yang Yong, Yao Yilin, Yu Qiuli. The two alternates are Qiao Shi and Hao Jianxiu (f). The former man received more votes in the CC and would have the first chance to replace someone in the full ranks. On January 15, 1983, Yang Yong died, and Qiao Shi became a full member. All members are elected by the 1st plenum of the 12th CC under Article 21, par. 1 of the Statute. By comparison, the CPSU has never had a chairman and it abolished the alternate secretary after the 20th Congress in February 1956. Among the 9 full Chinese members only Wan Li, Xi Zhongxun and Yu Qiuli are concurrently Politburo members, while Yao Yilin is an alternate member in both bodies.

Central Advisory Commission

This is a new body which was instituted by the 12th Congress. Article 22, par. 2 describes it as the "political assistant and consultant to the Central Committee." Just like the latter and the Central Commission for Discipline Inspection, it is elected by the Congress (Article 19, cl. 6). Its tenure is the same as the CC. Although nothing about this is said in the Statute, the tenure coincides with the Congress. That is to say, if the latter is elected either prior to or later than the statutory five years under Article 18, par. 1, the term of the Commission in question is adjusted accordingly. At a plenary session, the Commission elects the chairman and vice-chairmen and other members (Article 22, par. 2). However, they must be approved by the CC which presumably can veto any of the names. The number of the vice-chairmen and members is fixed by the CC. On September 12, 1982, the Commission chose Deng Xiaoping as chairman and the following four vice-chairmen: Bo Yibo, Xu Shiyou, Tan Zhenlin, Li Weihan.[60] There are 172 ordinary members. As qualifications for all members Article 22, par. 1 lays down: a) they must have a party standing of at least 40 years, b) have rendered "considerable service to the party," c) possess "fairly rich experience in leadership and enjoy fairly high prestige inside and outside the party." Except for a), the leaders in power are quite free in the matter. What kind of experience is "fairly rich"? What kind of prestige is "fairly high"? If a dispute arises, what agency is empowered to review the decision of the Commission? (Vice-chairman Tan Zhelin died on Sept. 30, 1983)

If the 40-year rule is strictly adhered to, all the 172 commissioners would have to be joining the party before 1942, the year of the famous

---

[59] *The twelfth national congress of the CPC* (September 1982), Beijing: Foreign Languages Press, 1982, p. 154; also in *Beijing review*, September 20, 1982, p. 6, cols. 1-2.

[60] *Beijing review*, September 20, 1982, p. 6, col. 2. *ibid.*, April 4, 1983, p. 8, col. 1, mentions Deng Xiaoping as vice-chairman. This is apparently a mistake.

rectification (see next chapter). They are the Jiangxi soviets, the Long Marchers and the ancestral Yananites. All but a handful of them are now septuagenarians or octogenarians. The Commission, it is pretty clear, is a dumping ground for superannuated revolutionaries. Three points are worth mentioning here. First, not all worn-out leaders are consigned to it. Among the six-man Standing Committee of the Politburo five should have gone there, but did not. Second, the chairman of the Commission is an ex-officio member of the said Standing Committee. Third, the Statute in Article 22, par. 2, requires the voice of other members to be heard in the policy-making councils. To be more specific, members a) may attend plenary session of the CC as non-voting participants, b) vice-chairmen may take part, again without vote, in the Politburo meeting, and c) other members of the Standing Committee of the Commission may do the same, if the CC wants them to. These provisions indicate the important role of the Commission.

On the other hand, though, the Statute in Article 22, par. 3 relegates it to a secondary position. It is "assistant and consultant" to the CC. Working under the latter's leadership, the Commission "puts forward recommendations on the formulation and implementation of the party's principles and policies and gives advice upon request." Also it aids the CC in investigating and handling "certain important questions," and "in doing other tasks." One cannot, of course, expect the Statute to spell out these questions and tasks. It shows that the leaders desire the experience and prestige to push through their programs, particularly those which may encounter opposition from the public or from within their ranks. It is to this end perhaps that the Statute orders the Commission to perform some propaganda functions inside and outside the party (Article 22, par. 3). One may observe, as a footnote here, that two purged leaders, Chen Xilian and Wu De were elected to the Commission, and that Xu Shiyou, a late opponent to Deng Xiaoping and a former Politburo man, is vice-chairman of the Commission.

No stipulation in the Statute prohibits concurrent posts in the Commission and other bodies. This fact and the free choice of the members (except the 40-year rule) give the top leaders much room to maneuver. Besides those who are too senile to be of any use to the regime, political rivals, provided they are not so stubborn as to warrant liquidation, may be appointed to the Commission. The aforesaid Wu De and Chen Xilian, expelled by the 5th plenum of the 11th CC in February 1980, found their way to the Commission. They were supporters of the falling Hua Guofeng. This man, no longer in the Politburo, would have been tossed onto the Commission, if he had fulfilled the requirement of the 40-year rule. We have no doubt that he will be placed there from the CC where he is now, as soon as he accummulates that many years' standing in the party. However, another supporter of Hua Guofeng, Wang Dongxing, who was purged by the 5th plenum of the 11th CC, was not elected to the Commission, but to the CC as candidate (the last of the 138 candidates).[61] Probably such a candidate has the same status as a member of the Commission. Both are subsidiary positions. On the other hand, Politburo members and members of the Standing Committee of the Commission are probably on the same level as far as formal protocol is concerned. Is it for this reason that Xu Shiyou shifts from the Politburo to the vice-chairman of the Commission? By going there, Xu actually loses nothing. For him, it is not a matter of demotion.

Party discipline and disciplinary bodies

The 1982 Statute pays the closest attention to the problem of how well a member should behave and what consequences would be entailed if he did not. Chapter I on membership is both hortatory and remonstrative. A set of rigorous rules of conduct for party cadres as distinct from the rank-and-file members are laid down in Chapter VI. Punitive measures and still more guidelines on correct action and thinking are written down in Chapter VII. All of these culminate in Chapter VIII which sets up the machinery to enforce the rules. All counted, twenty-one of the fifty Articles in the Statute bear on discipline.

The disciplinary agency is provided for in the 1956 Statute, but the 1969 and 1973 Statutes deleted it. Although revived in the 1977 document, it is given only a very brief mention in one article (13). The agency was set up in 1980, but only at the center. It was not until 1981 that the disciplinary bodies began to appear on the sub-national level and in the army above the regiment. The system authorized by the 1982 Statute takes a pyramidal shape. The Central Commission for Discipline Inspection, as the organization is now translated, acts under the CC. A local commission acts under the leadership of the party committee on the same level, and under the leadership of the next higher commission. The term of office of the commission coincides with that of the party committee on the corresponding plane (Article 43, cl. 3). The Central Commission is chosen by the National Congress (Article 18, cl. 6). The plenary session of the Commission produces a Standing Committee, a secretary and deputy secretaries. Their names are, however, to be transmitted to the CC for approval. Similarly, a local commission elects the same officials. The slate is reviewed by the party committee and afterwards reported to the next higher party commission for approbation. Whether a primary party committee should establish a commission or just appoint a single commissioner is determined by the next higher party organization, but the committee of a general party branch or party branch can have only a commissioner. (Article 43, par. 3).

The first secretary of the Central Commission for Discipline Inspection is required by Article 43, par. 3 to be a member of the Politburo's Standing Committee. On September 12-13, 1982, the 1st

---

[61] The twelfth national congress of the CPC (September 1982), p. 148.

plenum of the Commission chose Chen Yun and Huang Kecheng as first and second secretaries respectively. The former in fact took the post in 1980,[62] while the latter was previously a standing secretary of the Commission, a post presently filled by Wang Heshou. The September plenum also chose the following secretaries: Wang Congwu, Han Guang, Li Chang, Ma Guorui, and Han Tianshi. Even though the Statute does not state this fact expressly, the Standing Committee is composed of all secretaries, no matter what rank they hold. There are now 132 members of the Commission, compared with former membership of 100.[63] Note that before the 1982 re-organization, the Commission's second secretary was Deng Yingchao and its third secretary Hu Yaobang. Hu, at the time, was also the General Secretary of the CC, a powerful figure.

What are the functions of the Commission? It upholds the Statute and other important rules and regulations of the party, renders help to the various party committees in the rectification of the party style, and checks up on the execution of the line, principles, policies and decisions of the party (Article 44, par. 1). Also, it educates party members about observance of party orders. The Commission disposes of "significant or complicated cases" involving breach of the Statute and decrees of the party or the laws and ordinances of the state by party organizations or individual members. Also within its purview is the power to decide on the punishment of members after hearing their cases and personal complaints. Both the central and local commissions must make reports to the party committees in respect to the handling of matters of extraordinary importance; local commissions must submit their decisions to the higher commission for review. If the Central Commission for Discipline Inspection finds that a member of the CC has violated party discipline, it may send the case to that body which "must deal with the case promptly" (Article 44, par. 4).

A higher commission has the right to oversee lower commissions and to approve or modify their actions. If the actions so modified have already been ratified by the party committee, they ought to be sanctioned by the next higher party committee. If a local commission does not concur with the party committee, it may request the commission at the next higher level to re-examine the issue in question. If a local commission discovers a breach of party discipline or the laws and ordinances of the state by the party committee or by its members, and if the party committee fails to deal with them properly or does not deal with them at all, it can appeal the case to the higher commission (Article 45, par. 2).

As a matter of historical interest, the 1956 Commission consisted of 60 individuals. After the Cultural Revolution, all but six were disciplined and purged.[64] This happened because the enforcement

---

[62] *Zhong guo shou ce*, Hong Kong: Da gong Bao, 1980, p. 133.

[63] James Wang, *Op cit.*, p. 76; *Zhong guo shou* ce, p. 139.

[64] D.J. Waller, *The government and politics of communist China*, London: Hutchinson University Library, 1970, p. 80.

of discipline always involves personal or sectoral grudges and revenge. As well, discipline may have to do with ideology which shifts unexpectedly from one extreme to another. This invariably brings groups into confrontation. The Commission has been fairly active for the past several years. For example, *Renmin ribao* of August 7, 1980 (p. 1) and of November 23, 1981 (p. 1), printed its order to "ban protective relations (Russian blat) between economic and administrative organs purported to evade the law."

Local organizations

The congress of a province, an autonomous region, a centrally ruled city, a city which has districts in it, or an autonomous prefecture, is held once every five years. The congress of a county (qi in an autonomous region), an autonomous county, a city not divided into districts, or a municipal district meets once every three years. The congress is called by the party committee. In exceptional circumstances, subject to the approval by the next higher party committee, it may be called before or after the fixed date. The number of delegates to the local congress, and the procedure of election, are determined by the party committee and are reported to the next higher party committee for sanction (Article 24).

The congress is authorized to hear the report of the committee and of the commission for discipline inspection. It can deal with major issues in the area, elect the party committee and commission for discipline inspection, and send delegates to the congress at the next higher level. Moreover, it chooses the party advisory commission and receives and examines its reports.

The party committee of a province, an autonomous region, a centrally ruled city, a city divided into districts, or an autonomous prefecture, is elected for five years. The members and alternate members of such a committee must have a party standing of at least five years (Article 26, par. 1). The party committee of a county (qi in an autonomous region), an autonomous county, a city not divided into districts, or a municipal district is mandated for three years. Members and alternate members on this type of committee may have a party standing of only three years. When a local party congress is convened before or after the due date, the tenure of the committee elected by the previous congress is correspondingly shortened or extended. The number of members and alternate members of a local party committee is fixed by the next higher committee. Vacancies on the local party committee are filled by the alternate members according to the number of votes they were accorded. The local party committee meets in a plenary session at least once a year. It carries out, during the recess of the congress, the directives of the next higher party organizations and the decisions of the congress on the same level. It also directs work in its own area and reports on it to the next higher party committee at regular intervals.

A local party committee elects a standing committee, a secretary, and deputy secretaries, then submits the results to the next higher party committee for approval. The standing committee exercises the powers of the local party committee when the latter is not in session. It continues to handle the day-to-day affairs when the next party congress holds its meeting, until the new standing committee has been elected.

The party advisory commission of a province, an autonomous region, or a centrally ruled city functions as the political assistant and consultant to the party committee. It functions under the control of the latter committee and in the light of the provisions of Article 22 of the Statute. The qualifications of the members are laid down by the party committee in keeping with these provisions and by taking into consideration the conditions in a given area. The party advisory commission has the same tenure as the party committee. It chooses a standing committee, its chairman, and vice-chairmen; the panel must be endorsed by the party committee and then the names sent to the CC for final review. Members of the advisory commission may attend plenary sessions of the party committee, although they have no voting rights (Article 28).

A prefectural party committee, or an organization similar to it, is the representative body dispatched by a provincial or an autonomous regional party committee to a prefecture, which embraces a number of counties, autonomous counties, or cities. It exercises leadership over work in the area as authorized by the provincial or autonomous regional party committee (Article 29).

Primary party organizations

These are formed in factories, shops, schools, people's communes, offices, city neighborhoods, co-ops, farms, townships, towns and troop units. A primary organization must exist wherever there are three or more party members. With the approval of a higher party, such an organization may have, a) a primary party committee, b) a committee of general party branch, or c) a committee of party branch, depending on the type of work done and the size of the membership. The a) committee is elected by the general meeting or delegate meeting, but b) and c) are elected by the general meeting (Article 30, par. 2). Normally a primary organization convenes a general meeting or delegate meeting once a year, while a general branch holds meetings twice a year, and a party branch once every three months. As regards tenure, the first committee sits for three years, while the other two committees sit for two. Each type of committee elects a secretary and deputy secretaries whose names must be reported to the higher party body for approval.

The primary organization is described as a "militant bastion" of the party in Chinese society. It is responsible for eight tasks. 1) It carries on propaganda and executes the party line, principles and policies, the decisions of the CC and other high organizations of the party, and implements its own resolutions. The organization is called to give full play to the vanguard role of party members, and to unite the cadres and the rank and file both inside and outside the CCP in order to accomplish the work of the units. 2) It organizes members to study Marxism-Leninism and Mao Zedong Thought, to learn everything about the party, and to acquire technical and scientific knowledge. 3) It educates and supervises party members, ensuring that they participate regularly in the function of the organization. 4) It maintains intimate touch with the masses whose views are solicited about the party members and their work-style. In the meantime, the organization must "correct the erroneous ideas and unhealthy ways and customs that may exist among the masses and properly handle the contradictions there." 5) It admits new members, evaluates them, and collects membership dues. 6) It conducts criticism and self-criticism in party meetings. The organization has to make sure that all cadres strictly observe the laws and administrative orders, and respect financial and economic discipline, i.e., not steal public money. 7) It encourages the initiative and creativeness of the cadres in order to stimulate innovations and inventions. Finally, 8) the organization cultivates members' revolutionary vigilance and resolute struggle against counterrevolutionaries and saboteurs.

In an institution or enterprise, the primary party organization, general branch committee, or branch committee spearheads the work. It discusses major questions and at the same time ensures that the administrators fully exercise their authority, yet it must refrain from taking over their jobs. Its responsibility, in other words, is to guarantee the production quota or operational tasks of the institution or enterprise. To quote Article 33, par. 2 of the Statute, the organization is "to assist the office heads to improve work, raise efficiency and overcome bureaucratic ways, keep them (office heads) informed of the shortcomings and problems discovered in the work of these offices, or report such shortcomings and problems to the higher party organization."

All communist systems are plagued by the duplication of the functions of party and government. In theory, the former oversees the latter in the effectuation of plans handed down to it. However, the apparatchiks always find it necessary to interfere with the actual working out of the plans. They not only force bureaucrats to change the course of action, but issue minute details for them to adhere to. This cannot but result in confusion and waste. *Renmin ribao* of December 18, 1981 (p. 5) printed a critical article about this practice calling for its rectification so as to achieve smooth and economic work at the basic levels of the system. The CPSU Statutes in Rule 42, cl. (c), be it noted, not only orders that a party organization may not act in place of government, but that it may not act in the place of a trade-union agency, a co-op or other public body. The merging of the function of party and other organizations or undue paralellism is outlawed. It is obvious that the Chinese communists are not prepared to go that far because the Statute forbids merely the taking over by the party of the government work.

CHAPTER IV
Power Struggle

Introduction

In order to understand the CCP, it is not enough to study its doctrines, its policy, and its apparatus. Equally important is an assessment of the level of solidarity of the leadership. From the outset we must note that the CCP is far from monolithic as is claimed by some. It is not a "united front" itself, although it initiated and noisily yelled that slogan a couple of times in the past.[1] Any communist party, as is known to all, forbids internal cleavage as vehemently as it denies outside competition. However, the truth has been that this is an aspiration rather than a fact. Throughout the world, there is no compact communist party just as there is no compact democratic one. Human nature as it is, discordance has to prevail in all groupings, political or otherwise. Lenin was so foolhardy that he had the 10th Congress (1921) outlaw factionalism. His effort was bound to be futile, and the anti-faction stipulation of the CPSU Statutes (Rule 1 (f), and Rule 26) indeed came to be honored by breach rather than by observance. Aping the Russian party, the CCP in its Statute (Article 3, cl. 4) commands all members to "uphold the party's solidarity and unity, to firmly oppose factionalism and all factional organization and small-group activities." This provision is as pious a prayer as the CPSU provision just mentioned.

Before the earthquake of the Cultural Revolution, several Western scholars suspected that the CCP leaders had some Confucian corpuscles in their blood because they were said to exhibit a great sense of cohesiveness in the pursuit of the goal to build up a perfect society. These leaders were alleged to be bound by a politico-ethical code, submerging their personal difference for the common good. The historian O. Edmund Clubb admired the "stable" rulership,[2] and Allen S. Whiting talked about the "incredibly united and durable elite" of Beijing.[3] This view was taken by them long before the Cultural Revolution. As a matter of fact, though, dissension in the CCP started from its birth, although at that time the seeds of altercation were sown in Moscow. Later sporadic chasms arose in the party fold. This chapter is to examine the patterns of argument among the top men from the inception of the CCP to the Deng Xiaoping era.

Escalation of the Kremlin rift

The founding fathers of the Chinese party were not Chinese but the Russians and for seven years (1921-1927) the latter directed them and made the CCP an offshoot of their own party.[4]If it was not for

---

[1] Joseph W. Esherick, *Lost chance in China*, New York: Random House, 1974, pp. 362, 366, 382.

[2] O. Edmund Clubb, *The 20th Century China*, 2nd ed., New York: Columbia University Press, 1972, p. 313.

[3] Allen S. Whiting, "Political dynamics: the Communist Party of China," *Government of Communist China*, edited by George P. Jan, San Fransisco: Chandler Pub. Co., 1966, pp. 129-155 at 142.

[4] Shanti Swarup, *A Study of Chinese Communist Movement*, Oxford: Clarendon Press, 1966, pp. 13ff.

them, the CCP would have to arise, if at all, later than it did. No sooner was it organized than the Comintern ordered it to align with the Guomindang (GMD). The first secretary, Chen Duxiu wrote that the Comintern agent Maring "had forced the decision of the United Front upon the Chinese Communist Party by asserting the authority of the Soviet (communists)."[5] On that Front, Stalin pinned a great hope of converting China into a proletarian dictatorship. When it broke down following the ejection of all Russian comrades from that country in July 1927, he unjustifiably blamed the Chinese comrades and had Chen Duxiu fired as a right-wing opportunist. He, Stalin, even averred that the Front should not have been formed except for the insistence of Chen.[6] On his part, Trotsky was always critical of the GMD-CCP marriage. According to him, the CCP should go it alone to embark upon a mass revolution, and the GMD was an impossible partner, standing as it did for the interests of the compradors, landowners and bureaucratic capitalists. In the debate, Stalin was put in an embarrassing position. After banishing Trotsky in 1927, he thought it safe to order the dissolution of the said marriage, an action which precipitated the purge of the communists by the nationalists. Stalin now charged that Secretary Chen committed an error of "not following all instructions" of his.[7] In fact, this man was virtually his errand-boy, doing all he could to execute the instructions. Chen was replaced by Ju Qiubai on August 7, 1927 by a resolution of the CCP's emergency conference.[8] Now it was this man's turn.[9]

From the Kremlin, Stalin saw the revolutionary waves surge in China. He was now resolute to out-Trotsky Trotsky in starting a world revolution, beginning in China. The CCP was made busy with staging armed attacks wherever he imagined sanguine. There was the Swatow (Shantou) insurrection on September 23-24, 1927 and the Hunan revolt in the fall. Later (December 12-13) there was the bloody Guangzhou commune.[10] These attempts flunked quickly and they sealed the fate of the incumbent secretary, Ju Qiubai. At the expiration of one year's office, he was fired. The decision came from the 6th Congress of the CCP held in Moscow (June - July 1928). Ju was accused of unwisely plunging into revolts against the cities. The label pasted on him was leftist opportunist. The replacement was a certain Xiang Zhongfa. He served as proletarian symbolism, but little more. One is wondering whether Stalin thought that he was even easier to order around than his predecessors, the rightist and leftist opportunists?

[5] Zhang Guotao, *Wo de hui yi*, Hong Kong: Ming bao chu ban she, 1973, vol. 2, p. 670.

[6] Shanti Swarup, *op. cit.*, p. 228.

[7] Lucian W. Pye, *China*, Boston: Little, Brown, 1972, p. 157.

[8] Ilpyong J. Kim, *Politics in Communist China*, Berkeley: University of California Press, 1973, pp. 88-89.

[9] Lucian W. Pye, *loc. cit.*

[10] Richard C. Thornton, *China, the Struggle for Power 1917-1972*, Bloomington: Indiana University Press, 1973, p. 21; Shanti Swarup, *op. cit.*, pp. 73, 85.

The new secretary was a boatman. In Marxist lexicon, he cannot be classified as either a worker or a peasant. Because of his low intellect, he was intended to be a custodian rather than a boss in the secretariat. His function, although not the title "secretary", went to Li Lisan, a member of the CC.[11] During the second half of 1928 and in the next couple of years Li, too, could not achieve the Comintern objective of winning urban revolutions a la Russia's October coup.[12] Like Ju Qiubai, he was told by Stalin to envisage an actually non-existing revolutionary crisis all over south China. The communists' storming of Changsha which they occupied ten days, of Jian (Jiangxi province), Wuhan and Nanchang met with disasters. All this was attributed to what is calumniously called "Li Lisan line." An investigation was decreed at once by the Soviet dictator in order to determine the responsibility. Ju Qiubai was sent by Stalin from Moscow where he stayed to China to indict Li Lisan at the third plenum of the CC in September 1930. Ju found himself in an awkward situation because what Li had done was decided in the Soviet capital. The plenum first backed Li up, but the Comintern sacked him two months later for committing "revolutionary adventurism."[13] In March 1931, Li was summoned back to Moscow "for consultation."[14] He lived there until the communist victory in 1949 when he went home to take over a number of odd jobs in the new regime.[15]

In August 1927, Mao was ordered by the CCP (following instructions of Stalin) to take Changsha.[16] Failing this putsch and suffering heavy losses, he was to be blamed. All important posts, including membership in the Party Front Committee, were forthwith taken away from him.[17] Several months prior to the Changsha fiasco, however, Mao had fallen out with the majority of the fifth Congress of the CCP (April 1927).[18] In that Congress, he advocated "peasant confiscation" and the destruction of "local bullies and bad gentry." The proposal won no support. Thereupon he was discharged from the Politburo where he had a seat since 1923.[19] No record was found showing his later reinstallation. Really, he did not care less, because

[11] Sam C. Sarkesian and James H. Buck, *Comparative Politics*, Sherman Oaks, California: Alfred Pub. Co., 1979, p. 211.

[12] Ilpyong J. Kim, *op. cit.*, pp. 183-184.

[13] O. Edmund Clubb, *op. cit.*, p. 192.

[14] Peter S.H. Tang and Joan M. Maloney, *Communist China: The Domestic Scene 1949-1967*, South Orange, New Jersey: Seton Hall University Press, 1967, p. 52.

[15] "Li Lisan," *Bol'shava sovetskaya entsiklopediya*, 3rd ed., Moskva: Izdatel'stvo "sovetskaya entsiklopediya," vol. 14 (1973), cols. 1313-1314.

[16] Richard C. Thornton, *op. cit.*, pp. 11ff.

[17] *The Chinese Communist Movement*, Stanford: Stanford University Press, 1968, p. 26. This is the report of the US War Department of July 1945.

[18] Lucian W. Pye, *China*, p. 156.

[19] Peter S.H. Tang and Joan M. Maloney, *op. cit.*, p. 78.

soon he established a firm base in Ruijin whither the CCP headquarters had to move from Shanghai in March 1933.[20] The
source just cited mentions a very interesting point to evidence Mao's
departure from the Kremlin path during this period. In Jiangxi the Reds
committed no violence toward the well-to-do as Stalin wanted them
to. Their regime avowed to be one of all people, including the rich
peasants and landlords. These and the poor peasants were allowed
to serve the government. Obviously, that government was neither a
proletarian dictatorship nor a Soviet system which would have to
preclude the exploiters. It deviated stoutly from the Russian model.
The CCP thus came to establish its own identity by proclaiming its
declaration of independence.

Struggle among the Jiangxi Soviets

A. Chen Shaoyu
The Chinese Soviet Republic was officially proclaimed on
November 7, 1931 and, as its first act of "state," it declared war on
Japan. The leadership of the "state" was not monolithic as merely
meets the eye. It experienced many cleavages which occasionally
escalated into carnage. For example, on tactical problems, even Zhou
Enlai took strong views different from and opposing Mao Zedong.[21]
The first intra-CCP controversy relates to Chen Shaoyu, alias Wang
Ming.[22] Officially succeeding Xiang Zhongfa as the party secretary
in June 1931 after the latter's execution by the National
Government,[23] Chen was one of the "returned students from Russia,"
better known as the 28 Bolsheviks. They were ardent Russophiles,
more theory- than action-oriented. Refused cooperation by the
pragmatical majority of the CC hierarchy, Secretary Chen became
a frustrated man.[24] Feeling more at home in the workers' fatherland,
the USSR, he got himself appointed as the Chinese Soviet's
ambassador to that country in 1932. In the communist polemics, he
was a Li Lisan liner, accused of a) pursuing a policy of isolation from
the masses and b) refusing Mao Zedong's leadership.[25] However,
c) he was also castigated as taking a "rightist approach." This
assertion was based on his alleged giving too much credence to the
United Front.[26] Since that policy called for a close tie with the GMD,
Chen felt naively that the CCP had indeed embraced the GMD as

[20] *The Chinese Communist Movement*, p. 26.

[21] Harold Hinton, *An Introduction to Chinese Politics*, 2nd ed., New York: Holt, Rinehart and Winston, 1978, pp. 141, 146, 147.

[22] "Van Min," *Bol'shaya sovetskaya entsiklopediya*, 3rd ed., vol. 4 (1971), cols. 858-859.

[23] Ilpyong J. Kim, *op. cit.*, pp. 61, 89.

[24] Richard Thornton, *op. cit.*, pp. 39ff.

[25] Peter S.H. Tang and Joan M. Maloney, *op. cit.*, p. 54.

[26] K.S. Karol, *The Second Chinese Revolution*, translated from the French by Marvyn Jones, New York: Hill and Wang, 1973, pp. 39, 288.

its comrade-in-arms.[27] During the early months of 1942, Mao initiated the Zhengfeng (see below). Its main target was he.[28] Chen was said to commit dogmatism and slavish imitation of the Russians. The CPSU's answer to this assertion was that Secretary Chen was a deviator from January 1931 to January 1932, but not after the latter year.[29] It appears that Chen first disputed Mao's authority and the Russians backed him up. When they saw his chance was gone, they quietly withdrew their support and took him back to the Soviet Union. Then in 1935 they returned him to China to again challenge the leadership of Mao Zedong.

B. Zhang Guotao

He was one of the delegates to the first Congress of the CCP on July 1, 1921, supposedly sent thither by Li Dazhao to represent him.[30] He was active, but had little success, in the labor movement.[31] In 1922, he attended the Lenin-presided Conference of the Toilers of the East in Moscow, and along with Mao Zedong was elected on September 15, 1923 to the GMD Central Executive Committee when the United Front was in its initial stage.[32] On account of this kind of vitae, he prided himself on a par with Mao and would not concede to the latter's takeover of the party leadership.[33] Another factor which prompted his rivalry is that while Mao had his base in Jiangxi, Zhang had his own in Oyuwan straddling on the intersection of Hubei, Henan and Anhui, an area bigger than Mao's.[34] In October 1934, both men were disgorged of their territory by the nationalist and warlords' armies. Westward all the Reds escaped, with Mao undertaking the over-blown Long March and Zhang the less publicized scurry.[35] Via different route, Zhang headed for west Sichuan where he, commanding a larger army than Mao, arrived seven months earlier. Mao's procession reached Zungyi (Guizhou province) in January 1935.[36] While there Mao called a CCP conference on January 6-8. Out of it he successfully clenched his hegemony of the party. However, this was looked on with disdain and scorn by Zhang Guotao. He telegrammed a protest to that conference.[37]

Views on strategy, in addition to personality conflict, separated the two. In August 1935, their forces joined in west Sichuan. A meeting

[27] Harold Hinton, *op. cit.*, pp. 65, 68.

[28] J.D. Waller, *The Government and Politics of Communist China*, London: Hutchinson University Library, 1970, p. 37.

[29] "Van Min," *Bol'shaya sovetskaya entsiklopediya*, 3rd ed., vol. 4 (1971), cols. 858-859.

[30] Lucian W. Pye, *China*, p. 150.

[31] *Ibid.*, p. 151.

[32] *Ibid.*, pp. 152, 153.

[33] A. Doak Barnett, *Uncertain Passage, China's Transition to the post-Mao Era*, Washington: The Brookings Institution, 1974, pp. 183, 336 (note); Ho Kan Chih, *A History of the Chinese Revolution*, Beijing: Foreign Languages Press, 1960, pp. 70, 107.

[34] J.D. Waller, *op. cit.*, p. 30.

[35] Franklin W. Houn, *A Short History of Chinese Communism*, Englewood Cliffs, New Jersey: Prentice-Hall, 1967, pp. 43, 48, 94.

[36] Ilpyong J. Kim, *op. cit.*, p. 3.

[37] Lucian W. Pye, *China*, p. 162.

was held at Maoergai seeking to compose their differences.[38] It was not a success, however. Zhang proposed that a new base be set up in Xikang (a province at that time). Against this, Mao opted for a base in northern Shaanxi, where Liu Zhidan and Gao Gong already constructed a Red pocket.[39] Northern Shaanxi, moreover, is near the Soviet Union. In case the nationalist troops closed in, the communists were able to cross over Mongolia to enter that country, coming home to the socialist fatherland. Mao's motion carried, but Zhang was not to obey. After some month's recalcitrance, however, he gave up his original plan and led his force toward Shaanxi. The 6th enlarged plenum of the CC reaffirmed on October 12, 1938 the Zungyi resolution, thus finalizing the position of Mao. It was this plenum which isolated Zhang completely. Prior to it, he served briefly (until late 1936) as a vice chairman of the military council of the Shaanxi Soviet.[40] Gradually, he saw his former troops either dispersed or reassigned. Then he decided to leave Yanan. By the skin of his teeth, he fled to a government-controlled town. Thereupon, Mao promptly expelled him from the party. Zhang was the most acridly criticized of all the communist mavericks. He is said, among others, to engage in serious sectarianism and revolt against the authority of the CCP. Possibly the main reason for this castigation was that he later went over to the GMD and worked for it.[41]

C. Tan Pingshan

This individual was a free thinker. The communists are hateful of this sort of people more than straightforward enemies. He started out as a Marxist at the same time as Chen Duxiu, Li Dazhao, Ju Qiubai, Zhang Guotao and Mao Zedong.[42] Together with the latter four, he entered the GMD under the pennant of United Front. By the decision of the GMD's first congress of 1924, each of them got a grand stand within that party. Tan's was the directorate of the Orgburo, to borrow a Soviet term. Mao, incidentally, became the chief of the propaganda department. The importance of Tan in the GMD is evidenced by the fact that when the Front was dissolved and the communists were officially driven out on February 6, 1928, Jiang Jieshi, the Supreme Commander of the National Revolutionary Army, arrogated the Orgburo to himself.[43] Prior to the dismissal from the GMD, however, Tan was ousted from the CCP (November 1927) as a result of that party's own purge which took place after the termination, not yet made official at the time, of the Front. Then he

[38] *Xin hua ci dian*, Beijing: Shang wu yin shu guan, 1980, p. 570, col. 1.

[39] K.S. Karol, *op. cit.*, pp. 111, 304.

[40] Peter S.H. Tang and Joan M. Maloney, *op. cit.*, p. 99.

[41] *Ibid.*, p. 99, note 18.

[42] Franklin W. Houn, *op. cit.*, pp. 25, 36.

[43] O. Edmund Clubb, *op. cit.*, p. 131.

organized a third party only to be disbanded, and la\
GMD. In 1945 he created the San Min Zhu Yi Friend\
a tiny group within the GMD. Three years later it mer\
number of other picayune parties to form the GMD Revo\
Committee. Tan was rehabilitated by, but not re-admitted in, the\
The communist press is charitable on him. His was, after all, n\
formidable figure while in the party, and still less outside it.[44]

D. Unknown mavericks

We must mention here some lesser men involved in the battle for power before entering the Yanan period. An important incident, not widely written about, is the Futian insurgence of 1930.[45] In this event, Mao Zedong showed his full revolutionary wrath for the first time against adversaries.[46] During the early Jiangxi period, the Soviet leadership consisted of many incompatibles who were either mutineers or plain thugs, or Robin Hoods of sorts. There were some sterling Reds, to be sure.[47] Mao alleged to have discovered Li Lisan roaders venturing to erode Jiangxi from within. There was allegedly an attempt to set up an anti-Soviet base within the Soviet base. He was determined that the plotters be destroyed. Mao's assertion seems to have some grounds because the followers of Li Lisan organized the Jiangxi Provincial Action Committee.[48] Mao ordered the Central Front Committee, a counterpart of the KGB of the USSR, to arrest many suspects, charging them of working for the GMD's ABC (Anti-Bolshevik Corps). This provoked a swift retaliation on February 8, 1930 by a political commissar in a battalion, Liu De, of the 20th Red Army.[49] He hoisted the revolt flag at Tonggu and led several hundred men to storm the communist stronghold Futian. They freed the leaders of the Jiangxi Provincial Action Committee, yelling the slogan "down with Mao Zedong!" They ransacked the offices of the Jiangxi Provincial Soviet Government, forced out its staffers and detained Liu Teqiao, commander of the aforesaid 20th Red Army together with other supporters of Mao. Mobilizing his forces from other parts of Jiangxi, Mao quickly isolated the insurgents. It was not, however, until two months later that they were completely disposed of. According to one source, Mao had 3,000 of them executed in the end.[50] This

[44] Hsiao Tso-liang, *Chinese Communism in 1927, City vs. Countryside,* Hong Kong: The Chinese University of Hong Kong, 1970, pp. 41, 82, 83.

[45] Franklin W. Houn, *op. cit.,* p. 42.

[46] Zheng Xuejia, *Zhong gong fu tian shi bian zhen xian,* Taibei: Guo ji gong dang wen ti ying ju suo, 1976, pp. 170ff.

[47] Roy Hofheinz, "The Economy of Chinese Communist Success: Rural Influence Pattern, 1923-1945," *Chinese Communist Politics in Action,* edited by A. Doak Barnett, Seattle: University of Washington Press, 1969, pp. 3-77 at 35.

[48] James Harrison, *The Long March to Power, a History of the Chinese Communist Party, 1921-1972,* New York: Praeger, 1972, p. 214. Franklin W. Houn, *loc. cit.*

[49] Franklin W. Houn, *loc. cit.*

[50] J.D. Waller, *op. cit.,* p. 39.

first and only time that the CCP leader was threatened by a
war in his domain. The battalion commissar, Liu De, wanted in
effect to set up a rebeldom inside a rebeldom. All other communist
mavericks are famous, but Liu De is not.[51] Yet his non-entity is fully
made up by the bloody suppression by Mao.

Zhenfeng and its aftereffect

Zhenfeng took place during 1942-1944.[52] Mao's objective was to
a) "eliminate Wang Ming and leftist tendencies, and b) to purge the
party of subjectivism."[53] Since we already mentioned the former, only
the latter is analyzed here. The victim is Wang Shiwei.[54] A fairly known
author and versed in Russian literature, Wang first made his name
by translating some Marxist writings into Chinese. Later he
demonstrated his talent by producing a goodly number of tracts and
earned respect among fellow authors. Not bent to fawning or
sacrificing his integrity for a price, he was no ideological timber. He
may well be described and deplored as too outspoken to be in Yanan.
The whole story started with the flocking to the Red capital of left
belletrists throughout China in the early forties, some from the
government area, while most from the Japanese-occupation zone.
The pilgrims made their way to Shaanxi right after Pearl Harbor of
December 1941. They all thought that the communist regime was
there to stay. It wouldn't be overrun by the nationalist troops. These
individuals were already inclined toward Marxism and Yanan became
their beacon light. To them the Border Government emblazoned a
revolutionary romanticism.

Mao, however, thought that the leftists' convergence could not be
looked on with comfort. Initially he was elated by the open recognition
given his regime by such an articulate segment of the public, but on
a second thought, he came to the conclusion that the new arrivals
were a mixed bag.[55] They were not all expected to serve the Red
cause correctly. He found it vital to cleanse them of the "putrids,"
or at least to minister them a belated catharsis. With this in mind,
Mao began in 1942 a move with the code name Zhenfeng, or
rectification. It can be called Little Proletarian Cultural Revolution,
a pre-figuration of the Great one (1966-1969). The principal executor
was Liu Shaoqi,[56] who was himself cleansed in that Great one, but
de-cleansed in 1981. Early in 1942, Mao sent out an invitation to all
Chinese artists and men of letters to attend a forum in Yanan (many

---

[51] Shanti Swarup, op. cit., pp. 247-249.

[52] John Wilson Lewis ed., Major Doctrines of Communist China, New York: Norton, 1964, pp. 15, 17-18.

[53] Xin hua ci dian, p. 969, col. 2.

[54] Zhang Xiaocu, et alii, Yanan hui yi lu, Haerbin: Heilongjiang renmin chu ban she, 1958, pp. 20-22.

[55] James Chieh Hsiung, ed., The Logic of Maoism, Critique and Explication, New York: Praeger, 1974, pp. 62, 75.

[56] Peter S.H. Tang and Joan M. Maloney, op. cit., p. 111.

were there already) on May 3. He presided over the forum, and gave two speeches which go into his works as "Talks on art and literature."[57] He offered the confreres an olive branch that no coercion should be used to mold people's minds. "A patient," he said, "naturally expected his discomfort cured by pills and regimen prescribed by the physicians." However, he ordered that the audience abandon the idea of art for art's sake, and literature for literature's sake.[58] Mincing no words, he said both must serve the aim of politics.

To those who knew little about communists, the position of Mao sounded rather strange. They never realized that this was the way their walk of life was to be treated under communism. According to a report, all but one confreres were silent. He was Wang Shiwei.[59] It is out of question that Mao's view won virtually assured subscription because an overwhelming number of the audience already made up their minds before trekking to Yanan in response to Mao's call. This very fact makes it easy for one to understand why Zhenfeng was a complete success. The defiant Wang Shiwei was berated for "refusal to amend his error and reform at party's behest."[60] He said that "even on the sun there are spots" and that only criticism can help to expurgate them.[61] Dangerously candid were these statements: "Many youths were disenchanted because they came to Yanan in search for warmth and beauty, (but) they cannot but complain when they see its ugliness and coldness."[62] With sharp barbs, Wang denounced the dark side of the "holy center," and bemoaned the inequality which he saw prevailed in the Soviet. He said all this was un-communist.[63]

 Wang was labelled a subjectivist. Because the CCP had expelled him as an undesirable member, he needed not to concede to his sin and indulge in the gruelling self-criticism. Through this sort of criticism, according to the party rules, all mistaken partisans would have to go.[64] However, Wang had another price to pay. He was first ordered to a match factory to labor as a menial and then was shot. It is interesting to note that there are documents to show that Mao Zedong later regretted to have him put to death. He is said to have written that capital punishment was uncalled for in the case.[65]

[57] Delivered on May 2 and 13, 1942, *Mao Tse-tung hsuan chi*, Beijing: Renmin chu ban she, 1969, vol. 3, pp. 804-835.

[58] Franklin W. Houn, *op. cit.*, pp. 112-117.

[59] K.S. Karol, *China, the Other Communism*, translated from the French, New York: Hill and Wang, 1967, p. 263.

[60] Mark Selden, "The Yanan Legacy, the Mass," *Chinese Communist Politics in action*, pp. 91-151 at 106-107.

[61] K.S. Karol, *China, the Other Communism*, p. 261.

[62] James Harrison, *op. cit.*, p. 339.

[63] Chin King and Dennis Bloodworth, *Heir Apparent, What Happens When Mao Dies?* New York: Farrar, Straus and Giroux, 1973, p. 5.

[64] K.S. Karol, *China, the Other Communism*, p. 263.

[65] James Harrison, *op. cit.*, pp. 240-241.

Regional challenge

After the seizure of the mainland, the CCP had gone through a number of leadership crises, beginning with the Gao-Rao episode. This turns on the charge of regional buildup for personal ambitions: Gao Gong in the northeast, Rao Shushi in the east. The accusation is an admixture of facts and imagination, more of the latter. Comparing the two leaders, we find that the case of Rao is even less credible, for he did not have a compact area as Gao had in which to operate, or, to use the communist saying, to realize the private kingdom. Born in Shanghai, Rao acted exclusively within the east part of the country.[66] His first important post was that of a deputy secretary of CCP's Central China Bureau, headquartered in Yancheng on the coast, 350 kilometers north of Shanghai. The first secretary was Liu Shaoqi. In February 1949, the third field army of Chen Yi fought in the east provinces and Rao became its political commissar. After the CCP divided the nation into six regions to intensify the martial rule, it appointed, rather appropriately, Rao head of the east China region. There he wielded absolute power, as did his counterparts in all other regions. However, whether he had defied Beijing by capitalizing on his position cannot easily be substantiated.

Regarding Gao Gong, the assertion of regionalism is somewhat more plausible.[67] For one thing, his relation with the party center was never as intimate as Rao's. For another, his domain neighbors a foreign power, even though a friendly one at that time.[68] Gao was born in Manchuria, but before 1949 he operated entirely in north China, more precisely upper Shaanxi. Parallel in time to the Jiangxi Soviet, a Shaanxi Soviet made up of three counties was set up by him in league with Liu Zhidan.[69] The two collected many mutineers and organized them into their private army.[70] Mao Zedong's Long March, be it recalled, chose Shaanxi as its destination. After it ended there in October 1935, Gao seemed to be willing to play a second fiddle in the now expanded Soviet realm. His star was rising fast after the Japanese surrender in August 1945.

Manchuria ranked the highest on the Red Army's table of conquest. The situation there was extremely propitious for the communists. There was the Russian occupation, there was the abundant weaponry handed over by the Guandong horde of Japan, and there was the short route from Yanan. In anticipation of the victory, Mao thought that the best ruler there was the native son, Gao Gong. In 1948, the Reds won an easy triumph in Manchuria. Gao came there as the first secretary of the Northeast Bureau of the CCP, a bureau which unlike

[66] Franklin W. Houn, *op. cit.*, pp. 95, 103, 104.

[67] Richard C. Thornton, *op. cit.*, pp. 226-229.

[68] George P. Jan, ed., *op. cit.*, pp. 141, 142, 147. 142, 147.

[69] Richard C. Thornton, *op. cit.*, p. 87; Ho Kan-chih, *op. cit.*, p. 272.

[70] James Harrison, *op. cit.*, p. 193.

other bureaus elsewhere in China enjoyed a large measure ⌣ autonomy.[71] On account of its situs, the region was very delicate. There the Russians' privileges and rights secured by the controversial Yalta secret deal of 1945 and their ransacking of industrial and rail facilities almost compelled the new communist regime of Beijing to give the Northeast Bureau a free hand to manage its own affairs, not the least of which was the on-the-spot negotiation with the Soviets on such matters as regional economy and trade. In 1949 and 1950, Gao concluded a great number of treaties with the USSR in the name of Manchuria, but not the People's Republic of China. This event may well have prompted Beijing to take a careful look at the irregular status of the northeast. The later suspicion of Gao's construction of an independent realm has its basis here.

Both Gao and Rao were said to engage in factionalism and in anti-party scheming. They were accused of forging an alliance to defy Beijing.[72] It is highly interesting to observe that they were given important posts in the Central People's Government during the investigation of their cases: Gao as State Planning Commissioner; Rao, Head of the Organizational Department of the CCP. In the meantime, they were still first secretaries of the respective regions. It is sure that their grips on the base areas became loosened because they had to stay away from there most of the time to run huge offices in the capital. Although the real motivation of Mao in removing the two individuals remains unexplained, the fact is that they were expelled from the party by a CC plenum in February 1954. Soon Gao committed suicide and Rao vanished without a trace.[73] On the heels of the episode, the CCP proceeded to liquidate the regional-bureau system in an avowed attempt to bring the provinces closer to the center.[74] The bureaus were revived in the early sixties only to disappear again. Once more they re-emerged in 1977, but they are a pale image of their former selves.[75]

Military challenge

Peng Dehuai and company were the *dramatis personae* here. Mao Zedong's wrath on them stemmed from their criticism of the commune system. The latter system, we shall remember, involved an extensive use of the armed formation in agriculture. First of all, Peng felt that soldiers' morale was seriously affected. They saw with their own eyes the dislocation of family relation, the overworking of the peasants, the hardship of life and the general discontent in the countryside.[76]

---

[71] A. Doak Barnett, *Uncertain Passage, China's Transition to the Post-Mao Era*, pp. 188, 213, 214.

[72] Peter S.H. Tang and Joan M. Maloney, *op. cit.*, p. 102.

[73] *Ibid.*, p. 93.

[74] John Wilson Lewis, ed., *op. cit.*, pp. 36-38.

[75] K.S. Karol, *The Second Chinese Revolution*, pp. 224-225, 404-405, and last section of Chapter IX (below).

[76] *Ibid.* pp. 148-149, 348.

When the recruits received letters from their home telling of the plight of parents and relatives, they must have had a sense of dejection. With demoralized troops, how could the officers lead them in combat in a war, for example, with India or Taiwan? The relation with both, it is to be noted, was very tense at that time (1956-1959). Apart from the morale issue, the employment of uniformed personnel in dam-building, planting, harvesting and whatnot deprived them of the time for training and indoctrination. A contemporary army, Peng maintained, must be professionalized.[77] The People's Republic could not go back to the Yanan days when a soldier had to be laboring in the field during the day, but fighting the GMD troops at night. He insisted that China must "concentrate on the modernization of the conventional forces along the Soviet line which he had inaugurated in 1954."[78] In his opinion, the CPR could not but rely on the People's Liberation Army (PLA) for traditional battle and on the USSR's thermonuclear arms for non-conventional war. The help of that country was essential because China had not yet developed these means. On account of this line of thought, Peng counseled, in effect, against offending the Soviets, an action which Beijing apparently was doing from 1958 on. Late in April 1959, Peng made a trip to the Soviet Union and Eastern Europe. It could not have been made at a worse time. Probably it was intended to be a trap for the politically naive marshal. To all semblance, he, Mao, had made up his mind to move away from the Soviets following the breach of numerous agreements by them. The journey of Peng served only to dramatize his Russophilia.

As if lending support to that impression, Nikita Khrushchev on June 20, 1959, a week after Peng's return to China, rejected Beijing's asking for a sample of an atomic bomb, officially rescinding the treaty of October 27, 1957 on such aid. All this made it plausible that there had been a collusion between the Russian leadership and the Chinese defence chief, who just finished talks in the Kremlin. Some years later, the Chinese media were to write: "In his conversation with the delegation of the CCP, Khrushchev . . . even expressed undisguised support of the anti-party elements in the CCP."[79] They seem definitely to implicate Peng Dehuai.

At the 8th plenum of the 8th CC held at the famous summer resort Lushan from August 2 to 16, 1959, attended by high officials both CC members and non-members, a clash erupted. Buttressed by Huang Kecheng, the General Chief of Staff, Defense Minister Peng Dehui launched a broadside on Mao Zedong in regard to his agricultural policy.[80] The action was more revengeful than preventive, because the Great Leap Forward had by that late date been under

---

[77] James Townsend, *Politics in China*, Boston: Little, Brown, 1974, pp. 98, 123, 126.

[78] Harold Hinton, *op. cit.*, p. 46.

[79] *Hongqi*, and *Renmin ribao*, September 6, 1963; see also Peter S.H. Tang and Joan M. Maloney, *op. cit.*, p. 103.

[80] Peng Dehuai is said to differ from Mao on the Li Lisan policy, see Shanti Swarup, *op. cit.*, p. 246 note.

review and been found wanting. In fact, it was revoked four months before Lushan. The debate is of great historical import. It is the first time after the celebrated Zungyi rendezvous of January 6-8, 1935 that Mao was directly challenged. On the previous occasion, we shall remember, Zhang Guotao assaulted Mao from a distance of 2,300 km and through a telegram, but this one was a face-to-face confrontation. In both instances, Mao won easily. Peng and Huang had to bow out to be replaced by Lin Biao and Luo Ruiqing respectively. Interesting enough, Lin was forced to flee China in September 1971 and died in a plane crash and Huang, in August 1969 in an attempt to escape the Red Guards, jumped out of a window and seriously wounded himself. Gone with Peng and Huang were a group of VIP's, including General Su Yu and vice foreign minister Zhang Wentian. Peng was tortured to death by the Gang of Four on November 29, 1974.[81] The verdict of Peng following his dismissal by Mao says that the marshal was "failing to pass the bourgeois-democratic stage of revolution," and that he had never been a real communist.[82] At present, both individuals, Peng and Huang, are fully rehabilitated, in the case of Peng post-humously. Huang, as mentioned in the preceding chapter, is the second Secretary of the CC's Central Commission for Discipline Inspection.

The party-apparatus challenge

Liu Shaoqi and Deng Xiaoping came to join the rank of power contenders from the party and state apparatus. The former man is the highest of all the mavericks to Mao, if indeed he can be considered a maverick. Head of state from 1959 to 1968, and reputed successor to Mao, Liu had been carrying into execution the latter's order to purge others both in the Zhenfeng and in the Gao-Rao affair. Now came his turn. It followed upon several years' development beginning in the post-Leap recovery and culminating in the storm of the Cultural Revolution.[83] A few pages cannot summarize what has happened. We can merely highlight the campaign against Chairman Liu and General Secretary Deng Xiaoping. The economic malaise caused by the commune and the Leap must have struck so painfully the conscience of Mao Zedong that he decided to retire from state office. "I no longer have the courage to stand upright before the suffering millions," he probably had said to himself. Nineteen fifty-nine saw him surrender the chairmanship to Liu Shaoqi, his righthand man since 1942. Having taken office at such a depressing time, Liu proceeded quietly to restore the public trust and readjust the economy by steering away from extreme centralism and egalitarianism. He set out to keep at arm's length the specter of class struggle which haunted

[81] *Xin hua ci dian*, p. 635, col. 1. "Written judgment of the Special Court under Supreme People's Court of the People's Republic of China, January 23, 1981," *Beijing review*, February 2, 1981, pp. 13-28 at 17, col. 1.

[82] Peter S.H. Tang and Joan M. Maloney, *op. cit.*, p. 103.

[83] James Chieh Hsiung, ed., *op. cit.*, pp. 26, 28, 115.

everybody in the nation.[84] With the cooperation of the pragmatical bureaucrats at the top echelon of the party and government, particularly Premier Zhou Enlai and Deng Xiaoping, he managed to repair the damage of the previous years. He indeed had quite a great mess to clean.[85] His strategy was to cut down on the commune and to lessen the scale of heavy industry. More emphasis came to be placed on the production of consumer items and foodstuff. Within three years (1959-1962), China convalesced nicely and began to forge ahead. Coincidentally, the Soviet Union was also implementing the same reform at that time, with accent on material incentive and managerial autonomy. Liu's new course which seven years later was dubbed a "counterrevolution" brought measurable prosperity to the urbanites; and agricultural production was up. In the latter, it was helped to no small degree by good weather. Tourists back from the People's Republic reported well-stocked stores and cheerful moods of the people. Law and order obtained throughout the country, and workers had high morale. Characteristic of the enterprises were rationalized planning and sound stewardship. Another indication of the improved economy was the sharply reduced refugee stream into Hong Kong. Its volume was not to augment until the Cultural Revolution. In short, China had leaped over the crisis and regained her health.[86]

This state of affairs, however, displeased Mao Zedong.[87] He came to fear that the revolution which he had achieved after one third of a century's struggle was gone with the wind. He saw the bourgeoisie stalk the country. They put high premium on material value and forgot the Marxist legacy of sacrificing the present for the future, of dedication to internationalism and democratic dictatorship, and of combating revisionism. Everywhere in the CPR there was the worship of money and creature comforts. All this he imputed to the Liu-Deng dispensation. In the meantime, Mao allegedly envisaged the same situation in the Soviet Union. No news was good news, he apparently sighed![88]

What disturbed Mao even worse was the prospect of the young. He claimed to have descried the total lack of effort to educate them in the communist world view. Those born after the victory of 1949 knew about that revolution only through books. The toughness and endurance which made possible the Jiangxi Soviet, the Long March and the Border Government, no longer characterized the rising

[84] Hungdah Chiu, "Criminal Punishment in Mainland China: a Study of some Yunnan Province Documents," *The Journal of Criminal Law and Criminology*, no. 3, 1977, pp. 334-398 at 391, col. 2.

[85] Richard C. Thornton, *op. cit.*, pp. 243, 249.

[86] A. Doak Barnett, *China after Mao*, Princeton, New Jersey: Princeton University Press, 1967, pp. 82ff.

[87] Hans Granqvist, *The Red Guard, a Report on Mao's Revolution*, translated by Erik J. Friis, London: Pall Mall Press, 1967, pp. 3-11.

[88] Tang Tsou, "Revolution, reintegration and crisis in communist China: A framework for analysis," *China in Crisis*, edited by Pinti Ho and Tang Tsou, Chicago: University of Chicago Press, 1968, vol. 1, book one, pp. 337-364 at 339.

generation. What appealed to them was not the Olympian ideal of revolution, but vulgar materialism. Mao was anxious that after his death ("going to see Marx," he said to Edgar Snow) the foundation which he laid would evaporate. Who was to blame for this sorry situation? It was, he insisted, the lackadaisical men in the high places. There was Liu Shaoqi, Deng Xiaoping, Lu Dingyi (propaganda chief), Yang Shangkun (administrator of culture), Peng Zhen (Beijing mayor), Wu Han (Beijing vice-mayor), Chen Boda (Mao's amanuensis), Kang Sheng (secret police chief), Tian Han (man of letters), and nearly every university president. They were all taken to task. The youth, he thought, would have found their way except for these misguided officeholders.[89]

How could the CPR be saved? How could the bourgeois decadence be arrested? Only the youth themselves, felt Mao, were able to provide the answer. Among them, moreover, only those who were born around 1949 were the most hopeful. In 1966, they found themselves in high schools. This explains why that age group became the backbone of the Cultural Revolution. To channel their energy, Mao gathered around himself a team of confidantes and gave it the humble title of Cultural Revolution Group. In reality, it was almighty. One may call it Mao's kitchen Politburo. It was comprised of five individuals. Setting out to work to get rid of the undesirables, they were soon found to lack energy and ardor to do his bidding. Mao dismissed all but one, who was none other than his wife, Jiang Qing. One woman, of course, could not constitute a team. Within a month a new group came into being. There were eighteen in it. Four months later, however, Mao fired thirteen of them for similar reasons. This was in May 1966, the morrow of the greatest of all upheavals in the history of the CCP, the rampancy of the Red Guards or Red Rebels, who were to revolutionize China's culture. Thereafter, Mao took personal command of the Revolution, helped, as is known now, by the Gang of Four. No one else was able to win his trust, still less to stand in his way.[90]

Communist propaganda traced Liu Shaoqi's "duplicity" forty years back, beginning in the late twenties. In 1944, he allegedly encouraged some comrades to "give themselves up to the GMD and turn against the CCP."[91] Later he even rewarded them by giving them promotions. Another charge pictured him as in favor of private ownership of means of production and as opposing class struggle.[92] It is also stated that Liu's booklet *How to be a good communist* advocated the absolute obedience of minority to majority. There is, we suppose, nothing wrong with such a well-known plank of democratic centralism. Yet Beijing's organs saw in it a sinister intent of Liu. Sensing perhaps

[89] *Ibid.*, pp. 338-339.

[90] John Wilson Lewis, "Leader, commissar, and bureaucrat: the Chinese political system in the last days of the revolution," *China in Crisis*, vol. 1, book two, pp. 449-481 at 473, 474.

[91] Peter S.H. Tang and Joan M. Maloney, *op. cit.*, p. 115.

[92] *Ibid.*, p. 113.

that Mao was actually in the minority in the Cultural Revolution, these organs found it imperative to dispute that plank. Liu was described as mistaken in urging the subordinating of the lesser number of people to the greater number, but in fact, the media asserted, the lesser number had truth on their side. Blinded obedience was to be objected, it was warned.

As if all these counts were still inadequate to convince the masses of Liu's crime, the press resorted to more sensational reports of the discovery of a military coup of the capitalist roaders to be implemented in February 1966. On the 23rd of that month, Liu was said to have flown to Xinjiang in order to secure the support of Wang Enmou, a strongman there. Meanwhile, Deng Xiaoping is alleged to have disappeared from Beijing and turned up in Xian to solicit Liu Lantao's backing.[93] Similarly, the Beijing mayor, Peng Zhen, was said to have been going to southwest China to confer with the VIP there, Li Jingchuan. The plot reputedly aimed at seizing central and east China.

Still another accusation painted Liu in an unpatriotic color.[94] It said he was in communion with Khrushchev. He was China's number one revisionist.[95] Although no direct contact was discovered between the two, the synchronical move of the USSR and CPR toward decentralization of economy, or what is called capitalist revival, was not seen as a mere coincidence. A pro-Soviet clique, according to Mao's mouthpiece, was formed by Liu. Many facts were dug out of the archives to prove the point. Here are a few. Liu joined the CCP in Moscow.[96] He attended the Red Army Academy there and accompanied the Soviet troops entering Manchuria in 1929.[97] What is more, Liu went to the Soviet Union more frequently than any other Chinese leader: 7 times.[98] On two occasions, the sojourn was protracted. There were more and more stories about the CPR Chairman to show his wickedness. Western students and now the Chinese communists themselves dismissed them as mendacious. The defamation was indicative of Mao's desperate attempt to stage a comeback after being phased out in 1959 following the Leap fiasco. It is also possible that now in his dotage, Mao simply hankered after some revolutionary quixotism which might bring a modicum of solace.[99]

The victims of the Cultural Revolution in contrast to the accused in the previous purges, are distinguished by a) their eminent status,

[93] *Ibid.*, pp. 116-117.

[94] John Wilson Lewis, "Leader, commissar ...," p. 479. C.K. Yang, "Cultural revolution and revisionism," *China in Crisis*, vol. 1, book two, pp. 501-524 at 501.

[95] Harold Hinton, *op. cit.*, p. 66.

[96] Peter S.H. Tang and Joan M. Maloney, *op. cit.*, p. 110.

[97] *Ibid.*, p. 111.

[98] The years are 1920, 1922, 1927, 1928, 1929, 1937 and 1963, see *Ibid.*, Harold Hinton, *op. cit.*, p. 189.

[99] Benjamin I. Schwartz, "China and the West in the thought of Mao Tse-tung," *China in Crisis*, vol. 1, book two, pp. 365-396 at 375-376, 384.

b) their sheer number, and c) the groundlessness of the stories. A reasonable individual can hardly imagine that Chairman Liu Shaoqi and General Secretary Deng Xiaoping were intent upon the destruction of the People's Republic. Today the imprecations against them were officially declared null and void. Liu was post-humously rehabilitated in May 1981. Although the legacy of the Cultural Revolution was still paid homage by the one-time strongman Hua Guofeng,[100] the 1977 Party Statute ("General Program") and the 1978 CPR Constitution (Preamble), both the 6th plenum of the 11th CC, meeting from June 27 to 29, 1981, and the 1982 Party Statute denounced it as disastrous.[101]

Armed coup

The central man here is Lin Biao, a mighty figure in the Reds' Sanhedrin. Probably born in 1907, he graduated from Jiang Jieshi's Huangpu Academy in 1927.[102] The following year he rebelled in southern Hunan together with the much older comrades Zhu De and Chen Yi.[103] The latter two were to be outshone by him some four decades later. At the youthful age of about 28, he led the 3rd army corps during the Long March.[104] In September 1937, the 8th route army destroyed two Japanese divisions at Ping-xing Pass, a victory commonly attributed to him, and a German military journal described it as a "classic of mobile warfare."[105] From then on, he remained obscure until the capitulation of Japan which led at once to the GMD-CCP racing for Manchuria. During this crucial contest, Lin Biao displayed his ability and audacity in routing half a million government troops out of the southern part of that region. In the last leg of the civil war (1947-49), he was instrumental in winning an array of battles in central and east China.[106] No other man in the entire PLA did so much to help bring the CPR into being. These credentials are dazzling and they are indeed earned by bravery and devotion. It is natural that they boosted his political career. There is, however, a lot of manipulation and luck in his meteoric rise.

Mao Zedong, as said before, deplored the lax atmosphere in the country, being horrified by the obdurate officials and aimless youth. To counter all this, he decided to hold up the PLA as the model for all to follow. Here, Lin Biao's ship was coming home. Who in the country can symbolize that model except the Defense Minister? In

[100] His report to the 11th Congress of the CCP, *Keesing's*, December 16, 1977, p. 28720.

[101] *Renmin ribao*, July 1, 1981, pp. 2, 3.

[102] Louis Barcata, *China in the Throes of the Cultural Revolution, an Eye Witness Report*, New York: Hart Pub. Co., 1967, p. 118.

[103] James Harrison, *op. cit.*, p. 142.

[104] *Ibid.*, p. 163.

[105] *The Chinese communist movement*, p. 45.

[106] "Lin Piao," *Current History*, New York: Wilson, 1967, pp. 250-253.

fact, the ascendancy of the PLA in the political spectrum pre-dated the Cultural Revolution which commenced in 1966. Three years before that, the craze of the "si qing" move to purify politics, economy, organization and thought had already lionized the role of the armed forces and placed it above other subsystems.[107] Yelled loudly by Mao Zedong was the slogan of "learn from the army."[108] He insisted on the absolute control of the thinking and activity of the masses in order to make them good students of Marxism and good continuators of the Chinese revolution. He wanted to impose on the people the duty of subscribing to the will of the central authority. An unswerving loyalty to Mao, in effect, was a must of each and every citizen. In the socialist education campaign (1962-1965), all offices, communes, factories, schools, stores or construction sites were to set up a political bureau staffed by army-appointed lecturers. They were to imbue men and women with unadultered communist doctrines, as distinct from what Mao believed to be the bogus versions as practiced in the Soviet Union.[109]

Because Lin represented the military machine, he was looked up to as the paradigm. Against him all Chinese, except Mao, ought to measure. In fact, Mao did not realize that he was creating a Frankenstein's monster. The "si qing" was likened to the Renaissance in European history and was drummed up by the media in the most diligent way. Like a prairie fire, it burned everywhere and caught everyone. In it, Lin Biao as the number one soldier, enjoyed the greatest visibility and popularity.[110] Taking an unprecedented step, Mao had the CC plenum of August 8, 1966 endorse his desire of naming him the sole vice chairman of the party.[111] Previously there were six vice chairmen. Lin's ambition to be the heir apparent of Mao was realized. Today, it is clear that the support by Lin of the socialist education move was the quid pro quo for the number two spot of the CCP hierarchy. By the time the just-said plenum met, Lin was getting out of Mao's hand. In private, he must have stated to himself: "I can hardly wait for that man's death."

Leaving some of the details of the Cultural Revolution for the next section, we propose to analyze how Lin has become the beneficiary of that event and how the armed coup came about. The Red Guards set out to annihilate the apparatus leaders from Liu Shaoqi and Deng Xiaoping down and they met with counter-Red Guards undoubtedly organized by these leaders. Had Lin cast his lot with Liu-Deng groups, Mao would surely be the loser, just as if Yuan Shikai threw his weight with the Manzhou the fate of the 1911 Revolution was sealed. Lin,

[107] Harold Hinton, op. cit., p. 53.

[108] Xin hua ci dian, p. 742, col. 1.

[109] Franz Schurmann, "The attack of the Cultural Revolution on ideology and organization," China in Crisis, vol. 1, book two, pp. 525-564 at 562.

[110] Chou Yi-min, "The Mao-Lin faction's deadlocked power-seizure," Asian Outlook, 2 (July 1967), pp. 11-16.

[111] Harold Hinton, op. cit., p. 64.

however, found it to his advantage to back up Mao (after promised the number two post) and ordered the army to provide the Red Guards with all sorts of help. However, ever savager battles continued to rage between factions and workers' collectives each allied with Red Guards and each claiming to fight for Mao Zedong. Turmoil and anarchism obtained through the length and breadth of the CPR and among the Chinese communists in Rangoon and Hong Kong. This state of affairs was completely unforeseen by both Mao and Lin. It was clear to both that the internecine war might well spell the end of the revolutionary gain which they set out to consolidate in August 1966. Facing them was the alternative of either curbing the excesses of the youth or risking the total collapse of the socialist order. Sobriety ultimately prevailed.[112] All of a sudden Mao was angered that his own Red Guards had betrayed him, but it is known to all that it was Mao who ordered them to embark upon the rampage.[113] In order to be successful, Mao's new course must obtain the cooperation of Lin Biao who had control over the armed forces, the only organization left intact in the universal chaos. The cooperation he was only too glad to offer, because he needed Mao's unqualified support of his successorship.

From January 1967 onward, troops went into action and quickly curbed the excesses of the Red Guards of whatever brand. The public began to breathe a sigh of relief. With peace and order restituted, Mao Zedong formally appointed Lin Biao his heir apparent. This was provided in the 1969 CCP Statute and was to be provided in the next CPR Constitution. Now the "successor Lin" was to encounter difficulties. His dual-adversary policy against the USSR and the US, according to one author,[114] collided head-on with Zhou Enlai's dual-friend policy, which aimed at building up a rapprochement with both nations. It was suggested that it was Lin who actually engineered the Damansky incident of March 3, 1969, designed to get his point across that Russia was dangerous to China.[115] In addition to the Lin-Zhou conflict, there must have been the Lin-Mao suspicion. Mao may well have been compelled by Lin to name him his heir apparent both at the inception and at the end of the Cultural Revolution. In 1970-1971 when the country became calm, thought Mao, Lin had outlived his usefulness. He was disposable, that is. Being faced with a suspicious Mao and a disagreeable Zhou, Lin acted. Hence the reported attempt at armed coup, seeking to kill Mao and seize power. According to the Special Court's judgment, the coup was as follows.[116]

In 1970, Lin Biao, having been designated to succeed Mao, saw that Jiang Qing, Zhang Chunqiao and company grew ever more

[112] Y. Kosyukov, "Winding up the Cultural Revolution," New Times (Moscow), March 12, 1969, pp. 8-11.

[113] Chen Chien-chung, "New situation of the Maoist power seizure struggle," Asian Outlook, 3 (September 1968), pp. 13-22.

[114] Harold Hinton, op. cit., p. 77.

[115] Ibid., p. 73.

[116] Beijing Review, February 2, 1981, p. 19.

formidable. He felt it vital for him to take over the hegemony right away. While cognizant that that group might not succeed in its ambition, he also believed Mao would never permit his premature succession of him. He thought it imperative then to take his life. As early as October 1969, Wu Faxian, commander of the air force and one of the 10 defendants during the trial of November 1980-January 1981, handed over to Lin Liguo (Lin Biao's son) all his authority. The young Lin organized an action group to execute the coup nicknamed joint fleet. In March 1971, a plan was developed by him together with Zhou Yuchi and others. It was known as Project 571. In Chinese it sounds "armed righteous uprising." In order to set up a command post, Lin Liguo called to a secret meeting in Shanghai on March 31, the following men: Jiang Tengjiao, an air force political commissar of the PLA's Nanjing units and one of the ten defendants; Wang Weiguo, a political commissar of the PLA unit 7341; Chen Liyun, a political commissar of the PLA unit 7350; and Zhou Jiangping, a deputy commander of the air force stationed in Nanjing. Acting as liaison was Jiang Tengjiao. He was to see to it that the forces in Nanjing, Shanghai and Hangzhou be coordinated. On September 5 and 6, Lin Biao and his wife Ye Qun, after being apprised first by Zhou Yuchi and then by Huang Yongsheng (General Chief of Staff) about Mao Zedong's intimation that he knew of Lin Biao's plot, decided to assassinate him on his inspection tour to the south by the use of planes, explosives, missiles, bombs and flamethrowers.[117] On September 8, Lin Biao issued a handwritten decree reading: "Expect you to act according to the order transmitted by comrades Liguo and Yuchi." The two then gave detailed assignments to Jiang Tengjiao and Wang Fei, a deputy chief-of-staff of the air force, and other key members of the aforesaid joint fleet. While this scheme was being hatched, Mao Zedong was alerted. He called off the tour and returned to Beijing on September 12. Failing in the conspiracy, Lin Biao made preparation for an escape, together with Huang Yongsheng, Wu Faxian, Li Zuopeng and Qiu Huizuo (the four were among the ten defendants), to Guangzhou where a counter-government was to be established.

Lin Biao ordered Hu Ping, a deputy chief-of-staff of the air force, to get eight planes readied for taking off to Guangzhou. On September 12, Hu Ping dispatched the special plane 256 to Shanhaiguan for use by Lin Biao, Ye Qun and Lin Liguo who were at that time in Beidaihe. A few minutes past 10:00 that night, Premier Zhou Enlai asked about the Shanhaiguan-bound plane and ordered it flown back to Beijing at once. Hu lied to him, saying that the plane went to Shanhaiguan on a training exercise and that it experienced engine problems. Meanwhile, he phoned Zhou Yuchi that the Premier had inquired about the said plane. Zhou Yuchi reported this to Lin Liguo. While giving instruction to those in charge of the navy aviation corps' Shanhaiguan airport, first at 23:25 on September 12 and then at 00:06

117 Renmin ribao, December 22, 1981, p. 5, col. 1; also Beijing Review, January 5, 1981, p. 22, col. 1.

next day, Li Zuopeng distorted Premier Zhou's directive that the plane "cannot take off without a joint order from these four: Zhou Enlai, Huang Yongsheng, Wu Faxian, Li Zuopeng," by stating it could not be allowed to fly out unless one of the four gave the order. At 00:20 on September 13, when Han Hao, director of the navy aviation corps' Shanhaiguan airport had discovered the strange circumstances at the time, he phoned Li Zuopeng and asked him what to do if the plane were to leave forcibly. Li took no steps to prevent it from flying out. This made it possible for Lin Biao, Ye Qun and Lin Liguo to take off. Knowing of Premier Zhou Enlai's inquiry about the plane 256, Lin Biao felt it was impossible to go to the south to set up a government there. Thereupon they went north. The machine left Shanhaiguan at 00:32 on September 13. It crashed in Mongolia, killing all aboard.

The Gang of Four

Mao Zedong was universally recognized as the Godfather of the Cultural Revolution, but there were many who supported it on their own accord. In fact, it was one of the Gang of Four who fired the initial shot which enkindled the young hearts. He was Yao Wenyuan, a youthful writer of Shanghai. On November 25, 1965, he wrote an article in *Wen hui bao,* attacking Beijing's vice-mayor Wu Han for his supposed innuendo criticism of Mao Zedong.[118] The latter, says the article, was criticized by Wu in a novel *Hai Rui ba guan.* Hai Rui, a beloved magistrate of Ming dynasty, flourishing from 1514 to 1587, was unjustly removed by the emperor, Shen Zong. This piece of literature is allegedly levelled at Mao's dismissal of Peng Dehuai as Defense Minister in 1959.[119] Possibly, Yao was instructed by Mao to author it. Mao was in Shanghai at the time of the publication of the article. He went there because he was unable to get control of the party machine in the capital, a machine which he charged refused to listen to him. Immediately after the appearance of Yao's writing, a cultural revolution group of five was organized by Mao within the CC. The most loyal and most effective backers of the revolution were Mao's wife, Jiang Qing, Zhang Chunqiao, Yao Wenyuan and, at a later stage, Wang Hongwen. These are the Gang of Four, arrested on October 6, 1976.[120] When Deng Xiaoping visited the US in late January 1979, some anti-Deng demonstrators, apparently not knowing the derogatory import of the collective sobriquet, shouted at him that they supported the Gang of Four.

What the four Gangsters set out to combat was revisionism. The latter, averred they, represented peace with the imperialists, friendship with neutral states, bourgeois wage system, material enjoyment,

[118] Y.T. Hsiung, *Red China's Cultural Revolution,* 1st ed., New York: Vantage Press, 1968, p. 34.

[119] S.H. Ahmed, "China's Cultural Revolution," *International Studies* (New Delhi), 9 (July 1967), pp. 13-54 at 15; Brian Hook, "China's Cultural Revolution," *World Today,* 23 (November 1967), pp. 454-464 at 455.

[120] C.P. FitzGerald, "Reflections on the Cultural Revolution in China," *Pacific Affairs,* 41 (Spring 1968), pp. 51-59 at 51.

expedient economy and universal relaxation. They opposed all these,[121] and clamored obstreperously "politics in command," "down with Soviet and Yugoslav revisionism," "assist the colonial revolts," "help the democratic elements in Western countries," and "liberate Taiwan." Besides, the Gangsters urged the reinstitution of the original (1958) rural commune, egalitarianism, rededication to proletarian internationalism, consolidation of world revolutionary movement. What is more, class struggle was to be intensified; and to achieve this objective, the Chinese were to be categorized into five bad and five good groups.[122] All rewards or penalties were graded in accordance with the social stations of the people concerned. In short, the Gang of Four were determined to make the CPR a true communist polity and they pointed their fingers at the USSR as the apt example of a spurious socialism.[123] To them, the Kremlin leaders were degenerates of the old Bolsheviks.

As related above, Mao somehow became disillusioned in early 1967 when it was dawning upon him that the youngers whom he himself enkindled to action, were to ruin the Chinese revolution. Losing no time, he instructed Lin Biao to get rid of them. In the groove, this man executed his order. Lin ruthlessly broke them up and "exiled" them to the countryside. There began the still continued *Xiafang* (downward move) which, inter alia, was aimed at alleviating the mounting unemployment in the cities. However, there still lurked in the party hierarchy the friends of the Cultural Revolution. They never reconciled themselves to the about face. No doubt, Lin's downfall in September 1971 pleased them to no end, but the pragmatists like Zhou Enlai irked them just as much. However, Zhou was too popular to attack. The only people the radicals (as the Gang of Four began to be known) could get at were his top aides. One of them was Deng Xiaoping.[124] He had been reviled and sacked during the Cultural Revolution, but Zhou took him back in the spring of 1973, given no less a job than that of the First Vice Premier.[125] We may note en passant that although Liu Shaoqi was officially ousted from state and party organs, Deng was not. In a legal sense, Zhou's reappointment of him was indisputable, but we cannot say for one moment that Zhou acted in fact on that basis. The year 1974 saw Deng take a seat in the Politburo,[126] and 1975 brought him to its inner circle, the Standing

[121] Lowell Dittmer, "Bases of power in Chinese politics: a theory and an analysis of the fact of the Gang of Four," *World Politics*, 31 (October 1978), pp. 26-60 at 31.

[122] See Chapter XV, section on "Equality before the Law."

[123] Jürgen Domes, "The gang of four and Hua Kuo-feng, analysis of political events in 1975-1976," *China quarterly*, September 1977, pp. 473-497. Yao Meng-hsuan, "Peiping's political situation after Teng's rehabilitation," *Asian Outlook*, 12 (September 1977), pp. 38-46.

[124] Gregg Benton, "China after the events at Tien an men," *Inspector*, April 29, 1976, pp. 7-12.

[125] *Encyclopedia of China Today*, 1st ed., compiled by Frederick M. Kaplan, Julian M. Sobin and Stephen Andors, New York: Harper and Row, 1979, p. 113, p. 1.

[126] Harold Hinton, *op. cit.*, p. 137.

Committee. The second move was sanctioned by the second plenum of the 10th CC. In the meantime, the fourth National People's Congress voted him as one of the twelve vice-premiers. This made his position constitutional.[127]

Deng's comeback was extraordinarily swift and was, without question, viewed with dismay and disdain by the restive and vengeful radicals.[128] Mao was now obviously too senile to attend to state affairs which were discharged entirely by Zhou Enlai. The latter's hospitalization from May 5, 1974 (until his death on January 8, 1976) logically made Deng premier de facto. It seems certain that the radicals were facing a difficult future. Not only had they lost active protection from the withering-away patron, but they were confronted with an enemy in the premier-to-be. Thus from 1974 to 1976 there was a resurgence of the radical force which took the form of anti-US and anti-USSR propaganda, the persistent stand of the radicals.[129] Ignited against Deng was a barrage of assault in the press. However loudly the radicals may have cried, they could not achieve anything concrete because the odds against them were too much. Zhou's modernization plan as enunciated at the fourth National People's Congress apparently struck the cord of the people's heart. A return to radicalism appeared to be hard, if not entirely impossible.[130]

Zhou Enlai's demise emitted a ray of hope for the Gang of Four, however. Their leader, Zhang Chunqiao, was aspiring to the vacancy against the other First Vice Premier. In terms of seniority, the two stood an equal chance. The choice would logically lay with Mao, who however, had retired then. His last public appearance in fact was made in 1971.[131] This circumstance threw the selection to the Politburo's Standing Committee. It is very likely that Jiang Qing, Mao's wife, asked him to personally interfere, but he refused. An indication of a deadlock in the said Committee is the sidetracking of the two senior vice-premiers, Zhang Chunqiao and Deng Xiaoping.[132] And it reached "into the regular Politburo members for the only vice premier in that body who held a political portfolio (in charge of public security), Hua Guofeng."[133] Being a passable administrator, and more importantly, on nice terms with both sides, he had long claimed Zhou Enlai's attention.[134] It is even possible that he was intended by Zhou

[127] Ibid., p. 91.

[128] "Teng Hsiao-ping," Current Biography, 1976, pp. 398, 401.

[129] Harold Hinton, op. cit., pp. 90, 93.

[130] Ross Terrill, "China after Mao," Worldview, 19 (March 1976), pp. 14-16.

[131] Harold Hinton, op. cit., p. 95.

[132] Michail Galin, "Maoist merry-go-round: the political struggle in China," New Times (Moscow), 14 (April 1976), pp. 26-28.

[133] "Mao's surprise: the unexpected choice of Hua Kuo-feng as acting prime minister," Economist, 258 (February 14, 1976), pp. 15-17; Chiu Kung-yuan, "The new political storm on the Chinese mainland," Asian Outlook, 10 (May 1975), pp. 6-21.

[134] "Hua Kuo-feng," Current Biography, 1977, pp. 209-212. New York Times' Biographical Service, July-December 1976, pp. 1416-1417.

to be "a fallback replacement for Deng if necessary. Hua was informally announced in early February 1976 as temporary acting premier."[135] In the capital there prevailed a subdued tension between the contesting parties, the moderates and radicals, which did not flare into the open until April 5, 1976, the Qing ming, a Chinese version of the Memorial Day in respect of the deceased.

The incident now takes the historical appellation of "Tian an men outburst" after the name of the city square in Beijing where it occurred.[136] On April 4, the public placed spontaneously wreaths in honor of the late premier. Manifestly his pragmatic policy endeared him to the masses. To the radicals, this display of love appeared to be incited by their enemy, the moderate faction whose standard bearer was Deng Xiaoping. Next morning all the wreaths disappeared. It is suspected that the radicals ordered them carted away, for they hated to see Zhou's image revived. At once anger and indignation drove the citizens into riot. Fights erupted during the entire day between groups on the square until the troops, backed by police, moved in to disperse them, but by then the whole square was unsightly. There was massive destruction of public buildings and property.[137] The crisis was attributed by the radicals to Deng and company. The next day (April 6), the Politburo issued three decrees to a) release Deng Xiaoping of all posts, holding him responsible for what it called the counterrevolution in Tian an men, b) name Hua Guofeng first vice premier and c) account for what had happened on the previous day. Thus gone was Deng for the second time (first time November 1967).

Hua Guofeng and Deng Xiaoping

Why did not Hua back up Deng? He may have believed that the removal of him was blessed by Mao. However, he must have known that Jiang Qing and company would never accept him as the leader. Having neutralized Hua, they schemed to get rid of the moderates and even of him. Indeed, later official statement says that they attempted a coup against Hua and had him shot on October 6, 1976.[138] Hua was aware of this and planned accordingly. Many have suspected an anti-radical alliance being formed soon after the Tangshan earthquake of July 28, 1976. Hostility kept mounting as the two sides began to watch each other's next step. Matters came to a head on September 10, when Beijing announced the death of Mao. Now the Gang of Four demanded Hua to give the premiership to Zhang Chunqiao by an understanding of April 7. Hua refused, however. They reacted by inserting a phrase in various editorials (commencing on September 16): "Act according to the principles laid

135 Harold Hinton, loc. cit.

136 David Bonavia, "Anti-Teng campaign," East Asian Review, 4 (Summer 1977), pp. 143-157.

137 New York Times, April 5, 1977, p. 12, col. 4; April 6, 1977, p. 1, col. 8.

138 Harold Hinton, op. cit., p. 97.

down.''[139] In a speech to the 1st session of the newly elected National People's Congress (fifth since 1956) on February 26, 1978, Hua Guofeng said that there were no such principles.[140] However, many scholars think otherwise. The principles referred to probably envisaged Zhang Chunqiao to be premier and Hua Guofeng chairman of the party.[141] There is also the speculation that the principles would have Jiang Qing to succeed her husband as chairman. This would leave Hua in the cold.

Certainly after consultation with other like-minded individuals, Hua Guofeng who had the advantage of being Minister of Public Security acted swiftly after the expiry of the month-long mourning. On October 6, 1976, Beijing radio enunciated the arrest of the widow of Mao, Jiang Qing along with Zhang Chunqiao, Yao Wenyuan and Wang Hongwen. They were kept incommunicado until late November 1980 when they were brought to semi-public trial. The four, and another six including five generals were charged with committing counterrevolution (see Chapter XV). In the past few years, the Chinese press blamed everything, however trivial, on them. The disconnection of an electric cord in a theater, e.g., was said to be their doing. The ouster of them has signaled the abandonment of "politics in command" and ideological escapade.[142] This escapade, we should emphasize, was characteristic of the late Mao Zedong and the Gang who acted on his order and in full accord with him.

A re-evaluation of Mao began after the 3rd session of the 5th National People's Congress (August 31-September 6, 1980).[143] The (unofficial) General Secretary of the party, Hu Yaobang castigated him severely for having fomented the Cultural Revolution which he deplored had ruined China's economy. The grading of Mao's achievement cannot be all bad, as would be expected, because it is impossible for the Reds to attack him without at the same time scolding the communist drive for power. The CCP's official comment on Mao has been that he perpetrated serious mistakes but that his contributions to the Chinese revolution remain great.[144] It says that he was 70 percent right, but only 30 percent wrong. He received a B minus. The CCP did not treat Mao as the CPSU did Stalin.[145]

[139] *Ibid.*

[140] *Keesing's,* September 8, 1978, p. 29181, col. 2.

[141] Kenneth Lieberthal, "China turmoil: ghost of Mao?" *Wall Street Journal,* 192 (December 1, 1978), p. 22; Andres D. Onate, "Hua Kuo-feng and the arrest of the Gang of Four," *China Quarterly,* September 1978, pp. 540-565 at 551.

[142] Susan L. Shirk, "Going against the tide: political dissent in China," *Survey,* 24 (Winter 1979), pp. 82-114; Ross Terrill, "China enters the 1980's," *Foreign Affairs,* 58 (Spring 1980), pp. 920-935 at 930.

[143] Hsin Chi, "Is it possible that the CCP will launch a movement to criticize Mao Tse-tung?" *Chinese Law and Government,* 12 (Winter 1979-80), pp. 3-23.

[144] *Renmin ribao,* July 1, 1981, pp. 2, 3.

[145] "Deng: cleaning up Mao's feudal mistake, an interview by Oriana Fallaci with Deng Xiaoping," *The Guardian,* September 21, 1980, pp. 17-18, at 17, col. 3.

After the arrest of the Gang of Four, Deng Xiaoping came back as quickly as he departed in 1976. He was stated to be sheltered in the south where his longtime chums, Xu Shiyou and Wei Guoqing, ruled supreme,[146] the former being commander of military region in Guangzhou, while the latter, First Secretary of the Guangdong party apparatus. It is quite likely that Hua was forced to take Deng back. Xu and Wei patently wanted to restore him in the central leadership, but did not insist on the kind of job he would get. Perchance, they found it impossible to ask more for Deng. No politican gives up, *sans force majeure,* something already in hands, and Hua cannot be an exception. Was he requested by Xu Shiyou and Wei Guoqing that he surrender either the premiership or the party chairmanship to Deng? If he was, he would have lectured them something like this: "I, Hua Guofeng, have the right to enjoy the fruit of the coup, because I have risked my life to get the Gang of Four out of the way." On his part, we suppose, Deng was contented, for the time being, with running the State Council in a secondary but familiar capacity of a vice premier of whatever rank, first or last. Thus, on the seventh day of the seventh month of 1977 (when Deng began to assume that post), the situation is: the two most powerful jobs of the chairmanship of the CCP and the premiership went to one man, a potential contender sat at the vice-premier's desk, and four mighty figures languished in the detention house.

Upon the demise of Zhou Enlai, we will recall, Mao vested Hua Guofeng with acting premiership. He said to Hua that "with you in command, I am at ease." This, in fact, is the only credential of Hua's. Unfortunately for him, the credentials became, with the erosion of the image of Mao, a liability. Hua's association with and benefiting from the Cultural Revolution definitely mars his luster. He stood quite unfittingly in a pragmatical regime, for he was the only man whose star arose thanks to that upheaval and who was still around and thriving at that. His anti-Liu Shaoqi diatribes vibrated as late as February 1978,[147] and criticism of Deng Xiaoping kept on until the eve of his return to the State Council.[148] The position of Hua waxed vulnerable as the public became more angered by the ten sad years. In what was to all intents and purposes the regime of Deng Xiaoping, Hua Guofeng became anachronistic. In every state event, Hua was eclipsed by him. Probably he, Hua, had a guilty conscience, but certainly he did not build up a counter-force in or out of the highest councils. The general moods of the country are unmistakably moving away from the stifling Maoist atmosphere toward relaxation and "personal ease of mind and liveliness," to borrow a phrase from the Preamble of the 1978 CPR Constitution. The easy mind is cherished by the victims of the Cultural Revolution, victims, of whom Hua

---

[146] *Facts on file,* October 1, 1979, p. 734, D1.

[147] *Keesing's,* September 8, 1978, p. 29182, col. 1.

[148] "Deng: cleaning up Mao's feudal mistake...," *loc. cit.*

Guofeng is not one. Who questions that the nation is angry with a leader who symbolizes the hedious Maoism?

True enough, Hua does not intend to follow the ancien regime, but he has committed the errors of a) investing too much resource to impractical projects not directly related to the people's livelihood and b) promoting a cult of personality à la Mao Zedong. His power is rapidly contracting. First the premiership was divested on September 5, 1980 by the 5th National People's Congress. Zhao Ziyang, a Deng Xiaoping protégé, came to take it over.[149] Then the chairmanship of the party was deprived during the 6th plenum of the CC which met from June 27 to 29, 1981. The position went to Hu Yaobang, another protégé of Deng Xiaoping. In the meantime, the chairmanship of the Military Affairs Committee of the CC was grabbed away from him by Deng Xiaoping himself.[150]

Prior to the just-mentioned plenum, Hua Guofeng was not officially criticized. The silence is now broken. The plenum passed the resolution on a number of historical problems in which Hua is attacked. He is said to make grave aberrations. He belongs to the Fanshi school, namely, a school of infallibility. "Whatever Mao Zedong decides receives our support and whatever he directs gets our observance."[151] It is, therefore, known as two whatevers (Fanshi). Yet, the leaders, in view of his contribution to the right cause by incarcerating the Gang of Four, did not cast him away. He was offered in June 1981 the last spot of a 7-man politburo (1 chairman and 6 vice chairmen) of the CC. However at the 12th Congress of the party (September 1-11, 1982), he was criticized acrimoniously, and this, in spite of his support by Ye Jianying and Li Xiannian.[152] Disappearing he is now from the Standing Committee and the Politburo after that Congress.

The criticism of Deng Xiaoping's leadership has ominously appeared in the August 28 (1982) issue of the *Liberation Army Daily* and the *Shanghai Liberation Daily*. Zhao Yiya, an advisor to the first publication, contributes an article on "communist ideology, the core of socialist spiritual civilization." He accused the current party hierarchy of pushing the country toward bourgeois road. Socialism, he was afraid, would be jeopardized if the trend is not arrested. Wei Guoqing, the PLA's head of general political department under whose jurisdiction the papers fall, was forthwith relieved of his post (even though he is elected to the Politburo). This opposition to Deng Xiaoping appears to be the only outspoken voice. One cannot know just how widespread the dissent is, but certainly it does not augur well to the contemporary oligarchy.

[149] *Facts on file*, March 7, 1980, p. 171.

[150] *Renmin ribao*, June 30, 1981, p. 1.

[151] *Ibid.*, July 1, 1981, p. 3., col. 3.

[152] *Globe and Mail*, September 13, 1982, p. 1, col. 1.

CHAPTER V
The State
Principles and Policies

Introduction

In one of the greatest contrasts with the Soviet party, the CCP found itself a political shareholder of the country before acquiring a full title to it by violently displacing other holders, the GMD and the warlords. The year 1949 saw the culmination of a protracted struggle for that title by a ruthless army-cum-civil juggernaut. Until then, the communist portion of China was a sovereignty in all but name. It had a territorial domain just as Nanjing and various regional leaders had theirs. In no way is the occidental term "party out of power" applicable to the CCP during the twenty years from 1929 to 1949. First in Jiangxi and then in northern Shaanxi, the party possessed the complete panoply of bureaucracy and military formation. In the first decade (1929-1939), the Chinese Soviet regime was striving for sheer survival, but in the second (1939-1949), it grew rapidly. The Reds mobilized the total resources in their realm to destroy the so-called *national* government.[1] Within the GMD area, they organized student protests and demonstrations, threatened with assassination of high officials, overblew administrative errors of the regime and clamored all sorts of freedoms despite the wartime situation.[2] In their anti-Nanjing (later anti-Chongqing) hullabaloo, their own authoritarian stripes escaped the attention of foreign journalists. In the Reds' areas, the party apparatus wielded martial and civilian control which was so pervasive that no possibility could develop for opposition to surface, except for the occasional squabbles within the hierarchy. On the contrary, there were, in the nationalist controlled provinces, the communist-fomented unrests, critical press (CCP's *Xin hua ribao* published in Chongqing), and the complaints of hardship associated with material scarcity. Whenever the regime took steps to deal with these, the American papers would loudly condemn it, alleging that it lost touch with the people.

Mao and company forged a combating mechanism which defended, lorded over, and widened its territory. There was little distinction between party and state instruments, or between these and the military. Together the three imposed a draconian rule which the US newsmen and the State Department regarded as democracy because things were awfully quiet there. The trinity of party, government and army are always linked up in one breath by the press when mention is made of the "major institutional actors."[3] The relation among the

---

[1] *Zhong guo renmin jie fang zhan zheng he xin zhong guo wu nian jian she,* Beijing: Renmin chu ban she, 1954, pp. 46-50.

[2] Richard C. Thornton, China, *the struggle for power 1917-1972,* Bloomington: Indiana University Press, 1973, pp. 78-95.

[3] Sam C. Sarkesian and James H. Buck, *Comparative politics,* Sherman Oaks, California: Alfred Pub. Co., 1979, p. 215, col. 1.

trio is prescribed in the 1978 constitution. This document refers to the CCP nine times,[4] indicating in so many ways its dominant position. Article 22, clause 4, for example, says the National People's Congress (NPC) appoints the premier upon the nomination of the Central Committee (CC) of the party and Article 46 compels all Chinese to accept the latter's leadership.[5] By the former provision, the legislature has no right of its own to recruit a premier and by the latter, non-party citizens are captive communists. Come to the military, it is stipulated in April 19, par. 1 that the CCP chairman "commands the armed forces of the CPR." The Constitution does not use the term "commander-in-chief" perhaps in order to avoid the "wrong" thinking that there can be a "commander-in-second". The armed forces, in other words, must be placed under one and only one man, the supreme boss of the party. Moreover, par. 2 of the same Article says expressly that the army is led by the party. It lies beyond the purview of the legislature.

The 1982 Constitution changes all this. Detailed regulations will be introduced later in various parts of this book. Suffice it to state here that Article 24 still enjoins the government to educate the people in the spirit of communism and that although institutionally there is a separation of power between the state and the CCP, the role of the latter remains supreme. Things abide as they always were.

Interestingly enough, the hierarchical tandem of party, government and military is not seen in the Russian Constitution. The Soviet elite do not consider it legally proper to a) demand every citizen, communist or non-communist, to follow the CPSU and b) require nomination of the Chairman of the Council of Ministers by the Central Committee of the party. On the other hand, in neither Russia nor China has the belief obtained that the state organs should be replaced by the party apparatus. With the latter country, this institutional segregation was not achieved until after 1949. Now that the enemy threat was gone, the pre-1949 jack of all trades, that is, cadre-soldier-administrator, has lost its raison d'être. A traditional state, Mao Zedong came to feel, needed the kind of setup in which each body is entrusted with a portion of the ruling chore; and to this end, he sorted out the three functional entities of party, government and PLA and gave each a field of operation. He did this, of course, not for the sake of deconcentration of power, but to achieve efficiency of the grand system. Such an arrangement, thought he, would further the legitimacy of the CPR.[6] Little wonder he decreed the organic laws (see below) no sooner than he rode triumphantly into Beijing in September 1949 after the garrison general Fu Zuoyi waved the white flag to him.

Since the principles and policies of the state are laid out in the

[4] Constitution, Preamble (three times), Articles 2, 19 (two times each), and Articles 22, 56 (one time each).

[5] W.W. Rostow, The prospects for communist China, London: Chapman and Hall, 1954, p. 72: Frank Moraes, Report on Mao's China, New York: Macmillan, 1953, pp. 146-147.

[6] Zhong guo renmin jie fang zhan zheng he xin zhong guo wu nian jian she, p. 105.

Constitution, let us examine them in this chapter, leaving the government institutions to the next, but at this moment we must say something about the whys and wherefores of the constitution. Under a parliamentary democracy the supreme law of the land intends to delineate the political organizations on the one side of the coin but to guarantee the people's rights on the other.[7] At the core of that regime is the restricted area of action of the policy-makers. These men must rotate from time to time through mandating by the people in free elections. Nothing is more alien to the communists than this practice (although a lip service is paid it in the 1982 Constitution). Strange may it sound, they actually build on the assumption of the divine right of king. Having fought to the seat of power, in the way an incoming Chinese emperor defeated the last ruler of a decaying dynasty, they consider it a sacrosanct trophy. All communists the world over, once taking the reign of government by force of arms, would proceed helter-skelter to enshrine it in a fundamental instrument. It is directed not at limiting the will of the party, but at reinforcing its monolithic sway.

There are a number of uses of a "communist constitution", to employ a rather bemusing term. First, it records the accomplishment of the people's struggle (CPR Constitution, Preamble). Second, it "defines the basic systems and tasks of the state" (*ibid.*). Third, it sets down "basic norms of conduct of officials and individual citizens" (*ibid.*). The Soviet Constitution (Article 65) is purported to foster among the people "an uncompromising attitude toward an anti-social behavior." Fourth, the constitution dishes out authorities to diverse organs such as the bureaucracy, the representative assembly, the judiciary, local administration, the procuracy, the public security office, the armed forces and the militia. How great a mess would it be if there were no differentiation between and among all these bodies! Fifth, it seeks to strengthen the autocracy by a) outlawing any opposition which the CPR Constitution (Article 28) calls either counter-revolutionary or treasonous and b) decreeing all citizens to be led by the CCP (Preamble). Sixth, it proclaims state policy which is a mixed bag of programs and dogmas. Seventh, it puts down the rights of workers and peasants, declaring their "dictatorship." Eighth, it aims at dramatizing the claim of the CCP as a system ruled by law but not by a man, however wise and saintly. Such claim, as known to all, has no basis whatsoever while Mao Zedong was alive. After his departure, the rule of law is slated to be refurbished by the practice of socialist legality (Preamble and Article 5). We think it is an elusive hope unless communism is abandoned lock, stock, and barrel.[8]

Through the thirty-three years of its history, the Chinese regime has written four Constitutions (same as the USSR). The present one

---

[7] Kenneth C. Wheare, "Constitution," *Chamber's encyclopedia,* new rev. ed., London: International learning system, 1966, vol. 4, pp. 45-46.

[8] See a comment on this by Jerome Cohen, "Will China have a formal legal system?" *American bar association journal,* October 1978, pp. 1510-1515 at 1510, col. 1.

is dated from December 4, 1982. A Revision Committee of one hundred was appointed on September 7, 1980 by the NPC to develop a draft.[9] Before the convocation of the NPC on November 30, 1981, there was the expectation that a new Constitution would be promulgated. However, the just-said Committee asked for a delay of the draft for another full year.[10] On April 21, 1982, it finished the job and had it published in Beijing review (May 10, 1982, pp. 19-47). The document was endorsed by the NPC Standing Committee in its 23rd session on April 22.[11] Before analyzing the present Constitution, let us briefly look at its earliest predecessor.

The CCP drew up what may be termed a pre-constitution in 1949. The instrument is made up of three parts, rubber-stamped by the mouthful Chinese People's Political Consultative Conference (CPPCC). They are a) the Common Program, b) the Organic Law of this body, and c) the Organic Law of the Central People's Government.[12] The three remind us of the equal number of basic laws (written in 1875) of the Third French Republic, likewise produced during a national upheaval. Similar to them, the Chinese documents are poorly articulated, hastily put together and too skeletal to be a guideline for the government.[13] There is no room nor the need to narrate them here, but it is interesting to see what kind of state the CPR is made to be. The Common Program (Article 1) says it is a "new democracy" which means people's democratic dictatorship: democracy among the people but dictatorship over the enemy (the non-people).[14] Into the definition of people, the Program puts the workers, peasants, petty and national bourgeois, while the non-people are said to embrace landlords, feudalists, bureaucrats, capitalists and the hybrid of bureaucratic-capitalists, rich peasants and those bourgeois who had foreign connection. The Common Program alleges to see China to be traversing from semi-feudalism and semi-colonialism to the proletarian dictatorship.[15] During such a transition, the CPPCC acted as an interim parliament made up of 585 delegates and 77 candidates. It was authorized to enact the fundamental rules of the state, namely the three organic laws just mentioned.[16] According to Article 3 of the Organic Law of the CPPCC, disagreeable delegates have the right to get out.[17] But nobody disagreed and none got out.

[9] Bryan Johnson, "China kills 10 Year Plan," Globe and Mail, September 8, 1980, p. 3, col. 4.

[10] Ibid., November 30, 1981, p. 14, col. 4: Renmin ribao, December 3, 1981, p. 1.

[11] "Draft of revised Constitution made public," Beijing review, May 3, 1982, p. 5.

[12] Zhong hua renmin gong he guo kai guo wen xian. Hong Kong: Wen hua zi liao gong ying she, 1978, pp. 236-274.

[13] Harold W. Jacobson, "The political system," People's Republic of China, a handbook, edited by Harold Hinton, Boulder, Colorado: Westview, 1979, pp. 99-173 at 99-100.

[14] Xin hua ci dian, Beijing: Shang wu yin shu guan, 1980, p. 703, col. 1.

[15] Common Program, Article 3, Zhong hua renmin gong he guo kai guo wen xian, p. 262.

[16] Ibid., p. 18; Zhong guo shou ce, Hong Kong: Dan gong bao, 1979, p. 118.

[17] Zhong hua renmin gong he guo kai guo wen xian, p. 237.

The CPPCC ceased to exercise the legislative function after the coming into being of the NPC on September 15, 1954.[18] However, it is still kept as a "united battle formation," to use the official description of it.[19] The members are all communists and sympathizers. The latter are particularly in evidence and it is mainly through them that the communist propaganda is spread far and wide. This is what the 1982 Constitution (Preamble) intends the CPPCC to be. The CCP is portrayed as having the broadest appeal not only to the faithful card-carriers but to non-party people inside and outside the CPR. Up to now there have been six CPPCC's and since April 17, 1959, its members are given the right to sit but not vote in the NPC.[20] The following shows the duration and related data on the six convocations at their first (one time the only) sessions.[21]

First session	Honorable chairman	Mem.	Standing cmt.	Times met
1st Sept. 1-30, 1949	Mao Zedong	662	180	4
2nd Dec. 21-25, 1954	same	493	65	3
3rd Apr. 17-29, 1959	same	1071	143	4
4th Dec. 24, 1964				
- Jan. 5, 1965	same	1199	159	1
5th Feb. 24-Mar. 8, 1978	Deng Xiaoping	1988	243	5
6th June 4-22, 1983	Deng Yingchao	2036	297	1

The fifth (5th) CPPCC held its 4th session from November 29 to December 13, 1981, and its fifth session from November 25 to December 11, 1982. Both had Deng Xiaoping as honorable chairman, and both had a membership of 2,054 and a standing committee made up of 270 deputies. The first session of the sixth CPPCC (June 1983) has 2036 members and a standing committee of 297. Among the members are 11 foreigners (*Renmin ribao,* May 8, p. 4; June 4, p. 2, 1983). Communist membership is said to be 40 percent, in comparison with 60 percent of the preceding CPPCC (*ibid.,* May 8, 1983, p. 1). Overseas Chinese representatives, 75 strong (44 from Hong Kong and 31 from other parts of the world), make for 3.7 percent of the total membership (*ibid.,* pp. 2, 3). The CPPCC does not have a constitutional standing until the 1982 Constitution whose Preamble makes a brief reference to it. It is an unvarnished political expediency. Needless to say, both this body and the NPC are consultative in nature, but the CPPCC has to be more so (if that is possible) than the NPC because it is not an elected organization as the latter is, according to the term of the Constitution.

18 *Zhong guo shou ce,* p. 118; Preambles of the 1978 and 1982 Constitutions.

19 *Ibid.* A new CPPCC Statute was adopted on December 11, 1982, *Beijing review,* December 20, 1982, p. 4.

20 *Zhong guo shou ce,* p. 119.

21 *Ibid.,* pp. 117-119. The 16th session of the Standing Committee of the CPPCC held on November 23, 1981 decided to add 70 new members, *Renmin ribao,* November 24, 1981, p. 1. The total would have to be 2,158.

The tripartite pre-constitution was in effect for five years. It was replaced by the first Constitution on September 20, 1954. The latter gave way to the second on January 15, 1975 and the third and fourth were proclaimed on February 26, 1978 and December 4, 1982 respectively. Regarding their length, they have each 111, 106, 30, 60 and 138 articles.[22] In general, one may assert that the pre-constitution is a hodgepodge. It has many policy specifics seasoned with strong Marxist-Leninist spices, the first constitution goes on, as it were, ideological diet and has some positive stuffs; the second summarizes the experience of the Cultural Revolution by considerably cutting down civil rights; the third seeks to preserve the odor of that Revolution but adds a modicum of legalism; and the fourth embarks on a new course and yet reputedly patterns itself after the first because, to use the words of Peng Zhen (vice-chairman of the Revision Committee), "the 1954 Constitution was relatively flawless" and hence is followable.[23] One most notable aspect of the several documents is that the pre-constitution, more specifically Articles 26-30 of the Organic Law of the Central People's Government, has five articles on law and justice, the 1954 Constitution 12 articles (73-84), the 1975 Constitution only one article (25), the 1978 Constitution three articles (41-43), but the 1982 Constitution thirteen articles (123-135) on them.[24]

All the Constitutions entitle the CPR a democratic dictatorship which is equated to proletarian dictatorship.[25] Since the latter expression is, in turn, equated to "dictatorship by the working class founded on the alliance of workers and peasants," the CPR is a class state. This is so, in spite of the fact that the term "whole people" (quan min) is employed to describe the ownership of the socialist sector of the economy.[26] In contrast, while the Stalin Constitution (1936) in Article 1 labels the USSR a state of workers and peasants, the Brezhnev Constitution (1977) in Article 1 marks it as a state of all people. On paper, the Russians have outwitted the Chinese in this department because class state is generally deemed as an old fashioned concept.

Sovereignty

Where lies the sovereignty of the CPR? Article 2 of the Constitution lays it in the people, because it says that they wield "all power of

[22] The Organic Law of the CPPCC has 20 articles, the Organic Law of the Central People's Government 31 articles, and the Common Program 60 articles, Zhong guo renmin gong he guo kai guo wen xian, pp. 236-274.

[23] Peng Zhen, "Explanation on the draft of the revised Constitution of the People's Republic of China at the 23rd session of the Fifth National People's Congress Standing Committee on April 22, 1982," Beijing review, May 10, 1982, pp. 18-26 at 18, col. 1.

[24] Section 7 of Chapter 3 of the 1982 Constitution deals with courts and procuracy of the CPR.

[25] This outright equation is seen in "Guan yu jian quo yi lai dang de ruo gan li shi wen ti de jue ji" (A resolution on several historical points since the founding of the CPR), by the sixth plenum of the 11th CC, Guangming ribao, July 1, 1981, pp. 1-5; also in Renmin ribao, same date, pp. 1-5 (we use the latter source). From now on, this source will be cited as "Guan yu jian guo yi lai."

[26] The 1982 Constitution, Articles 6-8.

the Chinese People's Republic.'' According to the con
''people'' (*ren min*) means not the whole populace, but only
masses;[27] and ''people's power'' means their dictatorship. ᵣ ᵤ
sovereignty is just a different expression of dictatorship of workers
and peasants. The Preamble unequivocally equates people's
democratic dictatorship with dictatorship of the proletariat, as does
the aforesaid CC Resolution of June 27, 1981.[28] In China, therefore,
sovereignty or dictatorship resides in the working class. Those who
do not belong to that class, of course, cannot exercise it. Being enemy
to the sovereign class, they are not ''people''. This dichotomy of ''we
the people'' and ''they the non-people'' was utilized during the early
years of the CPR to justify the suppression of the so-called exploiting
segment of the society. However, as time goes by, one hears less
and less of this rhetoric until it is all but gone. By a simple logic,
dictatorship cannot exist any longer than its target. If the latter
vanishes from the scene, it is nonsense to speak of dictatorship. What
has happened is that the Reds ''have annihilated''[29] the landlords,
rich peasants and grand bourgeois (as distinct from the petty ones
whom they decided to save). In this way the communists cut the
ground from under the dictatorship of the proletariat.

However, the Reds do not adhere to this reasoning, since they keep
on talking of class struggle which boils down to be an exercise of
sovereign power over the enemy class. The fundamental question
is whether class struggle can go on after that class is destroyed? To
this, the present ideologues first answered negatively. Mao Zedong
was roundly upbraided on this very point. It was held that he in his
dotage wrongfully waged war with the enemy class when this class
no longer lived.[30] Most recently, however, they answered the question
affirmatively. Manifesting this new stand, the Constitution (Preamble)
asserts that following the abolition of the exploiting class in the CPR,
''class struggle will continue to exist, within certain limits, for a long
time to come.'' In early 1978, we will remember, the CCP passed a
resolution to de-class the ''landlords and rich peasants.''[31] From then
on, enemy class in the traditional sense was gone. However, a fresh
class emerges. Lumped in it are ''forces and elements both at home
and abroad which are hostile to China's socialist system and try to
undermine it'' (Constitution, Preamble). Peng Zhen sees the ''forces
and elements'' in spies and special agents, serious criminals like
embezzlers, bribers, smugglers, speculators, swindlers and thieves
of state property. Class war, he insisted, must be fought as

---

[27] *Xin hua ci dian*, p. 699.

[28] ''Guan yu jian guo yi lai'', p. 3, col. 1.

[29] These two words are acutally used in ibid., p. 5, col. 2.

[30] *Ibid.*, p. 3, col. 1.

[31] ''Zhong gong zhong yang zuo chu guan yu di zu fu nong fen zi zhai mou wen ti he di fu zi nu cheng fen wen ti de jui dian'' (The CC resolution on the problem about de-capping the landlords and rich peasants and about the status of their children), *Renmin shou ce*, Beijing: Renmin chu ban she, 1979, p. 235.

indefatigably as ever.[32] Therefore, although the dictator-class consists of workers and peasants (loosely interpreted, see Chapter on the CCP), the dictatee-class has different characters. After all, China is a class state and the proletariat still exercises class sovereignty. The above analysis is kept strictly within the legal context. However, if we understand sovereignty as the ultimate power to decide state policy, it is in the hand of the party, or more precisely, the apex of the party hierarchy. The assertion that all power emanates from the workers and peasants is, we believe, little better than a myth. In this respect, the Stalin Constitution of 1936 and its 1977 successor are more candid than the Chinese Constitution in conceding the sovereign role to the CPSU. The 1936 document says in Article 126 that the party is the "vanguard of the working class," and the 1977 one states in Preamble that "the leading roles of the Communist Party of all the people has grown" and in Article 6 that the party leads and guides the people and is the nuclear force in the Soviet society. The CPR Constitution however never mentions the CCP in the main part of the text, even though it refers to it four times in the Preamble, all within historical framework.

Nature of the state

Socialist

Apropos of the nature of the Chinese body politic, there are a couple of ways of considering it. From the economic angle, the CPR is a socialist system as clearly declared in Article 1, par. 1, which is to be distinguished from a communist system. The name of Communist China, although popular, is technically wrong. Here we find it interesting to observe that the 1954 Constitution (Article 1) calls the country a people's democracy, not a socialist state. This is so perhaps as its new rulers, transported by the victory in the just-ended civil war, were not sure of the appropriate appellation for the big prize, even though they all seemed to be determined to take the CPR straight to the communist paradise. But after thirty years, the paradise is still a never never land because the hallmark of communism, i.e., abundance of goods and distribution according to one's needs, is not in sight. "We might as well settle with socialism and forget communism for the time being," the Beijing oligarchs must have said to each other in 1978. This explains why that year's Constitution (Article 1) describes China as socialist. The USSR, further thought the oligarchs, has travelled much longer on the road to the workers' Eden, but not yet closer to it in 1978 than in 1936 when Stalin said socialism was completed and communism was begun. A confession of socialism in the Chinese Constitution of 1978 is seen in Article 6 which writes: "The economic system applies the principle from each according to his ability, to each according to his work." This saying was coupled with another one: "he who does not work shall not eat"

[32] Peng Zhen, "Explanation on the draft of the revised Constitution of the People's Republic of China," *Beijing review,* May 10, 1982, pp. 18-26 at 20-21.

in Article 10, par. 1. The two are also in the 1936 Stalin Constitution (Article 12). Strange enough, the second sentence disappears from both the Soviet Constitution of 1977 and the Chinese Constitution of 1982.

If communism suffers a verbal setback by the deletion of the statement "he who does not work shall not eat," humanism must have gained. Both the Russians and Chinese from now on would not deny food to one simply because he takes up no job. But we would hasten to add that the Russians nevertheless keep that statement in the CPSU Statutes (Rule 59 (h)). This means that as far as party members are concerned, no quarters are to be given to idlers, and this in spite of the humanitarian requirement for being good communists (also provided in the same Rule) that "man is to man a friend, comrade and brother." Can a brother refuse to hand out food to another hungry brother in any case? Why the Chinese drop the saying "he who does not work shall not eat" from the 1982 Constitution is perhaps because they do not want to be outdistanced by the Soviets in this principle matter. The CCP Statute (often called CCP Constitution), be it noted, has no humanism provision as the CPSU Statues' Rule 59 (h). Obviously that ism is not the Chinese communists' admired behavior. As if for the sake of compensating for this, they create the phrase "love of men" in the new Constitution (Article 24), a phrase missing in the Soviet counterpart. In standing up against the Russians, the Chinese may well comfort themselves by thinking that although they lose the statutory battle, they win the constitutional war.

Unitary

In terms of division of power between the center and province/region, the CPR is a unitary state (Preamble). According to Article 4, par. 3, all the national autonomous areas are inalienable parts of the Republic. This is to say, they cannot "secede" (par. 3). The unitariness of the system is reaffirmed in five ways: a) the declaration of Article 96 that local people's congresses at various planes are local "organs of state power", b) the veto power of the State Council over the local administration as provided in Article 89, cl. 14, c) the authority of the NPC Standing Committee to annul statutes, decisions of provinces, autonomous regions and municipalities directly under the Central People's Government as envisaged in Article 67, cl. 8, d) the review by the State Council of the formation of the units just mentioned, plus the autonomous prefectures, counties, autonomous counties and cities, in accordance with Article 89, cl. 15, e) by Article 110, par. 2, local people's governments are "organs of state administration" (nominally different from "organs of state power") under the unified leadership of the State Council and subordinate to it. None of the local units has its territorial integrity, a most salient feature of federalism. True, there is provided in Article 3, par. 4 the geographical "division of functions and powers." But the division is one between central and local state institutions. This provision is extremely misleading, because the Constitution says nothing about the local administration's functions and powers at all, but those of the Central People's Government are found galore.

The Chinese unitary regime is in perfect consonance with a communist polity. Its rulers, we may suppose, find it just too dishonest to cloak totalitarianism with a federal garb as the Kremlin does. Should the CPR form itself into a federal state, its federal divisions (i.e., Han people's republic or Hui people's republic as the Reds undoubtedly would call them) would have a better territorial and populational balance than the union republics of the USSR. In the latter country, the Russian Soviet Federal Socialist Republic with its 17,075,000 sq km is 300 times bigger than the smallest Armenian Soviet Socialist Republic with its 59,800 sq km. In the case of the CPR, the Han area having 5,167,300 sq km is 86 times the Ningxia-hui Autonomous Region with a little over 60,000 sq km. Population-wise, the Russian Republic inhabited by 137,552,000 is 900 times the least populous Estonian Republic embracing 1,466,000 souls. Against this, the Hans, 936,703,824 strong, are 240 times the Ningxia-huis numbering only 3,895,578.[33]

Ideological behests

In the old Constitution, the hook-ups of Marxism-Leninism and Mao Zedong Thought parade four times (one each in the Preamble, Articles 2, 14, 16), and Mao Zedong appears five times (all in the Preamble), but in the new Constitution (Preamble), the hook-ups show only twice and Mao comes out also twice. More notable perhaps is the fact that the old Constitution mentions the CCP seven times: three in the Preamble and 4 in Articles 2, 19, 22, 56. Against this, the new Constitution (Preamble), although speaking of the CCP four times, never refers to it in its main body.

Can one argue that the leaders have reduced the role of the party? Hardly. This is because the Preamble of the Constitution enjoins the citizens to abide by the order of the party, Marxism-Leninism and Mao Zedong Thought, people's dictatorship and socialist road (in that sequence). These are loudly sung as *si ge yuan ze* (four principles). Actually the Constitution does not have the word four. It is supplied by the propaganda mills in order to come up with a slogan easy to cry out. The four are ideological absolutes, and no communists can afford not to mouth them. Originally they were written into the Preamble of the 1978 Constitution. The carryover seems to be intended to appease the diehard followers of Mao Zedong and the friends of the ousted Gang of Four. The term socialism, in the draft Constitution, be it observed, does not always stand alone. In two instances (Preamble and Article 21), *modernized* socialism is

33 "The 1982 census results," *Beijing review*, November 8, 1982, pp. 20-21. Also in *ibid.*, January 3, 1983, p. 25.

employed. It is, in other words, not the brand of socialism as practiced by the hegemonic (no longer the epithetic revisionist) Soviet Union. The final text of the Constitution does not qualify socialism with modernized.

It is as important to know what the new oligarchs do not stand for as it is to know what they advocate in ideology. In 1978 when the Gang of Four were locked up in jail and the dust was not yet completely settling down, the new elite were taking, as it were, a deep sigh. On the one hand, they were gladdened that all was over, but on the other, they were still confused, having no firm direction. Undoubtedly many were torn between the nostaliga of the Cultural Revolution and a gleam of renaissance. As it turned out, Hua Guofeng was only a transition leader, China's Malenkov perhaps. In 1981, he was charged of dragging his feet in setting things straight and reinstating the fallen cadres.[34] At the commanding heights there was sitting the Fanshi faction, a faction which swore that "whatever Mao Zedong decides gets our support, and whatever he directs gets our observance."[35] Giving this circumstance, it was no surprise that many cultural-revolution vagaries found their way into the 1978 Constitution. Held high is Mao Zedong's banner of permanent revolution. And the Cultural Revolution of 1966-1969 is said to be only the "first." China would be "continuing the revolution under the dictatorship of the proletariat" (Preamble). The whole nation was to work on the "three great revolutionary movements of a) class struggle, b) struggle for production and c) strife for scientific experiment. A solemn pledge was made to "oppose revisionism and prevent the restoration of capitalism" (ibid.) Furthermore, the 1978 Constitution enshrines the refrain of the Cultural Revolution in Article 10, par. 2: "Put proletarian politics in command." Firmly riveted in Article 15, par. 2 were the five requirements for successors of the proletarian cause: a) to conscientiously study the works of Marx, Lenin and Mao Zedong, b) to always serve the collective interests of the people and never work for private gains, c) to strive for united-front work, d) to consult the masses, e) to be willing to make criticism and self-criticism.[36] Last but not least the triadic principle of staffing state organs, i.e., cadres must come from the age-groups of the old, the middle-aged and the young, is written in Article 15, par. 2. All of these, except the struggle for production and scientific experiment, are now regarded, although not in so many words, as "mistakes" of Mao Zedong.[37] They are jettisoned for good.

In making a cursory and self-righteous survey of history, the Preamble ventures to periodize the years from 1840 to 1949. By

[34] "Guan yu jian guo yi lai", p. 3, col. 3.

[35] Ibid., see also Chapter II, note 150.

[36] The constitution does not actually mention the five perhaps for short of space. These can be found in James Wang, Contemporary Chinese Politics, An Introduction, Englewood Cliffs, New Jersey: Prentice-Hall, 1980, p. 86.

[37] "Guan yu jian guo yi lai", p. 2, col. 3. The Preamble of the Constitution talks of unspecified "mistakes."

following what is being said there and by taking into account Mao Zedong's writings we get this historical timing:

(in the Preamble)

Year	
1840	China was feudalism
1841	gradually became semi-feudalism
1911	feudalism (Sun Yat-sen overthrew feudalism)
1912	gradually became semi-feudalism

(in Mao Zedong's writings)[38]

Year	
1930	feudalism
1931	semi-feudalism (Japan's invasion of Manchuria in September 1931 turns feudalism into semi-feudalism)
1939	feudalism (from 1840 to 1939, China under feudalism)
1940	semi-feudalism

(in the Preamble)

Year	
1949	feudalism (CCP overthrew feudalism)

Thus feudalism and semi-feudalism hopped back and forth in modern annals of China. Even a single event, that of foreign (Japanese) invasion, can direct China from feudalism to semi-feudalism! The Beijing oligarchs should tell us more about all this nonsense. We will have more to say about the ideological position in the discussion of social and cultural control later in this chapter.

Direct and indirect democracy

In the history of political theory, there is a never ending debate on the merits and shortcomings of direct or indirect participation of the masses in decision-making. While we can hardly imagine the Chinese leaders have ruminated on this issue by reading books and taking notes, their Constitution does seek to balance the two and adds more "to boot." On the three levels of administration below the county, the election is direct, but on the three levels above it, it is indirect. The former are a) town (township) congress, b) commune congress and c) county congress; the latter are d) prefectural congress, e) provincial (regional) congress and f) the NPC (see also section on election in Chapter VI). Such a double-track approach, it is to be noted, was adopted by the 1970 election law of Hungary;[39] and a Russian dissident would like to see the Soviet Union follow suit.[40]

Going further than this, the Chinese democracy requires leading cadres of workers' collectives to be chosen by their members according to Article 17, par. 2. It is provided in Article 16, par. 1 that "state enterprises have decision-making power in operation" and they "practice democratic management through congresses of workers

[38] Mao Zedong, *Zhong guo ge ming yu zhong guo gong chan dang* (The Chinese revoltion and the Chinese Communist Party), Han Dan: Xin hua shu ju, 1949, pp. 5-7.

[39] Roy Medvedev, *On socialist democracy*, New York: Norton, 1975, p. 146.

[40] *Ibid.*, p. 145.

and staff." To implement this right, there was issued in July 1981 provisional regulations on the said congresses.[41] From what has taken place in plants and shops, it is clear that the party secretaries and government-backed men are always elected as managers or directors of the enterprises. Noteworthy too is that the right to manage the factory affairs and elect the chiefs is not placed in Chapter two of the Constitution on Fundamental Rights of Citizens. Certainly it is not regarded by the Beijing oligarchy as fundamental. Both the Soviet and Chinese Constitutions (strangely enough in Article 3 of each document) set forth democratic centralism, with the minor difference that while the former enumerates the several planks of it, the latter elects to be silent about them. Citizens' participatory role is summarized in the Chinese document (Article 2) by considering it as their "right to administer the affairs of the country," and in the Soviet document (Preamble) by depicting it as the people's "running of the state" and in Article 48 as their "management and administration of state and public affairs." To further the socialist democracy, both documents (Chinese Constitution Article 41, Russian Constitution Articles 49 and 58) grant the citizens the privilege of making complaints, filing charges in case of violation of the law by state officials regardless of whether their action inflicts damage on their rights. If the latter, they are to be compensated, however.

General policy
Four modernizations

The loudest-cried slogan of Beijing is that of the four modernizations of industry, agriculture, the military and science and technology. Although both the 1978 and 1982 Constitutions (Article 11, par. 2 and Preamble respectively) write of them, the latter no longer declares agriculture to be *fundamental* and industry *leading* of the four. These adjectives are dropped because, the hierarchy has perhaps found out, the dictionary does not say which is foremost. Why is modernization limited to these four? The famous dissident-convict Li Yizhe (actually three young men) propounded democratization as the fifth. In their opinion, without this, the others cannot do much good for the people. It seems that the 1982 Constitution has taken such proposal into account, because the Preamble talks, in one breath, of four modernizations and *democracy and legalism*. The Preamble, to be exact, does not have the word four. Like the four principles already introduced, it is the propaganda mills which supply it so as to make the slogan "four modernizations" easy to yell.

Taiwan annexation

All but the first Constitution avow to take Taiwan. However there is a change of wordage regarding the technique. While the 1975 and 1978 documents speak of "liberation," the 1982 document mentions

---

[41] *Beijing review*, October 4, 1982, p. 20, col. 2.

"unification." This, of course, sounds much less offensive to the people there. What is more, the present Constitution makes reference to *zhong hua min guo* (Chinese republic), the 1911 revolution and Sun Yat-sen. Of course, it is intended by Beijing to hypnotize the GMD elite in Taiwan because that italicized title is their traditional state and because that medical doctor-turn-revolutionary their revered idol. There are two other equally tendentious provisions. (A) Article 31 and Article 62, cl. 13 are an indirect appeal to the island by promising it an autonomous status to be called "special administrative (actually economic) zone." It is to be governed by a special law of the NPC. We will remember that under the 9-point proposal offered by Ye Jianying (see chapter on diplomacy, relation with US), Taiwan can keep whatever it has even, perhaps particularly, armed forces and capitalist economy. The CPR has presently established four *jing ji te cu,* meaning literally unusual quarters of economy, along the southern coast. To be more specific, three are in Guangdong: Shenzhen, Zhuhai and Shantou; and one is in Fujian, namely Xiamen.[42] They are intended to be a bait for the Taiwan fish.

(B) Article 50 is to court the overseas Chinese, said to be 20,000,000 (God knows how many, because there are no statistics). By that article (also Article 89, cl. 12), the Chinese Government is now obliged to protect their legitimate interests while abroad whether as sojourners or citizens of the adopted countries (the clause mentions "Chinese nationals residing abroad). Meanwhile they enjoy "lawful rights" while finding themselves in the CPR. Especially noteworthy, in the light of what occurred in the past, is the constitutional assurance that their relatives in the CPR are also taken good care of, that is, they are to have "lawful rights and interests." As is known to all, such relatives were persecuted, harassed, dispossessed, tortured, extorted, imprisoned or executed on the simple reason that they had "foreign connection" (*hai wai guan xi*). As a result, overwhelming numbers of overseas Chinese are distrustful, hostile, skeptical or outright hateful of the Red regime. An overwhelming majority of them are pro-Taiwan. In order to win them over, Article 50 is written. It amounts to a clarion-call: "Behold! dear brethren, your rights and those of your beloved ones are granted constitutional safeguard. From now on you have no reason to stand on the other side of the strait."

To get the island, Beijing has left no legerdemain unplayed. It resorts to nerve war, armed threat, cajolery, letter-writings, exertion of pressure upon the US Administration to force the Taiwan regime to submit to the CPR's ultimatum.[43] Frequently it signals Moscow a desire of rapprochement in the hope that the US would be so scared that it would soften its stand on the Taiwan issue. Further, the Red authorities engage in subversive actions carried out by infiltrators,

[42] *Ibid.,* April 12, 1982, p. 5; *The China reporter,* October 1982, p. 8, col. 3.

[43] Stanley Oziewics, "US averts diplomatic rift by limiting Taiwan arms sales," *Globe and Mail,* August 18, 1982, p. 9, cols. 2-6 at 5-6 where President Reagan denied such pressure.

bogus deserters and refugees from the province of Fujian. There are, in addition, sympathizers who, although not stooges of Beijing, are inspired by it. At times they engineered conspiracy and bloody uprisings. What they dream for is that if they succeed, the Red regime would award them with fat jobs on the island. All the moves described above have failed to topple the Taiwan government. As a final attempt of accomplishing this objective, Beijing is now trying a fresh approach of constitutional hoax to see if it works.

Civil rights

Compared with the 1978 Constitution, the 1982 one shows much more care about these, an obvious contrition, on the part of the CCP leaders, of their tyranny in decades. A prima facie proof of the importance attached by them to the freedoms and well-being of the masses is that civil rights make up Chapter 2 of the 1982 Constitution, while the 1978 text places them in Chapter 3, an uplifting also seen in the 1977 Soviet Constitution which advances such rights to Chapter 2 from the 1936 predecessor's Chapter 10.

The drafters are bounty, even lavish, with the provisions on civil rights. Altogether they assign 27 articles to them out of a total of 138.[44] Because of limited space here, it is impossible to list, let alone discuss, all of them. Suffice it to mention the salient ones. There is the responsibility of the government to provide social assistance and social insurance against old age, illness or disability (Article 45, par. 1) and against unemployment (Article 42, par. 4). There is the equality before the law and the familiar freedom of speech, the press, assembly and association. And there is the less familiar freedom of procession and demonstration (Article 35). Although these freedoms were at one time abolished by the third plenum of the 11th CC in late 1978,[45] the new Constitution sees it fit to restore them.

Article 37 declares that freedom of person is inviolable. Extra-legal detention of citizens, or extra-legal deprivation or restriction of that freedom is prohibited, as is extra-legal search of citizens. Also worth mentioning is Article 38 upholding personal dignity of citizens and forbidding insult or slander of citizens in any form. These are not in the 1978 Constitution whose Article 47 does not go beyond the perfunctory saying of freedom from unlawful arrest. However there is a setback in the new document in that it withdraws the freedom of strike as provided in Article 45 of the 1978 Constitution. Moreover, neither Constitution revives the 1954 document's (Article 90, par. 2) freedom of movement. This deletion is understandable in the light of the government policy to bar the peasants from migrating to the cities to look for jobs, cities already crowded and plagued with problems of employment and food supply. During the time when the 1954 Constitution was in force, the courts were quite busy with cases

---

[44] Articles 33-50, Article 2, par. 3; Article 4, par. 4; Article 9, par. 1; Articles 14, 116, 117, 121, 122, 134.

[45] "Guan yu jian guo yi lai", p. 4, col. 1.

144   GOVERNMENT OF SOCIALIST CHINA

where the police compelled the peasants to go back to the villages, but their lawyers cited the aforesaid article to defend their constitutional right.[46] Repeating verbatim the Soviet Constitution (Article 39, par. 2), the CPR Constitution prohibits the exercise of the civil rights regarded as counterrevolutionary (Article 28), or detrimental to public order, and to the interest of work collectives or individuals (Article 51). However, we cannot find in the Chinese document the limitations set forth in the Russian counterpart (Article 47) that the various freedoms must be for the sake of communism. Truly there is no need to spell this out, because a citizen of the CPR is a quasi-communist (he ought to observe the *si ge yuan ce*, one of these being the belief in Marxism-Leninism and Mao Zedong Thought), if he does not have the party card already. There is, finally, a restriction on the freedom of religion which Article 36, par. 4 writes must not submit to foreign influence. According to the draft constitution (Article 35, par. 4), we must observe, religious activities are not to be dominated by any foreign *state*. The change is certainly prompted by the fear that in the case of the Roman catholicism, it can provoke a legal argument. Because the Vatican is not a state, it can control the catholics in China by appointing church officials for them without violating the terms of the Constitution. Now such argument is forestalled.

Rotation of office

One of the phenomenal changes is the compulsory pensioning of the highest mandarins after two consecutive terms in office with each term lasting five years. Leaving the specific regulations to the next chapter, we may point out here that this system was introduced by the 3rd plenum of the 11th CC in December 1978, a plenum which incidentally, is regarded by the CC itself as one of the "most significant watersheds of the party's history."[47] It resolved that the "de facto life-tenure of leaders cease and desist."[48] However, we cannot but think that the principle itself is more important than the reality and that democrats should not get excited by it, neither should the upholders of the Parkinson law that if a superior stays in his post too long, his lieutenant would lose his ability to take over. It is because the current aristocrats cannot physically hang on much longer than 10 years. Given their already advanced age, they will be octogenarians upon finishing their term; and the successors, when finishing theirs, will also be in their eighties. The law of nature, but not the 1982 Constitution, acts to force them to quit.

Separation of state from party

As referred to somewhere else in this book, three deliberate attempts are made on this matter: (1) the nomination of the premier

[46] Lin Ziqiang, "Che di pi pang ren min lu shi gong zuo zhong de zi chan jie ji si xiang" (To criticize thoroughly the capitalist thinking in the work of the people's lawyers), *Fa xue*, no. 1 (1958), pp. 39-43 at 40, col. 2.
[47] "Guan yu jian guo yi lai", p. 3, col. 3.
[48] *Ibid.*

is now made, not by the CCP chairman, but by the CPR president, (2) the chairman is not made commander of the PLA, (3) the PLA is described as belonging to the people, not to the party. On the lower plane, however, separation of party apparatus and state administration is not ordained by the constitution. The press has come to advocate such separation. A commentator in *Renmin ribao* came out as early as December 1980 with an indignant plea.[49] His article details the sorry result of the mixing up of the two organs. Going to the heart of the problem, it deplores the overriding authority of the CCP secretaries at the local levels where they have set out to run the entire show. During the past two years, a strong pressure has built up to remedy the situation and it culminates in the separation principle. It goes without saying that in a communist regime, one cannot expect the government to be autonomous, but the 1982 Constitution does take a step, however formal and limited, to stop the blatant interference of the CCP in public administration.

Economy and ownership patterns

There are two sectors of economy: socialist and individual. The latter is given only two articles (11, 13), while the former six (6-10, 12). The two sectors are to be linked together. The individual economy was not allowed until the ouster of the Gang of Four. It purports to provide the most essential items for the consumers in the first place and to create jobs in the second. From criminal offenses, individuals' economic activities have gone a long way to becoming a constitutionally dignified function. They are made an ally of the socialist economy to be helped out by the government.

The socialist sector assumes two forms: a) state economy which is owned by the whole people, b) collective economy. The second embraces i) rural and ii) urban economy. There are two subdivisions of i), namely, rural people's communes and agricultural producers' co-ops. Individual villagers can engage in private economy; they are given the "right, within the limits prescribed by law to farm plots of cropland and hilly land, to undertake household sideline production and to raise livestock" for their own needs (Article 8, par. 1). From now on, the commune is made an economic unit, having no responsibility as a government body.[50] While rural co-ops perform only restricted operation on account of simplicity of life there, urban co-ops carry on extensive trade. Article 8, par. 2 says they can do "handicraft, industrial, building, transport, commercial and service trades." Such activities are very brisk and the government is mighty pleased for reasons just stated. Instead of prohibiting, the administration is ordered by the Constitution to foster them (Article

[49] "Lun dang zheng fen gong" (Separation of work between the government and the party), *Renmin ribao*, December 18, 1980, p. 5. See also *ibid.*, July 11, 1983, p. 3.

[50] Song Dahan and Zhang Chunsheng, "Important change in the system of people's commune," *Beijing review*, July 9, 1982, pp. 15-17 discussing the separation of government administration from commune's management of economy.

8, par. 3). Incidentally the same holds true with the Soviet Constitution (Article 13, par. 2). Obviously bureaucratic capitalism of both countries is modified.

Sanctioned by the 1982 Constitution is the linkage economy under which socialist production is to be reinforced by trading and manufacturing done by workers' collectives or individuals. The system is ascribed to Mao Zedong and Deng Xiaoping.[51] On account of this credibility alone, it is here to stay. Little wonder, unlike the old Constitution (Article 5, par. 2) which calls upon the authorities to guide them "step and step onto the road of socialist collectivization," the new Constitution (Article 11) says that "individual economy of the urban and rural working people is a complement to the socialist sector of the economy." The CPR, in other words, is to be a tripartite body economic.[52]

From the point of view of orthodox Maoists, this course may well be dubbed revisionist. The current pragmatists, we suppose, have admitted this, because Article 1, par. 2 uses the word "basic" to describe China's socialist system. As long as the fundamentals remain unchanged, that is, some alterations can be introduced. Deng Xiaoping's statement that no matter black or white, if a cat is capable of catching the mice, that is enough may better be interpreted to mean systems than to mean red or expert individuals. The contemporary economy of China reminds us of the NEP of the Soviet Union during 1921-1928. In both cases, it is a tacit concession to the virtue of capitalism. As some scholars remarked, modernized socialism cannot offer anything new besides absorbing some elements of free enterprise.

Now turning to types of ownership. Classified as state property are mineral resources, waters, forests, mountain lands, grasslands, beaches and other natural resources of the sea and land (Article 9). Under the original draft of the Constitution, legislation may vest forests, mountain lands, grasslands, underdeveloped areas and beaches to collectives (ibid.), but it is deleted from the final text. Although land in the cities is owned by the state, that in the villages, towns and suburban districts is the property of the collectives except the portion which by law belongs to the state (Article 10, par. 2). It is also envisaged that lots for building houses on or tilled for personal needs are not owned by the individuals, but by the collectives (ibid., par. 2). Upon the exercise of eminent domain, the state may take over tracts for its own use to meet the demands of the general public in accordance with the provisions of law. To combat the widespread disposal of land title by enterprises and individuals, the Constitution (Article 10, par. 4) commands: "No organization or individual may appropriate, buy, sell or lease land or unlawfully transfer land in other

51 "Guan yu jian guo yi lai", p. 4, col. 2 (Mao Zedong), p. 2, col. 2 (Deng Xiaoping).

52 "Brief summary of the draft of the revised Constitution," Beijing review, May 3, 1982, pp. 18-20 at 19, col. 1.

ways."[53] Individuals have the right to the earned income, savings, houses and other lawful property (Article 13). The Constitution protects the inheritance of private property (*ibid.*) but this provision is not in the 1978 predecessor. Private property, however, does not include copyright and patent which are placed in the hands of the state. It is to be noted that the draft constitution in Article 41, par. 3 creates right of invention, but the final draft drops this provision. The basic assumption is that under socialism "an individual's talent is not just his own personal possession but also belongs to the whole people" (Roy Medvedev, p. 227). Special legislation of the NPC has, however, provided for the safeguarding of the interests of the inventors.[54] In connection with state, collective or individual ownership, we may mention foreign ownership under the rubric of open door policy.

By this policy the regime seeks to rejoin the rest of the world and to welcome foreigners bringing money and technology with them, regardless of their odious ideology. "The future of China is closely linked with that of the whole world," says the Preamble of the Constitution. After having been in practice for several years, the solicitation of outside investment is now elevated in 1982 to a constitutional requirement (Preamble and Article 18). This policy of opening the CPR for business is not mentioned in the 1978 Constitution, a document which largely reflects the seclusive value of the Cultural Revolution. By the end of 1983, the CPR's foreign loan will be 4 billion US dollars, reported Wang Bingqian, Finance Minister, to the Fifth session of the Fifth NPC on December 1, 1982.[55] This fact alone shows that the said value is buried. The open-door plan, according to a commentator, will not be deflected by problems involving "cases of graft, corruption and smuggling in China."[56] Potential investors are expressly assured that trade and economic concession for the Reds "is not an expedience but a strategic decision taken after careful consideration." Beijing would never retreat from a settled course like this. Again we quote the Chinese: "Not a single country in the world, no matter what its political system, has ever modernized with a closed-door policy. International cooperation and exchange are increasingly necessary in today's world."[57] The Russians, it is interesting to observe, have ridiculed this policy of China's by alleging that Beijing is currying the favor of the imperialists at the expense of the Chinese people.[58]

[53] Many cases of selling and buying of lands are reported in *Renmin ribao*, March 21, 1981, p. 4; December 9, 1981, p. 3: November 11, 1981, p. 3; May 13, 1982, p. 3.

[54] "Zhong hua ren min gong he guo fa ming jian li tiao li" (Regulations on the encouragement of inventions of the People's Republic of China), *Zhong guo bai ke nian jian*, Beijing: Zhong guo da bai ke quan shu chu ban she, 1980, pp. 425-426.

[55] Wang Bingqian,"Report on the implementation of the state budget for 1982 and the draft state budget for 1983 (excerpts)," *Beijing review*, January 17, 1983, pp. 13-17 at 17, col. 1.

[56] Wang Dacheng, "More on prosecuting economic criminals," *ibid.*, March 15, 1982, p. 3.

[57] *Ibid.* See Hu Yaobang's address to the 12th Congress of the CCP, *Globe and Mail*, September 2, 1982, p. 10, col. 1.

[58] B. Barakhta, "Kitai: politika otkrytykh dverei" (China: on open door), *Pravda*, June 25, 1982, p. 5, cols. 5-8.

Social control

In the Constitution there are many ethical aspirations. Grown-up children, runs Article 49, have the duty to support and assist their parents. This obviously disavows the erstwhile practice under which rabid communists abetted the youngsters to inform on their fathers and mothers said to be reactionary or counterrevolutionary. In return for the filial regard, parents are enjoined not to "mistreat" their offspring. Love does not end here. The same article teaches kindness to old people and women. As related before, Article 24 writes of love of men. Disciplinary education is also placed *ibid*. Similar inculcation is envisaged in Article 46, par. 1. Don't insult or slander others! and maintain your personal dignity! (Article 38). Banned by Article 4, par. 1 is discrimination against or oppression of minor races. Han and local national chauvinism must go, it is stressed in the Preamble.

To be combatted are the "capitalist, feudalist and other decadent ideas" (Article 24, par. 2). Hu Yaobang stresses this point in his speech to the 12th Congress of the party on September 1, 1982, and Zhao Ziyang does it in his speech to the 5th session of the 5th NPC on November 30, 1982. The Constitution and the two men, however, do not say what these ideas are. The old basic law in Article 16 forbids state officials to deceive people or to exploit their position and power for personal ends. This stipulation, interestingly enough, is not repeated in the new. Here we must note that nepotism has beset the communist, as much as all previous, governments of China. That is why the CCP Statute has an advise in the "general program" to the effect that the "party must conscientiously follow the proletarian line on cadres, the line of 'appointing people on merit' and oppose the bourgeois line of 'appointing people by favoritism.' " Although the Constitution does not have a similar commandment, the party and state mandarins are obliged to observe it.

In close connection with the hortatory messages is the personal responsibility in work imposed by Article 27 (same in Article 3 of the USSR Constitution). The Chinese *Gong zuo ze ren zhi* carries a much more imperative tone than the translated "system of socialist responsibility" (Article 14, par. 1). The original expression exerts psychological as well as legal pressure on the individuals and calls for efficiency and combat against bureaucratism (Article 27). Personal accountability, in the political culture of the CPR, involves faith in the masses. One must seek and heed the opinions and suggestions of the constituents, be they colleagues in an office, audience in a courtroom, or members of a production team in a ricefield. If something goes wrong, the leading cadre may be charged either of unwillingness to accept the supervision of the people there, or failure to use one's initiative. Individual activeness is required by many provisions (Article 2, par. 2; Articles 16, 17, 27). All this sets on a constitutional basis the workers' participation in the management of state enterprises and units of the collective economy. In these units, let it be reiterated here for the sake of emphasizing the point, the managerial personnel are to be elected or removed by the "entire body of their workers and staff members" (Article 17, par. 2); although in reality, ordinary workers do not control the hiring and firing of officials, they share the decision in other matters relating to the plants (Article 16).

The above management system is much more developed than what is provided in Articles 8 and 16 of the Soviet Constitution because the Russians do not demand workers to choose the directors of their units. It is rather close to the Germans' co-determination (Mitbestimmung). Says one Chinese source that it is Mao Zedong and Deng Xiaoping who invented it,[59] and that it was reaffirmed by the Central Working Conference convened in April 1978 by the CCP.[60] Behind the system is the fundamental principle that masses are bosses and owners of the plants. We quote Article 42, par. 3: "All working people in state enterprises and in urban and rural economic collectives should perform their task with an attitude consonant with their status as masters of the country." Stated somewhat differently, they are the sovereigns or dictators. The call for the respect of the masses on the one hand, and on the other for the observance of the "guidance of the state plans" (Article 17, par. 1) or "unified leadership of the central authorities,"[61] besides the 35 statements in the Constitution that officials can do this or that except otherwise provided by law, creates difficulties for these officials. It places them between the Scylla and Charybdis. Wouldn't they pass the buck upward or sideways? Wouldn't they just play it safe by doing nothing at all? The stormy campaign waged in the last couple of years to lay off millions of cadres is partly to remedy this situation. Some speculate that it is undertaken also to get rid of the left extremists.

Come to the cultural regulation, one indication that this matter figures pretty large in the eyes of the Beijing oligarchy is that the word *wen hua* (Culture) appears 20 times in the Constitution touching on it in so many ways. Article 14, for example, speaks of the state's responsibility to gradually improve the cultural life of the citizenry and to enhance their technical skill. There is the pledge, made in Articles 19 and 22, of developing education, science, public health and sports, culture, art, publishing, broadcasting, press, libraries, museums, and cultural centers and other cultural undertakings. In light of the wanton destruction of ancient and bourgeois objects by the Red Guards during the Cultural Revolution, the present leaders are quite resolved to preserve China's past treasury. Hence the stipulation of Article 22: "The state protects places of scenic or historical interest, valuable cultural relics and other cultural items of China's historical and cultural heritage." Persons who "steal and ship valuable relics out of the

[59] "Guan yu jian guo yi lai", p. 4, col. 2 (referring to Mao Zedong), p. 2, col. 2 (referring to Deng Xiaoping).

[60] *Ibid.*, p. 4. col. 1.

[61] This statement in slightly different forms appears in Article 3, par. 4: Article 16, par. 1; Article 89, cl. 2 and 3; Article 110, par. 2; Article 118, par. 1.

country" can be punished by 10 years to life imprisonment or death.[62] As important as preserving cultural formations is the freedom to work in cultural and cognate fields. To further this, the Constitution (Article 47) declares that citizens of the CPR have the liberty to engage in scientific research, literary and artistic creation and other cultural pursuits. In the meantime, the state encourages and assists creative endeavors, which are conducive to the interests of the people and human progress, by citizens in education, science, technology, literature, art and other cultural work (ibid.). Endeavors of this sort in the CPR, as one would expect, cannot be immune from the government hand. True, the present Constitution has expunged the Wagnerian soprano of "proletarian politics in command" (1978 Constitution, Article 10), but it substitutes the tenets of Marxism-Leninism and Mao Zedong Thought (Preamble).

In the Preamble, the Chinese culture is described as "splendid" (Red Guards had said it stinks) and "cultural exchanges" are to be carried out with other peoples. Yet Article 24 calls upon the citizens to rinse themselves of the lingering feudalistic and degenerate thought and it warns them of the capitalist influence. Hu Yaobang (loc. cit.) brought up this point in the September 1 (1982) speech to the 1600-man Party Congress. The elite, we must know, esteem none other than what they consider as the "valuable" or "important" culture (Article 22), or culture which is "creative" or conducive to the interests of the people (Article 47). The Constitution in Article 119 tells the minority nationalities that the state is to "cull through" their cultural heritage in order to pick up the good parts of it for support. In other words, the Chinese culture would not admit of what are regarded as backward or un-creative or non-people's. This constitutional command lodges the autocracy with an unlimited police power to set up the standards it sees fit.

Conspicuous in the old but absent in the new Constitutions are Mao Zedong's teachings: a) correctly handle the contradictions of the people, b) "let one hundred flowers blossom, and let one hundred schools of thought contend," and c) achieve the unity of will and personal ease of mind and liveliness.[63] Why? These are disagreeable to the pragmatic coterie who consider them an outright wishful thinking and therefore unworthy of constitutional recital. Strange enough, though, the first teaching is dragged into the new party statute.

Foreign and military affairs

Neither the *four* modernizations nor the *four* principles, as stated previously, are so numbered, but the *five* concepts (so many corollaries of state independence) of peaceful co-existence are in fact enumerated in the Constitution (in the party statute as well). Actually

---

[62] *Beijing review*, March 15, 1982, p. 6, col. 2

[63] The first two are all well-known; the third is attributed to him in "Guan yu jian guo yi lai," p. 2, col. 2.

the five are immediately followed by another (sixth) dictate: "development of diplomatic relations and economic and cultural exchanges with other countries." This stance of the CPR compels one to think that there can no longer be the expression of "self-reliant" in the document. That expression, which is in the 1978 Constitution, was predicted by *Renmin ribao* of November 27, 1981 (p. 5) to be dropped from the forthcoming Constitution. However, it is kept there (Preamble). One cannot say that China will take up again an abandoned policy of isolation. The expression of self-reliance may not be more than the didactic that the CPR must not totally depend on foreigners for the modernization drive. Hu Yaobang (*loc. cit.*) says China will not become a vassal of any state. By no means does self-reliance imply a closed-door orientation. Another provision in the Constitution about diplomacy, which is in keeping with modern practice,[64] is the investiture of the State Council with the authority to conclude and enforce less important treaties. These do not have to wait until the ratification by the NPC Standing Committee before taking effect. Our interpretation derives from the wordage of Article 67, cl. 14 and Article 81. All these stipulations say that only "important" international agreements are to be approved by the just-said Committee.

As regards military policy, we must point out first the doctrine of civilian supremacy. Article 93 says that the Central Military Commission is to lead the armed forces and Article 66 that the Commission and its Chairman are responsible to the NPC Standing Committee. Further the NPC has the power to recall or to remove the Chairman and other membersof the Commission. Finally it is the State Council which "directs and administers the building of national defense" (Article 89, cl. 10). Second, we find it interesting to note the provision in Article 32 of the Soviet Constitution, by which the "state supplies the armed forces of the USSR with *everything necessary*" to carry out their mission. The CPR Constitution, however, does not have such a statement, as if declaring to the entire world that the Government of the People's Republic would not engage in an all-out armament as the Russian regime does.

Third, the Chinese Constitution (Article 65, cl. 18) plagiarizes the USSR document (Article 121, cl. 17) in providing that when the NPC (Supreme Soviet) is not in session, the Standing Committee (Presidium of the Supreme Soviet) can decide on the declaration of a state of war in the event of armed attack on the country or in the fulfilment of international treaty obligations concerning common defense against aggression. In international law, the second part of the provision is tantamount to the delivery of a preemptive assault. According to many authors, such a move is sanctioned by conventional international law,[65] provided one's own country is under

64 J.L. Brierly, *The law of nations, an introduction to the international law of peace*, 6th ed., edited by Humphrey Waldock, New York: Oxford University Press, 1963, p. 321.

65 *Ibid.*, p. 415: Gerhard von Glahn, *Law among nations, an introduction to public international law*, 4th ed., New York: Macmillan, 1981, p. 581.

imminent threat of invasion. Whether nation A can initiate a strike at nation B simply because its ally, nation C, is menaced with attack is not so sure. Why does the CPR have such an article in the Constitution? Since the termination in 1979 of the Sino-Soviet treaty of 1950, the People's Republic has no military alliance yet. This provision may well be seen as an "ad" for one. The prospective partners are told, in essence, that Beijing can be a faithful friend because its basic law, the Constitution, authorizes it to take armed action against a common enemy, regardless of whether China itself is subject to an impending aggression.

CHAPTER VI
The State
Institutions

After setting forth the principles and policy matters of the state, the Constitution moves on to the institutional actors in charge of implementing them. There are eight such actors: a) the National People's Congress, b) the Standing Committee, c) the President of the Republic, d) the State Council, e) the provincial and other local governments, f) the procuratorates, g) the courts and h) the Central Military Commission. This chapter will analyze all but the last three. These are to be studied in the chapters on the army and law.

National People's Congress

Of the eight, the most august is this one. That is why the Constitution has it head all other seven bodies. The NPC is said to be the "highest organ of state power" (Article 57). Here the text simply repeats Article 108 of the USSR Constitution which applies the phrase to the Supreme Soviet. At the opening of the Chinese basic law (Article 2, par. 2), the NPC is described as the medium through which the "people exercise the state power." In Article 3, par 3, it is deemed the source of administrative, judicial and procuratorial authorities. Thus, the NPC acts as the vox populi or repository of sovereignty, but it is indirectly mandated. In fact, counting from the grass roots, or what the Constitution (Article 111, par. 1) calls primary level, we get these rungs: villagers' committee (*ibid.*), town (zhen), township (xiang), county (xien), province (Article 102). In Beijing, Shanghai and Tianjin, the rungs are: residents' committee, district (cu), county, municipality. Deputies to the NPC are chosen from 21 provinces, 5 autonomous regions and the three cities just named (Article 59, par. 1); and their numbers are rated to the population of each constituency (see also section on election). In addition, the army is reserved an undetermined number of seats (*ibid.;* Election Law, Article 5).[1] This last arrangement again copies the Russian system, but there it is dropped following the seventh convocation of the Supreme Soviet in 1966.[2] The keeping of it by the CPR intimates the high regard of the Chinese Reds for that instrument of violence.

Different from the Soviet prototype but imitating the French National Assembly is the quota offered the overseas Chinese. One possible explanation for this is that an unusually large horde of the CCP leaders sojourned in France. Zhou Enlai, Deng Xiaoping and Chen Yi, for example, were part-time students and part-time workers there not long after the First World War. They seem to appreciate the token presence in a nation's parliament of citizens abroad. Hence, the 1954

---

[1] The Election Law can be found in *Ren min shou ce,* Beijing: Ren min ribao chu ban she, 1980, pp. 400-403.

[2] L.G. Churchward, *Contemporary Soviet Government,* American ed., New York: American Elsevier pub. co., 1968, p. 118.

Constitution (Article 23) empowers the government "to invite overseas Chinese" and in the 1975 Constitution (Article 16) authorizes it "to name a certain number of personages to the NPC."[3] However, this provision is not in the 1978 and 1982 Constitutions. But it appears in Article 6 of the 1979 Election Law as amended in 1982. All the invitees to the NPC are said to be elected by the more than 20 million Chinese in foreign land. In reality, they are none other than the Reds, or their communicants, or front-organization men of the CCP. There are also a sprinkling of intellegentsia with crimson heart and GMD capitulationists, civilian as well as military.

The 6th NPC was chosen in 1982-1983 from 31 constituencies, namely, the above-mentioned 29 units plus the PLA and Taiwan. The people's congress of each province supposedly picked up one deputy for every 800,000 inhabitants and that of each city elects one for every 100,000. The Congress's first session was convened in June 1983. Sichuan province has the biggest number of deputies: 202; and Taiwan the smallest: 13. The 13 are named by the communists, of course. Coming from the PLA are 267 deputies.[4] The Chinese media does not refer to the size of overseas Chinese representatives, but it writes of such people (*Renmin ribao,* June 20, p. 5; June 21, p. 4, 1983). They probably number between 25 and 30.

By the Election Law (Article 12), the deputies are distributed by the NPC Standing Committee in accordance with the principle that the number of people represented by each deputy in the rural area be eight times the number represented by each deputy in a city. This rural under-privilege, we should note, is abandoned by the 1936 Stalin Constitution. Do the Chinese find it hard to get rid of Marx's image of rural idiocy?[5]

In accordance with the Local Government Act (Article 4) and the Constitution (Article 97, par. 1), the congresses of provinces, autonomous regions, centrally-controlled cities, autonomous prefectures and cities with districts in them are elected by the lower-level congresses; but county congresses, congresses of autonomous counties, cities without districts in them, city districts, people's communes and towns are elected by people directly. The indirect method, although not appropriate to create the highest authority in the nation, does have its justification because given the electors' unfamiliarity with the names of the candidates other than the great stars like Deng Xiaoping, Hu Yaobang and Zhao Ziyang, direct franchise savors just too much of a hoax. The old Constitution in Article 21 lays down a unique process of democratic consultation and secret ballot, but the new constitution leaves this to the law. The Election Law in Article 33, par. 1 retains the second (secret ballot),

[3] Chun-tu Hsieh, "The new Constitution of the CPR," *Problems of communism,* 24 (May-June 1975), pp. 11-19.

[4] *Renmin ribao,* May 11, 1983, pp. 2-3.

[5] Marx and Engels, "Manifesto of the communist party," in *The Marx-Engels reader,* 2nd ed., edited by Robert Tucker, New York: Norton, 1978, pp. 469-500 at 477.

and in Article 28 the first (democratic consultation). It would be interesting to find out what this "consultation" looks like.

In practice, delegates were "swapped" during an election campaign between rival bosses in Beijing. Each wanted to garner as many delegates as possible, because they represented big political "capital." It is widely assumed that after Lin Biao became the successor of Mao Zedong, the deferral of the 4th NPC (held in 1975) was due to the leaders' haggling for the share of the "capital." That NPC was not called until after the death of Lin Biao. This man, it is to be noted, had his successorship riveted in the CCP Statute of 1969. However, this fait accompli, in order to be binding, must be legitimated by the Constitution. It has not materialized, however, owing to the mystical plane crash on September 13, 1971 which took Lin's life.

The statutory term of the NPC is five years (Article 60, par. 1). Its membership is on the increase, and one time it took a high jump as is shown below.[6].

NPC	date of 1st session	chairman	mem.	yrs.	times
1st	Sept. 15-28, 1954	Liu Shaoqi	1226	5	5
2nd	Apr. 18-28, 1958	Zhu De	same	5	4
3rd	Dec. 21, 1964- Jan. 4, 1965	same	3040	11	1
4th	Jan. 13-17, 1975	same	2885	3	1
5th	Feb. 26- March 5, 1978	Ye Jianying	3497	3	5
6th	June 6-22, 1983	Peng Zhen	2978		

The fifth congress had met annually. In the 1980 (3rd) session from August 31 to September 3, the delegates increased from 3497 to 3525.[7] This exceeds by 25 the legal 3500, a ceiling set up by Article 13 of the Election Law.[8] The 4th session from November 30 to December 13, 1981 was attended by 3453,[9] and the 5th from November 26 to December 10, 1982 attended by 3421.[10] The size is thus brought within the law. The first session of the 6th congress cut back the number by more than 400. There is the noticeable usage that before the convocation of a Congress, the CC holds a plenum. The fifth session of the fifth NPC, from November 26 to December 8, 1982 for example, was preceded by the 12th Congress of the CCP which convened from September 1 to 11, 1982. This shows that the CC makes decisions which are then tabled in the NPC for endorsement. We should point out, too, that all CC members are in the NPC. Virtually the CC is a steering committee of the NPC.

---

[6] *Zhong guo shou ce*, Hong Kong: Da gong bao, 1980, pp. 99-101.

[7] *Globe and Mail*, September 3, 1980, p. 1, col. 3.

[8] *Keesing's*, October 3, 1980, p. 30493, col. 1: *Ren min shou ce*, Beijing: Ren min ribao chu ban she, 1979, p. 401, col. 2

[9] *Renmin ribao*, November 30, 1981, p. 1; *Globe and Mail*, same date, p. 14, col. 1

[10] *Beijing review*, December 6, 1982, p. 17.

Almost always, the NPC came out with some sensational decisions. The 1st and 4th Congress adopted each a Constitution in 1954 and 1975 respectively, but the 5th, doing better, produced two of them (one in 1978 and one in 1982). Again the 1st and 2nd elected each a CPR chairman, namely Mao Zedong in 1954 and Liu Shaoqi in 1959, and the 3rd re-elected the latter man in 1964. Although the 2nd wrote no constitution, both it and the 3rd Congress functioned as important sounding boards. The former heard Mao Zedong speak, for the first time in his life, of absorbing Western technique and the latter heard Zhou Enlai trumpet his Four Modernizations. Despite all these sensational developments, the 3rd Congress was pushed aside for eleven years (1965-1975); during this interval there was neither election to nor convocation of the NPC.

The five-year term, interestingly enough, is envisioned in the 1975, 1978 and 1982 Constitutions (Acticles 16, 21 and 60, par. 1 respectively), but the 1954 Consitution (Article 24) provided a quadrennium. As the above table indicates, the 1st and 2nd Congresses sat each one year too many, because they can only sit four, but not five, years. The 4th, elected in 1975 for a term of five years, was dissolved in 1978. Its life was thus shortened by two years. In fact, the CCP hierarchy is within its power to do whatever it wishes with the congressional tenure. And this is because the four Constitutions each invest the NPC Standing Committee with the authority to delay or to advance the convocation and the Committee is made up of the top elite of the CCP. Although all the four documents call for annual sessions,[11] only during the chairmanship of Liu Shaoqi was this requirement nearly met (there was no session in 1961). Both the 3rd and 4th held one session each, and the latter's session was behind the door. From January 1965 to December 1982, for a period of 16 years, the NPC assembled only five times. This "highest organ of state power" is certainly not regarded in the highest manner by the Chinese communists. Special sessions are envisaged by the 1954 Constitution, whose Article 25 runs that the "Standing Committee or one-fifth of its NPC deputies" may request such meetings. However, this never happened. The 1975 and 1978 Constitutions realistically deleted the special-session clause, but the 1982 document revives it. Since the Reds feel the regular meetings to be something of a nuisance, why should they bother with the irregular ones?

What powers reside in the NPC? Article 62 counts down 15, but other stipulations in the Constitution grant more to it. This conjures up a strong but wrong impression that the body under review is uncheckable. As if reinforcing such an impression, clause 15 of Article 62 enables the NPC to assume additional authorities as exercisable by the "highest organ of state power." However, such statement is significantly different from the corresponding (now deleted) statement in clause 10 of Article 22 of the 1978 Constitution which says that

[11] The 1954 Constitution, Article 24; the 1975 Constitution, Article 16; the 1978 Constitution, Article 21; the 1982 Constitution, Article 58.

the NPC can take up other functions and powers as it deems necessary itself. Apparently, the new Constitution confers no similar discretion on the NPC. If our interpretation is correct, the Congress, however potent, has no other rights than those in Article 62 and in related stipulations. The CPR, to put it in another way, has a parliament which possesses only enumerated functions. Let us have a look at them presently. They appear in our discussion at random, that is, not arranged according to the order of importance to the operation of the system. The Congress has a supervisorial power over the Standing Committee (Article 69), over the Supreme Court (Article 128) and over the Supreme Procuratorate (Article 133). As behooves a sovereign body, it can amend the basic law and legislate (Article 62. cls. 1 and 3; Article 64, par.1). However, in re amendment to the Constitution, the NPC is limited to a role of deliberation because it is not this body, but the Standing Committee, or one-fifth of the NPC deputies, which is enclothed with the competence to propose it. When the proposal gets a more than two-thirds backing of the Congress, it becomes effective.

The Constitution grants the NPC the great power of recruitment. Most important is the finding of a premier, but he has to be recommended by the President of the CPR. Under the previous Constitution (Article 30, par. 2) the premier was nominated by the Central Committee. This change is prompted by the idea of separation of the state from the party, as said in the preceding chapter. The alteration, we must add, is more apparent than real. From where else can one expect the candidate for the premiership than the CC? Upon this offical's recommendation, the NPC names others in the State Council: the vice-premiers, state councilors, ministers in charge of ministries or commissions, general auditor and general secretary (Article 62, cl. 5). Also appointed by the NPC are a) the chairman of the Central Military Commission, b) upon his recommendation, the other members, c) president of the Supreme Court, d) Procurator General, and e) the NPC Standing Committee. Strange enough, the Constitution is mute on the nominators of all but b), even though the original draft text (Article 90, cl. 4) grants the State Council the right to recommend them to the NPC.

All the mandarins just referred to are also removable by the NPC (Article 63). Must the recall of vice-premiers and other members of the State Council be made at the advisory of the premier? Does the removal of members of the Central Military Commission require his recommendation too? For no good reason, we think, the Constitution should be silent on this point. In re the Central Military Commission, we may note that the premier has no control, direct any way, on its members and would surmise that since their hiring is made upon the request of the chairman, their firing would follow the same procedure.

The NPC seems to be powerful in recruiting and dismissing high dignitaries. However, this is not true. There is a constitutional restriction. The CPR basic law, in imitation of that of the United

States, adopts the two-term system but extends it to more posts than one. Although such NPC-sanctioned officials like the general secretary of the State Council, the general auditor, ministers (Article 87, par. 2) may remain at the job upwards of ten years, the CPR President and vice-president (Article 79, par. 1), premier, vice-premiers, state councillors, supreme court president (Article 124, par. 2) and chief procurator (Article 130, par. 2) may not. Perhaps this limitation should also apply to the ministers and governors of provinces, because life-tenure is bound to perpetuate their obduracy and obfuscation as much as others. Their exemption from it is to be explained by the fear, on the part of the Beijing lordship, of arousing their suspicion and resistance.

The approval and superintendence over the execution of budget and social and economic plans appertain to the NPC (Article 62, cls. 9 and 10). The confirmation of the setting up of provinces, autonomous regions, and cities having provincial status was vested by the old Constitution (Article 22, cl. 8) in the NPC, but it is now in the hand of the State Council (Article 89. cl. 15). All local divisions, we may note at this juncture, remained unchanged from 1949 to 1956. The ensuing Great Leap brought in its wake a shuffling of them by splitting many counties and, in this way, creating scores of new ones. Coming within the purview of the NPC is the question of war and peace (Article 62, cl. 14). However the fact that the teaching to Vietnam a punitive lesson in February-March 1979 was not deliberated by the NPC attests to the vacuity of the constitutional restraint (1978 Constitution, Article 22, cl. 9). Further, the NPC can pass laws in order to establish special administrative zones (Article 62. cl. 13). The enumeration of actions in the CPR basic law should not be seen in the same light as the US and French systems where the doctrine of limited power prevails if for no other reason than that there lacks in China a Supreme Court capable of overruling executive or congressional decisions as in the US or a Constitutional Council vested with the right to examine the organic laws to determine their constitutionality as in France. Other powers jointly exercised with the Standing Committee are to be discussed later.

Now turn to the organizational matters. The NPC is convened by the Standing Committee at least once a year (Article 61, par. 1). Two months before the term of the NPC expires, says Article 60, par. 2, the Committee must ensure that the election of the succeeding NPC be completed. If, however, circumstance should thwart the election, the incumbent NPC may sit until the next NPC is open. The prolongation of the term ought to be approved by more than two-thirds of the said Committee. During the session, the NPC elects a presiding corps to conduct business (Article 61, par. 2). Past practice shows that this strange body has several hundred deputies in it (see below).

In order to examine bills, the NPC sets up six special committees on: (1) nationalities, (2) finance and economy, (3) law, (4) education, sciences, culture and public health, (5) overseas Chinese, (6) foreign affairs (Article 70, par. 1). Others can be added. For the sake of comparison, the Supreme Soviet of the USSR has 14 standing committees, even though the Constitution itself refers only to the following six: credentials (Article 110), conciliation (Article 115), inter-cameral (Article 125, par. 1), inquiry, audit (*ibid.*, par. 2), people's control (Article 126). It is implied in the CPR Constitution (Article 70, par. 1) that the six committees are also standing bodies in that they operate during the recess of the NPC. The congress and the Standing Committee (but not the special committees) are authorized by Article 71, par. 1 to appoint commissions of inquiry for the investigation of particular matters and to make relevant decisions in the light of the reports of these commissions. All organs of state, public entities and citizens are ordered to supply information to the commissions when they request it (par. 2). Legislative proposals may be submitted by deputies (Article 72) and the State Council (Article 89, cl. 2). Inspired by Western usage, the Beijing hierarchs introduce a modified question-and-answer technique for the NPC. Article 73 writes that deputies are entitled to "address questions, in accordance with procedures prescribed by law, to State Council, or ministries and commissions under the State Council." The original draft text (Article 72) allows questions to be put to the Supreme Court and the Supreme Procuratorate. All questions are to be replied. In constitutional amendment, declares Article 64, par. 1, the NPC acts by two-thirds plus, but in laws and bills, by a simple majority (par. 2).

Both legally and factually, the NPC is a paper tiger, but it performs a useful function of formalization. No bill can become law without going through it or its Standing Committee (Article 58). Previously, the congress in question had only a budget committee and the deputies always sat in a mass gathering, something like a couple of battalions of PLA. The newfangled committee system, however, cannot be expected to do much to animate a robot. The handpicked congressmen are brought to Beijing to listen to the communist celebrities and to applaud in unison. Criticism of the Red regime is out of the question. It is as rare as it is risky. The Constitution does not demand that the Congress be open to the public. All but three of the 17 sessions (1962, 1963, 1975) were indeed open. The secret rendezvous, it is safe to say, were frank and they must have gotten reports which were unpalatable to the general citizenry. In the interest of analogy, whereas the Supreme Soviet adopts bicameralism and collects every six months, the Chinese counterpart is unicameral and is a yearly affair (legally at any rate). Why unicameral is because the CPR is a professed unitary system against the USSR's federalism. As a matter of theory, therefore, the Russian parliament contains some elements of checks and balances, but this is totally alien and horrendous to the Chinese. Moreover, the NPC is by far larger than the Supreme Soviet: 3,500 to 1,500 deputies. We should note, too, that over the Beijing throng is a chairing corps or presidium of 164,[12]

[12] *Renmin ribao*, June 5, 1983, p. 1.

but over the Kremlin crowd are just two men (USSR Constitution, Article 111). This extremely odd 164-man body should not be confused with the Standing Committee of the NPC to be discussed below. Presumably it is in charge of arranging the session. In 1954, the Chinese legislature comprised 1,266 at a time when the Supreme Soviet had 1,316. Since then Beijing increased the size to more than double the soviet mob. Does the CCP clique wish to outsmart the Russians by saying that their rule-making organ is more democratic because it is more massive?

Just a few words about the deputies at this juncture. Their number is to be determined by the Election Law (Constitution, Article, 59, par. 3). Although a deputy is recallable, this happened only twice in the history of the CPR (see election later in this chapter). With these exceptions, all congressmen have been well behaved. This must have satisfied the Beijing elite greatly. Common to legislators of other nations, there is the provision that no deputy may be arrested or placed on trial without the consent of the presiding corps of the NPC or, when the NPC is not in session, the consent of the Standing Committee (Article 74). To the end of guaranteeing their freedom in discussion, they are exempt from legal investigation for speeches or votes at its meetings (Article 75). On the other hand, the deputies, according to Article 75, par. 2 must exercise mass line, that is, maintain close contact with the people, listen to them and report their opinions and demands. Finally, most deputies are ordinary workers, peasants, low-ranking cadres and military men. Only the hierarchs of the CCP can be called full-time politicians.

Standing Committee

The NPC, as the reader has known by now, makes only a brief annual debut, as it were. It acts through another vessel, the Standing Committee. Elected by the Congress for the same term as itself, the Committee is a "permanent body" (Article 66, par. 1). The 1st session of the 6th NPC, elected a chairman, 20 vice-chairmen, and 133 members, although neither the old nor the new Constitutions (Article 24 and 65, par. 1 respectively) specifies the number of the personnel. To all these the new Constitution adds a general secretary. In order to make the Committee representative of all nationalities, it is envisaged in Article 65, par. 2 that "appropriate representation" be accorded minorities. Among the 20 vice-chairmen are two Tibetans, one Zhuang, one Uygur and 16 Han. And among the 133 members, all but 13 are Han. Article 67 of the original draft text, it is interesting to note, requires the attendance in its session by the chairman or vice-chairman of the standing committee of the congress in each province, autonomous region and city with provincial status. There is set up a chairmanship conference by Article 68, par. 2 consisting of the "chairman, vice-chairmen, and the general secretary to handle the important day-to-day work of the Standing Committee of the National People's Congress."

The committee is intended to be more than a miniature NPC. It has far-reaching legislative and decree powers.[13] For this reason and in consideration of the propriety of separating rule-making, rule-execution and rule-adjudication, the party leadership felt compelled to prevent all the committee members from taking concurrently "posts in state administration and the judicial and procuratorial organs" (Article 65, par. 4). This fact is stressed by Peng Zhen, vice-chairman of the Revision Committee in his report to the 23rd session of the NPC Standing Committee on April 22, 1982.[14] The same consideration is behind the limitation of the term of the chairman and vice-chairman of the Committee to ten years (Article 66, par. 2). In accordance with Article 66, par. 1, the Committee continues to function until its successor is elected by the next NPC. The relation between the two bodies, as hinted before, cannot be likened to one of proxy and its principal, due to the reason that the Committee may legally do much more than the parent NPC, a situation holding true with the Supreme Soviet and the Presidium (USSR Constitution, Article 121). Placed under the Committee are 21 responsibilities (Article 67), the last one being a catchall which says it attends to others as "assigned to it by the NPC." This clause, incidentally, also appears in the 1978 Constitution (Article 25, cl. 13). In broad terms, the functions may be grouped into (A) those which are proxy in nature on account of the fact that they may be done only in the recess of the Congress, (B) those which are concurrent, because of the use of the conjunctive and/or in the text, and (C) those which are exclusively the Committee's. While sorting them out this way we bear in mind the directive of Article 69 that the Committee is responsible to the NPC. Short of constitutional practice, one cannot be sure as to whether this directive amounts to investing the parent body with a veto over the action of the Committee.

There are four referrals under (A). The Committee (a) adjusts and partially amends programs of national social and economic development and budget in the course of their implementation (Article 67, cl. 5). As customary in all countries, financial authority belongs to the supreme body, and yet some unforeseen events may force a revision of the spending pattern already laid out. Because the Congress meets once a year only, the contingency ought to be met by a "permanent body" like the Committee. (b) Clause 9 of the same article grants the latter the power over the appointment and removal of ministers, general auditor and general secretary at the suggestion of the premier. The vice-premiers, however, are not mentioned here. Article 62, cl. 5 declares that these officials' appointment is made upon the recommendation of the premier, but it does not speak of their removal; this, however, appears in Article 80 where it is provided that the CPR president appoints and removes vice-premiers (along with premier, state councillors, ministers in charge of ministries or

[13] Hu Sheng, "On the revision of the Constitution," *Beijing review,* May 3, 1982, pp. 15-18 at 16, col. 1.

[14] Peng Zhen, "Explanation on the draft of the revised Constitution of the People's Republic of China," *Beijing review,* May 10, 1982, pp. 18-26 at 24, col. 2.

commissions, etc.) in pursuance of the decision of the NPC and Standing Committee. Thus, only the CPR president is within his right to initiate the removal of the vice-premiers. The drafters of the Constitution, we think, have made an error here. Is there any reason why the premier cannot recommend the removal of his understudies? Similar to ministers, etc., the ordinary members of the Central Military Commission may be recalled by the Standing Committee as recommended by the chairman of the Commission (Article 67, cl. 10).

(c) The Constitution, taking into account the international situation, ordains that the Committee may declare a state of war in the event of armed attack on the country or to fulfil international agreement of common defense (cl. 18). Finally, (d) in view of the long hibernation of the Congress, Article 92 makes the State Council accountable to the Committee. In light of the proxy situation, legalists would argue that should the Committee act on the various matters while the Congress is in session, it would overstep the constitutional bounds.

Let us take up (B) concurrent jurisdiction. We find no less than six circumstances. Both bodies can issue directives to the special committees (Article 70, par. 2), institute commissions of inquiry (Article 71, par. 1), hand down guidance to the State Council (Article 89, cl. 18), and exercise supervision over the same organ (ibid.; Article 67, cl. 6), the Supreme Court (Article 128), the Supreme Procuratorate (Article 133). The remaining two are the enactment of laws and decrees (Article 58), and the partial amendment of and supplement to the basic laws passed by the Congress (Article 67, cl. 3).

Group (C) concerns the realms where the Committee acts alone, whether or not the parent body is in session. In effect, the Constitution bars the Congress from entering there. A rigid interpretation of that document dictates that neither can trespass the other's authority. We classify these functions into constituent action, legislative and decree rights, supervision, finance, veto, recruitment, international relations, military affairs, reward and pardon.

Although the NPC is within its competence to revise the Constitution under Article 64, par. 1, it cannot act until it gets a proposal from the Committee, a point previously brought up. Election to the Congress is called and conducted by the Committee (Article 59, par. 2; Article 60, par. 2). It is anticipated by the latter stipulation that the election may have to be advanced or deferred due to "exceptional circumstances." The NPC itself cannot decide on this. Instead it is done in the Committee by a more than two-thirds majority. Furthermore, an extraordinary session of the Congress can be convened by the Committee. What majority decides this is not specified by the Constitution, however. What is more, an exclusive power to interpret and enforce this basic law, says Article 67, cl. 1, resides in the Committee, but not in the NPC. So much for the constituent role of the Committee.

In the rule-making area, we first note that although the Committee and the Congress are both declared competent (Article 58), only the former can construe the laws and decrees, even those which are enacted by the latter (Article 67, cl. 4). For unstated reasons, the supervision over the Central Military Commission is left by Article 67, cl. 6 to the State Council, in contrast to the co-supervision by the NPC and the Committee over the Supreme Court and the Supreme Procuratorate. With reference to the supervision over the State Council, there is an inconsistency in the Constitution. On the one hand, Article 67, cl. 6 gives it expressly to the Committee but on the other, Article 92 says the supervision is exercised only during the adjournment of the Congress. Should there arise a dispute on this issue, we suppose, the Committee can invoke Article 67, cl. 1 (constitutional interpretation) to dissolve it. The Constitution stipulates a couple of vetoes in Article 67, cls. 7 and 8. Under the first, the Committee can annul "administrative rules and regulations, decisions or orders" of the State Council, if they are in conflict with the Constitution, laws and decrees, and under the second, it can do the same with the regulations or decisions issued by the provinces, autonomous regions and the cities of Beijing, Shanghai and Tianjin, if they are in violation of the Constitution, etc.

Coming under its purview are also the setting up of military, diplomatic and other titles and ranks, the establishment of state orders, medals and titles of honor and the conferment thereof, and the grant of special pardons. (Article 67, cls. 15-16). All military ranks we should note here, were abolished as un-proletarian at the inception of the Cultural Revolution and therefore the 1978 Constitution (Article 25, cl. 10) refers to titles of honor only. The committee determines the general or partial mobilization (1982 Constitution, Article 67, cl. 19), declares and executes martial law in the entire nation or in some provinces, autonomous regions or the cities of Beijing, Shanghai and Tiajin (cl. 20). In accordance with Article 116, statutes on local autonomy and the separate rules drawn up by autonomous regions shall be submitted to the Committee for sanction before they can take effect.

Exclusive rights in foreign affairs involve the sending of plenipotentiary representatives abroad (cl. 13) and the ratification and nullification of treaties and "important agreements concluded with foreign states" (cl. 14). Strange enough, the provision does not also refer to international organizations as does the comparable Article 73, cl. 10 of the USSR Constitution. The Committee enjoys an exclusive recruitment power over a great many second-string mandarins who are not subject to the three-term ban. Included here are the Supreme Court's vice-president, judges, members of the judicial committee, at the suggestion of the president, in accordance with Article 67, cl. 11; and the deputy chief procurators, ordinary procurators, and members of the procuratorial committee, at the suggestion of the chief procurator in accordance with Article 67, cl. 12. Similarly the Committee approves the appointment and removal of chief procurators of the provinces, autonomous regions and Beijing,

Shanghai and Tianjin. In the original draft text there are mentioned the deputy general auditors and ordinary auditors whose appointment and removal is made upon the recommendation of the general auditor; and the Committee reviews the appointment and removal of chief auditors of the lower level of government just mentioned.

The above is a textual exegesis of the Constitution. In actuality, usages come to frustrate the Committee. By no stretch of imagination can one think that a weak body like the NPC may have a strong arm in the Committee. In particular, we like to punctuate the fact that both the NPC and the Standing Committee are not active bodies. They can only act upon submission of proposals (Article 72; Article 89, cl. 2). Logically, if no agency comes to it with an idea, they would be left in the cold.

However, allowance being given to the decision of the highest policy by the party hierarchs, the Committee which at any rate contains the most important ones of these, cannot be brushed aside as of no use at all. For one thing, it legitimates the CPR's treaties and, for another, it oversees the state bureaucracy. Government bodies have to report to it. The fact that it convenes very frequently is a good indication that it is kept extremely busy. The first Committee met 109 times, second 137 times, and third 32 times.[15] The fifth Committee dating from February 1978 held the 20th session on September 4-5, 1981, the 21st on November 20-24, the same year,[16] the 23rd during a 15-day period from April 22 to May 8, 1982, and the 26th on February 28 to March 5, 1983.[17] Occasionally the Committee announces highly important actions and this leads us to conclude that it has played a helpful, although not a crucial, role in the Chinese system of government. A party organ, think the ruling cliques of Beijing, may not rightfully make decisions binding upon the citizens, and this, in spite of the fact that every Chinese is actually a communist because a) the CCP imposes its Marxism-Leninism and Mao Zedong Thought upon him, b) he is duty bound to follow the party leadership and c) he ought to accept the proletarian dictatorship as commanded by the Constitution (Preamble).

Let us cite a few concrete examples of the operation of the Committee. Zhou Enlai stated to the Committee on April 25, 1964 that the Chinese aid of $100 million to such countries as the Congo (Brazzaville), Ghana and Ceylon (Sri Lanka) had no strings attached and that it was intended purely to help the recipients to increase their national income and reach the goal of financial independence.[18] The

---

[15] Harold Hinton, *An introduction to Chinese politics*, 2nd ed., New York: Holt, Rinehart and Winston, 1978, p. 187.

[16] *Renmin ribao* and *Guangming ribao*, September 4, 1981, both on p. 1; *Renmin ribao*, November 21, 24, 1981, both on p. 1. *Guangming ribao*, November 21, 1981, p. 1. We have no statistics about the 4th Committee, however,

[17] *Beijing review*, March 15, 1982, p. 5, col. 1. Another information says the 23rd Committee sat from April 22 to May 4, *ibid.*, May 10, 1982, p. 3. The 26th session mentioned in *ibid.*, March 14, 1983, p. 9.

[18] Peter S.H. Tang and Joan M. Maloney, *Communist China: the domestic scene, 1949-1967*, South Orange, New Jersey: Seton Hall University Press, 1967, p. 413.

78th session of the 1st Committee approved on August 1, 1957 the "decision concerning the offenders ordered to be reeducated through labor" and the supplmentary provisions to this decision.[19] A session of the 4th Committee resolved on October 23-24, 1977 to convene the 5th NPC in the spring of 1978. The then strong man Hua Guofeng reported to this session that a new revolutionary committee would be elected in each province, region and centrally ruled city. Yu Qiuli, chairman of the State Planning Commission, spoke to the Committee that the wages of the lower-bracket workers had been increased. He also made a lengthy talk on the state of the economy.[20] The Committee's legal affairs commission headed by Peng Zhen developed seven laws on the people's congresses of local governments, election, court system, procuracy, criminal code, criminal-procedure law, and joint Chinese and foreign venture legislation.[21] They were promulgated on July 1, 1979 and the first six went into effect on January 1, 1980, but the last one took force immediately.[22] Another example is the setting up by the Committee on October 5, 1980 of a special procuracy and a special bi-cameral (one civil and one military) court to try the Gang of Four and six others charged with counterrevolution, killing of countless innocents and with the attempt on Mao Zedong's life on September 12, 1971. The aforesaid 23rd session of the fifth Committee, a session of 15 days (unprecedentedly long), heard one report on the draft Constitution and another on the economic situation.[23] The Committee took decision to restructure the State Council.[24] The most recent case was the 26th session which accepted the request of Ye Jianying for retirement from the forthcoming 6th NPC on February 25, 1983.

President of the CPR

In the 1954 Constitution, the Chinese Reds, with one single deviation, well-nigh xeroxed the 1936 Stalin Constitution. The USSR was considered then as their elder brother. The deviation concerns the CPR chairmanship. While the young brother's document (Article 39) provides a normal chef d'état, the elder's (Article 48) envisages a chairman of the Presidium of the Supreme Soviet. Why the difference? We may answer that the collectivism which symbolizes

---

[19] *Keesing's,* December 16, 1977, p. 28727, col. 1

[20] *Ibid.*

[21] *Zhong guo shou ce,* p. 102, also in *Britannica book of the year,* 1980, p. 247, col. 2; *Renmin shou ce,* pp. 397-427.

[22] Jerome Cohen, "The year of the law and end of arbitrary courts," *Far Eastern economic review,* October 5, 1979, p. 54, col. 3; Article 15 of the Law on the Joint ventures, in *Renmin shou ce,* pp. 426-427 at 427, col. 2. The laws on local people's congresses, and on election were revised by the Fifth NPC Congress on December 11, 1982, see *Beijing review,* December 20, 1982, p. 4.

[23] Yao Yilin, "Report on the draft 1982 economic and social development plan (excerpts)," *Beijing review,* May 24, 1982, pp. 14-15.

[24] "NPC Standing Committee decisions on the restructuring of the State Council and other questions," *ibid.,* March 15, 1982, p. 5.

the presidium is not the cup of tea for the Chinese. Second, a Confusian tradition of rectification of names inclines the communists to call a spade a spade. They feel it wrong not to confer on the party chairman the mantle of the head of state. Third, in the excitement of the 1949 victory which put Mao Zedong on the imperial dais, he would settle for nothing less than the honorable and respectful appellation of zhuxi (translated either as chairman or president) of China. Besides, he was chairman of the Supreme State Conference (Article 43) and of the Council of National Defense (Article 42). More important still, he was the commander-in-chief of the military force (*ibid.*). There is no comparable panjandrum in the USSR.

After the Cultural Revolution, the Chinese effectuated an about-face. Both the 1975 and 1978 Constitutions abandoned the presidential in favour of the presidial office of the Soviet Union by making the chairman of the NPC Standing Committee a de facto head of state. As a point of law, the CPR did not have a zhuxi or chef d'état, a unique situation among the world's nations.

Mao Zedong was Chairman from September 1954 to April 1959. He was succeeded (later he said it was against his will) by Liu Shaoqi, After the latter's denigration and unconstitutional removal (unconstitutional because it was not done by the NPC but by the 12th plenum of the 8th CC on October 24, 1968), one of the two vice-presidents Dong Biwu (the other Song Qingling) acted as chairman until his death on April 2, 1975.[25] Then Zhu De stepped in. Upon his demise on July 6, 1976, Wu De (not Song, a non-communist) was named acting chairman. When he was purged on March 5, 1978, Ye Jianying took over by a resolution of the Standing Committee of the Fifth NPC.[26] On February 25, 1983, Ye turned in his resignation on account of old age, and Peng Zhen temporarily replaced him on order of the same Standing Committee.[27] Song Qingling, two weeks before her death on May 29, 1981, was appointed by the Politburo (not the Standing Committee of the NPC!) to be an honorific president.[28] This is an extra-constitutional office. At the same time, she was admitted to the CCP, the membership of which is said to be repeatedly denied her since 1949. On June 19, 1983, the 6th NPC elected Li Xiannian as president.

Liu Shaoqi was charged with trying to build the chairmanship into a stronghold of his. Following the Cultural Revolution the leaders thought it best to have only a figure head of state, so that any incumbent would be unable to challenge the party chairman. However, in the 2nd plenum of the 9th CC (August 25-September 6, 1970), Lin Biao supported by Chen Boda advocated the restoration of the 1954 presidential setup, but he could not prevail against a

25 *Xin hua ci dian*, Beijing: Shang wu yin shu guan, 1980, p. 189, col. 1.

26 *World almanac*, 1981, p. 525, col. 1; *Facts on file*, March 10, 1978, p. 153, cl.

27 *Globe and Mail*, February 24, 1983, p. 19.

28 *Renmin ribao*, December 16, 1981, p. 4.

stubborn Mao who stuck to a weak chairmanship. This helped to widen the cleavage between Lin and Mao, a cleavage leading eventually to the former's perdition. *Zhuxi* was brought back by the 1982 Constitution. The reasons are said to be that "practice in the years after the founding of the People's Republic proves that the post of chairman of state is necessary for improving our state system and it also conforms to the habits and wishes of the peoples of all nationalities in our country."[29] We are in agreement on the second part of the assertion, because the Chinese for thousands of years apparently enjoyed having an emperor. However we would like to know what "practice" came to "prove" the need for that post. The part-time chairman of the CPR, that is, one whose main function was heading the legislative branch of the regime (NPC) was doing quite well. Nothing inconvenient seems to take place during the thirteen years from 1969 to 1982. One official sees the office in question as being able to exert "an important and positive influence on the political life of the nation."[30] The newly installed chairmanship has to work hard, we think, in order to meet this high expectation, but in the light of the "rights" given him, his role is bound to be a feeble one. It is unlikely that he can have any "positive influence" at all.

The 1982 Constitution is admittedly patterned after the 1954 text said to be "relatively flawless," but not after the 1975 and 1978 documents which are "rather imperfect."[31] However, when one makes a circumspect collation of them all, he would readily see that the new Constitution has many features of the predecessors with some changes of course. One of these pertains to the CPR president. He was made, we will remember, a potent figure in 1954 because Articles 40, 42 and 43 vest in him the rights to convene the Supreme State Conference, to chair the Council of National Defense and to command the army. On the contrary, the new Constitution abolishes the first two bodies and deprives him of the military authority. By Article 1 of the draft text of the Constitution, he is a symbol of the state, inside and outside. This description, interestingly enough, is deleted from the final draft. By Article 81, he receives foreign diplomats, apparently on his own initiative. However, in re appointment and recall of CPR's plenipotentiary representatives, ratification and abrogation of treaties, he acts "in pursuance of the decisions of the NPC Standing Committee." This quoted phrase also qualifies his appointment and removal of the premier, vice-premiers, state councillors, ministers in charge of ministries or commissions, the general auditor, and the general secretary of the State Council, the conferment of state medals and titles of honor, the issuance of special pardon, the proclamation of martial law and of a state of war,

[29] *Peng Zhen, op. cit.,* p. 25, col. 1.

[30] *Hu Sheng, op. cit.,* p. 16.

[31] Peng Zhen, *op. cit.,* p. 18, col. 1.

and the decreeing of mobilization (Article 80). This exhausts the list of his rights. A hamlet of sorts, the chairman is truly a pale image of its 1954 self. Yet the new Constitution still deems it necessary to limit his term and the term of the vice-president to ten years (Article 79, par. 3). Do the drafters of the document mechanically copy Article 54, cl. 2 of the Basic Law of the Federal Republic of Germany whose president, although powerless, cannot serve more than two terms? Any citizen who has the right to vote and stand for election and who attains the age of 45 (40 in German Basic Law, Article 54, cl. 1) are eligible for the two highest offices of the land (Article 79, par. 2). Election is done by the NPC. Should the office of the president fall vacant, the vice-president succeeds (Article 84, par. 1), and should that of the vice-president fall vacant, the NPC holds a by-election to choose a new vice-president (Article 84, par. 2). If both fall vacant, the NPC similarly fills them. The Constitution (Article 84, par. 3), in order to avoid an interregnum vacuity, ordains the chairman of the NPC Standing Committee to be the acting president of the CPR until the new head of state assumes the post.

State Council

Known as Government Administrative Council in Article 5 of the Organic Law of the Central People's Government of September 27, 1949,[32] the State Council is one of the only two agencies of the country which do not bear the magic word "people" (the other: jail). Probably the ideologically tepid Zhou Enlai does not like the shingle, "People's State Council," hanging on his office. Even so, the constitution clearly says that the state Council is just another name of Central *People's* Government (1954 Constitution, Article 47). This equation repeats itself in all the later Constitutions. What kind of role is assigned to the body in question? The Chinese rephrase, quite awkwardly, Article 64 of the 1936 and Article 128 of the 1977 USSR Constitutions to label the Council the "executive body of the highest organ of state power [and] the highest organ of state administration" (CPR Constitution, Article 85). This is not as understandable as the Russian "highest executive and administrative body of state authority."

The State Council underwent a major "surgery" in May 1982, and the Constitution in Chapter 3, section 3 registers this fait accompli. By Article 86, par. 1, the Council members are the "premier, vice-premiers (original draft text specifies 2 or 4 of these), state councillors, ministers in charge of ministries, ministers in charge of commissions, general auditor and general secretary." The exact composition is to be governed by law (par. 3). Such law was enacted by the Fifth NPC on December 11, 1982.[33] On the eve of the above-said surgery, the Council had a total membership of 112: the premier, 13 vice-premiers, and 98 others (ministers and the like). The number, interestingly

[32] *Zhong hua ren min gong he guo kai guo wen xian*, Hong Kong: Wen hua zi liao gong ying she, 1978, p. 246.

[33] The Organic Law of the State Council mentioned in *Beijing review*, December 10, 1982, p. 4.

enough, is identical to the Council of Ministers of the USSR. The March 1982 reorganization cut the size down to half. It left 55 offices filled in by 49 individuals.[34] Under the new Constitution which went into effect on December 4, 1982, the Council for the first time was elected by the NPC on June 20, 1983 in accordance with its Article 62, cl. 5. Now it consists of the premier (Zhao Ziyang), four vice-premiers (Wan Li, Yao Yilin, Li Peng, and Tian Jiyun), ten State Councillors (Fang Yi, Gu Mu, Kang Shien, Chen Muhua (f), Ji Pengfei, Zhang Jingfu, Zhang Aiping, Wu Xueqian, Wang Bingqian, and Song Ping), one general secretary and 34 ministers. Also included are the president of the People's Bank of China, the general director of *Xin hua* news agency, the commissioner of physical culture and sports, and the commissioner of family planning. These four, however, are not specified in Article 86 of the Constitution which names all other offices of the Council. If each individual grabs one post apiece, the Council would have 53 people.[35] But nine of them wear two hats each and this makes it a team of 44. Due to much administrative ado, no two ministries are taken over by one man. Instead, a majority of non-ministrables (to use a French term) are given two portfolios. Thus the premier is put in charge of the commission of restructuring economic system; vice-premier Tian Jiyun, of general secretariat; councillors Wu Xueqian, of foreign ministry; Zhang Aiping, of national defense; Song Ping, of state planning; Zhang Jingfu, of economics; Fang Yi, of science and technology; Wang Bingqian, of finance; and Chen Muhua, of foreign economic relations and trade. In comparison with the March 1982 Council which operated under the old Constitution, the June 1983 one has two more vice-premiers, one more commission (science, technology and industry for national defense), *Xin hua* news agency, and one more ministry (state security). This newcomer appeared just on the eve of the NPC session, avowedly a counter-intelligence body (*Beijing review,* July 4, 1983, p. 6). No doubt it is the carbon copy of the KGB of the USSR. There are three females against two in the preceding Council. Also interesting is that there are 15 new faces. Leaving the Council are such heavyweights as vice-premier Bo Yibo, foreign minister Huang Hua and defense minister Geng Biao (the latter two left in 1982). Finally, all members of the body under consideration are from the Han race, the minorities being given no representation, but one Yang Jingren, minister in charge of nationalities affairs, is portrayed as a Hui *(Renmin ribao,* June 18, 1983, p. 3).

The term of office of the Council is five years, the same as the NPC (Article 87, par. 1). Whether vice-premiers, ministers, state councillors, heads of commissions, general secretary and general auditor must come from the NPC is not said in the Constitution, but practice shows that they are all deputies. In accordance with the principle of rotation

[34] "NPC Standing Committee decisions on restructuring the state Council and other questions," *ibid.,* March 15, 1982, pp. 5-6 at 5, col. 1. *Ibid.,* May 10, 1982, p. 4, col. 1.

[35] *Ibid.,* June 27, 1983, pp. 9, 12.

of office, the "premier, vice-premiers and state councillors shall serve
no more than two consecutive terms" (Article 87, par. 2). This assures
them 10 years. We think this ban is un-Chinese and it would not work.
Another Constitution (soon perhaps) will certainly delete this provision.
Following the Soviet model (USSR Constitution, Article 132), the
Chinese document (Article 88, par. 3) writes of the so-called
"executive meetings" attended by the premier, vice-premiers, the
state councillors and the general secretary," and the "plenary
meetings" attended by all these, plus the ministers and the general
auditor. The Russians use the term presidium for the Chinese
executive meetings, but do not mention plenary meetings in their basic
law. The Chinese Constitution in Article 86, par. 2 introduces the
premier and ministerial responsibility system in imitation of the Soviet
edinonochalie (one-man management). It is the premier and nobody
else, the Constitution obviously stresses, who is accountable for the
affairs of the entire Council to the NPC or the Standing Committee,
and it is the mininster who is accountable for the affairs of his domain
to the same (Article 90, par. 1). This explains why a minister is
oustable. If our interpretation makes any sense in a totalitarian system
like the CPR, the Beijing leadership envisages both individual and
collective responsibility à la parliamentary custom.

Let us quickly go through the ministries and commissions. Some
are common to democratic nations, i.e., defense, foreign relations,
education, communications, posts and telecommunication, justice,
trade (adding foreign economic relations), agriculture (adding animal
husbandry and fishery), commerce, public health, labor (adding
personnel), railways, and finance. Others are less common or at least
not made into separate ministries in other countries. They deal with
state planning, urban/rural construction/environment protection,
culture, family planning, physical culture/sports, radio/television,
geology/minerals, water conservancy/power, and forestry. Then there
is the familiar ministry of public security and the not so familiar ministry
of civil affairs which supervises elections, and does spy work. Rarely
or not seen at all in a Western cabinet are the even dozen industrial
ministries of metallurgy, machine-making, nuclear industry, aviation,
electronics, weaponry, space industry, petroleum, chemicals, textiles,
coal, light consumer articles. The weaponry ministry is making nuclear
arms, besides conventional ones. The government of the CPR, like
other socialist systems, arrogates to itself the tasks of providing the
daily necessities of the citizens. No wonder the Chinese yamens are
legion. In March 1982, they numbered 127 under the roof of the State
Council.[36] After consolidation, they still number 100.

We now come to the functions of the Council. This body is the
workhorse of the government. The areas mentioned in the preceding
paragraph and many others are all planned and directed by it. Article
89 enumerates 18 tasks and Article 91 adds one more. We will not
catalogue all of them. Suffice it to refer to the economic and social

[36] "Reforming the cadre system," *ibid.*, March 1, 1982, p. 3, col. 2.

development, the budget, the overseeing of the bureaucratic web staffed by 20 million men and women,[37] the conduct of foreign affairs, the control of the four million plus armies, the stockpiling of nuclear-missile weapons, the auditing (through an independent agency within the State Council) of the over 250 billion yuan spending.[38] Certainly, not every activity has to be envisaged by the text of the Constitution. It possesses immense discretion as behooves any executive machine. In April 1978, for example, a drought hit hard a great part of China. An extraordinary session of the Council was called on the 25th of the month. It came out with a declaration of war on heaven and promptly mobilized 100 million people to water the dying crops by buckets and to construct reservoirs by hand.[39] Further, the council enjoys a right in treaty-making (Article 89, cl. 9). Here the Constitution grants, in Article 67, cl. 14, the reviewing authority to the Standing Committee only in repsect of *important* agreements with foreign states. But what are important and what are not would, we think, have to be decided by the Council because only the agency which concludes them is in a position to pronouce judgement on the matter.

The Constitution twice (Article 67, cl. 14; Article 89, cl. 9) mentions agreements of the State Council with foreign states. A strict interpretation would have to be that agreements with international agencies are not brought to the Standing Committee for sanction. The UN Charter, for example, refers to a) arrangement made between member states and the Security Council concerning the supply of armed forces to help with enforcement action assumed by the Security Council to maintain or restore international peace (UN Charter, Article 43), b) member states may set up specialized agencies by inter-governmental instruments (Article 57), c) trusteeship plans can be reached between member states and the United Nations (Articles 75-77). In re these agreements, the State Council can act independently.

In the history of the CPR, the Council is more stable than the party, army or judicature. The individual who headed it for a quarter of a century is Zhou Enlai. He is commonly considered a moderate man. However, we are not prepared to laud this man, because, among others, he failed to use his influence to check the massacre orgy of the Reds during the land reform of the early fifties, and the killing of god knows how many good persons in the Cultural Revolution. Yet the fact that he was left alone to manage his constituency for so long, particularly amidst the turmoil of that Revolution and the further fact that the communists heaped little invectives upon him seem to reflect a spark of conscience of theirs. Solely due to the quiet work of the Council, the ship of state was kept afloat and was able to sail through the choppy China sea.

---

[37] *Ibid.*

[38] *Ibid.*, December 20, 1982, p. 19, col. 1.

[39] *Keesing's*, September 8, 1978, p. 21293, col. 2.

The CPR, it is important to note, has had only three premiers: Zhou Enlai, 1949-1976; Hua Guofeng, 1976-1980; Zhao Ziyang since the latter year. In contrast, there have been 8 chiefs of state variously called:

Mao Zedong	1954-1959	chairman	resigned
Liu Shaoqi	1959-1968	same	removed
vacant	1968-1970		
Dong Biwu	1970-1975	acting chairman	died
Zhu De	1975-1976		died
Wu De	1976-1978	chairmen of NPC	removed
Ye Jianying	1978-1982	Standing Committee	resigned
Li Xiannian	1983-		

Song Qingling was honorific chairman from May 15 to 29, 1981.

Six defense ministers:

Peng Dehui	1954-1959
Lin Biao	1959-1971
Ye Jianying	1971-1975 (acting)
Xu Xiangqian	1975-1981
Geng Biao	1981-1982
Zhang Aiping	1982-

six general chiefs of staff (one man held the office twice):[40]

Huang Kecheng	1954-1959
Luo Ruiqing	1959-1966
Yang Zhenwu	1966-1968
Huang Yongsheng	1968-1971
(vancant)	1971-1973
Deng Xiaoping	1973-1975
(vacant)	1975-1977
Deng Xiaoping	1977-1980
Yang Dezhi	1980-

and six presidents of the Supreme Court:

Shen Junyu	1949-1955
Dong Biwu	1955-1959
Xie Juezai	1959-1965
Yang Xiufeng	1965-1975
Jiang Hua	1975-1983
Zheng Tianxiang	1983-

The Hua Guofeng Council sought to prevent the country from lapsing into another cesspool; and to this end, he felt it essential to resort to the favorite three-in-one technique. Hua placed himself at the head of the administration, the army and the party. As premier, as CCP chairman and as commander-in-chief (this under Article 19 of the 1978 Constitution), he wielded an absolute stick, even

[40] Regarding the vacancy, see *Encyclopedia of China today,* 1st ed., compiled by Frederick M. Kaplan, Julian M. Sobin and Stephen Andors, New York: Harper and Row, 1979, p. 113, col. 1. However, *Yearbook on international communist affairs,* 1976, p. 261 mentions wrongly a vacancy from 1971-1975.

unmatchable by Mao Zedong, because he did not assume the first named post (premiership). The role of Hua Guofeng ran into collision with Deng Xiaoping. He was forced to retreat from the premiership on September 4, 1980 which went to Zhao Ziyang, a pragmatist and one of Deng's supporters. Zhao, as related above, administered the largest province, Sichuan, with "success" according to the mouthpiece of Beijing.[41] He was said to promote productivity of labor by offering incentive wages and by fostering local initiative.[42] In April 1980, Zhao was elevated to the vice-premiership,[43] and five months later he grabbed the premier's chair.

Local government
Division

By the definition of the Constitution (Chapter 3, section 5), provinces and their subdivisions are local regimes. The Chinese ape the Russian Reds in the organization of these. Parallel to the quadruplet of union republic, autonomous republic, autonomous region and autonomous area (before 1977 called national area), they display a foursome of autonomous region, autonomous prefecture, autonomous county and autonomous qi (all but the last are in the Constitution). In the Great Russian and Han parts of the countries, territorial divisions do not carry the word autonomous. Indeed they are not intended to be autonomous. The Han reside in 21 provinces and 3 cities with provincial status (Beijing, Shanghai, Tianjin). Any publication which need to mention all these are ordered by the State Council to follow a sequence like this: 1, Beijing, 2, Tianjin, 3, Hebei, 4, Shanxi, 5, Neimenggu, 6, Liaoning on down to 26, Gansu, 27, Qinghai, 28, Ningxia-hui, 29, Xinjiang and ending with 30, Taiwan.[44] Each city consists not only of the metropolis, but the vast periphery, because a number of counties are incorporated in it. Shanghai has 10 of them, Beijing 9 and Tianjin 5.[45] Driving 4 or 5 hours without meeting any soul, you are still within the city of Beijing! A county or autonomous county is made up of townships (xiang) and towns (zhen). An autonomous prefecture consists of counties, autonomous counties and cities (Article 30, par. 2). This level (prefecture), we want to remind the reader, is specifically for the minority races and throughout the Constitution the word prefecture is always coupled with autonomous, but occasionally loose talks and even media refer to this or that prefecture in Han areas.[46] Up to January 1983, the numbers of

[41] Tian Yun, "More authority for enterprises revives the economy," *Beijing review*, April 6, 1981, pp. 21-26.

[42] Ren Tao, Sun Huaiyang and Liu Jinglin, "Investigation report: enterprises in Sichuan province acquire greater independence," *Social science in China*, 1 (1980), pp. 201-215.

[43] *Globe and Mail*, September 4, 1980, p. 3, col. 1.

[44] *Renmin ribao*, January 7, 1981, p. 1.

[45] *Zhong guo shou ce*, p. 19

[46] *Beijing review*, June 21, 1982, p. 7, col. 3 refers to four prefectures in northwestern Shandong province. Even Premier Zhao Ziyang is not very restrict in the use of the term prefecture, see his speech to the Fifth NPC Congress on November 30, 1982, *ibid.*, December 20, 1982, p. 32, col. 2.

administrative echelons are as follows:[47]

provincial level	cities	city districts	prefectural level	county level
30	230	514	208	2,136

22 provinces			164 prefectures	2,001 counties
5 autonomous regions			30 autonomous prefectures	69 autonomous counties
3 cities			1 administrative area	54 qui (banner)
			9 meng (league)	3 autonomous qi
				9 autonomous townships

Organization

The above table shows the confusing names which number no less than a dozen. However, the compensating feature lies in the structural simplicity. The administration was known as the revolutionary committee from 1966 to 1977 which was Mao Zedong's proud brainchild charged with perpetuating the Chinese revolution. Only a few months following his death and the ouster of the Gang of four, the revcom (to use the once affective abbreviation) was on the way out, but it took over two years before it was legally dead. This came to pass by a constitutional amendment in the second session of the 5th NPC on June 26, 1979, in accordance with Article 25, cl. 13 of the 1978 Constitution. The reason given was that as the CPR was embarking on socialist construction in the new era, it was essential first to separate the organ of state power (people's congress) from the administrative agency (people's government), and second to establish the standing committee in the congress at and above the county plane. (From this point on, we will omit the word people's when mention is made of these organizations) The revcom is no longer able to answer the needs of the modernization drive. In particular it is alleged that the rechristening of the revcom to government not only helped further socialist democracy but reinforce the bond between the government and the masses.[48] This assertion is far from convincing. It is hard to know how the bond can be reinforced by a change of name-calling. In fact, Article 37 of the 1978 Constitution clearly says that the revolutionary committee *is* the government. There is no need, we think, for the change, except for the fact that nobody takes the trouble to read the Constitution.

Like the regime in Beijing, a local regime has three bodies, namely

[47] *Beijing review*, January 3, 1983, p. 25. The four types below the provinces do not include Taiwan's units. Administrative units were reshuffled in late 1983, see *Ibid.*, Oct. 28, 1983, p. 3.
[48] David Bonavia, "Hua spells out Deng's brave new world," *Far Eastern economic review*, no. 27, July 6, 1979, pp. 10-11 at 10, col. 1.

the congress, the standing committee and the government. Take the congress first, the tenure is five years in a province, a city directly ruled by the central government and any other large city (one divided into *cu* or districts), but the tenure is three years in a county, a small city (one not so divided), a township, a nationality township or a town (Article 98). The size of a congress is fixed by the Election Law (Article 100, par. 2). Regarding the manner in which deputies are produced, it is envisaged in Article 97, par. 1 that those of the five-year congress are elected by the congresses at the next lower level; at and below the county level, mass voters elect the deputies. All deputies, no matter how chosen, are recallable any time by the electors (Article 102, par. 2). Underlying this practice is that deputies are simply a proxy. It rejects the Burkian theory of representation. A congress enjoys a great scope of power. In a given district, says Article 99, par. 1, it ensures the observance and implementation of the Constitution, laws, decrees and general administrative rules, and in accordance with its authority as prescribed by law, it adopts and issues decisions and plans social, economic and cultural development and public utilities. By the term of the Constitution (Article 99, par. 2), only the county or provincial congress examines and approves the plans for economic and social improvement and budgets of their respective administrative areas, and examines and approves reports on their execution. It has the power to alter or annul inappropriate decisions of its own standing committee. Whether units below the county level have budgetary rights is not stated in the Constitution.

The congress, whether the five-or three-year variety, is within its right to appoint or remove the leading cadres of the government, be he the governor or vice-governor of a province, mayor or vice-mayor, head or vice-head of a county, or a township or a town. As if flying in the face of the proclaimed judicial independence (Article 126), the congress names and dismisses the president of the court and the chief procurator at the same level; but with respect to the latter official, a report must be made to the chief-procurator at the next higher level, who in turn sends the report to the standing committee of the congress at that level for approval (Article 101, par. 2)

Each congress chooses a standing committee whose members it can recall. The committee consists of a chairman, unspecified number of vice-chairmen and others. All are responsible to the congress at the corresponding level (Article 103, par. 1). "No one on the standing committee of a local people's congress at and above the county level," says par. 3, "shall hold any post in state administrative, judicial and procuratorial organs," This, incidentally, is not in the original draft text. The size of the committee is fixed as follows: province, autonomous region and cities ruled by Beijing directly, 35-65; autonomous prefecture and city, 13-35 (in the most populous city the ceiling is 45); county, autonomous county, and city, 11-19 (in the most populous city, the ceiling is 19).[49] The election to a higher congress

49 Election Law, Article 36, par. 3, *Renmin shou ce*, p. 399, col. 1.

is conducted by the standing committee. Within the latter's competence fall the deliberation of major issues concerning the work in the district and the overseeing of the work of the government, court and procuratorate. On the inappropriate decisions and orders of the government at the corresponding level and of the governments at the next lower level, the standing committee is directed to exercise veto. The same holds true with the inappropriate decisions and orders of the lower-level congresses. What is more, the committee controls the administrative personnel of the district. When the congress is not in session, it holds by-elections of deputies to the congress at the next higher level, and it recalls them, too. The standing committee of a city with districts in it or a county conducts election of deputies to the congress of municipal districts, township, nationality township and town (Article 104). So much for the standing committee.

The government administers the economy, education, science, culture, public health, physical culture, urban and rural construction, finance, public security, civil affairs and family planning (Article 107). It is within its right to appoint, remove, train, reward and sanction the cadres. It is further stipulated in Article 108 that the government directs the work of the various departments and the work of lower-level governments. Also lodged with it is the amendment and nullification of inappropriate orders and directives of these departments and governments. There are auditing bodies at and above the county level, which exercise auditorial and supervisory authority independently in accordance with the law, but are responsible to the governments at the corresponding levels and the auditing bodies at the next higher levels (Article 109). A government is made accountable to the congress or, when it is not in session, to the standing committee.

The above are applicable to the Han areas. Section 6 of Chapter 3 of the Constitution is devoted to the minority races. By Article 113, par. 1, they are entitled to representation in the regional congress as specified by legislation. Chairman of the autonomous region, head of an autonomous prefecture or autonomous county must be from the nationality in question (Article 114). The congress in the national area is within its power to draw up statutes on autonomy and other regulations in the light of the political, economic and cultural characteristics there (Article 116). The statutes and regulations of a region have to be submitted to the Standing Committee in Beijing for review, however, but those of an autonomous prefecture or autonomous county are to be submitted to the standing committee of the provincial or regional congress for approval. They need be reported to the Standing Committee in Beijing just for the record of it.

Different from a Han province or county, an autonomous region or any of its subdivisions has financial autonomy by Article 117. It is stated there that all revenues accruing to the autonomous areas shall be used in accordance with the arrangements made independently by the organs of self-government in those areas. On the matter of economic construction, education, culture, public health and physical culture (Article 119), the competent authorities are subject to the guidance of the state plan (Article 118, par. 1). In keeping with the military system of the CPR, so says Article 120, the organs of self-government may have their security forces to maintain public order, but the State Council must give its sanction. Language right is provided by Article 121 which declares that organs of self-government can employ the spoken and written language or languages in common use there. What about the Han language? Article 19, par. 5 orders the state to promote the nationwide use of *Putonghua* (common speech based on Beijing pronunciation). The original draft text (Article 19, par. 4), it may be noted, mentions Han language instead of *Putonghua*. Will this lead ultimately to a compulsory requirement for all nationalities to practice Guoyu? Finally, the autonomous areas may implement state law by taking into account local conditions and Beijing promises to give financial, material and technical assistance to minorities, including the training of "large numbers of cadres at different levels and specialized personnel and skilled workers of different professions and trades from among the nationality or nationalities" (Article 122, par. 2) Something like a foreign aid program!

Beneath the bottom layer of the administrative cake, in both Han and non-Han parts of the country, are the residents' or villagers' committees which are considered as "mass organizations of self-government at the primary level" (Article 111, par. 1). A committee has a chairman, vice-chairmen and others, all directly elected by residents. They are also recallable. The committee can establish mediation, security, public health, and other commissions. These are to relay people's opinions and demands to the government and to make suggestions to, and exercise supervision over, the administration. The relation between such mass bodies and the organs of state power at the primary level is to be specified by law. The residents' or villagers' committees are as old as the communist regime. They keep an eye on what is happening in the locale. Any strange face turning out there is immediately tipped off to the police.[50] Besides, they recruit the literary people for bull sessions to study Marxism-Leninism and Mao Zedong Thought, manage small factories, engage in welfare work and set up noodle restaurants. On the average, a committee covers an area inhabited by 20 families. It is also instrumental in birth curbing. Meetings of neighbors decide how many babies are to be produced and who may do it and when.[51] Such an all-purpose organization has been a long-standing custom. Of all the Constitutions, only the 1982 one finds room for it.

[50] "Our neighborhood revolutionary committee," *China reconstructs*, vol. 22, no. 8 (August 1973), p. 3, cited in James Wang, *Contemporary Chinese politics, an introduction*, Englewood Cliffs, New Jersey: Prentice-Hall, 1980, p. 143, noe 23.

[51] James Wang, *op. cit.*, p. 140.

Election[52]

Equality before the law heads the "bill of rights" in the Constitution (Article 33, par. 2). Supposedly it is the number one right of the Chinese citizens. Upon the exercise of election, one segment of the population (rural) is expressly made inferior to another (urban). Witness the following situations. a) In the congress of prefecture (the Constitution by the way does not mention this kind of congress), county or autonomous county, one town deputy represents one-fourth of the inhabitants as represented by his rural counterpart (Election Law, Article 10). b) In the congress of a province, autonomous region or city directly controlled by the central government it is one-fifth (Article 12), and c) in the NPC it is one-eighth (Article 14). Such prejudice is not justified at all in the light of the peasants' contribution to the conquest of power by the Reds. Do they know that this unequal franchise adopted in the USSR Constitution of 1924 was even deleted by Stalin from that of 1936?

A procedure is provided for nomination of the candidates and for compiling a list of names following repeated exhange of views, "from bottom up and from top down" (Article 28, par. 1). Vested with the right to nominate are the CCP, various democratic parties which number eight presently,[53] mass bodies, and any elector or deputy who can solicit no less than three citizens to endorse a nominee (Article 26, par. 2). The final slate is reached "after many times of deliberation and discussion and democratic consultation among the electors or their deputies" (Article 28, par. 1). Whenever necessary, a straw vote can be taken on the candidates (par. 2). In the past, the CPR followed the Soviet practice of one aspirant per seat. The new dispensation brings in a regulated contest by demanding more candidates than the spots to be filled. The number of candidates, in the case of direct election, should double the number to be chosen; the number of candidates to be elected by a congress should be one fifth or one half more than the vacancies to be filled (Article 27, par. 2). If the nominees are quite many, "a preliminary election may be held to determine the formal list of candidates" (Article 28, par. 2). There are special provisions for the multi-racial areas (Articles 16-19). The details need not to detain us here.

When a congress elects deputies to the higher congress, the candidates are not necessarily from it (Article 29). An elector has the right, by Article 34, to vote for or against the nominee, to choose another man, or to relinquish his right altogether. If the ballots cast are more than the electors, the election is automatically null and void, but if they are less, it is valid (Article 37, par. 1). Similarly, a ballot is not to be counted should there be more names on it than the

---

52 See also the preceding chapter, section on direct democracy.

53 They are the Revolutionary Committee of the Guomindang, China Democratic League, China Democratic National Construction Association, China Association for Promoting Democracy, Chinese Peasants and Workers Democratic Party, China Zhi Gong Dang, Ju San Society, and Taiwan Democratic Self-Government League, *Zhong guo shou ce,* pp. 141.-142.

required number, but it is good should there be less names (par. 2). As a basic principle, a candidate who garners more than one half of the ballots is elected. But if the candidates getting this majority are more than the fixed-up number only those who obtain the most ballots become deputies (Article 38). The list of the eligibles in direct election must be made known to the public 30 days before the election, and they are issued certificates of their qualification (Article 24). In case different opinion arises on the list, a protest may be filed with the election committee which is to decide it within three days. Against the committee's holding, an appeal may be made to the court. Its judgment is final (Article 25).

Citizens and electors in congress can recall deputies as related before. If the recall election gets approval of the majority, the deputies are removed (Article 40). Does this happen very often? Once in a blue moon, so to say. According to the press, an NPC deputy, one Fan Delin, from Hebei province was de-mandated in 1981 by the people's congress of that province,[54] and one unnamed NPC deputy was similarly disqualified by the people's congress of Anhui province in 1979.[55] We have, however, no record of the recall of a directly elected deputy.

Civil Affairs Minister Cheng Zihua (replaced by Cui Naifu in May 1982) submitted an interim report to the Standing Committee on the local election which dragged on from September 1979 to March 1982.[56] He says that out of a total of 2,756 units of government, 2,365 finished their election by August 1981. A total of 1,925 units with a population of 743,760,575 produced 595,345 deputies. On the average, 1,249 inhabitants have one deputy. He also states that among the deputies there are:

    10.56% workers
    47.61   peasants
    25.53   cadres
     8.44   intellectuals and armymen
     7.86   patriots, overseas citizens
    21.89% women
    33.15   non-communists

His conclusion is that the result "fully expresses the proletarian dictatorship of our country which is led by the workers' class and based on an alliance of that class and peasants." We would ask the former minister: Since the workers have only 10.56%, on what account can they claim the leadership?

---

54 *Renmin ribao,* November 27, 1981, p. 1; *Guangming ribao,* same date, p. 3.

55 *Renmin shou ce,* Beijing: Renmin ribao chu ban she, 1980, p. 239, col. 1.

56 *Renmin ribao,* September 12, 1981, pp. 1, 4.

CHAPTER VII
The Army

Gun, the Almighty!

The three important subsystems of the Soviet State are the Central Committee of the Communist Party, the Supreme Soviet and the Council of Ministers. In the CPR, the big three are the CCP, the government and the army. They are handily shortened in speeches and writings as Dang-zheng-jun. One author considers them as forming "a single Gestalt."[1] During the rebellion, the functional boundary among the trio almost blurred to the vanishing point. From top to bottom in the communist regime, an official was duty bound to be a warrior, a civil administrator and a party apparatchik.[2] It is only after 1949 that the three came to have each distinguishable institutions, and the problem arises as to which is the premus inter pares. Beijing's doctrinal stance dictates the precedence of the *Dang* over *Zheng* and *Jun,* particularly the second (*Jun*).[3] Some writers regard the army to be the third subsystem of the Chinese state.[4] They hold that it carries less weight than the other two authorities (*Zheng* and *Dang*). This way of looking at the matter does little justice to truth. To a greater degree than Nazi Germany, the People's Republic has fused the three powers in one and the military factor bulks preeminent.[5] The PLA is the sine qua non of the existence of that state. It is the armed triumph which crowned the Reds' struggle with the national government. Their tactics and brutality, but by no means their principle appeal, ensured their fortune. This point seems to escape many observers; these and the dyed-in-wool communists have elected to view history as a living god pushing China by means of dialectics toward the workers' Elysium. Without military control of the masses, we think, the Beijing oligarchy would probably have been toppled.

Little wonder, therefore, Article 19, par. 2 of the 1978 Constitution concedes the PLA to be "the pillar of the dictatorship of the proletariat."[6] This notion was hammered home by Mao Zedong in the famous saying that "political power comes out of the gun barrel."

---

[1] "Chou En-lai and Chinese politics," *Governments and Leaders,* Boston: Houghton Mifflin, 1978, pp. 437-533 at 452, col. 2.

[2] Shao Hua, "Zhong guo gong chan dang yu zhong guo renmin jie fang jun," *Qing zhu zhong guo gong zhan dang dan sheng san shi zhou nian wen xian,* Nanchang: Zhong gong jiangxi sheng wei hui, 1951, pp. 132-142.

[3] Paul Elmqvist, "The internal role of the military," *The Military and Political power in China in the 1970's,* New York: Praeger, 1972, pp. 269-290 at 278-280.

[4] James Townsend, "Politics in China," *Comparative Politics Today, a World View,* 2nd ed., Boston: Little, Brown, pp. 381-432 at 405, col. 1.

[5] Alexander L. George, *The Chinese Army in Action, the Korean War and its Aftermath,* New York: Columbia University Press, 1967, pp. 39-41, 51, 66.

[6] Harold Hinton, *An Introduction to Chinese Politics,* 2nd ed., New York: Holt, Rinehart and Winston, 1978, p. 215.

It is also reified in a less cited but equally remarkable expression of
his: "Where there is army there is power. War solves all problems.
This view is taken by Jiang Jieshi, and rightfully so. We must learn
from him in this regard. Jiang Jieshi and Sun Yat-sen are our
teachers."[7] There is then the jingoistic editorial of *Renmin ribao* of
June 24, 1964 (p. 1) that "political authority, independence, equality,
liberty, all emanate from armed forces."[8] One is wondering if there
is more vibrant militarism.

It is the very awareness of the armed parentage of power which
prompts Mao Zedong to maintain that the CCP must get hold of the
gun and must make sure that it not be snatched away. This worship
of Mars has come to color the military-civil relations of the People's
Republic from its inception and keeps intensifying as the system
unfolds. Now that the gun is so crucial, the top man ought to see to
it that every part of it be within his firm grip.[9] This is most graphically
demonstrated by the 1978 Constitution, Article 19, par. 1 of which
gives the CCP chairman the supreme command of the army. There
is no comparable stipulation in the USSR Constitution, although Yuri
Andropov is the de facto c-in-c of the Soviet hordes. Chiefly
responsible for vesting the CCP chairman with the military robe is
the Cultural Revolution. Before that, it was the CPR chairman who
donned it. Liu Shaoqi, we will recall, assumed the chairmanship in
1959. Under the then Constitution (Article 42), he was the c-in-c. The
disclosure of his crimes by the Red Guards made the radicals fear
that a possession of the military power can make the chef d'état
irresistible. Hence, they were determined to deprive the future
officeholder of that power, thinking that the CCP chairman should
have it.[10] This decision was subsequently written into the 1975 and
1978 Constitutions.[11] One may query why the two documents do not
make the CCP chairman concurrently the CPR chairman and in this
way Article 42 of the 1954 Constitution may be retained? A possible
explanation is that the Chinese were deliberately anti-Soviet in this
matter. Simply because Leonid Brezhnev (from 1977 to his death in
1982) wore the two diadems of party chief and head of state, they
must separate them.

As constitutionally ordained supreme commander, the party
chairman is placed in an unchallengeable position. But what about
the defense minister? According to Article 22, clause 4 of the 1978
Constitution, the premier has to be recommended by the CC for the

[7] Mao Zedong, "Zhan zheng he zhan lue wen ti," November 6, 1938, *Mao Zedong xuan ji*, Beijing: Ren min chu ban she, 1969, vol. 2, pp. 506-521 at 511.

[8] This statement is also noted by John A. Harrison, *China since 1800*, New York: Harcourt, Brace & World, 1967, p. 232, where the date of the Chinese source is wrong, however.

[9] Richard Walter, *China Under Communism, the First Five Years*, New Haven: Yale University Press, 1955, p. 31.

[10] James D. Jordan, "The Maoist vs. the professional vision of a people's army," *The Military and Political Power in China in the 1970's*, pp. 25-45 at 26, 27.

[11] Articles 15 and 19 respectively.

NPC to appoint. In the next clause, he is given the right to recommend ministers, including the defense minister to the NPC. Can one expect the CC to nominate a non-communist premier? or the latter recommend a non-communist defense minister?

Besides the defense establishment, there was the Military Affairs Committee under the old setup. This body is both unique and normal; unique because it does not exist in the CPSU Statues of which the CCP Statute is otherwise a carbon copy, normal because a warlike party like the CCP should have it to enforce its will. The 1978 CPR Constitution and the 1977 CCP Statute were both silent on the committee. Its existence is a matter of what the British call a convention. More of this body later in the instant section.

From 1949 to 1954 there was a People's Revolutionary Military Council. This body and the Military Affairs Committee existed side by side and their functions were duplicating. Obviously on account of this reason, the Council was abolished in 1954. Yet a new machine, the Council of National Defense, was created. It was presided by the CPR chairman, according to Articles 27 and 40 of the 1954 Constitution. Under the then setup there were three cognate agencies: a) the defense ministry, b) the Council of National Defense, c) the Military Affairs Committee. Of the three, the most important is the last-named which is however a party body, but the second was nevertheless considered indispensable. It was utilized to accommodate the GMD generals and warlords who went over to the Reds. A fanfare of propaganda was made with the communist humanity. It appealed to the leaders of Taiwan that if they surrendered, the Council but not the execution ground was their place. This agency has a counterpart in the Chinese People's Political Consultative Conference (CPPCC), mentioned at the beginning of Chapter V, which was utilized to accommodate the renegading high civilians of the nationalist regime, as well as the sympathizers. With all the GMD generals superannuated, the Council of National Defense is let to wither away. The 1975 and 1978 Constitutions drop it altogether, but it is brought back in the Central Military Commission in the 1982 Constitution.

This Constitution introduces a number of changes in the military establishment. Under it the CCP General Secretary does not command the army. Instead, the Central Military Commission comes "to direct the armed forces of the country" (Article 93, par. 1). The text, it is noteworthy, uses the words *ling dao* (lead), but not *tong shuai* (command). The latter term is in Article 42 of the 1954 Constitution. Article 89, cl. 7 of the new Constitution again talks of *ling dao,* this time by the State Council. Thus the Council and the Central Military Commission both lead the armed forces (!) but there is no commanding organ in the Constitution. By contrast, the Soviet Constitution (Article 121, cl. 14) speaks of the Council of Defense, and mentions high command to be appointed or dismissed by the Presidium (equivalent to the NPC Standing Committee of the CPR), besides referring to the direction of the forces by the Council of Ministers (Article 131, cl. 5). The 1982 CPR Constitution is perhaps the only kind in the world which is silent on the high command of the armed formation.

The Central Military Commission (a state body) is intended by the leaders to be a) collectively and b) individually accountable to the NPC Standing Committee, with an emphasis however on b). We call the reader's attention to the fact that all authorities mentioned in the Constitution, except a) the highest body provided in Chapter 6 on autonomous areas of the CPR and b) the general auditor of the State Council (Article 69, cl. 9) are provided with an understudy. There is, to enumerate, the vice-president of the CPR (Article 79, pars. 1 and 2), vice-premiers (Article 86, par. 1), vice-president of the Supreme Court (Article 67, cl. 11), deputy chief procurator (cl. 12), vice-governor of a province (Article 101, par. 2), and vice-head of each lower-level government (*ibid.*) Even the neighborhood or villagers' committee has its vice-chairman (Article 111, par. 1). Contrary to all these, there is no vice-chairman of the Central Military Commission mentioned in the Constitution.

The Constitution in Article 93, par. 3 speaks of the "overall responsibility for the Commission" placed in the hands of the chairman. He is not subject to third-term ban (although he was, under Article 96 of the draft text of the Constitution). This shows the significance of the post. Is the Commission plural or singular in composition? Section 4 of Chapter 3 of the Constitution devoted to this body says nothing about this, but section 1 of the same chapter devoted to NPC indicates it is plural. To be precise, Article 62, cl. 6 writes of "other members of the Commission" to be chosen upon the recommendation of the chairman. Similarly Article 63, cl. 10 states that such "other members" can be appointed and removed by the Standing Committee upon the same chairman's recommendation when the NPC is not in session.

On June 20, 1983 the 6th NPC elected a chairman, four vice-chairmen (identical with chairman and vice-chairmen of the party's Military Commission, see below) and four ordinary members. The latter four are (1) Yu Qiuli, chief political commissar of the armed forces, (2) Zhang Aiping, defense minister, 3) Yang Dezhi, general chief of staff, and (4) Hong Xuezhi, logistical commander.

The new system separates the party from the state in military affairs. While Article 19, par. 1 of the 1978 Constitution was vague on the troops' belonging, Article 29, par. 1 of the new minces no words that the "armed forces of the People's Republic of China belong to the people." A semantic difference between the documents is that the term PLA appears in the former (Article 19, par. 2), but armed forces or national defense appears in the latter (Article 29, par. 1; Article 89, cl. 10). A further change is that Article 19, par. 2 of the 1978 Constitution says that the PLA is workers' and peasants' own armed forces "led by the Communist Party of China." This quoted phrase is now dropped. Moreover, the present Constitution stresses that military power is in the hand of the Central People's Government because Article 120 grants only the government of national autonomous areas the right to "organize their local public security" in conformity "with the military system of the state and concrete local needs and with the approval of the State Council." By implication, a province cannot have a similar right. The present armed formation no longer "combines" the so-called field army and militia as envisioned in Article 19, par. 3 of the 1978 Constitution. However, while field army disappears completely from the 1982 Constitution, militia is referred to in its Article 52, par. 2, and citizens are enjoined to serve in it.

In contrast with the 1977 party Statute which mentions army in three of a total of 19 articles, the 1982 Statute refers only once to it in a total of 50 articles (in connection with the establishment of a primary organization in a company). Probably the Beijing aristocrats sought to lower the profile of the naked force in their system. However, one cannot for one moment conclude that the CCP would henceforth give up the gun or relax the hold on it. The current control pattern is that every unit has a party branch staffed with a secretary, a committee and several bureaus. Under their charge are soliciting and disciplining members, collecting dues, organizing the study of Marxism-Leninism and Mao Zedong Thought, engaging in criticism and self-criticism, discussing party-related issues, hearing of complaints, and carrying out party line. During meetings, from which non-party people are barred, all are equal irrespective of the positions held (military ranks being done away with from the inception of the Cultural Revolution but to be revived soon). Party congress from regimental level up must convene every three years. Under special circumstances, it may meet before or after the due date, subject to the approval of the next higher party committee. Below the regimental level, a congress is to take place every other year. The apparatus of the lowest unit (platoon) reports and is responsible to the next top rung and so on up the ladder. The apex is the Military Commission (to be distinguished from the Central Military Commission, a state body).

The Military Commission is envisaged in Article 21, par. 4, but its size and responsibility are not laid down there. All members are elected by the Central Committee. On September 12, 1982, the first plenum of the 12th CC chose Deng Xiaoping as its chairman and Ye Jianying, Xu Xiangqian, Nie Rongzhen and Yang Shangkun as its vice-chairmen.[12] The Commission was originally founded in 1930 and headed by none other than Mao Zedong after that year until 1976 when he died.[13] From 1976 to 1981, it was chaired by Hua Guofeng. In the latter year, Deng Xiaoping took over from him. Besides chairman and vice-chairmen, the Commission has a standing

[12] *The twelfth national congress of the CPC* (September 1982), Beijing: Foreign languages press, 1982, p. 154.

[13] Harold Hinton, *op. cit.*, pp. 100-101; James Wang, *Contemporary Chinese politics, an introduction*, Englewood Cliffs, New Jersey: Prentice-Hall, 1980, p. 76.

committee, a general secretary and an advisor who is ex officio head of the general office.[14] Although it has existed for so long, it is not until 1982 that it appears in the party Statute. As to be expected, the Commission makes the highest military policy,[15] but at times it assumes responsibility in matters which are operative in nature. Early in 1967, for example, it acted jointly with the State Council and the Cultural Revolution Group of the CC to pacify, by the use of force, the Red Guards.[16] And on January 1, 1981, it ordered the "preparation for war" and the "taking good care of military men's dependents by the general public."[17]

Unlike the CPSU Statutes (Rules 65 and 66), the CCP Statute says nothing about the political agency in the army, even though it is a very important part of it. On the surface, the party branch and political commissariat deal with different things, but in reality they complement each other. While the former (party branch) occupies itself with such routines as calling sessions and handing out membership cards, the latter (political branch) is to improve the ideological standing, keep the men and officers abreast of current events and in general enhance political awareness on their part. There is a division of labor here. However, a more obvious distinction of the two bodies resides in the fact that a party organization is by definition for the card-carrying communists only, but a political machine is for everybody in the unit.[18] Each army and division has a political bureau, while each regiment and subordinate unit a political office. A political commissar works alongside a commander.[19] The former is responsible to the higher political bureau and through it to the General Political Department whose head since September 1982 has been Yu Qiuli (formerly Wei Guoqing). By practice, although not under statutory instrument, political cadres may not tamper with the operational decisions of commanders, but they must make sure that these men are loyal to the communist regime. A party committee of each unit includes three keymen: the commander, the commissar, the party secretary.[20] Frequently the first two are the same individual, and this undoubtedly avoids discord. If, however, a conflict should develop among the trio, the party secretary surely enjoys the upper hand.[21]

[14] *Zhong quo shou ce,* Hong Kong: Da gong bao, 1979, p. 303.

[15] James Townsend, *Politics in China,* 2nd ed., Boston: Little, Brown, 1980, p. 94; James Wang, *op cit.,* p. 75.

[16] James Wang, *op. cit.,* p. 155.

[17] *Guangming ribao,* January 1, 1981, p. 1.

[18] V.I. Elizarov, "Kommunisticheskaya partiya kitaya," *Bol'shaya sovetskaya entsiklopediya,* 3rd ed., Moskva: Izdatel'stvo "sovetskaya entsiklopediya," vol. 12 (1973), cols. 1604-1607.

[19] A.A. Martynov, "Kommunisticheskaya partiya kitaya," *ibid.,* 2nd ed., vol. 22 (1953), pp. 200-205.

[20] James Townsend, *loc. cit.*

[21] David F. Roth and Frank L. Wilson, *The Comparative Study of Politics,* 2nd ed., Englewood Cliffs, New Jersey: Prentice-Hall, 1980, p. 336.

Responsibility of the armed forces

a) Win the civil war

In technical terms, it is the PLA, not the Red Army, which scored the final "touchdown" in the protracted struggle of the communists with the legitimate government. The name change occurred, for unknown reasons, in 1948.[22] That year marked the last leg of that struggle, and the PLA was engaged in a mopping up action.[23] To make a long story short, the government troops in Manchuria were hard pressed early in 1948. In order to relieve the pressure, a powerful armored division landed on the Liaodong peninsula. It was to fight through to Shenyang but was quickly surrounded and wiped out by the newly labeled PLA under Lin Biao. Meanwhile the garrison units of that city forced their way out to relieve the division. They met the same fate. Falling victim to the PLA were more than 500,00 men and their equipment. In January 1949, Beijing capitulated.[24] General Fu Zuoyi opened the gate of the city for the Reds. In return for his deeds, Mao Zedong offered him a portfolio in his establishment soon to be organized. From then on, the communists conducted a veritable Blitzkrieg. Nanjing, the seat of the National Government, was taken in April 1949,[25] and Shanghai fell in May.[26] Hainan Island was evacuated by the nationalist army late in April 1950.[27] Tibet was invaded by the PLA in 1951.[28] One hardly needs a better proof that political power comes from the gun barrel. Sympathetic writers should take to heart this maxim and cease asserting that the Nanjing regime lost the support of the people, as if there was a popularity contest between the two sides. In 1948-1949, province after province changed hands in a matter of weeks at the order of a governor going over to the victors.[29] Did the public have the chance to manifest their free will in making the choice? Swift military success is easily but simplistically taken to mean their gaining the people's heart. The forces of Japan, incidentally, ran over 11 provinces of China during July 1937-April 1938. Who dared to say that one half of the Chinese population loved the Japanese?

[22] Harold Hinton, p. 206; J.D. Waller, *The Government and Politics of Communist China*, London: Hutchinson University Library, 1970, p. 40. However, F.F. Liu mentions July 1946, *A Military History of China*, Princeton, New Jersey: Princeton University Press, 1956, p. 243.

[23] Nan Hui, comp., *Zhong guo renmin jie fang jun guang hui shi ji*, Hong Kong: Qiao yang chu ban she, 1970, pp. 181-197 at 190.

[24] Dork Badde, *Peking Diary, 1948-1949, a Year of Revolution*, Greenwich, Connecticut: Fawcett Publications, 1950, p. 121.

[25] Zhang Zenggao, *Zhong guo gong chan dang li shi jiang hua*, Beijing: Qing nian chu ban she, 1962, p. 270.

[26] *Di san ci guo gong nei zhan da shi yue biao*, Hong Kong: Wen hua zi liao gong ying she, 1978, p. 88.

[27] *Ibid.*, p. 100.

[28] *Renmin ribao*, July 3, 1981, p. 2, col. 4.

[29] Hu Hua, comp., *Zhong guo ge ming shi jiang hua*, Beijing: Zhong guo ren min da xue chu ban she, 1962, pp. 551-553.

b) Pacification

Although the twenty years' civil war was won, the Reds were still civil warriors, because now and then they went to action to squelch the resisting citizens.[30] For several years after 1949, the communists ruled over China not as administrators in their own country, but as conquerors of a foreign land. To facilitate the pacification, the nation was divided into six regions of martial rule, each under a commission armed with both civil and military power. This "viceroyalty" endured from the end of 1949 to the end of 1952.[31] On November 19 of the latter year, Beijing ordered civilians to take over the regions, but it was not until 1954 that armed control of the people was lifted.[32] It is generally true that regional commissioners did not employ troops in formal combat. Yet they were ordered to smash opposition of the former police or suspected persons.[33] The latter were liquidated because of their bourgeois thought or for the bare fact of owning some land. At a time when the Red militia and security networks had yet to be organized, the units under the authority of the regional administration conducted search, seizure and execution. The public were awed by their ruthlessness. The Beijing Military Commission was set up in January 1949 under the command of Ye Jianying.[34] His was a reign of terror in the capital-to-be.

During the Great Leap, troops were used to break up the mass revolts in the central Yangzi region.[35] In 1964-1965, pacification took place along the coast.[36] In the second year of the Cultural Revolution (1967), armies were kept busy suppressing the Red Guards. At that time, such cities as Beijing and Guangzhou were placed under direct armed sway, so were some provinces. Instead of loving the Red Guards as his worthy successors, Mao Zedong now dismissed them as trouble-makers. Pacification also took place in the summer of 1975.[37] There was serious labor unrest in Zhejiang. Wang Hongwen was sent there to effect a settlement by persuasion. He failed. Armed forces were rushed to that province to do the job. This decision, according to one author, was made by Deng Xiaoping, a decision which was held against him the next year.[38] In the spring and summer

[30] Jonathan R. Adelman, "The Soviet and Chinese Armies: their post-war roles," *Survey*, 24 (Winter 1979), pp. 57-81.

[31] J.D. Waller, *op. cit.*, p. 116.

[32] *Ibid.*, p. 87.

[33] Angus A. Frazer, "Military Modernization in China," *Problems of Communism*, 28 (September-December 1979), pp. 34-49.

[34] J.D. Waller, *op. cit.*, p. 91.

[35] *Ren min shou ce*, Beijing: Da gong bao, 1965, pp. 221-222.

[36] Harold Hinton, *op. cit.*, p. 197.

[37] *Ibid.*, pp. 91-99.

[38] *Ibid.*, p. 92.

of 1976, riots erupted in the industrial cities of Zhengzhou, Wuhan and Baoding, due to wage disputes and general dissatisfaction of the workers with their lot. Thanks to the PLA, peace was restored.[39] On February 27, 1977, a broadcast from Hebei province told of military intervention to crush the followers of the Gang of Four.[40]

In the minority areas, the troops went into action at one time or another. The revolt of Xinjiang in mid-1968 saw General Long Shuqing lead units from Hunan province to that region to subdue it.[41] In 1959, the PLA quelled mass uprisings in Tibet and drove the Dalai Lama and tens of thousands out of that land. As a general rule, in either minority or Han areas, armed action occurs only if the normal civil authorities were found inadequate to grapple with the situation. The infrequent uses of the PLA attest to the efficiency of the security arms of the state. Owing to the tight police surveillance and fast repression, the regular forces are spared much troubles.

c) Mobilization

This role was performed most admirably by PLA's predecessor, the Red Army, for within the various rebeldoms the commands helped the administrative cadres to coerce the able-bodied for all sorts of work, military or otherwise. The political commissars of the forces were very active in making propaganda, writing wallposters, printing flyers and putting up shows to entertain the public and soldiers. The CPR adopted the system of conscription in 1955 and this gives the PLA the responsibility to indoctrinate and train a substantial portion of the young citizenry. The regular troops are utilized to spearhead major economic and social drives. They went to the villages to organize the peasants in conjunction with land reform and with the inauguration of the commune system.[42] Needless to add, the Defense Ministry must formulate contingency plans of total or partial mobilization for war.

d) Frontier work

This includes (A) the guard against unauthorized border crossings. Such tasks keep the troops stationed between Hong Kong/Macao and Guangdong province extremely busy. Both motor boats and foot patrols are on duty day and night; and they are armed with small-caliber weapons and watchdogs. They shoot refugees like ducks. (B) In the mid-1950's, the PLA along the Burmese frontier carried on political indoctrination among the tribesmen allured from Burma in order to imbue them with communism. Broadcasting was beaming from Yunnan province in the language of the aboriginals and training centers were set up to teach them guerilla technique. (C) Toward

[39] *Keesing's*, December 16, 1977, p. 28718, col. 2.

[40] *Ibid.*

[41] Harold Hinton, *op. cit.*, p. 274.

[42] J.D. Waller, *op. cit.*, p. 115.

the end of the 1950's, Chinese troops were engaged in road construction on territories claimed by adjacent countries. The most notable is the building of military highways leading to the Pakistan-held Kashmir, the Aksai Chin area, Nepal and northern Laos. This activity has the purposes of defense and communication.[43] It does not appear to be motivated by offensive strategy.

e) Politicizing and revolutionizing

During the social-education movement and the ensuing Cultural Revolution, Mao Zedong sought to remake the people in his image, that is, one of a devout revolutionary. To this end, he set the PLA to be the exemplar for them in 1963.[44] The slogan is "to learn from the army." Orders were issued by him to organize departments in all institutions whatsoever to teach politics. It was only logical that the PLA supplied the instructors. In this way, China would remain a Marxist system after he departed from the scene. The crusade had many stout soldiers abroad. In one of the universities of an English-speaking country, a professor of Chinese stock diligently transmitted Mao's message on a TV network for several months. It was not, however, more than a decade later that the legislators of that country criticized the TV authorities for not identifying that man as a Maoist. The PLA has operated radio and publishing services and this makes it an effective tool to keep the masses cognizant of the stand of the leadership and to convey to them the necessary directives. Due to such effort, millions upon millions of uniformed men and masses are fully politicized.

f) Production

Throughout its history, the PLA finds itself doing a sort of moonlighting. After gaining the victory in 1949, the CCP thought of either demobilization or keeping the troops but putting them to work.[45] The latter idea proved attractive to its leaders. Some of the explanations are: a) the Red Army and the PLA are always made up of soldier-peasants, and therefore, agricultural chore is familiar to them,[46] b) the manpower of several millions should not be let idle when they no longer have formidable enemy to fight, c) they are a financial burden to the state, over 10 percent of the GNP being spent to keep them.[47] Their productive labour may well be turned into good use so as to defray the cost. d) To set them to work can improve the civilian-

[43] Harvey Nelson, "Regional and paramilitary ground forces," *The Military and Political Power in China in the 1970's*, pp. 135-152 at 149-150.

[44] Sam C. Sarkesian and James H. Buck, *Comparative politics, an introduction*, Sherman Oaks, California: Alfred Pub. Co., 1979, p. 263, col. 2.

[45] Angus M. Frazer, *op. cit.*, pp. 23-24.

[46] Ai-li Chin, "Value themes in short stories, 1976-1977," *Moving a Mountain, Cultural Change in China*, edited by Godwin C. Chu, and Francis L.K. Hau, Honolulu: University of Hawaii Press, 1979, pp. 27-56 at 49.

[47] *Countries of the World*. Toronto: Coles Pub. Co., 1980, section on China, p. 8.

military relations whether on the farm or in the factory.[48]

The assignment of production work did not start in earnest until after the cessation of the Korean war. In 1956-1958, the instituting of the rural commune and the Great Leap aimed at the mobilization of the entire population made it necessary to call the soldiers for help in such things like dam construction, factory work, harvesting and sowing, deforesting, flood control, canalization, earth moving, road paving, grain milling, repairment of dikes, and fertilizer making.[49] In 1958, the total manhours donated by officers and men were 59 million.[50] When they were not helping with farm work, they grew vegetables, raised hogs, and made simple instruments for themselves. Except weapons and ammunition, the units were completely self-sufficient, costing the government practically nothing for their maintenance. A number of state farms were run by the troops stationed nearby.[51] Slack a little after 1959, the work participation resurged during the campaign of social education and Cultural Revolution. There was now the added reason that the PLA was to serve as a model for the people of China. Again, nothing was heard of work assignments until the mid-1970's. It was stated that in July 1975 the regime sent 200,000 troops to factories to assist with the production which was stalled due to the disturbance of the bourgeois elements.[52] When a drought developed early in 1977, the PLA units were ordered on March 22 to support the local effort of combating the calamities. The airforce and artillery went into shelling and bombing action in order to bring about artificial rainfall.[53] The armed forces also did production work in friendly nations. In 1965, they laid out roads for the government of Nepal and Laos.[54] The engineering troops numbering 50,000 repaired the bombed out rails in Vietnam during the late sixties and early seventies.

g) Deterrent

The PLA purports to be the CCP's armory against formerly the US, and now the USSR. In the past four years, the first country became, in the Chinese press, a peace lover, but the second an international criminal. China used to declare that if the imperialists dare to attack her, she would fight a people's war to the last man. The outside world was served the warning by Beijing that she would retaliate and carry the war into the enemy's territory if need be. The phrase "a war

[48] J.D. Waller, op. cit., p. 115.

[49] James D. Seymour, China, the Politics of Revolutionary Integration, New York: Thomas Crowell, 1976, p. 123.

[50] Sam C. Sarkesian and James H. Buck, op. cit., p. 265, col. 2.

[51] Economic intelligence unit, "China: The national economy," New Encyclopedia Americana, Chicago: Encyclopedia Americana, 1979, vol. 4, pp. 276-277 at 277, col. 1.

[52] Encyclopedia Yearbook, 1976, p. 115, col. 1.

[53] Keesing's, December 16, 1977, p. 28727, col. 1.

[54] John A. Harrison, China Since 1800, p. 238.

without boundaries" appeared in the Chinese propaganda during 1965 when the Vietnam war just began escalating.[55] China's nuclear capacity grows ever mightier and puts teeth in the deterrent policy. It is somewhat of a phenomenon that as her retaliatory muscle waxes sturdier, the threat of using it is less brandished. In May 1980, Hua Guofeng said in Tokyo that the CPR would not be the first country to hurl an atomic bomb onto others. Does a sense of responsibility come with the increase of the power of destruction?

h) Forward defense

From 1949 to 1981, the Chinese army struck out from the CPR territory 10 times.[56] Five of them can be considered as major; and in point of time, they are evenly distributed: 1950, 1956, 1962, 1974, 1979. The so-called volunteers in the Korean war of 1950-1953 were PLA regulars under the supreme command of, first, Lin Biao and after his being wounded, Peng Dehuai. The two were communist generals of long standing. The decision to militarily aid North Korea can only be explained by Beijing's concern, unnecessary we must add, with the territorial integrity of China. The UN forces never intended to touch Manchuria, but the threat of Douglas McArthur precipitated Beijing into action. As is generally agreed, the action cannot easily lend support to the assertion that the CPR was intrinsically aggressive. It is described by most scholars as defensive in nature.[57] The same holds with Chinese thrust into an area on the Sino-Indian border in 1962 (and a similar but smaller act in 1959). The area, in fact, was never determined to be India's. Western press, it is only fair to argue for the CPR, cried out loudly but wrongly about the "Chinese invasion." They already presumed India's sovereignty in the disputed place. In both instances Chinese troops broke the engagement and left.

Another forward defense occurred in 1956. The Chinese intrusion into Burma's Kachin province was for the main purpose of putting pressure on the Rangoon authority to ensure that no arms move through there to the Khamba guerillas in east Tibet.[58] In reality, the Chinese have refrained from launching punitive onslaughts against them in spite of their seeking refuge in north Nepal since 1959. It is from there that the Khambas made sorties into Tibet. The next defense was undertaken on January 20, 1974 to recover what the CPR elected to call its territory, the Parcacels and Spratly islands, 280 km southeast of Hainan. Although the operation was short, it took the form of a triphibian attack on a handful of south Vietnamese.[59]

---

[55] Y. Semyonov, "Beijing's policy constitutes a military threat," *International Affairs* (Moscow), April 1979, pp. 64-74.

[56] Angus M. Frazer, *op. cit.*, pp. 33-38; Harold Hinton, *op. cit.*, p. 211.

[57] Angus M. Frazer, *The People's Liberation Army, Communist China's Armed Forces*, New York: Crane Russak, 1973, pp. 56-57.

[58] Harold Hinton, *op. cit.*, p. 198.

[59] *Encyclopedia Yearbook*, 1975, p. 164, col. 2.

China officially annexed the islets on January 30, 1980 by proclaiming sovereignty over them.[60] The Vietnamese apparently did not concede to the CPR's claims. Now and then, they attempted to assert their authority. In February 1980, Beijing reaffirmed its rights to the islets.[61] In July 1980, it warned Hanoi and the Soviets to keep hands off them when they sent teams to explore oil resources there. The latest assertion of Chinese sovereignty was made in September, 1983 *(Beijing review,* September 26, 1983, p. 8.)

The first and final major operation took place in north Vietnam on February 17, 1979. The Chinese troops withdrew on March 5.[62] From the very beginning of the campaign, Beijing stated that it would be limited in scope, purported to teach Vietnam a lesson and to scourge her for the alleged invasion of Yunnan province and for the offensive war in Kampuchea. On the day the Chinese armies were withdrawn, the mouthpiece of Beijing declared that "having attained the goal in self-defense counterattack against the aggressors," the Chinese evacuated the enemy territory.[63]

i) Foreign aid

The PLA has ministered military assistance to others in the manner of arms or training. Throughout the years, the beneficiaries have been North Korea, Vietnam, Pakistan, Tanzania and Albania. Receiving similar type of help are many guerillas fighting imperialism. With them, Beijing regarded itself as forming a united front. In Asia, the Chinese aid went to insurgents in Vietnam (south), Laos, Kampuchea, Malaysia, the Philippines, Indonesia, Burma and Thailand. Besides, Beijing sent materiel to the Arab groups operating in Palestine and along the Persian Gulf, to mobile forces acting in South Africa, Angola and Mozambique. Although the high policy was decided by the Politburo, the PLA was to assess the needs in each case, dispatch the military hardware, provide instructors, print propaganda circulars, do the broadcasts and arrange liaison with the recipients. This kind of activity has abated considerably after 1976.

j) Taiwan liberation

This objective is placed in the 1978 and 1982 Constitutions. It was repeated times without end by the CCP oligarchs. Peng Chen, Politburo man, spoke of it in an address to the 5th session of the 5th NPC on November 26, 1982.[64] However, less frequently was the PLA ordered to get ready for an attack. Back in 1950, it is to be recalled, the communist troops were prepared for landing on Taiwan. Save

---

[60] *Facts on File,* February 1980, p. 132, C3.

[61] *Beijing Review,* February 18, 1980, pp. 15-24.

[62] *Britannica Book of the Year,* 1980, p. 249, col. 1.

[63] Angus M. Frazer, "Military modernization in China," pp. 39-40.

[64] "Report on the draft of the revised constitution of the People's Republic of China," *Beijing review,* December 13, 1982, pp. 9-23 at 20, col. 2.

for the Korean war which compelled President Truman to defend it, they may well have taken it. Now the problem is whether the PLA can accomplish the task so solemnly entrusted to it. After January 1, 1979, the US was legally not committed to the aid of Taiwan if the CPR is to conquer it. Many authors concur that that country is much superior in military power. Yet the PLA, according to experts, has no capability of conducting an amphibian action across a channel of 150 km. One of the important factors is that the US still provides some defensive means to the government of Taiwan. Until further change of balance of strength between the CPR and that government occurs, the insular regime does not have much to fear.

The command structure

The supreme direction, according to Article 93, par. 1 of the Constitution, is vested in the Central Military Commission. Although par. 3 does not explicitly say so, the chairman of this commission is the c-in-c. On the party side, there is the Military Commission (CCP Statute, Article 21, par. 5). Under the Central Military Commission is the defense minister (Zhang Aiping), and under him are echeloned the general chief of staff (Yang Dezhi), the general logistics command (Hong Xuezhi), and the general political commissariat (Yu Qiuli). There is no command of land army as such. Presumably it is invested in the chairman of the Central Military Commission. In the field the PLA units are headquartered in Shengyang, Beijing (including garrison there and Tianjin garrison), Jinan, Nanjing (including Shanghai garrison), Fuzhou, Guangzhou, Wuhan, Chengdu, Kunming, Lanzhou and Urumqi. Each group of units has a commander, from one to five deputy commanders, one first political commissar, one or two deputy political commissars.

Within the General Staff there are three departments: armament, signal, military training.[65] The General Political Department also has three departments: propaganda, culture and mass work. There is only one department, that of public health, under the General Logistics Department. The PLA Navy is staffed by 1 commander, 1 first deputy commander and 5 (plain) deputy commanders. Besides, there is 1 first political commissar and 1 (plain) political commissar. The navy has three fleets called North, East and South China Sea Fleets.[66] The PLA Air Force is under 1 commander (no first deputy commander), 7 deputy commanders, 1 political commissar and 3 deputy political commissars. There are six service bodies for the ground force:

PLA Artillery
2nd Artillery
Armored Force
Railway Corps
Capital Construction-Engineering Corps
Engineering Corps

---

[65] All the following information appears in *Zhong guo shou ce*, pp. 303-312.

[66] *Ibid.*, p. 307 mentions only the first two fleets, however.

The above, interestingly enough, do not include missile or strategic corps. There is the speculation among scholars that the 2nd Artillery is a nickname for it.[67] In the State Council (see Chapter VI), the reader is reminded, there is a ministry of weaponry. Here we have a camouflaged arm. There are, in addition, ten auxiliary organizations:
Science and Technology Commission for National Defense
Office of National Defense Industry
Military Academy
Academy of Military Science
PLA Political Academy
Command College of the PLA Navy
PLA General Hospital
PLA Arts College
PLA Army Men's Association
Liberation Army Daily

China is divided into eleven military regions, each named after the city where the regional command has its headquarters. Subordinate to them are 26 military districts, each named after the province or autonomous region it controls. The number of regions was reduced from the previous twelve, but that of districts increased from 24 in 1964 to the present 26 after the Cultural Revolution. Neimeng and Tibet used to be military regions, but demoted to districts in 1969 and 1972 respectively.[68] Apart from regions and districts, there are three garrisons of Beijing, Tianjin and Shanghai. The divisions are like this:

Regions	Districts	Garrisons
Wuhan	Henan	Beijing
	Hubei	Tianjin
Urumqi	Xinjiang	Shanghai
Shenyang	Heilongjiang	
	Jilin	
	Liaoning	
Beijing	Hebei	
	Neimeng	
	Shaanxi	
Lanzhou	Gansu	
	Ningxia	
	Shanxi	
	Qinghai	
Kunming	Guizhou	
	Yunnan	
Fuzhou	Fujian	
	Jiangxi	
Chengdu	Sichuan	
	Tibet	

---

[67] James Townsend, *Politics in China*, p. 92. Harold Hinton, *op. cit.*, pp. 274-275.

[68] James Townsend, *Politics in China*, p. 92n; Harold Hinton, *op. cit.*, p. 274.

Guangzhou . . . . Hunan
                                    Guangxi
                                    Guangdong
Nanjing . . . . Anhui
                                    Zhejiang
                                    Jiangsu
Jinan . . . . Shandong

The need for special garrisons of the three cities indicates the kind of concern of the Beijing oligarchy with the aggregated millions there. What would happen, they may be asking themselves, if popular uprising should erupt in those metropolises? Neimeng and Tibet, as just said, were regions. Obviously because they are sensitive areas, the CCP decided to bring them under the regional commands of Beijing and Chengdu respectively. The military-district setup is a successor to the system of regional commissions which had both civil and military authority when created in 1949. Five years later, the system was abolished, with civil power either transferred to the provinces or recentralized, but military control was left to the troop commands located throughout the country. The current arrangement harked back to the reorganization effected in 1954-1955. The heads of the regions and districts are all top professionals. Presently, two of the 11 regional commanders, namely Li Desheng (Shenyang area, a full member), Qin Jiwei (Beijing area, a candidate) are in the Politburo. And all district commanders are in the CC.

All regions are approximatley equal in size,[69] with the exception of Jinan, which for unstated reasons has one district in it only. The region facing Taiwan embraces Fujian and Jiangxi, instead of Fujian, Guangdong and Zhejiang. The latter grouping would perhaps pose a wide marine front toward Taiwan, but have a shallow hinterland.[70] The current arrangement is apparently intended to construct an in-depth defense.[71] All military districts are coterminous with the provinces whose boundaries date back to the Tang dynasty (618-906 A.D.) Do these boundaries meet the needs today? This is a moot question. The concept of the so-called people's war implies alluring the foe and fighting him on one's familiar homeland.[72] The regions or districts are to serve as combat zones. One final comment is that the pairing of provinces is not new. Under the Manzhou, every two provinces formed a Zundu, but unlike the communist system, the Zundu was not for the single purpose of armed control. The Nanjing government did away with the Zundu and in fact none of the warlords during 1927-1949 lived on the fat of more than one province. The

[69] Harold Hinton, op. cit., p. 223.

[70] Gerard H. Corr, The Chinese Red Army, Campaigns and Politics since 1949, New York: Schocken Books, 1974, pp. 159-160.

[71] Harold Hinton, op. cit., pp. 199, 205.

[72] J.D. Waller, op. cit., pp. 124-125.

Reds' nostalgia, en passant, is also manifesting in the restoration of the prefectures of the Qing dynasty, although they set them up for the minorities alone, but not for the Han. Article 19 of the 1978 Constitution says that "our armed forces are a combination of the field armies, the regional forces and the militia." Although one may not argue that both navy and airforce have no constitutional standing, the quoted phrase does point to the principal interest of the Chinese communists in foot soldiers. The mention of field armies is an anachronism. Such armies, five in number, existed from February 1949 to December 1954.[73] They consisted of sizeable surrenderers of Nanjing and independent provincial forces. When field armies were found cumbersome by the Reds, they were replaced with a system of army corps which are the highest organization (a former field army had several of these). We doubt very much if the draftsmen of the 1978 Constitution ever consulted the military staff regarding the term "field armies." However, we are sure that those of the 1982 Constitution did consult it, because the term is no longer used.

Presently the Chinese main force is directly under the General Chief of Staff in Beijing; and it is to be distinguished from the regional force.[74] The latter comes under the 11 military regions and 26 military districts mentioned above. The main force has two-thirds of the military strength and is stationed in each province and autonomous region. The bulk of it is found on the northern border confronting the Soviet army, where the PLA carried out a much propagandized maneuver in the fall of 1981.[75] A sizeable body of troops is located in Fujian and Yunnan facing the Nationalists and the Vietnamese respectively. It has been surmised that a little less than 1/3 of the army, most of the air force and about a third of the navy are placed under Shenyang and Beijing regions.[76] They are to mount an assault "beyond the gates" of China, if need be.[77] On the other hand, the regional force is to fulfil the task of putting down riots, assuring frontier security, providing for local protection and serving as reserve pool for the main force.[78] Under the regional command is also the direction of the militia and of the so-called production and construction corps. These operate principally in Xinjiang region and Yunnan province.[79] They are estimated to be 4 million strong,[80] and are engaged in factory work, road building, land reclamation and farming.

---

[73] Harold Hinton, op. cit., pp. 206, 207, 214.

[74] Kenneth R. Whiting, The Chinese Communist Armed Forces, Maxwell Air Force Base, Alabama: Air University Institute for Professional Development, 1974, pp. 74-79.

[75] Renmin ribao, September 27, 1981, p. 1. The troops involved are those under the Beijing military region.

[76] Keesing's, December 16, 1977, p. 28726 (55 of the estimated 136 divisions).

[77] J.D. Waller, op. cit., p. 126; James Townsend, loc. cit.

[78] James Townsend, loc. cit.

[79] Hungdah Chiu, "Criminal punishment in mainland China: A study of some Yunnan province documents," The Journal of Criminal Law and Criminology, no. 3, 1977, pp. 374-396 at 396, col. 1.

[80] Statesman's Yearbook, 1979-1980, p. 337.

The militia mentioned in Article 19 of the 1978 Constitution is no longer classified by the 1982 Constitution as a military establishment, because Article 29, par. 1 makes the militia and the military two separate bodies. The policy of revolutionization, regularization and modernization is specifically aimed at the military (par. 2). The militia has a great deal of historical import, harking back to agrarian revolt of the Jiangxi and Yanan days. When the Red Army engaged the government troops, the militia fulfilled the duty of garrison to ward off attacks and to defend the villages. On their part, the government troops had to do both attack and defense.[81] During the Korean war, the militia was expanded because the PLA depended on it as a source of recruitment. Afterwards it suffered a decline only to be revitalized in the Leap of 1957. The size of the militia rose from 22 million to a whopping 220 million from 1953 to 1958. With the retreat of the Leap in 1959, it was shrinking. In 1964, its strength was about 10 million. Then it received fresh momentum in the Cultural Revolution, thanks to the policy of making "everyone a soldier." The advocates of militia, Lin Biao and the Gang of Four, assigned it four tasks: a) assist the PLA regulars in repelling foreign aggressors, b) help maintain social discipline as an auxiliary police and a public security arm, c) serve as the ultimate recruiting source for the PLA (citizen soldiery makes up the reserve of the regional force, and the regional force makes up the reserve of the PLA), d) assure the absolute safety of the communist regime. In the pre-1949 days, the National Government organized no militia. When its forces were defeated in major campaigns which always took place in and around large cities, the Reds just walked in to take control of the countryside. They met with no resistance whatsoever. Now the communists came to learn a great lesson. For them, it is a must to arm the villagers. Even if the PLA units were compelled to evacuate a city in a war, they figure, the militia can hold on.

The militia idea does not go without opposition among the Beijing leaders.[82] First, the Defense Minister Peng Dehuai in 1958 and then the General Chief of Staff, Luo Ruiqing ten years later, did not support it.[83] Both were persuaded that the scheme was a waste of time, that amateur police were not much of a fighter, and that resources otherwise needed for modernization of the regulars were spent for nothing. In their view, the most objectionable part of the militia related to people's war. This kind of war was, they felt, obsolete and dangerous to the CPR. It relied on ancient tactics and made use of outmoded means; and to let the enemy march in before destroying him would result in tremendous damage to the country.[84]

---

[81] Franz H. Michael and George E. Taylor, *The Far East in the Modern World*, rev. ed., New York: Holt, Rinehart and Winston, 1964, p. 447.

[82] Gerard H. Corr, *op. cit.*, pp. 162-163.

[83] Robert Trumbull, *This is Communist China*, New York: David McKay, 1968, pp. 217-220.

[84] J.D. Waller, *op. cit.*, p. 126.

Propounded by Mao Zedong, the organization of civilian troops was pushed hard by the radicals. According to the charges leveled against them, they controlled most of the militia. The trial of ten in November 1980-January 1981 revealed that the defendants used them to stage a coup d'état in Shanghai.[85] The present leaders have jettisoned the people's war completely, but the militia system is retained along with the regional force. There are three species of militia. First there are the armed militia, *wu zhuang min bing,* numbering between 7 and 9 million.[86] Regularly drilled and provided with fairly modern weapons, they can be converted into combat units and made part of the PLA at once. Unarmed and getting less training are the approximately 100 million common militia, *pu tong min bing.* In between there are 15-20 million basic milita, *ji ben min bing.* These are given some training, and like the common militia, they have no arms. As in military service, the enlisting in militia is described in Article 55, par. 1 as the "honorable duty of citizens." People can join it without having to leave their employment or study. They are, however, subject to summons for military lessons from time to time. With respect to armed militia, the drilling is a weekly routine. Instructors come from the nearby PLA units. The voluntary age ranges from 18 to 50.[87] Both sexes are acceptable. Due to the more than one billion population, even the common militia (100 million) constitutes only 10% of the total.

Strength

Army is by far the most important of the several kinds of the PLA units. The communist leaders rose to power through battlefield victory. That power truly derives from the gun barrel, and it is to be maintained by it too. It is no surprise that Article 19 of the 1978 Constitution says that "the state devotes major efforts to the revolutionization and modernization of the PLA." The same is repeated in Article 29, par. 2 of the 1982 Constitution which adds "regularization." There is no sure way to assess the degree of all these endeavors, particularly modernization,[88] but an attempt will be made in this section to give an estimate, necessarily rough, of the nuclear strength and sizes of the principal branches of the forces.

The PLA reached its peak size in 1950. At that time, it was in the neighborhood of 5 million, expanding considerably by the flocking in of the capitulating forces of the Nationalist regime.[89] Although there

[85] *Beijing review,* February 2, 1981, p. 21, col. 1.

[86] *Statesman's Yearbook,* 1979-1980, p. 337; *Countries of the World,* p. 8, col. 2. *Renmin ribao,* April 6, 1983, p. 1 mentions armed police combining militia and voluntary soldiers.

[87] John A. Harrison, *op. cit.,* p. 233.

[88] Leo Yueh-yun Liu, "The modernization of the Chinese military," *Current History,* 79 (September 1980), pp. 9-13; Thomas A. Mark, "Two Chinese roads to military modernization," *Strategic Review* (Summer 1980), pp. 18-28.

[89] *Renmin ribao,* July 3, 1981, p. 2, col. 4 mentions the elimination of 8,004,000 troops by the Reds from July 1946 to June 1950. They must also include the capitulationists.

is no exact figure of such forces, they may well number 1 million, of which half were in Manchuria, 300,000 in north China (under Fu Zuoyi) and 200,000 in central China (under Cheng Qian and Chen Mingren). Nearly all of them were "volunteered" by Beijing to fight in Korea, because of their better weapons than the PLA's and of their doubtful loyalty to it. The latter point was proved by the refusal of 2/3 of the CPR's POWs to repatriate after the cessation of hostility in Korea in 1953.[90] Mobilization proceeded fast from that year on. By 1955, Beijing felt it necessary to introduce the draft system, imposed upon the 18-year olds to replenish the ranks.[91] The law fixed the service years of the army, airforce and navy at 3, 4 and 5 respectively. After the Cultural Revolution, these were reduced each by one year. On March 7, 1978, the NPC Standing Committee issued a decree restoring the 3-4-5 scheme in order to "modernize" them.[92] The communists wanted to assure the "continuous development of our army's technical equipment" by placing "higher demands on the fighters' military and political quality and their technical standards."[93] The prolonging of the service years is not expected to augment the size of the forces. China can only take a few percentile of the eligible draftees because of their big number.

The army is divided into main and local forces. The former, administered by the military regions but commanded by the Defense Ministry, are available for operation anywhere and are better equipped, but the latter concentrate on the defense of their own areas. The size of the forces is given differently from source to source. Most publications place it at 4,325,000.[94] This is mighty close to the official figure of 4,238,000.[95] The component army, navy and air formations are also variously estimated. All recent statistics never go down to 3,000,000 for the army.[96] This branch includes the just-stated main and local forces, the latter sharing about one-third of the total.[97] There are, according to one source, 261 divisions. Among these are 40 artillery, 12 armored, 121 infantry, 3 airborne and 70 local divisions.[98] Regarding personnel, an armored division consists of about 10,000 men and 270 tanks; a mechanized division, 12,000 men and 30 tanks; an airborne division, 9,000 men.[99] This source does not mention the un-mechanized divisions which may, according to one study, have

[90] Harold Hinton, op. cit., p. 212.

[91] Keesing's, September 8, 1978, p. 29196, col. 1.

[92] Ibid.

[93] Ibid.

[94] World almanac, 1981, p. 525, col. 1.

[95] Beijing review, November 8, 1982, p. 21.

[96] James Townsend, loc. cit.; Countries of the World, loc. cit. Statesman's Yearbook, 1979-1980, p. 337; Financial Times, September 14, 1977, cited in Keesing's, December 16, 1977, p. 28726, col. 1.

[97] James Townsend, loc. cit.

[98] All the following statistics, unless otherwise indicated, derive from the Financial Times, loc. cit.

[99] Information Please, 1979, p. 392.

each 15,000 men.[100] In addition, there are the para-PLA forces of 300,000 security troops, 4,000,000-man production and construction corps (referred to above), and 300,000 military police.[101] There are 67 military colleges of various sorts.[102] At least two works consider the Chinese navy as "the world's third largest.[103] Probably they mean the number of craft, but not the strength or armament. The CPR's navy is a coast defense formation, very much an adjunct of the local militia as viewed by one writer.[104] From 1960 to 1972, it is reported, the construction program which was initiated as early as 1954 was expedited, especially in the modernization of the navy yards and port facilities. Since 1972 the tempo slackened, probably due to difficulties in getting materials and naval architects. It may even be impacted by political decisions shifting the priority to land armies. The present naval composition is as follows:[105]

900	coast and river defense craft	25	fast patrol craft
470	landing craft	25	oilers
380	fast gunboats	25	survey and research ships
280	fast torpedo boats	23	ocean minesweepers
200	missile boats	20	large patrol boats
120	coast patrol craft	16	frigates
100	conventional subs	12	destroyers
80	mine warfare craft	12	patrol escorts
40	supply ships	6	boom defense vessels
40	tugs	2	nuclear subs
37	landing ships	2	repair ships
		1	sub with ballistic missile tubes

Active personnel in 1983 are more than 300,000, including 28,000 marines and 30,000 naval airpilots.[106].

The CPR has only half a dozen naval bases. They are, in descending order of importance, Qingdao (one-time US base), Lu Shun (Hq. North Sea Fleet), Shanghai, Zhoushan (Hq. East Sea Fleet), Huangpu, Zhanjiang (Hq. South Sea Fleet). The navy's airforce has more than 700 aircraft including MiG-19 and MiG-21 fighters, 150 IL-28 torpedo bombers, Madge flying boats, Hound M14 helicopters and communications and transport aircraft. It is worth mentioning that the communists constructed their navy almost from scratch. While the

[100] J.D. Waller, op. cit., p. 112.

[101] Statesman's Yearbook, 1982-1983, p. 348.

[102] John A. Harrison, op. cit., p. 233.

[103] World Almanac, 1981, p. 526, col. 1; Countries of the World, loc. cit.

[104] John A. Harrison, op. cit., p. 233.

[105] Statesman's Yearbook, 1982-1983, pp. 348-349.

[106] Ibid., see also Financial Times, loc. cit.; Angus M. Frazer, People's Liberation Army, pp. 7-8.

Nationalist regime had some aeronautics industry and training facilities, its naval establishment was negligible. In February 1949, two battleships and in the following April, some craft of the second fleet of the National Government defected to the Reds.[107] They were their nuclear sea power.

Compared to the navy of the USSR or that of the US, China's is a laughing affair.[108] Her fleet is bound to limit its activity to the immediate vicinity of the coast, not far out from the continental shelf.[109] Efficient enough to shoot the freedom seekers swimming to Hong Kong, it is no good to fight a battle. The CPR's slow development of a navy is thought to have been caused by her seeing no Soviet threat from the waterfront.[110] The inability of her fleet to stage an amphibian operation against the tiny Taiwan and the restriction of it to self-defense has, we suppose assured peace in that region. Because the buildup of a navy is a long process and involves the highest technology, the communists have far to go before they can come up with anything deserving the name of a modern navy. In November 1981, the CPR launched a nuclear submarine, but its full operation is believed to be three years away.[111]

Thanks to missiles and the delivery system (see below), the CPR's "space army" (Chinese term for airforce) fairs better than the navy. Prior to the USSR withdrawing the industrial assistance in 1960, it grew rapidly. During the Korean War, the Soviet Union provided Beijing with an unspecified number of planes which, however, were not flown to challenge the UN airpower or even to assist the infantry in action. Major efforts, stimulated no doubt by the fear of the counter-attack seen to be likely by the National Government from Taiwan, were exerted to construct the branch of arms in which that government still held superiority. Up to 1956, the support of the Soviets to Beijing was both sincere and gigantic in this as well as in all other departments. China had between 2,000 and 2,500 planes by 1960, and they were of the MiG-15, -17 and -19 series.[112] It was the Russian help which made this possible.

A fatal blow was dealt to the CPR by the refusal by the Soviets of further help in 1960. Short of aviation fuel and spare parts, nearly all the planes were grounded. "What kind of airforce is it if the machines cannot fly?" exclaimed a Chinese airman.[113] The betrayal

[107] *Zhong hua ren min gong he guo kai guo wen xian*, Hong Kong: Wen hua zi liao gong ying she, 1978, p. 220.

[108] Donald C. Daniel, "Sino-Soviet relations in naval perspective," *Orbis*, 24 (Winter 1981), pp. 787-803.

[109] Gerard H. Corr, *op. cit.*, pp. 163, 164; Kenneth R. Whiting, *op. cit.*, pp. 79-80.

[110] *Financial Times, loc. cit.*

[111] CBC Broadcast of November 5, 1981, quoting the journal *Combat Fleet*.

[112] Franz J. Moglis, "The role of the Chinese communist air force in the 1970's," *The Military and Political Power in China in the 1970's*, pp. 253-266.

[113] Bernard Brodie, *Escalation and the Nuclear Option*, Princeton, New Jersey: Princeton University Press, 1966, pp. 40, 41, 44.

by the older brother now left the younger brother with no alternative but to rely upon himself.[114] A crash program was set in motion to solve the fuel problem and top priority was placed on aviation technology. By 1964, the number of planes which could be flown reached 2,500 after about 500 of the unflyables went into mothballs. The planes were copied from the MiG-17 and -19 types. However, the usable bombers numbered only about 100. At that time (1964), the CCP planned to skip the man-bomber stage and it undertook the development of the missile system for the nuclear bomb ready to be exploded. During the turmoil of the Cultural Revolution, China's nuclear schedule suffered very little, as did her aeronautics industry, because as said elsewhere in this book, Zhou Enlai demanded from the fanatics the promise that scientists be unharassed. That they were indeed left alone is proved by the detonation of atomic bombs in 1966-1969.[115] Meanwhile, the airforce was supplied with a large number of machines, although their quality may not be excellent in comparison with the product of the superpowers.

The CPR possessed, as of 1983, 5,300 front-line planes.[116] They are organized into over 100 regiments of jet-fighters and about 12 regiments of tactical bombers. In addition, there are reconnaissance, transport and helicopter formations. Each regiment consists of 3 to 4 squadrons. Each of the latter is made up of 12 planes, and 3 regiments make a division. Regarding the type of craft, there are 250 J-7 (MiG-21), 3,000 J-6 (MiG-19) and 300 (MiG-17) home-defense interceptors, about 450 H-5 (IL-28) jet-bombers, nearly 100 H-6 Chinese-built copies of the Soviet Tu-16 twin-jet strategic bomber, and a few piston-engined Tu-4 (Soviet type of Boeing B-29) strategic bombers plus a growing number of Q-5 twin-jet fighter-bombers, evolved from the MiG-19. Transport aircraft include about 300 Y-5 (An-2), Y-8 (An-12), An-24/26, 100 Li-2, 30 IL-14, 10 IL-18 and a few three-turbofan Trident fixed-wing types, plus 300 Mi-4 and Mi-8 helicopters and 13 French-built Super Frelon heavy transport helicopters. The MiG fighters and Antonov transports have been manufactured in the CPR, initially under license, and other types have been assembled there, including several hundred JT-5 (2-seat MiG-17) trainees. Air personnel were 490,000 in 1983, of which 200,000 belonged to the air defense organizations.

In assessing the capability of a nation's military hardware, emphasis should not be placed on the quantitative dimension. It is true that the Chinese inherit from the Russians a sense of sheer mass. The latter's doctrine of "large number"[117] became the former's mass-line. Both mean the more the better. As time goes by, however, the Chinese

[114] Harold Hinton, op. cit., p. 211.

[115] J.D. Waller, op. cit., p. 121.

[116] Statesman's Yearbook, 1982-1983, p. 349 provides the following figures.

[117] Ts. A. Yampol'skaya, Social Organization in the Soviet Union, Political and Legal Organizational Aspects, Moscow: Progress Publishers, 1975, p. 162, note 1.

have come to modify the stand. Witness a statement in the *Jie fang jun bao* of October 1, 1977 that "quantitative quota [of arms] must be fulfilled, but quality is even more important."[118] In the face of the USSR challenge, the Chinese regime knows where its shortcomings lie. According to the CIA testimony before the US Congress which was released on August 16, 1977, China's military set-up was heavily imprinted with the Soviet mold of the 1950's, and in most weapons, it was 15 to 20 years behind the USSR.[119] Another source says that the Chinese arms were seriously lacking, that there were only an estimated 10,000 tanks patterned after the Russian make and that most of the artillery pieces were antique.[120] Lastly, majority of the planes were dated and the navy was very poor. Now the US seems to be quite willing to help China out in this regard. In January 1980, the US defense secretary, Harold Brown, went to the CPR and took a good look at the facilities of the PLA. It was announced, upon his return, that the Carter Administration would send to China military transport and communication means. The Chinese vice-premier, Geng Biao visited Washington in mid-1980 and asked the US Government to supply auxiliary facilities to the PLA. There began the real attempt to bring the armed forces of the CPR up-to-date. The Reagan Administration declared that it did not rule out the possibility of selling quality weapons to China in light of the Soviet misbehavior in Afghanistan and elsewhere in the world.[121] From mid-1981, China began to acquire these weapons.

Nuclear buildup

In May 1965, the *Military review* carried an article on the "progress of nuclear weapons in communist China."[122] In it the author, a Sinologist with specialty in economy, stated that "the Chinese communists have given priority to the nuclear weapons program, but continuing development would be limited if the general economic condition does not show substantial improvement." Hindsight, however, shows that the first part of the assertion is correct, but the second falls flat. Throughout the years, the Chinese economy kept worsening, but her missile and nuclear strength is growing. Rather than use the scarce resources to improve the people's livelihood, the oligarchy is hellbent toward the manufacturing of extreme arms. The problem involves the simple policy-option. In both the USSR and the CPR, it weighs heavily, if not exclusively, on guns, but not on butter! We have here a fallacy. Socialist economy placing the means of production in the hands of the public and abolishing the exploitation

118 *Keesing's,* December 16, 1977, p. 28726, col. 2.

119 *Hammond,* 1981, p. 548, col. 2.

120 *Financial Times, loc. cit.*

121 *Time,* June 29, 1981, p. 12, col. 3.

122 Cheng Chu-yuan, "Progress of nuclear weapons in communist China," reprinted in *Government of Communist China,* edited by George P. Jan, San Francisco: Chandler Pub. Co., 1966, pp. 543-550 at 550.

of man by man does not assure welfare and happiness. In Russia and, to a much greater extent, in China, there coexist a primitive consumer industry and an ultra-modern military enterprise.[123] The two countries are both developed and undeveloped. The CPR's nuclear program, leveled at the two superpowers and purported to exert its influence in Asia,[124] began as early as 1953 according to the afore mentioned Sinologist.[125] An effort of twelve years, from that year to the testing of an A-bomb on October 16, 1964, should have been sufficient for any nation, be it a Mexico or a Lebanon, to produce some horrible things, given a lavish funding, an obdurate heart of the rulers to the hardship of people and a banning on critical press. Beijing's first nuclear step was the organizing of an Atomic Energy Commission within the Academy of Sciences. This was followed by a Sino-Soviet agreement of April 1955 envisioning the supply to China of a reactor and technical data. The same year saw the inauguration of the Five-Year Plan which significantly assigned the said Academy the main responsibility of developing atomic energy. Then a twelve-year plan of science and technology was drafted in 1956, placing the center of gravity on that type of energy. During 1955-1957, the scientific cadres were greatly increased and by the end of the period, the Institute of Physics recruited more than 200 researchers. This agency, now renamed Institute of Atomic Energy, was to concentrate working on the reactor. In December 1957, Moscow agreed to offer Beijing a prototype nuclear bomb and the method of producing it. As a result, the first reactor went into operation in 1958. It is revealing enough that by that year the CPR's investment in science increased nine times the sum of 1955.[126] No doubt, most of it went into the nuclear area.[127]

Up to that stage, the Chinese depended heavily on the Soviet Union for nuclear research and indeed for any other development. However, this was destined to change. Khrushchev's new deal of peaceful coexistence and improvement of light industry and agriculture to better the civilian economy led him to repudiate China's wasteful Great Leap and her dangerous bombardment of Jinmen and Mazu which he felt would provoke a strong reaction by the US. It was patent to the Kremlin that China was determined to become a great power and that she had begun an independent policy toward America. No alternative was left for the Russians but disavowal of the treaty commitment. They unilaterally withdrew all personnel from China and would no longer assist her in any respect whatsoever. Thence, the CPR was bound to depend on herself entirely. Premier Zhou Enlai

[123] Robert Wesson, *Modern Governments*, Englewood Cliffs, New Jersey: Prentice-Hall, 1981, p. 308, col. 1.

[124] J.D. Waller, *op. cit.*, p. 122.

[125] Cheng Chu-yuan, *op. cit.*, p. 543.

[126] *Ibid.*, p. 544.

[127] Kenneth R. Whiting, *op. cit.*, pp. 86-87.

declared that "China would develop nuclear weapons with her own scientists."[128] In this field, she was to succeed.[129] Beijing's resolve was most eloquently attested by the fact that "in 1960 the state budget for scientific purposes rose to 459 million dollars, a figure nearly three times that of 1958 and almost 28 times the amount allocated in 1955."[130] Mincing no words about the military import of their program, Liu Shaoqi, the then CPR chairman, said that it was for war as well as peace![131]

The Chinese nuclear development is a free one.[132] Beijing can test fissionary weapons wherever it sees fit, uninhibited as it is by the 1963 Test Ban Treaty and the 1968 non-proliferation agreement. In fact, the Chinese press attacks these instruments to be a plot of superpowers to lord over the world.[133] Pushed vigorously, Beijing's thermonuclear schedule progresses by leaps and bounds. The following tests have been carried out.[134]

	no.		no.
October 16, 1964	1	June 27, 1973	12
May 14, 1955	2	June 17, 1974	13
May 9, 1966	3	October 27, 1975	14
October 27, 1966	4	January 23, 1976	15
December 28, 1966	5	September 26, 1976	16
June 16, 1967	6	October 17, 1976	17
December 27, 1968	7	November 17, 1976	18
September 23, 1969	8	September 17, 1977	19
September 29, 1969	9	March 15, 1978	20
November 18, 1971	10	October 16, 1980	21
January 7, 1972	11		

The CPR has put out 12 articifial satellites:[135]

	no.		no.
April 24, 1970	1	August 30, 1976	6
March 3, 1971	2	December 7, 1976	7
July 26, 1975	3	January 31, 1978	8
November 26, 1975	4	September 20, 1981	9,10,11
December 16, 1975	5	September 9, 1982	12

[128] Cheng Chu-yuan, op. cit., p. 545.

[129] Ellis Joffe, Party and Army, Professionalism and Political Control in the Chinese Officer Corps 1949-1964, Cambridge: Harvard University Press, 1965, pp. 91-100.

[130] Cheng Chu-yuan, op. cit., p. 543.

[131] Ibid., pp. 544-545.

[132] Communist China and Arms Control, Palo Alto: Hoover Institution, 1968, pp. 149-155.

[133] Dev Kinandan, How China May Use Atom Bomb, 7 Military Scenarios, Delhi: Gandhinagar, 1974, pp. 75-143 at 100.

[134] From 1 to 20, Zhong guo shou ce, pp. 236-237. The last test is in Facts on File, October 31, 1980, p. 828, A3.

[135] From 1 to 8, Zhong guo shou ce, p. 238; all these and 9-11, in Renmin ribao, September 21, 1981, pp. 1, 4. The 12th is in Beijing review, September 20, 1982, pp. 6-7.

Finally a brief paragraph about the missile situation. The CPR is said to have 160 missile boats, 2 guided missile destroyers under construction, unspecified number of 8,000-km intercontinental ballistic missiles and multi-stage 4,800-km ICBM's.[136] Medium-range and intermediate-range missiles with a maximum range of 2,821 km were deployed, and about 40 of the latter were positioned in hardened silos in the northeast.[137] It is estimated that the Chinese missiles were still liquid-fueled which would mean considerable delay in getting them ready for launching.[138] On October 16, 1982, China for the first time fired a submarine-based carrier rocket.[139] As for the MRBM's (medium-range ballistic missiles) and IRBM's (intermediate-range ballistic missiles), one author put them at 80 and 40 respectively.[140] The former can reach 2,601 km and the latter somewhat longer. Up to now the USSR has 5,737 and the US 3,503 missiles of various kinds,[141] and their combined nuclear tests were estimated totaling more than 500 by the Peruvian delegate to the International Atomic Energy Conference held in Geneva in August 1980.[142] Further, the Soviet Union has launched 600 artificial satellites and the US 700, according to a Soviet count in 1974.[143] A study of the Swedish military institute Hagorfs gives the following figures of the underground atomic detonation, in 1981 and 1982, of the five countries:[144]

	1981	1982
China	0	0
France	11	5
UK	1	1
US	16	18
USSR	21	31

In comparison with other nuclear powers, the record of China is negligible indeed. For this reason, Beijing proposed the mutual destruction of nuclear weapons and delivery systems by all nations. If its proposal were accepted, the CPR can overwhelm every country with conventional arms and ten of millions of militia and regular units of the PLA.

---

[136] *Financial Times, loc. cit.*

[137] *Ibid.*

[138] Harold Hinton, *op. cit.,* p. 204.

[139] *Beijing review,* October 25, 1982, p. 5.

[140] Harold Hinton, *loc. cit.* Different estimate is made by Angus M. Frazer, *The People's Liberation Army,* p. 5.

[141] *Hammond,* 1981, p. 733.

[142] *Globe and mail,* August 13, 1980, p. 14.

[143] M.P. Erpylev, *et alii,* "Iskusstvennye sputnik zemle," *Bol'shaya sovetskaya entsiklopediya,* Moskva: Izdatel'stvo "sovetskaya entsiklopediya", 3rd ed., vol. 10 (1972), cols. 1398-1405 at 1398. For English version, see *The Great Soviet Encyclopedia,* 3rd ed., New York: Macmillan, 1976, vol. 10, pp. 9-12 at 9, col. 1.

[144] *Kanada kurier,* February 17, 1983, p. 2, col. 3.

CHAPTER VIII
Diplomacy

Constitutional basis

The foreign relation of the CPR has made a turn of one hundred and eighty degrees. This change is not just an expedient. Truly it represents a purposive direction. The Chinese may argue, with some cogency, that it is not they but the other countries which have made the turn. Not going into the interesting controversies as to whether the Chinese are right or wrong, the change in diplomacy is really remarkable and surprising. Once China's friend, the USSR has become her enemy; and the reverse is the case of the US. To this nation she was most hostile, and now she can hardly wait to sign a military pact.[1] From a diplomatic spouse, Albania is divorced from China.[2] Beijing's most hated Tito turned out to be a warmly welcomed guest when he flew to that famous city on August 30, 1977.[3] After a couple of years' intimacy with Cuba (1959-1961), the latter has since kept China at arm's length. All the leaders of Europe were berated in the Chinese press as history's rubbish and the US Government's lackeys. Now the Beijing elite fly there in droves to shake their hands.[4] Another about-face is the stand toward India, a country which was the loudest supporter of the Beijing oligarchy in its first decade of existence. Today the two nations are extremely cool to each other. A similar case is the Sino-Indonesian situation. President Suekarno literally vied with Nehru for Zhou Enlai's love. Currently, Djakarta and Beijing do not even exchange ambassadors. Perhaps the most dramatic development is the relation with Vietnam, which came all the way from Beijing's darling to an object of punishment.

After 1970, particularly since the demise of Mao Zedong, the CPR has come to make more friends and create less enemies. Her policy orients her away from ideological stricture to pragmatical embracing of many a statesman. The leadership's dedication to the modernization program can be taken as a vow to abandon the insular and repugnant attitude. A new deal of toleration at home is fully matched by an accommodating diplomacy. Thrown to the wind is the erstwhile xenophobia. A joint editorial of the three big mouthpieces on September 10, 1977 declared that "we must not mechanically apply quotations from Chairman Mao in disregard of the concrete time, place and circumstances, but we must grasp the essence of his works as a whole."[5] Wholly or partly, these works have no

---

[1] Richard A. Aliano, *The Crime of World Power, Politics Without Government in the International System*, New York: Putnam, 1978, pp. 13, 220.

[2] Robert Wesson, *Modern Government*, Englewood Cliffs, New Jersey: Prentice-Hall, 1981, p. 305, col. 1.

[3] *Facts on File*, September 17, 1977, p. 710, B1.

[4] Raymond Aron, *Peace and War, a Theory of International Relations,* translated from the French by Richard Howard and Annette Baker Fox, Garden City, New York: Doubleday, 1966, p. 120.

[5] *Renmin ribao*, September 10, 1977, p. 3. The other two are *Hongqi* and *Jie fang jun bao*.

relevance to the contemporary world whose music the contemporary cast of stars led by Deng Xiaoping, Zhao Ziyang and Hu Yaobang are facing.

As if emulating the Soviet Constitution of 1977 (Articles 28-30), the Chinese Constitutions of 1978 and 1982 regulate foreign policy. In their Preambles, we find the five planks of peaceful coexistence which are nothing more than so many corollaries of the single idea of state independence. The five are "mutual respect of sovereign right and territorial integrity, mutual non-aggression, non-interference in each other's internal affairs, equality and mutual benefit, and peaceful coexistence,"[6] originally embodied in the treaty between China and India signed on April 29, 1954. Comparing the two Constitutions, we find that the 1978 one was a great deal more bellicose. Let us take a look at that Constitution first. The CPR's peace pledges are seriously compromised by the three-world concept written so large in the Preamble and declared so boisterously by Hua Guofeng in the 11th Congress of the CCP on August 8, 1977.[7] The Constitution mentions no countries by name. It refers to the first world's "superpowers" which means the "social imperialist" USSR and the plain, or regular, imperialist US. The socialist countries are placed alongside (not inside) the "third world." The document does not tell us who are in that world. Of the second world, the aforesaid Hua Guofeng speech cites European nations and Japan as examples. Neither the Constitution nor Hua Guofeng cares to be specific on the components of the third world, but both are articulate on the policy toward it and toward the other two worlds.

Characteristic of the US and the USSR are colonial exploitation, oppression and intimidation. They are said to "bully" the third world. Nations of the "second world," to quote Hua Guofeng, "have a dual character." On the one hand they oppress, exploit and control the third world, and on the other, they are controlled, threatened and bullied by the first world in varying degrees. Placing itself in the third world, the Chinese government is said to be duty bound to side with it in the just struggle to achieve and defend national independence, safeguard state sovereignty and develop its economy. With respect to the second world, the CPR will help it to stand up against the dominant nations. As the Preamble of the Constitution states, Chinese diplomacy is aimed at forming "the broadest possible international united front against the hegemonism of the superpowers and against a new world war" and at striving "for the progress and emancipation of humanity," China, it is stressed, is resolved not to live in friendship with the "oppressive states."[8]

[6] According to *Xin hua ci dian*, Beijing: Shang wu yin shou guan, 1980, p. 337, col. 2, it first appeared in Sino-India Treaty of April 29, 1954.

[7] *Keesing's*, September 16, 1977, p. 28721, col. 2.

[8] Roland Felber, "Der Alp einer reaktionären tradition, chinesischer Grossmachtehegemonismus und Sinozentrimus in vergangenheit und gegenwart," *Deutsche Aussenpolitik* (Berlin), 24 (1979), no. 6, pp. 84-97 at 85.

The three-world thesis, which was brought up by Mao Zedong in 1974,[9] harks still further back to the stand he took in 1927 during the village struggle in Hunan province.[10] There he sorted out the peasants into rich, middle and poor categories. The first were said to bully the second and the third, and the second to both bully and be bullied. Only the third are bullied but not bully. Mao said it was the policy of the communists to assist the poor, and to ally them with the middle in order to destroy the rich. Now this tactic came to apply to the world politics. In neither case is there a sincere desire for peace.[11]

The CPR's trichotomous formula was put into operation from the time of her admission to the United Nations in 1971 to 1978 when the Constitution was promulgated. In fact, that document was outdated the moment it appeared. It came out a few months before the US recognition of the Beijing regime. What Harold Hinton calls duo-adversary policy of that regime has since then given place to a uni-adversary one. Hua Guofeng in a speech to the 5th NPC on June 18, 1979 attacked ferociously social imperialism (n.b. not regular imperialism).[12] Conspicuously absent in his speech is the criticism of the US or Japan, or west European countries. What has been left in the diplomatic pouch of the CPR is the occasional voicing of support of the endeavors of the third-world nations to preserve their natural resources, particularly those of the marginal sea and continental shelf, from foreign exploitation. Beijing's delegate vetoed repeatedly, in November 1981, Kurt Waldheim in favor of candidate Salim Ahmed Salim for the General Secretary of the UN, clearly in championship of the cause of the third world.[13] In the 1982 Constitution, the three-world slogan is deleted. The overtone is sober and conciliatory. The status of China is said to be "closely linked with the bright future of the whole world," and this is because her "achievements in revolution and construction are inseparable from the support of" others. Coupled with this spirit of cooperation is, however, the avowal to oppose imperialism, hegemonism (which replaces the social imperialism of the 1978 Constitution) and colonialism. The Chinese government goes on the constitutional record to back up the oppressed and developing countries in the just fight for their independence and economic development. Here Beijing keeps the three-world slogan alive. In practice, its leaders, while meeting statesmen from the developing systems, still flaunt with it in spite of dropping of the term from the Constitution.

[9] *Keesing's*, September 16, 1977, p. 28721, col. 2.

[10] Mao Zedong, "Report of an investigation into the peasant movement in Hunan," *Government of Communist China*, edited by George P. Jan, San Francisco: Chandler Pub. Co., 1966, pp. 38-61, *passim*.

[11] Alastair Buchan, *The End of the Postwar Era, a New Balance of World Power*, New York: E.P. Dutton, 1974, pp. 80-81.

[12] *Facts on File*, 1979, p. 484, F2, *Britannica Book of the Year*, 1980, p. 247, col. 1.

[13] *Globe and Mail*, December 4, 1981, p. 1, col. 4; *Renmin ribao*, November 22, 1981, p. 6.

The United States

In the pamphlet *On the people's democratic dictatorship* (June 30, 1949), Mao Zedong maintained that China had no other alternative but to lean toward one side, the Soviet Union.[14] This view has the ideological basis that between imperialism and socialism, there was no choice, or, in his expression, "a third road."[15] In 1954, Mao Zedong wrote this view in the Constitution (Preamble), intimating that it was to be a durable course of the Chinese Government. Although not in so many words, the policy was opposing the US. Under the circumstances of 1949, he might have made the right decision, because the USSR was truly China's "chum" and the CPR felt so much at home with her. On the other hand, the US had rendered help, however far from all-out, to the Nationalist Government in its life-and-death struggle with the Reds. Mao's one-sided diplomacy was a costly one. Were it not for that, Taiwan would not have been an issue for all these years. Any fair-minded individual, we think, readily concedes that the US is the least abominable of all imperial aggressors of China. We do not have to traverse the history of Sino-US relation to find evidence to prove the argument. Suffice it to point to the Burlingame mission of 1867 or John Hay's Open Door Notes of 1899.[16] Perhaps the most conspicuous demonstration of America's attitude toward China is that unlike all other powers, she held no leased territory, staked no sphere of influence and established no settlement in Chinese ports. On the other end of the scale, incidentally, is Japan which almost strangled Cathay. Had it not been for her, the Reds would not have arisen.

The anti-US venom of Mao and company was solely derived from the transport by that country's marine corps of the troops of Jiang Jieshi immediately after the V-J day to the Japanese-held areas.[17] During the Marshall Mission (December 20, 1945-January 7, 1947), the US played a role which favored what it considered to be an underdog, the CCP. The simplistic communists were not aware of Washington's readiness to recognize whatever side of the Chinese civil war represented the people.[18] This side, in the opinion of the State Department, was the CCP. President Truman's White Paper of 1949 makes the point abundantly manifest. Before the Korean war, Taiwan was not within the American defense pale in Asia.[19] If the Red Army continued the drive by landing on the island, it could easily

---

[14] Written "In commemoration of the twenty-eighth anniversary of the Communist Party of China," in *Selected Works of Mao Zedong*, Beijing: Foreign Language Press, 1961, vol. 4, pp. 411-424 at 415.

[15] J.D. Waller, *The Government and Politics of Communist China*, London: Hutchinson University Library, 1970, p. 154; John A. Harrison, *China Since 1800*, New York: Harcourt, Brace & World, 1967, p. 240.

[16] *Xin hua ci dian*, p. 577, col. 2.

[17] *Di san ci guo gong nei zhan da shi yue biao*, Hong Kong: Wen hua zi liao gong ying she, 1978, pp. 14, 21, 23.

[18] E.J. Kahn, *The China Hands, America's Foreign Service Officers and What Befell Them*, New York: Viking, 1975, pp. 141, 176.

[19] Inis L. Claude, *Power and International Relations*, New York: Random House, 1962, pp. 166, 171.

have destroyed the troops of the nationalists. The turning point is the Korean conflict.[20] During the three years (1950-1953) of fighting on the peninsula, the anti-American campaign was whipped up to the zenith. From 1953 to the close of the Cultural Revolution, the Beijing regime was truculently against the US. In the meantime, the two countries, almost entirely at the latter's initiative, held "ambassadorial talks" first in Geneva and then in Warsaw intermittently for fifteen years (1955-1969).

The volte-face of Beijing's America policy came after the winding up of the Cultural Revolution. The reasons are threefold. First, there is the scheme of the USSR to isolate China, a step made possible by her wilful cessation of diplomatic activities. In 1966-1968, all but one of the emissaries (Huang Zhen in Egypt) were recalled. Russia was thus able to carry out an anti-China propaganda in all capitals where Beijing was no longer represented. Second, China was convinced by Richard Nixon that the US had no intent to endanger her security and that a peaceful solution of the Vietnam problem would reduce America's military presence there.[21] Third, more importantly, the Sino-Soviet border clashes in March 1969 had awakened the Chinese oligarchy, and their sense of fear was reinforced by the 1968 Warsaw Powers' invasion of Czechoslovakia.[22] Russia was posing a real danger to the CPR as it did to that European country. This anxiety, although not justified, forced the Beijing elite to seek outside support. Meanwhile, the US was fully aware of the weakness of China, debilitated as she was by internal tumult and divided leadership.[23] The two parties, therefore, had held a common view and saw mutual benefit to be gained by a rapprochement. Just which party went farther than the other on the meeting ground is subject to speculation. The noteworthy fact, however, is that they both looked with disdain at the Soviet Union, and they both felt the need for cooperation in checking it and in maintaining a warless southeast Asia. With the US troops gone, thought Beijing, a fraternal North Vietnam with or without annexing the south, was saved, just as North Korea was some twenty years ago.

The need of one for the other, particularly America's need of China, was urgent and ardent.[24] A positive step toward improving the relation was taken by Nixon in the manner of withdrawing the Seventh Fleet from the Taiwan strait in March 1969, and immediately before this, he proposed the resumption of the ambassadorial rendezvous in

[20] Philip W. Buch and Martin B. Travis, *Control of Foreign Relations in Modern Nations,* New York: Norton, 1957, pp. 378, 379.

[21] Thomas B. Larose, *Soviet-American Rivalry,* New York: Norton, 1978, pp. 209-210.

[22] Henry A. Kissinger, *American Foreign Policy,* 1st ed., New York: Norton, 1969, p. 129.

[23] Richard Moorsteen and Morton Abramowitz, *Remaking China Policy, U.S.-China Relations and Governmental Decision-making,* Cambridge: Harvard University Press, 1971, document section, pp. 87-131.

[24] James C. Thomson, "The United States and China in the Seventies," John H. Gilbert, *The New Era in American Foreign Policy,* New York: St. Martin's Press, 1973, pp. 140-150, *passim.*

214   GOVERNMENT OF SOCIALIST CHINA

Poland. In February 1970, Beijing hinted its willingness to have direct contact with the US by inviting Nixon to China. Instrumental for the linkage was President Nicolae Ceausescu of Romania who visited America during October 13-27, 1970.[25] While he was there, Nixon for the first time called Mao and company "Chinese People's Republic." On April 14 the following year, the famous pingpong team of the US was hosted in Beijing by Zhou Enlai.[26] The relation between the two countries appeared to be very close, but it required another trip of the Romanian official to get things actually rolling. He went to Beijing on June 9, 1971,[27] and soon after, Henry Kissinger's disguised tour was made (July 9-11). On the heels of this tour, Nixon announced in a nationwide address (July 15) that he was asked by Zhou Enlai to visit China. Showing gratitude, the US Government in October 1971 tacitly endorsed the admission of the CPR into the United Nations and the exclusion of the Chinese Republic. The historical Nixon mission was made in February 21-28, 1972.[28] Several months before that, a stream of American sightseers went to that country, now open ajar, to gratify their wanderlust and curiosity. Galore of Sinophiles repaired just to pay homage to the leaders with whom they had long been in communion.

The Shanghai Communiqué signed in that Westernized city climaxed the Nixon tour.[29] It laid down the foundation for the future China policy of the American Government and it affected profoundly the diplomacy of many a country. The US, so says the document, acknowledges that "all Chinese on either side of the Taiwan strait" held that "there is but one China and that Taiwan is a part of China."[30] This seems to be an indirect way of conceding to the CPR's title to that province and a direct disavowal of America's intent to interfere in a China-Taiwan war. The US set high hope on the rapprochement. Ultimately, the Communiqué says, the US would take its military personnel out of Taiwan as tension in that area eases up. Adumbrating a decision to void the 1954 mutual-defense treaty between Washington and Taibei, the instrument was a signal victory of the communist regime which won everything it wanted at that time but lost nothing. While Nixon meekly spoke of self-determination for the people of South Vietnam, the CPR expressed the unswerving commitment to the succor of Hanoi in its drive to conquer that nation.

On February 22, 1973, Kissinger took another unheralded flight to Beijing where another communiqué appeared pledging both

[25] *Facts on File*, October 22-28, 1970, p. 767, G1.

[26] *Ibid.*, April 8-14, 1971, p. 261, A1.

[27] *Ibid.*, June 10-16, 1971, p. 448, A1.

[28] *United States Foreign Policy for the 1970's, the Emerging Structure of Peace*, Washington: Government Printing Office, 1972, pp. 26-37.

[29] A. Kokorev, "Kitaya, vneshnyaya politika," *Ezhegodnik*, 1973, p. 379.

[30] The Communiqué is in *Beijing Review*, 9 (March 3, 1972), pp. 4-5; also in appendix C of James Wang, *Contemporary Chinese Politics*, Englewood Cliffs, New Jersey: Prentice-Hall, 1980, pp. 295-298.

countries' plan to institute liaison offices in each other's capitals. Quickly, such offices were opened. On November 4, 1973, Kissinger journeyed to see Mao once more. Not unexpectedly, one more communiqué developed. It reaffirmed the one-China policy of the American Government as if the Shanghai document is not articulate enough on this point. From that time on, trade and cultural intercourse between Washington and Beijing were dramatically stepped up. In the first eight months of 1973, the commodity exchange of $500 million was reported.[31] Many sympathizers were flown to Beijing at China's expense. Wined and dined, they were jetted to many other designated locales for amusement as well. In the last leg of the Nixon Administration, he was diverted from the China mania by the famous Watergate scandal. Although no diplomatic ploy was made by the worn-out president, the Congress got excited. Senators Henry Jackson and William Fulbright and many House members made their way to Beijing, as did hundreds of citizens. Some paid their fare, but many were invited by the Chinese institutions of various descriptions, most notably the Foreign Affairs Association.

The year 1974 saw some frigid periods in the Sino-American atmosphere because the liaison officers Huang Zhen and David Bruce were absent from their posts for a considerable length of time. A month after Gerald Ford took over the presidency, he appointed George Bush to Beijing to succeed the US-staying Bruce, indicating the new administration's will to befriend China. The indefatigable Kissinger journeyed to see Mao Zedong on October 19, 1975, to arrange a Ford visit later in the year. The visit took place from December 1 to 5. Nothing, however, came out of it in spite of Ford's pledge to normalize the relation with China prior to his departure for Beijing. Meanwhile, the Chinese rulers showed a tremendous interest in purchasing high technology from America. They indicated for the first time a shift from traditional trade to military equipment. In that year, the US sold China three million tons of wheat, making the CPR her greatest grain customer.[32] Although Ford desired to court Beijing, he also spoke of America's commitment to Taiwan in a policy speech on May 6, 1975.[33] This stand of his was prompted by the objection of many leaders to further concessions to the rulers in Beijing.

The China issue exercised greatly the US presidents from Nixon on, if for no other reason than that it is an easy matter to handle. To sacrifice a helpless Taiwan is not much of a problem. No sooner did Carter enter the White House than he talked of normalization with the regime of Mao. When Secretary Cyrus Vance went to China to see its leaders from August 22 to 26, 1977,[34] Hua Guofeng and Deng Xiaoping presented him with three demands of a) withdrawal of US

[31] *Encyclopedia Yearbook*, 1975, p. 163.

[32] *Ibid.*, 1978, p. 153.

[33] *Ibid.*, col. 2.

[34] *World Almanac*, 1978, p. 942, col. 2. A. Kokorev, "Soedinennye shtaty ameriki," *Ezhegodnik*, 1978, p. 358.

troops from Taiwan, b) abrogation of the 1954 defense treaty and c) severance of diplomacy with the government there. Vance's counterproposal of letting Taibei and Washinton set up a liaison similar to the one already existing between Beijing and the latter was rejected by the CPR. That Carter would yield to the three points was evidenced by his lauding of the Vance trip as a great success.[35] He, Carter, was ready to drop the counterproposal and accede to the communists' wishes.[36]

Throughout 1978, the US Government sought earnestly to further the tie with Beijing without, however, granting it full diplomatic protocol. The two countries agreed to expand trade and the CPR was assured of America's aid in technology. In July, a group of US scientists headed by Frank Press, Carter's science advisor, jetted to Beijing. At exactly the same time, the CPR bought an airborne exploration system for oil discovery and 3.9 million tons of wheat from the US. Furthermore, the Chinese signed on November 20, 1978 with the Pan American World Airways a contract of $500 million both to build and administer a chain of hotels in such cities like Beijing, Shanghai and Tianjin. Toward the end of the year, the Coca Cola Firm was granted a franchise in the CPR beginning on January 1, 1979. On December 5, finally, there broke out the simultaneous announcements in Beijing and Washington that the US was to cut off relation with Taiwan and that China and the US would give each other diplomatic recognition from January 1 and exhange ambassadors on March 1 the following year.[37]

The Chinese ruling coterie obtained all they asked for. To the American public, whose opinion was overwhelmingly against the recognition in the polls,[38] Carter said he had tried to get from the Reds the pledge not to use force to take Taiwan, but failed. He stated the negotiation which led to the denouement gave him grounds to assume that Beijing had yielded on that point. In an invited trip to Beijing (August 24-28, 1981), he repeated to foreign newsmen that assumption.[39] Up to this moment, Carter is wrong because Beijing has persisted that it does not rule out the use of force to get the island.

Defensive means, the US proposed, be given the government of Taiwan, but this was opposed by Beijing. To satisfy the latter, Carter explained that the arms deal was concluded before the normalization. Any further delivery of them was to be reviewed periodically. Whatever goes to Taiwan since then, according to officials there, is outdated. If Beijing should employ violence to "emancipate" the island, the US,

[35] Encyclopedia Yearbook, 1978, p. 153, col. 1.

[36] Paolo Boenio-Brochieri, "Normalizzaione fra cina i usa," Relazioni internazionali (Milano), vol. 42, no. 51-52 (1978), pp. 1139-1140.

[37] World Almanac, 1981, p. 526, col. 1. A. Kokorev, "Soedinennye shtaty ameriki," Ezhegodnik, 1980, p. 344.

[38] Harold Hinton, An Introduction to Chinese Politics, 2nd ed., New York: Holt, Rinehart and Winston, 1978, p. 321.

[39] Renmin ribao, August 25, 1981, p. 1.

needless to say, has no obligation to defend her. It is scarcely credible that in the face of the steady threat from the mainland, Carter should have been so "confident that the people of Taiwan face a peaceful and prosperous future,"[40] and that the "normalization . . . will not jeopardize the well-being of the people" there.[41] Frequently he opined that it was not in Beijing's interest to attack Taiwan. Who can be cocksure that Beijing thinks the way he does? The existence of Taiwan, we would argue, is thankful to the USSR. The moment that country moves away its more than 500,000 hordes from the Chinese border, Taiwan will be gone.

Deng Xiaoping, the then first vice premier, came to the US on January 28, 1979 for nine days' visit. He was taken to Washington, Houston, Atlanta and Seattle. The intent of this man was not so much the solicitation of American aid in order to realize his four modernizations, as the involving of Carter in an anti-USSR united front with him. To the press, Deng objected to the pending US-USSR strategic arms accord. He clamored for blocking Russian expansion. With much truth, we think, he told the White House host that China understands the Soviets better than the Americans because she has had long intimate contacts with them. Apparently yielding to him on this score, Carter in the joint statement of February 1, 1979 agreed that they opposed efforts by any country to exercise "hegemony or domination" over others.[42] Several documents were signed on January 31 between the US and China on technology, culture, space and high-energy physics. An interim protocol envisioned the establishment of consulates by the CPR in Houston and San Francisco. The ice once broken, contacts waxed more cordial and more often. In February 1979, Treasury Secretary Michael Blumenthal flew to China to settle the outstanding credit claims between Washington and Beijing. His mission was followed by Secretary of Commerce, Juanita Kreps. Hers was to help further trade relations. An agreement providing a most-favored nation deal to China which entitled her to low-interest Export-Import Bank credits was signed on July 7, 1979 in Beijing by Ambassador Woodcock and the Chinese Trade Minister Li Qiang.

Reciprocating the Deng visit, Vice-President Walter Mondale arrived in Beijing on August 25, 1979. This trip produced an agreement on cultural exchange and another on hydro-power projects which obliged American investment of $2 billion in five years.[43] On the political side, Mondale reiterated the familiar slogan of the time that a strong and modernized China was in the best interest of the US and that Beijing and Washington had many parallel strategical and bilateral concerns. On January 8, 1980, Defense Secretary Harold Brown arrived at the

[40] US statement of December 15, 1978, in James Wang, *op. cit.*, p. 308.

[41] President Carter's address to the nation, December 15, 1978, *ibid.*, p. 307.

[42] *Encyclopedia Yearbook*, 1979, p. 170, col. 2.

[43] *Ibid.*, 1980, p. 249, col. 1.

Chinese capital. He watched an airforce maneuver and armored-carriage mock attacks. Coinciding with the Soviet invasion of Afghanistan, the Brown mission promised the CPR logistic and communication systems for the PLA. Returning his visit, the Chinese Vice Premier Geng Biao came to America in May. He was the second highest figure among the Beijing elite to come to the US. Treated with a 19-gun salute, he was given an audience with Carter, an honor not usually granted to an official of that rank.

The China policy of President Reagan deviates little from that of his predecessor, except in the way the Taiwan officials in the US are treated. While under Carter, all contacts with them took place in a restaurant, or a parking lot, or a government building not yet designated as such (just to satisfy the term "unofficial relations" in the Joint Communiqué),[44] the current administrators can give them audience in their offices. With respect to the arms sale to Taiwan, Washington assumes an extremely halting attitude, lest Beijing should be offended. The regime is considered by the US as moderate and as worthy of supporting. Any large-scale backing of Taiwan can arouse opposition by the radical elements in China. Late in 1981, Beijing staged an energetic campaign of peaceful liberation of Taiwan. Chairman Ye Jianying of the NPC Standing Committee offered a nine-point proposal to President Jiang Jingguo of the Chinese Republic envisaging a free communication and an unalteration of economic and military regime of the island.[45] President Reagan may take this campaign seriously. It was even speculated at that time that he might act as a go-between for the Beijing and Taibei leaders. Former Secretary of State, Alexander Haig said that the CPR's suggestion deserved consideration.[46] To this author, such thinking is naive. The two united fronts in the past were bad enough for the GMD. Who can trust the Chinese communists, or for that matter, any communists? What alliance with the communists has succeeded in history? An admission of the CPR agents into Taiwan would certainly lead to subversive activities there. For a long time these activities have been directed by the CPR's machinery in Japan and Hong Kong. In the past couple of years, Taiwan officials discovered such conspiracies masterminded by the Reds. President Jiang Jingguo's refusal of the suggestion of Ye Jianying is well-grounded.

In front of President Reagan is the option of an all-out military aid to the CPR or a limited assistance in view of the displeasure of the Asian countries with the prospect of a powerful China. Spokesmen of the State Department hinted that the US decision on the matter depends on the behavior of the Kremlin. There have already been arms sales to the CPR following Alexander Haig's visit to Beijing (June 14-16, 1981). He said in the Chinese capital that the "Reagan

[44] James Wang, op. cit., p. 305.

[45] Renmin ribao, October 1, 1981, p. 1.

[46] Ibid., November 16, 1981, p. 6.

administration would remove restrictions to permit China to buy US weapons and high-technology equipment."[47] In mid-June, 1981, US officials admitted that for the past year, America and China had run an electronic listening station in Tianshan (Xinjiang Autonomous Region.)[48] It monitors missile tests the Soviets conduct in the proving ground of Leninski and Sary-Shan of Kazakhstan. The station was built by American technicians but was manned by the Chinese. US officials frequently go there to pick up data and check on the facilities.

Sino-American interests, after all, are not as identical or even parallel as many think; Washington plays the China card just as hard as Beijing plays the US card, each striving to improve its respective bargain with a third power. We will have more to say about the Chinese diplomacy towards that power, but at this point attention must be directed to the serious question confronting the policy-élite of the US and the CPR in re Taiwan. According to the Taiwan Relations Act enacted by the US Congress, the American Government will continuously sanction the sale of defense weapons to Taiwan as situations warrant. President Reagan, after weighing the balance of strength of the CPR and the National Government, decided on January 11, 1982 to approve the sale of F-5Es.[49] These are, however, not the advanced F-5Gs favored by the Taiwan authorities.[50] The Beijing aristocracy, prior to the announcement of the sales, threatened to lower its diplomatic ranks in the US. It is undoubtedly thanks to this pressure that President Reagan took such a middle stand which he hoped would lay the fear of Beijing on the one hand, and meet the criticism expressed in the US Congress for his administration's back away from help to the island republic, on the other.

The reaction of the Chinese communists to Washington's decision was unexpectedly mild, for they signaled nothing more than verbal anger.[51] Vice-President George Bush's visit to Beijing (May 5-9, 1982) did very little to mollify the Reds.[52] Nor did that of Howard Baker, Senate majority leader (June 1-3, 1982), although he promised to Deng Xiaoping his blessing of the one-China policy.[53] When the new Secretary of State, George Shultz, during the Senate confirmation hearings in July 1982, promised to abide by the Taiwan Relations Act, Beijing saw a self-contradictory position of his and indicated great displeasure with him.[54] Behind-the-scenes pressure continued to

---

[47] *Information please,* 1982, p. 154.

[48] *Time,* June 29, 1981, p. 12, col. 3.

[49] *Facts on file,* January 15, 1982, p. 11, D1.

[50] W.A. Henry, "Anger over arms to Taiwan," *Time,* January 25, 1982, p. 23.

[51] *Beijing Review,* April 26, 1982, p. 6.

[52] *Facts on File,* May 14, 1982, p. 341, G3.

[53] *Facts on File,* June 18, 1982, p. 443, A1.

[54] *Beijing Review,* July 26, 1982, p. 2 carries a translated commentary on *Renmin ribao* of July 18, "Hostile policy will not sabotage Sino-US relation."

mount from Beijing to stop the US arms sales to the nationalists. "An uneasy compromise" was declared simultaneously in Beijing and Washington on August 17, 1982. The US agreed first not to exceed the sales level already reached in recent years and second to eventually "come to a complete solution" which means total cessation at a fixed time. But what that time will be is not stated in the communiqué.[55] Meanwhile, the Reagan administration "formally announced, only two days after Shanghai II [second Shanghai communiqué] was issued, the sale of 60 F-5E fighters, worth some $240 million, to Taibei."[56] From the Washington commitment, Beijing derived the satisfaction that the weapons sale will be finally cut and will not surpass the 1982 amount. This indeed represents a diplomatic victory for the CPR, as in no previous agreement did the US go that far. It must be noted that the concession runs contrary to the balance-of-strength assumption of the Taiwan Relations Act. The opposition to the concession was very strong, and this forced the State Department to back down quite a bit by saying that there was no time-limit for the final stop of the sale, that peaceful resolving of the Chinese unification was the condition for the stop and that Shanghai II has to be read within the context of the various Sino-US treaties. In further meeting the criticism in the US, the Reagan administration sold more arms to the national government of Taiwan in 1983 than in 1982: from $600 million to $800 million; and the planned 1984 sale amounts to $780 million.[57] This cannot fail to infuriate the Reds.[58]

Secretary of State George Shultze repaired to Beijing for a four-day "diplomatiquing" (February 2-5, 1983). No breakthrough was effected. This time the American official made it quite clear in a news conference in the Chinese capital that the US has definite commitment to Taiwan which cannot be disavowed, and in the meantime both he and the host (Premier Zhao Ziyang) talked of "mutual trust" to improve the relations of both countries.[59] The latest events troubling the Beijing and Washington detente concerns an old debt of China to US citizens.[60] In 1911 the Qing Government, in order to obtain loans from a consortium of foreign banks to construct the Guangdong-Hankou Railway, issued them bearer bonds. In November 1979, nine Americans holding the bonds filed a suit against the CPR in the US District Court for the northern district of Alabama in demand of repayment of the principal and interest of the bonds. The Court gave a "default judgment" on September 1, 1982 ordering the Beijing regime to defray the plaintiffs more than $41.3 million.

[55] *Globe and mail*, August 18, 1982, p. 9, cols. 2-6.

[56] *Time*, August 30, 1982, p. 19, col. 1.

[57] *Ibid.*, April 18, 1983, p. 30.

[58] *Beijing Review*, March 28, 1983, p. 9.

[59] *Ibid.*, February 14, 1983, pp. 8-9.

[60] *Ibid.*, February 21, 1983, p. 8.

The Chinese refused this judgment in an aide memoire handed by the foreign minister (Wu Xueqian) to George Shultze during the latter's stay in Beijing. It is alleged in the aide memoire firstly that China as a sovereign state cannot, by international law, be subject to the juridical authority of the US or its subdivision, and secondly, by the "long-established international law odious debts are not to be succeeded to." The first argument, it seems, is plausible, but the non-succession to the "odious debt" was in effect established by the Chinese Reds. International law does not have that rule.[61]

Gravely straining the fragile Sino-US diplomacy is the according of political refuge to a tennis-player Hu Na who during a tournament in July 1982 slipped out of a California hotel and went into hiding at a friend's home. For eight months no decision was made on her application for a stay in the US. The Chinese communists even resorted to outright false charge of collusion of Washington and Taibei in alluring her into defection.[62] The asylum was finally granted on April 4, 1983 and the reaction from Beijing was swift. On the 7th, its spokesman declared null and void 10 athletic agreements (all events to take place in US)[63], and 8 cultural exchanges.[64] The affected programs are all one year in duration, but the 1984 Los Angeles Olympics will not be boycotted. In the Hu Na case, there was serious dissention among officials of the State Department and the Immigration and Naturalization Service. It appears that the White House has exerted a decisive influence upon the final determination to refuse the communist demand. With the appeasement-prone Carter administration, we would argue, the woman would have been forced to go back to the system which she denounced as coercive.

The Soviet Union

China's diplomacy with the USSR as well as with the US came back to square one. At the inception of the Maoist regime in 1949, America was her first and foremost enemy, and Russia her "elder brother." The 1954 Constitution, already noted, riveted this sweetness in the Preamble. On August 24, 1973, by contrast, the reputed moderate Zhou Enlai declared to the 10th Congress of the CCP that "the Soviet revisionist ruling clique from Khrushchev to Brezhnev [became] new czars." In the same breath, he compared them to Hitler.[65] On April 1, 1974, first vice premier Deng Xiaoping reviled on the rostrum of the UN General Assembly the USSR as the worst of all imperialists. He used the words "vicious and unscrupulous" to describe it.[66] On

[61] Fu Zhu, "US court trial violates international law," *ibid.*, March 14, 1983, pp. 24-27, 30.

[62] *Renmin ribao*, April 6, 1983, p. 1; *Beijing review*, April 18, 1983, pp. 4-5.

[63] *Renmin ribao*, April 8, 1983, p. 1.

[64] *Kanada kurier*, April 21, 1983, p. 1, col. 3.

[65] *Facts on File*, September 2-8, 1973, p. 739, C2; *Encyclopedia Yearbook*, 1974, p. 175, col. 1.

[66] *Encyclopedia Yearbook*, 1975, p. 164, col. 1. *Facts on File*, April 20, 1974, p. 299, E3.

another occasion, he avowed that the "warming up" of Sino-Soviet relations was out of the question not only for this but for the following generations.[67] In 1976, the Chinese press spoke of the Soviet Union as CPR'S "main enemy."[68] In a speech delivered on May 29, 1978 at the UN General Assembly's special session on disarmament, Foreign Minister Huang Hua called Russia the "most dangerous source of a new world war."[69] Hua Guofeng, addressing the 11th Congress of the CCP on August 18, 1977 said the Soviets acted on bad faith in their dealings with other nations and are betrayers of Marxism-Leninism.[70] Except for Hua Guofeng's criticism, the other abusive expressions just cited were hurled at the Americans before the Shanghai Communiqué of February 28, 1972. Since then the US, an inveterate foe of China's, has become her friend. What more eloquent testimony can there be to show the volatility of the Beijing oligarchy? Who can be absolutely sure that they will not someday change their mind? Will China, once powerful and self-assured, fulfil the Carter Administration's wish to be a stabilizing force to help keep the peace in the world? All depends, in a dictatorship, on the stripes of the leadership. If the present moderates were to be swept away by radicals, of whom the CPR still has lots, the chances are good that the US would be once more rebuked and the USSR once more their "elder brother." Things would start all over again.

Stalin pooh-poohed the Chinese communists,[71] and so did Lenin, whose emissary Adolf Ioffe, we shall remember, agreed in the Shanghai Communiqué of January 26, 1923 with Sun Yat-sen that China was not ripe for communism. In effect, the two were saying that the few communists there were visionaries. In the name of the Comintern, Stalin found it necessary to thrust a united front strategy on them in the belief that these visionaries may have to abide their time, and do so within the GMD fold.[72] During the Jiangxi and Yanan periods, Soviet aids to the Reds were nil due to geographical and, perhaps, ideological factors. Like the Yugoslavs and Albanians, the Chinese comrades came to power almost entirely on their own, except at the last, but crucial, leg of their struggle, the race for Manchuria. At that time, the USSR offered operation bases to the Chinese Reds in its territory across from the Amur.[73] As late as 1945, Stalin showed no interest in support of these Reds.[74] Without

---

[67] A statement made to a visiting German delegation on September 25, 1977, *Encyclopedia Yearbook*, 1978, p. 153, col. 2.

[68] *Ibid.*, 1976, p. 156, col. 2.

[69] *Ibid.*, 1979, p. 157, col. 2.

[70] *Keesing's*, December 16, 1977, p. 28721, col. 1.

[71] Chiang Chung-cheng, *Soviet Russia in China, a Summary at Seventy*, New York: Farrar, Straus, 1957, pp. 150-151, 190.

[72] Zhang Guotao, *Wo de hui yi*, Hong Kong: Ming bao yue kan she, 1973, vol. 2, p. 527.

[73] A.G. Yakovlev, "SSSR i bor'ba kitaiskoga noroda protiv yaponskoi agressii, 1931-1945 gg.," *Leninskaya politika SSSR v otnoshenii kitiya*, Moskva: Izd-vo "nauka," 1960, pp. 68-120 at 119.

[74] Franz H. Michael and George E. Taylor, *The Far East in the Modern World*, 2nd ed., New York: Holt, Rinehart and Winston, 1964, p. 749.

expressly saying so, Beijing regarded this indifference as Stalin's mistake alongside other mistakes, like the removal to Russia of industrial equipment in Marchuria soon after Japan's capitulation there, and the Soviet backing of the GMD regime throughout the Second World War. Then there was the so-called Shanghai massacre of April 12, 1927 perpetrated by Jiang Jieshi.[75] All these were made possible by the Kremlin's China policy.[76] The first half dozen years of the CPR was marked by cordiality with the CPSU. Moscow gave back the railway rights in Manchuria to China. Khrushchev and Bulganin, in an effort to eliminate the last suspicion of China, went to Beijing on October 1, 1954 to take part in the celebration of the fifth anniversary of the founding of the Chinese People's Republic, and to sign a treaty there handing over Port Arthur to Mao. It also dissolved the four joint companies originally set up to develop the resources of the Chinese Turkestan and commercial opportunity in Manchuria, because they savored too much of imperialist exploitation.

However, the Sino-Soviet concord was not to endure. With the 20th Congress of the CPSU in February 1956 came the turning point. Zhu De, the then Vice-President of the CPR, attended the congress as the head of the Chinese entourage. He listened to the unpleasant (to him) attack by Khrushchev on Stalin in the secret session. This gathering is now officially referred by the Soviet press as devoted to the problem of "personality cult and its consequences."[77] Three theses were brought up by Khrushchev: peaceful coexistence, avoidability of war, parliamentary approach to socialism. Electing to uphold the position which Lenin took in 1919 on non-coexistence,[78] but to forget his teaching on coexistence in 1918,[79] the Beijing elite insisted that capitalism must be dispatched by the flaming swords of the proletariat, that the bourgeois legislature could not be used to achieve socialism, and that war was the only road to victory of the communist nations. On this last theme, it is reasoned that even if the East bloc would not fight, the Western countries would. To top over all these polemics, the Chinese media despised the unilateral and arbitrary defaming of Stalin. An important course like this, the CCP thought, ought to be taken after a consultation with all fraternal parties, but it was not. China felt slighted by the Kremlin masters.

Believing itself entitled to make a common policy for the socialist camp, the CPSU claimed to possess a better view of the world

[75] *Xin hua ci dian*, p. 412, col. 2; *Beijing Review*, 38 (September 20, 1963), pp. 9-10.

[76] J.D. Waller, *op. cit.*, p. 158.

[77] "Kommunisticheskaya partiya sovetskogo soiuza," *USSR entsiklopedicheskii spravochnik*, Moskva: Izdvo "sovetskaya entsiklopediya," 1979, cols. 484-504 at 500.

[78] Lenin, "Iz 'otcheta tsentral'nogo komiteta," *O voine, armii i voennoi nauke*, Moskva: Voen. izd-vo, 1965, pp. 562-566.

[79] *Idem*, "Strannoe i chudovishchnoe," *Sochineniya*, 4th ed., Moskva: Izd-vo polit. lit-ry, 1947-1957, vol. 27 (1952), pp. 46-53 at 49.

situation than the CCP. It maintained that the global balance of power was shifting to the East's favor and that no other country than the Soviet Union knew where the West stood. Khrushchev was not saying that the West was actually behind the East. If anything, he thought the latter had a long way to go before being able to catch up with the former. Thereupon he counseled a prudent stand in international politics. On this point, Mao differed sharply. He felt that the USSR with the nuclear bombs and the sputnik launched on October 4, 1957 was far superior to the US. In an armed showdown, the latter would be crushed. This rationale was expressed by him in an informal talk to the Chinese attending the Moscow University on November 7, 1957 while he was in the Russian capital for the celebration of the 40th anniversary of the Bolshevik revolution. It is there that the well publicized phrase of the east wind prevailing over the west wind was coined.

One meaning of this phrase, we think, was not caught by any commentator. In fact, the Chinese leader was more prudent than merely meets the eye. According to his estimate, the Soviet Union was indisputably mightier, but she must take advantage of it by striking timely at the enemy, because the advantage cannot be kept for long. It is a matter of time that the other side may enjoy it. Because wind is seasonal by nature, the west wind is bound to prevail over the east one. In military strategy, which Mao had written so much on, one must take the offensive while he is stronger. With all this argument, Khrushchev could not concur.[80] A surprise nuclear assault, he thought, on the imperialists was too much a gamble. Whether the USSR were in a position to win the war was a moot question after all. Therefore, he put stress on the deterrent policy, trying to convince Mao that the East camp had become so formidable that the aggressors dared not enkindle a fight and in this way, preemptive war was unnecessary. Thus war was averted.

On his part, Mao was obsessed with winning out on the battlefield. The Soviet Union, he insisted, was capable of destroying the US and she should therefore lose no time in doing just that. Here we have two brave men each seeking to outbid the other. One (Mao) brags that he is so strong that he can gain the upper hand in a bout with the enemy, but the other (Khrushchev) declares that he is so strong that the enemy does not even dare to dig up the hatchet. Mao's stance was put to a couple of tests. The first was the Taiwan issue. Both in 1954 and 1958 he ordered the bombardment of the off-shore islands and this in spite of America's determination to make Taiwan safe.[81] Khrushchev never backed up Mao, for he saw his intent of dragging

[80] Alvin Z. Rubinstein, The Foreign Policy of the Soviet Union, 2nd ed., New York: Random House, 1966, p. 248.

[81] The shelling of the islands by the Chinese Reds was criticized by Moscow as undertaken without obtaining its consent, O. Borisov i B. Koloskov, "Politika sovetskogo soiuza v otnoshenii NR," Leninskaya politika SSSR v otnoshenii kitaya, pp. 159-256 at 174.

the USSR into the trouble.[82] The second test was the Sino-Indian difficulty in October 1959 and October 1962. On both these occasions, the Chinese troops were engaged on their border.[83] The Soviet Union did not side with the Chinese despite their being the younger brothers and despite their being faced with a hostile bourgeois nation. In the 1962 clashes, the Beijing leaders were infuriated by the favoritism shown by Russia to India and Russia's supply of jetplanes to strengthen the latter's forces in anticipation of the next round of fighting.[84]

A confrontation of the CPR with the US would certainly involve the Soviet Union and a skirmish in the Taiwan area may well escalate. At Khrushchev's side was indeed an untoward ally. With determination he was a) to bring it into line through international pressure and b) to keep it weak and subordinate to Moscow. To these ends, he called the 12-ruling party conference on November 14-16, 1957, the 61-party conference on the next two days,[85] and the 81-party conference on November 1, 1961.[86] He schemed to condemn China and/or exclude her from the socialist camp, but she fought back tooth and nail. Amassing a sizeable support, she succeeded in keeping herself in and forcing some ideological kowtow from the Kremlin.

However, Khrushchev was able to deal a severe blow to the ambition of the CPR to become a nuclear and industrial power. In 1958, he broke treaty commitments by refusing Beijing a sample A-bomb and three years later he recalled nearly all Soviet Union's and East European experts from China. This move could not come at a worse time because Mao and company had entertained ambition of becoming a strong state. After the Great Leap of 1958, disillusion prevailed among the Beijing rulers. Among them the pragmatists assumed the leadership. They scaled down, although not yet jettisoned, many gigantic construction projects in favor of consumer-oriented enterprises. A policy of "walking on two legs" was inaugurated to simultaneously foster native handicraft and modern manufacture.[87] Parallel with this new course was an excruciating assault on the Soviets whose repudiation of contractual obligations to the CPR was resented to no end. As the sixties wore on, China's pragmatists came in for criticism. They and the Soviets were denounced by Mao and company as revisionists intent upon taking the capitalist road. Diplomatic ties with Russia were severed in

[82] *Ibid.*, p. 180.

[83] Ishwer C. Ojba, *Chinese Foreign Policy in an Age of Transition, the Diplomacy of Cultural Despair*, Boston: Beacon Press, 1969, pp. 154, 168.

[84] O. Edmund Clubb and Eustace Seligman, *The International Position of Communist China*, Dobbs-Ferry, New York: Oceana Publications, 1965, pp. 18-19.

[85] *KPSS, spravochnik*, Moskva: Izd-vo polit. lit-ry, 1976, pp. 290-291.

[86] *Ibid.*, p. 391.

[87] Morton H. Halperin and Dwight H. Perkins, *Communist China and Arms Control*, New York: Praeger, 1965, pp. 28-29.

1963.[88] The Soviet embassy and its personnel were seized in Beijing and the Chinese in Moscow were harassed in return. The Russians and Chinese were outright foes by the time the Cultural Revolution unfolded. On August 20-21, 1968, the CCP suddenly was waked by the five-power invasion of Czechoslavakia.[89] The latter country sought to go its own way by initiating some domestic reform and foreign-policy change. In this deviation, she was not to succeed. The attack and occupation could not fail to drive home a lesson to the Chinese, a lesson which they were to experience in a few months' time.[90] On March 3, 1969, an armed clash erupted on an islet called Damansky in the middle of the boundary river, Ussuri. The true picture is still clouded, but there is reason to suppose that the Russians were the culprits. Following the first fight, they ignited a second one on March 15 at the same location, and the Chinese were reported to take heavy casualties. It is from the latter part of 1968 that the Soviet Union stepped up the defense along the entire border with China. In August 1969, Moscow appointed a missile expert, Colonel-General V. Tolubka, to be the new commander of the Far Eastern Military District. Shortly afterwards, a consolidated command was formed along the central Asian front.[91] The message of the Kremlin could not be missed by Beijing: the annihilation of the nuclear facilities in Xinjiang and/or the detachment of that region. China's response was two-pronged. First, in the face of the threat she could not afford to be continuously defiant. She came to the negotiation table on October 6, 1969 with the Soviets, willing to discuss the boundary issue by taking as the basis the unequal treaties between imperial Russia and imperial China; and this put off indefinitely the territorial claims of the CPR. Ambassadors were returned to each other's capitals in 1970,[92] and both agreed to improve commercial intercourse.[93] Second, Beijing quietly approached (more likely, was approached by) the US. Here was a country, but no other, Beijing felt, which was able to lend her assistance in more ways than one and which was equally resolved to resist the Russians. Hence, the pingpong diplomacy, the invitation of Nixon and the rest of the story appearing in the preceding section.

Whether or not in response to the improved Sino-US relation, the USSR proceeded in earnest to beef up her position in the Far East.[94] Reports estimated her troops along the Sino-Soviet border to be

[88] *Information Please*, 1979, p. 158, col. 2.

[89] *World Almanac*, 1969, p. 88, col. 1.

[90] *China and U.S. Foreign Policy*, 2nd ed., Washington: Congressional Quarterly, 1973, pp. 73-74.

[91] Harvy G. Gelber, "Sino-Soviet Relationship and the United States," *Orbis*, Spring 1971, pp. 118-133 at 118.

[92] *World Almanac*, 1980, p. 525, col. 2.

[93] Harold Hinton, *op. cit.*, p. 301.

[94] O. Snegin, "Militarizatsiya kitaya, ugroza azii." *Aziya i afrika*, 8 (1978), pp. 39-41.

between 45 and 48 divisions by 1973.[95] In the meantime, the Russian Government accelerated the peasant re-settlement in the disputed territory, that is, territory which China claimed; and many places saw their names changed so that they sound Russian rather than Chinese. At boundary talks both sides hardened their stand.[96] There was absolutely no progress. More on this anon. Even though the Soviets made little threat, Zhou Enlai urged the Chinese to be prepared for their surprise assault.[97]

Antagonism remained unabated in 1974. Beijing and Moscow kept on piling up abusives against each other. On May 23, the CPR was served a warning by the Russian Foreign Office that unless it recognized the USSR sovereignty over a certain island at the confluence of the Amur and Ussuri, Chinese ships would be barred from plying the Soviet inland waterways. When the CPR counter-proposed a mutual withdrawal of troops along the border and the signing of non-aggression pact, she was rebuffed unceremoniously. A couple of incidents occurred to aggravate the tension of the two countries. On January 19, 1974, Beijing expelled five Russian diplomats, charging them with improper activities. In retaliation, one Chinese agent was ordered out of Russia on similar accusations. Then on May 14, a Russian military helicopter landed in the Chinese Turkestan and the machine and crew were captured. While the Soviet spokesman said the helicopter strayed into China by accident, Beijing insisted that they were spying on the nuclear establishment of Xinjiang. After almost a year's detention, the crew and the ship were handed back.[98]

At the top of their voice, the CCP demanded, prior to the 1975 military debacle of South Vietnam and Kampuchea that the US get out of there. On the morrow of America's retreat, the Chinese had a second thought on the matter, however. Now facing the clear and present danger of their northern neighbor whose forces they always exaggerated to have reached one million (actually about half of that), they wished the US to stay in the Pacific region. Witness the repeated expression the Beijing elite made to American reporters and Congressmen that the US should "maintain armed forces in Asia as a deterrent to Soviet expansion."[99] How to relieve herself of the burden of confronting the USSR alone has become, from 1975 on, the CCP's diplomatic center of gravity. In order to combat that "main enemy," China has sought to gain broad succor everywhere possible, particularly in Europe and at the same time, she whipped up anti-

---

[95] *Encyclopedia Yearbook*, 1974, p. 175, col. 1.

[96] "Kitaya," *Ezhegodnik*, 1976, pp. 307-308.

[97] Dieter Heinzig, "Neuer Tiefpunkt zwischen Peking und Moskau," *Aussenpolitik*, 27 (1976), heft 3, pp. 298-307 at 299.

[98] *Encyclopedia Yearbook*, 1975, p. 164, col. 2.

[99] *Ibid.*, 1976, p. 156, col. 2.

GOVERNMENT OF SOCIALIST CHINA

Soviet propaganda. In it she exhausted all conceivable synonyms of "evil" to characterize the Russians.

On the surface, the downfall of the Gang of Four might reverse the "hate-USSR" policy which was linked with them, but Deng Xiaoping dispelled that speculation.[100] In fact, he pledged that policy not only for this but for the next generations (see above). Such inveterate phobia does not, however, exclude some minor corrections in Sino-Soviet contacts. For example, on October 7, 1977, an agreement was made regarding the navigation on the Ussuri, stipulating among other things that "at times of low water Chinese ships can use a channel near Khabarovsk."[101] The impassioned courting by the US during 1978 had the effect of emboldening the Chinese in their standup against the Soviets. Seeing their hands strengthened, Beijing launched a vigorous diplomatic drive on Brezhnev. When he offered to conduct dialogue with a view to ameliorating their relation, Beijing spurned it as sheer talk.[102]

The nerve war escalated from words to deeds. Border skirmishes on both the Far East and Xinjiang fronts were reported now and then from 1976 to 1979.[103] On May 7, 1978, thirty Soviet troops backed up by a helicopter and river flotilla crossed the Ussuri into Hulan district of Heilongjiang province in the wee hours. According to the Beijing media, a number of inhabitants were shot or wounded. The Soviet government, while not denying the military move, refuted the casualty assertion of China.[104] The incident, like so many others, remains unexplained by either party. Probably it is the CPR which invoked the Soviet action, now that it was made ever braver by the impending US recognition and by the almost sure support of that country should a collision flare up between the two communist neighbors. With the incident in mind, the head of China's delegation to the UN General Assembly dubbed the Soviet Union the "most dangerous source of a new world war" (see above). Perchance the extremely hostile step taken by the CPR is the announcement of September 6, 1978 that it would terminate the 1950 Sino-Soviet treaty of alliance and mutual defense, now that the target of that instrument, the then detested US, has become a dear friend of Beijing. This resolve was reaffirmed on April 3, 1979 by the Chinese Government whose spokesman stated that the treaty "has long ceased to exist,"[105] and that by April 11, 1979 it would become null and void. So it did.

There is the possibility that the Beijing-Washington rapprochement

[100] N. Kapchenko, "Geopoliticheskie raschety i politicheskie proschety pekina," *Mezhdunarodnaya zhizn'*, 6 (1979), pp. 37-47 at 41.

[101] *Encyclopedia Yearbook*, 1978, p. 153, col. 2.

[102] *Ibid.*, 1979, p. 157, col. 1.

[103] *Information Please*, 1979, p. 525, col. 2.

[104] *Encyclopedia Yearbook*, 1979, p. 157, col. 1.

[105] *Britannica Book of the Year*, 1980, p. 249; *Encyclopedia Yearbook*, 1980, p. 171, col. 2.

has stimulated the balancing Russo-Vietnamese alliance which was embodied in a treaty of November 2, 1978. The instrument purports to eliminate, through consultation, an attack (or threat thereof) on either side by a third power.[106] China's military offensive in Vietnam starting from February 17, 1979 prompted the USSR to order her to cease and desist "before it is too late." However, although Russian planes and vessels were rushing materiel to Hanoi, no Soviet armed attack on the CPR took place. In mid-1979, there was a short exchange of friendly notes between Moscow and Beijing, indicating their willingness to compose their differences and to improve relations in trade and culture and in boundary problems. Significantly, China dropped in June her long-insisted term of having Soviet troops taken from unspecified places as preliminary conditions of settlement. Yet three months later, border clashes erupted in west Xinjiang,[107] but Beijing offered to talk. She refuted the Soviet accusation of her territorial aggrandizement.[108] On September 26, Beijing dispatched Vice Foreign Minister Wang Youping to Moscow to meet the Soviet counterpart Leonid Ilyichev to develop an agenda and procedure for a boundary parley. For all this move and trade agreement signed in August, the CPR never let off her verbal abuse of the Soviet hierarchy. Not unexpectedly, Russia replied in kind.[109]

The boundary difficulties constitute a serious problem which almost assures the two countries to be bad neighbors. Settlement efforts were made in 1964, and resumed in 1969 and 1979. All are to no avail. China claimed that czarist Russia grabbed from her, by the unequal treaties, 1,500,000 sq km which is described as big as three Frances or thirteen Czechoslovakias, but said that she was willing to let bygones be bygones.[110] Still there are many undetermined lines. The Soviet Union, it is asserted, maintained two positions which make the situation "smell gunpowder."[111] The Kremlin mouthpiece argues the boundary is not only fixed up by the treaties but by a) "de facto position" and b) historical crystallization.[112] These would include vast areas outside the treaty-stipulated zones. It is the insistence of the Soviets that China recognize all these as belonging to them. Most ominous to Beijing is the Soviets' rejection of its demand of withdrawing each other's troops from the controversial places as a modus vivendi. As the situation stands today, unless the CPR makes substantial concessions, that is, let the Soviet Union take the extra-

[106] Encyclopedia Yearbook, 1979, p. 158, col. 1.

[107] Britannica Book of the Year, 1980, p. 249, col. 2.

[108] A. Platonov, "Kurs, ugrozhaiushchii miru; gegemonist., ekspansionist. politika pekina, istochnik mezhdunar. napryazhennosti," Sovetskie profsoiuzy, 13 (1980), pp. 44-45.

[109] V.N. Borisov, "Peikin, destruktivnaya politika," Problemy dal'nego vostoka, 2 (1980), pp. 44-54.

[110] Renmin ribao, June 17, 1981, p. 7, col. 1.

[111] Ibid., col. 3.

[112] Ibid.

treaty land, the issue will remain thorny and truly dangerous. On June 16, 1981, Afghanistan and the USSR signed a boundary agreement which, asserts Beijing, affects the territory of the CPR. The latter's Foreign Office declared that the CPR is not going to be bound by it.[113] The size of the territory in question is more than 20,000 sq km. The CPR, it is pertinent to comment here, has concluded no less than five boundary treaties: with Burma (October 1, 1960), with Nepal (October 5, 1961), with Mongolia (December 26, 1962), with Pakistan (March 2, 1963), with Afghanistan (November 22, 1963).[114] Each time, it is the Chinese who generously conceded junks of territory. Why wouldn't they do the same with the Soviet Union?

A late development in the otherwise stationary Sino-Soviet relations is the Tashkent speech of President Leonid Brezhnev delivered on March 24, 1982.[115] It recognizes the sovereignty of the CPR over Taiwan and offered to discuss ways and means to improve friendship with it. Such a position was however rejected by Beijing as inane.[116] It said the soviet leader was playing a division trick during a time when the Sino-American diplomacy was at a low ebb due to the arms sales to Taiwan. Brezhnev was accused as hypocritical because the Chinese asserted the best manner to better the relations is for the USSR to demilitarize the strip abutting on China, but it does not do it. This attitude of the Chinese, however, changed a few months later in response to the US policy toward Taiwan. Being unable to get the Reagan administration to abrogate the Taiwan Relations Act, Beijing decided to play its USSR card. The occasion was Nixon's fourth visit to the CPR (September 8-11, 1982). As usual, he praised the Chinese oligarchs for their instrumentality in providing peace and stability in Asia. In the meantime, he was just as enthusiastic in blaming the USSR for warmongering. But the Chinese press never reported the latter rhetoric, and foreign minister Huang Hua, in greeting Nixon, said nothing about the Soviet hegemonism.[117] The US government is served the warning of the possible review of China's diplomacy, a review which some US senators, particularly the late Henry Jackson of Washington were worried about. By capitalizing on this fear on the part of American politicians, Hu Yaobang made a speech during the 12th Congress of the CCP that China and the Soviet Union can come to terms. But his proviso is the removal of Russian troops from the Chinese border. We would argue that the rift between Moscow and Beijing is deeper than merely meets the eye and the latter's threat to rechart the course toward the US must not be taken at its face value.

---

[113] *Ibid.,* July 23, 1981, p. 1, also September 1, 1981, p. 4.

[114] *Zhong guo shou ce,* Hong Kong: Da gong bao, 1980, p. 317.

[115] "Rech' tovarishcha L.I. Brezhneva" (Speech of comrade L.I. Brezhnev), *Pravda,* March 25, 1982, pp. 1-2 at 2, columns 6-8.

[116] *Beijing Review,* April 5, 1982, p. 11.

[117] *Globe and mail,* September 8, 1982, p. 10, columns 2-4.

Early in 1982, the Soviet government sent the Chief of General Staff, Nikolai Ogarkov for an intensive tour "to Hanoi, Phnom Penh and Vientiane to hold secret talks."[118] It also dispatched "a massive soviet military (80 people) delegation led by Defense Minister D. Ustinov to India" on March 20 of the same year.[119] These activities are viewed in Beijing as indicative of Russian expansionism.[120] The Chinese called attention of the ASEAN countries to the USSR's espionage carried out in them to collect "information about the sea lane," saying it constituted a military threat.[121] It also stated that it is the USSR in league with Vietnam which came to disturb peace and order in that region.[122] This sort of propaganda probably will diminish in light of the USSR card played by the Beijing oligarch from at least 1982 on.

At Brezhnev's funeral on November 13, 1982, Foreign Minister Huang Hua had cordial conversations with Yuri Andropov and he said to reporters that there cannot be a serious block to Sino-Russian detente. And on the 60th founding anniversary of the USSR (December 22, 1982), China's Standing Committee of the NPC and State Council sent a message of greetings to the Presidium of the Supreme Soviet and the Council of Ministers of the Soviet Union.[123] The sincerity of these moves, we hold, should be judged against the persistent demands of China that the USSR get out of Afghanistan, withdraw her troops from the Chinese border and stop supporting the Kampuchean regime.

The above survey of the Sino-Soviet relation shows how drastically and dramatically the CPR has reshaped its attitude toward the USSR.[124] Both national interest and ideology have played their parts in straining the friendship, and some argue that the latter (ideology) is a facade. Moscow and Beijing, they say, are never united by it (in fact divided by it), while the only bone of contension centers on nationalism and all that involves. We think such assertion is sharable, judging from the latest round of argument in which the blaming of each other for deviation from Marxism-Leninism is completely gone. Deng Xiaoping must be given a great deal of credence when he said that the relation between Beijing and Moscow will be irreparable for several generations.

[118] Mai Zhenmin, "Soviet Chief of General Staff tours Indochina," *Beijing Review,* March 1, 1982, pp. 11-12.

[119] Yu Ying, "Why was Ustinov in India?" *ibid.,* April 5, 1982, p. 13. *Facts on File,* March 26, 1982, p. 216, G2.

[120] Song Fusheng, "Soviet drive into southeast Asia," *Beijing Review,* March 1, 1982, pp. 15-17.

[121] Xie Wenqing and Zhang Junli, "Soviet drive into southeast Asia," *Beijing Review,* March 1, 1982, pp. 15-17.

[122] Song Fusheng, *loc. cit.*

[123] *Beijing Review,* January 3, 1983, p. 8.

[124] Steven I. Levine, "China und die sowjetunion, unuberbrückbare feindschaft oder eine anfang?" *Europaarchiv* (Bonn), 34 (1979), heft 20, pp. 611-622.

Asia

The CPR was recognized diplomatically by all but one communist state within 10 days of Mao Zedong's proclamation of its founding on October 1, 1949. That one is Albania which followed suit on November 11.[125] India shared the honor with Burma to be the first non-communist polities to do the same on April 1, and June 8, 1950 respectively. Jawaharlal Nehru showed his dedication to the Beijing oligarchy by persistently sponsoring its entry into the UN from 1949 to the year he died (1964). Brimful with animus against imperialism and having a lethal neighbor of Pakistan, India found it essential to befriend the CPR. In 1951, both governments signed a trade agreement, followed three years later by a protocol conceding China's sovereignty over Tibet. This protocol (April 29, 1954) contains the so-called Pancha Shila (five principles of coexistence) orchestrated by Nehru and Zhou Enlai in later international politics. The Indian statesman, in carrying out the terms of the instrument, refused Tibetans and Kazaks seeking refuge in India at that time.[126]

Beijing, however, soon found out that Nehru was after all not as anti-American or anti-USSR as he was thought to be. This resulted in cooling off of the Sino-Indian relation. It was not long before a crisis occurred. In 1956 the Indians discovered that China had built up a military road across their territory in the Aksai Chin plateau in the Ladakh region of northwest India. A border fight flared up on October 20, 1959.[127] The crisis was compounded by the Chinese army's suppression in the preceding month of the Tibetan revolt, and by India's granting of asylum to tens of thousands of the participants.[128] China laid claim to a substantial portion of the Ladakh region and the Northeast Frontier Area neighboring on Tibet. With or without justification, China would not accept the 1913 McMahon line as the demarcation. A bigger clash broke out on October 20 (!) 1962 when the PLA launched a surprise attack in Ladakh and in the disputed Area.[129] It took the territory which the CPR stated to be hers. Then, the Chinese Government declared a unilateral ceasefire on November 24 and withdrew its troops.[130] The situation remains unchanged ever since.[131]

The Beijing-Delhi relation can only be portrayed as correct up to the Cultural Revolution.[132] At one time during that turmoil the Red

[125] Zhong guo shou ce, p. 318.

[126] D.G. Stewart-Smith, The Defeat of Communism, 1st ed., London: Ludgate Press, 1964, p. 144.

[127] World Almanac, 1960, p. 122, col. 1.

[128] Ibid., p. 99, col. 1.

[129] Ibid., 1963, p. 124, col. 1.

[130] Ibid., p. 126, col. 1.

[131] V. Borisov, "Peking: Hegemonism in Action, China's Policy in southeast and south Asia," International Affairs (Moscow), January 1981, pp. 34-42.

[132] A.G. Noorani, "India and China start talking," New Leader, 62 (February 12, 1979), pp. 8-9.

Guards carried out demonstration and harassment of the Indian embassy in Beijing and the Indians retaliated in kind in Delhi. Diplomats were recalled from each other's capitals. On November 30, 1972, India offered to negotiate on the boundary issue but China declined,[133] and in order to render some comfort to Pakistan, she vetoed Bangladesh's admission to the UN on August 25, 1972.[134] Sino-Indian diplomacy was not to show signs of improvement until 1976 when ambassadors were exchanged and Indian ships were allowed to enter Chinese ports. Yet the Tibetan question and the alleged support by India of Tibetan refugees' demand of secession of their homeland from China continued to vex the relation.[135] During a September 1978 visit to the Soviet Union, External Affairs Minister Vajpayee assured his hosts that India would make no deals with China at the expense of the USSR. In the previous month, a Chinese trade delegation, the first ever coming to India since the 1962 border war, was courteously treated. Beijing invited Vajpayee to visit there.[136] After a couple of delays the journey was made, but no concrete result was achieved. On June 22, 1980, the CPR formally requested a settlement to be effected on the troubled boundary. India responded coolly. Delhi and Beijing seem to have their eyes on their respective allies, namely the Soviet Union and Pakistan. These two nations, each for its own reasons, were not willing to see a detente between India and China. The latter's Foreign Minister Huang Hua paid a visit to Dehli from June 26 to 30, 1981.[137] A Chinese paper describes the friendship of the two nations as inexhaustible and everlasting as China's Huanghe and India's Ganges, but Indian press was excited little by the event.[138] Nevertheless, the two neighboring nations held rounds of talks with a view to improving the situation. The first round occurred on December 9-14, 1981.[139] The second round began on May 15 and ended in a deadlock five days later,[140] as failed the third round from January 28 to February 2, 1983.[141] Spokesmen for the two sides always stated that the differences were still very great, even though there had been some similarity of opinion over how the dispute should be solved and both sides agreed to meet again.[142] Russia, needless to say, did not approve of their rapprochement, and the TASS news

133 *Facts on File*, December 3-9, 1972, p. 981, F2.

134 *Ibid.*, August 27-September 2, 1972, p. 675, A1; *Encyclopedia Yearbook*, 1973, p. 251, col. 1.

135 *Facts on File*, March 10, 1978, p. 154, G2; *Encyclopedia Yearbook*, 1978, p. 154, col. 2.

136 *Encyclopedia Yearbook*, 1979, p. 245, col. 2; *Facts on File*, February 16, 1979, p. 123, D1.

137 *Renmin ribao*, June 27, 1981, p. 4.

138 *Ibid.*, June 24, 1981, p. 4.

139 *Facts on File*, December 25, 1981, p. 949, G3.

140 *Ibid.*, May 21, 1982, p. 369, D1.

141 *Beijing Review*, February 14, 1983, p. 9, col. 3.

142 *Facts on File*, May 21, 1982, p. 369, D1.

agency accused China of "occupying large portions of Indian territory" and suggested that the just way to solve the border problem was for China to return to India the land it occupied and to renounce its territorial claims. Renmin, however, saw this as "Moscow's attempts to sow discord between India and China."[143]

In late 1982, Beijing accused India of annexing a huge territory of China and forming it into a state called Arunachal Pradesh. The territory is said to be in the Chinese domain south of the McMahon line at the eastern section of the Indo-Chinese border. "It has been illegally encroached by India ever since the country's independence in 1947."[144]

Regarding Pakistan, China felt that a good relation with her was to her best interest, although for many years she criticized its government for taking up a membership in the now defunct SEATO.[145] On her part, Pakistan was only too glad to ally with the CPR, facing as she was an unfriendly southern neighbor. On March 2, 1963, a Sino-Pakistan agreement settled a long-standing land demarcation. Relation between the two countries remained warm despite the xenophobic Cultural Revolution and despite the leadership change in Islamabad. China's veto of Bangledash's bid for UN membership had greatly pleased Pakistan. President Ali Bhutto visited Beijing three times during his term in office (1971-1977). By sheer coincidence, each time he was there, China blew out a nuclear bomb as if to salute him.[146] His successor and overthrower, General Mohammad Zia ul-Haq, was a frequent guest of the Beijing elite. The two countries seem to have close consultation in aiding the freedom-fighters of Afghanistan after Babrak Karmal took power there in a coup of December 27, 1979.[147] The official exchange of visits between Beijing and Islamabad has been on the increase. China's vice-premier, Ji Pengfei on March 23, 1982 flew to the Pakistani capital to take part in celebration of that country's national day,[148] and Pakistan's foreign minister, Sahabzada Yagub Khan to Beijing on April 23.[149] Deng Xiaoping toasted the latter with the following warm words: "Sino-Pakistan relations have always been good, our friendship has stood the test of time. Our mutual support on the basis of mutual trust is praiseworthy. We have cooperated very well also in international affairs. This close relationship will be further consolidated and remain so in the future."[150] From october 17 to 23, 1982, President Zia ul-

[143] Renmin ribao, May 21, 1982, commentary translated in Beijing Review, May 31, 1982, p. 11.

[144] Beijing Review, December 20, 1982, p. 9.

[145] G.W. Choudhury, "China's policy toward south Asia," Current History, vol. 76 (1979), pp. 155-158.

[146] During the 10th test, November 18, 1971; 12th test, June 27, 1973; 13th test, June 17th, 1974.

[147] Duan Lian, "Afghanistan must not be forgotten," Beijing review, March 29, 1982, p. 7.

[148] Ibid.. April 5, 1982, pp. 3-4.

[149] Ibid., May 3, 1982, p. 2, col. 1.

[150] Ibid.

Haq visited China. He and Zhao Ziyang called for the withdrawal of foreign armies from Afghanistan and Kampuchea.[151]

Not to the USSR, but to Japan, the CCP should give the sincerest thanks. Japan, it is to be recalled, persistently harassed the GMD and prevented it from establishing an effective rule. This had the distinct effect of weakening the regime's ability to deal with the Reds. The latter, we suspect, entrapped Nanjing in a war with the Japanese. Without their aggression and military defeat of the National Government, the Chinese communists would probably have been wiped out. In the first two decades of the existence of the CPR, Japan was execrated as an ally of the imperialistic US and an enemy of China.[152] The situation was bound to change with the detente between Beijing and Washington.[153] After the visit of Nixon to Beijing, Prime Minister Eisaku Sato tried to jump on his wagon only to be spurned by the Chinese who considered him as an opportunist. His successor, Kakuei Tanaka, was liked by the CCP, of which he was a long-time admirer. On September 29, 1972, he, while visiting China, pronounced a decision to sever relation with Taibei and recognize the host country.[154] January 11, 1973 saw the exchange of ambassadors between Japan and the CPR.[155]

Japan hoped to win the CPR's cooperation in curbing the Soviet influence in the Far East. Publicly Beijing buttressed her demand of the return by Russia of the four islands which she illegally annexed in August 1945.[156] Even though official relation was restored, a peace treaty still waited to be concluded. Beijing repeatedly urged such an instrument, but insisted on an anti-hegemony article in it. This the Japanese refused because it would amount to an anti-Soviet declaration. Unwilling to offend the USSR, Tanaka was not prepared to rush into a treaty in spite of much pressure from Beijing. The latter sought to convince the Japanese Government of the mean behavior of the Kremlin. It pointed to the Soviet troops stationed in eastern Siberia which it held were posing a threat to Japan and the US as well as to China. Therefore, the Chinese propaganda said it behooved the three powers to form a united front toward the USSR.[157] When the latter country took the step to make agreements with Japan in order to get her help in the development of oil and gas resources in Siberia, Beijing offered at once to export more oil to Nippon. The CPR's attempt to isolate Russia in the northwest part of Asia, it is

[151] *Ibid.*, November 1, 1982, p. 8.

[152] Donald C. Hellman, *Japanese Foreign Policy and Domestic Politics*, Berkeley: University of California Press, 1969, p. 31.

[153] *Encyclopedia Yearbook*, 1973, p. 154, col. 1.

[154] *World Almanac*, 1973, p. 1021, col. 2.

[155] *Facts on File*, January 14-20, 1973, p. 37, F3.

[156] *Renmin ribao*, January 8, 1981, p. 4; June 12, 1981, p. 6.

[157] *Encyclopedia Yearbook*, 1978, p. 153, col. 2.

clear, depends for its success on the willingness of Tokyo to go along, but Beijing cannot be assured of this. Japan can hardly afford to comply with China's anti-hegemony demand unless she felt it safe to do so. Throughout 1975, when the Sino-Japanese peace treaty was discussed feverishly in both Beijing and Tokyo, the Soviet press served the notice that it must not contain the anti-hegemony clause. Signed on August 12, 1978 in the Chinese capital, that treaty, however, did contain it.[158] In doing so, Japan was in effect encouraged by the US.[159] Mincing no words, the governments of the CPR and Japan concurred to resist efforts of any country to assert domination in the Asian-Pacific region or anywhere else. Another successful step in diverting the Nipponese from Russia's course was taken on February 16, 1978 when China and a group of Japanese trading companies signed a $20,000 million eight-year agreement whereby China was to export oil and coal to Japan in exchange for Japan's industrial plants and technology.[160] A new era was open with Deng Xiaoping's stopover in Japan on February 6, 1979 on his return from the US. On that occasion, the Japanese Government lent to China more than $10,000 million for development.[161] Beijing's Japan policy is a two-pronged one: the outspoken anti-soviet appeal to the Japanese people and the attracting of financial and technological investment of big Japanese companies. In regard to the former, the success is only marginal since Tokyo cannot afford to be too offensive toward Moscow, but the latter effort has had remarkable results. Nevertheless, there are difficulties due to the curtailment in China's capital consumption which caused appreciable cancellation of contracts concluded by the Chinese Government and Nipponese firms. Evidence to prove the importance attached by Beijing to its Japan policy is that included in China's delegation to Tokyo are the highest ranking mandarins of the CPR. In 1982, vice premier Bo Yibo went to Japan for a two-week visit from April 1 to 14,[162] as did Premier Zhao Ziyang (May 31-June 5).[163] The latter made a major policy speech in Tokyo in praise of Sino-Japanese friendship and touching many aspects of CPR's diplomacy in general.[164]

A crisis, certainly the only crisis, flared up on July 5, 1982. It related to a school textbook apropos of Japan's aggression on China. The textbook used to be factual and straightforward, but on June 26, the

[158] A. Ivanov, "Yaponiya, vneshnyaya politika v 1978 g.," *Ezhegodnik*, 1979, p. 381.

[159] Giseda Bonn, "Der chinesisch-japanische vertrag," *Indo-Asia, vierteljahreshefte für politik, kultur und wirtschift indiens*, bd. 20, 1978, heft 4, pp. 404-406.

[160] *Encyclopedia Yearbook*, 1979, p. 158, col. 1.

[161] *Britannica Book of the Year*, 1980, p. 249, col. 1.

[162] *Beijing Review*, April 26, 1982, pp. 6-7.

[163] *Ibid.*, June 14, 1982, pp. 1-6.

[164] "Premier Zhao Ziyang on Sino-Japanese relations and other questions," *ibid.*, May 21, 1982, pp. 1-5.

Japanese Education Ministry ordered the revision of it. A change was made from "invasion" to "advance of troops," and the "Nanjing massacre" of December 1937 was described as provoked by the residents. In spite of the strong protest by the Chinese Foreign Ministry, the Japanese Government did not apologize for the textbook.[165]

The Chinese communists, it is to be noted, have thanked the Japanese for their invasion of China and for their help in bringing down the GMD regime. However, the utter brutality of the Japanese toward the innocent civilians in that country shocks the conscience (!) of the Reds.

According to a soviet source, the Chinese Ambassador in Tokyo recently visited the Chief of Japanese defense force.[166] This, says the Russian paper, is the first such development ever since the normalization of Sino-Japanese relation in 1972. Nipponese media are said to have widely reported the event. They wrote it as the initial step in the forging of military linkage of Tokyo and Beijing. Some local papers, *Pravda* continues, state the defense department has planned a special scheme for regular meetings of armed circles of the two countries in order to discuss the military and political situation in Asia, exchange information and engage in "active cooperation in diverse fields."

China was instrumental in effecting the ceasefire in Vietnam as governed by the accord of January 24, 1973.[167] Beijing's purpose is not only to avoid a strained relation with the US, but to checkmate the soviet influence there. Wanting to draw away Hanoi from the USSR toward herself, the CPR entered into a treaty with North Vietnam promising it substantial aid for reconstruction.[168] In 1978 it was revealed that China had granted the North Vietnamese over $10 billion during the past twenty years.[169] As has been noted, the Chinese persistently sought to get the US out of Vietnam, but when that country began to pull out, they felt a danger from the Soviet penetration and a Vietnamese hegemony in south Asia. Kampuchea and Laos would be under the thumb of Hanoi. The year 1975 brought a change of heart by the Beijing regime. Now it would not like to see the US go. It was also in that year that China established a closer relation with the Kampuchean insurgency under Pol Pot. Through the CPR's pressure, he accepted Prince Norodom Sihanouk to be the titular head when Pol Pot became the actual ruler of that nation. However, his regime was overthrown in 1979 by another group headed by Heng Samrin backed up by Hanoi.

[165] For portrayal of Nanjing massacre, see *Xin hua ci dian*, p. 605, col. 2.

[166] "Ukreplyaiut svyazi" (To strengthen the ties), *Pravda*, July 29, 1982, p. 5, col. 7.

[167] *World Almanac*, 1974, p. 985, col. 1.

[168] *Encyclopedia Yearbook*, 1974, p. 175, col. 1.

[169] *Information Please*, 1979, p. 159, col. 2.

In March 1978, Hanoi ordered a suppression of private enterprise. Ethnic Chinese in the southern part of Vietnam, mostly businessmen, suffered heavily. By mid-July, 140,000 of them fled to China. Beijing demanded that Hanoi cease and desist from its persecution. On July 3, Beijing ended its economic aid to Vietnam and frontier clashes occurred on August 25 and November 1. The invasion by Vietnamese troops of Kampuchea in 1978 to topple the government of Pol Pot, and the eviction of Chinese from Vietnam were China's casus belli in her intrusion into Vietnam from February 17 to March 5, 1979.[170] Beijing used between 200,000 and 300,000 men supported by planes and artillery "to punish the Vietnamese" and "to teach them a lesson."[171] Since China and Kampuchea do not have a common border, Chinese supplies to the overthrown Pol Pot guerillas must go through Thailand which, however, would not allow them to pass. Meanwhile, the Chinese and the Vietnamese have not been successful in their boundary talks. Such talks actually began in March 1979, alternately taking place in each other's capitals. On June 20, 1980, they changed sharp words, indicating that no progress has been made. Vietnam and the USSR formed an alignment on November 2, 1978 and the Heng Samrin regime was recognized by several communist states, including the USSR. It is clear that the Beijing leadership cannot do very much to sweep their stooge Pol Pot back into office as Kampuchea's dictator. Recently, Hanoi proposed to Beijing an ending of hostile action along the border, resuming as soon as possible the third-round talks between the two countries, and concluding a Sino-Vietnamese treaty of non-aggression. It also promised "to pull some of the Vietnamese troops out of Kampuchea."[172] The Chinese, however, brushed these aside as simple propaganda and deserving no attention.

One reason for the difficulty in overthrowing the Heng Samrin regime and in getting the Vietnamese out is that the opposition forces are badly dispersed among different factions and leaders. In May 1982 there emerged a unifying force of Kampuchean resistance which is planning to form a coalition counter-government. Beijing supports it whole-heartedly,[173] and it urges the United Nations to make efforts to force the Vietnamese to leave Kampuchea.[174]. Beginning on March 31, 1983, the Vietnamese troops mounted a major offensive against the insurgents in Kampuchea.[175] The battle spilled over into Thailand, as the Vietnamese forces were engaged in hot pursuit of the rebels. Apparently in response to this plight of their friends, the Chinese leaders ordered their troops into action by firing upon the Vietnamese

[170] R. Khamudlin, "V'etnam, vneshnyaya politika v 1979 g.," *Ezhegodnik*, 1980, p. 227.

[171] *Hammond*, 1980, p. 549, col. 1.

[172] Je Ying, "Hanoi peace offensive," *Beijing Review*, March 8, 1982, p. 15.

[173] *Ibid.*, June 25, 1982, p. 17.

[174] Mu Youlin, "True nature of the Kampuchean issue," *ibid.*, April 19, 1982, pp. 3-4.

[175] *Ibid.*, April 11, 1983, p. 11.

border guards. Both sides suffered considerable casualties.[176] It is unlikely, though, that the CPR would invade its southern neighbor as it did in the spring of 1979, remembering that its forces fought very badly on that occasion.

China used to consider Thailand as a dangerous country on account of its partnership in the SEATO and of the US military bases and personnel there. During the Vietnam conflict, these were employed to strike at the forces of Hanoi. Because no common boundary exists between the CPR and Thailand, the Chinese had to engage in subversive activities against it by helping the Thai communists. They supplied them with small arms which, however, had to pass through the Burmese-Laotian territory of about 150 km. This geographical difficulty, plus Beijing's reluctance to offend these two nations which wished to maintain normal relation with Thailand, made the Chinese effort not very effective. The CPR was constrained to focus on the training of Thai Reds in mobile warfare and the stepping up of propaganda on behalf of them. To this end, it set up radio stations in Yunnan province beaming into Thailand in native language the communist message to incite revolt there. Beginning in 1974, relation between the two countries improved appreciably thanks to Thailand's closure of American bases. In June, the last B-52 bombers were flown out and this was followed by Bangkok's declaration of all Thai-US military agreements null and void before or on March 20, 1975.[177] In February 1975 China pledged herself not to support the Thai rebels. All hindrances between Beijing and Bangkok had been removed and diplomatic recognition resulted on July 1, 1975.[178] A month earlier, the Philippines established relation with the CPR. In both cases, Taiwan was recognized as part of China from which Bangkok and Manila withdrew their ambassadors.

It appears that since then the CPR has stopped aiding the insurgents in Thailand. The Thai Government, however, has to worry about the Reds along the border with Malaysia. Through most of 1978, a large-scale pacification campaign was jointly undertaken by the two powers.[179] The Chinese shed no crocodile tears for their comrades butchered by the thousands in the jungle. The Thai Prime Minister Kriangsak visited Beijing and was lavishly treated there for a whole week beginning on March 29, 1978. Undoubtedly his was a thankful trip.[180] In return, Deng Xiaoping visited Thailand on November 5, 1978. The Chinese Foreign Minister Huang Hua, on June 25, 1980, pledged his regime's support of Thailand in repelling the Vietnamese incursion. Hua Guofeng met the Thai Prime Minister on July 9, 1980,

---

[176] *Renmin ribao*, April 17, 1983, p. 1.

[177] *Encyclopedia Yearbook*, 1975, p. 508, col. 2.

[178] O. Borin, "Thailand," *Ezhegodnik*, 1976, p. 391.

[179] *Encyclopedia Yearbook*, 1978, p. 491, col. 2.

[180] *World Almanac*, 1980, p. 914, col. 2.

while both attended the funeral of the Japanese Prime Minister, Masayoshi Ohira and told him the CPR would surely come to the aid of the Thais if attacked by the troops of Hanoi. In late January 1981, the CPR Premier Zhao Ziyang flew to Bangkok to confer with Thai officials in regard to technical and economic cooperation.[181] In short, the Sino-Thai relation turned from estrangement and hostility to accommodation following the US disengagement in southeast Asia. Formerly, Beijing piled up lots of derogatory words such as "fascists" or "military junta" upon the Bangkok regime. Now these quietly disappear from the Chinese press. The Thai Prime Minister Prem Tinsulanoda was invited to visit China from November 17 to 20, 1982. Zhao Ziyang stated to him that should the Vietnamese authorities dare to invade Thailand by force, the Chinese Government and people will stand firmly by the side of Thailand and give all support to the Thai people in their just stand of opposing aggression.[182]

While the lack of geographical propinquity makes the Chinese intervention in Thailand hard, if not impossible, the situation is different with Burma which is unfortunately the adjacent neighbor of China. The aid of the Burmese insurgents by the Chinese has been persistent since 1949. Adopting the same kind of technique as used to assist the Thai Reds, Beijing accords the Burmese comrades all facilities, not the least of which is asylum. Given this situation, the Sino-Burmese diplomacy cannot be warm. Nevertheless, Burma maintains correct relation with Beijing. It signed a boundary treaty with the CPR on October 1, 1960. China even offered economic assistance to the Rangoon Government, while in the meantime, it does not quit interfering in Burma's internal affairs. The former Burmese strongman, General Ne Win, earnestly wished to improve the relationship. He made no less than six trips to China. All but one were taken after he assumed the presidency on March 2, 1962. The first journey occurred when he was Prime Minister.[183] On that occasion (March 4, 1959), he initialed a protocol of friendship with the CPR.[184] Beijing, however, elected to pursue a double course. It keeps on abetting the Burmese communists.[185] The Chinese Premier Zhao Ziyang went to Rangoon on January 26, 1981.[186] He is the first highest official of the CPR to return the visit of the Burmese Prime Minister or President to the Chinese capital. In a recent journey to the Philippines, he said that in the future, China will not provide assistance to communist insurrection in Thailand, Indonesia, Malaysia and the Philippines.[187] Significantly, Burma is not mentioned: why this

[181] Renmin ribao, January 27, 1981, p. 1.

[182] Beijing Review, November 29, 1982, p. 7.

[183] He was appointed Prime Minister on February 13, 1958, see World Almanac, 1960, p. 342, col. 1.

[184] Wang Gungwu, China and the World Since 1949, London: Macmillan, 1977, p. 150.

[185] Encyclopedia Yearbook, 1976, p. 134, col. 1.

[186] Renmin ribao, January 27, 1981, p. 1.

[187] Kanada Kurier, August 27, 1981, p. 2, col. 5.

omission in the light of the CPR's seemingly sincere effort to brighten her image in the eyes of the south and southeast Asians?

Although Israel swiftly recognized the CPR (1950),[188] the relation between them was and remains nil, a fact the Beijing regime has conceded to.[189] The regime poured military hardware into the Palestinian units, besides arming the guerillas along the Persian gulf.[190] On October 18, 1981, the CPR, however, made it known that it would no longer provide arms for the Palestinians, and that instead, the aid would be of an economic nature.[191] On June 19, 1982, the PLO representative Tayeb Abdul Rahim Mahmond met with China's vice-foreign minister in Beijing. The latter promised one million US dollars in aid to that organization. It is noteworthy that there is no specified use of the money.[192]

During the three-power landing of troops in the Suez zone in Octobr 1956, China promised 250,000 volunteers to Egypt to help her to "kill off" the imperialists, and in the Cultural Revolution, all of China's diplomats except Ambassador Huang Zhen to Cairo were recalled. It accused Israel of aggression in the Arab-Israeli war in October 1973. The CPR's delegation to the UN declined to support the US-USSR resolution in favor of a ceasefire. The Chinese press assailed the Soviets for betraying the Arabs by withholding aid from them. In the energy crisis of 1974, China praised the Arab nation's use of oil as a means to fight foreign exploitation.[193] In November 1981, China denounced the Knesset (Israel's legislature) for its refusal to accept the eight-point proposal put forth by the Saudis to settle the Middle East problem.[194] The Israeli invasion of Lebanon from June 4, 1982 is scathingly attacked in the Chinese press.[195] Premier Zhao Ziyang voiced his support of Arabs' claim for their territory during his journey of 11 African states in late 1982 and early 1983. However, he also spoke of the right of existence of the Jewish country.[196]

Except Saudi Arabia, the Chinese Government has established relation with all the countries of the Middle East. The visit of Hua Guofeng with the Shah in 1978 was perhaps a year too soon. What goodwill was generated by it leaves no dent on the Islamic revolution of Iran.

[188] Wang Gungwu, op. cit., p. 146. It is extremely strange that two important Chinese sources which list all the countries giving recognition to the CPR omit Israel, Zhong guo shou ce, pp. 317-320 and Xin hua ci dian, pp. 1221-1231.

[189] Beijing review, July 28, 1980, p. 8.

[190] Harold Hinton, op. cit., p. 307.

[191] Toronto Star, October 19, 1981, p. 17, statement by CPR's deputy foreign minister, He Yiang.

[192] Beijing Review, June 28, 1982, p. 5.

[193] Encyclopedia Yearbook, 1975, p. 164, col. 2.

[194] Renmin ribao, November 5, 1981, p. 6.

[195] Beijing Review, June 14, 1982, p. 4; Zhong Tai, "Israel's expansion into Lebanon," Ibid., June 1, 1982, pp. 10-11.

[196] Ibid., January 3, 1983, pp. 6-7.

Other countries

Although England recognized China on January 15, 1950[197] and France on January 27, 1964,[198] and Federal Republic of Germany on October 11, 1972,[199] the contacts between them were minimal. It was not until the early seventies that they became brisk. In China's view, an Europe with its own identity can provide a counterpoise to both superpowers, and from the mid-1970's, to one of the two, the USSR.[200] To western Europe, in return, the CPR is a great help in drawing away some Soviet pressure from it. In 1973, the Chinese diplomats exerted great effort to cultivate the Europeans' goodwill.[201] The people of London and Paris, for the firt time, were treated, in May of that year, with a valuable collection of archaeological exhibits by the Chinese. Next month, Foreign Minister Ji Pengfei journeyed to Britain and France for a diplomatic debut. He asked Prime Minister Edward Heath and President Georges Pompidou for a state visit to his country. The latter man went on September 11, 1973 and remained there for seven days. To him, Mao Zedong and Zhou Enlai expressed their support for France's endeavor to develop European unity, but the Chinese objected to the establishment of an East-West detente. In the Sino-French communiqué of September 17, both sides opposed "all hegemony," a pet idea of China's, an idea suiting the French leader just as well.[202] A strong Europe, thought the Chinese, would impel the Soviet Union to move more troops out of the Far East. Beijing, therefore, gave its blessing to the European Economic Community.[203] In the meantime, it labeled as a plot the USSR-sponsored European security pact said to be designed to keep Russian interests supreme.

The then vice premier Deng Xiaoping arrived at Paris for a six-day (May 12-17, 1975) visit.[204] He held several audiences with President Valery Giscard d'Estaing and premier Jacques Chirac and invited them to China in 1976. The result of the talks was the agreement on holding regular consultation and the setting up of a Sino-French Joint Economic Commission to promote trade.[205] President Valery Giscard d'Estaing flew to China early in 1980. In August 1982, foreign minister

[197] Wang Gungwu, op. cit., p. 146.

[198] Xin hua ci dian, p. 1223.

[199] Ibid., p. 1224.

[200] F. Primorskii, "Kitai," Ezhegodnik, 1974, p. 309.

[201] F. Primorskii, "Kitai," Ibid., 1975, p. 318; Peter J. Opitz, "Westeuropa in der globalstrategi Pekings," Zeitschrift für politik (Berlin), 25 (1978), heft 3, pp. 223-238.

[202] Encyclopedia Yearbook, 1974, p. 174, col. 2.

[203] Iu. Dimov, "Za oruzhiem k 'varvaram,' ukhishcheniya maoistov i blizorukost' zapada," Novoe vremya, 32 (1978), pp. 18-19.

[204] Facts on File, May 31, 1975, p. 383, D3.

[205] Encyclopedia Yearbook, 1976, p. 156, col. 2.

Cheysson jetted to Beijing for a friendly visit,[206] as did the president of the National Assembly, Louis Mermax.[207] On the non-governmental level, the CCP and the French Communist Party restored their relationship after 17 years' severance when the latter party's General Secretary George Marchais led a delegation to Beijing upon the CCP's invitation in mid-October 1982.[208] President Francois Mitterrand is a three-time China visitor. In 1961 as Senator he went as a guest of the Chinese People's Institute of Foreign Affairs.[209] Mao Zedong recevied him in Hangzhou. In their conversation, the Frenchman stated that he would work for severing France's diplomatic relation with Taiwan and for recognizing the CPR. Also he supported China's legitimate seat in the United Nations. Twenty years later, in February 1981, Mitterrand stayed six days in China as head of a large Socialist Party delegation. Deng Xiaoping hosted the delegation warmly. Mitterrand said that only by closing ranks and becoming strong could the European nations deal with the challenge from the USSR and build an equal partnership with the US. It was during this visit, the French Socialist Party and the CCP decided to establish official party-to-party relations. On May 5, 1983 he journeyed to Beijing as President. Remaining there for five days, he was honored by the people of the capital city and embraced the hosts. Except the basic ideological ligament, Mitterrand and the autocrats of China have nothing in common.

The British conservative leader, Margaret Thatcher was invited to China on April 11, 1977. At the banquet in her honor, vice premier Li Xiannian ferociously rebuked the Soviet Union. However, she made no comment, let alone echo him. Once more, she visited China, from September 22 to 26, 1982, this time as Prime Minister,[210] with a view to discussing the possible reversion of Hong Kong to the CPR in 1997. As of this writing, the issue remains unsolved, with England insisting on sovereignty based on the Nanjing treaty of 1842. China's relation with West Germany is marginal; the only notable event is the visit to Beijing of that country's titular head of state, Karl Carstens from October 11 to 17, 1982.[211]

The flying of Tito to China on August 30, 1977 washed off once and for all the foulmouthed sayings about him during the early sixties.[212] The renegade and scab of Mao suddenly became a great hero. Sino-Yugoslavian diplomacy remained on the verbal level until 1982 when a committee for economic, scientific and technical

[206] Beijing Review, August 9, 1982, p. 9.

[207] Ibid., September 13, 1982, p. 9.

[208] Ibid., October 25, 1982, p. 9.

[209] Beijing Review, May 9, 1983, p. 4.

[210] Ibid., October 4, 1982, p. 9.

[211] Ibid., October 25, 1982, p. 8.

[212] I. Gusev, "Iugoslaviya," Ezhegodnik, 1978, p. 403.

244 GOVERNMENT OF SOCIALIST CHINA

cooperation was organized. Its third meeting was held in the Chinese capital from March 10 to 12, 1983. On this occasion, Premier Zhao Ziyang and Vice-President Mijat Sukovic pledged themselves to opening various channels of contacts beneficial to both sides.[213] The People's Republic, on May 1, 1975, formally recognized the European Economic Community; in the meantime, she signed the first trade deal with it, both for the purpose of straight business and for the support of Europe against the USSR. The year 1978 saw the flourishing of merchantile activity in China. The firms of the Federal Republic of Germany initialed a $4,000 million contract to rejuvenate her coal mines, and Dutch concerns concluded deals to expand her harbor facilities. A number of French companies contracted a $12,000 million loan for the purchase of French hydro equipment. More of this development will be seen in Chapter XI.

Championing for the European solidarity to counter the Soviet Union, the CPR did not overlook that country's backyard," the eastern sector of Europe.[214] In the northern tier of East Germany, Czechoslovakia and Poland, China does not think it worth the candle to try her hands, but she wants to do a bit of arms twisting in Romania and Yugoslavia which had refused to side with the USSR in its feuds with China.[215] With this in mind, Hua Guofeng set out for a tour there in the summer of 1978. He arrived at the capital of the first-named country on August 17 for a four-day stay, talking with leaders and doing some sightseeing. He declared at a dinner that those who tried to dominate the world would be "crushed under the iron fists of the masses," a shopworn shibboleth of the Chinese communists. In Yugoslavia from August 21 to 29, he was embraced by Tito. Alluding to a possible Soviet invasion of that country in the eventual death of the latter, he remarked that "Yugoslavia is ready at all times to repel the enemy."[216] Undoubtedly, the hosts were quite charmed. "That enemy is also China's," Hua Guofeng was saying in effect.

The next round of his trip came in late 1979, this time to the south and west parts of Europe. On October 15, Hua Guofeng flew to Paris to start a 23-day, 4-country itinerary. To his hosts in France, he pointed out "Europe's pivotal role in international affairs," urging it "to strengthen itself to smash foreign aggressors." On the Chinese leader's route, Bonn was the next station. Anxious to better the relation with Moscow, the German press said that he should ease up his Sovietphobia while a guest of the Federal Republic. In Munich, however, Hua Guofeng called for a united Europe facing up to Russia's threat.[217] It was, however, in Margaret Thatcher that he found the strongest disliker of the Soviets. Little wonder Hua Guofeng made

[213] *Beijing Review*, March 21, 1983, p. 9; also January 31, 1983, p. 9.

[214] M. Galin, "Otravlenoe sladkorechie pekingkogo vizitora," *Novoe vremya*, 47 (1979), pp. 14-15.

[215] *Encyclopedia Yearbook*, 1979, p. 204, col. 1.

[216] *Ibid.*, p. 179, p. 158, col. 1.

[217] V. Krasheninnakov, "Federativnaya respublika Germaniya," *Ezhengodnik*, 1979, p. 351.

in London the bitterest slap at them. On October 28, he indirectly compared the USSR to Nazi Germany and referred to it as the culprit of a third world war. As if fatigued from singing in high pitch of the anti-Soviet song, Hua Guofeng was quiet in his rendezvous with the Italian Prime Minister Francisco Cossiga on November 3.[218] Tourism now became his main enjoyment, although he did not forget comrade Enrico Berlinguer, the first secretary of the communist party of Italy, with whom he had a tête-à tête. Before flying home, Hua Guofeng came to see the house of Marco Polo. Undoubtedly he had in mind the ambition of building up his country, by means of the four modernizations, into a fairyland which the famous Venetian so romatically (we think, flatteringly) depicted in his travelog.

Undergoing a change as drastic as China's relation toward the USSR is hers toward Albania.[219] The Soviet Union, it is to be noted, broke diplomatic ties with the latter country at the same time as Khrushchev took the Soviet experts out of China. No sooner did he announce the ending of the Soviet assistance to Enver Hoxha in 1961 than Mao rushed to his side. From that moment on, Beijing and Tirana sang in chorus the "down with Russia" and "down with Tito" notes until 1972, when the Sino-US rapprochement began. Enver Hoxha viewed this situation with anger. Cemented by an identical ideology and fortified by a firm anti-Sovietism, the Beijing-Tirana alliance was none too closer from 1960 to 1971. Economically and militarily, Albania was the beneficiary of it simply because she is such a poor country. It was only through China's magnanimous help that that country's first and second five-year plans were successfully completed, the latter plan winding up in 1972 on the eve of the deterioration of relation between them.[220] In spite of China's abominable (to Tirana) attitude toward the US, the Albanians still approved the leadership change and policy alteration announced at the 10th Congress of the CCP (August 24-28, 1973).[221] However, Tirana, sensing the Chinese reorientation toward the imperialists, began to show anxiety. Exercising Enver Hoxha and company was the dependability of Beijing as an ally. In particular, they worried about what would happen if Albania could not acquire anything from China, now that she was so much reliant on her.

Since 1973, tension commenced to build up between China and Albania. Both, however, tried to present a façade of unity until the bubble blew up. In July 1977, an editorial of the Albanian party daily accused the CCP of betraying the world revolutionary movement because it said it had courted favor with the US and non-communist countries of the third world. The two former allies moved on to

[218] P.S., "Italiya, vneshnaya politika v 1978 g.," *ibid.*, 1979, p. 260.

[219] Geoffrey Stern, "Chinese-Albanian Relations: the End of an Affair?" *Millennium*, 6 (winter 1977-1978), pp. 670-674.

[220] *Encyclopedia Yearbook*, p. 78, col. 2.

[221] *Ibid.*, 1974, p. 87, col. 2.

compete for the support of Marxist-Leninist parties everywhere. Irritating the Albanians was the CCP's moderate course of domestic reform. In January 1978 China officially declared that she would review her Albania policy in light of that country's open criticism of her. At the same time, such words like "blackmail" and "pressure" emerged in the Albanian media, indicating that Beijing had used economic leverage to bring Tirana into line. Undaunted, Enver Hoxha scored the Chinese for their taking side in the Vietnam-Kampuchea conflict and recalled all Albanian students from China. In addition, he dissolved unilaterally the Joint Sino-Albanian Shipping company. Trade ties virtually ended.

Further escalation by Tirana of the dispute took the form of labeling the CPR social imperialist and revisionist, terms which Beijing had hurled at the Kremlin for more than twenty years. The cantankerous Albanian press scathingly assaulted Hua Guofeng for his touring of Yugoslavia, Romania and Iran in 1978.[222] It is in this year that ambassadors of China and Albania were recalled.[223] On July 13, 1978, China cut off all aid to Albania.[224] The latter was not deterred, however. Enver Hoxha's long commentary on the Sino-Albanian relationship between 1962 and 1977 chided the Beijing regime in the most acrid terms.[225] Hoping to step into China's shoes, the Soviet Union tendered an olive branch to Tirana. It was promptly rejected.[226] In the eyes of the Albanian leaders, all communists, except themselves, have sold out the lofty Marxism-Leninism for mundane materialism at home and appeasement abroad.

In the remaining pages, let us highlight the CPR relation with some third-world powers not already mentioned. Cuba recognized Beijing on September 28, 1960,[227] but the latter has not taken kindly to the pro-Soviet stand of Castro and this results in a very cool relation between the two countries. Frequently, Chinese diplomats staged walkouts from state occasions in Havana when Castro taunted the CPR.[228] In 1978, China shrilled at the Soviet-Cuba interventions in Africa and offered aid to Somalia and Zaire.[229] On February 22, 1982 a *Xinhua* commentary criticized Cuba as being built into a "Soviet military stronghold in Latin America." It describes that country as a military state which has one million troops in reserve, 200,000

---

[222] *Ibid.*, 1978, p. 88, col. 1; p. 158, col. 1.

[223] *Ibid.*, 1979, p. 88, col. 1; 1980, p. 96, col. 1.

[224] *Information Please*, 1982, p. 132, col. 1.

[225] Enver Hoxha, *Reflections on China*, Toronto: Norman Bethune Institute, 1979, 2 vols., see also *Encyclopedia Yearbook*, 1978, p. 96.

[226] *Encyclopedia Yearbook*, 1979, p. 88, col. 1.

[227] *Zhong guo shou ce*, p. 318.

[228] *Facts on File*, January 12, 1979, p. 20, col. 1.

[229] *Information Please*, 1979, p. 159, col. 2.

standing army, and 20 military academies[230]. China and Indonesia were friendly before 1966; the renowned Bandung Conference was held there in 1955, but the help of the CPR to the communists of Indonesia to stage a coup in 1966 prompted the authorities to sever diplomatic ties with Beijing. Up to the present there is no indication of willingness on either side to restore it. Toward North Korea, the CPR has played a restraining role. Deng Xiaoping told the visiting Kim Il Sung, President of that country, on April 18, 1975 that peaceful unification should be the goal, strongly hinting at the CPR's disapproval of another war on that peninsula.[231] China entered into diplomatic ties with Malaysia on May 31, 1974.[232] The fact that that nation has an overwhelming number of ethnic Chinese caused it anxiety and Beijing found it necessary to allay it by counseling the Chinese there and indeed anywhere else to be law-abiding citizens of the adopted countries.[233]

Even though a developing system itself, the CPR has a politically motivated program of foreign aid. Most credits and grants are interest-free. The total was $3,500 million covering the period of 1958-1974. Approximately sixty percent of the aid went to Africa where it was used to make small projects, although the Tan-Zam railway connecting Lusaka (Zambia) with Dar-es-Salaam (Tanzania) is by far the most impressive and costly ($400 million). The period of 1970-1974 saw Pakistan receive $250 million and Ethiopia $84 million, Somalia $111 million, Zaire $100 million, and Sri Lanka $114 million from Beijing.[234] A noticeable feature of the Chinese foreign aid is that it is declining as time goes by. On November 15, 1971, Qiao Guanhua in a speech to the UN General Assembly conceded that "China is still a developing country. Its economy is relatively backward. Hence the material assistance we can offer is limited, and our support will primarily be a political and moral one." For example, in 1970, the Chinese aid amounted to $710 million, but four years later it shrunk to $200 million.[235] In 1977, grants were made to Equatorial Guinea and Niger when the chiefs of state of the two nations, Francisco Macie Nguema Negue Ngong and General Seyni Kountché respectively paid a visit to China.[236] According to Chen Muhua, Minister of Foreign Economic Relations and Trade, the Chinese foreign aid was $540 million in 1982.[237] However, she did not say who the beneficiaries were. The more recent aid took the form of a waiver by Premier Zhao

[230] Reprinted in *Beijing Review*, March 15, 1982, pp. 10-11.

[231] *Encyclopedia Yearbook*, 1976, p. 156, col. 2.

[232] M. Mikhailov, "Malaiziya," *Ezhegodnik*, 1975, p. 339.

[233] *Encyclopedia Yearbook*, 1975, p. 164, col. 1. Hua Guofeng's speech of February 26, 1978 to the 5th NPC, *Keesing's*, September 8, 1978, p. 29181, col. 2.

[234] *Countries of the World*, p. 7, col. 3.

[235] *Ibid.*

[236] M.K. "Ekvatorial'naya gvineya," *Ezhegodnik*, 1978, p. 400; A. Nizskaya, "Niger," *ibid.*, p. 319.

[237] *Beijing Review*, February 7, 1983, p. 14, col. 1.

Ziyang of a whopping debt of $100 million owed by Zaire since 1973 when he visited that country on January 3, 1983 and personally offered it to President Mobutu Sese Seko. Making quite a bit of propaganda, he said that while certain (unidentified) nations had "let the burden of their economic crisis fall on shoulders of others, China would reinforce its solidarity and cooperation with countries of the third world."[238] It is true that the Chinese cannot compete with the Soviets in the dimension of assistance, but their emphasis is on light industry and the results are palpable to the populace. This is in contrast to the heavy things envisaged by the Russian aid which have no direct effect on the livelihood of the masses.

In the past, the CPR sent arms to tribal insurgents and guerilla bands in sub-Sahara Africa, aimed particularly at the "white redoubt" countries such as South Africa, the then bourgeois Rhodesia, Angola and Mozambique.[239] This action has stopped completely due to the changing circumstances. China had once said that she did not send arms to guerillas in El Salvador, but news kept coming out contradicting that statement.[240] Premier Zhao Ziyang visited eleven African states (Egypt, Algeria, Morocco, Gabon, Guinea, Congo, Zaire, Zambia, Zimbabwe, Tanzania and Kenya) from December 20, 1982 to January 17, 1983. Besides pledging the CPR's support in fighting racism of the South African Republic, he talked exclusively of technical and economic cooperation with the regimes of these countries.[241] The diminishing dose of ideology in Beijing's diplomacy has inclined others to accept the CPR as a non-revolutionary, conventional regime and they are willing to enter into relation with it. For a period of 22 years, from September 1949 to September 1971 (on the eve of China's admission to the UN), 63 countries recognized the CPR, but for a period of 12 years, from the latter date to April 30, 1983, 62 did the same.[242] The last five recognizing socialist China are:

Vanuata	March 26, 1982	a
Antigua and Barbuda	January 1, 1983	b
Angola	January 12, 1983	c
Ivory Coast	March 2, 1983	d
Lesotho	April 30, 1983	e

a *Beijing review*, April 15, 1982, pp. 7-8.
b *Ibid.*, January 10, 1983, p. 8.
c *Ibid.*, January 24, 1983, p. 9, col. 2.
d *Ibid.*, March 14, 1983, p. 12.
e *Ibid.*, May 23, 1983, p. 6, col. 3.

[238] *Facts on File*, January 1, 1983, p. 6, col. 2.

[239] Harold Hinton, *op. cit.*, p. 199.

[240] The Chinese disavowal was made in *Beijing Review*, March 9, 1981, p. 3, but the CBS news of February 12, and April 10, 1983 said that Chinese arms were in the rebels' hands.

[241] *Beijing Review*, January 3, 1983, p. 6; January 24, 1983, pp. 7-10.

[242] *Zhong guo shou ce*, pp. 317-320.

CHAPTER V

Following the entry into the world body, China has d'
top of the voice her union with the downtrodden of ev
particular, she pledges to help the colonies and depe
struggle for equality and sovereignty. Her official goal is ͟ͅ
a broad anti-imperialist common front. In order to emphasize ͟.
government's determination to pursue this goal, the Constitution
(Preamble) fixes it as one of the prime obligations of the state. The
CPR's representatives in international organizations have endeavored
to rally the third world nations under its banner. For example, on July
2, 1974, at the UN Law of the Sea Conference, held in Caracas of
Venezuela, Cai Shufan who headed the Chinese delegation
enthusiastically championed the proposal of 200-mile maritime zone
favored by those nations. The Chinese support of the third world stand
on the 12-mile territorial waters and 200-mile economic zone, as
developed from the Jamaica law-of-the-sea conference on December
10, 1982, was voiced with a great deal of ardor by their delegation.[243]
The Chinese communists, in order to improve the credibility of their
stand, have driven home the assertion that the CPR belongs to the
third world, because like them she is in the process of developing.[244]
However, the CPR sits in the most powerful organ, the Security
Council. Apparently, she is not embarrassed by this anomaly. Here
we see Mao Zedong's mass-line approach being extended to
international politics. China intends to compensate what she lacks
in such vital symbols of national strength as high GNP and industrial
output by producing nuclear bombs in the first place, and by dragging
onto herself the mass of nations in the second.[245]

---

[243] *Beijing Review*, December 27, 1982, p. 7.

[244] Hua Guofeng's speech to the 11th CCP Congress on August 18, 1977, *Keesing's*, December 16, 1977, p. 28720, col. 1.

[245] Hua Guofeng's speech to the 5th NPC on February 26, 1978, *ibid.*, September 8, 1978, p. 29183, col. 2.

CHAPTER IX
Agriculture

The peasants and land reform

Marxism-Leninism teaches that workers and peasants would form an alignment to stage the proletarian revolution and that the alignment would be led by the workers. The Chinese revolution, as known to all, relies entirely on the masses of the countryside, because there were hardly factory hands in the communist hide-outs. Even today the workers are only a pitiful fraction of the vast soil-tillers. If the theorists of the CCP are less imprisoned by the Marxist saga, they should abandon the fiction of the leadership role of the proletariat and grant that role to the farmers. After the break-up of the united front in July 1927, the Comintern-controlled CCP followed the Soviet recipe of proletarian revolution aimed at seizure of power in the cities by organized armed workers there. However, one after another, the attempts fizzled out.[1] Mao Zedong had to lead a band to the Jiangxi mountains where he built up a base. Quite a few scholars praised him for this "genial" move. In reality, it did not take a genius to choose that course. Following half a dozen abortive urban uprisings during 1927-1929, was there an alternative? The choice of Mao is all the more compelling in view of the lax rule of the warlords in the godforsaken areas of their provinces where Mao's force struck roots. Only a numskull would try armed revolts in the China of the late twenties by taking a leaf out of the Marxist book. The former Chinese dictator can scarcely be regarded as an innovator or as a conscious reviser of the traditional tactic of proletarian revolution.

Some students have made the assertion that the CCP-ruled peasants were "receptive to communist revolutionary mobilization."[2] This cannot be any more convincing than the credit given to Mao for his amending the revolutionary method. In the first place, the Reds were not begged by the mountain people to mobilize them. While intruding there, they imposed their control and gave them no opportunity to vote on their stay or leave. In the second place, the illiterate masses, utterly devoid of political sense or ideology, cannot, except by the wildest imagination, be seen as switching their loyalty from the warlords to the new masters. For the peasants, whoever came to assume the authority were their dominators. In fact, they were freer before the advent of the communists. Because of the marginal rule of the warlords, they were neither forced to report for military duty nor to pay tax.[3] Owing to the extirpation drives by the National Government in conjunction with the several provinces, the inhabitants

---

[1] Zhang Guotao, *Wo de hui yi,* Hong Kong: Ming bao chu ban she, 1973, vol. 2, p. 887.

[2] Thomas P. Bernstein, "The government of the People's Republic of China," *Government and Politics,* 2nd ed., New York: Random House, 1971, pp. 227-260 at 237.

[3] *Yi jiu si jiu shou ce,* Hong Kong: n.p., 1950, p. 62.

of the rebeldoms were totally mobilized for war. As a result, their fate was infinitely sadder than before.

Not the vote of thanks of the villagers, but their natural submissiveness and the superb skill of organization of the communists made it possible for the CCP to gain victory in battle after battle during the civil war and this only at the last phase of it. To the peasant army, the Reds can never pay enough gratitude. In all fairness, they should give something in return. That something is land. Its traditional system of ownership has indeed wrought a great deal of injustice, but we think in so enormous a country like China, this is inevitable. What is a fair rent or what is an equitable holding has no national standard, and the judgment on either of these cannot but vary. It has been too well known that the communists are wont to condemn what they elect to call feudal practice of land possession, and they would not abide by the practice, except for the sake of expedience. This happened immediately following their conquest of China. In any society there is bound to exist, more or less latent, a cleavage between segments or neighbors and such cleavage is often reinforced by personal enmity. The communists are extraordinarily capable of fomenting inter-group and inter-personal grudges and doing this in the name of class-struggle. A brief survey of the land reform of the Reds testifies to their Machiavellianism and animal brutality.[4]

The land program of the CCP has featured many zigzags since the 1920's.[5] The period of 1921-1927 saw a policy of moderation. A change to radicalism came with the setting up of the Soviet in Chaling (Hunan province) in November 1927, and the agrarian law promulgated the following year called for takeover of all land by the Soviet. This move could not fail to frighten the rural population. On January 1, 1931, the communists issued another decree which confiscated only the holdings previously belonging to the feudalists, warlords of varied ranks, country gentlemen, Buddhist temples and other big proprietors.[6] It left intact those of the middle and poor holders. The Jiangxi Soviet adhered to this course. After the Reds transferred their base to the northwestern part of China, the same policy continued until the inauguration of the united front in 1937.[7] That year saw the proposal by the CCP and acceptance by the GMD of a common platform which envisaged a new land policy. According to this, there was to be a complete stop of confiscation by the border government.[8] Is this pledge of the CCP meaningful? Up to 1937, one

---

[4] N.A. Vaganov et alii treat the 1947 land reform in "Agranye reformy," Bol'shaya sovetskaya entsiklopediya, 2nd ed., Moskva: Gosudarstvennoe nauchnoe izdatel'stvo "bol'shaya sovetskaya entsiklopediya," 1949-1958, vol. 1 (1949), pp. 320-337 at 333.

[5] Xie Fuye, Zhong gong pi ping, Taibei: Zheng zhong shu ju, 1952, p. 51.

[6] Peter S.H. Tang and Joan M. Maloney, Communist China: the Domestic Scene, 1949-1967, South Orange, New Jersey: Seton Hall University Pres, 1967, p. 337.

[7] A. Nove, "Collectivization of agriculture in Russia and China," Economic and Social Problems of the Far East, ediction by E.F. Szczepanik, Hong Kong: Hong Kong University Press, 1962, pp. 16-24.

[8] Peter S.H. Tang and Joan M. Maloney, op. cit., p. 63.

must remember, the communists had had more than two
carry out their agrarian reform. Given their dedication and effi
in doing things, all confiscation was already completed. The prom
they made in the common platform was an empty gesture to the
National Government in Chongqing. Further expansion of the Soviet
realm, prior to Pearl Harbor of December 1941, does not seem,
however, to be attended by ruthless dispossessing of the owners, and
this moderation was obviously calculated to assuage the fear of most
of the farmers who did have some land.[9] Yet as soon as the Axis
Powers lost their hope of victory in the Second World War, the CCP
changed its attitude toward what they catalogued as rich peasants.
These were forced to surrender their deeds to the poor. When a Red
hamlet was retaken by the government troops, there was invariably
a re-disgorgement waged by the prior owners against those given
land by the communists. Such seesaw struggle was reported in the
Chinese papers of that time, but, it does not seem to attract attention
of students in the West.

One indication of the highest priority given to the land problem by
the communist government is that it proclaimed the Agrarian Reform
Law on June 28, 1950 when the Red power was not yet fully
consolidated.[10] The PLA had still Tibet to conquer and pockets of
resistance to eliminate in China proper. It was four years before a
new Constitution appeared on September 20, 1954. Obviously, the
communist leaders could hardly wait until then to put the reform into
effect by invoking the authority of the People's Congress, the highest
organ of state power under that Constitution. If the CCP were legally
minded, or behaved a little patiently, it should defer the land bill to
1954. The deferment is particularly necessary in view of the gravity
of the provisions and the way they were executed. In reality, the Land
Reform Law amounts to death warrants to tens of millions of innocent
citizens.[11] It was announced as a decree of the Central People's
Government Council, with the initials of Mao Zedong. Its declared
aim, interestingly enough, is not to provide charity to the peasants,
but to free the rural production forces from the shackles of the feudal
owners or the landlord class. It is to develop agricultural production
and pave the way to rapid industrialization.[12] This proves that
individual proprietorship of the proletarians is not the government's
concern.[13]

Article 2 of the Law calls for the confiscation of land, beasts of
burden, farm tools and surplus grain of the landlords, and Article 10

[9] Thomas P. Bernstein, op. cit., p. 238.

[10] Gong fei bao zheng er shi nian, mao fei jie ju da lu er shi nian de zui xing, Taibei: Guo min da hui bi shu chu, 1969, pp. 8-16.

[11] Mao fei bei zhan yu dui nei kong zhi, Taibei: Guo min da hui bi shu chu, 1970, pp. 38-53; Eric Axilrod, Mao, Lenin and the Two Revolutions, Hong Kong: The Chinese University of Hong Kong, 1972, p. 11.

[12] Articles of the Land Reform Law, cited in Peter S.H. Tang and Joan M. Maloney, op. cit., pp. 338-339.

[13] J.D. Waller, The Government and Politics of Communist China, London: Hutchinson University Library, 1970, p. 129 where Liu Shaoqi's statement is cited.

an equal share of the redistributed land to in honest living.[14] The communists classify the

	owning, not working
ants	owning, hiring labor, working
easants	owning, working
asants	tenancy, working
orers	working, not owning

As to the size of the five groups, it is said only that the landlords are four percent of the peasantry, but no figures are given for each group.[15] Omitted in the Law is such a vital problem as how much land should a person have in order to be placed in a given category. This left the local cadres with arbitrary decision making. As J.D. Waller put it, rather mildly, "there was considerable confusion because of variation in the criteria for differentiation applied in different areas" of the country.[16]

The Law was implemented leniently at first. The leadership, no doubt, was determined to rid the countryside of the landlords.[17] As for rich peasants, the Law (Article 6) provides protection, pledging that the land owned and cultivated by them or by their hired laborers, as well as other kinds of property of theirs, was not to be infringed. Those who executed the legislation too harshly were denounced as leftist and punished.[18] It calls to our mind Stalin's famous charge, made in March 1930, of the Land Captains' dizziness with success in collectivization.[19] In the Soviet Union, it is worth noting, the collectivization was discontinued from June to October of 1930, when the farmers were allowed to withdraw from the kolkhozy.[20] In the CPR, however, this did not come to pass, as indurate as the CCP was toward the rural "exploiters". Although there was a brief interval of readjustment in the administrative machine looking toward decentralization, there was no suffering of individual withdrawal.[21] After the Beijing regime got its soldiers volunteered to the Korean

[14] V. Ya. Avarin, "Kitai: ekonomiko-geograficheskii ocherk," *Bol'shaya sovetskaya entsiklopediya,* 2nd ed., vol. 21 (1953), pp. 181-197 at 187; G.K. Efremov, "Azia: fiziko-geograficheskii ocherk," vol. 1 (1949), pp. 519-526 at 523.

[15] Lowell Dittmer, "Chou En-lai and Chinese politics," *Governments and Leaders, an Approach to Comparative Politics,* Boston: Houghton Mifflin, 1978, pp. 437-533 at 488, col. 1; J.D. Waller, *op. cit.,* p. 129; and Peter S.H. Tang and Joan M. Malony, *op. cit.,* p. 339.

[16] J.D. Waller, *loc. cit.*

[17] A.M. Gurevich, "Sel'skoe khozyaistvo," *Bol'shaya sovetskaya entsiklopediya,* 2nd ed., vol. 38 (1955), pp. 431-438 at 432.

[18] Franz H. Michael and George E. Taylor, *The Far East in the Modern World,* 2nd ed., New York: Holt, Rinehart and Winston, 1964, p. 459.

[19] *KPSS, spravochnik,* 4th ed., Moskva: Izd-vo polit. lit-ry, 1978, p. 213.

[20] Jerry F. Hough and Merle Fainsod, *How the Soviet Union is Governed.* rev. and enlarged ed., Cambridge: Harvard University Press, 1979, p. 150.

[21] Franz H. Michael and George E. Taylor, *op. cit.,* p. 467.

war in October 1950, the Land Reform was enforced with extreme sadism. In the following year, the entire country was plunged into a frenzy of partition.[22] The persecution, first, of landlords and, soon, rich peasants together with their families took the form of kangaroo trials and summary death by shooting. This was justified in the interest of class struggle. Day in and day out, the villagers were hurled onto the open field to witness the process. They shouted in chorus the verdict of kill and cheered and applauded as the victims wallowed in a pool of blood high on the platform on which the executions took place.

The following scenario repeated itself in hundreds of thousands of hamlets.[23] There walked in a man called Land Commissioner, his entourage and a squadron of riflemen. Immediately he got hold of a few individuals who were known to begrudge the well-to-do. They were to be assigned as accusers. In most cases, they were tenants, with or without a score to settle with the landlords. The next task of the commissioner was to file the peasants into the aforesaid five groups by whatever standard he improvised. Having done this, he went on to conduct the trial rehearsal with his comrades, and they pre-determined who were to be shot and who were to have lesser forms of penalty. It was a common drama that friends and family members bitterly abused each other in the hope of pleasing the communist cadres and of escaping the worst fate. The victims of the land campaign mounted quickly. When it officially ended in 1952, according to one source, "between one and two million landlords, few of whom could have owned more than a dozen or so acres, were executed."[24] This is a ridiculously low assertion. The toll ran into 10-15 million according to many other sources.[25] At this tragic price, China suddenly became a country of smallholders, each homestead having perhaps a couple of mu (one mu equals 0.7 hectares). None of these holders, the supposed beneficiaries, probably knew much about the Land Reform Law. If they did, they had little joy in becoming instant "landlords." Before very long, what they got from the commissioner was grabbed away in the collectivization which followed. Truly the Reds played the role of a Robin Hood. After giving the money to the poor, they lost no time in robbing it back.

Collectivization

The Land Reform, as seen above, was not designed at all to relieve the peasants. Yet they received each a piece of real estate to be called

[22] Z. A. Muromtsev i L.A. Volkova, "Politika kitaiskogo rukovodstva v derevne na razlichnykh etapakh ekonomicheskogo razvitiya strany," Sel'skoe knozyaistvo KNR 1949-1974, Moskva: Izd-vo "nauka" 1978, pp. 26-77 passim.

[23] Cathleen Douglas, "The death penalty, Chinese style," Trial, no. 2, February 1977, pp. 44-46 at 45, col. 1.

[24] Lucian W. Pye, China, Boston: Little, Brown, 1972, p. 186; Sam C. Sarkesian and James H. Buck, Comparative Politics, Sherman Oaks, California: Alfred Pub. Co., 1979, p. 288, col. 1.

[25] Franz H.Michael and George E. Taylor, op. cit., p. 459.

his own and tilled it individually. This is clearly incongruous with the fundamental thesis of the regime that all means of production be socialized. However, the ruling elite were unable to agree on the immediate action following the completion of the reform. There are reported to be two lines of thinking. One counseled a Fabian move toward the final goal of collectivization, while the other pressed for an uninterrupted agrarian revolution. This division of opinion has its Soviet precedent during the period after the death of Lenin in January 1924 when Kamenev, Zinoviev and Trotsky argued for the termination of the New Economic Policy in opposition to Rykov and Bukharin. The difference between the Russian and the Chinese case is that in the former, the opponents are identified by name, but in the latter, they are not. What scholars have definite evidence to prove is that a split of view had indeed taken place in the party councils.[26] It is speculated that Zhou Enlai, Liu Shaoqi and some others were moderates. They were in favor of gradual divesting of the peasants of their holdings. Before China mechanized the agriculture, they maintained, it was pointless to change the land-tenure right away. Others led by Mao Zedong were more ideologically disposed. It was their stand that the revolutionary momentum must not be slowed down. The petty owners, they feared, would develop a sense of solidarity and they would be hard to convince of the desirability of collective economy once their taste of private proprietorship was sharpened beyond the point of no return. In that case, there would have to be another round of agrarian reform with all the attendant tumult and executions. Happily, the hardliners softened and considered it inexpedient to proceed too fast. It was the best policy, they realized, not to offend the beneficiaries in such a short time. The result of the argument of the two sides was a compromise. Progress toward collectivization, it was agreed, had to be made but must not be too precipitate or disrupting.[27]

The prelude to the so-called people's commune consists of several stages. Although each stage was brief, moderation characterized its course, and there were no mass trials and shootings. A Chinese village was made to undergo the following phases:[28]

A. Mutual-aid team
1. Temporary type
Prevailing for about 18 months from late 1951 to early 1953, the team was comprised of 3-5 households. They joined forces helping each other with sowing and harvesting. All their previous status was left intact. Such change has no precedent, however. It was the communists who imposed it, as anything else, for that matter, upon the masses. Western writers always assert the team to be the practice

[26] Lowell Dittmer, *loc. cit.*

[27] *Mao fei bei zhan yu dui nei kong zhi,* p. 39-53.

[28] *Zheng zhi chang shi du ben can kao zi liao,* Beijing: Xue xi za zhi she, 1952, pp. 232-237.

in Chinese tradition.[29] However, truth speaks otherwise. China's agriculture was individualistic out-and-out. It never had a collectivist tinge and the work was done by hired labor during busy times. The mutual-aid regime was totally alien to this author's native province (Hunan) which is said to be a granary of that country. We are not saying that the idea of reciprocal assistance is not an attractive one, but only that to consider it a general usage in China is incorrect. Throughout the provinces and regions, the teams under review numbered about 197,000,000 in February 1953.

2. Permanent type
Beginning in the summer of 1953, the above setup was going through a process of consolidation. Government pressure came to be more in evidence.[30] Not only the households were increased (now 6 to 10 per team), but they came to have formal structure; with this, they waned less voluntary. Even though the means of production were still privately possessed, they were pooled together for common employment. All families joined in work year around, not just sporadically as before. It is here that the seeds of socialism were sown. On everybody's mind was imprinted the motto "from each according to his labor." The team authority took charge of the capital invested. In theory, entry into the team was not compulsory and families could get out. In practice, however, the system was ordered by the Reds. They considered it a forward step to the ideal communist paradise. There were about 90,000,000 teams at the inception of 1954.[31]

B. Agricultural producers' co-op (APC)
3. Elemental type
On the average, each co-op contained around 40 homesteads. It can be a natural neighborhood.[32] There were 20,000,000 of co-ops in 1955, covering 95 percent of rural China.[33] Like the team, a co-op claimed no ownership of property. Each family remained theoretically a proprietor of the land and other property. These were merely put under the management of the APC. The sharing of the year-end income was calculated according to the labor and acreage each homestead brought in. As the problems of control, distribution of work and record-keeping multiplied, an administrative body had to be set up to take charge of them. In the village there was some measure of direct democracy in the manner of consultation among the

[29] Sam C. Sarkesian and James H. Buck, op. cit., p. 229, col. 2.

[30] Yang Mengwen, Zhong gong shi nian, Hong Kong: Yu lien chu ban she, 1964, pp. 141-146.

[31] Lun Qiao, Wei da de zu guo, Hong Kong: Ji wen chu ban she, 1956, pp. 169-170.

[32] Sam C. Sarkesian and James H. Buck, op. cit., p. 230, col. 1.

[33] M.N. Gorbunova, "Prirodnye usloviya provintsii shan'dun i razvitie sel'skogo khozyaistva," Voprosy narodnoi respublik, Moskva: Izd-vo akademii nauk CCCR, 1959, pp. 47-77 at 61-62.

members on what was to be done in re investment, buying and selling of produce, instrumentation, capital outlay and discipline. Some co-ops, particularly those near the big cities, were engaged in extensive cultural, recreation and sports functions by arranging with various departments of the city administration.

4. Advanced type

Further escalation toward socialism was the advanced type of APC. Now each co-op had about 80 families.[34] By mid-1956, the total co-ops were some 10,000,000. An advanced co-op was a true collective entity, now that the individuals could not claim separate holdings. Thus ended the home ownership of the means of production which existed in all the foregoing rural regimes. With this alteration, "the burden of the agricultural tax was shifted from the individual and became the collective obligation of the advanced APC."[35] One of the obvious requirements for this kind of co-op is the more elaborate management scheme; and sizeable personnel are needed to perform a thousand and one duties, not the least of which is the minute bookkeeping, not only of finance, but of work-records. The family still retained a small plot on which it could plant whatever it wished. Coming to distribution of the fruit of labor, the co-op followed outright the principle: "to each according to his work." The administrators were nominally elected by the co-op members. In truth, they can do more than endorse the appointment made by the local party secretary.

Progression from the team to the co-op regime coincided with the first Five-Year Plan, 1953-1957 (see next chapter). Both industrial and farm products were up, but the first more dramatically. The crops ranged from poor to mediocre in the early stage of the Plan. Insofar as progress was concerned, industry presented much less of a problem. The success here was largely due to the simple fact that heavy or rather coarse things, for example, pig iron, mineral ore and cement, were easy to make and it was on them that the nation's effort was concentrated. Less attention was spent on farm production, which was improving but not impressively. The lack of manufactured goods for sale in the villages, however, led the farmers to "raise their own consumption and reduce the surplus available to the state."[36] This and many other factors compelled the Reds to proceed to the people's commune no sooner than the Five-Year Plan ran its full course.[37]

The commune
1. The decision
Whether to stop, for the time being at least, at the APC or to

[34] N.A. Kulagin, M.A. Kraev i. V.P. Tikhomirov, "Krest'yanstvo," Bol'shaya sovetskaya entsiklopediya, 2nd ed., vol. 23 (1953), pp. 371-378 at 377; "Soiuz rabochego klass i krest'yanstva," vol. 40 (1957), pp. 225-231 at 230.

[35] Sam C. Sarkesian and James H. Buck, loc. cit.

[36] J.D. Waller, op. cit., p. 131.

[37] Liu Shi-tsi, Geografiya sel'skogo khozyaistva kitaya; perevod s kitaiskogo V.P. Iliushchkina et alii, Moskva: Izd-vo inostrannoi literatury, 1957, pp. 43-49.

bulldoze ahead toward the commune was an issue on which the communist hierarchs were divided. Here again the moderates represented by Zhou Enlai in the State Council, preferred going it slow. All along he counseled against rapidity and dislocation on the rural front. At the third session of the first NPC (April 1956), he defended ardently the reasonable income-differences and pleaded that no radical change be undertaken. "As a result of the opposition to adventurism put up by Zhou and his cabinet in the summer of 1956, the Leap Forward approach to development was firmly rejected at the eighth Congress (of CCP) in September 1956." [38] The Leap, to be discussed in the following chapter, is a concomitant of the commune campaign. We think it almost certain that Zhou's insistence on a steady but orderly process in the solution of agricultural problems forced Mao to defer the commune for at least two full years.[39] It was not until August 1958 that the CC approved the establishment of it "all over China."[40] Uncertainty among the elite still continued for several more months. Finally on December 10, 1958, the 6th plenum of the CC adopted the "Resolution on some questions concerning the people's communes."[41] For the advocacy of the deferment of the commune, Zhou Enlai was later to express his apology in these words: "I bore the responsibility for the opposition to adventurism in 1956 (and) I made an examination" of myself.[42] In fact, the appearance of the commune was six months before the adoption of the resolution just quoted. What is often called the first model commune named Sputnik originated in Xinyang county (Henan province) in April 1958.[43] In the previous month, Mao announced in Chengdu (Sichuan province) the consolidation of the APC's into fewer units. Here is a signal of the inauguration of communization.

What are the considerations on which Mao Zedong based his decisions[44] First, he was "hellbent" toward communism which the commune semantically emblematizes. In July 1955, interestingly enough, he promised in the first Five-Year Plan to usher in socialism within 15 years.[45] In December, however, he shortened it to 3 years.[46]

---

[38] Lowell Dittmer, op. cit., p. 491, col. 1 (note).

[39] George McTurnan Kahin, Major Governments of Asia, Ithaca, New York: Cornell University Press, 1958, p. 61.

[40] Franz H. Michael and George E. Taylor, op. cit., p. 486.

[41] Text in George P. Jan, ed., Government of Communist China, San Francisco: Chandler Pub. Co., 1966, pp. 421-444.

[42] Lowell Dittmer, op. cit., p. 490, col. 2. Biographical Dictionary of Chinese Communism, 1921-1965, Cambridge, Massachusetts: Harvard University Press, 1971, vol. 1, pp. 210-219 at 218.

[43] Peter S.H. Tang and Joan M. Maloney, op. cit., p. 375.

[44] "Ying jie ren min gong she de gao qiao," Hongqi, September 1, 1958, pp. 13-15.

[45] Countries of the World, Toronto: Coles Pub. Co., 1980, Chinese section, p. 6.

[46] A remark made by Mao in an introduction to the pamphlet The surging tide of socialism in the Chinese rural areas, cited in Peter S.H. Tang and Joan M. Maloney, op. cit., p. 374.

GOVERNMENT OF SOCIALIST CHINA

..cates how impatient he was in transforming the CPR. In this
...t, Mao resembles Stalin. In February 1931, we may recall, the
...t dictator spoke of his determination to complete the Five-Year
Plan in these words: "Sometimes people ask whether it is not possible
to slow the pace somewhat, to hold back the movement. No!
comrades, it is impossible to reduce the rate."[47] Second, Mao was
deeply convinced of the "natural socialism" of the farmers.[48] The
collectivist mode of life was not new to them. In socialism, he was
sure, they should feel at home. Third, Mao was resentful that some
of his subordinates not only did not share his agricultural policy, but
actually undermined it. Deng Zihui, for one, had ordered the
dismantling of 200,000 APC's,[49] and this "sabotage" may well have
been cleared with Zhou Enlai, because he was Zhou's deputy in the
State Council.[50] This resistance to Mao would not fail to incur his
wrath. He must have feared that the Council could wreck the
commune program if it were not carried out quickly enough. Fourth,
the APC's, as stated above, had begun to expand their consumption
pattern and in this way would diminish the resources otherwise usable
for capital investment. Fifth, the Five-Year Plan had shown a steady
increase of farm output, in per capita kg, like this:[51]

1952	283
1953	281
1954	278
1955	295
1956	302

The upswing, except in 1954 (due to bad weather), must have
enheartened Mao Zedong greatly, thinking that his gradual
socialization beginning with the mutual-aid team was chiefly
responsible for it. A further move in the same direction would certainly
increase the productivity.[52]
Sixth, Khrushchev's de-Stalinization in 1956 had the effect of
inclining the Chinese leader to hasten the program of true
communism. The Soviet Union since the demise of Stalin, the Chinese
supposed, had made little progress toward socialism. Mao was
resolved to outstrip that country in the race for the workers' paradise.
Seventh, China was to furnish an exemplar for the underdeveloped
nations the world over, one of revolutionary transformation of a

[47] quoted in Jerry F. Hough and Merle Fainsod, op. cit., p. 163.

[48] Harold Hinton, An Introduction to Chinese Politics, 2nd ed., New York: Holt, Rinehart and Winston, 1978, p. 243.

[49] Sam C. Sarkesian and James H. Buck, op. cit., p. 231, col. 2; Lowell Dittmer, loc. cit.

[50] Bill Brugger, Contemporary China, London: Croom Helm, 1977, p. 419.

[51] James Townsend, "Politics in China," Comparative Politics Today, 2nd ed., Boston: Little, Brown, 1980, pp. 381-432 at 393.

[52] Zhong hua ren min gong he guo shi gao, Hebei, Beijing shi fan xue yuan li shi xi san nian ji ji ti bian xie, Beijing: Renmin chu ban she, 1958, pp. 362-364.

backward agricultural economy to a most advanced regime. Eighth, his country was in earnest need of capital for a swift industrialization and a new type of farming would surely be able to turn out lots of things for export.[53] With this, foreign exchange would pour in, Mao hoped. Ninth, by 1958 the deterioration of the Sino-Soviet diplomacy was almost beyond repair. Now that the only source of foreign aid was gone, no other country could grant China credit and technical help. Therefore, the CPR was impelled to depend on herself. A reorganization of the rural structure and mass employment of villagers was, therefore, to be the solution of the problem. Tenth, during the hour of decision on the commune in mid-1957 the entire nation was plunged into the anti-rightist hysteria in response to the short-lived liberalism of the "hundred flowers." Criticism, first, of communist cadres, and then of communism itself, became the keynote of the rightists. Looking around him, Mao saw hostile forces closing in which, if unchecked, would rock the whole boat. How vital it was for the CCP to rectify the situation! The commune was admirably suitable for the purpose. Eleventh, manpower would be multiplied if all the able-bodied were put to work; and a total mobilization would accomplish the twin objectives of Great Leap in industry and the communization in agriculture.[54] The final reason is that the full use of men and women in the hamlets had the effect of preventing migration to the already congested cities.[55] No one single explanation seems sufficient to account for the commune decision of Mao, but adding the above together, we can get a better idea of the motivation behind his plan.

NB

2. The operation
Communization, or what is really the fullest collectivism of agriculture, started in mid-1958.[56] As an immediate prelude to it, there was the feverish merging of the APC's. At the beginning of 1957 there were about 20,000,000 of the latter. In the spring of 1958 these formed themselves into 740,000 units.[57] With the formal début of the commune signified by the aforesaid Sputnik in April that year, the movement of consolidation went apace.[58] Toward the end of 1958, the peak time of the drive, there were 26,425 communes.[59] "The smallest embraced about ten times the land and population as contained in an advanced APC."[60] One should not be led to think

---

[53] Xu Lichun, "Cong shi fou yi jing dao le gong chan zhu yi shuo qi," Hongqi, no. 12, November 16, 1958, pp. 20-28 at 21.

[54] V.I. Potanov, "Zernoe khosyaistvo," Sel'skoe khozyaistvo KNR 1949-1974, pp. 247-285 at 263.

[55] David F. Roth and Frank L. Wilson, The Comparative Study of Politics, 1st ed., Boston: Houghton Mifflin, 1976, p. 417.

[56] Rene Dumont, Revolution dan les campagnes chinoises, Paris: Editions du Seuil, 1957, p. 345.

[57] George P. Jan, ed., op. cit., p. 447.

[58] Li Yujiu, "Henan xin yang lai xin," Hongqi, no. 7, September 1, 1958, pp. 22-23.

[59] Peter S.H. Tang and Joan M. Maloney, op. cit., p. 376.

[60] Lowell Dittmer, op. cit., p. 495, col. 1.

that the APC's had been abolished. They simply became the subunits of the new giant which had on the average 24 of them. The APC's now took up the name of brigade, while their own subunits became known as production teams still numbering some 3,000,000 in 1959.[61]

From the co-op to the commune there was a smooth passage devoid of the havoc characteristic of the Soviet Union during its collectivization.[62] The reason may be advanced that fresh coming to power and behaving as conquerors the Chinese Reds had, in the land reform, already got rid of tens of millions of farmers. Only thereafter did they proceed to institute the step-by-step change of the rural structure which culminated in the commune in 1958-1959. Stalin, let's make a comparison, did not eliminate the kulaks right away prior to the Five-Year Plan (1928). They were executed or exiled in the midst of collectivization. It is also noteworthy that the Russian dictator had the vast Siberia to banish the peasants, but Mao Zedong resorted to direct disposal of them by shooting, since he had no Chinese Siberia to accommodate that enormous number. In each case, interestingly enough, collectivization took seven year: the USSR 1929-1936,[63] the CPR 1953-1959.

In the majority of cases, the boundary of a commune coincided with the administrative *xiang* which was the lowest rung of the political ladder of the state.[64] Below was the brigade and further down the production team. However, only the commune at that time (1959) was designated the basic accounting unit.[65] It was responsible for work assignment, harvesting and dividing of the produce and for bookkeeping. It reaped its own profits and at the same time absorbed its own losses.[66] Under the charge of the commune administration were economic planning, police, the military, culture, education, and large agricultural, commercial and industrial enterprises.[67] Water conservancy was another task. There was a party apparatus in each commune and brigade consisting of a secretary and six departments dealing with organization, propaganda, youth, women, military and political problems.[68]

As to be expected, the boundary concomitance of a commune and a *xiang* resulted in the takeover of the latter's function by the former. This was rationalized by the good Marxist ideology of withering away

[61] Peter S.H. Tang and Joan M. Maloney, *op. cit.,* p. 379.

[62] Y.C. Chang, *Factional and Coalition Politics in China, the Cultural Revolution and its Aftermath,* New York: Praeger, 1976, pp. 3-6.

[63] Jerry F. Hough and Merle Fainsod, *op. cit.,* p. 151.

[64] Li Xiannian, "Ren min gong she suo jian," *Hongqi,* no. 10, Octover 16, 1958, pp. 4-8.

[65] Jon Sigurdson, "Rural industry and the internal transfer of technology," *Authority, Participation and Cultural Change in China,* London: Cambridge at the University Press, 1973, pp. 119-233 at 200.

[66] James Townsend, "Politics in China," *op. cit.,* p. 391.

[67] Sam C. Sarkesian and James H. Buck, *op. cit.,* p. 233, col. 2.

[68] *Ibid.*

of the state. In a commune, the sovereign authority was a representative body called congress. It was made up of delegates of the brigades. There was an Administrative Committee charged with the execution of policy, making of plans, control of finance and management of production and other matters. The Committee had a director, several vice directors and ordinary members. Paralleling the aforesaid party departments were the following functional bureaus: agriculture, water, forestry, animal husbandry, transport, industry, accounting, food, trade, culture, education, labor, defense, planning, research, well-being, general affairs.[69] Similar to the commune, the brigade was provided with a congress, an executive agency, and a host of cadres. The production team was a smaller organization but it had all the bureaus just mentioned. In 1959, there were 500,000 brigades and 3,000,000 teams,[70] each of the former having from 200 to 300 households and each of the latter having from 30 to 50. In size, a team was the same as the lower APC, and a brigade the same as the higher APC.

Although the commune was communistic in that family plots were turned to the state and that egalitarianism was the objective, the rule demanded that each person work to the utmost of his ability but receive according to labor and, on a much lesser degree, to his needs.[71] One's workpoints would determine his worth, with the result that the harder workers would get more out of the common labor-fruit both in kinds and in money. There lacked the "complete equality in rewards" as alleged by one author.[72] Depending on the type of economy in various parts of the country, four methods of recompense were identified: a) meals plus small cash, b) grain plus some cash, c) grain alone, d) all daily necessities plus cash.[73] The fourth was adopted in prosperous areas, but the third in poor regions. No matter what payment, the system of mess hall was the absolute rule. There was to be no private cooking. It was calculated to utilize the entire labor force, female and male.[74]

Women had traditionally been immobilized by the household chore. If they were relieved of this, manpower would be automatically doubled. With this in mind, the CCP ordered the liberation of them. People had to eat in the common kitchen; and pots and pans of the families were collected as scraps to be converted into steel by the backyard furnace. Quartered in two barracks, men and women marched out to the field at reveille and returned at nightfall. During

[69] Yao Yuanfang, "Qian xian de yi ge ren min gong she," *Hongqi*, no. 14, December 16, 1958, pp. 38-41.

[70] Peter S.H. Tang and Joan M. Maloney, *loc. cit.*

[71] H.D. Waller, *op. cit.,* p. 136; A.A. Volkova, "Organizatsiya proizvodstva, raspredeleniya i oplaty truda v sel'skom khozyaistve," *Kel'skoe khozyaistvo KNR 1949-1974*, pp. 108-140 at 109.

[72] Thomas P. Bernstein, *op. cit.,* p. 253.

[73] Peter S.H. Tang and Joan M. Maloney, *op. cit.,* p. 253.
[74] Zhang Yusan, "Guan yu ren min gong she shi xing ban gong jie ban gong zi de diao cha," *Hongqi*, no. 12, November 16, 1958, pp. 38-41.

the meager sparetime, they had to attend political lectures. Military drill, however, was placed in the regular work-schedule. Each commune was formed into an army division, and below it were the brigade and regiment. The last-named comprises the workers of a production team. To look after the aged and the young, the authority set up happy homes and various schools up to senior high. The whole system was featured by centralization. It was intended to be a minutely regulated mechanism in control of all phases of life. An adult was at once a soldier, a worker and a peasant.[75] In short, the Chinese commune reached the nth degree of governmental interference. Very aptly, the Soviet press depicted it as a military bureaucratic dictatorship.[76]

3. The failure

The CCP had obviously overestimated the socialistic proclivity of the Homo sapiens. Having defeated the Guomindang's several million troops, the Reds felt themselves on the top of the world. They could almost do anything with equal success. In the eyes of Mao, where there is a communist will, there is a communist way. It looks as if he can produce a test-tube baby in the Marxist lab. Mao, we shall remember, used to cherish the legend of "a foolish old man who intends to move a mountain." Unwittingly he set out to rival him. We shall remember too that Mao taught that a society needs *luan* (chaos) to move forward.[77] This is not unlike Thomas Jefferson's thinking that a state should go through a revolution once in a while, except that the Chinese plumped for autocracy, but the American craved for democratic freedom and basic rights. Had the commune been carried further, the Chinese as a nation would have been destroyed. It is no small measure of the CCP's prudence that the whole idea was quickly jettisoned. As a matter of fact, it was in operation for just a year, from August 1958 to August 1959.[78]

What are the causes of its failure? a) For the first time in the history of the CCP, there erupted an open chasm between the top men.[79] Defense Minister Peng Dehuai, as seen above, challenged Mao Zedong at Lushan conference of August 1959, for he considered the commune as undermining the military strength and the morale of the peasant-soldiers. b) The communist oligarchy was downright foolhardy because they put too much faith on willpower to the neglect of sound judgment.[80] Vast resources were simply squandered. In 1959, "the hopes for a leap in farm productivity were so high that

[75] Fu Qiutao, "Quan min jie bing," *Hongqi*, no. 10, October 16, 1958, pp. 21-24; Zhong gong min hou xian wei hui, "Gong nong shang xue bing jie wei yi ti," *Hongqi*, no. 10, October 16, 1958, pp. 24-27.

[76] I. Aleksandrov, "Vopreki interesam Kitaiskogo naroda," *Pravda*, August 16, 1967, p. 4.

[77] Harold Hinton, *op, cit.*, p. 7.

[78] George P. Jan. ed., *op. cit.*, pp. 421, 463.

[79] Harold Hinton, *op. cit.*, p. 243.

[80] Gong Mianren, *Zhong gong shi nian*, p. 77.

the cultivated acreage allocated to food production was reduced by nearly 30 percent."[81] Climatic or soil conditions were not adequately surveyed before projects of giant magnitude were undertaken. c) Pretending to know everything in connection with farming, Beijing poured out order after order having no relation to reality. In effect, it overstretched itself. Minute directives handed down to the local cadres served only to stifle their initiative. They preferred compliance with the authorities to the assuming of responsibility in running the economy. d) Very frequently the first set of schemes was scarcely brought to fruition than the second set was officiated. The cadres, ardent to push forward, did not take the trouble to check upon or repair the projects at hand, with the consequence that many existing schemes were falling apart while fresh ones were catching fire with the officals.

e) "Mismanagement of labor was perhaps one of the most serious defects of the commune."[82] The organization of huge mobile teams comprising upwards of 100,000 men each, sent here and there at a moment's notice, contributed to the disarray of peasant life. These teams were shifted around endlessly in the countryside. Lacking transportation, they had to walk miles to the assignments. Much time was lost in this way, and complaints were mounting.[83] f) The dearth of skilled functionaries gravely hampered the commune operation. The ignorance of the cadres was hardly conducive to the Leap's popularity. With little training or expertise, for example, they were often commissioned to do extremely technical jobs, such as planning, survey, accounting and zootechnique. Unable to apply the central policy expediently, such amateurish officials were prepared only to stick to the letter of the law. g) The natural disaster of 1959-1960 came to assure the flunk of the commune. More than 60,000,000 hectares of land were reported to have been affected by natural calamities.[84] Only six provinces and regions of a total of 26 were free from them.[85] Such disaster was also man-made.[86] For example, the zealous cadres had ordered cotton planted in swamp areas, or dams erected on loose ground which gave way to very slight rise of water level. h) The dissolution of private plots and home life visited hardship on the public and i) the semi-free supply system diminished the incentive of the workers. Loud grievances were aired by those who had small families, saying that they labored themselves hard only to feed the big families.[87] j) Statistical scheme collapsed under the bureaucratic

[81] *Countries of the World*, p. 6.

[82] George P. Jan, ed., *op. cit.*, pp. 455-456.

[83] Fang Yuan, "An lao fen pei he deng jia jiao huan," *Hongqi*, no. 7, 1979, pp. 19-20; Hong Xin, "Ren min gong she de ji lei he shi dang," *Hongqi*, no. 7, 1979, pp. 21-22.

[84] *Xinhua news*, December 2, 1960, cited in George P. Jan, ed., *op. cit.*, pp. 456-457.

[85] *Renmin ribao* (editorial), December 29, 1960, p. 1.

[86] George P. Jan, ed., *op. cit.*, p. 457.

[87] Wang Lu, "Nong min zong yang yi lun an lao fen pei," *Hongqi*, no. 1, 1959, pp. 34-36.

pressure to report more optimistic results to the higher-ups. Most of the figures showing the increase of output were later admitted as a fake.[88] At the Lushan Conference in August 1959, mentioned above, it was conceded that the previous year's estimate of grain produce was "somewhat too high."[89] k) Finally the peasants were simply overworked. They were laboring from 5 am to 9 pm.[90] In December 1958, a twelve hour a day for eating and resting was decreed by the government.[91] "Eventually an eight-hour minimum for rest" had to be guaranteed.[92]

Modification
The rush into communism brought the public to physical and mental trauma. If the regime were to continue with the course, its fate could be dark indeed. Either by on-the-spot checks or by indirect information, the authorities came to realize that something had gone seriously wry. Gradually, they were disillusioned, in spite of the piles of reports from their subordinates that agricultural output had increased ten-or twenty-fold.[93] All independent studies agree that farm produce suffered a slump consequent upon the communization. Lowell Dittmer, for one, writes that the economic depression was China's worst since 1929.[94] Another research tells that agricultural production descended from 1957 on until it recovered in 1965. It says if the 1957 index for industry and agriculture is 100, the 1959, 1960 and 1961 indexes would be 83, 78 and 77 respectively.[95]

The grain harvest in million tons are:[96]

1958	200
1959	165
1960	160
1962	160

The same deterioration can also be expressed by taking into account the per capita grain produce, this time in kg, as follows:

1958	315
1959	256
1960	229
1962	242

[88] Cao Bi, "Guan yu nong cun ren min gong she shi xing de shang chuai," *Hongqi,* no. 6, 1979, pp. 42-49.

[89] George P. Jan, ed., *op. cit.,* p. 465; *Food and Agriculture in Communist China,* edited by John Lossing Buck, *et alii,* New York: Praeger, 1966, pp. 48, 76.

[90] George P. Jan, ed., *loc. cit.*

[91] J.D. Waller, *op. cit.,* p. 137.

[92] Franz H. Michael and George E. Taylor, *op. cit.,* p. 488.

[93] Sam C. Sarkesian and James H. Buck, *op. cit.,* p. 233, col. 2.

[94] Lowell Dittmer, *op. cit.,* p. 496, col. 1.

[95] *China, a reassessment of the Economy,* Washington: Government Printing Office, 1975, p. 23.

[96] *Ibid.,* Sam C. Sarkesian and James H. Buck, *op. cit.,* p. 231.

The 1958 record remains unsurpassed until 1979 when the figure was 348 kg (see below). In 1982 it became 332 kg.[97] This is far from adequate. According to our calculation each healthy person needs 450 kg unmilled grain per year (this amounts to 268.9 kg milled one)[98] China's 6th Five-Year Plan (1981-1985) adopted by the fifth session of the Fifth NPC on December 8, 1982, envisages 360,000,000 tons of grain in 1985.[99] By then the population will be 1,060,000,000.[100] The required grain should be 455,800,000 tons. Thus the end of the current plan will see a shortage of 95,800,000 tons. To put it in another way, 200,000,000 Chinese would have to go hungry two years from now.

To combat the inauspicious climate and other adverse conditions, the leaders have resorted to rural reorganization. In the commune, one was paid according to needs and labor, much more the former rather than the latter. This is ill-suited to the encouragement of men to work. Egalitarianism, impeccable as it may be from the Marxist point of view, runs afoul of the individualist ethos of human beings. Even on the collective basis, it is just as bad. A commune has a great number of brigades, with quite different natural endowments. Some are better than others. It is reported that peasants in well-to-do brigades complained of having to share their profits with those in the less fortunate ones.[101] This grunting must have been brought to the attention of the hierarchs by some conscientious cadres. Given such criticism and the unwieldly and wasteful commune administration, it was only a matter of time before Beijing came to its senses by amending the scheme.[102]

Beginning in the spring of 1959, there was set afoot a modification.[103] In the place of the commune as a managerial and accounting unit, there was decreed, initially the brigade, and two years later, the production team.[104] Such decentralization was accompanied by a policy to substitute "agriculture first" for the "walk on two legs" of agriculture and industry.[105] The readiness to change on the part of the communists must be imputed to their guerilla orientation which

[97] See the section on current performance

[98] *Beijing review*, February 14, 1982, p. 22, col. 2 says one county reached the 400 kg mark.

[99] *Ibid.*, December 20, 1982, p. 12 (table).

[100] *Ibid.*, p. 18, col. 2.

[101] Sam C. Sarkesian and James H. Buck, *op. cit.*, p. 234, col. 2.

[102] L.A. Volkova, "Formy sobstvennosti v kitaiskoi derevne," *Sel'skoe khozyaistvo KNR, 1949-1974*, pp. 77-107 at 100.

[103] George P. Jan, "Failure of the Chinese Commune Experiment," in his edited book, *Government of Communist China*, pp. 453-474 at 462, 463.

[104] Lowell Dittmer, *op. cit.*, p. 496.

[105] D. Bonavia, "Changes down on the farm," *Far Eastern Economic Review*, no. 97, September 30, 1977, p. 28.

is characteristic of constant improvisation. When an irresistible enemy (in this case, both nature and human errors) advances, they retreat. The decision to flinch was officially reaffirmed in the 10th plenum of the CC in September 1962 by declaring "agriculture as the foundation of the national economy."[106] Afterwards, it was tabled in the NPC for rubber-stamping. This body in its 1962 secret session produced a ten-task document; and in its 1963 *in camera* rendezvous it developed a seven-point program.[107] In both cases, agriculture tops the list. "To strive for increased agricultural production, especially the production of grain, cotton and oil-bearing crops" is the first task, while "to strive for a still better harvest" appears as the first point. Failure to provide such items like grain stuff, the leadership must have thought, would constitute a breach of its prime mandate. To win bread for the masses, has, therefore, to be the foremost job, and light and heavy industries can only lay the second and third claims to the national resources. This priority ranking held true in the early sixties. Later when the policy of "agriculture as the foundation and industry as the leading factor" of economy appears in Article 11 of the 1978 Constitution, the communist literature and many Western analysts regarded it as in favor of agriculture. However, whether it is so cannot be certain, because the dictionary does not say which of the two words "foundation" and "leading" is more basic. Hence the 1982 Constitution drops the quoted words. On the other hand, we find it very difficult not to see heavier weight on agriculture. After all, the four modernizations are headed by it. In reality, the Chinese have now four legs to walk on. The recent development toward readjusting the economic regime by placing accent on pragmatism on the one side, and by constitutional echeloning of agriculture, industry, military and science/technology on the other side, has definitely shown "agriculture first."[108]

From the viewpoint of the peasants, perhaps the most meaningful change is the restoration of the garden plots to them in 1962, plots which were withdrawn by the government in 1953 and returned the next year, only to be withdrawn again in 1958 with the adoption of the commune.[109] From 1962 to the onset of the Cultural Revolution, the peasants apparently possessed the tracts of land to develop their sideline farming and to expand their income.[110] To what extent does this activity contribute to the recovery of China's economy in those years is nowhere analyzed by students, but it no doubt has some recuperative virture, just as the NEP helped Russia to regain her

[106] J.D. Waller, *op. cit.*, p. 138.

[107] George T. Yu, "The 1962 and 1963 sessions of the National People's Congress of communist China," George P. Jan, ed., *op. cit.*, pp. 255-266 at 258-259.

[108] Hu Yaobang's speech, *Beijing review*, September 13, 1982, pp. 11-40 at 18, col. 1.

[109] J.D. Waller, *op. cit.*, p. 137.

[110] Subramanian Swarmy, *Economic Growth in China and India, 1952-1970*, Chicago: University of Chicago Press, 1973, p. 21.

economic health during 1921-1928. However, the impact of the Cultural Revolution shook the foundation of the CPR. From it agriculture, as anything else there, was not to be immune. The private plots were once more outlawed, although not entirely, in 1968.[111] The Gang of Four, by one account, were responsible for this.[112] It was stated that the said plots, constituting five percent during the Cultural Revolution, became one percent in the early seventies. On the contrary, Hua Guofeng pointed to the reverse direction, saying that the Gang of Four had interfered in agriculture by parceling out land for peasants' household use.[113] There is no way for us to check on the veracity of these conflicting assertions.

Both the 1975 Constitution (Article 7, par. 2) and its 1978 successor (Article 7, par. 3) speak of the peasants tilling "small" tracts. It is stated that they may make use of these. Since use is not title of ownership, the government can withdraw, if need be, the tracts, as it has done several times. In doing so, it cannot be charged with violating the basic law. In the 1982 Constituion, Article 8, par. 1 regards peasants to be in their right to develop agricultural and hilly land. For one thing, this policy is in keeping with the incentive system which is the thrust of China's new economic course.[114] Now the nation's press accused bitterly the Gang of Four of confiscating the garden holdings, of forbidding the peasants to raise pigs and chickens, to plant fruit trees, or to garner wild berries there.[115] Since 1978, the Chinese mouthpieces invariably defend the private sideline farming and free market of agricultural goods. They deny it being "capitalist vestige." Such subsidiary means of developing the rural economy is seen as helpful to modernization and socialist construction.[116] Chinese writers talked about expansion of the garden possession to 15 percent, saying that this still left 85 percent in the collectives' hand.[117]

The new basic regime in rural China is the production team, equivalent to the lower APC with 20 to 30 households.[118] Its area covers a traditional settlement. Undoubtedly, such size is optimal, because members there know each other well and work assignment is done in a convenient neighborhood. The life of the team centers on a little market-town. In general, the economy is self-sufficient and the people make almost all of the articles of daily use. Being an

[111] Harold Hinton, *op. cit.*, p. 247.

[112] *Keesing's*, September 8, 1975, p. 29190, col. 1.

[113] Speech to the 5th NPC on February 26, 1978, *Ibid.*, 29181-2.

[114] Sam C. Sarkesian and James H. Buck, *op. cit.*, p. 236.

[115] *Keesing's*, September 8, 1978, p. 29193, col. 2.

[116] *Ibid.*, p. 29192, col. 2.

[117] *Renmin ribao*, June 17, 1981, p. 2.

[118] *Countries of the World*, p. 6; Lowell Dittmer, *op. cit.*, p. 496; Thomas P. Bernstein, *op. cit.*, p. 254.

accounting unit, the team has a general assembly, a board of directors and several sectors dealing with records, distribution of supply and job specification. There is apparently a division of function in that the team organization is concerned with production, while administrative affairs are vested with the regular local government which in the 1982 Constitution (Article 95, par. 1) is called *xiang*. The commune and the brigade still exist, but they take up an overseeing and coordinate responsibility over the production team in regard to school system, irrigation, afforestation, reclamation of land and other big projects. The unpopular mobile working contingents, mentioned above, are dissolved.

All that a team has earned belongs to it and is not to be shared with other teams. Due to geographical diversity, some brigades can be made accounting units and they are usually larger than teams. The much drummed up Dazhai, discussed below, is a brigade.[119] There are 710,000 brigades,[120] 55,000 communes, and 5,600,000 teams.[121] As to the size of a team, it seems that it cannot be made smaller. For one thing, a little community consisting of 10-15 homesteads would, to the communists, look like a clan, or a cluster of extended families with all the outmoded and abominable habits such as the fondment of private ownership and cherishing of privacy, habits which the communists are determined to destroy.[122] We find it interesting to note that in the Soviet system there has developed since at least 1971, the link regime, an aggregate of a few rural families empowered to farm with a great deal more autonomy than what a kolkhoz can enjoy.[123] The regime still remains in the experimental stage. Little is written about it in the Soviet press. Apparently, the Kremlin has harbored the same fear as the Beijing oligarchy regarding any sub-team units.

Is the old style of commune gone with the wind? Or, is the scaled-down operation a tactical retreat? The three-layered system of commune, brigade and team is reaffirmed in Article 7 of the 1978 Constitution. It is stated that although the team is made an accounting unit, the brigade (n.b., not commune) may become one "when the conditions are ripe." The commune is obviously precluded from becoming such a unit because it is just too big to manage the farming effectively. In the 1975 Constitution (Article 7, par. 2), it is said that only the team, not even the brigade, is an accounting body.[124] Against all this, the 1982 Constitution (Article 8, par. 1) mentions no brigade

[119] *Facts on File*, December 31, 1976, p. 999, D3.

[120] *Beijing Review*, January 14, 1980, p. 7, col. 3.

[121] *Ibid.*, June 23, 1980, p. 20, col. 1; *Zhong guo jian kuang*, Beijing: wai wen chu ban she, 1983, p. 2.

[122] Alain Jacob, "China's new economy: profits and viability," *Manchester Gardian Weekly*, September 24, 1978, reprinted in *Le monde*, September 15, 1978. James Townsend, "Politics in China," p. 398, col. 1.

[123] Hedrick Smith, *The Russians*, Quadrangle/The New York Times Book Co., 1976, pp. 212-214, 496.

[124] Kuan-i Chen, "Agricultural modernization in China," *Current History*, 449 (September 1979), pp. 85-86.

or team. Instead, it writes of "rural people's commune" and other agricultural producers' co-ops. Probably the specific kinds of such co-ops are left to the legislation. Otherwise a change of them would entail a constitutional amendment. As a matter of historical interest, after the promulgation of the 1975 Constitution, Hua Guofeng took an unconstitutional stand. On September 15, 1975, he delivered a speech in which he emphasized the interim nature of the decentralization of the rural structure. The allusion was that recentralization was intended.[125] The speech was made by him as vice premier to a 3,700-delegate conference a little less than four months before the death of Zhou Enlai. His statement on the potential role of the brigade to be the accounting unit enters the 1978 Constitution, but the suggestion that communes may also be reactivated "when the conditions are ripe" is abandoned. Hua's stand was close to that of the Gang of Four. The latter were accused of seeking to weaken the "production team and to strengthen the production brigade and people's commune.[126] In Hua's speech, ideology clearly carried him away. "In the still more distant future, the people's commune will undergo the transition from the system of collective ownership, i.e., commune, to the system of ownership by the whole people, i.e., state farm." The pre-1976 Hua Guofeng was every inch a Marxist, nay, a Soviet. Witness the expression of "whole people," an expression acquiring so much currency in Russian media of recent years. Mao Zedong, we shall remember, in his Ninth Letter, dated July 14, 1964, to the CPSU listed fifteen points as the main contents of the theories and policies advocated by the Chinese leadership. One of the fifteen is the transition from "collective ownership" to "ownership by the whole people."[127] An interesting question posed itself: If Hua were the top man in China now, would he recentralize the rural organization by bringing back the commune as the basic accounting unit and thus push the CPR toward a whole people's state? We think he would, belonging as he does to the "whatever school", the Fanshi faction, as the Chinese say it.

After going through a state of hybridization of economic and administrative body,[128] the current commune, as hinted above, becomes one of the rural co-ops. It has nothing to do with govenment affairs (Constitution, Article 95, par. 1). Today's decentralization scheme has increased the number of teams as autonomous entities. It has also led to the shrinking of the size of the communes and, correspondingly, their number is on the increase. In 1958, it was 25,000,[129] but in April 1983 it grew to 55,000. On the average, each

[125] Keesing's, April 9, 1976, p. 27670, col. 2.

[126] Ibid., September 8, 1978, p. 29190, col. 1.

[127] Harold Hinton, op. cit., pp. 245-246.

[128] P.B. Kapralov, A.M. Kruglov i A.V. Ostrovskii, "Nekotorye tendentsii v sotsial 'no-ekonomicheskoi politike kitaiskogo rukovodstva," Problemy dal'nego vostoka, 4 (1980), pp. 105-116.

[129] James Townsend, "Politics in China," op. cit., p. 394, col. 1.

county has 25 communes. However, their size is anything but uniform. Some contain no more than a few thousand people, cultivating a couple of hundred hectares, but some have more than 10,000 hectares and upwards of 100,000 inhabitants.[130] The present commune, a pale image of its 1958 self, is supposed to be more efficient and more of a coordinating nature.[131] As before, it sets up a delegate conference, an executive committee and an array of departments.

Like in the USSR, there are also state farms which are a sort of grain factories.[132] The difference between these and the collective farms is a matter of theory. The latter are co-ops and enjoy some measure of autonomy, while the former enjoy none because they are government organs. In truth, all farms are regulated in the greatest of details by the agricultural bureaucracy.[133] However, a household on the collective farm can have a plot, which is denied to members of the state farms. In 1960, these farms numbered 2,500 with 2,800,000 employees tilling almost 6,000,000 hectares. In 1964, they numbered 6,400, of which 2,000 are described as "big."[134] More recent information about these is lacking. If the former strongman Hua Guofeng were able to redeem his promise made in the September 15, 1975 speech, this type of farming would be the wave of the future. Increasingly the leaders come to appreciate the productive sentiment of individual farmers. Now a farmer or rather his family is given the privilege to acquire a plot from the collective to work on. It is known as bao chan dao hu to be discussed presently.

It is a household-contract system of responsibility. It has been designed to enhance productivity. Based on tripartite participation of the state, the collective and the peasant family,[135] the system requires, first, the state developing an overall plan of production. A given amount of crops is to be put out by a certain region. On this calculation, the production team contracts out the acreage to a tiller and his household who concur to grow a specified product. Beasts of burden and farm implements are distributed to the peasants by the team. It is the latter which legally owns the land and which operates the big machines and water conservancy facilities. Under this arrangement, the household is levied agricultural taxes and it sells a prescribed quota of harvest to the state. The team keeps a share of the sale for its own use, with the remaining going to the household.

[130] Economic intelligent unit, "China: the national economy," New Encyclopedia Americana, Chicago: Encyclopedia Americana, 1979, vol. 4, pp. 276-281 at 277, col. 1.

[131] Beijing review, July 19, 1982, pp. 15-17.

[132] Zheng zhi chang shi du ben can kao zi liao, pp. 229-231. Renmin ribao, December 9, 1981, p. 3 very briefly describes the state farm.

[133] Iu. V. Minolov, "Organizatsiya proizvodstva, raspredeleniya i oplaty truda v sel'skom khozyaistve, gosudarstvennyi sektor," Sel'skoe khozyaistvo KNR 1949-1974, pp. 124-127.

[134] Economic intelligent unit, loc. cit.

[135] Lu Baifu, "The way for agriculture," Beijing review, January 24, 1983, p. 14.

To fulfil this contractual obligation, the household is allowed to organize more freely the production than previously. No longer was the peasant's work determined arbitrarily by the state cadres. The system abolishes the principle of equal pay. It puts into effect the socialist tenet of reaping one's fruit of labor by actual engagement in work. Peasants who produce more receive more, but produce nothing receive nothing. A gradation of compensation is the policy guide for reward. A recent Chinese press calls for "farewell, big public pots.''[136] It writes that eating from the big pot is the popular metaphor for absolute egalitarianism in distribution, one of the undesirable practices that China seeks to get rid of as part of its contemporary rational economic reform.

At one time, it was held that socialist agriculture by the nature of things was undertaken by big collectives. The bigger the better. The initiation of the responsibility system purports to alter this mentality. Management by the household has now come to reduce the size of the accounting unit and this is alleged not to violate the socialist public economy. The press describes it as "an appropriate route for socialist agriculture (because) it conforms to China's specific conditions and offers broad prospects for further development.''[137] The explanation is advanced that the contract regime requires public ownership of the basic means of production. In the meantime, the household control is premised on the co-ordinate plan of collective cultivation. And the team exercises unified supervision over the use of large farm machinery and other tools. Furthermore, the peasants have the privilege to develop the tracts but no right to sell, lease or transfer the title. And they are duty bound to deliver the agreed-on quantity of things to the state and retain enough for the collective before they can claim the remainder.

Just a paragraph or two on the Dazhai model. In the communist terminology, it is a brigade, not a commune as seen in some writings. The Chinese media made a good deal of fanfare about it, but presently it is found to be overblown and a hoax of the Gang of Four[138] The importance of Dazhai is said to be comparable to such landmarks as the agrarian reform of 1949-1952, the rural co-op setup of 1954-1956 and the communization of 1958-1959.[139] Situated in Xiyang county (Shaanxi province), some 400 km southwest of Beijing, Dazhai is a mountain settlement of 450 souls. Formerly it was penurious, with 4,700 plots of land in gullies and ridges. The plots were amalgamated into 1,500 terraced fields during the Great Leap. In 1971-1975, the peasants allegedly leveled off 33 small mounds, filled up 15 big trenches and carted away 700,000 cubic meters of earth. In the

[136] Ibid., February 14, 1983, p. 4.

[137] Lu Baifu, op. cit., p. 16, col. 1.

[138] New York Times, October 4, 1979, p. 6, col. 5. Such important books do not mention Dazhai at all, Xin hua ci dian, Beijing: Shang wu yin shu guan, 1980; Zhong guo shou ce, Hong Kong: Da gong bao, 1980.

[139] The description of Dazhai is in Keesing's, April 9, 1976, p. 27670.

meantime, two huge ponds were dug up and 40,000 fruit trees planted on the barren uplands. All these measures pushed up the grain harvest from 40 tons in 1949 to 385 tons in 1974. Thanks to this, income of the farmers increased 11 times during the same period. Further trumpeted by the Reds is the new housing development on the farms. Dazhai has, in addition, such industries as cement works, chemical fertilizer plants and collieries.

In recognition of Dazhai, its chairman, a "model" farmer and secretary of the party branch there, Chen Yonggui, was made a member of the Politburo in 1973.[140] He was reelected to that body at the 11th Congress of the CCP (in session from August 12 to 18, 1977).[141] A month-long National Agricultural Conference on "learn from Dazhai" was held in September-October 1975[142] The meeting started right on that farm, but later moved to Beijing, apparently because most of the 3,700 confreres were high mandarins who could ill-afford to stay away from their yamens at Beijing for so long. Chairing the "jamboree," Hua Guofeng (vice premier then) asserted that the entire Shaanxi province and 300 of China's 2,200 counties greatly benefited by following the example of its distinguished brigade. He cited fantastic figures of production of this or that thing. He assured that total mechanization of the country's agriculture would be completed by 1980. This date was postponed by the same Hua Guofeng to 1985, the final year of the 10 year plan, in a speech of February 26, 1978 to the 5th NPC.[143] On December 10, 1976 there was called a second agricultural conference on learning from Dazhai. This time the attendants augmented to 5,000. Nothing new developed out of it, and it only rehashed the programs outlined by the first conference a year before. Thereafter, this farming model becomes a matter of disillusion, and its symbol, Chen Yonggui, was removed from the Politburo after the 12th Congress of the CCP in September 1982.

Current problems

First of all let us survey the agricultural records by taking into consideration the population size and the concrete measures currently carried out to increase the output of grain, the single most vital thing.[144] As the following table shows, grain production, which in some years includes soya bean, was on the upswing during the entire history of the CPR, with a few exceptions.

[140] Harold Hinton, *op. cit.,* p. 246; *Facts on File,* September 25, 1976, p. 712, BI.

[141] *Facts on File,* August 20, 1977, p. 645, GI.

[142] Rüdiger Machetzki, "Die zweite Tachai Konferenz, bestätigung der neuen Führung und ihrer landlichen Wirtschaftspolitik," *China aktuell,* 6 (1977), februarheft, pp. 25-29.

[143] *Facts on File,* March 10, 1978, p. 154, DI.

[144] Hu Yaobang's speech emphasizes this, *Beijing review,* September 13, 1982, pp. 15-16.

1952	161 million tons	1976	285
1957	191	1977a	283 down
1965	194	1978b	305
1970	243	1979c	332
1971	246	1980d	317 down
1972	240 down	1981e	345
1973	266	1982f	335 down
1974	275	1983f	342.5
1975	284		

Source: from 1952 to 1976, James Townsend, *Politics in China*, 2nd ed., Boston: Little, Brown, 1980, p. 364. Other years from
a *Keesing's*, September 8, 1978, p. 29193, col. 2.
b *Hammond*, 1980, p. 547, col. a.
c *Ibid.*, 1981, p. 548, col. 1. Yao Yilin, "report on the arrangements for the national economic plans for 1980 and 1981," *Main documents of the third session of the fifth NPC of the CPR*, Beijing: Foreign languages press, 1st ed., 1980, pp. 5-47 at 7 mentions 332.12 million tons.
d Yao Yilin says grain production was down by 15 million tons in 1980, *Zhong yang ribao*, March 8, 1981, p. 1.
e *Beijing review*, December 20, 1982, p. 20, col. 1, the figure was given by Zhao Ziyang.
f These are estimates, in *Beijing review*, January 3, 1983, p. 4, col. 1.

Let us convert the above figures into per capita kg.[145]

1952	283	1972	273	1977	334
1957	298	1973	297	1978	303
1965	259	1974	300	1979	348
1970	289	1975	304	1980	333
1971	286	1976	300	1981	353

Taking the 1979 per capita kg for consideration, we should note that it does not mean that every Chinese has 348 kg to eat. The consumable amount is less. Western statistics for grain and wheat refer to the produce in the natural or non-milled form. The Chinese call it *gu*. Shedding the husk it becomes *mi*. When it is ready to serve after being cooked, it assumes the name *fan.*, The husks of the grain are of course unedible. The milling rate is 65 percent for rice, 80 percent for wheat and 82 percent for other cereals.[146] The 1979 per capita kg of 348 (*gu*) turns out to be only 251.3 in terms of *mi*. This is actually cookable. Then we calculated that each able-bodied person should eat 0.747 kg a day. In a twelve-month period, he requires 268.9 kg. This leaves a shortage of 17.6 kg. China has to go abroad for it.[147] How much came from this source (in million tons)?[148] From 1972 onward, the record is as follows.

1972-1973 6.4(a)	1977-1978 3.9(b)
1973-1974 7.8	1978-1979 4.4(c)
1974-1975 6.2	1979-1981 40.0(d)
1975-1976 6.2	1982 10.2(e)
1976-1977 8.0	

145 We take the population figures for 1952-1979 from *Hammond* and *Stateman's Yearbook* and those for 1980 and 1981 from *Information Please*, 1981 (p. 172, col. 2) and 1982 (p. 151, col. 1.).
146 *Europa*, 1979, vol. 2, p. 120.
147 *Information Please*, 1979, p. 159.
148 *Europa*, 1979, vol. 2, p. 123 gives the figures for 1972-1977, and the *Encyclopedia Yearbook*, 1979, p. 157, col. 1 offers the figure for 1977-1978.

276   GOVERNMENT OF SOCIALIST CHINA

(a) Figures from 1972 to 1977, *Europa*, 1979, vol. 2, p. 123.
(b) *Encyclopedia yearbook*, 1979, p. 157, col. 1.
(c) *Facts on file*, November, 24, 1978, p. 902, Al.
(d) *Beijing review*, November 8, 1982, p. 7, col. 1.
(e) The 1982 figure includes 6 million tons from US, and 4.2 million tons from Canada. For the first figure see *Facts on file*, October 24, 1980, pp. 801, B2; for the second figure, *ibid.*, May 21, 1982, pp. 366-367.

How many persons can, for example, eight million tons of imported grain feed? After milling, the amount is reduced to 520,000 tons. By the standard of 268.9 kg per capita, it is capable of feeding 1,907,000, less tha 0.2% of the population. The supplying countries are, in the ranking of importance, Canada, Australia, US and Argentina. These capitalist regimes are supporting a country whose leaders used to be boastful of their superior socialist economy.[149]

The thorny problem for China's agriculture turns on the size of the population. Before the 1982 census disclosed the official figure, each press in the West made its guess, the larges estimate being that of the Central Intelligence Agency of the US. In mid-1978 it put the figure at 1,004,000,000.[150] The 1982 census reveals that as of July 1, mainland Chinese numbered 1,008,175,288.[151] How close is it to the CIA estimate! Hua Guofeng, it is interesting to note, spoke of 700,000,000 peasants of China (n.b. not rural population) in an address to the NPC on February 26, 1978[152] It surely takes demographers agog to multiply that number by 4.5 per family so as to get the total rural residents.

Village population, according to the 1964 census, made for 81.6 percent of the total, but it came down to 79.4 percent in the 1982 census.[153] Most studies maintain that about 11 percent of the territory is arable.[154] Practically all Chinese (Han) and good soils are in the eastern half of the country.[155] The communist regime must be able to feed over 20 percent of the world's population with less than 7 percent of the world's agricultural land.[156] How much of this does each Chinese have? One Western reference gives 0.39,[157] whle

[149] Zhao Ziyang repeats this boast in the speech to the fifth session of the Fifth NPC, *Beijing review*, December 20, 1982, p. 23, col. 1; p. 33, col. 2.

[150] Cited in James Townsend, "Politics in China," p. 397.

[151] *Beijing review*, November 8, 1982, p. 20, col. 1.

[152] *Facts on file*, February 26, 1978, p. 154, Bl.

[153] *Beijing review*, November 8, 1982, p. 21, col. 2.

[154] J.D. Waller, *op. cit.*, p. 125 (gives 15 percent however).

[155] James Townsend, "Politics in China," p. 398, col. 1.

[156] *Keesing's*, December 16, 1977, p. 28724, col. 1.

[157] *Europa*, 1979, vol. 2, p. 118.

CHAPTER IX   277

another gives 0.3 acres.[158] Besides, there is a Chinese figure. Hua Guofeng's speech of February 26, 1978 (cited above) mentioned 700,000,000 peasants but only 500,000,000 mu. By converting the mu to acres (6:1), we arrive at 0.12 acres per capita. The now abandoned 10 year plan (1976-1985) envisaged one man one mu toward the end of the plan. That is to say, it has to be in 1985 that each Chinese would have 0.16 acres, i.e., one mu. Within 10 years, the increment is from 0.12 to 0.16, a gain of 0.04 acres. From the above, there are three statistics of per capita arable acres at the present time: 0.12, 0.3, 0.39. Which is nearer to the truth?

For farming doldrums, a whole array of cures are tried. The earliest but the least fruitful is the enlargement of the harvesting area. Hua Guofeng, as stated above, envisaged the goal of one man one mu in ten years' time (1985). Ever since the 1957 Leap, we have scanty information on the effort of the government to open up more area for planting cereals. Even the hysterical drive of reclamation during the Leap produces no figures about land brought under cultivation.[159] Hu Yaobang deplored the "huge population" but "insufficient arable land,"[160] as did Zhao Ziyang in their respective speeches to the 12th Congress of the CCP and the Fifth NPC Congress. The latter man spoke of expanding the "total area of artificially sown pastures from the 32 million mu in 1980 to 100 million mu in 1985."[161] No new lands are planned to be opened, however.

Then there is the attempt, very reluctant though, to leave "small" garden tracts to the peasants. The quoted adjective, incidentally, was used in the 1975 and 1978 Constitution (both in Article 7), but dropped from the 1982 one. At one point in our early discussion, mention was made of the reduction of these tracts from five to one percent of the farming acreage due to the influence of the Gang of Four in the early seventies. The Gang, it is alleged, thought it contrary to socialism to allow the peasants to till even a little piece of backyard. Criticizing such radicalism, a long article in a Beijing media held that "there has never been a class conflict without a material base, nor a revolution unconnected with economic interests."[162] The media extolled the peasants' private produce sold at the communal plaza as a boost to livelihood. In 1978, the Chinese press began to place greater stress on the development of garden plots by rural residents. This it called sideline production.[163] The Xinhua news agency holds that such production does not have a capitalist stench as the Gang of Four tried

[158] World Almanac, 1981, p. 525, col. 1.

[159] There are, however, planned areas to be cultivated, Owne L. Dawson, "Irrigation developments under the communist regime," John Lossing Buck, et alii, ed., op. cit., pp. 149-167 at 161.

[160] Beijing review, September 13, 1982, p. 15, col. 1.

[161] Ibid., December 20, 1982, p. 14, col. 2.

[162] Renmin ribao, September 16, 1978, pp. 1, 3.

[163] Keesing's, September 8, 1978, p. 29193, col. 2.

to make it up to be. It is one way to meet the demands of the working masses and "a necessary means to supplement the socialist economy."[164] Furthermore, the plots can multiply the resources and prevent their being squandered.

Several months prior to the *Xinhua* commentary, Hua Guofeng had said the sideline labor must be supported.[165] The private area, having dwindled to one percent of the farming acreage in the early seventies, went up to seven percent in 1980 and the government plans to raise it to fifteen percent before long.[166] Many journals editorialized their backing of it. *Hongqi,* for example, wrote that these "legal family occupations carried out on the side" could help diversify products in rural China.[167] An item in the *Xinhua* news agency of April 24, 1978 emphasized that at a time when the collective economy had not yet prospered enough to assure the peasants a good life and to satisfy the needs of cities and countryside, the ancillary production of the villagers should not be despised. It is vital, said *Xinhua,* to positively prop it up toward the development of individual but non-exploitative engagements.

The 1982 Constitution (Article 9, par. 1) creates the "right" for the individual peasants to till plots in accordance with legislation. It also encourages household sideline production and livestock for their own use. Speaking to the 12th Congress of the CCP on September 1, 1982, General Secretary Hu Yaobang reiterates this line.[168] Now the Chinese no longer equate "individual farming" to speculation and profiteering.[169]

In order to augment the output of agriculture, Beijing bulldozes ahead with mechanization and fertilization.[170] A *Xinhua* release of September 8, 1977 mentioned a high jump in the importing of farm instruments, insecticides and fertilizers.[171] With regard to the last-named item, one author notes that substantial fertilizing industry was developed in the entire sixties. However, the needs must be met by foreign supply and the Chinese output is only a small portion of it. In 1979, for example, the Chinese themselves manufactured 8,693,000 tons of fertilizers,[172] and in 1982 and 1983, 12,550,000 tons

[164] *Ibid.*

[165] Speech before the 5th NPC on February 26, 1978, *Ibid.*, September 8, 1978, p. 29182.

[166] *Facts on File,* February 22, 1980, p. 132, A3.

[167] *Ibid.*, March 19, 1977, p. 200, C3.

[168] "Create a new situation in all fields of socialist modernization," *Beijing review,* September 13, 1982, pp. 11-40 at 14, col. 1.

[169] *Facts on file,* March 19, 1977, p. 200.

[170] Z.A. Muromtseva, "Material'no-tekhnicheskaya baza sel'skogo khozyaistva," *Sel'skoe khozyaistva KNR 1949-1974,* pp. 141-177 at 141.

[171] *Facts on file,* October 13, 1978, p. 773, D3.

[172] *Britannica Book of the Year,* 1980, p. 246, col. 1.

annually.[173] Compare these figures with the historical import figures below.[174]

(million ton)

1965	7.6	1973	24.8
1970	14.0	1974	24.9
1971	16.8	1975	27.9
1972	19.8		

The Chinese statistics on the item under consideration are rare, but western ones are fragmentary, inconsistent and, for the most part, outdated.[175] In this circumstance, we cannot have an intelligent understanding of the problem, except the general conclusion that fertilizers are increasingly used in the CPR to better the crops.

In respect to mechanization of agriculture, the now discarded 10 year plan envisaged 85 percent completion by 1985.[176] As in the case of fertilizers, the CPR must go abroad for it. A publication reports recent years' import of tractors as follows (in thousand 15-horsepower units.)[177]

1965	23.9	1973	166.0
1970	79.0	1974	150.0
1971	114.6	1975	180.0
1972	136.0	1976	190.9

The leaders seem to have realized that too rigid control over the farm management tends to stifle the initiative of the local regime and individual peasants. Lately (only lately) the provincial authority is empowered to give more leeway to the team in deciding what to grow. This is particularly true in the biggest province, Sichuan. There, the garden tracts are expanded by more than one-third.[178] For the alleged achievement of productivity in Sichuan, Secretary Zhao Ziyang was catapulted to the premiership of the CPR in September 1980, bypassing many bright stars. This decentralization is admittedly a belated but wise step, because the local conditions are so diverse in that country that it is just impossible to lay down a hard and fast rule for all to follow. A recent article in the party organ stated the structural variation from region to region and from village to village. Yet it suggested the observance of uniform principles throughout the

---

[173] *Beijing review,* January 3, 1983, p. 8, col. 1.

[174] "China: economic indicators," reprinted in James Townsend, "Politics in China," pp. 364-365.

[175] For example, the 1979 domestic product of fertilizers is 8,693,000 tons (see main text), but *Hammond,* 1980, p. 547, col. 1 mentions 14,000,000 tons for that year. Harold Hinton (*op. cit.,* pp. 250-251) and Economic intelligent unit (p. 279, col. 2) alleged that China produced 14,000,000 tons in 1970. Moreover, the *Britannica Book of the Year,* 1976, p. 192 said that in 1973-1974 the Chinese agriculture was supplied with 4,070,000 tons of fertilizers. The publication does not specify whether the sum was an import or domestic output. The *Europa,* 1979, vol. 2, p. 123 tells that in 1973 and 1974, China used 4,200,000 tons of fertilizers each year and in 1975, 4,100,000 tons.

[176] Speech to the 5th NPC, February 26, 1978, *Keesing's,* September 8, 1978, p. 29182.

[177] "China: Economic indicators," reprinted in Townsend, *loc. cit.*

[178] *Facts on File,* February 22, 1980, p. 132, C3.

nation.[179] The totalitarian mode of thinking is hard to get rid of. To stimulate production, Beijing decided to raise the state payment for grain. Starting from the summer of 1979, according to a CC resolution of December 22, 1978, peasants would be given 20 percent higher for that item.[180] The previous year (October 23, 1977) Yu Qiuli, the then planning czar of the CPR, declared to the NPC Standing Committee the government policy of assuring the "peasants higher income and more consumer goods."[181] This step, as officially recognized, was to overcome the scissor-situation in which the farm output brought less and less return, while the manufactured items soared in price. The aim of the CCP, allege the Chinese, is not to ground down the peasants, as the CPSU did, but to make them happy.[182].

Another help to the farming folks is the *xiafang* movement. There were two earlier editions, one in the sixties and one in the fifties. During the Cultural Revolution, the higher cadres in the party and administration were decreed to spend a month or so a year at the bottom levels of the government, mainly villages, to perform manual duties. During 1958, bureaucrats and intelligentsia were ordered to do physical labor as members of the mass workers.[183] At the end of the Cultural Revolution (1968-1969), more than 30 million former Red Guards were forced out of the cities.[184] For unknown reasons, *xiafang* was abruptly halted after the Sino-Soviet border clash on March 3, 1969,[185] only to be quickly resumed. The years 1975 and 1976 saw 2,000,000 and 2,700,000 dispatched respectively to the hamlets. The idea of *xiafang* was originated by Mao Zedong. He assumed that the youth were willing to integrate with the broad masses. Thankful to *xiafang*, a "profound socialist revolution" was said to be achieved, with the resulting elimination of the differences between town and countryside, between workers and peasants and between menial and mental labor.

Xiafang, however, does not fulfil the task perceived by Mao. It is really an act to turn the adolescents into rural employees. The state virtually sets no service time. Once sent to the countryside, a youth remains there for the rest of his life. It is a one-way alley. As such *xiafang* is harsher than the system of labor conscription which Leon Trotsky instituted in 1922-1923 for the Russians. If the young people are experts of some sort, their stay may be useful there, but they are not. They come fresh from the classroom and have no special training

[179] *Renmin ribao*, September 12, 1978, pp. 1,3.

[180] *Facts on File*, December 31, 1978, p. 1015, Bi.

[181] *Ibid.*, October 29, 1977, p. 823, Bl.

[182] *Renmin ribao*, September 12, 1978, pp. 1, 3.

[183] James Townsend, "The politics of China," p. 392, col. 2.

[184] Harold Hinton, *op. cit.*, p. 72.

[185] *Ibid.*

whatsoever. Is every high school graduate *xiafanged?* Apparently not. In 1977, for example, high school graduates were 59,079,000,[186] and in 1980, they numbered 65,000,000,[187] but approximately ten million had been *xiafanged* in each of the two years. Except for *xiafang,* several millions would have been jobless. Modernization is still in the infancy stage. Before it picks up momentum, industries are in no position to absorb all the young adults. In this situation, rural China has to be the dumping site of them. The flow from the countryside to the cities is now totally blocked since industries there cannot take more labor force. The government moved to lower the wage of the unskilled workers in the city in order to make it less attractive. There are elaborate rules to prevent the peasants from going to town. If they succeed in entering, they find it impossible to remain. There are mass evictions of rural migrants.[188] For the first time in the CPR history, a frank confession of unemployment was expressed in 1979 by a high mandarin, Li Xiannian, the then vice premier. He said China had 20,000,000 people without jobs and 100,000,000 people underfed.[189] Unless industrialization is stepped up, the vast army of school-leavers are candidates for unemployment and a sizeable number of them are village-bound. An unforeseen problem arises that the *xiafang* youth, for understandable reasons, are unable to integrate with the peasants as Mao supposed they could. Even with the tight surveillance of the communist police, many youngsters are able to sneak back to the cities where life is more pleasant and opportunities are greater. However, they cannot be given residential permits and they are not entitled to rations. This leads to the logical consequence: crime. Yet severity of law does not ensure peace and order in a Chinese city (see Chapter XV).

Organization reform, as stated above, has devolved responsibility on the lowest echelon to enhance the productivity. The centerpiece is now the working team, a self-financing juridical person. As a consequence, Beijing has to deal with several millions of such units. This kind of remote control cannot be very effective. This, along with the fact that different parts of the country have quite distinct economic patterns led the government to think of establishing six regions in the northeast, north, east central, south, southwest and northwest, to act as a sub-national rung with the responsibility to monitor the team activities.[190] Although such a plan was revealed in early 1977, it was not to be effected until 1985, according to Hua Guofeng.[191]

---

[186] *Ibid.*

[187] *Britannica Book of the Year,* 1980, p. 246, col. 1.

[188] Dwight H. Perkins, "China: economy," *Americana,* internatinal ed., New York: Americana Corporation, 1976, vol. 6, pp. 515-523 at 520-521.

[189] *Britannica Book of the Year,* 1980, p. 248, col. 1; *Americana Annual,* 1980, pp. 167-171 at 170, col. 1.

[190] *Keesing's,* December 1977, p. 28723, col. 2.

[191] *Facts on file,* March 10, 1978, p. 154, DI.

The explanation of the deferment is not hard to find. Regions as administrative cadres, we shall remember, were set up in 1949, but two of them, the northeast under Gao Gong and the east under Rao Shushi, were reputedly defying the central authority. This ended in the abolition of all the regions. Revived in 1961 to meet the need of restoring the economy after the debacle of the Leap, the system disappeared at the inception of the Cultural Revolution.[192] The 1977 decision to revive it intimates the dilemma facing the leadership who want an efficient economy as well as a firm grip at the top. The future regions are avowedly economical in nature. They are, in other words, to stay away from politics. A warning is thus served to a Gao Gong or a Rao Shushi that he should act within the prescribed ambit.[193]

It has been claimed that thanks to the various measures in rural China, gross agricultural output value has increased at an annual rate of 5.6 percent over the last four years.[194] Grain estimates for 1982 were as high as 335 million tons, cotton 3.3 million tons, oil-bearing crops 14.185 million tons. They represent increases of 9.9, 52.3 and 171.8 percent respectively over the 1978 figures. Peasants' income has increased fairly fast. Per capita net income in 1981 was 223.4 yuan, a 66.7 percent rise over the 134 yuan in 1978. The collective pays 116.2 yuan of this sum and the remainder is from their private plots and household sideline occupations. These occupations produced in 1981, a sum of 29,780 million yuan worth of output which is 17.3 percent of the total value of CPR's agricultural product.[195] It is stated in the Chinese papers that with the exception of a few destitute areas where natural conditions are difficult, the quality of food, clothing and housing in rural China has improved. The percentage of marketable agricultural goods has increased, as has the quantity of raw materials supplied to factories.[196]

Rice is the staple food on the Chinese table. When they eat three rice-meals a day, the demand upon it is understandably enormous. The same holds true with wheat in many areas of China. If the diet varies a little, for example, by adding fruits or dairy products, the pressure on these two things (rice and wheat) would be leveled out and the problem would become less acute. One can also suggest that more cash crops may be planted. By selling these on the world market, the government could use the exchange to buy food stuffs overseas. Probably it is less expensive to get them that way than

---

[192] Keesing's, loc. cit.

[193] K.N. Chernozhukov i E.V. Martygina, "Pochvenno-klimaticheskie usloviya, zemel'nyi fond, struktura i razmeshchenie sel'skokhozyaistvennogo proizvodstva," Sel'skoe khozyaistvo KNR 1949-1974, pp. 178-227 at 220-22.

[194] Lu Baifu, op. cit., p. 15, col. 1.

[195] Beijing review, February 7, 1983, p. 27.

[196] Lu Baifu, loc. cit.

invest money in agriculture.[197] Although not expressly stating so, the Soviet Union until the 1982 Brezhnev food program, had preferred paying cash for foreign grain to laying out capital in farming.[198]

In re the kinds of plantation, northern China produces wheat, barley, corn, sorghum, millet and cognate cereals. There are also beans and peas. In the south, rice, sugar and indigo are the most important articles. The Yangzi basin is the country's grain basket and tea is grown in the central upland, along the coast and particularly in Sichuan province. Soybean and cotton are not negligible. Others include fibers, tobacco, vegetables, oils, cane sugar and many sorts of herbs and spices. Before the seizure of power by the communists, there were no huge plantations to produce these things. It was the itinerant hawkers who collected them from rural people and sold them to big merchants. Now the government has enjoyed the advantage of being the organizer and enterpreneur of agricultural output. Better techniques can be introduced and soil survey may discover many terrains more usable for one plant than another. Provided the leadership is stable and does not channel all the resources to the weapons development, and provided radicalism is given a final death knell, the agricultural problem can be somewhat assuaged, though not solved.

---

[197] Theodore Shabad, *China's Changing Map, a Political and Economic Geography of the Chinese People's Republic,* New York: Praeger, 1956, pp. 70-72.

[198] In the comment on the Food Program, *Pravda* pointed out that to buy foodstuff abroad gives imperialist powers a great diplomatic lever in their dealings with the USSR, 'Vo imya narodnogo blaga,'' *Pravda,* May 26, 1982, p. 1, col. 1.

CHAPTER X
Industry

Rehabilitation

In 1949, the GMD was driven out of power by force of violence. To the conqueror-communists was left a dilapidated economy. In military prowess, they proved mighty, but other endowments of theirs failed to pass the severest of tests. After decades of civil strife and Japanese invasion, what remained was nothing but shambles and poverty.[1] Even in Manchuria, the most developed part of the nation (thanks to the Japanese), the picture was bleak. In addition to the ruins caused by the fighting there, the Russians eviscerated all industrial facilities worth having and shifted them across the Amur and Ussuri. In China proper, livelihood of the masses was everywhere below the subsistance line. Inflation soared from one hour to another and price tags of any commodity were marked by the thousands of million yuan.[2] The plummeting of the morale in the GMD provinces contributed to the triumph of the Reds many times more than the setback at the front. A little noticed fact in the civil war is that the communists printed astronomical amounts of bogus money both to finance their war and to destroy the state currency. This counterfeit was poured out in militarily contested areas only, because the "liberated" districts, mostly in the north and Manchuria, had their own currency. In order to battle the government forces, the guerillas tore off trunks, derailed trains, detonated dams, blocked rivers, blew up air transport, dynamited highways, fire-bombed busses, exploded plants, etc. Besides, they fomented strikes, stirred up student demonstrations, burned down public buildings and engaged in assassinations. In all these, the Chinese communists rehearsed, as it were, for the Vietcongs during the Indo-China conflict some 25 years later. Fiscal as well as military assault on the power that be stands the Reds in good stead.

Having acquired full domination over China, the Reds set out at once to construct a nation in the image of their ideal system, or truer yet, in the image of the Soviet Union.[3] During the first three years, however, their measures were rather mild, judging by their standard of course.[4] There was, after all, no communism in the shortest order.[5] Industry no less than agriculture moved from private to public footing

---

[1] Solomon Adler, *The Chinese Economy,* New York: Monthly Review Press, 1957, pp. 16-20.

[2] Albert Feuerwerker, *The Chinese Economy,* 1912-1949, Ann Arbor: University of Michigan, center for Chinese studies, 1968, p. 60.

[3] M. Ya Sonin, "Rabochii klass, stran narodnoi demokratii," *Bol'shaya sovetskaya entsiklopediya,* 2nd ed., Moskva: Gosudarstvennoe nauchnoe izdatel'stvo "bol'shaya sovetskaya entsiklopediya," 1949-1958, vol. 35 (1955), pp. 436-448 at 448.

[4] "Smeshannye obshchestva," *Ibid.,* vol. 38 (1956), p. 461. "Ekspropriatsiya ekspropriatorov," vol. 48 (1957), p. 421.

[5] Robert Gillain, "Tod einer alten Zivilisation," *Gegenwart,* 11 (1956), no. 4, pp. 109-111.

step by step. Before long, the regime stabilized the financial market, checked the inflation and brought down the prices. In doing this, it employed draconian means, such as mass execution of "profiteers." Meanwhile, major articles were hoarded by trading concerns which had the power to dump or to withhold so as to maintain the fixed charge on customers. "By controlling both the credit and a decisive amount of commodities, the government in effect related the currency to goods rather than to gold."[6] At the same time, the authority employed tax as a weapon to regulate what was perforce a modified bourgeois economy.[7] Contributing to the financial normalcy were the deflationary policy instituted by the People's Bank, and a crash program of re-opening the lines linking Beijing to Guangzhou in the south and to Shanghai in the east, lines which had been put out of use by the roving and ruthless Reds during the war. Free from the mass destruction as suffered by the GMD and backed by capital punishment for disturbance of the fiscal order, the economy began to breathe some life, but it was not until after the wiping out of the undesirables like landlords, shopowners and industrialists did the government push for a socialist program.[8] Having studied the collectivization in the previous chapter, we now look at how the business circles had fared.

The regime found it expedient to go slow. At first, it left traders and entrepreneurs operate as before.[9] The policy was to make use of the private enterprises which it hoped may help to rejuvenate the economy. In the two years (1949-1951), China seems to opt for a sort of New Economy Policy which characterized the Soviet Union of 1921-1928.[10] Then followed the period of restriction featured by repression and bloodshed. Beginning in April 1953 the Reds commenced to unmask themselves. The bourgeois had to go. Even though the CCP made a great noise with the "joint revolution of the bourgeois and the toiling masses" for the purpose of broadening its appeal, it did not hesitate to break its word. Once the communists were firmly nestled, they found the verbal alignment with the exploiters losing the raison d'être, and they were determined that this kind of men were to be tossed to the trash of history.[11]

A major punitive action was the five-anti campaign, starting out in

[6] Franz H. Michael and George E. Taylor, *The Far East in the Modern World*, 2nd ed., New York: Holt, Rinehart and Winston, 1964, p. 458.

[7] T.J. Hughes and D.E.T. Luard, *The Economic Development of Communist China, 1949-1960*, London: Oxford University Press, 1961, pp. 29-31.

[8] Feng-hwa Mah, "The first Five Year Plan and its international aspects," *International Economics of Communist China*, edited by C.F. Remer, Ann Arbor: University of Michigan Press, 1959, pp. 33-34.

[9] "Derevnaya," *Bol'shaya sovetskaya entsiklopediya*, 2nd ed., vol. 14 (1952), pp. 57-65 at 64.

[10] "China, Wirtschaftliche Erfolge des Jahres 1952," *Aussenhandel*, 3 (1952), p. 87; "Die wirtschaftliche Entwicklung der Volksrepublik China," *Ibid.*, 3 (1953), p. 589.

[11] Maurice Meisner, *Mao's China, A History of the People's Republic of China*, New York: Macmillan, 1977, p. 81.

October 1951 and winding up in June 1952.[12] The five objects are tax evasion, bribery, cheating in government contracts, theft of economic intelligence and stealth of state property. Any shopkeeper could be charged with one or several of these, because there were no legal definitions of, for example, what is economic intelligence or what constitutes a tax evasion. Numerous tribunals quickly sprang up to prosecute the suspects. At the beginning, only a small number of the merchants and factory owners were arrested, but the cases grew apace from day to day. The victims were subject to summary procedure and were led to incriminate each other. Associates of many years' standing, and fathers and sons often knocked in oral combat in the "court." Each tried to please the Reds and hopefully to save his skin. Many were jailed or shot and the death toll increased by waves of suicides. Some were lucky enough escaping the firing squads, but they were heavily fined or lost their property completely. As there was no bankruptcy law, the firms were not allowed to be declared insolvent.[13] Thereupon, the state came to grant high-interest loans to enable them to carry on. This onerous burden then led to the "partial transfer of the business capital to government ownership."[14] Moreover, the firms were to take communists either as supervisors or board directors; soon the government came to manage them, while hiring the former owners as aides and advisors.[15]

The next step was the outright takeover of the enterprises by the state. It goes by the slogan of "transformation of private property", lasting from 1954 to 1957. Sometimes it is known as "buying off the bourgeois." They were paid five percent, in lieu of dividend, on the value of the capital and were in a few cases retained as executives of their lost companies.[16] As the collectivized peasant received pay for his labor and the land he put in, so the manager obtained a wage plus the dividend. However, while the recompenses for the land were soon abolished,[17] the five percent profit continued until 1961. It was then decreed to be further defrayed because the government needed the managerial skill and it found it wise not to alienate the ancient entrepreneurs.[18] Even though dispossessed of their property, the reformed businessmen were very glad that they did not get shot. In fact, there were only a handful of them left and their position,

[12] A.Kh. Chekalin, "Perekhodnyi period ot kapitalizma k sotsializmu" Bol'shaya sovetskaya entsiklopediya, 2nd ed., vol. 32 (1955), pp. 468-470 at 470; "Staat und Gesellschaft in Rotchina," Ostproblem, 5 (1953), pp. 423-442.

[13] Franz H. Michael and George E. Taylor, op. cit., p. 461.

[14] Ibid.

[15] "Das volk regiert in China (Po Ji-po)," Gesellschaft, 1952, heft 11, pp. 823-830.

[16] J.D. Waller, The Government and Politics of Communist China, London: Hutchinson University Library, 1970, p. 132.

[17] "China, kollektivizierungswander," Rundschau (Köln), 7 (1957), no. 2, p. 20.

[18] Franz H. Michael and George E. Taylor, op. cit., p. 476.

subordinate as it was, prevented them from doing any harm to the regime. By 1957, China eliminated utterly the vestige of the bourgeois proprietorship in the city as well as in the countryside.[19] Although not explicitly stated, the aforesaid five percent interest was suspended during the Cultural Revolution. It was not until 1979 that the payment was restored.[20]

What was the economic achievement during the period of rehabilitation?[21] The period, we must remember, saw China fight a war in Korea. She had to finance it. The weapons her volunteers used came from Soviet Russia, but she paid for them. Exact information is scarce on how much the Soviets received from the arms sale. One thing is certain: the war was a high burden to Beijing. The state acquired a lot from the private sector during the period under review. Most assets of this sector were confiscated. A study shows that in 1952 the government budget indicated a revenue of over $8 billion compared to an expenditure of $6,895,000,000. The surplus of over one billion was believed derived from the capital fines imposed on the companies.[22] No matter what use, military or otherwise, the regime had put it, it was a great help to the state.

Even though the takeover from the bourgeois was a noteworthy exploit, economic recovery was mainly due to such measures as financial stabilization, transport repairment, etc. Beijing claimed that by 1952, the "output of 33 major industrial products had risen to 26 percent above pre-war peak level: 16 percent in capital goods and 32 percent in consumer goods."[23] One author saw the claim as an overstatement, but he and a host of other writers agreed that at the end of the Korean war, if not earlier, the economy of the People's Republic had fully healed itself from the destruction wrought by the Japanese and by the civil war.[24] In respect to revenue, while in 1949, 15.5 percent of industrial production derived from the state enterprises, in 1950 it rose to 43.8 percent and in 1952, 67.3 percent.[25] Communist sources say that in the latter year, 80 percent of heavy industry and 40 percent of light industry came to be owned by the state, as were 90 percent of the facilities of international trade. In fine, the year 1952 marked the end of recuperation, and some of the

[19] Ho Kan-chih, A History of the Modern Chinese Revolution, Beijing: Foreign Languages Press, 1960, p. 613.

[20] Statesman's Yearbook, 1979-1980, p. 338.

[21] Yuan-li Wu, An Economic Survey of Communist China, New York: Bookman Associates, 1956, pp. 238ff.

[22] Franz H. Michael and George E. Taylor, op. cit., p. 461.

[23] A. Doak Barnett, "The economic development of communist China," George P. Jan, ed., Government of Communist China, San Francisco: Chandler Pub. Co., 1966, pp. 374-396 at 375-376.

[24] Ibid., p. 376. Thomas P. Bernstein, "The government of the People's Republic of China," Government and Politics; under the editorship of John C. Wahlke and Alex N. Dragnich, 2nd ed., New York: Random House, 1971, pp. 227-260 at 242; Lowell Dittmer, "Chou En-lai and Chinese politics," Government and Leaders, an Approach to Comparative Politics, Boston: Houghton Mifflin, 1978, pp. 437-533 at 488, col. 1; Countries of the World, Toronto: Coles Pub. Co., 1980, Chinese section, p. 6.

[25] Franz H. Michael and George E. Taylor, loc. cit.

claimed attainments of the regime, which were recognized in the West as generally credible, had enabled the CPR to embark upon a new course, one of planned economy.[26] This step coincided with the termination of the Korean war and the annihilation of the alleged hostile forces in the rural and urban areas.

Modernization, Russian style

As early as 1950, China commenced to think of projected development of her economy,[27] but the leaders showed a great deal of hesitation. Rightfully so, because they did not have the resources the USSR had in 1928 when she started her Five-Year Plan. Although Beijing was said to go on planning early in 1953, it had, in fact, only a vaguely conceived scheme which was projected from one year to the next.[28] It was not until mid-1955 that a set of planks was published and this came after the Soviet aid was granted and the foreign war concluded.[29] The document was subjected to extensive emendation late in 1955 when a bold move was undertaken to score an agricultural breakthrough. Aimed at making the CPR tomorrow's USSR, the plan was virtually identical to that of the latter country. Both regimes put accent on heavy industry, consequent upon rural collectivization.[30] One author remarked that "despite . . . obvious differences between the two societies in economic development and revolutionary history, the Soviet model seemed the best, indeed the only, guide for socialist development."[31] Mao Zedong, looking at the future, was moderately sanguine. He spoke of fifteen years before China became socialist. From 40 to 50 years were required for her to become a powerful industrial complex.[32] In this "tea-leaf reading," he was saying that China would not be industrialized before the year 2000, and that not until 1965 could she reach the Soviet level of 1942. Today, although the year 2000 is marked as the completion date of the modernization,[33] the Soviet model is officially repudiated in favor of a Chinese one featured by pragmatism and consumer- or rather food-oriented system.

The first Plan channeled by far the most resources toward the

---

[26] V. Ya. Avarin, "Kitai, ekonomiko-geograficheskii ocherk," *Bol'shaya sovetskaya entsiklopediya*, 2nd ed., vol. 21 (1953), pp. 181-197 at 182.

[27] A. Doak Barnett, *loc. cit.*

[28] "Rotchinesische Planwirtschaft," *Ost-problem*, 5 (1953), pp. 896-904 at 900; "Staatsplan für 1952 in China," *Presse-forum*, 6 (1952), no. 30-31, p. 24.

[29] J.D. Waller, *op. cit.*, p. 133.

[30] Ernst Nagel, "Die Wirtschaftsziele der Chinesischen Volks-republik," *Deutsche Woche* (München), 8 (1958), Sonderblatt zur Deutschen Industriemesse, 1958, p. 5.

[31] James Townsend, "Politics in China," *Comparative Politics Today: a World View*, 2nd ed., Boston: Little, Brown, 1980, pp. 381-432 at 390, col. 1.

[32] J.D. Waller, *loc. cit.*

[33] *Beijing review*, December 20, 1982, p. 10, col. 2.

advancing of heavy industry.[34] Such concentration was, of necessity, at the expense of light goods and foodstuffs. The leaders thought little of the alternative that capital accummulation in an agricultural society is best done in the rural sector. The neglect of the latter is bound to hamper the priority (heavy) industry, because there just isn't enough export to get foreign exchange with which to buy machines and fertilizers abroad. Perhaps the Chinese were too obsessed with the Soviet aid to think of that option. The reorganization of the farming structure gave the CCP the only and unwarranted hope to boost production and to finance industrialization.[35] In 1953-1957, the allocation of the investment gives 56 percent to industry, 18.7 percent to transport and 8.2 percent to agriculture, forestry and irrigation. Of the 56 percent, heavy industry has a lion share of 87 percent with only 13 percent going to consumer enterprises.[36] Respectable progress was made in such items like steel, electric power, fuels (other than petroleum), raw materials, big machines, trucks, aeronautics and ships. During the Plan, according to one scholar, the late T.C. Liu, the "average annual increase in net domestic product . . . expressed in 1952 prices, amounted to 6.9 percent."[37] This is seen by A. Doak Barnett as "close to double the rate of 4 percent which India achieved between 1951 and 1956."[38] Even though the overall growth is striking, the rates in industry and agriculture are glaringly discrepant.[39] They reflect the preference for the former by the leadership. While industrial production went up annually from 14 to 19 percent, agricultural output did so by 4.5 percent only.[40] Poor performance in the latter led to less export of foodstuffs and ultimately to reduced import of machinery and equipment.[41] A drawback for the Plan was the low harvest in two successive years (1953, 1954); as a result, industry fared the worst in 1954 and 1955,[42] indicating the impact of one (agriculture) on the performance of the other (industry). Good crops, that is, boost manufacture, while poor ones drag it down.

This type of development, as related in the preceding chapter, took the form of a pair of scissors, an analogy used in the early twenties by Leon Trotsky to depict the price behavior in agriculture and industry

[34] Ho Kan-chih, *op. cit.*, pp. 587-589.

[35] Audrey Donnithorne, *China's Economic System,* New York: Praeger, 1967, pp. 458-459.

[36] J.D. Waller, *loc. cit.*

[37] Cited in A. Doak Barnett, *op. cit.*, p. 380.

[38] *Ibid.*

[39] Maurice Meisner, *op. cit.*, pp. 121-122; "China, Wirtschaft, ende 1954," *Welt-Wirtschaft* (Kiel), 1954, no. 2, pp. 58-64.

[40] J.D. Waller, *loc. cit.*

[41] Ulrich Rühmland, "China auf dem Wege zur wirtschaftlichen Grossmacht?" *Aussprache* (Bonn), 7 (1957), pp. 13-16.

[42] J.D. Waller, *op. cit.*, p. 134.

in Russia. The Chinese crisis, like the Russian one, was artifically headed off by a policy of collectivizing the agriculture and of forcing deferment of consumption on the masses. Although the regime was niggardly toward the peasants, it set out to extract from them as much as it could in the manner of savings and above-quota production. To use an analogy, without feeding the cows, the leaders ordered that they provide plenty of milk and meat nevertheless. Toward the end of the Plan, it was clear, agriculture represented a serious bottleneck. Lying at the root of the difficulty were not only the "anger" of nature like drought or flood, but the madness in producing babies by 13,000,000 a year.[43] It is agriculture which must keep the huge population from famishment, which must turn out materials for light industry, which must pay for the import, and which must provide for savings for capital investment.[44]

In early 1957, the momentum of the Plan had been slacking.[45] Beijing had to act by tailoring its policy to meet the difficulty. It decided to expend more attention on the rural front. The so-called "walk on two legs" was developed to achieve a more balanced economy. A change was effected from industry first to a parity of industry and agriculture. This came as a result of many reasons, not the least of which was the reluctance of the Kremlin to further support the Chinese.[46] The Soviet action itself reflected that country's trouble with East Europe which was restive, nay recalcitrant, toward the post-Stalin hierarchy.[47] Other considerations were the reaction against the rightist criticism of the Beijing rulers, the condemnation of the collectivization and the resolve of Mao Zedong to challenge the CPSU on the leadership of the world communist movement. All this drove the CCP to a different course, known as the Great Leap Forward. It is a shorthand expression of China's effort to create for herself a fresh path of modernization.[48] It represented in the industrial sector what the communization did in the agricultural. Both aimed at plunging the CPR into communism.

In every respect, the Leap was a comedy. On the farm, as we said in the preceding chapter, each adult was at once a peasant of a team, soldier in a squadron and worker in a factory. In the last-named capacity, he has the responsibility of engaging in one or two of numerous activities involving tannery, artifacts, sericulture, tea-planting and packing, weaving, upholstery, furnishings, embroidery,

[43] A. Doak Barnett, *op. cit.*, p. 388.

[44] "Die Wirtschaftsplannung tritt in eine neue Phase ein," *Bulletin der Botschaft der Volksrepublik China in der Deutschen Demokratischen Republik* (Berlin-Karlshorst), 1955, no. 3, *passim.*

[45] "Wirtschaftsschwierigkeiten in der Volksrepublik China," *Aussenhandelsdienst* (Berlin), 13 (1959), no. 13, pp. 18-19.

[46] Claude Cadart, "Les relations sino-soviétiques de la création des communes populaires à la conference des 81," *Revue française de science politique* (Paris), 11, 1961, h. 1, pp. 60-88; h. 3, pp. 569-608.

[47] Franz H. Michael and George E. Taylor, *op. cit.*, p. 488.

[48] Arthur W. Just, "Chinas wirtschafts- und sozialprogram," *Volkswirt* (Frankfurt/Main), 8 (1954), no. 41, pp. 18-19.

garments, footgears, appliances, insecticides, kitchen wares, cutlery, glasswares, ceramics, crockery, simple herbs for medicine, needles and threads, lacquer, cooking oil, grain milling, paper pulp, commercial cannery, knitwear, umbrellas, ink and brushes, typesets, book- and newspaper-printing, bookbinding, etc. On the heavier side are cement making, roadbuilding, canal digging, irrigation projects, housing construction, energy industry, river channeling, reclamation, reforestation, lumbering, quarrying, earth work and excavation, the laying of bridges, dams and dikes and ironworks. However, the wildest and also the widest noted was the homemaking of steel. Crisscrossing the countryside were several millions of blast furnaces (actually kilns) belching out smoke twenty-four hours a day. People took turns poking the coal or feeding it with twigs and leaves. The chore was scheduled for each and every person, be he a physician, a barber, a blacksmith, a librarian, a writer or a professor. Furnaces dotted the cities as well as the villages. China was literally a nation of steelworkers.

The ruling coterie of Beijing thought that since steel was the symbol of industrialism, what was more fitting and proper than to mass-produce it? Should the CPR outpace the US, for example, in this single prestiged thing, she would be the most industrialized of all countries. In 1958 the communists claimed that there were 50,000,000 steelmen who worked spare-time at that. A veritable metal-fever caught the whole body politic. In Beijing alone, 6,000 furnaces were built in a few weeks, one to be worked by the staff of a newspaper, another to be worked by the clerks of a store, etc.[49] In the city of Changchun in Jilin province, 2,855 furnaces were said to have been erected in two days.[50] Publications bristled with success stories of this or that team. All original targets of output were raised again and again in a matter of days by factories or shops. Such statistical victory was utilized to justify the continuous and extraordinary demand on labor and resources. The claims of achievement were prompted by the cadres' yearning for preferment and careerism. The quota set up by Beijing as maximum was exceeded many times, because when it was transmitted through the province and county to commune, each level marked it up in order to please the higher ups. Out of this adding process there emerged an impressive but incredible record of performance.

The reported figure for grain in 1958, for example, was 375,000,000 tons, a figure that later was said to be 125,000,000 too many.[51] The latter sum, in effect, was produced by the several layers of bureaucrats in their offices by the stroke of pens. Getting back to the steel, the 1958 claim was 11,080,000 tons, but later in the year the revised version was 8,000,000 tons. In this case too, the bureaucrats

[49] Franz H. Michael and George E. Taylor, *loc. cit.*

[50] *Ibid.*

[51] *Ibid.*, p. 489; Harold Hinton, *An Introduction to Chinese Politics* 2nd ed., New York: Holt, Rinehart and Winston, 1978, p. 47.

pushed their pens to forge 3,080,000 tons.[52] Even the lower counts of the grain and steel were questioned by students. They agreed that most of the steel was just useless scrap. Probably the grain included a sizeable portion suitable only for animal consumption. The result is that instead of "happiness and abundance" for the peasants and workers, as described by the leaders, there was hardship and famine. On this the media all blamed the inclement weather. However, natural disaster only explained in part the difficulty. During the same period, all the Far Eastern countries except China made great strides in agriculture, according to the study of competent scholars.[53]

Whether China's plight was caused by policy or by climate, it is a fact that the policy had contributed to the natural disasters.[54] There were the unscientific methods like deep plowing and close planting, the putting up of dams on sandy grounds, the sowing of crops in unfitting soils, the brutal deforestation to gain acreage for seedlings, the alkalinization of land, the overirrigation and the man-made floods. The last is because dikes were often built where no geodetic study was undertaken. The collapse of agricultural economy seriously impacted on industrial growth.[55] The failure of cash crops led to the deterioration of the consumer sector, so that "by 1961, 50 percent of all light industrial plants had ceased production."[56] This situation created urban unemployment and it was further aggravated by the Soviets' boycotting of the Chinese economy.[57] Khrushchev, having been so belittled by Mao and company for his denunciation of Stalin, for his detente with the imperialist US, and for his ridiculing the Beijing monocrat, was determined to teach the Chinese a lesson.[58] Hence, the withdrawal in the summer of 1960 of nearly all Soviet and East European advisors and technicians from the People's Republic and ordered them to take back with them each and every blueprint.[59] As a result, most Chinese constructions were forthwith halted and most factories were bolted. Is there an option for the CCP leadership except striking out in a new direction? To this, we now turn.

Restoration and setback

To begin this analysis, we should note that during 1956 and 1957 as the first Plan was nearing completion, the CCP laid out the second,

[52] A. Doak Barnett, op. cit., p. 392.

[53] Franz H. Michael and George E. Taylor, loc. cit.

[54] Klaus Terefloth, "Spring vorwärts, Sprang rückwärts, wechselndes und konstantes in den Volkskommunen Chinas," Aussenpolitik (Stuttgart), 10 (1959), pp. 807-814.

[55] Gottfried Missbach, "Volkschina weiter auf dem Grossen Sprang," Finanzwirtschaft (Berlin), 13 (1959), heft 18, p. 425.

[56] J.D. Waller, op. cit., p. 137.

[37] J. Schütze, "Der Grosse Sprung des Riesen China," Die Nation (Berlin), 9 (1959), pp. 692-713.

[58] "China, uberspringt der sowjetunion," Der aktuelle Osten (Bonn), 5 (1959), no. 22, pp. 6-9.

[59] Hugh Seton-Watson, "Die Grosse Spaltung, die Geschichte des chinesisch-sowjetischen Konflikt," Der Monat (Berlin), 15, 1962-1963, heft 178, pp. 7-18 at 10.

slated to be ended in 1962. It called for continuing high rate of investment, rapid industrial growth and enhancement of the total national income by 50 percent. This amounted to an average annual increase of about 9 percent.[60] The gross output of industry and agriculture combined was to be up by 70 to 75 percent in 1962. To attain this goal, the authority was to collect 30 percent of national income as government revenue and to route 40 percent to capital construction.[61] These objectives were considered in the West as reasonable. However, in the spring of 1958, Mao Zedong wanted to take his country to instant communism by throwing the second Plan to the wind, with the hysteria of the Leap and the consequences outlined above as well as in Chapter IX. There is then no alternative but retreat. This, thought Mao, should not be called "planned economy," a term reserved for a more worthy approach. The government felt reluctant to promise anything according to the book, because it was afraid of failing to deliver it on time. Therefore, there was no plan from the end of the Leap to 1966. It is little short of irony, though, that the economy behaved a great deal better during this planless period. Mao Zedong, perhaps overcome by embarrassment and shame, elected to stay away from the administration. He quit the CPR chairmanship in April 1959 and remained fairly quiet for several years. With no fanfare, the pragmatists led by Liu Shaoqi (now the CPR chairman), Zhou Enlai and Deng Xiaoping, proceeded to salvage whatever they could. They launched an energetic drive toward a balanced growth and adopted a rational approach to resource allocation.[62] There were two objectives: readjustment (1961-1963) and advance (1964-1965).[63] The "unplanned" economy placed priorities on agriculture, light industry and heavy industry in that order.[64] All this was spelled out in the decisions of the CC of November 1960 and of September 1962 and in the legislations of the NPC of 1962 and 1963.

The readjustment is outlined in the 10 tasks of 1962 and 7 points of 1963 which were sanctioned by the NPC and the CC. There are no control figures for such and such things to be turned out at such and such times. Instead, the hierarchy declared a set of advisements. All the cadres in the economic field were admonished to "work hard and thriftily and calculate with the greatest care, spending money cautiously" (point 7).[65] This is a direct repudiation of the extravagancy of the Leap. Due to the cancellation of Russian aid, capital projects were retrenched, and material equipment and manpower were utilized

[60] A. Doak Barnett, op. cit., p. 380.

[61] Ibid., p. 381.

[62] "La situation économiqué en Chine," Problèmes économiques (Paris), 708 (1961), pp. 15-20 at 19.

[63] Countries of the World, loc. cit.

[64] George T. Yu, "The 1962 and 1963 sessions of the National People's Congress of Communist China," George P. Jan, ed., op. cit., pp. 255-266 at 259, col. 1.

[65] Ibid., pp. 258-259 lists the ten tasks and seven points.

only "where they are most urgently needed" (task 3). In particular, it was instructed that the enterprises take careful inventory and examine the amount of funds for each project so that "unused materials and funds may be used where they are needed most" (task 5). Remembering that the Leap created maldistribution, the 1962 NPC resolution called for good management of purchasing and supplying of commodities and improvement of marketing procedure (task 6). In addition, expenses were to be reduced, revenues increased (task 9), science, education and culture bettered and urban population curbed (task 4). On this very last point, it has been surveyed that city-residents decreased from 150,000,000 to 110,000,000 during 1961-1963.[66] The returnees had previously flocked to the metropolises to look for jobs, or escape economic hardship. Even though they were to be persuaded to leave the city, actually force had to be used to get them out.

It has been studied that the retrenchment policy as enunciated by the national legislature was strictly executed. Many giant constructions were discontinued and resources so saved were budgeted for lesser but more manageable undertakings.[67] Put in charge of the various enterprises were experts, dedicated cadres, technicians, economists or research workers. Following the principles of cost account and balanced payment and the adage of reward according to work, they were able to normalize the economy. With good weather and a favorable harvest in 1962, the production swang up in 1963.[68] Owing to the efficacious organization and technology, a still higher result was attained in 1964-1965.[69] There was in the cities and countryside a substantial improvement in the quality of life through a coordinated control of labor and produce. Other measures of restoration involved the gradual modification of self-reliance and birth restriction. From 1960 on, China was to buy grain from the West to the tune of 5,000,000 tons per annum on the average.[70] Although, as pointed out before, this sum fed only a pitiful portion of the huge population (between 0.1% and 0.2%), at least part of the armed forces and central bureaucrats were provisioned.

By 1966, the gross national output was about 30 percent above that of 1957.[71] Most of the increase was in the industrial sector, with agriculture slightly above the pre-Leap plane. It is written that in 1966 the "industrial production had reached a level nearly 70 percent greater than that of 1957."[72] This recovery, nay upsurge, was

[66] Countries of the World, loc. cit.

[67] Maurice Meisner, op. cit., pp. 278-283.

[68] Countries of the World, loc. cit.

[69] Robert Michael Field, "Chinese industrial development, 1949-1970," People's Republic of China, an ·Economic Assessment, Washington: Government Printing Office, 1972, pp. 61-85 at 64-65.

[70] J.D. Waller, op. cit., p. 139.

[71] Countries of the World, loc. cit.

[72] Ibid.

achieved by "diligence" and "thrift," to use the expression of the aforesaid ten tasks and seven points.[73] Apparently, it laid the foundation for another Five-Year Plan, the third. It was to begin in 1966 and end in 1970.[74] However, just as the second Plan was disrupted by the Leap, so the third was thrown into confusion by the Cultural Revolution.[75] This time the damage was not as serious, but the upheaval inevitably made the Plan's smooth operation impossible. Had it not been for the pandemonium, China's economy would undoubtedly have faired much better. In 1978, Hua Guofeng was to hint at the effect of the Red Guards, a point to be taken in the following section. Let us pause a little here by asking: What was in Mao Zedong's mind when he set in motion the pandemonium? The answer is to be sought in his obsession with the idea of "politics in command." It seems certain that the improvement of people's livelihood pleased everyone, but horrified Mao. The period of readjustment exactly coincided with the period of the squabble between the CCP and the CPSU in which Mao Zedong scoffed at Khrushchev and company for taking the capitalist road. In the Soviet Union, as he saw it, it was economics not politics that took command. Commercial materialism, but not dialectical materialism, eroded the system bequeathed by Lenin and Stalin. Mao taunted them as a degenerate bunch. He asked in effect that what good would physical comfort do if the proletarian soul is gone?

To Mao and company, the Chinese pragmatists were wrong men.[76] They set out to kill the revolution. Together with the Soviet revisionists they conspired to torpedo the communist state of affairs. Losing hope in these men, Mao set it on those who were born at the time of the "liberation," and who were attending high schools in 1966. Galvanized by his call, they were only too ardent to respond. Tens of millions of them were swept off their feet and were ready to do battle for him. What came to hurt the economy most was not the kind of vandalism they might play, but their jamming of the nation's railway traffic.[77] The flow of goods and raw materials from factory to factory or from region to region was gravely impaired. Many workers were driven out of the shops; and assembly lines were disrupted simply because supplies were not forthcoming. Forced to cease production, the employees and cadres came to divide illegally whatever the enterprises had produced. Another effect on the economy stemmed from the embroilment of the workers in the struggle. With a view to

---

[73] George T. Yu, *op. cit.*, pp. 258-259.

[74] Marianne Bastid, "Levels of economic decision-making," *Authority, participation and cultural change in China,* London: Cambridge at the University Press, 1973, pp. 159-197 at 192-193.

[75] Eric Axilrod, *The Economic Theory of the Two Tendencies in the Cultural Revolution,* Hong Kong: Chinese University of Hong Kong, 1971, 22 pp.

[76] Leo Goodstadt, *China's Search for Plenty, the Economy of Mao Zedong,* 1st ed., New York: Weatherhill, 1973, pp. 65ff.

[77] Jan Deleyne, *The Chinese Economy,* translated from the French by Robert Leriche, New York: Harper and Row, 1973, p. 131.

repelling the Red Guards who carried the Cultural Revolution onto the plants or construction sites, they got themselves organized and acted as true Red Guards. Equally detrimental to the industry was the dragging out of the managers and charging them with practicing bourgeois economy. Suffering from beatings and insults, they were demoralized. Decision-making fell into the hands of the revolutionary committee. Its members were all amateurs, knowing no management ABC's. This was hardly conducive to productivity.

The amount lost in monetary terms as a consequence of the dismissals of competent administrators must have been great. As said elsewhere, Zhou Enlai sought to protect industry by advising the Red Guards to leave the technical and administrative personnel alone, provided they "are patriotic, work energetically, are not against the party and socialism, and maintain no illicit relations with any foreign country."[78] However, the young rabids found it very easy to argue that they did not do things right and, therefore, were subject to correction. Thanks to the relatively short duration of the rampancy, the economy was able to escape total breakdown. Fortunately too, little affected was farm output; and there was propitious climate in 1967 and again in 1970.[79] By late 1968, industrial growth was above the 1967 record. It averaged about 20 percent a year during 1969 and 1970. Although sliding back somewhat in 1971, industry still sustained an impressive rate of 10 percent.[80] In effect, the third Five-Year Plan (1966-1970) had only one and a half bad years. The Cultural Revolution, to sum up, was unleashed by Mao Zedong to bring the proletarian virtues to his subjects. The whole nation, and particularly the youth, were to rededicate to the cause of communism. It is better for one to be poor than to have an easy life, which would lead astray to the bourgeois way. Sensing the chaos and the infighting about to endanger the nation, Mao flinched, guerila style. Both the Great Leap and Cultural Revolution were forsaken by him with the same alacrity as he hit upon them. Here one finds his strength as a politician. From 1969 to his sudden death on September 10, 1976, he seems to be content with the reigning, leaving the ruling to others.   *NB*

Modernization, Chinese style

The fourth Plan started in 1971 and wound up in 1975.[81] The regime did not reveal much of it and Western researches on it are nil. One source casually notes an economic slowdown in 1974-1976[82] and another writes that the "economic growth rate was around 8 percent

[78] "The CC resolution of August 8, 1966," A. Doak Barnett, China After Mao, Princeton, New Jersey: Princeton University Press, 1967, pp. 263-287.

[79] Countries of the World, p. 7.

[80] Ibid.

[81] John G. Gurley, China's Economy and the Maoist Strategy, New York: Monthly Review Press, 1976, pp. 223ff.

[82] James Townsend, "Politics in China," p. 396, col. 1.

during 1972 and 1973 but slided to below 4 percent in 1974."[83] The
Joint Economic Committee of the US Congress has appraised that
the rate was 6.8 percent during 1971-1975.[84] This is to be compared
with the first Plan's 7.1, the second Plan's 3.8 and the third Plan's
7.0 percent.[85] Looking at these statistics, one must say the fourth
Plan was not a poor one. However, the Chinese leaders did not
consider it satisfactory, judging by their decision to embark upon a
new strategy of development after 1975.[86] It is possible, too, that the
fourth Plan was not as desirable as merely meets the eye. When the
Plan still had one year to run, Zhou Enlai in an address of January
13, 1973 (to the NPC) pointed a) to 1980 as the year for the CPR to
become "an independent and relatively comprehensive industrial and
economic system" and b) to the turn of the century when it would
find itself at the forefront of nations.[87] c) He propounded the now
famous four modernizations.[88] These were placed in the 1975
Constitution (Preamble). Hua Guofeng was to reiterate the whole idea
on August 18, 1977 at the 11th Congress of the CCP,[89] and on
February 26, 1978 at the Fifth NPC.[90] Both premiers set out to chart
a new economic course, having found the old one not gratifying. Hua
did some name-calling. The economy, according to him, was
"sabotaged by Liu Shaoqi [at that time not yet refamed], Lin Biao
and particularly the Gang of Four."[91] The most lurid and frank
confession of the sad shape of economy during the fourth Plan was
made by none other than the then chairman of the Planning
Commission, Yu Qiuli.[92]

The report which Yu Qiuli presented to the NPC Standing
Committee on August 23-24 was gloomy. First it declared the growth
of agriculture and light industry to be far short of the requirement of
the "country's construction and the people's life." Second, the
"development of the coal-power industries and the primary-goods
industry did not keep pace with the need of the whole nation." Third,
the consolidation of economic management, then under way, had
made no appreciable strides. In particular, he called attention of the
Committee to the poor produce, enormous consumption of materials,

[83] Countries of the World, loc. cit.

[84] Arthur G. Ashbrook, "China: Economic Overview 1975," China, a Reassessment of the Economy, Washington: Government Printing Office, 1975, pp. 20-51 at 27.

[85] Countries of the World, loc. cit.

[86] Arthur G. Ashbrook, loc. cit.

[87] Countries of the World, loc. cit.

[88] Harold Hinton, op. cit., p. 91.

[89] James Townsend, loc. cit.

[90] Facts on File, March 10, 1978, p. 154, D1.

[91] Keesing's, September 8, 1978, p. 29182, col. 1.

[92] Ibid., December 16, 1977, p. 28727, col. 1.

low productivity, excessive overheads, and the tying up of too much funds. Fourth, he leveled the by now universal charge at the Gang of Four. Interestingly enough, he mentioned no Liu Shaoqi. We quote him: "[The Gang] undermined our planned economy so seriously that for the last few years [the fourth Plan period], the national economy was in fact developed in a semi-anarchical fashion." Fifth finally, a significant part of the economic activities was allegedly not placed in the unified system. Some of them so placed did not function strictly in tune with the schedule.

Several months later, Hua Guofeng made the same allegation, but documented it with figures. On February 26, 1978, he reported to the NPC that sabotage and interference during 1974-1976 by the radicals had caused a loss of about 100 billion yuan in total industrial value, 28 million tons of steel and 40 billion yuan in state revenue.[93] In some regions and departments where the "bad elements" were in control, factory activities came to a standstill. He deplored: "The whole country was on the brink of collapse." Hua Guofeng bandied out these figures, but did not speak of the percentage in each of the three categories. We calculate that the annual industrial loss amounts to 8.5%, revenue loss to 17.8% and steel loss to a whopping 57%. If we give full credit to the statement of Hua Guofeng which appears in the first part of the speech in question the Gang of Four are trully ruinous. However, the Chinese authorities do not tell us how their statistics are derived and how vandalism of such dimensions can happen in the first place.

Although the Gang of Four were in the powerhouse, the Politburo, no administrative departments were assigned them. All were plain members of that body, only Zhang Chunqiao concurrently holding the post of the directorship of the PLA's General Political Department. We seriously doubt that they were able to command the lower-level bureaucrats and workers to boycott the operation of enterprises and to bring the People's Republic to the threshold of bankruptcy. Hua Guofeng stated that in some provinces and administrative bodies dominated by the "bad elements," production ceased completely. Yet he did not say which provinces or which administrative bodies. Devoid of better allegation of the four persons' misdeeds than the criminal offences "proved" by the extraordinary prosecutor Huang Huoqing during the two months' trial (November 20, 1980 to January 25, 1981),[94] the accusation against them in the economic sphere cannot be taken at face value. It may well be an *ipse dixit*.

Hua Guofeng's indictment in the first portion of the February 26, 1978 speech is compromised, nay taken back, in the second portion. The economy of the CPR during these years (1974-1976) was not bad after all. He asserted that in the eleven years (1966-1976), despite the sabotage and interference by the Gang, output still showed a yearly increment of 4.3 percent in one third of the provinces,

[93] *Facts on File*, March 10, 1978, p. 154, G1.

[94] *Guangming ribao*, January 26, 1981, p. 2, col. 1.

municipalities and autonomous regions. The maximum was 5.5 percent. The value of industrial produce, he moved on, went up yearly by more than 12 percent likewise in one third of the provinces, municipalities and autonomous regions. The maximum was 18.5 percent.

In presenting the Sixth Five-Year Plan to the Fifth NPC on November 30, 1982, Premier Zhao Ziyang declared that "during the decade between 1971 and 1980, our industrial enterprises, not including those run by production brigades and teams in the rural areas, increased from over 195,000 to more than 377,000, almost double the 1970 figure."[95] The growth in the twenty-eight years, from 1953 to 1980, according to him, "was not low."[96] Two researchers in the Economic Study Centre of the State Council made the assertion that the annual growth of industrial and agricultural output from 1950 to 1981 was 9.2 percent and that the 1958-1977 average was 7.4 percent.[97] By comparison, the Sixth Five-Year Plan envisages 4-5 percent.[98] Premier Zhou Ziyang conceded the development to be at "a slower" tempo.[99] In foreign trade, Chen Muhua said, China scored a 12.3 percent average annual increase between 1950 and 1980. "This is slightly higher than the world average," alleged she.[100] Besides all these (communist) sources, one Western study maintained that the "industrial growth averaged about 10 percent from 1952 to 1977.[101] Another Western publication held that as regards such important things as steel, crude oil, grain, and coal, the Fourth Five-Year Plan (1971-1975) was a success."[102] The foregoing presentation impels us to conclude that the Gang-inflicted damage was not crippling. The CPR did not wither away. Indeed she was hale and sound. The Beijing lordship, we think, must produce more evidentiary proofs to substantiate the outcry against the Gang of Four's economic crime.

The Fifth Five-Year Plan (1975-1980) received scanty attention of students because its data are too few. The table below presents a broad view on it.[103]

	1975	1976	1977	1978	1979
GNP, billion 1977 US$	342	342	370	404	375

---

[95] *Beijing review*, December 20, 1982, p. 26, col. 1.

[96] *Ibid.*, p. 12, col. 1.

[97] *Ibid.*, February 28, 1983, p. 13, col. 1.

[98] *Ibid.*, December 20, 1982, p. 12, col. 1.

[99] *Ibid.*

[100] *Ibid.*, February 7, 1983, p. 15, col. 1.

[101] James Townsend, *"Politics in China,"* p. 398, col. 2.

[102] David F. Roth and Frank L. Wilson, *The comparative study of politics*, 2nd ed., Englewood Cliffs, New Jersey: Prentice-Hall, 1980, p. 421.

[103] Figures for 1975-1978 from James Townsend, "Politics in China," p. 397; the figure for 1979 from *Hammond*, 1981, p. 548, col. 1.

Per capita					
income (yuan)	363	355	377	407	370
Agricultural production					
1957:100	148	148	146	141	n.a.
Industrial production					
1957:100	502	502	572	646	n.a.

The inter-Plan year, 1975-1976, is marked by stagnation, but not deterioration,[104] except that there was a downward per capita income from 363 to 355. In general, all the indicators point to an upward trend from 1976 to 1979.

One reference book notes the official release showing that the 1978 output in several key industries rose appreciably over the 1977 one.[105] "Steel production increased 55.3 percent from 20,460,000 to 31,780,000 tons." Coal was up 28 percent to 618,000,000 tons; crude oil heightened by 19.5 percent to 104,000,000 tons and electric power reached 256 billion kwh, a gain of 26 percent. Yu Qiuli declared on October 23, 1977 that the country's industrial production was again on the upswing after a period of decline.[106] Three months later, however, he backed down. On January 26, 1978, he stated to a conference on agriculture that rural development was slow in the last few years because of the low pace of mechanization. This he attributed to the drop in steel output.[107] Later, this output was up from 31.7 million tons in 1978 to 34.4 million tons in 1979. The following year witnessed a two-million-ton drop, however.[108]

In a few years, several plans appeared; there was the Zhou Enlai Five-Year Plan and there was the Hua Guofeng Five-Year Plan, the former was announced by its author on January 3, 1975 to the Fourth NPC's annual session,[109] and the latter by its on August 12, 1977 to the 11th CC.[110] Hua modified Zhou's version looking toward heavier investment in basic industries. Not content with this, he came out with a 10 year plan which he proclaimed to the NPC Standing Committee on February 26, 1978.[111] Before this one got off the ground, he presented a new 10 year plan in an address to the NPC on September

---

[104] Keesing's, December 16, 1977, p. 28727, col. 1. He addressed the NPC Standing Committee in session on October 23-24, 1977.

[105] Britannica book of the year, 1980, p. 248, col. 1.

[106] Facts on file, October 29, 1977, p. 823, A2.

[107] Keesing's, September 8, 1978, p. 29193, col. 2.

[108] The figure for 1978 from Britannica book of the year, 1980, p. 246; that for 1979 was calculated from Main documents of the third session, p. 9. The 1980 figure of 32 million tons derived from B. Barakhta, "Kitai: starye problemy" (China: an old problem), Pravda, February 1, 1982, p. 6, cols, 2 and 3.

[109] Countries of the world, p. 6.

[110] Keesing's, December 16, 1977, p. 28721. The congress was in session from August 12 to 18, 1977.

[111] Facts on file, March 10, 1978, p. 154, D1.

5, 1980.[112] The new deal said to consist of two five year plans got nowhere, but according to the old 10 year plan, no less than 120 gigantic projects were provided.[113] Among them were 10 iron and steel plants, 9 non-ferrous metal centers, 8 coal mines, 10 oil and gas fields, 30 power stations, 6 mainline trunks and 5 ports.[114] As to be related below, all these are now scored as "blind" actions.

The erosion of the Fanshi faction headed by Hua Guofeng in the power struggle paved the way for the new masters, the pragmatists. By mid-1981, that faction was decidedly elbowed out. The State Council now under Zhao Ziyang in the report on the work of the government delivered at the 4th session of the NPC (in November-December 1981) put forward 10 principles for the development of the national economy centered on better achievements. The State Council then mobilized the relevant quarters to discuss major issues. Out of this came the Sixth Five-Year Plan. This is a fresh approach to the building of the country. There was no fear on the part of the elite for its plan's possible defeat in another shift of power. The Sixth Plan was to begin in 1981. However, according to Premier Zhao Ziyang in a speech to the 5th session of the Fifth NPC on November 30, 1982, the government owing to the lack of "objective conditions" was not able to go ahead with it right away.[115] It had to wait for a comprehensive study and compiling of data, with the consequence that the first two years failed to develop any definitive scheme or forecast, except some target figures to be achieved in 1985. The Premier sought, wherever possible, to make a comparison of the Sixth to the Fifth Plans. In general, the current plan aims at "economic result and efficiency rather than swift construction."[116] It envisages a gross value of industrial and agricultural production to be increased by 21.7 percent. The total investment in fixed assets came to 360 billion yuan. Funds for education, physical culture, science, culture and public health are 96.7 billion yuan, an increase of 68 percent over the 57.7 billion yuan of the Fifth Plan. The per capita consumption in urban and rural areas will rise by 22 percent, averaging an annual rise of 4.1 percent. The statistics of the last year of the Fifth and final year of the Sixth Plan in key items are as follows. (Compiled from figures given in Beijing review, December 20, 1982, pp. 10-35).

	1980 (million)	1985	percentage
gross value of agr. & industrial prod.	715,900	871,000	21.7
grain (ton)	320.56	360.00	12.3
cotton (ton)	2.71	3.60	33.0

[112] Globe and mail, September 8, 1980, p. 3.

[113] Information please, 1979, p. 159, col. 1.

[114] Facts on file, March 10, 1978, p. 154, D1; Keesing's, September 8, 1978, p. 29182, col. 2.

[115] Beijing review, December 20, 1982, p. 10, col. 1.

[116] Renmin ribao, September 18, 1981, p. 1.

yarn (ton)	2.93	3.59	22.8
sugar (ton)	2.57	4.30	67.3
coal (ton)	620.15	700.00	12.9
electricity (kw)	300,600	362,000	20.4
steel (ton)	37.12	39.00	5.0
import & export	56,300	85,500	52.0
import	29,100	45,300	55.6
export	27,200	40,200	47.7
investment in capital			
construction	230,000	same	0
state revenues	108,500	127,400	17.4
state expenditures	121,200	130,000	7.2
retail sales	174,000	290,000	7.0
peasant annual			
income (yuan)	191	255	6.0
workers & staff payroll	77,300	98,300	4.9

Pragmatic orientation

The keynote of the current plan is "drastic" retrenchment which implies readjustment, restructuring, consolidation and improving.[117] How much or how drastic is the retrenchment? How does the contemporary plan stack against the previous one? Needless to say, one cannot judge the result until 1986. It behooves us to observe however that the total capital outlay remains the same as in 1975-1980. There is no clear ground for Premier Zhao Ziyang to assert that investment has been cut and to criticize that "the past capital construction was too large in scale."[118] Looking at the number of projects to be completed by the government, one cannot but be impressed by its vastness. Zhao Ziyang referred to 890 large and medium undertakings including 28 big coal mines with an annual capacity of over one million tons, 132 deep-water berths to be laid out in 15 harbors, 15 hydroelectric stations each with an installed capacity of 400,000 kw or more (these are in addition to the presently undertaken 20 stations with a total capacity of 10 million kw),[119] 45 thermal stations each with 200,000 kw or more, upwards of 310 million square meters of residential housing, 2,000-kilometers of rails, double-tracking 1,700 kilometers of the present rails and electrifying 2,500 kilometers, and an increase of the area for fresh-water aquaculture by 16 million mu and that for sea-water aquaculture by 800,000 mu. In addition, there are a great number of inland navigation projects along Changjiang and other river systems.[120] Compare all these with the list cited in the preceding section (120 projects which was

[117] *Beijing review,* December 20, 1982, p. 11, col. 1; January 17, 1983, p. 13, col. 2.

[118] *Ibid.,* December 20, 1982, p. 12, col. 2.

[119] *Ibid.,* December 6, 1982, p. 7, col. 3.

[120] *Ibid.,* December 20, 1982, p. 14, col. 2.

contemplated by the Hua Guofeng plan), one gets the impression that the Zhao Ziyang ambition is just as enormous and perhaps as unrealistic. The state revenues, it is particularly significant to note here, are said to be on"continuous decrease over the years" (in fact, three in a roll),[121] and this decline will not change until 1982. And after that year, the increase cannot be very fast.[122] Unless, we think, this trend is reversed through (a) expansion of production,[123] (b) favorable balance of trade or (c) massive floating of foreign loan which in 1983 is 400,000,000 yuan above the 1982 level,[124] where do the projects receive their funds?

How much progress is envisaged in the Sixth Plan over the past? It is far from spectacular. Zhao Ziyang tells the NPC that in the 28 years from 1953 to 1980, the gross value of agricultural output was up by an average of 3.4 percent a year, but the Sixth Plan is to bring this to 4-5 percent. More noteworthy is that this Plan anticipates an industrial production lower than the average of the preceding decades. Conceded Zhao Ziyang: "The rate of the industrial growth in the previous 28 years was not low."[125] As far as the overall achievement is concerned, the past compares favorably with the Sixth Plan.

The contemporary ruling clique set out to attain "an independent and relatively comprehensive industrial and economic system."[126] Hua Guofeng, we will recall, brought up this line before the CCP Congress on August 12, 1977.[127] However agreeable this was to Zhao Ziyang and company, the way it was carried out was considered as leaving much to be desired. Particularly it is accused that the former plan was lack of sense of direction. Too much priority went to the kind of undertakings with no "economic result." Zhao Ziyang repeats his criticism of "blind extension of capital construction,"[128] or "blind expansion."[129] Under the new dispensation, there is envisioned an intensification of light industry to boost food and consumer items. In the meantime, it calls for a circumspect capital outlay. Declares Zhao Ziyang that "compared with 1980, the gross output value of light industry increased by 14.1 percent in 1981 and is expected to go up by another 5.1 percent in 1982. This indicates an average increase

[121] Stated by Finance Minister Wang Bingqian, *Beijing review*, January 17, 1983, p. 14, col. 1.

[122] *Ibid.*

[123] *Ibid.*, p. 13, col. 1.

[124] *Ibid.*, p. 16, col. 1. See also *ibid.*, February 7, 1983, p. 14, col. 1 where Chen Muhua, Minister of Foreign Economic Relations and Trade said foreign debt of China was $1,630 million in 1983.

[125] *Ibid.*, December 20, 1982, p. 12, col. 1.

[126] *Countries of the World*, p. 7.

[127] *Keesing's*, December 16, 1977, p. 28721, col. 2.

[128] *Beijing review*, December 20, 1982, p. 24, col. 2.

[129] *Ibid.*, p. 26, col. 1.

of 9.6 percent for these two years."[130] Retail sales volume for 1981 registered a 9.8 percent increase over 1980 and the estimated increase for 1982 is 8.9 percent over the preceding year. Heavy industry had been on the decrease. Its gross value was down by 4.7 percent during 1981 compared with 1980. However, beginning with 1982, it is to pick up. The estimate is that there will be a 9 percent increase in 1982 over 1981 "so that the average annual increase for these two years will be 1.9 percent."[131] More important, heavy industry is no longer serving its own expansion to excess and is now designed to provide a larger portion of its products to agriculture and light industry in the manner of raw and semi-finished things and tools for technical transformation. Many heavy enterprises are now manufacturing durable consumer articles.

The State Council coordinates all capital investments to ensure the proper use of funds and to get greater returns. It is demanded, in the first place, that the investment in fixed assets including those covered by the state budget, self-collected funds or bank loans, are subject to overall balancing by the State Planning Commission or its sub-offices. No unit is allowed to make ultra-plan investment without prior sanction from a competent agent. A warning is served that any violator of this rule will be called to account and punished. In the second place, all large and medium projects are to be reviewed by the State Planning Commission. No organization can decide on these projects except through checking with the planning bodies. In the third place, all projects must be carried out in strict accordance with the procedures for capital construction. Nothing shall be included in the annual construction program, still less shall it be started hastily, without a feasibility study and technical and economic appraisal. In the fourth place, while a project is contemplated, care must be taken to (a) fix its scale, assess the amount of money and time required for its completion and the returns and (b) to arrange co-operation with other agencies. In the fifth and final place, investments are to be put under the control of the Bank of Construction of China which is authorized to supervise their use according to plan.

To be curtailed are those enterprises which are heavy consumers of materials, put out poor products and incur a loss over the years due to bad operation, those with large overstocks of goods, and inefficient undertakings which contend with the efficient ones for energy, resources, transport facilities and markets, and especially those set up without justification in the first place, and hampering production of the better enterprises. It is directed that regions and departments draw up two-year plans for closing, suspending or amalgamating undesirable establishments. And all enterprises which have suffered big losses because of sub-standard technique must commence to earn profit within a certain time and those which fail to do so must cease and desist.

[130] *Ibid.*, p. 21, col. 1.

[131] *Ibid.*

The pragmatic economy aims at a mixed system in which workers' collectives, state bodies and individuals come to assume the operation of various types of business.[132] This system is allowed by Article 9, par. 1 of the Constitution. It is theorized that to the extent that one does not squeeze fellowmen, it is perfectly legitimate to enter sideline production. This point is emphasized in Hu Yaobang's speech to the 12th Party Congress on September 1, 1982.[133] Surpassing the Soviet Union today, China has her "second economy" run by tailors, beauty salons, restaurants, tutorial schools, repairmen, porters, traders of many sorts. In big metropolises, plumbers, for example, make fabulous money, because it takes several months for the municipal administration to dispatch its plumbing cadres to one's apartment which belongs to the city to fix broken pipes. Of course, the tenant cannot afford to wait that long.

Under the planned economy, an unmistakable emphasis is on centralization. Zhao Ziyang's address to the Fifth NPC has a critical paragraph on the disorderly situation.[134] "To this day," he says, "quite a number of enterprises have still not matched their best past technical and economic norms; nearly 30 percent of the state-owned industrial enterprises practicing independent business accounting incur losses, the total sum of which may well exceed 4 billion yuan this year." He deplores that the irrational organization of plants and shops and their foolish operation have made it impossible for them to work at full capacity. The consequence is that large numbers of such deplorable plants have found it all right to rely for their survival on the fruit of others' labor. Implied in his critique is that autonomous operation of enterprises had led to near-anarchism. Early in 1977 there was a move toward decentralization of industrial management. Directors had the right to order the production independently and the right to acquire raw materials and fuel.[135] Associated with such a course was Sun Yefang who in fact suggested (very bravely, we may add) such change as early as 1957 when he was the head of the Institute of Economics in the Academy of Social Sciences.[136] During the Cultural Revolution, he was berated as rightist. The Red Guards said he was a worshipper of money, holding contempt of "politics in command."

Following the ten disastrous years of 1966-1976, the oligarchy of the CPR has been zigzagging between:

decentralization	1976-1977	recentralization	1979-1980
recentralization	1977-1978	decentralization	1980-1981
decentralization	1978-1979	recentralization	1981-

[132] *Ibid.*, p. 18, col. 1.

[133] *Ibid.*, September 13, 1982, p. 18, col. 2, and p. 19, col. 2.

[134] *Ibid.*, December 20, 1982, p. 26, col. 2.

[135] *Keesing's*, September 8, 1978, p. 29192, col. 1.

[136] Harold Hinton, *op. cit.*, p. 54.

In decentralization the local regime and plants had large margin of operational right in locating resources and financing, but in centralization, all powers belonged to the State Council, with very little left to the discretion of sub-units. The 1977-1978 recentralization was inaugurated following a major policy review made in September 1977,[137] and the subsequent decentralization was commenced with the unqualified rehabilitation of the aforesaid Sun Yefang. The current recentralization, featured by "stricter financial supervision and control" (to use Finance Minister Wang Bingqian's expression),[138] was preceded by free investment by plants and their lack of financial discipline, as related above. Centralization is not what Sun Yefang has advocated. But why the same Sun was praised by Premier Zhao Ziyang in his November 1982 speech? It is for quite different reasons, or rather for quite a different theory propounded by him. This economist wrote an article for the *Renmin ribao* in support of the premier's promise to quadruple the gross annual value of industrial and agricultural output at the end of the century.[139] Sun suggested, rather tritely, the improvement of production skill as the basis of achieving the objective. We quote Zhao: "Production will definitely grow at a faster rate, he (Sun) said, if we no longer 'freeze technologies,' but systematically undertake technical transformation of the existing enterprises in their hundreds of thousands."[140] On this premise, Sun asserted that the rate of depreciation for fixed assets should be raised gradually to shorten the depreciation period. This certainly is not much of a theory or "remarkable proposition" as the premier thinks it is. While extolling such stand of Sun's, the other really important or innovative view, namely cost accounting of enterprises, Zhao ignored totally. Interestingly enough, that view is not in the *Renmin ribao* writing. (Sun died on May 10, 1983).

The Constitution has a weird provision in Article 16, par. 1 on this autonomy issue. On the one hand, it says that state enterprises have decision-making power in operation and management, but on the other, they must act within the law and must submit to the unified leadership of the state and fulfil their obligations under the state plan. What a give-and-take legerdemain!

This yes-and-no stand applies equally to the provincial administration. The Constitution in Article 100 speaks of non-contravention of local statutes with the "laws, decrees and general administrative statutes" of the state. Supposedly a local regime can act on its own, but it ought to function within the ambit of specification of the central decision.

---

[137] *Encyclopedia Yearbook*, 1978, p. 152, col. 2.

[138] *Beijing review*, January 17, 1983, p. 13, col. 2; p. 17, col. 1.

[139] Sun's article appears in *Renmin ribao*, November 19, 1982, p. 5 entitled, in translation, "Quadrupling the value of agricultural and industrial production is guaranteed not only politically but economically and technically." Premier Zhao Ziyang praised the article in *Beijing review*, December 20, 1982, p. 10, col. 2 and p. 28, col. 1.

[140] *Ibid.*, p. 28, col. 1.

The tenet of self-reliance is watered down in the pragmatic economy.[141] Under present conditions no system can benefit from autarky. The Constitution in the Preamble concedes to this by stating that the CPR ought to pursue a policy of mutual advantage with others and that trade and cultural exchanges with them are essential to the construction of the country. Hu Yaobang stresses that the self-reliant stand means that we "Chinese depend mainly on our own hard work" to achieve modernization.[142] The word "mainly" is used studiedly. The new open-door stance militates against isolationism in a world of inter-dependence and reciprocal dealings.

Finance

The Chinese published no data about government finance from 1961 to 1977 (inclusive). During these years, they considered such data as state secret.[143] Some students suggested that even the published budget is not complete because according to them, the "annual budget covers 80 to 85 percent, but not 100 percent of the total receipts and expenditures." Another feature is that the budget includes the spending of local authorities.[144] This situation is thankful to the fact that China is a unitary state whose subdivisions possess no power over finance. In 1979 the Beijing regime published details of the budget for the first time since 1960,[145] although national expenditure and revenue were revealed for 1978 and a modest budgetary surplus was officially declared in 1973. The figures below are in million yuan:

	Expenditure	Revenue	Surplus	Deficit
1960a	70,020	70,029		
1978b	111,093	112,111	1,018	
1979c	120,300	137,360	17,060	
1980d	121,270	108,520		12,750
1981e	108,580	105,860		2,720
1982f	113,690	110,690		3,000
1983g	126,200	123,200		3,000

a *Statesman's Yearbook*, 1979-1980, p. 338.

b *Ibid.*, 1980-1981, p. 341. *Britannica Book of the Year*, 1980, p. 247, col. 2 gives (by citing Yu Qiuli) revenue and expenditure for 1978 as $70,770 million and $70,130 million respectively. Both revenue and expenditure for 1979 were $72,000 million each.

c *Main documents of the third session*, pp. 50, 51.

d *Renmin ribao*, December 15, 1981, p. 3; *Guangming ribao*, same date, p. 2, from a report of Finance Minister Wang Bingqian to the NPC's annual session.

e *Renmin ribao* and *Globe and Mail*, loc. cit.

f *Beijing review*, January 17, 1983, p. 13, col. 1.

g *Ibid.*, p. 14, col. 2.

[141] *Renmin ribao*, November 27, 1981, p. 5; see also Hans Heymann, "Self-reliance revisited, China's technology dilemma," *China's changing Role in the World Economy*, New York: Praeger, 1975, pp. 15-35 at 31.

[142] *Beijing review*, September 13, 1982, p. 20, col. 2.

[143] *Britannica Book of the Year*, 1980, p. 247, col. 2.

[144] Economic intelligent unit, "China: the national economy," *New Encyclopedia Americana*, Chicago: Encyclopedia Americana, 1979, vol. 1, pp. 276-281 at 279, col. 2.

[145] *Statesman's Yearbook*, 1979-1980, p. 338 for this and the next statement.

The most detailed account of the income and outgo of the state treasury so far is the one made by Finance Minister Wang Bingqian in the budget speech to the NPC on December 1, 1982. The former is categorized into six, while the latter eleven rubrics. Neither the *Beijing review* of January 17, 1983 nor the *Renmin ribao* of December 2, 1982 prints the full text of Wang Bingqian's report. And therefore some items are given no figures. Below we present the revenues and expenditures by following the speech. The bracketed statistics are supplied.

Revenues

	in million yuan	
	1982	1983
1. funds raised from key projects in energy and transport	n.a.	6,000
2. foreign loans	7,600*	8,000*
3. receipts of state treasury bonds	4,200	4,000
4. basic depreciation funds turned in by enterprises to central departments	n.a.	2,200
5. receipts from enterprises	31,100	32,390
6. tax receipts	67,950	72,970

* "By the end of 1983," said Wang Bingqian, "the total of outstanding foreign loans borrowed as part of state revenue will be an estimated 4 billion US dollars" (*Beijing review*, January 17, 1983, p. 17, col. 1). He also stated on p. 16, col. 1 that the "investments using foreign loans amount to 5.4 billion yuan, an increase of 400 million yuan over the 1982 estimate." As of April 1983, one US dollar is close to 2 yuan.

Expenditures

	in million yuan	
	1982	1983
1. capital construction	30,270	36,180
2. technical transformation	5,470	6,570
3. circulation funds for enterprises	[2,250]*	2,250
4. aid to rural people's communes	[7,750]*	7,750
5. culture, science, education, public health service	19,000	20,400
6. national defense	17,870	17,870
7. administrative expenses	8,000	8,500
8. funds for the disabled	2,400	2,400
job creating funds	380	300
9. repayment for principal and interest on foreign loans	4,970	5,100
10. general reserve funds	n.a.	2,000
11. other expenditures	n.a.	n.a.

* The two years' estimates are almost the same, *Beijing review*, January 17, 1983, p. 14.

The present regime's financial policy of readjustment has curtailed the revenues and expenditures, particularly the latter, from 1981 onward. There is a deficit for each of the four years of 1980-1983, a fact that the government conceded to with some regret.[146] The

146 *Renmin ribao*, December 1, 1981, p. 1; also in *Globe and mail*, December 1, 1981, p. 13, col. 1.

reasons for the deficit are offered by an economist of the Beijing authority, Xue Muqiao, as a) over-commitment to heavy industry, b) higher payment for agricultural goods by the state, c) wage increment, d) inflation, e) plain waste, and f) unreasonable price policy.[147] One of the methods to reduce the deficit from 12,750 million yuan (1980) to 2,720 million yuan (1981) is the curtailment of foreign contracts worth $1,700 million.[148]

The 1979 revelation of more detailed budget was animated mainly, if not exclusively, by the resolve to oust Taiwan from both the World Bank and the International Monetary Fund. According to the rules of the two bodies, an applicant for membership must disclose its fiscal conditions before giving consideration. Beijing did it in December 1979. Consequently, on April 17, 1980 the CPR entered the IMF,[149] and on May 15, she joined the Bank.[150] Western studies show that as state enterprise expands, the portion of receipt from this resource is on the increase, while the portion from agriculture is correspondingly on the decrease:

	from agricultural goods	from state enterprises
1950	41.50%	17.10a
1954	13.43	63.58b
1979	10.00	90.00c
1980	10.00 (minus)	90.00d (plus)
1981	10.00 (minus)	90.00e (plus)

a Peter S.H. Tang and Joan M. Maloney, *op. cit.*, p. 366.
b *Ibid.*, p. 367.
c *Statesman's Yearbook*, 1980-1981, p. 341.
d *Ibid.*, 1981-1982, p. 346 where it says less than 10 percent from the agricultural goods.
e *Ibid.*, 1982-1983, p. 350.

Until 1980, China levied no income tax.[151] She seemed to try to outscore the Soviet Union where citizens are not free from it (an industrial family pays 4.1 percent of its income as tax and a collective-farm family pays 1.4 percent of its as tax).[152] However, in the fall of 1980, the following scheme of taxation was approved by the NPC:[153]

grade	range	rate in %
1	monthly income of 800 yuan and less	0
2	that part of monthly income from 801 yuan to 1,500 yuan	5
3	that part from 1,501 to 3,000 yuan	10
4	that part from 3,001 to 6,000 yuan	20
5	that part from 6,001 to 9,000 yuan	30
6	that part from 9,001 to 12,000 yuan	40
7	that part above 12,000 yuan	45

[147] Xue Muqiao, "Wei shen mo sheng chan xing shi hen hao, cai cheng hui you chi zi" *Dang qian wo guo jing ji wen ti*, Beijing: Renmin chu ban she, 1980, pp. 180-189 (reprinted from *Renmin ribao*, September 2, 1980).

[148] *Globe and Mail, loc. cit.*

[149] *New York Times*, April 18 (VI), 1980, p. 1, col. 6; *Facts on File*, April 25, 1980, p. 302, C2.

[150] *New York Times*, May 16 (V), 1980, p. 4, col. 6; *Facts on File*, May 23, 1980, p. 389, C1.

[151] *Statesman's Yearbook*, 1979-1980, p. 338.

[152] *The 1978 Yearbook of the USSR*, Moscow: Novosti Press, 1978, p. 156 (table).

[153] *Main documents of the third session*, p. 245.

The legislation applies to everyone in the CPR (foreigners included) who earn more than 800 yuan ($400) a month.[154] Only about 20 people among that country's one billion population make that amount, hence subject to levying. It has been written that the two topmen at that time, Deng Xiaoping and Hua Guofeng, drew a monthly salary of 1,200 yuan. Under the law, they pay tax on the four hundred yuan above the minimum. In fact, the law is simply a way to meet the objection of foreign residents who have complained that it was discriminatory for them to pay income tax when Chinese citizens do not.

The CPR's fiscal power is exercised by the People's Bank, which has a network of 30,000 branches,[155] and the Finance Ministry. The first took over the former Central Bank in 1950 and absorbed many private monetary establishments. The Bank issues notes, regulates circulation, grants loans to enterprises and audits the spending of government bodies. Besides, it does conventional transactions and serves as a savings outlet for the public (masses is the better word in the CPR). Moreover, it takes charge of such routines as accounting, payments and receipts from factories and administrative organizations, a function which enables it to monitor their financial activities in light of the Five-Year Plans. Also within its purview are foreign trade and cognate overseas operations such as the enormous remittance of the Chinese. However, in this case it acts via the Bank of China with its scores of branches in many parts of the world.[156]

The Finance Ministry collects tax, prepares fiscal statements and distributes investment resources, but agricultural economy finds itself under the authority of the Agricultural Bank. Throughout the vast land there are mushrooming rural credit co-ops. They derive funds from this bank and deposits of the peasants. For the purpose of investing in, or financing of, construction and communication works, there are the People's Construction Bank and the Bank of Communication.[157] In addition to the already mentioned five banks there are several others.[158] They are the China & South Sea Bank Ltd., China International Trust & Investment Corporation, China State Bank, Guangdong Provincial Bank, Jincheng Banking Corporation, National Commercial Bank Ltd., Xinhua Trust, Savings and Commercial Bank Ltd., and Yian Yie Commercial Bank Ltd.

At the end of the second quarter of 1982, China's gold reserves totaled 12.67 million troy ounces, and foreign exchange reserves $7,059 million, 1,854 million more than at the end of March.[159] The

[154] This and the following information are from the *Globe and Mail*, September 3, 1980, pp. 1, 5.

[155] *Statesman's yearbook*, 1979-1980, p. 338; 1980-1981, p. 341.

[156] Nicholas H. Ludlow and James B. Stepanek, "Inside the Bank of China," *Chinese business review*, 7 (July-August 1980), pp. 9-13.

[157] "China's financial institutions," *ibid.*, p. 15-18.

[158] *Europa*, 1982, vol. 2, p. 134.

[159] *Beijing review*, November 8, 1982, p. 7.

country's total deposits were 202,176 million yuan, 4,153 million yuan more than at the end of the first quarter and the total loans were 268,133 million yuan, a 1,855 million yuan increase. Circulation funds were 35,250 million yuan, 2,537 million yuan less than at the end of March.[160]

Transport

Basic to industrialization are transport and energy, the former being considered essential because it brings the latter to the site of construction and manufacture. Avows Premier Zhao Ziyang: "We must first of all ensure investment in key energy and transport projects."[161] He says these are the desiderata to realize China's hope to be a great power. The two, regrets he, are the weakest links in the current modernization campaign.[162] To strengthen them, the Sixth Five-Year Plan provides 38.5 percent of the total investment funds.[163] Inadequate transport, he asserts, is partly responsible for the energy shortage. In 1981, for example, more than 17 million tons of coal were waiting to be shipped out of Shanxi, the richest of all the provinces in this item. Some coal mines are forced to fix their production quotas in keeping with the transport capacity. In this section we take up transport, leaving energy to the next.

When the civil war came to a close in 1949, China, according to one communist source, had 26,129 km of railways,[164] but another says it was 20,000 km,[165] still another gives 10,000 km.[166] This indicates, incidentally, that the communist statistics are so inconsistent. If we take the first figure which seems to be close to the fact, half of the total were in Manchuria and they were in operational condition, but the other half in China proper were destroyed by the Reds. The new regime encountered no difficulty in restoring each and every line to use as early as 1952, thanks to its brutality toward even a negligible breach of regulations. Since then roughly 24,000 km are added. At present there are 70 main and 140 subsidiary trunks.[167] Four of the 70, totaling 3,021 km, were substantially finished before 1949 but the Reds have come to claim full credit for having built them.[168] There are three new lines: a) Beijing-Tongliao, the latter a town on the border of Waimeng and Neimeng,

[160] Ibid.

[161] Ibid., December 20, 1982, pp. 24-25.

[162] Ibid., p. 25, col. 1.

[163] Ibid., p. 12, col. 2.

[164] Zhong guo di tu ji, by Lin Chong and Huang Jiushun, Hong Kong: Xin yu chu ban gong si, 1980, pp. 38-39.

[165] Beijing review, January 31, 1983, p. 18, col. 2.

[166] Ibid., December 27, 1982, p. 5, col. 1.

[167] Zhong guo di tu ji, p. 38.

[168] Zhong guo shou ce, Hong Kong: Da gong bao, 1980, p. 207.

b) Lanzhou-Urumqi, c) Xining-Lhasa reaching Germu in 1975.[169] In length they are 870, 1,892 and 834 km respectively.[170] An interesting fact is that Japan has nearly the same mileage of railways, but she is only 1/25th of the CPR.[171] A second noticeable contrast is that while 97 percent of Japanese lines are electrified, a mere 3 percent of China's are.[172] The CPR's Sixth Five-Year Plan anticipates electrifying 2,500 km in 1985. At that time China would have a total of 53,900 km of rails.[173]

Many short spurs of the rails are for factory or mining use only. There is absolutely no passenger traffic on them. Some of the most important trunks for this traffic are Beijing-Guangzhou, Tianjin-Shanghai, Manzhouli-Suifenghe, Shanghai-Hongzhou, Beijing-Haerbin (also spelled Harbin), and Lanzou-Baotao. All these, one should note, were built before the communist takeover.[174] The Manzhouli-Suifenghe railway was completed back in 1903.

In view of the significance of transport to China's modernization, it surprises no one when Premier Zhao Ziyang reported to the Fifth NPC on November 30, 1982 that the Sixth Five-Year Plan assigns 29.8 billion yuan to it (along with telecommunications).[175] In 1980, there were, according to one Chinese source, 51,900 km of rails,[176] but another source in the same media gives the figure 50,000 for the year 1981. Thus, the Chinese lost 1,900 km of rails somewhere in the country! The Sixth Five-Year Plan, made known in 1982, will add 2,000 km to the present total, besides doubling the tracks of 1,700 km and electrifying 2,500 km. Estimates show China's capacity to transport coal from the major coal fields in Shanxi, western Neimeng and Ningxia will increase from 70 million tons in 1980 to 120 million in 1985; and coal taken to the northeast industrial base will be at least twice the present level.[177] Railways handle 70 percent of the nation's total volume of freight and 60 percent of the total passengers. The freight the trains carried is asserted to reach 1,048 million tons in 1981, that is 10.5 times the 1950 record; and the number of passengers was 940 million, that is 6 times as many as in 1950. The People's Republic, it is alleged, ranks second in the world in railway freight and passenger transport density per km.[178]

[169] *Ibid.*, p. 209.

[170] *Ibid.*, pp. 206, 209.

[171] *Hammond*, 1982, p. 601, col. 1.

[172] *Europa*, 1979, vol. 2, p. 137.

[173] *Beijing review*, January 31, 1983, p. 18, col. 2.

[174] *Europa*, 1979, vol. 2, p. 124.

[175] *Beijing review*, December 20, 1982, p. 14, col. 1.

[176] *Ibid.*, January 31, 1983, p. 18, col. 2.

[177] *Ibid.*, January 31, 1983, p. 19, col. 1.

[178] *Ibid.*, December 27, p. 5, col. 2.

The second important transport means are motorways. In 1980 there were said to be 885,200 km of these (again there are quite a few conflicting figures),[179] in comparison with 20,000 km in 1950.[180] All are gravel roads. It is notable that four roads lead to Tibet from Xinjiang, Sichuan, Qinghai and Yunnan.[181] They are military in nature, being constructed by troops themselves. Another (open in 1983) strategic line runs from Dushanzi, a tribal town north of the Tianshan, to Kuqa another tribal town which is a fruit center on the old Silk Road south of her. This is reported to be an asphalt artery and 532 km in distance and 6 meters in width. It is the first passway ever to cross the heretofore uncrossable snow-capped ranges.[182] "Previously it took nearly four days to transport oil [if the Reds were honest, they should say armies] by trucks from Dushanzi to Kuqa on a circuitous 1,014-km route via Urumqi and Korla."[183] The new road which shortens the distance by half has reduced the travel time to a little more than one day.

The third important means are waterways. There are, by one account, 140,000 km of inland waterways of which 33 percent, that is, 46,400 km are open to steamships,[184] but by another account the total becomes 430,000 km of which 108,500 km are navigable.[185] The latter source does not tell us navigable by which means, steamship or wooden boat. The Sixth Five-Year Plan contemplates 132 deep-water berths for 15 coastal ports which will increase the handling capacity of the nation's harbor by 46 percent from 217 million tons in 1980 to 317 million tons in 1985.[186] The Yangzi is navigable by vessels of 10,000 tons as far as Wuhan, while smaller ones can continue to Chongqing in Sichuan province. More than one third of the internal freight tonnage is carried on rivers.[187] China will build its long coast and the Changjiang into two trunk lines of transport, the first north-south and the second east-west, and gradually link them with other rivers to form a complete water-transport network.

The fourth are airways. Domestic lines number 160 connecting more than 80 cities.[188] China has 12 air routes to 18 countries, with

179 The figure 70,000 km appears in F. Divov, op. cit., p. 279. Hammond 1982, p. 547, col. 2 gives 551,800 miles, i.e., 887,200 km.

180 Beijing review, January 31, 1983, p. 18, col. 2.

181 Zhong guo di tu ji, p. 39.

182 Beijing review, January 31, 1983, p. 7, col. 3.

183 Ibid.

184 Zhong guo di tu ji, loc. cit.

185 Beijing review, January 31, 1983, p. 18, col. 1.

186 Ibid., December 20, 1983, p. 14, col. 2; ibid., January 31, 1983, p. 19, col. 1.

187 Europa. 1979, vol. 2, p. 137.

188 Zhong guo shou ce, p. 212.

a mileage of about 600,000 km.[189] The Beijing oligarchy has signed navigation treaties with 38 states.[190] Finally, the People's Republic has 8,700 km of oil pipelines in 1980.[191]

Energy

Modernization depends on two keys, transport and energy.[192] Having analyzed the problem of the former, we now come to look at the latter. The difficulty in energy supply is being painfully felt as the country makes strenuous efforts toward industrial revolution. It is studied that the shortage of energy has idled 20 percent of the industrial equipment in the last few years, resulting in an annual loss of 70,000 million yuan of output value.[193] Many enterprises had no alternative but to plan their quotas in accord with the available energy. One research analyst explains it this way. In the first place, there has been a policy of one-sided focus on extraction and neglect of exploration. It led to imbalance between mining and tunnelling and between extraction and augmentation of the known reserves. In the second place, the magnitude of construction has been very small and it created no need to expand the energy base. In the third place, there was and is the squandering of energy owing to an ancient equipment and unscientific management.[194] From now on, it is suggested, priorities will be placed on opening of more coal mines and hydro power. Natural gas and nuclear energy will also be explored. Plans are made to provide incentive for locality to prospect and operate new mines or build power stations. The locality is to receive the sales of such power. In the remaining three years of the Sixth Plan (1983-1985), a 20,000 million yuan construction fund for energy and transport is to be raised by local administration and enterprises. On its part, the government will earmark 60,000 million yuan during the Sixth Plan for the exploitation of energy, a sum constituting one-fourth of the total capital outlay. Besides, "China is actively introducing foreign advanced technology" in helping solve the difficulty in this department.[195]

In regard to the coal and hydro situation, it has been speculated that as high as 85-90 percent of the nation's energy need is met by coal.[196] Its output and that of electricity are on the increase as

[189] Ibid.

[190] Ibid.

[191] Beijing review, January 31, 1983, p. 18, col. 2.

[192] Ibid., p. 16.

[193] Ibid., p. 16, col. 2.

[194] Ibid.

[195] Ibid., p. 20, col. 2.

[196] Economic intelligent unit, loc. cit.

316   GOVERNMENT OF SOCIALIST CHINA

indicated in the following table (coal in million tons, electricity in 100 million kwh).

year	52a	57	65	70	76	78b	79c	80	81	82d	83
coal	66.5	130.7	230	295	450	618	500	610	620	649	670
electricity	7.3	19.3	45	75	125	256	na	300	312	325	338

a 1952-1976 figures, *Europa*, 1982, vol. 2, p. 121.
b 1978 figure, *Britannica book of the year*, 1980, p. 246, col. 1.
c 1979-1981 figures, *Main documents of the third session, pp. 9, 25*. The China trade report put out by the Far Eastern economic review, 4th quarter, March 1981 gives the figures for electricity and coal as 360 and 600 respectively for the year 1981. A *Pravda* article of February 1, 1982, p. 6 mentions the two figures as 306 and 600.
d 1982 and 1983 figures from *Beijing review*, January 3, 1983, p. 8, col. 1.

The collieries will get 17.9 billion yuan investment during 1981-1985. It is mainly for exploiting reserves in Shanxi, northeast China and eastern Neimeng; at the same time, coalfields in western Henan, Shandong, Anhui, Jiangsu and Guizhou are to be developed. Scheduled in the plan are 28 super pits, each with an annual capacity of one million tons plus.[197] They, in addition to the projected small and medium mines, are expected to increase the total capacity of the coal industry by 220 million tons. Provisions are made for production capacity of 80 million tons to be available before the end of 1985, with work continuing during the next five-year plan period for the remaining 140 million tons. To expedite the expansion of the resource in question, the government concentrates firstly, on exploiting the giant open-cast mines and, secondly on inaugurating five such mines at Huolinhe, Yiminhe, Pingshuo, Yuanbaoshan and Jungar. Technical amelioration of the mining facilities presently in operation is also contemplated.

A big sum of 20.7 billion yuan is allocated to the power industry by the Sixth Plan. Exploitation of hydraulic potential will be carried out along the upper Huanghe, the upper and middle Changjiang and in the Hongshui basin. Envisaged is the laying out of an array of power establishments in the coal-rich Shanxi, eastern Neimeng, Huainan and Huaibei areas, western Henan, Weihe region and Guizhou. Thermo-energy generation will be started in Shanghai, Liaoning, Jiangsu, Zhejiang, Guangdong and Sichuan. The end of the Sixth Plan will see the building or continued building of 15 hydroelectric stations and 45 thermo-energy installations, each of the former having a capacity of 400,000 kw or above and each of the latter 200,000 kw or above. Added to the lesser projects to be erected, this amounts to a total increase of 36.6 million kw. Twelve point nine million kw of this is available by 1985, with the remaining 23.7 million kw available during the next plan period. The past several years saw the CPR earnestly seeking foreign mining and hydraulic technology in the form of concessions or joint ventures. In 1978, a West German consortium of Krupp, Demag, Thyssen and Rhurkohle signed a $4.2

197 *Beijing review*, December 20, 1982, p. 13, col. 2.

billion deal for five mines and for the extension of a sixth in Hebei.[198] The agreement also envisioned the construction of a factory making equipment to modernize some fairly efficient pits.[199] Beijing also entered into contract with Japan's Mitsui Mining Concern and several others to develop two signifcant mines in Shandong and Shanxi. Infusing in petroleum industry during the Sixth Plan is 15.4 billion yuan. Efforts are focused on prospecting work in the Songliao region of the northeast, the Bohai bay, the Puyang district of Henan and the Eren basin of Neimeng. Exploration will also be executed in the Jungar basin of Xinjiang and the Caidam basin of Qinghai. Similar activities will be going on steadily for present oil and natural gas fields in east China. In the five years (1981-1985) production capacity for oil will be up by 35 million tons and for natural gas by 2.5 billion cubic meters. This would help to make up for the depletion as a result of continued exploitation of oil wells now functioning and to maintain the annual oil output level at 100 million tons during the Sixth Plan.[200] The country's deposit of oil and natural gas, according to a Western journal, is from 40 to 75 billion barrels.[201] "Even at the present very dim state of knowledge, that is about a third of the equally conservative figure cited for Saudi Arabia," the journal asserts. Likewise a reference book says China's resources of oil ranks it possibly with that of that Arab state.[202] Starting from 1976, oil figures begin to appear in either Western or Chinese press. The previous recorded statistics are for 1949 and 1952. It is known that in 1976, China's oil production increased by 13 percent over the preceding year and it was 7.6 times that of 1965.[203] The annual barrels are as follows:

1949a	889,529,690	1979e	773,800,000	
1952a	3,205,283,520	1980e	771,610,000	-0.3%
1975b	545,329,000	1981f	736,887,550	-4.5
1976c	616,120,000	1982g	735,156,771	-0.3
1977c	652,620,000	1983g	735,156,771	
1978d	764,930,000			

a *Renmin shou ce,* 1979, Beijing: Renmin ribao chu ban she, 1980, p. 1109. We change the given tons into barrels. One barrel equals 299.8 pounds; one ton 2,204 pounds.

b It is calculated from the 1976 figure, less 13 percent, *Encyclopedia yearbook,* 1979, p. 156, col. 2.

c *Information please,* 1979, p. 344.

d *Britannica book of the year,* 1980, p. 246, col. 1 gives 104,050,000 tons. We change them into barrels, see note "a" above.

e *World almanac,* 1982, p. 130.

f Premier Zhao Ziyang says the output in 1981 was down by 4.5 percent from 1980, *Beijing review,* December 20, 1982, p. 21, col. 2.

g *Ibid.,* January 3, 1983, p. 8, col. 2 writes that in 1982 and 1983 the annual product is approximately 100,000,000 tons. We change them into barrels.

198 *Encyclopedia yearbook,* 1979, p. 157, col. 2.

199 *The economist,* October 14, 1978, p. 115, col. 1.

200 *Beijing review,* December 20, 1982, p. 13, col. 2.

201 *The economist,* October 14, 1978, p. 115.

202 *Britannica book of the year,* 1980, p. 246, col. 1; see also "CPR ready to move skills offshore," *Offshore,* 40 (June 20, 1980), pp. 180-181.

203 *Encyclopedia yearbook,* 1979, p. 156, col. 2.

The decrease of oil output is due to progressive exhaustion of the deposit presently explored, or to the deliberate restriction of quota on account of the inadequacy in refining and transport facilities, a point alluded above. In the 1970's, according to Zhou Enlai, China needed 20 million tons of oil (147 million barrels) per annum.[204] Naturally, with modernization in full swing, the requirement has been much greater, and the amount produced is now five times that figure. Besides supplying to domestic enterprises, the government has been exporting oil in order to build up the foreign exchanges. But the quality leaves much to be desired, because the Chinese oil is very waxy. It is just too crude. Only Japan and a handful of other nations are taking it.[205] The Nipponese are reluctant and some of them even refuse to purchase the waxy stuff from the People's Republic. Yet, because Japan depends almost entirely on foreign energy and due to the fact that oil is about all China has to offer Japan in return for technology and machines, the Japanese have no alternative.[206] Unfortunately for the Chinese, their oil output constitutes only 3.6 percent of the world's total.[207] China is therefore not much of a competitor in that commodity.

The Beijing autocracy has earnestly sought to involve foreigners in energy exploration. On January 6, 1982, the government enacted the Regulations on the Exploration of Offshore Petroleum Resources in Cooperation with Foreign Enterprises.[208] There are 31 articles in it covering very comprehensively both technical and financial problems. A number of Western companies have entered into agreements with Beijing in the past two years. The latest contract is one initialed with the Atlantic Richfield of California on September 19, 1982. The firm got the franchise to prospect the oil deposit of the continental shelf along the southern coast. The estimate is that the deposit is between 80 to 130 billion barrels.

Because of serious handicaps, the CPR's energy industry cannot develop very rapidly.[209] It is calculated that by the end of this century, the total energy output can double itself from 600 million plus tons in 1980 to around 1,200 million tons.[210] This being so, how can the People's Republic quadruple the gross annual value of industrial and agricultural production in the year 2000? The first two years of the Sixth Plan are anything but encouraging. The output of fuels, power and some important raw and semi-finished things has gradually picked

---

[204] Economic intelligent unit, p. 278, col. 1.

[205] The economist, October 14, 1978, p. 114.

[206] David Lewis, "Japan and the West sharing the China market," New leader, June 4, 1979, pp. 10-12 at 11, col. 2.

[207] World almanac, 1982, p. 130.

[208] Beijing review, February 22, 1982, pp. 14-18.

[209] Ibid., January 31, 1983, p. 17, col. 2.

[210] Ibid.

up following the stagnation or even decline of 1981-1982. In comparison with 1980, the 1981 record of coal was up by 0.2 percent, electricity by 2.9 percent and cement by 3.8 percent, while the output of crude oil dropped by 4.5 percent and steel products by 1.7 percent. It is estimated that compared with 1981, the 1982 production of coal will rise by 4.6 percent, crude oil by 0.5 percent, electricity by 5.1 percent, steel products by 1.9 percent, and cement by 8.6 percent.[211] Although Zhao Ziyang was talking (unjustifiably, we would argue) of the upward trend, the growth is too marginal to fulfil the quadrupling expectation.

The Chinese press has stressed the economizing of the available energy by enterprises. It regards this as important as making investments in brand new areas. The problem involves energy efficiency. One communist mandarin pleads that "we must send every ounce of coal, every watt of electricity and every drop of oil we have to places where it is most needed in renovation and production."[212] And Premier Zhao Ziyang placed "saving energy" as the number one guidepost toward technical transformation.[213] China's energy problem is critical, according to a writer. Even though her output of energy ranks fourth in the world, its gross national product ranks eighth due to the low energy utilization rate. Energy authorities say the CPR's rate is only 30 percent, whereas Japan's and America's are 57 percent and 51 percent respectively.[214] He moved on to assert that in terms of total output value and national income produced from consuming one ton of standard coal, Japan, France and West Germany are more than five to six times higher than the CPR, and India is more than twice China's figure. The following table compares energy efficiency (in percent):[215]

	China	developed nations
thermal power plants	29	35-40
industrial boilers	46-60	80
furnaces and kilns	20-30	50-60
home stoves	15-20	50-60
locomotives	6-8	25
	steam	diesel or electric

Within China, energy consumption varies considerably from place to place. Studies show that in 1980, Shanghai consumed only 29,000 tons to produce 100 million yuan of value, but Tianjin, Zhejiang and Jiangsu consumed 40,000 to 43,000 tons. Many provinces and regions go above 100,000 tons. Premier Zhao Ziyang promises to

[211] Ibid., December 20, 1982, p. 21, col. 2.

[212] Facts on file, March 19, 1977, p. 200, C3.

[213] Beijing review, December 20, p. 15, col. 1.

[214] Ibid., January 31, 1983, p. 18, col. 1.

[215] Ibid., p. 20, col. 2.

raise energy utilization rates of the less-developed provinces and regions by shutting down outdated enterprises that contend with advanced ones for energy and transport.[216] This step will hopefully move the country's average energy consumption towards the level of Zhejiang for example. It may lower the energy consumed in producing a value of 100 million yuan from the 1980's 91,000 tons to 45,000 tons. The Chinese have claimed that more than 60 million tons of energy are saved in 1980 and 1981. The energy used to turn out 100 million yuan of value in 1978 is 100,400 tons, in 1979, 94,700 tons; in 1980, 91,000 tons; and in 1981, 86,200 tons.[217]

Just a paragraph on technical transformation. In the Sixth Plan, the state makes an investment of 130,000 million yuan for this purpose. It represents 36 percent of the total investment in fixed assets. In the 28 years between 1953 and 1980, such funds made for about 20 percent.[218] Premier Zhao Ziyang almost considers the updating of the existing enterprises as a third key (two other keys: energy and transport) to China's economic growth.[219] China has about 400,000 industrial and transport enterprises. Only 20 percent of them are equipped with pretty good machinery.[220] In another 20-25 percent, although the equipment is maintained well, the technology is dated. As for the remaining 50-60 percent are concerned, they are backward. All their machines are due to be replaced. It is thought that new enterprises are indispensable, but the investment for them is much greater than that for renovation of the existing ones. The strategy adopted is both building new plants and modernizing the old ones.

Daqing

The biggest oilfield is located at Daqing in the Songliao basin of the northeast, where extraction commenced as early as 1951, but it was not until May 1960 that a grand-scale scheme was put in motion.[221] Within three years the work was brought to completion "thankful to one of the three red banners of Chairman Mao Zedong."[222] From 1976 to 1982 the annual output was stated to be 55 million tons.[223] This represents more than one half of the nation's total.[224] The growth rate in Daqing is said to be 28 percent a year.[225]

[216] *Ibid.*, December 20, 1982, pp. 26, 27.

[217] *Ibid.*, January 31, 1983, p. 18, col. 2.

[218] *Ibid.*, December 20, 1982, p. 13, col. 1; *ibid.*, January 31, 1983, p. 20, col. 1.

[219] *Ibid.*, December 20, 1982, p. 13, col. 1; pp. 14, 15.

[220] *Ibid.*, January 31, 1983, p. 20, col. 1.

[221] *Xin hua ci dian*, Beijing: shang wu yin shu guan, 1980, p. 140, col. 2. *Zhong guo bai ke nian jian*, Beijing: Zhong guo da bai ke quan shu chu ban she, 1980, p. 320, col. 2.

[222] *Xin hua ci dian, loc. cit.*

[223] *Beijing review*, March 28, 1983, p. 24, col. 1.

[224] *Ibid.*, p. 23, col. 1; *Zhong guo bai ke nian jian*, p. 320, col. 3.

[225] *Zhong guo bai ke nian jian*, p. 320, col. 2.

Just as Dazhai is flaunted as model for agriculture, so Daqing is boasted as one for industry, "a pace-setter," as it is called.[226] There was held, from April 20 to May 13, 1977, a "Learn from Daqing Conference" attended by a throng of 7,000. It was opened on the site, but soon moved to Beijing and adjourned there.[227] Song Zhenming, secretary of the Daqing party organization and chairman of the revolutionary committee, portrayed his constituency in fantastic figures. The output was valued in 1976 as 4.4 times that of 1965. From 1960 to 1979, Daqing turned to the state 17.8 times the money invested by it.[228]

The city has a population of 760,000. Sixty industrial-agricultural villages, imitating the Russian agrogorod, and 164 potential settlements, have grown up there; and over 40,000 people are engaged in farming, forestry, factory and fisheries. In the period from 1977 to 1981, they drilled 133 percent more than the total for the 16 years between 1960 and 1976.[229] In addition, they built a reservoir and a waste-water treatment plant, fractured and transformed 2,179 oil wells and put 709 new oil and water wells into operation. In 1979, there were constructed 133 residential houses of 400,000 square meters,[230] and in the two years that followed another 800,000 square meters were completed.[231] As of the beginning of 1983 plans were drafted for six small satellite towns and the construction of four was in advanced stages. The municipal administration has allocated 100,000,000 yuan annually to housing projects.

There are said to be 25 scientific academies and institutions in Daqing which utilize advanced oil technology and trained engineering and technical personnel. The research agencies are said to be well grounded in the realities of the oilfield and from 1960 to June 1982, they obtained satisfactory results in 38,800 separate projects. Each day sees 300,000 pieces of data turned over to these agencies by the work units.[232]

Daqing is said to have its own school system from nursery to university. The Daqing Petroleum College, a composite or key college in the Chinese terminology, is actually in Anda county of Heilongjiang province.[233]

On the above-mentioned (1977) conference, while Song Zhenming lauded the material side of the establishment, the luminaries like Ye Jianying, Li Xiannian and Hua Guofeng orchestrated with the

[226] *Beijing review, loc. cit.*

[227] *Keesing's,* December 16, 1977, p. 28728.

[228] *Zhong guo bai ke nian jian,* p. 321, col. 2.

[229] *Beijing review,* March 28, 1983, p. 24, col. 1.

[230] Harold Hinton, *op. cit.,* p. 246.

[231] *Beijing review,* March 28, 1983, p. 24, col. 2.

[232] *Ibid.,* p. 25, col. 1.

[233] *Xin hua ci dian,* p. 558.

laudation of the spiritual side. They considered Daqing as embodying the ideal of organizing industry, agriculture, commerce, culture, education and military activities into one unified mechanism. Driven home by them was the virtue of the commune which Daqing supposedly epitomized. An instruction of the Central Committee of the CCP in December 1981 affirmed Daqing's merit of self-reliance and hard work and its basic experience in managing a modernized enterprise. It says: "Daqing is worthy of the name of advanced model on China's industrial and transportation front."[234]

However, things do not seem to fare too well. First, the Chinese press admits that many primitive, or to use the original description, "earthen" dwellings have not been replaced with decent houses.[235] Second, it is acknowledged that "as time goes by, natural reduction in production of the oilfield is inevitable."[236] Just how much is the reduction is not stated. Judging by that confession, the claim of 28 percent increase of output must be taken with a pinch of salt. Third, reading between the lines, one gets a decadent situation in Daqing. Many veteran workers and veteran cadres are said to have left for other provinces and their places are taken by young and inexperienced hands. Very likely this is caused by the exhaustion of deposit in the field. The authorities may well think that it is better to put the skilled personnel to better use elsewhere. One team leader told the Beijing review correspondent that among the eighty-five men under him there were 68 young faces. They were engaged in fighting, gambling, burglary and embezzlement.[237] Probably these men do not have much to do on the job. Whether ideological and political education, which the management promised to carry out among the workers, can provide a remedy is not assured. Can Daqing offer anything worthwhile for others to learn? Can China's policy of "oil self-sufficiency" be achieve through the performance of Daqing?[238]

[234] Beijing review, March 28, 1983, p. 23, col. 1.

[235] Ibid., p. 23, col. 2.

[236] Ibid.

[237] Ibid., p. 25, col. 2.

[238] Xin hua ci dian, p. 141, col. 2.

CHAPTER XI
Foreign Trade
Leaning on the Russian trade

In discussing China's foreign commerce, one is beset by the difficulty that she "does not publish statistics" on it.[1] One has, therefore, to go by the log of her partners. From the beginning of the regime in 1949, the Chinese trading course has been parallel to their foreign policy. In both there is the reverse of direction, i.e., from East to West.[2] the CPR's economy was first tied to that of the socialist commonwealth for about ten years. Gradually it veered away from it, and after 1972, came to be bound up with the capitalist world's economy. For understandable reasons, the People's Republic took the Soviet path both industrially and politically in 1949. The vital prop to the new communist oligarchy was secured in a treaty signed on February 14, 1950 in the Soviet capital. It granted China a quinquennial credit of $300 million to pay for the Russian-supplied industrial equipment by exporting materials to the USSR.[3] The treaty, terminated in 1979, established four joint companies for the exploitation of oil and minerals in Xinjiang and for the operation of airlines and shipbuilding in Manchuria. Their stock was agreed on a fifty-fifty basis. In addition, a co-management was set up for each of the four.[4] A proposal, made after the death of Stalin, to establish a fifth company in south China was rejected by Beijing as compromising its independence.[5] The original treaty (of February 14, 1950) was supplemented in May by an appendix signed by the Soviet delegate and the authorities representing Manchuria and Xinjiang. The two regions were in fact separated from China proper.[6] Such a practice already had its precedent in the summer of 1949 when an official party of Manchuria concluded a special protocol with the USSR which obliged the latter to return some of the loot it carted away from there in 1945-1948. However, Manchuria was to ship to the Soviet Union unspecified agricultural produce. Thinly veiled was Russia's ambition of detaching parts of China, or at least, creating in them a sphere of influence à la traditional imperialism.

Before the communist takeover, the GMD made a Treaty of

---

[1] Economic intelligent unit, "China: the national economy," *New Encyclopedia Americana*, Chicago: Encyclopedia Americana, 1979, vol. 4, pp. 276-281 at 280, col. 1; *The economist*, October 14, 1978, pp. 114-115 at 114, col. 2.

[2] C.F. Remer, "International economics and the rise of Chinese communism," *International Economics of Communist China*, Ann Arbor: University of Michigan Press, 1959, pp. 7-29 at 23-25.

[3] Franz H. Michael and George E. Taylor, *The Far East in the Modern World*, rev. ed., New York: Holt, Rinehart and Winston, 1964, p. 368. Iu. N. Paleev, "Khronika vneshneekonomicheskikh svyazei," *SSSR, entsiklopedicheskii spravochnik*, Moska: Izd-vo "sovetskaya entsiklopediya," 1979, cols., 751-771 at 756.

[4] Chu-yuan Cheng, *Economic Relations between Peking and Moscow*, New York: Praeger, 1964, pp. 13-20.

[5] Franz H. Michael and George E. Taylor, *op. cit.*, p. 493.

[6] Mikhail Iosifovich Sladvoskii, *Ocherki ekonomicheskikh otnoshenii SSSR s Kitaem*, Moskva: Vneshtorgizdat, 1957, p. 14.

Friendship with the USSR on August 14, 1945, the day Japan capitulated. Thanks to this instrument, Russia came to co-own the facilities of Dairen, now declared an international free port, and Port Arthur, a Russo-Chinese naval base (actually Russian, since the GMD had a token navy). Moreover, the T-shaped network of the railways, running from Manzhouli to Suifenghe (thence to Vladivostok) and from Haerbin to Dairen was changed into a joint concern. Although China assumed the task of policing the lines, most of the subsidiary industries, mines and other concessions along the routes, were placed under a co-administration. We find it interesting that this fact is left out in a recent Soviet publication.[7] The entire arrangement was to continue until 1975.[8] The treaty in question, one may note, is traceable to the secret Yalta protocol of February 11, 1945 and it comes dangerously close to forcing the GMD to lean economically on Moscow. A related historical fact deserves mention here. The Chinese Eastern Railway which is the horizontal spur of the T-shaped network had czarist share in it during its construction in 1903. After the seizure of Manchuria by Japan in the fall of 1931, it perforce came under her (technically Manzhouguo).[9] In 1935, following a protracted bargaining, the USSR finally sold it to Japan for 170 million yen.[10] The Nanjing Government protested to Moscow only to be rebuffed that since it was unable to exercise jurisdiction over Manchuria, Japan had the de facto sovereignty there.[11] After the defeat of the Japanese in 1945, the Soviet Union grabbed the lines, as everything else, throughout Manchuria, thus reclaiming a right no longer hers.

Was the CPR to become Russia's appendage? Even at the early stage of its history, the Beijing regime had shown, however sub rosa, its displeasure toward Moscow. Had it not been for it, the Russians probably would not have handed over the rails to China in 1954. There was no alternative for the Chinese but leaning on their "elder brothers", the Soviets, now that the US had laid total embargo on Chinese import after Mao Zedong rushed his "volunteers" to fight on the side of North Korea.

Beginning in December 1953, the Soviet Union helped build up first 141 plants,[12] and a little later another 70 in China.[13] A large number

[7] Iu. N. Pavleev, op. cit., col. 755.

[8] Franz H. Michael and George E. Taylor, op. cit., p.360.

[9] Institut für Asienkunde, Die wirtschaftliche Verflechtung der Volksrepublik China mit der Sowjetunion, Frankfurt am Main: A. Metzner, 1959, pp. 90-91.

[10] Franz H. Michael and George E. Taylor, op. cit., p. 355; this is curiously not mentioned in Iu. N. Pavleev's book cited above.

[11] "Kitaiskaya chanchun'skaya zheleznaya doroga," Bol'shaya sovetskaya entsiklopediya, 2nd ed., Moskva: Gosudarstvennoe nauchnoe izdatel'stvo "bol'shaya sovetskaya entsiklopediya," 1949-1958, vol. 21 (1953), pp. 314-315.

[12] Franz H. Michael and George E. Taylor, op. cit., p. 466.

[13] A. Doak Barnett, "The economic development of communist China," George P. Jan, ed., Government of Communist China, San Francisco: Chandler Pub. Co., 1966, pp. 374-396 at 382.

of protocols were signed whereby the Chinese government was to hire Soviet personnel to operate the plants and to work in other capacities. Although the protocols do not mention the number, such personnel were 13,000 in 1960.[14] The 1950 treaty envisaged the laying out of two trunks linking China and Russia via Xinjiang and Mongolia. For all these, the USSR made two loans to China. The first was the aforesaid $300 million made in February 1950 and the second was made in October 1954 to the tune of $230 million.[15] They were not grants, but had to be repaid with interest.[16] China must also defray the training cost of about 7,000 Chinese in the USSR,[17] and the cost of military supplies which they got from the Russians in order to fight the war in Korea. All the above added up to $2 billion. Over half of it was for the military materiel.[18] Russia charged interest on every item it provided.

In 1956, China began to discharge her debts and by 1965 all were cleared up.[19] Although most Russian and East European experts left China in 1960, some continued to serve there until the Cultural Revolution. This means that the Chinese kept on paying them and providing service for them up to 1966. During the spring of 1961, it is interesting to note, a Russian delegation flew to Beijing to discuss further aid to the CPR. The Chinese later disclosed that the offer was rejected with thanks. Data given by the Soviet press revealed that in 1960, the CPR was delinquent by $300 million in her payment to Russia. An agreement then reached stated that the arrears were to be liquidated over a period of five years.[20] Meanwhile, the Soviet Union promised to continue oil shipment to China on which she depended so much for economic growth.

From 1955 on, China's export to Russia exceeded her import from her.[21] This was due to her payment of debt by sending Russia enormous foodstuffs, grain, vegetable oil and pig bristles. Of China's import in 1950, 87 percent were capital goods, and 12.8 were consumer articles. However, by 1958, 93.7 percent pertained to the first category, but only 6.3 percent to the second.[22] Capital materials such as machines, construction tools, heavy equipment, chemicals,

---

[14] Dwight H. Perkins, "China: economy," Americana; international ed, Chicago: Americana Corp., vol. 6, pp. 515-523 at 522, col. 1. David F. Roth and Frank L. Wilson, The Comparative Study of Politics, 2nd ed., Englewood Cliffs, New Jersey: Prentice-Hall, 1980, p. 420.

[15] However, Iu. M. Pavleev, op. cit., p. 370 mentions only $520 million of both loans. This seems to be a mistake.

[16] J.D. Waller, The Government of Communist China, London: Hutchinson University Library, 1970, p. 134.

[17] Dwight H. Perkins, loc. cit., David F. Roth and Frank L. Wilson, loc. cit.

[18] Ibid. (both sources).

[19] Ibid.

[20] Franz H. Michael and George E. Taylor, op. cit., p. 502.

[21] Harold Hinton, An introduction to Chinese politics, 2nd ed., New York: Holt, Rinehart and Winston, 1978, p. 251; Peter S.H. Tang and Joan M. Maloney, Communist China: the Domestic Scene, 1949-1967, South Orange, New Jersey: Seton Hall University Press, 1967, p. 364.

[22] Peter S.H. Tang and Joan M. Maloney, loc. cit.

and various raw stuffs were the backbone of China's first and second 5-Year Plans (1953-1962). Besides the Soviet Union, other countries also did some trading with Beijing.[23] Counting together all the nations of the East Bloc, one source reports that in 1954, their business with the CPR was 74 percent of that country's total with all foreigners.[24] Another source says that in 1955 it ascended to 82 percent.[25] Still another publication suggests, by taking a longer stretch of time into account, that for the first decade (1949-1959) about two-thirds of CPR's trade was with communist regimes, and one-third about equally halved between developing and advanced non-communist nations other than the US.[26] The latter country, as stated earlier, had severed trade with Beijing in 1950. The following table tells of the volume (in million dollars) of the top ten Chinese partners.[27]

```
Russia......................................2,054
East Germany...............................221
Hong Kong...................................201
Czechoslovakia.............................195
West Germany...............................191
UK...........................................121
Indonesia...................................111
Poland.......................................99
Malaysia & Singapore.......................88
Hungary......................................84
```

The total is $3,164 million. In the same year (1959), China's entire trade was worth $4,420 million.[28] Thus, the Soviet Union shared about 45 percent of it.[29] All the other countries, that is, those not in the top ten, had done only $1,256 million business with the CPR, that is 28 percent of the total.

"The year 1959 had marked a critical juncture for communist China's foreign trade policy," said one book.[30] As a result of the failure of the commune experiment and the bad harvest of that year, Beijing was impelled to reassess its policy. The crash program of heavy industry came to yield way to agriculture and manufacture of light goods. It is clear that the Soviet Union model was receding; and China was determined to cut back many ambitious constructions. The

[23] Feng-hwa Mah, "The first Five-Year Plan and its international aspects," *International Economics of Communist China*, edited by C.F. Remer, pp. 31-117 at 58-59.

[24] Economic intelligent unit, *op. cit.*, col. 1.

[25] Giovanni Breski, "China and Western Europe," *Asian Survey*, October 1972, p. 824.

[26] Harold Hinton, *loc. cit.*

[27] James Townsend, *Politics in China*, 2nd ed., Boston: Little, Brown, 1980, p. 370 where he cited Alexander Eckstein, *Communist China's Economic Growth and Foreign trade*, New York: McGraw-Hill, 1966, pp. 94, 280-285, 291.

[28] James Townsend, *Politics in China*, p. 368.

[29] Harold Hinton, *loc. cit.*

[30] Peter S.H. Tang and Joan M. Maloney, *op. cit.*, p. 410.

equipment which the USSR had heretofore provided was no longer appreciated, even if available. This new economic strategy reflected in the trade pattern with Russia. Starting from 1961, not only did the volume nose-dive, but also the composition underwent a transformation: less and less machinery southbound (to China) but more and more technical crops northbound (to USSR). The year 1961 saw a sharp deterioration of their commercial accord. Russia's exports to China were only 38.1 percent of the 1959 level (or 45 percent of the 1960 figure), and imports from China lowered to 49.6 percent of the 1959 record.[31]

Apropos of commodities, the Soviet Union sent the CPR in 1961 a ridiculous number of tractors (33) in return for an equally ridiculous amount of rice (2,300 tons). From 1961 onward, the Chinese found themselves in desperate need of foodstuffs. During that year, the CPR bought 6.5 million tons of grain from the West. In the early sixties, the People's Republic began to build up cash reserve through the sale of food coupons to overseas Chinese who had needy relatives in China. In Hong Kong and Macao, they could buy the over-priced coupons and mail them to such relatives. As regards trade with the Soviet Union, it fell by 25 percent in 1961-1962.[32] At this time, Beijing was fairly firm to steer away from the Russian direction. Looking around her, she found only Japan a hopeful and capable partner. There came the turning point of the CPR's trade, and the leaning on the Soviet Union was about over. Lying ahead was a fresh outlook of business relation with the capitalists whom the Beijing media was previously so abusive of but who were to be instrumental in helping modernize the Chinese economy in the future.

Period of transition, 1961-1970

This decade witnessed the passing from the exclusive trade with Russia to one with bourgeois countries. In the early sixties the CPR may be likened to a man who just separated from a long-time companion but who had not found a substitute friend. However, it was quite determined to face the new challenge by moving ahead, remodeling the economy and looking for partners. Such an orientation, maintained by overwhelming majority of the Beijing leaders, was in conflict however with the revolutionary psyche of Mao Zedong. His was to keep China apart from pollution, as it were, by the revisionists and imperialists. So long as the tough Mao and the moderates could not see eye to eye on the course China must take, her trading course and overall diplomacy were bound to remain uncertain. It is natural that no country would consider it safe to engage in commerce with a regime whose ruling elite were badly divided. It was thus difficult, if not impossible, for China to acquire help from abroad. First deserting the USSR and her satellites and then cooking

[31] *Ibid.*, p. 411.

[32] *Ibid.*, p. 412.

in the Cultural-Revolution stew for a couple of years, China was not able to carry on a thriving business with others. Whatever trade there existed was limited in scope and with only a few countries. Let us in the following pages summarize the situation of this transition period.

In the eighteen years after the advent of power of the communists, they received less than $1 billion in economic aid, by far the most from the USSR. By comparison, India obtained approximately the same amount annually in the same stretch of time. "China, therefore, more than any other underdeveloped nation, has had to rely on its own limited resources" in international commerce according to Dwight H. Perkins.[33] From 1949 to 1969, the CPR's trade reached about $4 billion per year and for the first decade nearly two-thirds of it were with the communist states. Although Soviet loans were no longer available after 1965, the CPR kept on trading with that country. With the dispute between the two nations erupting into the open in 1960, China almost rushed into repayment of her debt to the Soviets, once the "elder brothers." After 1965, Beijing contracted no further long-term external obligation with any country until the whopping $7 billion loans from 18 French bankers signed on May 9, 1979.[34] China's main source of hard currency exchange was (and is) derived from Hong Kong trade.[35] This is because the CPR bought so little there but that colony paid it several million dollars a year for food and water alone. This single exception apart, China was very much handicapped in her total trade balance. In the words of one writer, "this means that the rate of saving and taxation has continued to be high. The burden has further increased by China's going-it-alone foreign policy which necessitated large military expenditures."[36] The said saving derived from the peasants whose life was necessarily made hard by this onus and by the meager investment pumped into the rural economy.

After the Soviet trade fell sharply in 1970, Japan stepped in.[37] In fact, this was not unexpected. Almost from the moment the communists came to power, the Japanese trade started.[38] From a humble beginning, it kept growing ever since. By 1958, the Japanese export to the CPR reached $41 million and import $68.9 million.[39] The lack of formal diplomacy, however, proved very inconvenient, since all dealings were between the Beijing Government and private concerns of Japan. An incident took place in May, 1958 which involved the removal of the CPR flag by anti-communists from the Chinese trade exhibit in Tokyo. It resulted in the cooling off of the commercial

[33] Dwight H. Perkins, *loc. cit.*

[34] *Facts on File*, May 18, 1979, p. 370, G2.

[35] Harold Hinton, *op. cit.*, p. 252.

[36] Dwight H. Perkins, *op. cit.*, p. 522, col. 1.

[37] Harold Hinton, *loc. cit.*

[38] Alexander Eckstein, *Communist China's Economic Growth and Foreign Trade, Implication for U.S. Policy*, 1st ed., New York: McGraw-Hill, 1966, pp. 96, 97, 101.

[39] Peter S.H. Tang and Joan M. Maloney, *op. cit.*, p. 412, note 16.

relation. In 1961, after the exodus of the Soviet technicians from China, Japan's businessmen and the Chinese officials renewed contacts. An agreement was quickly arrived at, with the Japanese side headed by none other than Tatsunosuke Takasaki, one of the ruling Liberal Democrats and a former Minister of Industry.[40] It called for a trade volume of $450 million over a five year period, and China was to get the much-needed machines and fertilizers. The year 1962 saw the first sign of rejuvenation of China's trade which recorded the highest balance of $375 million. It was to be surpassed only by the 1976 balance of $945 million.[41] As agricultural and industrial produce scored in 1963 an increase of 3 and 5 percent respectively, the CPR was able to augment its trade by about 5 percent with a cash value of $2.9 billion. The sum included $865 million worth of import from non-communist quarters and the purchase of $5.7 million worth of grain. In the meantime, trade with the East accounted for about 43 percent of the CPR's total.[42]

In 1964, the CPR continued to improve her trade position. During the first six months, for example, it shipped $137 million worth of goods to Japan and imported $123 million from her. As said before, China's cash surplus was mostly from Hong Kong which was literally at her mercy, depending as it is on that country for vital necessities of daily life. In order to obtain foreign exchange, such Chinese goods as animal products and textiles were sold below the world price. In the mid-1960's, it stepped up exporting of these; and the CPR's outlets in Hong Kong were increased from a dozen to 31.[43] Trade balance went down from 1963 to 1964 by $99 million.[44] It continued to slide, largely due to the massive buying of grain. In 1965 and subsequent years, China's shopping list included such things as artificial fiber from Italy and copper from Chile. The 1965 export to non-communist states was about $880 million and import $825 million,[45] and during the year Beijing's trade with fellow-socialist nations dropped to 30 percent of the total. It was further down to just over 20 percent by 1970.[46] In 1966, CPR's transaction with non-communist governments increased 20 percent over the previous year.[47] Japan led them all.[48] One should not think that the CPR was

[40] *Ibid.*, pp. 412-413.

[41] James Townsend, *Politics in China*, pp. 368, 369.

[42] "Japan-China trade, 800 million customers," *The economist*, 244 (September 30, 1972), p. 91; "Japan, credit to China," 214 (January 23, 1965), pp. 162ff.

[43] Peter S.H. Tang and Joan M. Maloney, *op. cit.*, p. 314.

[44] James Townsend, *Politics in China*, p. 368.

[45] Peter S.H. Tang and Joan M. Maloney, *op. cit.*, pp. 413-414.

[46] Economic intelligent unit, *op. cit.*, p. 280, col. 1.

[47] Peter S.H. Tang and Joan M. Maloney, *op. cit.*, p. 414.

[48] Dwight H. Perkins, *op. cit.*, p. 522, col. 1.

a big partner. After a decade of fairly brisk activity, Beijing's trade in 1971 totaled only $4.5 billion which was about two-thirds that of Hong Kong.[49] From 1960 to 1969, the CPR put considerable stress on the earning of a surplus which was estimated at around $1 billion.[50]

Summarizing the trade situation of the ten years under review, we reproduce below four tables from the study of the Central Intelligence Agency.[51]

Table I: the total trade (million dollars)

	total	export	import	balance
1961	3,015	1,525	1,490	35
1962	2,675	1,525	1,150	375
1963	2,770	1,570	1,200	370
1964	3,220	1,750	1,470	280
1965	3,880	2,035	1,845	190
1966	4,245	2,210	2,035	175
1967	3,895	1,945	1,950	-5
1968	3,765	1,945	1,820	125
1969	3,860	2,030	1,830	200
1970	4,290	2,050	2,240	-190

This table tells of a) the slowness of export from one year to another, the rate averaging barely 10 percent; b) the irregular trend of import and export which we found closely correlated to the harvest. The good crops of 1963 and 1964 raised export for the next two years. c) The disaster of the Cultural Revolution is manifested in the deficit of $5 million and the 1970 imbalance was caused by the import of grain which was by far and away the highest before 1973. Witness the statistics below.

Table II: China's grain import
(million tons)

1966	5.6
1967	4.2
1968	4.4
1969	3.8
1970	4.6
1971	3.0
1972	4.8
1973	6.4
1974	7.8
1975	6.2
1976	6.2
1977	8.0

[49] Economic intelligent unit, *loc. cit.*

[50] *Ibid.*

[51] The four tables are made by the Central Intelligence Agency, reproduced in James Townsend, *Politics in China*, pp. 368-369.

d) The accummulated balance as shown in Table I was $1,745 million for 1961-1969. Since the 1960 deficit (Townsend, p. 369) was $70 million, the 1960-1969 balance has to be $1,675 million (not $1 billion as asserted by the CIA, see preceding paragraph).

Table III: trade with communist nations (million dollars)

	total	export	import	balance
1961	1,685*	965	715	250
1962	1,410*	915	490	425
1963	1,250	820	430	390
1964	1,100	710	390	320
1965	1,165	650	515	135
1966	1,090	585	505	80
1967	830	485	345	140
1968	840	500	340	160
1969	785	490	295	195
1970	860	480	380	100

* The 1961 total should be 1,680, and the 1962 total 1,405. There must have been errors somewhere.

Table IV: trade with non-communist nations (million dollars)

	total	export	import	balance
1961	1,335	560	775	-215
1962	1,265	605	660	-55
1963	1,525	755	770	-15
1964	2,120	1,040	1,080	-40
1965	2,715	1,385	1,330	55
1966	3,155	1,625	1,530	95
1967	3,065	1,460	1,605	-145
1968	2,925	1,445	1,480	-35
1969	3,075	1,540	1,535	5
1970	3,430	1,570	1,860	-290

Several points are worth noting. There is the crescendo of the non-communist and the decrescendo of the communist trade. As a matter of fact, the diminishing rate is more rapid than the increasing rate. Next, China's East trade was down by 12 percent in 1970 ($860 million) as compared with 1951 ($980 million). There was a slight upward trend after 1970 (see section on export below). In that year, it is important to observe, Russia and China concluded a trade agreement,[52] which raised the yearly value to over 100 million rubles (up to 40 million in 1969). The figure in the parenthesis was the lowest, but the first figure (100 million rubles) was far below the two billion plus level reached a decade earlier.[53] Third, all but three years (1965, 1966, 1969), ended in red letter. The entire deficit added up to $795 million. In order to retire them, the CPR had to build up cash reserve

[52] Harold Hinton, op. cit., p. 301.

[53] Thomas W. Robinson, "The view from Beijing: China's politics towards the United States, the Soviet Union and Japan," Pacific Affairs, fall 1972, p. 346.

by exporting all sparable (mostly unprocessed) materials which she really could not spare.[54] As one author points out, communist China has used trade as a form of foreign aid to serve its political ends, and such aid went to North Vietnam, Nepal, Kampuchea and Egypt. This activity was to continue for many more years. It is only after 1976 that Beijing began to show indifference toward national liberation wars, with the exception of the PLO. From 1981, Beijing would not be interested in providing arms for this organization, although in 1982, there is a modification of this attitude.

What countries were the big trading partners at the close of the decade under consideration? Among the Eastern nations, they were Romania, East Germany, Poland, Czechoslovakia and the USSR.[55] Japan headed the developed countries, followed by West Germany, UK, France, Italy and the Netherlands. The Japanese increased their sale to the Chinese by 75 percent between 1968 and 1970.[56] Standing out in the developing systems was Hong Kong. The table below is drawn from the OECD and national trade statistics for 1970.[57]

A developed nations	export to China	import from China
Japan	$568.9 million	253.8
West Germany	167.2	84.4
UK	107.0	80.5
France	80.7	69.9
Italy	57.0	63.1
Netherlands	21.9	26.7
B developing nations		
Hong Kong	10.6	467.0
Singapore	22.7	125.9
Pakistan	39.3	27.8
Sri Lanka	42.3	48.6
Egypt	22.6	16.2
Sudan	17.3	11.6
Morocco	7.2	11.0
C communist nations		
Romania	71.8	62.0
East Germany	42.0	35.7
Soviet Union	24.9	21.7

[54] Dwight H. Perkins, *loc. cit.*

[55] Economic intelligent unit, *loc. cit.*

[56] *Ibid.*

[57] *Ibid.*

It is interesting to see that the Soviet trade went down from as high as $2,054 million to $46.6 million (24.9 plus 21.7).[58] What a drop! The USSR and the CPR were unimportant to each other as traders.[59] The independence-minded Romania came to assume the role of a leading partner from the East. Probably it is because Moscow has exercised less influence over the Bucharest regime than over other satellites. Yet, East Germany is known to be the most loyal of the Kremlin allies and her place, next to Romania, may be explained by the fact that her economic and industrial pattern suited the CPR's needs nicely.

The US trade

Up to this point, we have concerned ourselves primarily with the development which is historical. From now, we shall focus on the most recent situation. First take up the US. An endeavor will be made here to examine the events leading to the opening of the commercial door of Cathay, to point out the difficulties attendant on such trade and to appraise the record. In the West's economic relation with Beijing, the US was a later comer. Informally the two countries kept on talking to each other, first in Geneva and then in Warsaw, although trade was severed by the US soon after the outbreak of the Korean war. When in the sixties the Europeans and Japanese did a pretty good business with the CPR, the US held aloof. It was not until November 22, 1972 that an about-face was executed by President Nixon with his lift of the government restriction on American planes and ships bound for China's mainland.[60] From then on, US industrial and farming interest groups became excited about the China market. Nixon's visit to Beijing greatly enhanced its future.[61] In September 1972, Washington announced the approval of the first sale of American wheat to China in 22 years.[62] It was a deal of 900,000 tons,[63] second only to Canada's 3.9 million tons China purchased in that year. In 1973 and 1974, the CPR acquired most of its grain from the US.[64] Trailing behind were, in descending order, Canada, Australia and Argentina. The next purchase of US grain took place in 1976. This time it was 3.9 million tons.[65] In monetary terms, Sino-American trade exceeded $500 million in mid-1973.[66] It climbed to nearly $1 billion

[58] The figure of $50 million was given in a reference book *Countries of the World,* Toronto: Coles Pub. Co., 1980, Chinese section, p. 8.

[59] Harold Hinton, *op. cit.,* p. 301 where he says that Sino-Soviet trade was negligible.

[60] *Encyclopedia Yearbook,* 1973, pp. 147-154 at 153, col. 1.

[61] Jan S. Prybyla, "The China trade," *Current History,* no. 373 (September 1972), pp. 109-113ff.

[62] *Encyclopedia Yearbook,* 1973, *loc. cit.*

[63] James Townsend, *Politics in China,* p. 369.

[64] *Ibid.*

[65] *Encyclopedia Yearbook,* 1979, p. 157, col. 1.

[66] *Ibid.*

the following year.[67] The principal item was, of course, grain. From 1974 on, there set in a setback. The year 1975 saw the Chinese cancellation of an order of 980,000 tons of grain. The reasons were not officially given either in Beijing or Washington. Probably the cancellation was used as a weapon to force the Ford Administration to recognize Beijing as the legal regime of China. Some analysts have also speculated the CPR's shortage of foreign exchange. There were other explanations like the better harvest of 1975 and the discovery of smut in the grain arriving from the US.[68]

As seen above, grain was the main and very lucrative article in the US dealings with China, but the latter country also obtained fertilizers, cotton and tobacco from it.[69] These items, however, were negligible. The non-grain dealers must, therefore, have felt that the refusal to recognize Beijing by Washington had thwarted the unfolding of better and broader intercourse with the CPR. With US economy in a slump in the aftereffect of the worldwide oil crisis, the China trade proved quite attractive, particularly to such sectors as heavy machinery, aeronautics and petro-chemical industry. As described by one source, China was deemed a fresh market.[70] Some of the biggest beneficiaries of this bonanza were the suppliers to the sectors worst hit by over-capacity at home and drowsy sales overseas, i.e., steel, chemicals, engineering stuffs and shipbuilding. Indeed, the Carter Administration's move to normalize its relation with Beijing was seen in many quarters as animated by pressure groups in the US. Asahi Shimbun of Japan wrote that "it is . . . surmised that there was prodding from American businessmen whose envy grew as they watched the development of Japan's and Western Europe's economic exchanges of China."[71] This point seems well taken.

In October and November 1978, Beijing initialed the most contracts up to that time (and at all times, as it turned out) with non-American companies. At that very moment, the behind-the-scenes parley leading to Carter's announcement of normalization went into the highest gear. Carter and company must have felt that before long China would have nothing left to be signed up with US firms. They decided, therefore, to act quickly, hoping to glean some crumblings. Unfortunately for them, by the time Commerce Secretary Juanita Kreps visited the Beijing hierarchy (May 1979), the latter had already quit granting contracts. In fact, it was in the process of beating a drum of retreat called by its mouthpiece "one step back, two steps forward."[72] Foreign Trade Minister Li Qiang told Kreps on May 9th

---

[67] World Almanac, 1980, p. 525, col. 2.

[68] Encyclopedia Yearbook, 1976, p. 156, col. 1.

[69] Ibid., 1974, p. 174, col. 1.

[70] The economist, October 14, 1978, p. 114, col. 4.

[71] Davis Lewis, "China and West sharing the China market," New Leader, June 4, 1979, pp. 10-12 at 10, col. 3.

[72] Beijing Review, July 21, 1980, p. 15.

that after his government re-examined the trade policy it had already ordered a halt.[73] It is little short of sarcasm that that very day saw the biggest credit deal that government ever signed with any foreigner: a $7 billion loan from 18 French bankers, to be drawn within five years.[74] Such a nice coincidence (Krep's visit and the loan) curiously escapes the attention of Western press.

The year of decision on normalization kept the Carter Administration very busy. "What a cornucopia Cathay was!" it must have thought. From the Americans she would not only get grain, but a thousand other things as well. Before the year was over, no less than seven VIP's flew to Beijing, including the second man of the US Government, the Vice-President. They were excited no doubt both by official sanguineness and personal curiosity, more the latter perchance. Leading the septet was Treasury Secretary Michael Blumenthal. At the so-called "people's hall" in the capital, he initialed on March 1, a draft agreement to settle the claims on the blocked assets pending since 1949. China would pay 41¢ on the dollar to American individuals and companies who demanded more than $196 million from the Chinese Reds for property expropriated by them when they assumed power in the just-mentioned year. This settlement capped four days of bargaining. In all, China promised to pay $80.5 million in cash to the US over the next five years (before October 1, 1984). The first payment was to be $30 million due on October 1, 1979. The balance was forthcoming in five installments of $10.1 million each.[75] The draft agreement was subsequently initialed on May 11 by Commerce Secretary Juanita Kreps,[76] the second VIP to go to China.

She spent two weeks there starting from May 7. After intensive talks between her and the Beijing authorities, a trade agreement was developed. It was initialed by the Foreign Trade Minister Li Qiang in the capital but done by her while she visited Guangzhou on May 14.[77] This was only a draft to be finalized and signed later. The signing was delayed, however, reportedly because Carter contemplated of reaching a similar deal with the USSR in the hope of concluding both at the same time. He had maintained all along that he would treat equally the two communist countries. American law barred most-favored-nation status to nations which did not allow free emigration; and progress on the Russian treaty was stalled by a refusal of the Soviets to offer assurances on the emigration question, but the Chinese Government had no objection to free emigration. A Washington official was quoted as saying that the "China agreement

---

[73] Facts on File, July 13, 1979, p. 423, C2.

[74] Ibid., May 8, 1979, p. 370, G2.

[75] New York Times, March 1 and 2, 1979, pp. 8 and 1 respectively. See also Statesman's Yearbook, 1981-1982, p. 347, US unblocked $80.5 million of Chinese assets.

[76] Lewis Young, op. cit., col. 1.

[77] Facts on File, May 18, 1979, p. 370, A1.

is going forward because it's ready, and there is no reason to penalize the Chinese because of the Russians."[78] On July 7, the agreement was signed in Beijing by Ambassador Leonard Woodcock and the aforesaid Li Qiang. The new tariffs set by the instrument lowered the average impost on Chinese goods to 5.7% of their value from the average of 34%.[79] The accord also contained provisions allowing the US companies to maintain offices in China[80] and afforded patent, trademark and copyright safeguard. On January 24, 1981, the deal was approved in the Congress: House by 294 to 88, Senate by 74 to 8.[81]

The third, fourth and fifth VIP's visiting the CPR were Energy Secretary James Schlesinger, Special Trade Representative Robert Strauss and Agriculture Secretary Bob Bergland. The first-named declared in the Chinese capital that the CPR agreed on several cooperative energy projects.[82] However, his two colleagues attained nothing tangible. The sixth VIP was Vice-President Walter Mondale. He reciprocated Deng Xiaoping's visit to the US, arriving at Beijing on August 25, 1979. After "extremely productive and friendly" talks with Hua Guofeng and Deng Xiaoping, he signed an accord on the details of the cultural exchange program and a protocol on hydropower projects that would involve as much as $2 billion in credit over five years.[83] The seventh VIP was Secretary of Health, Education and Welfare Joseph Califano. He signed nothing, however. It seems that J. Carter dispatched him to Beijing largely for the sake of watering down the mercantile character of all the previous missions.

Turning to the actual trading, most was done after the Carter Administration plunged into the China business. America had gained something, but it was not impressive. In 1978, several months before the normalization, David Rockefeller called a Chase Manhattan stockholders' meeting in Asia for the first time in its history. Then he deputed Chase president Willard Butcher to Beijing.[84] His was to talk the Beijing oligarchy into borrowing from that financial empire. Nothing developed, however. It must have been a shock to the Chase officials that in May 1979, Beijing announced its big loan from the French (see above). In November 1978, the CPR awarded a contract of $500 million to the Pan American Airways to build and manage an array of hotels in Beijing, Shanghai and Tianjin; and it made an agreement

[78] Ibid., July 13, 1979, p. 425, D2.

[79] Ibid.

[80] Lewis Young, op. cit., p. 132, col. 2.

[81] Facts on file, January 25, 1980, p. 46 E2. However, Hammond, 1982, p. 549, col. 1 mentions February 1, 1980.

[82] Encyclopedia Yearbook, 1979, p. 156, col. 2.

[83] Britannica Book of the Year, 1980, p. 249, col. 1.

[84] David Lewis, op. cit., p. 11, col. 1.

with the Coastal States Corporation to sell it 3,600,000 barrels of crude oil.[85] In December 1978, the Coca-Cola Company disclosed that it obtained the sales franchise in the CPR from January 1, 1979.[86] This drink became the first American product to be sold in China since 1949. In the same month, five US firms (Union, Exxon, Pennzoil, Gulf, Phillip) flew their representatives to the CPR to discuss the exploration of her offshore oil deposit, but came back with no contract.[87]

All the above were a pale image of the multi-billion dollar traffic done with the Japanese and West Europeans in the last few months of 1978 (see below). Statistics show that the 1978 Sino-American trade totaled a mere $1.2 billion,[88] less than $2 million estimated by US officials,[89] but $2 million above the 1973 and 1974 level.[90] By the end of China's (now abandoned) 10 year plan (1985), so goes an estimate, the trade figure may be between $10 billion and $12 billion, all depending on the Chinese ability to pay for the imports with hard currency. The currency, in turn, is to be raised through exports or outright borrowing.[91] Christopher H. Phillips, president of the National Council for US-China Trade, a quasi-government organization, maintained that in 1978 "US companies accounted for only six percent of China's worldwide trade. By 1985, the US share will roughly double that figure to between ten and twelve percent."[92] Statistics tell that the US-China trade was up at least three times from 1976 to 1978.[93] Of course, America enjoys ten to one advantage in the balance, simply because of China's large import of grain, cotton, corn and soybean from there.[94]

Sino-American trade flourished beginning in the mid-70's (see also next section). Bulking particularly large is China's shipment of clothing stuffs and textiles to US and her shipment of grain from it. Surveys show that between January and November 1982, China sold $825 million worth of textiles to America, that is, up 30 percent from 1981. This makes the People's Republic the fourth biggest textile supplier to that country, trailing not far behind Taiwan, Hong Kong and South Korea. However, unlike these countries which are willing to limit the

[85] *Encyclopedia Yearbook*, 1979, p. 156, col. 2.

[86] *Ibid.*, p. 157, col. 1.

[87] *Ibid.*, p. 156, col. 1.

[88] "A new trade pact with China," *Newsweek*, May 28, 1979, p. 72.

[89] *Hammond*, 1980, p. 547, col. 1.

[90] For 1974 figure, see *World Almanac*, 1980, p. 525, col. 2; for 1973 figure, see *Encyclopedia Yearbook*, 1974, p. 174, col. 1.

[91] Newsweek, *loc. cit.*

[92] Lewis Young, *op. cit.*, p. 133, col. 1.

[93] In 1976 it was $351 million, in 1977, $390 million, *State Department Bulletin*, March 1979, p. 18 (table). The 1978 figure, as cited in the text of this source, was $1.2 billion.

[94] *Encyclopedia Yearbook*, 1975, p. 163, col. 2. *Beijing review*, January 24, 1983, p. 10, col. 1.

growth rate of their textile shipments to one percent, the CPR has refused to follow suit. It contended that because it has run an annual trade deficit of $600 million with America, it should be entitled to a growth rate of 6 percent. The US textile industry objected to the Chinese position.[95] Washington requested Beijing to increase the number of restricted items to at least 28 categories. "The Chinese side," alleges a communist press, "made a major concession by agreeing to discuss expanding the coverage from 21 categories to 28."[96] But this did not satisfy the US negotiators, the press regrets. The Sino-US textile treaty lasted from January 1, 1980 to December 31, 1982. With a view to ironing out the differences, the two governments held four rounds of talk, the fourth round coming to a standstill on January 13, 1983. As a result, the US put a ceiling on 32 textile articles from the CPR, 14 of which, according to the Chinese, "were already limited through past agreement. The other 18 are newly restricted."[97] Quotas on the categories restricted by past agreement were reduced by nearly 30 percent through "unilateral" US action. And quotas on the major categories of Chinese textiles were cut by as much as 45 percent. In the newly affected items, the quantity set by the US was 16 percent lower than the present level of Chinese export. Following the US order of January 13, the CPR stopped, on January 19, any new contract to import cotton, chemical fibers or soybeans from the US and reduced its planned intake of the US agricultural produce this year. This determination was announced by Shen Jueren, director of the foreign trade and administration under the Ministry of Foreign Economic Relations and Trade.[98] The stalemate remained until July 30, 1983 when a compromise was reached in Geneva.

Import and the balance situation

It is interesting to note that the CPR imported the same sort of things like service, technology, factory plans as well as the tangible articles like machines in the seventies as in the fifties. (But from 1979, the pattern differed again, see Chapter XII, section on science and art). When the communists seized power in China, they regarded it vital to the survival of their regime to build up heavy industry and armament. To this end, they shipped in all kinds of metal and steel products. Due to the lack of native cadres to operate them, over 13,000 Russians and east Europeans were hired as guest workers. They continued working there until July 1960 when all but a few were withdrawn. During these early years, imports consisted of such things as weapons, naval vessels and military planes all made in the USSR.

[95] *Time*, January 23, 1983, p. 43, col. 3.

[96] *Beijing review*, January 24, 1983, p. 10, col. 3.

[97] *Ibid.*, January 31, 1983, p. 9, col. 3.

[98] *Ibid.*

There were no consumer items whatsoever. The Sino-Soviet quarrel from 1960 to 1964 and the subsequent Cultural Revolution stopped heavy stuffs coming from the USSR, but soon these came from Japan and Western Europe. The pattern of import is shown below:[99]

	1957	1965	1970	1975	1976
Food, drink, tobacco	25%	25%	16%	13%	10%
Raw materials, chemicals	35	30	32	25	25
Manufactured goods	30	45	52	62	65
Total	100	100	100	100	100

The table indicates that there is a closer balance among the three broad items for 1965, 1970 and 1975 than for 1957 and 1976. In the latter two years, there is a wider divergency between foodstuffs and manufactures.

During the past several years, the imports and their volumes are seen in three reports. (A) In 1976 industrial supplies made for 59 percent, capital goods 31 percent, foodstuffs 9 percent, and consumer merchandise 1 percent.[100] (B) Two years later, foodstuffs constituted 17 percent, primary commodities 43 percent, machinery and transport 18 percent, and manufactures 22 percent.[101] (C) In 1983, as revealed by none other than Chen Muhua, Minister of Foreign Economic Relations and Trade, "the imports of technology and equipment account for 37 percent, industrial raw materials 39 percent, materials for farm use 7 percent, market goods 9 percent and other items 8 percent."[102] The reader's attention should be drawn firstly to the overwhelming volume of machines. They are vital to the goal of modernization. Secondly, food things constituted a big portion of import in 1976 and 1978, but it is definitely down in 1983 (we subsume this item in "market goods" or "other items.") It is not our suggestion that in absolute quantity the import of these is declining. In fact it is on the increase. (See chapter on agriculture). The truth is rather that non-food items come to have a greater proportion in trade. Thirdly, consumer articles comprise a meager one percent in 1976. Both the 1978 and 1983 reports do not mention them. Judging by the admitted "drastic cut in the import of consumer goods," to use the expression of Chen Muhua, they must have been less than one percent.[103] Fourthly, all three reports do not indicate weapons. These, one may presume, are placed in such classification as industrial supplies, machines or technology. In the fifties, one may note at this juncture, China imported enormous arms from Russia for which she was known to be heavily indebted. Now that the Soviet Union has suspended

[99] *Europa,* 1979, vol. 2, p. 122.

[100] James Townsend, *Politics in China,* p. 371.

[101] *Europa,* 1982, vol. 2, p. 120.

[102] *Beijing review,* February 7, 1983, p. 17, col. 3.

[103] *Ibid.*

export of these to the CPR, the latter shows keen interest in acquiring them from other quarters. From mid-1981, Washington removed restrictions on China's purchase of US arms and high-technology equipment.[104] The *Business week* reported that NATO's Coordinate Committee on Export Controls was considering from June 1979 whether some prohibited items might be allowed to be sold to China by England, France and the US.[105] Beijing has been endeavoring to buy from the first country the harrier fighters, from the second the mirage planes, anti-tank and anti-aircraft missiles, and from the third all species of arms. The Chinese are in a good position to get these because there is a "worldwide scramble for lucrative China market."[106] Moreover, in the mind of the Western statesmen, Beijing can be a vitally needed military balance against the Soviets. We agree, however, with Alexander Sozhenitzyn that to foster the power of the Beijing autocracy is a dangerous gamble.[107]

With Western Europe, Australia and Japan, the CPR did big business, particularly in 1978, just on the morrow of the Sino-American normalization. The following is a sketchy survey of the import from these bourgeois nations the Chinese communists once scolded so vociferously. In 1972 they bought $25 million worth of Pratt & Whitney engines and spent $159 million for 20 Trident jets from the Hawker-Siddeley group.[108] On October 5, 1973, three years after China and Canada established relations, Zhou Enlai and Pierre Trudeau signed a wheat deal of $1 billion, the shipment to be made in three years beginning in 1974. Canada's trade with the CPR was $300 million in 1973. It further rose until 1977 (see table below). Another wheat contract was entered with Australia. On July 4 that year, the latter country's Wheat Board made the largest sale in history when it initialed a sale of three million tons to China within a year. In November 1976 the CPR acquired 500,000 tons and in March 1977 two million tons of wheat from Australia. The People's Republic had purchased over 11 million tons from the latter since 1976.[109] All these pushed Beijing's trade to just a little over the $1 billion mark.[110]

During 1978, Europeans flocked to Beijing to seek business. The months of October and November saw a "blizzard of signings" of contracts there.[111] West German companies acquired a $4,000 million

[104] *Information Please*, 1982, p. 154, col. 2. *Strategy for peace*, 1982, Muscatline, Iowa: Stanley Foundation, 1982, p. 34.

[105] J. Templeman, "Crumbling controls on trading with communists," *Business Week*, June 18, 1979, p. 75.

[106] *Ibid.*

[107] *Kanada Kurier*, November 5, 1981, p. 5, col. 5.

[108] *Encyclopedia Yearbook*, 1973, p. 153, col. 2.

[109] *Facts on File*, 1977, p. 576, F2.

[110] *State Department Bulletin*, March 1979, p. 18.

[111] Lewis Young, op. cit., p. 132, col. 1. Bernard Klinner "Entwicklung der aussenhandels der VR China," *Wirtschaftsdienst* (Hamburg), 11 (1979), pp. 573-577.

deal to build seven coalfields. British and West German concerns submitted bids for $14,000 million steel complex in Hebei province and French firms were to construct a $12,000 million power station.[112] *The economist* reported the following:[113]

a)   UK's Powell Duffryn and National Coal Board negotiated a deal producing 5 million tons of coal in Datong.

b)   The West German group of Krupp, Demag, Thyssen and Rhurkohle signed a $4.2 million project for five new mines,

c)   The Dowty group, Anderson Strathelyde and Gullick Dobson signed three agreements of $200 million to supply roof supports, cutting machines and conveyors,

d)   UK's Davy Powergas contracted for two oxo-alcohol plants worth $75 million,

e)   The Rolls-Royce got a contract of $158 million to build Spey engines for CPR's aviation industry, and

f)   British Davy's West German subsidiary, Zimmer AG, obtained $16 million for making a polyester plant producing 40,000 tons a year of that item.

In 1979, the biggest deal was the $7 billion loan by the French bankers, to which a reference was made in the preceding section. Thereafter contract signings petered off.

The superior traders are the Japanese.[114] In 1978 they sent more than 10,000 people on business missions to China.[115] On February 26, Beijing and the Japanese initialed a $20 billion deal by which "China undertook to export oil and coal to Japan in exchange for Japanese plants and technology."[116] Nippon Steel and other firms had a $3.2 billion agreement to put up a 10 million ton steel plant near Tangshan which suffered an earthquake on July 28, 1977 killing 800,000. Sumitomo Metal was to erect a seamless pipe plant for $500 million, and Nihon Kihatsuyu (with Marubeni Corporation) contracted a $130 million deal for an ethylene factory. For an artificial tannery, Kuraray was awarded $37 million. An $80 million deal went to Hitachi and Toshiba to produce color TV sets. For glass and cognate things, Asahi Glass obtained $65 million, Dai Nippon Toryo $9 million, Dai Nippon Screen and Nissho-Iwai $11 million, Toyota Motors $10 million in contracts. In addition, we must mention the Japanese cement-plant contract, the Danish technical and consultative services for harbor modernization and scores of European signings to build busses, ships, trains and tourist industries.[117] The latest and also the last big

[112] *Encyclopedia Yearbook*, 1979, p. 157, col. 2.

[113] *The economist*, October 14, 1978, p. 115.

[114] Alexander K. Young, "Japan's trade with China, impact of the Nixon visit," *The World Today*, no. 8 (August 1972), pp. 342-350.

[115] *The economist, op. cit.*, p. 114, col. 1.

[116] *Encyclopedia Yearbook*, 1979, p. 158, col. 1.

[117] *The economist, op. cit.*, p. 115.

deal was one totaling $1 billion entered with Nippon Steel on June 12, 1979 to put out a steel work near Shanghai.[118] Judging by the amount the Beijing authorities were willing to put out, their modernization plan was both firm and earnest, although as to be stated later, the pace has slowed down after 1979.

The next section will examine the export at great length, but let us view the trade balance here. Attention is first directed to that a) between China and non-communist states and b) between her and communist states. Then we go on to present a total picture. The figures for 1971-1976 are drawn from Townsend's book already cited,[119] while those for post-1976 years are garnered from various sources as indicated.

a) with non-communist states (million dollars)

	total	export	import	balance
1971	3,635	1,830	1,805	25
1972	4,645	2,345	2,300	45
1973	8,380	3,960	4,420	-460
1974	11,515	5,140	6,375	-1,235
1975	12,025	5,655	6,370	-715
1976	10,545	5,645	4,900	745

b) with communist states (million dollars)

	total	export	import	balance
1971	1,085	585	500	85
1972	1,275	740	535	205
1973	1,710	1,000	710	290
1974	2,435a	1,430	1,010	420
1975	2,360b	1,370	999	380 [371]
1976	2,340	1,270	1,070	200

a The total comes to be 2,440
b The total comes to be 2,369, and the balance has to be 371.

Looking at the "total" column, we perceive that the annual increase of communist trade was about 5 percent (except 1975) but that of non-communist trade was between 10 and 30 percent (except 1976). The first table's deficit is because China has not much to sell the non-communist partners, but she imported so much, particularly grain, from them. These things are simply not acquirable from fellow-communist systems.

In 1976 and 1979, the top ten trade partners and volumes of business (in million dollars based on partner-country statistics) are as follows:

[118] *Facts on File*, June 19, 1979, p. 484, F3.

[119] James Townsend, *Politics in China*, p. 369.

1976		1979	
3,052	Japan	4,048	Japan
1,620	Hong Kong	1,896	US
950	W. Germany	1,642	W. Germany
571	France	858	Canada
453	Romania	750	Australia
416	USSR	530	Romania
380	Australia	510	UK
351	US	385	Hong Kong
309	Canada	373	France
294	Singapore	365	Malaysia & Singapore

Sources: the 1976 figures from James Townsend, *Politics in China*, p. 370; the 1979 figures from *Europa*, 1982, vol. 2. p. 120.

In 1959, East Germany ranked second among the top ten (see first section of this chapter), but by 1976, she was out, and West Germany came into the table ranking third in that year and in 1979. One may be surprised by the USSR still taking the sixth spot in 1976, but she disappears from the top ten in 1979. As a matter of fact, that year saw her rank 12th behind Italy. Their business with China are $255 million and $285 million respectively.[120] In spite of the ill-feeling between the CPR and Russia, the latter and CPR traded more than the US and CPR in 1976. However, this situation has drastically altered. Now America came to replace Hong Kong as the number two best partner of China. The latter and the USSR concluded a trade deal in April 1982, raising their volume from $219 million in 1981 to $316 million in 1982.[121] The second figure compares with the US-CPR figure of $7,500 million,[122] and CPR-Japan figures of $10,000 million for the same year.[123] On March 10, 1983, Moscow and Beijing initialed a trade agreement, but details are not revealed.[124].

The table below shows the total trade and the exports and imports.

	total	export	import	balance
1971	4,720	2,415	2,305	110a
1972	5,920	3,085	2,835	250
1973	10,090	4,960	5,130	-170
1974	13,950	6,570	7,380	-810
1975	14,385	7,025	7,360	-335
1976	13,300	7,200	6,100	1,100b
1977	14,000	7,700	6,300	1,400c
1978	22,630	10,680	11,950	-1,270d

[120] *Europa*, 1982, vol. 2, p. 120.

[121] *Xinhua daily*, March 1, 1983, p. 13; *Facts on file*, June 18, 1982, p. 443, col. 2.

[122] *Beijing review*, October 4, 1982, p. 12.

[123] *New York times*, February 7, 1982, p. 1, col. 1; however *ibid.*, November 19, 1981, p. 5 mentions $7,200 million.

[124] *Beijing review*, March 21, 1983, p. 10, col. 3.

1979	28,966	13,670	15,296	-1,626e
1980	29,512	14,540	14,972	-432f
1981	32,079	15,717	16,349	-1,572g
1982	38,600	21,600	17,000	4,600h
1983	est 45,600	21,866	23,800	-1,934i

a. From 1971 to 1975, total is derived by adding export and import, James Townsend, *Politics in China*, p. 369.
b. *World almanac*, 1981, p. 525, col. 2.
c. *Statesman's yearbook*, 1979-1980, p. 340.
d. *Britannica book of the year*, 1980, p. 246, col. 1, figure given in yuan. We changed into dollars.
e. *Main documents of the third session of the fifth National People's Congress of the CPR*, p. 19 where figures are given in yuan which we converted into dollars.
f. *Renmin ribao*, January 10, 1981, p. 4 where yuan is given, we changed into dollars.
g. Figures are calculated from a report of Premier Zhao Ziyang, *Beijing review*, December 20, 1982, p. 17, col. 2. However, *ibid.*, November 8, 1982, p. 7, col. 1 stated that the total was $40,400 million, including 20,900 export and 19,500 import. *The China business review* of May-June 1982, p. 57 estimates the total as $43,126 million of which export was 21,560 and import 21,566.
h. Figures are given in US$ by Chen Muhua, Minister of Foreign Economic Relations and Trade, *Beijing review*, February 7, 1983, p. 14, col. 1. Usually such figures are given in yuan.
i. *Ibid.*, January 3, 1983, p. 8, col. 3, figures given in yuan, and we changed into dollars.

Trailing behind the West in technology, the People's Republic cannot be expected to produce things requiring high sophistication. Therefore, her "present export base is narrow and fairly typical of any less developed country: a mixture of commodities plus simple labor-intensive manufactures."[125] Yet these commodities do not necessarily create trade imbalance. The CPR can nevertheless enjoy an edge against her partners, if she sells them enough of raw materials or simple articles. However, China does not do so, as shown in the above table. Even if the CPR is able to outsell her partners in unsophisticated things, it cannot be regarded as an advantage in the long run.

Export

Regarding export, we should first of all notice that the communist regime has entered into large-scale borrowing under the open door policy set in motion by the plenum of the 11th CC in December 1978. As of 1982, that country borrowed $1,630 million in foreign capital for projects of one sort or another, and it absorbed approximately $700 million in foreign capital for government departments and regions and in direct foreign investment. China spent $1,700 million to import technology, $586 million in contracts for projects and labor service co-operation with other countries, and $29 million for production and technological co-operation with foreign firms.[126] Between 1950 and 1980, it is asserted, there was a 12.3 percent average annual increase in the total volume of China's foreign commerce, and in 1981, while the world export was in general decline, the export of the CPR was said to be up by 14.3 percent. Under the Sixth Five-Year Plan, the total import and export in 1985 is set at $51,500 million (for different figures see next section). It represents 51.8 percent above the 1980 figure and an annual average rate of 8.7 percent.

125 *The economist, op. cit.*, p. 115.
126 *Beijing review*, February 7, 1983, p. 14, col. 1.

As of 1979, the following fourteen countries traded with China in appreciable volumes, according to the International Monetary Fund's publication and Soviet information.[127] The figures, in million dollars, are based on partner-country's report.

2,985	Hong Kong
2,664	Japan
594	US
580	Malaysia & Singapore
560	Romania
485	West Germany
310	Italy
297	France
294	UK
229	USSR
166	Australia
143	Canada
90	Pakistan
60	Sri Lanka

We would like to point up the enormous trade deficit of Hong Kong (see preceding section). The CPR imports from it only $385 million, but exports to it $2,985 million. In this connection, one may note that it is through Hong Kong that the CPR earns one third of foreign exchange vital for economic modernization.[128] From Japan the CPR receives one and one half as much as it takes to it: $4,068 million against $2,664 million; and the Soviet trade is in good balance (import from it $255 million and export to it $229 million). A better equation prevails in the Romanian trade (import $530 million and export $560 million). The most unfavorable balance, that is, the anti-pole to the Hong Kong trade is the US trade. China ships from America $1,896 million, but ships to it $594 million.

China is said to hold a bright future of international commerce. According to Chen Muhua, there are several reasons for it.[129] In the first place, the CPR's total exports today are only one percent of the world's total of nearly two million million US dollars. Because the varieties of exports are small, the potential is great. In the second place, the world is experiencing a depression in imports and exports. Even though the supply of capital goods is reduced, the demand for consumer goods is on the increase. "China is well able to export such commodities." In the third place, China's exports of machinery, chemical, industrial and other products occupy a tiny portion of the world's total exports of these things. For example, the Chinese exports of mechanical and electrical products, instruments and meters are only 0.14 percent of the world's exports and chemical industrial

[127] *Europa*, 1982, vol. 2, p. 120.

[128] *New York times*, February 17, 1981, p. 12, col. 3.

[129] *Beijing review*, February 7, 1983, p. 15.

products (not including petroleum) 0.42 percent. Chen Muhua asserts that "we are able to rapidly increase our ability to export these goods." In the fourth and final place, the development of diverse forms of foreign economic activities will inevitably help bring more Chinese products to the international markets. Contracts for foreign projects and labor service cooperation are new undertakings. They will augment the export of building materials, mechanical, electrical and light industrial things.

During the period from 1953 to 1981, the mix of export has shown a downward curve in farm output and an upward curve in light stuffs and heavy products. We take the following table from *Beijing review* of February 7, 1983, p. 15:

year	farm & sideline products in %	heavy products in %	light items
1953	55.7	17.4	26.9
1959	37.6	20.5	41.9
1969	37.4	21.4	41.2
1979	23.1	31.9	45.0
1980	19.0	38.6	42.4
1981	17.6	43.4	39.0

The dwindling of farming products for export is explained by the high demand for these at home. The Chinese can hardly afford to ship them out at all. Yet they are compelled to make some food products for export, and their clients are overseas countrymen who are fond of native stuffs. Besides, the Beijing regime has used grain to win friends. Sizeable quantity of this is given to neighboring nations whose regimes are not overly hostile to the CPR. Among the light products the most profitable are textiles. The Beijing government trebled the sale of these in the US in a single year (1978).[130] Since then China's textile mills have operated under the 3-shift and 24-hour a day system.[131] Thanks to such dedicated endeavour, the People's Republic, as stated above, ranked in 1982 as the fourth largest textile exporter to America. Because Washington limited the import from China on January 13, 1983, the textile future in the US has suffered. On the Canadian market, Chinese textiles are also facing a rollback. Upon the lobbying of the Canadian Textile Industry Association, the Federal Cabinet has authorized trade officials to "seek new cut from China."[132] America, however, lifted the ban in July 1983.

Among the articles of heavy industry is oil, admittedly China's trump card. It accounts for the "largest single source of foreign exchange."[133] This fact attests why China has taken the most

[130] *The economist*, October 14, 1978, p. 115, col. 3.

[131] Wi Min. "1979: more than 7 million people employed," *Beijing review*, February 14, 1980, pp. 13-16 at 16, col. 3.

[132] *The China reporter*, October 1982, p. 20, col. 2.

[133] *Facts on file*, January 8, 1977, p. 2, A1.

vigorous steps to increase its volume.[134] As a foreign press noticed, the preliminary report of a discovery of oil and natural gas along the southern coast of China in 1976 immediately prompted the Beijing authorities to place large-scale orders of drilling equipments from America.[135] This "discovery" is later discounted. The Chinese oil, as known to all, is of low quality. It is taken only by the Japanese and a few other customers.[136] These include the less developed countries like Thailand.[137] The Chinese crude, when brought to Japan, must be refined before being used. Nippon's biggest oil company, Idemitsu Sekiyu, has to build a refinery in northern Kyushu just to process the Chinese stuff.[138] "Early in 1978, they [oil concerns] told the government that they were not eager to take on any more low-grade oil from the People's Republic."[139] The balking held on until the companies came to realize that oil is the only item China has to pay for the import needed for her ambitious modernization. It was said that if the Japanese did not take the Chinese crude, "with the normalization of relations, the US-based multinationals would take."[140] In return for this Chinese crude, the Japanese traded iron and steel which made up 40 percent of the CPR's import from Japan.[141]

The Beijing autocrats are very anxious to develop the offshore oil, according to a Western report, because the onshore production was rapidly declining.[142] Forty foreign firms were invited to the Chinese capital in March 1982 to bid for the drilling of offshore oil deposits.[143] *Xinhua* agency said that contracts would be negotiated immediately, with exploration of 150,000 sq km (58,000 sq miles) area to begin in 1983. The Atlantic Richfield Company signed, on September 19, 1982, an agreement with the CPR to allow it to start drilling for oil off the Chinese coast. Arco became the first US company to gain permission to start oil exploration and development projects in South China Sea (in the north, French and Japanese firms gained the concessions). The agreement gave Arco and its partner in the venture, Santa Fe Minerals, the right to explore for oil in a 9,000 sq km (3,500 sq miles) area south of Hainan Island.[144] The Chinese National

---

[134] *Encyclopedia yearbook*, 1976, pp. 155-156.

[135] *New York times*, May 6, 1978, p. 29, col. 1; p. 33, col. 5.

[136] "How will China alter the Far Eastern market?" *Business week*, March 5, 1979, p. 40, col. 2; *The economist*, October 14, 1978, p. 115, col. 2.

[137] *Encyclopedia yearbook*, 1975, p. 163, col. 2.

[138] Holger Dohman, "Handelvertrag bindet China an Japan," *China aktuell*, 7 (1978), Marzheft, pp. 132-133.

[139] David Lewis, *loc. cit.*

[140] *Ibid.*

[141] Economic intelligent unit, *op. cit.*, p. 279, col. 1.

[142] *Facts on file*, September 24, 1982, p. 710, col. 3.

[143] *Ibid.*, July 12, 1982, p. 477, col. 3.

[144] *Ibid.*, September 24, 1982, p. 711, col. 1.

Offshore Oil Corporation signed in early September 1982 its first joint-venture with the Norwegian Geophysical Company (Geco). The company's officials said the China-Geco Geophysical Company will be a 50-50 cooperation, providing survey services to international oil companies planning to drill off the Chinese coast. They expected it to be the only such company conducting survey work, although other joint ventures are likely to be formed to provide drilling helicopter and other services. The new company has a capital totaling $2.5 million. Drilling is scheduled to commence early 1983. However, oil is unlikely to flow in commercial quantities for at least another five years, according to Western oil sources.[145]

China possesses an estimated coal reserve of 5 trillion tons ranking behind only the US and the Soviet Union. Premier Zhao Ziyang met on November 3, 1982 the Sino-British Trade Council telling them that the Chinese welcomed foreign enterprises' cooperation in exploitation of energy, including the coal resources.[146] It is the Chinese Government's plan to double the coal export to 15 million tons by 1985 according to a report of the English-language *China daily* of Beijing.[147] In that year, the total output is to be 700 million tons.[148] The CPR in 1981 exported 6.6 million tons and in 1982 the figure was 7 million. The volume is about one percent of the country's total output. Poor transportation has hindered coal shipment tremendously. CPR's first deep-water coal harbor at Shijiusuo in Shandong province is scheduled to be operational in 1985. It is written that the port facilities will be able to handle 15 million tons of coal export a year.

The China National Technical Import Corporation will invite joint-venture bids from foreigners on the building of a 600-megawat power station in Yunnan province. The project, Lubuge Hydroelectric Power Station, would cost about $660 million. Construction starts in the first quarter of 1983 and is to be completed in six years. The project, by the description of the just-mentioned *China daily,* has several sections earmarked for foreign bidding. They are: a 9.4 kilometer power tunnel with an inside diameter of 18 meters, a different surge shaft with an upper chamber, two penstocks (or sluice gates) 519 and 583 meters in length, an underground powerhouse, and a tailrace tunnel 345 meters in length. The remainder of the project will be done by domestic contractors.[149] The Beijing authorities have applied for a loan from the World Bank to help finance the undertaking.

China will soon construct its first joint-venture nuclear power plants with Hong Kong's China Light and Power Company to provide the much-needed electricity in Guangdong province.[150] The nuclear

[145] *The China reporter,* October 1982, p. 8.

[146] *Beijing review,* November 15, 1982, p. 8, col. 1.

[147] *The China reporter,* October 1982, p. 7, col. 2.

[148] *Beijing review,* February 28, 1983, p. 11 (table).

[149] *The China reporter,* October 1982, p. 7, col. 3.

[150] *Beijing review,* April 4, 1983, p. 9, cols. 1-2.

power plant will be built some 60 kilometers east of the Shenzhen Special Economic Zone. The Chinese partner in the venture is the Guangdong Electric Company. Power generated will be shared by the province and Hong Kong. Guangdong officials stated that China is negotiating with two European companies to supply the reactors. One was French and the other English. US laws prohibit direct sales of energy plants by US companies to countries such as China that do not permit international on-site inspection of nuclear facilities. Canada is prepared to collaborate with the CPR in developing that country's nuclear energy. The Atomic Energy of Canada officials will be visiting the People's Republic in 1983 to maintain the contacts already established by visits of Chinese nuclear experts to Canada.[151] China was believed to have a total of about 40 nuclear reactors in operation at the end of 1966. We lack latest information on this. There are three agencies: Atomic Energy Institute, Atomic Research Center, Military Scientific Council in this field.[152] Not much is known about them.

What steps are taken to promote trade?

In order to facilitate trade, the Chinese communists have begun modernizing the procedure of business transaction in keeping with foreign practice and ideas. First and foremost, they dispense with the old line of self-reliance which would not fail in leading to economic stagnation. The determination to promote foreign contacts, as ordained by the Preamble of the Constitution, goes a long way toward the modernization drive. Witness the 11,000 (as of mid-1983) students who are really engineers-practitioners dispatched abroad. Ten thousand are in the US.[153] Cadres of trade administration no longer push their pens in Beijing all the time. In droves they set out to see the outside world. From 1978, foreign ministers, trade ministers and special "Chinese delegations are trotting around Australia, Finland, Austria, West Germany and southern Europe shopping for Western know-how."[154] Foreign business people, as stated previously, were pouring in. The most important ones were flown in in Beijing's own jets. There are, for example, the British steel and chemical contractors, Danish harbor experts, German electronics specialists, French shipbuilders, American aircraft salesmen, Nipponese bankers and rollingstock men, and EEC representatives. The climate rapidly warmed up for negotiation and for signing up of concessions.

By the very nature of things, foreign trade fo the CPR is a state monopoly. It is for this reason that the Constitution does not like the Soviet Constitution (Article 10) mention that fact. China's international commerce "is conducted through a number of corporations

[151] *The China reporter*, October 1982, p. 8.

[152] *Europa*, 1982, vol. 2, p. 136.

[153] *New York times*, December 13, 1982, p. 8, col. 2.

[154] *The economist, op. cit.*, p. 114, col. 1.

specializing in broad product groups."[155] No less than twenty-six bodies deal with that trade. All but the ones with astrisks below bear the title "China national," instead of the shopworn "people's." We will let the two words go.[156]

1) arts & crafts import & export corp.
2) cereals, oils & foodstuffs import & export corp.
3) chartering corp.
4) chemicals import & export corp.
5) China coal industry technology & equipment corp.*
6) China export bases development corp.*
7) China Jinshan associated trading corp.*
8) China silk corp.*
9) foreign trade storage corp.
10) foreign trade trasportation corp.
11) guoji shudian (international bookstore)*
12) instruments import & export corp.
13) light industrial products export corp.
14) machinery & equipment import & export corp.
15) machinery import & export corp.
16) metallurgical products import & export corp.
17) metals & minerals import & export corp.
18) native produce & animal byproducts import & export corp.
19) packing import & export corp.
20) Shanghai advertising corp.
21) Shanghai handkerchiefs import & export corp.
22) Shanghai international trust service corp.*
23) Shanghai toy import & export corp.
24) technical import corp.
25) textiles import & export corp.
26) Waiwen shudian (foreign-literature bookstore)*

These twenty-six are operating hundreds of companies in Macao, Hong Kong, all the coastal provinces and the entire Manchuria, but not in Xinjiang or Tibet.[157] There are no less than four superintending or coordinating bodies and two lateral bureaucracies of the trade networks. The four are: 1) Foreign investment control commission, 2) China international trust investment company, 3) China council for the promotion of international trade, 4) Ministry of foreign economic relations and trade. The last-named was formed in March 1952, but from that year to 1982, it was known as Ministry of foreign commerce. The two lateral bureaucracies are: a) General administration for industry and b) All China federation of industry and commerce.[158]

For financial activity, there is the Bank of China taking charge of

[155] Economic intelligent unit, op. cit., pp. 280-281.

[156] Europa, 1982, vol. 2, pp. 134-135; Beijing review, February 14, 1983 backpage.

[157] Zhong guo shou ce, Hong Kong: Da gong bao, 1979, pp. 354-387 lists the branches of companies.

[158] Europa, 1982, vol. 2, p. 135. These two deal with domestic trade.

foreign exchange and settlement. It was established as far back as 1912, the first year of the Republic of China; and in 1949 it went under the control of the CPR. The branches of this bank in many parts of the world receive deposits from traders and arrange international loans.[159] A Beijing publication reported agreements between this bank and the banks of the United Kingdom providing seven separate deposit facilities, totaling $1,200 million.[160] They were signed in London on December 6, 1978. Enabling the UK exporters of capital goods and associated services to finance trade with China, they are said to be the first inter-bank facilities of this kind concluded with the Bank of China supported by an official credit insurance organization. A number of foreign banks are maintaining offices in the CPR: Chartered Bank, Deutsche Bank of Frankfurt, Hong Kong & Shanghai Banking Corporation, Midland Bank Ltd., Overseas Chinese Banking Corporation.[161] Several other overseas Chinese banks also have branches in the People's Republic.[162] Until 1980, China's trade with the non-communist systems was done in pound sterling. Following the devaluation of the latter in 1967, the CPR began to use the French franc. When this also weakened the next year, pound sterling recovered at least some of its previous role. Since then, the US dollar has been used on a broad scale. Meanwhile, the Chinese yuan (*renminbi*) gradually comes into use.[163] In September 1983, the exchange rates were: 1 pound to 3.352 yuan, 1 US dollar to 1.968 yuan, 1 ruble to 1.30 yuan, and 1,000 yen to 7.711 yuan.

According to one estimate, the now abandoned 120 major projects enunciated on February 26, 1978 by Hua Guofeng would cost upwards of $250 billion.[164] The current modernization program costs at least as much. Clearly the CPR is not in a position to provide it except through borrowing; and by the beginning of 1983, as stated above, China borrowed $1,630 million in foreign capital. If the communist government was unwilling to incur a deficit of nearly $1 billion in 1979, its trade would have come to a halt.[165] The Red regime was formerly very reluctant to use the word "borrowing." It preferred the nicer expression of "deferred payment." Now this thinking is changing. One source writes well that the "government in Beijing is gradually getting over its political aversion to calling a spade a spade."[166] The regime has finally acknowledged that "China is now

---

[159] Economic intelligent unit, *op. cit.*, p. 279, col. 2.

[160] *Beijing Review*, December 15, 1978, p. 6, col. 2.

[161] *Europa*, 1982, vol. 2, p. 134.

[162] Economic intelligent unit, *loc. cit.*

[163] *Ibid.*, p. 280, col. 2.

[164] Lewis Young, *op. cit.*, p. 132, col. 1.

[165] *Americana annual*, 1980, p. 170, col. 1.

[166] *The economist*, October 14, 1978, p. 114, col. 4.

beginning to purchase on credit."[167] It has been noted that loan arrangements were made with Japanese and West German banks, and after 1979, French banks, and that the "would-be Western creditors are more keen to see the Chinese get into debt than are the Chinese themselves."[168] In order to implement the modernization, Beijing has to be practical. It did not flinch from what is described as "medium financing" of trade imbalance. China came to pay for higher imports with higher exports, thus eschewing a trade deficit. The most noteworthy fact is that the CPR has entered into a very brisk traffic with the bourgeois governments.

Besides borrowing, or, to use the formerly preferred term, deferred payment, Beijing revives the idea of joint project. During 1950-1954, as seen above, the CPR and the USSR maintained four companies (a proposal of a fifth was declined by China) to develop mineral resources in the region of Xinjiang, and to undertake some commercial activities in Manchuria. The dissolution of such firms was thankful to the nationalistic pride of the Chinese who undoubtedly equated the Russian involvement to colonial exploitation. The present leaders' pragmatism and their lack of capital for modernization has come to induce them to be less sensitive in the matter. Legally, the Preamble of the Constitution gives a green light to the new policy of joint venture in the expression of "mutual benefit" governing relation with other nations.

The policy has taken a definite shape. As things stand now, Beijing allows foreigners to both set up their own plants in China producing consumer items, e.g., the Hitachi and Toshiba TV establishment, and enter into joint contract with the Chinese involving heavy industry, e.g., the Sino-French deep-sea drilling along China's northern coast.[169] In 1978, as said before, five US companies have started negotiation to develop oil resources in the CPR; and in 1982 contracts were signed to develop these on the continental shelf. The Beijing regime has cooperated with Hong Kong to erect plants in China,[170] Hong Kong and Macao to make consumer articles.[171] It is reported that in 1982 Hong Kong financed China's first super highway at the cost of $400 million. It connects the British and Portuguese colonies to Chinese mainland.[172] Now foreign firms are permitted to keep offices in Beijing and they can employ outside managers, engineers and accountants.[173] Of course, the CPR wishes to foster its own industrial capacity and, in the long run, to be as self-sufficient as the capitalist

[167] *Encyclopedia Yearbook*, 1974, p. 174, col. 1.

[168] *The economist*, October 14, 1978, pp. 114-115.

[169] *Renmin ribao*, January 10, 1981, p. 4.

[170] *Business Week*, March 1980, p. 46, col. 2.

[171] *Encyclopedia Yearbook*, 1979, p. 156, col. 2.

[172] *New York times*, May 6, 1982, p. 6, col. 1.

[173] *Americana Annual*, 1980, p. 170, col. 1.

nations with which it now began to trade. Perhaps with this in mind, the regime has lately taken measures to step up its own output of iron ore and establish assembly plants to turn out lorries and aircraft engines, using Chinese-made parts.[174] Welcoming foreigners to invest their money and technology in the People's Republic, the Chinese communists have found it imperative to give them the necessary protection. When the US Commerce Secretary Juanita Kreps visited China in May 1979, she hammered the point home in her talk with Deng Xiaoping, hinting that without a prudent law to safeguard the firms from afar, no investment could be expected. Two months had barely elapsed before the 5th NPC at its second session enacted (July 1, 1979) the Law on Joint Ventures. A major concern of foreign firms operating jointly with the Chinese or individually by themselves has to do with their financial obligations to the government. To regulate them, a tax law was made by the 3rd session of the 5th NPC in September 1980.[175] Most of the provisions were not put into effect until the promulgation of detailed rules of application by the State Council on December 10, 1980, and these were declared in force four days later by the Finance Ministry.[176] In December 1981, the 4th session of the 5th NPC found it necessary to revise all the regulations.[177] More of this in Chapter VI.

The prospect of export appears to be moderately promising, if we give credence to the Chinese plans. According to these, the output of agricultural and industrial goods will be on the increase, as it has always been. Xue Muqiao asserts that during the Sixth Five-Year Plan (1981-1985) China strives for a five percent or higher annual increase, while in the following Plan six percent or higher is anticipated.[178] "After a solid foundation is laid, we will achieve an annual eight percent or higher increase in the 1990's. In this way, it is possible to attain the goal of quadrupling our production targets."[179] By expanding output, the country would have more things for sale. Against this rosy future, the communist leaders design an array of measures to meet the new task. First, commodity mix is to be adjusted in response to the market demand. To do this, market analysis would have to be undertaken, a work which the present research facilities of the Chinese regime do not appear to be able to perform. Second, the highest item of export, oil, will be maintained at the current level until marine oil is exploited. The government has also set great store in the export of non-ferrous metals, metal products and coal. Third, machinery goods, agricultural, sideline and special local stuffs are

[174] *The economist,* October 14, 1978, p. 115, col. 3.

[175] *Globe and Mail,* September 3, 1980, p. 2.

[176] *Renmin ribao,* December 18, 1980, p. 2.

[177] *Ibid.,* November 27, 1981, p. 1.

[178] *Beijing review,* October 4, 1982, p. 16, col. 2.

[179] *Ibid.*

important components in the mix. Particular attention is paid to mechanical stuffs, but presently the export of these accounts for only four percent of the nation's processed output. The Chinese consider these a big export potential.

Fourth, in order to attract buyers, Beijing has to improve the quality of wares. Since raw materials and primary products are China's main things to take out of the country in the year to come, the authorities have thought it extremely important to stress the processing of such materials to make quality goods. Designs and varieties of these are to be improved, as is the packaging technique. The goal is to sell better things at reasonable charges. Fifth, China expects to build production bases and factories which turn out marketable articles. The end of 1982 witnessed the laying out of 24 comprehensive bases and 90 single production bases for export commodities. Ninety-four factories and mines are in operation to manufacture such commodities.[180] It is interesting to note that a study by Douglas Stuart and William Tow finds that Chinese production and sale of strategic minerals to the US and other Atlantic alliance members may provide funds the country needs to begin military modernization.[181] Among the production bases are those which cultivate fresh-water fish and poultry in Guangdong and Fujian provinces and livestock breeding and aquatic products in other provinces. Sixth, the communist regime is maximizing the advantage of the coastal regions where plants are processing imported materials to make things for export. Shanghai, Tianjin and other big cities have a fine industrial foundation, a high level of technology, fast communications and rich experience in commerce. With these assets, they should be able to make optimal use of foreign capital in order to expand their activities.

Seventh, the problem of transport and storage will be tackled, it being realized that timely delivery is vital in trade. When two rival merchandises are of the same quality, the one that arrives promptly is more valuable. The ports of Nantong and Zhanjiagang are accessible to foreign vessels on the Changjiang. Local authorities, it has been urged, be permitted to appropriate their own funds or foreign investment to construct port facilities including wharves so as to facilitate shipment and simplify the procedure. Steps have been taken to enhance the holding capacity by introducing the system of enterprise management. Standardized charges for storage and independent accounting are instituted to encourage a more swift turnover in warehouses. Eighth, China will open new markets, while at the same time consolidating and developing trade linkage with others. Plan is being implemented to join efforts with third world nations to strengthen "South-South" cooperation in order to arrest the irrational and unequal international economic trend.

Ninth, an overhaul of the trade apparatus has been ordered since early 1982. Chen Muhua held a news conference in March 1982 to

---

[180] *Ibid.*, November 9, 1982, p. 7; February 7, 1983, p. 16.

[181] *New York times*, December 27, 1981, p. 9, col. 1.

reassure foreigners that the contemplated reform of her organization (trade ministry) would not impair commercial development. Rather it purported to streamline the transaction of foreign trade.[182] Toward the same goal is the creation of the China Investment Bank, specializing in collecting foreign funds.[183]

Tenth, finally, tourism is to be fostered. This industry seems to be quite hopeful and the regime has left no stone unturned to intensify it. The current open-door line is said to be adopted officially in December 1978.[184] Afterwards each year sees a conference on travel held in the Chinese capital which draws foreign as well as Chinese delegations. The 1983 rendezvous took place from February 28 to March 4. There many papers were read on tourism forecasting its prospects in Asia and the world. An exhibition of 3,000 sq meters familiarized the participants with the historical and scenic areas of China.[185]

The Chinese tourist authorities are carrying on a management reform and instituting an economic responsibility system which would integrate power, duty and profit. All service personnel are to take fresh courses to upgrade their qualifications. Interpreters who are now with the government and students of foreign-language schools are solicited by the tourist agencies. Furthermore, a publicity campaign is staged about the beauties of China. Many liaison groups are being sent to the UN, Japan and West European states to attract tourists. Beijing has been inviting many newsmen to come to China to report about her. Provisions will be arranged for individuals and small groups to tour the Republic for different purposes ranging from honeymoon to recuperation to special studies. The Chinese are welcoming international conferences to be held in the CPR. Rewards are given those who organize the most tours. More urgent than all the foregoing are the measures to improve the sanitation and general conditions of the guest houses and in and around the scenic areas.

By the mid-1980's, China would have hotels with 150,000 rooms.[186] As stated in the section on US trade, the Pan American Airways has been awarded a huge contract to develop tourism in China. In 1978, according to a Chinese source, there were 680,000 visitors, including 120,000 foreigners; and by 1982 the total number went up to 1,220,000, of which 300,000 were foreigners.[187] Among the latter Japanese accounted no less than 127,000.[188] The 1983 estimate is

[182] *Ibid.*, March 17 (IV), 1982, p. 3, col. 1.

[183] *Ibid.*, December 24 (IV), 1981, p. 8, col. 6.

[184] *Beijing review*, February 7, 1983, p. 14, col. 1.

[185] *Ibid.*, December 6, 1982, p. 15.

[186] *Business week, loc. cit.*

[187] *Beijing review*, February 7, 1983, p. 8, col. 1.

[188] *Ibid.*, October 5, 1982, p. 12.

356   GOVERNMENT OF SOCIALIST CHINA

1,300,000 including 400,000 foreigners.[189] In 1980, according to
Western press, tourism brought China $617 million, a rise of 35.6
percent over 1979.[190] This source has told that there were 5,700,000
tourists to China in 1980.[191] The information is obviously an
aberration. There are six principal bodies to develop China travel:
a) General Administration for Travel and Tourism,[192] b) Chinese
People's Institute of Foreign Affairs, c) The Chinese People's
Association for Friendship with Foreign Countries,[193] d) China Council
for Promotion of International Trade,[194] e) International Liaison
Department of the Central Committee of the CCP, f) China
International Travel Service (Lüxingshe). The penultimate draws
people from socialist nations. Of the six, the second and third are
most busy in collecting all manners of sympathizers for extended stay.
Besides, there are as many friendship societies as there are countries
with which the CPR has diplomatic relations. That means that in 1983
they number 125. In this group the most active is the China-Japan
Friendship Society founded on October 4, 1963.[195] This body is both
vocal and militant. It succeeded in selling China's charm to the
Nipponese, resulting in making them one third of foreign visitors to
China. Immediately after Nixon's Beijing tour in February 1972, the
Society exerted the greatest pressure upon the Japanese Government
to grant recognition to the CPR and to withdraw it from the National
Government in Taiwan. This was done on September 29, 1972. The
point is worth accentuating that all the invitees of the above bodies
are communicants of the Chinese Reds, while "most prospective
visitors unlikely impressed as desired are not admitted to the
country."[196]

As a form of foreign trade, we may mention the countless exhibits
done by the communists in foreign lands. Masterpieces of museum
collections are transported overseas to charm curiosity seekers and
fabulous receipts go to the Red treasury for sundry purposes, not the
least of which is the military. Similarly the Chinese oligarchy sent
acrobats overseas with the same objective.

The rugged trade route

The China trade has an uncertain prospect. One Western estimate
says it can reach $65 billion by 1985,[197] but another forecasts $85

[189] Ibid., February 7, 1983, p. 8, col. 1.

[190] Europa, 1982, vol. 2, p. 136.

[191] Ibid.

[192] Beijing review, February 7, 1983, p. 7.

[193] Europa, 1982, vol. 2, p. 136.

[194] Ibid., p. 134.

[195] Zhong guo shou ce, p. 334.

[196] Harold Hinton, op. cit., pp. 259-260.

[197] "Jardines: an old China hand for a new wave of trade," Business week, May 21, 1979, p. 108, col. 1.

billion for the same year.[198] The Chinese themselves put it sometime at $57.400 billion,[199] and sometime at $44 billion.[200] Such a wide range of suggestions shows how difficult it is to tell a business fortune. An old China hand believed correctly that "there is too much euphoria" of traffic with the People's Republic. "We will not have pots of gold dropping out of the sky in 1979 and 1980 [thereafter as well] because China is opening up," cautioned he.[201] Japan, the biggest partner of China, exported to her less than to Taiwan in 1977 and the export was less than the increase in Japan's trade with America for the same year.[202] In 1980, Japan exported to the CPR $5,078.6 million, but to Taiwan $5,145.8 million.[203] Up to 1983 the peak of the China contracts appeared only once, that is, in October and November 1978, with one exception which occurred in mid-1979 when the French loaned to the CPR $7 billion. Afterwards, there are no impressive contracts.[204] Many difficulties exist in the trade route, such as China's shortage of capital, next-to-nil savings from agriculture, negligible revenues from the domestic market, low level of productivity and the obsolete equipments.[205] There is a terrible squandering of resources. Finance Minister Wang Bingqian reported that the CPR had 13,000 industrial enterprises operating at a yearly loss of $2.8 billion because of waste, bad planning and incompetent management.[206] China's oil, as noted above, can be sold only to a few buyers and her textile sales had met difficulties in the US and Canada in 1982 and 1983. Beijing acquired the most-favored-nation privilege from the EEC on July 18, 1978, but that body set a ceiling on China's goods to its members, while cutting EEC tariffs on Chinese exports to an average value of 6.7 percent.[207] The protectionist West is unwilling to welcome Chinese things with open arms,[208] as the Minister of Foreign Economic Relations and Trade, Chen Muhua, has recently noticed.[209]

True enough, the Gang of Four are gone. This does not mean, however, the cessation of policy disputes. Judging from a) the

[198] Lewis Young, op. cit., p. 132, col. 1.

[199] Beijing review, December 20, 1982, p. 11 (table).

[200] Ibid., February 7, 1983, p. 14, col. 1.

[201] "Jardines . . .," op. cit., p. 108, col. 3.

[202] The economist, October 14, 1978, p. 114, col. 4.

[203] Europa, 1982, vol. 2, p. 652.

[204] Lewis Young, loc. cit.

[205] Vladimir Potapov and Yuri Dimov, "China-capitalist powers, from euphoria to disappointment," New times (Moscow), 25 (June 1979), pp. 18-20.

[206] New York times, December 15 (VI), 1981, p. 16, col. 2.

[207] Facts on file, July 27, 1979, p. 554, C3; February 17, 1978, p. 102, B1.

[208] The economist, op. cit., p. 115, col. 1.

[209] Beijing review, February 7, 1983, p. 15.

regime's denunciation of followers of the Gang allegedly entrenched in the provinces and in the central government's ministries, b) the official report of mass meetings all over China and of "political executions" of the Gang's supporters,[210] and c) the reputed destruction of nearly one tenth of the nation's economy by the Gang, the opposition to the new pragmatic hierarchy must have been very strong. During the visit to Beijing in 1979 Commerce Secretary Juanita Kreps was told by Deng Xiaoping that the leadership was in accord on the "broad" policy of the modernization program.[211] This came as an answer to a reporter on the circulated split in the CCP summit. Deng's reply can be taken as admitting the differences in the party councils on sub-policy or on how the broad policy was to be executed. At that time, it is to be remembered, five Politburo men were "removed from posts or detained," because they were all associates of the already weakened premier Hua Guofeng.[212] On the trade front, one can think of the divergent views on the pace in the granting to foreign companies of concessions, the priority of these, and the amount of investment. Such matters did not have unanimous decision in the Politburo. There is, too, the issue as to whether light industry should have a big bite of the budget. Deng Xiaoping revealed to Kreps that he was not personally in charge of China as speculated by the foreign press,[213] intimating that the decision at the top is a collective one and that he cannot order his colleagues around. In view of Deng's statement, who can be sure that the four modernizations will not be altered with respect to their tempo? No sooner were the massive contracts initialed in the fall of 1978 than Beijing decreed a "reassessment" of the entire policy. Obviously a majority in the Politburo came to feel that the drive has been pressed too far and that the country had overcommitted itself.[214] In late 1982, Premier Zhao Ziyang openly criticized the capital expansion in the preceding years as "blind."[215] The fact that the Maoists in 1978 and again in 1982 charged Deng Xiaoping and company of taking the CPR to capitalism,[216] shows the latent resistance to pragmatism.

Disagreement among the leaders has driven the China trade toward an irregular and unpredictable path. This situation enables one writer to comment that "China has not proved itself the most reliable of

[210] Keesing's, December 16, 1977, p. 28718.

[211] Lewis Young, op. cit., p. 133, col. 2.

[212] New York times, March 27, 1979, p. 23, col. 1.

[213] Lewis Young, op. cit., p. 133, col. 2.

[214] Frank Ching, "Long march home as China retrenches, many US companies cut their staffs there; some withdraw completely, often Chinese employees are left to hold the forts," Wall street journal, 197 (March 18, 1981), p. 1.

[215] Beijing review, December 20, 1982, p. 24, col. 2.

[216] Lewis Young, loc. cit., Leo Goodstadt, "The great Chinese economic retreat, China has retreated from the market economy, chopped some major external contracts and turned to Friedman's monetary theories to halt its economic slide," Euromoney (London), April 1981, pp. 73-74. See also Chapter on power struggle of this book.

trading partners."[217] He proves the point by citing the evidence that "on March 24, 1979, the People's Republic stunned the Japanese business circle by announcing that it was putting on hold, pending review, all plant contracts signed since the beginning of 1979 with Japanese firms." At that time, these firms had already a $3.7 billion assignment to be fulfilled by the end of 1980. Of that sum, $1.5 billion contracts were cancelled before the year was out.[218] Many US and other foreign companies were quietly curtailing operations in China, being frustrated by bureaucratic hindrance to trade transaction.[219] This situation militates against the opinion of many Westerners that the "Chinese are always scrupulous in observing the provisions of trade and loan agreements."[220] Up to mid-1981, the CPR has revoked more than $2 billion in contracts with Japanese and West German firms.[221] However, by the end of the year (1981), about $300 million were restored with the Japanese. Tokyo and Beijing signed a $1.38 billion agreement covering the former's financial aid to key Chinese projects and Japan extended $275 million state credit to China.[222] One author asserts that "Chairman Mao Zedong's longtime policy of economic self-reliance is still valid," but we agree with David Rockefeller that "China will retain open door policy despite economic cutbacks."[223] On March 2, 1981, Beijing borrowed from the International Monetary Fund $500 million to stabilize her economy,[224] after the IMF approved a total of $550 million when it was satisfied that the CPR had started the necessary program to halt inflationary pressures and trade deficits.[225]

The idea is entertained in some quarters that Beijing's development plan is bound to be affected by the kind of cadres coming into contact with the traders. China experts in Japan have long held that the Chinese do not have good managers and technicians to effectively administer the economy. During the Cultural Revolution of 1966-1969, the doors of the universities were closed. They graduated no single scientist, engineer, or business executive. Equally disconcerting is the fact that as many as one half of the personnel taking up the directive posts in the ministries and plants were chosen for their

[217] David Lewis, op. cit., p. 12, col. 2. Almost the exact sentence is used by the correspondent of Globe and mail, December 1, 1981, p. 13, col. 1 in view of China's curtailment or suspension of $1.7 billion foreign contracts.

[218] New York times, February 16 (IV), 1981, p. 1, col. 4.

[219] Ibid., February 24 (IV), 1981, p. 17, col. 1.

[220] Economic intelligent unit, op. cit., p. 281, col. 1.

[221] James B. Stepanek, "Beijing's continuing retrenchment," China business review, 8 (January-February 1981), pp. 16-18.

[222] New York times, December 17 (IV), 1981, p. 1, col. 3.

[223] Ibid., May 24, 1981, p. 7, col. 1.

[224] Facts on file, March 13, 1981, p. 162, G1.

[225] New York times, March 3 (IV), 1981, p. 1, col. 4.

redness rather than for their expertise. They still hold on. As noted above, Chen Muhau has proceeded to reform the trade organization which is her domain. There used to be something of a laissez-faire in the industrial control because individual ministries and chiefs of enterprises were allowed to make important decisions on their own. Consequently, a large number of projects were unleashed without anyone considering if there was enough budget to cover them and sufficient cadres to do the job even if the money was indeed available. Having this in mind, Deng Xiaoping spoke of the lack of balance among the various parts of China's economy. This sort of donnybrook has proved a drawback to the advance of trade. One is doubtful as to whether the reassessment after the "blizzard of signings" of contracts four years ago was not the result of the realization on the part of the leaders of such a chaotic situation. The ministers or department heads may have conceivably overstepped their sphere of action by pledging too much to foreigners. Upon discovering this state of affairs, the Politburo was alarmed. Therefore it found it imperative to call for readjustment of the capital expansion.[226] This readjustment has become the single most prominent idea in China's present economic policy. To the NPC Standing Committee meeting on March 1, 1981, Premier Zhao Ziyang declared that the government spending would be reduced by 15 percent. On November 30, 1981, he reported to the 4th session of the 5th NPC the curtailment and suspension of $1.7 billion of foreign trade.[227] From 1983 on, he declared to the 5th session of the same NPC, no ministry or local government is free to make investment except by permission of the Central People's Government, that is, the State Council.[228]

One author writes that "China conducts all its trade through just 20 (now 26) state corporations, while thousands of US companies import and export."[229] The Beijing oligarchy may have believed it fitting and proper to devolve the responsibility of commercial traffic upon the working echelons so as to expedite the process or to cut the red tape. No matter what has really happened, the fact which worries foreigners is that Beijing is taking a second look at the Western trade, or, at least some aspects of it. Although modernization is China's aim, "some businessmen [of the West] still fear that Chinese policy could take yet another lurch and wipe out the relaxation that is under way now."[230] Perhaps to allay this fear, Zhao Ziyang said to the fifth session of the Fifth NPC on November 30, 1982 that China would continue to encourage foreign trade and investment and import

[226] T.A. Sanction and R. Bernstein, "No search for quick results," Time, 117 (March 16, 1981), p. 69; D. Jones, "Power play behind China's trade fiasco," Business Week, March 9, 1981, pp. 38-39.

[227] Globe and mail, December 1, 1981, p. 13, col. 1.

[228] Beijing review, December 20, 1982, pp. 24-26.

[229] Lewis Young, loc. cit.

[230] Ibid.

advanced technology.[231] The once-trumpeted slogan of self-sufficiency is all gone.

Business transactions with Beijing can be greatly facilitated through men who have intimate knowledge on what agencies to keep in touch with or what types of goods are China's most wanted.[232] They know the entire system, the bureaucrats, the institutions and procedures. In other words, they are the ones who can find their way around in Beijing. It is their specialty to secure orders for outsiders. Such agencies are surprisingly similar to the mid-19th century cohongs which negotiated sales for the English ware (opium) in Guangzhou and the Chinese Hong Kong, and which are described in the history of China as imperialists' running dogs. Abolished by the Nanjing Treaty of August 29, 1842, cohongs seem to have reappeared today in such concerns like Jardines, Matheson & Company, Hutchinson Whampoa, the Swire Group, East Asiatic Company and Wheelock Marden. They become counselors or outright agents "for big foreign companies hoping to penetrate the Chinese market for the first time."[233] In them we have a sort of middleman, seeking to build up a workable combination of the alien firms' products and their own operational skill in dealing with the Beijing mandarins. Undoubtedly, personal contacts between these agencies and the CPR officialdom are essential to any successful negotiation. For fourteen years now, China has staged a trade fair in Guangzhou twice a year: from April 15 to May 15, and again from October 15 to November 15. This is the occasion for initialing of export agreements with merchants from abroad. However, imports are signed in Beijing after centralized bargainings there.

[231] Beijing review, December 20, 1982, pp. 17-18.

[232] Hugh Scott, "China's trade policy and practice, continuity and change," Journal of International Law and Economics, 13 (1979), no. 3, pp. 607-617; Yoshi Tsurumi, "Your check list for an approach to China: where and how can I begin to assess business opportunities in China?" Columbia Journal of World Business, 14 (summer 1979), pp. 8-15.

[233] Business Week, May 21, 1979, p. 108, col. 2.

CHAPTER XII
Education

An overview

The establishment of the communist regime in China is thankful to military muscle, as confirmed by Mao Zedong's dictum that political power comes from the gun barrel, but the durability of the regime has to depend on the conquest of the heart of man.[1] Education is basic to this latter endeavor. Mao likened the proletarian heart to a carte blanche on which one can inscribe the Marxist message. It is axiomatic that if a person is unable to read, he is not likely to get that message. Besides, education is vital to imparting technical skills with which to construct a socialist system. In the meanwhile, those who were regarded as uneducable or as dangerous were to be eliminated. All this purports to make the people's democracy not only safe but lasting.[2]

The developing of mass education was one of the topmost tasks of the communist leaders in 1949. Estimates show that, at that time, the Chinese over 7 years of age had an average of less than 2 years' schooling.[3] The decade of 1949-1959 marked a fourfold increase of enrollment in school. In the latter year, the students reached 1 million. Consequently, the average years of education went up from 2 to 3.5. Studies indicate that in 1959, primary education was virtually universal. At urban centers and in nearby villages the junior high system was widespread, but senior high and college education was limited. The government, meanwhile, resorted to stiff exams to bar all but a tiny fraction of high school graduates from entering the post-secondary institutions. The quality of schooling kept declining during the first ten years, but improved from 1959 to 1966; in the latter year, the average number of school years for all Chinese were five and a half. In 1966-1968, education deteriorated fast. Students were all getting out of the classroom. They travelled all over the country in order to compare their revolutionary notes. As a result, schools and universities were closed down. Although elementary education was resumed early in 1968, junior and senior highs were not open until the end of the year, and university doors remained shut for twelve months more, for it was only in the fall of 1970 that limited enrollment was adopted by a few institutions. As late as 1978, the majority of the CPR's colleges did not receive applications of admission. In that year, about sixty schools started to process these.[4] Several hundred others, however, recruited no students at all. All youth were expected

[1] Theodore Hsi-en Chen, *The Maoist Educational Revolution*, New York: Praeger, 1974, pp. 295ff.

[2] Gerald J. Roth, *A Conflict between Ideology and Expertise, Scientific and Technical Education in the People's Republic of China*, Maxwell Airforce Base, Alabama: Air War College, 1973, pp. 101-105.

[3] *Countries of the World*, Toronto: Coles Pub. Co., 1980, Chinese Section, p. 3. All statistics in this paragraph are from this source.

[4] *Beijing review*, August 4, 1978, p. 5.

to be both expert and red, more of the latter, during 1966-1976, and the universal value of orderly conduct was thrown overboard, as were the tests and measurements to evaluate the students. Technical schools, considered in these years as deviating from the political path, became a target of attack. They were denounced as reactionary. In one province, each and every one of them was dismantled.[5]

It was not until the ouster of the Gang of Four that things began to normalize. Beijing decreed in 1979 ten rules of conduct, each for grade and secondary schools, and the then Education Minister Jiang Nanxian put them into effect on September 1, 1981.[6] Strange enough, there is as yet no such canon for university students. The two sets of rules are almost identical and *Beijing review* summarizes them as follows:[7]

a) love the motherland and the people
b) take care of the collective and public property
c) study diligently
d) do physical exercise so as to keep fit, and pay attention to hygiene
e) engage in bodily labor, and lead a thrifty and simple life
f) respect rules of behavior and public order
g) be deferential to teachers, and keep close ties with schoolmates
h) be modest and honest, and be ready to correct mistakes

Conspicuously missing from the panel is the first and foremost rule: to love the Chinese Communist Party. Do the editors of that journal deliberately omit it?

The values embodied in the above planks are trite, for no country wishes its youth to be, e.g., dishonest, lazy, unpatriotic and the like. However, in the People's Republic, such return to the once negated conventionalism, like the respect of teachers, is something noteworthy. A review of moral outlook was conducted by the communists upon their assumption of power in 1949. They went all out to encourage the adolescents to be loyal to the regime by spying and informing on their parents. The assault on traditions was in abeyance during 1956-1966. Then the high-tide of the Cultural Revolution (1966-1968) saw the youth inbued with the spirit of defiance. Today the press condemns that development in no uncertain terms. More of this in the last section of the instant chapter.

The revamping of education is one significant phase of the modernization policy, based as it is on the commonplace that the rebuilding of the country needs trained cadres and that school is the sole agency to produce them.[8] The official call for the new course is an article in *Hongqi*.[9] In it the Gang of Four were in for vile treatment

[5] *Ibid.*, October 18, 1982, p. 24, col. 2.

[6] Complete list in *Renmin ribao*, August 29, 1981, p. 1.

[7] *Beijing review*, January 7, 1980, p. 23.

[8] Arthur Ashbrook, "China: economic review 1975," *China, a reassessment of the economy*, Washington: Government Printing Office, 1975, pp. 20-51 at 37.

[9] *Keesing's*, December 16, 1977, p. 28725, summarizing the article in *Hongqi*, August 1977.

for what came to pass during these "ten disastrous years," as it is now fashionable to use it to label the period 1966-1976. The school standards were down and the number of graduates were too few to meet the requirement of the nation. If this situation were to endure, the socialist revolution and the four modernizations would be thwarted. *Renmin ribao* reiterated the same line. In particular, it admonished the restitution of the status of teachers, a status which the Gang of Four had allegedly done so much to undermine.[10] However, we must say, it was Mao Zedong himself who declared for the youngsters the right to rebel and who unleashed them to do violence. It is pertinent to note that from October 1976 to September 1977, the then strong man Hua Guofeng was uncertain on the direction he should take: continue the Maoist heritage or strike for a different approach? Pragmatic education was not to take shape until the reappearance of Deng Xiaoping in summer 1977.

Late in September 1977, just two months after the comeback of Deng, a National Conference of Teacher Recruitment was convened in Beijing. The delegates piled up more invectives on the Gang of Four, as to be expected. Putatively due to their sabotage, school enrollment plummeted steadily. Entrance exams were abolished, as were the intramural ones. The exams were supposed to smack too much of bourgeois values, and were beneath the revolutionaries of China. Admission of students after 1970 was based on family origins, with preference formally given to those of proletarian background, but actually to children of superior officials. Meanwhile, a high school student could not apply for admission right away upon graduation. He had to labor at least two years in industry, agriculture or service in the army before doing so. Besides, he must secure a recommendation from his work collective. This procedure inevitably hurt the quality of learning. Loudly decried was the secret favoritism shown the ranking cadres' offsprings. *Renmin ribao* revealed that a number of hierarchs in Hebei and Henan provincial governments were dismissed from the CCP for enrolling their sons and daughters through the back door.[11] The above-mentioned conference urged the reversal of all these and it proposed matriculation of students aged 30 and older who had perforce left school in 1966-1967. An official press has reported in 1978 the resumption of intramural exams.[12]

An authoritative pronouncements on policy was made by Deng Xiaoping in early 1978 to a National Education Convocation. Three points were stressed in his speech: a) bettering the quality of education, b) strengthening of discipline, c) tailoring curriculum to the demands of modernization.[13] He said the government should not interfere with school management, force students to engage in

[10] *Ibid.*

[11] *Keesing's,* September 8, 1978, p. 29194.

[12] *Renmin ribao,* October 23, 1978, p. 1.

[13] *Keesing's,* September 8, 1978, p. 29194.

physical chores for long periods of time and set them against teachers as was done during the reign of the Gang of Four. For eleven years, Deng said, the removed leaders opposed strict assignment of work to students and diverted their interests away from study. "Although schools should attach prime importance to a correct political orientation, this does not mean devoting many hours in the classroom to political education." Mao Zedong, he asserted, had no objection to exams per se. The kind he disapproved of envisaged students as an enemy to be taken by surprise attack and compelled them to answer odd and catchy questions. Deng spoke of the Gangsters torpedoing education and leveling the students' achievement. They, he minced no words, made the "young people 'illiterate hooligans.' " To the confreres he orated that the government considered it "necessary to inculcate in the youth the revolutionary style of learning diligently and of respecting discipline." Regarding the expert-red issue, he said that if a specialist can further the cause of modernization, he is red. One does not have to be versed in ideology in order to be so. Deng Xaioping has indeed stretched the meaning of red quite a bit. In the current system of education, red loses its pride of place, even though leaders have frequently referred to ideology in their speeches on education.

Pre-secondary system

Literacy campaign

According to a western source, the CPR spends "about 10 percent of its annual budget" for education.[14] It was probably much lower than that. Premier Zhao Ziyang reported to the NPC on November 30, 1982 that during the Fifth Five-Year Plan (1975-1980), 11 percent of the government spending went to (a) culture, (b) public health, (c) physical culture, (d) education and (e) science but that the Sixth Plan envisaged 15.9 percent expenditure. In 1985, the last year of this Plan, it would reach 16.9 percent.[15] Elsewhere in the same address, he said funds for developing these five areas were 96.7 billion yuan during the Sixth Plan, which is an increase of 68 percent over the 57.7 billion for the Fifth.[16] Since there are no breakdowns in either the percentage or the lump sum given by the Premier, it is impossible to tell just how much goes to each of the five areas he talked about. Should we arbitrarily divide the money evenly, each area would share about 2.2 percent in 1975-1980 but 4 percent in 1981-1985.

A commendable service is rendered by the Reds to the education of the adult citizenry, particularly in the campaign against illiteracy. This no doubt makes their regime *moins désagréable*. At one time,

---

[14] David F. Roth and Frank L. Wilson, *The comparative study of politics*, 2nd ed., Englewood Cliffs, New Jersey: Prentice-Hall, 1980, p. 423; 1st ed., p. 421.

[15] *Beijing review*, December 20, 1982, p. 15, col. 1.

[16] *Ibid.*, p. 11.

they went so far as to claim 100 percent success.[17] Due to the subversion of the Gang of Four, it is alleged, "illiteracy increased again" during and after the Cultural Revolution.[18] Lately, however, the communists quietly rescinded the assertion. First, the 1982 census discloses that "illiterates and semi-literates (people 12 years of age and above who cannot read or can read only *a few words*) in the 29 provinces, municipalities and autonomous regions number 235,820,002."[19] In comparison with the 1964 census, the 1982 one further says, the percentage of illiterates and semi-literates in the total population has dropped from 38.1 to 23.5 percent. The strange category of semi-literacy should perhaps be classified as illiteracy, because "a few words" can hardly make one literate. Indeed, a communist lexicon has no entry of "semi-literacy," but identifies an illiterate as one who can recognize a small number of characters.[20]

Second, to a seminar of the UNESCO held in Foshan of Guangdong province in October 1982, the Chinese representative Yao Zhongda stated that his government had reduced illiteracy rate among people aged 12 to 45 from over 80 percent in the early post-1949 period to 25 percent today,[21] and that during the past 32 years, 137,700,000 adults had been taught to read and write.[22] Interestingly enough, comrade Yao did not blame the Gang of Four for the illiteracy, nor did he speak of semi-literacy. That sort of propaganda, he may have figured, would not make much sense to the confreres. Third, Premier Zhao Ziyang referred, in the report to the NPC on November 30, 1982, to the "illiteracy among young and middle-aged people," the elimination of which was confronting the educational workers throughout the country with a "most arduous and pressing task."[23] Again the Gang of Four were not accused for the illiteracy. Fourth and last, Education Minister He Dongchang declared in November 1982 that "there is still a considerable number of people who are illiterate or semi-illiterate."[24] Once more he held no one responsible for it. We think the Beijing authority was never close to the goal of 100 percent literacy.

What is the Chinese standard of literacy after all? Since a few words are not so powerful to make one literate, the Reds have to go higher than that. A rule is then laid down that a peasant must be able to identify 1,500 words and a city dweller 2,000 before they qualify as

[17] *Ibid.*, January 8, 1980, p. 10, col. 3.

[18] *Ibid.*

[19] *Ibid.*, November 8, 1982, p. 20, col. 2.

[20] *Xin hua ci dian*, Beijing: Shang wu yin shu guan, 1980, p. 879, col. 2.

[21] *World almanac*, 1982, p. 527, col. 1 estimates China's literacy rate to be 70 percent.

[22] *Beijing review*, November 22, 1982, p. 27.

[23] *Ibid.*, col. 2.

[24] *Ibid.*, p. 28, col. 1.

literate.[25] With this size of vocabulary, it is reasoned, a man can read simple papers and journals, write notes and keep accounts. The two numbers of characters are to be explained by the more complex life in the towns than in the villages in the first place, and in the second place by the probable consideration that if the peasants are also required to master 2,000 ideographs, the illiteracy rate would be pushed up uncomfortably in the nation as a whole. Do the Chinese rulers unconsciously inherit Marx's and Engels' contempt of the rural idiocy expressed in the *Communist manifesto?*

To facilitate the command of the basic words, the Reds have greatly simplified their structure. Many difficult ones are stripped of the unnecessary strokes and dots. Mostly these words are left out of the ordinary usage and sometimes they are replaced with easier ones. However, the sentential formation which seems to be the hardest part of the language is kept intact. The communists apparently are not concerned with this. Nor have they attempted to invent some grammatical rules to expedite the learning process. Functional literacy, when it comes to writing, has seldom been achieved by all but a few of the simple folks. It frequently happens that after cramming a few dozens of words, a man forgot them all. But statistically he had been counted as literate.

The Beijing clique heroically set out to sweep off the illiteracy. Throughout the width and breadth of the country there exists no one work collective where there is no learning class. This class is held during spare-time and is led by a literate who can always be found in that group and who may have barely escaped illiteracy himself in the recent past. According to the communist media, most of the illiterates are female, because, to quote it, "parents just do not want to spend money to educate their daughters."[26]

The literacy campaign is an urgent task of the regime. Equally urgent is the enhancement of the level of adult education. Indeed that campaign is directly related to the improvement of the work skill. It is recognized that men in possession of professional knowledge are indispensable to China's socialist modernization. Without them, the CPR "cannot fully utilize its rich natural resources, manufacture and use advanced equipment and develop production rapidly."[27] In order to upgrade the labor force, the administration has resorted to diverse means. There are the full- or part-time short courses. Radio lectures and correspondence instructions are widespread; many county governments set up experimental classes for the peasantry. In big cities and mining towns, there are extension divisions or evening departments of a school of higher learning. Galore are the so-called "universities" sponsored by plants, construction sites, collieries and shops of various descriptions. There are universities of this radio

25 *Ibid.*, p. 27, col. 2.

26 *Renmin ribao*, September 3, 1981, p. 3.

27 *Beijing review*, October 25, 1982, p. 3, col. 1.

channel or that TV network under the jurisdiction of education bureaus; and tens of thousands of schools are financed by civil organizations, even by groups of individuals.

The impressive and earnest mass education is disseminating Marxist messages and scientific know-how. It is trumpeted that in the period from 1950 to 1982, 38,640,000 adults, through spare-time effort alone, reached the level of primary education, 3,590,000 the level of secondary education and over one million the level of university education.[28] At present, it is further maintained, around 75 percent of the adult peasants are literate, and among them 25 percent have secondary school standard and above.[29] Each morning, writes an official media, some 790,000 adults are glued to TV sets watching university courses broadcasting across the airwaves.[30] All but 4,000 of them draw salaries from their units while they are full-time TV university attendants for one to three years. Many special institutions of advanced studies (all tuition-free) are organized for factory workers and staff members who are on full-pay leave. To encourage self-education, the State Council in 1981 empowered the municipal authorities of Beijing, Tianjin and Shanghai to issue certificates to those who have achieved university standard by self-study and passed a set of exams.[31]

An increasing number of employed people are taking time off for either full- or part-time education. Twelve percent of the workers in Liaoning province (970,000) are reported to involve themselves in some types of study. The 1982 Constitution in Article 46 guarantees the educational right of citizens. To implement this mandate, the state requires that work collectives continue to pay those accepted into educational programs and to offer them benefits such as health care. Some enterprises grant bonuses to worker-trainees, with larger amounts to the ones who do well in their courses. Because a few individuals are reluctant to study hard, it is stipulated that only those who pass their courses can be considered for promotion or pay hike. The flunkees would lose their bonuses. Even though the government is generally curtailing expenses, workers' educational funds (an average of 1.5 percent of payroll) are not affected. An enterprise is within its right to secure educational funds from a number of sources such as the profits it has made.

Just a paragraph on the above-said universities. The term (not even the less prestiged term college) is employed quixotically by the communists. The first and the most facetious was the Anti-Japanese University of Politics and Armed Affairs opened in Yanan in 1937.[32] Its "students" were frankly acknowledged to be just "production

[28] *Ibid.*

[29] *Ibid.*, col. 2.

[30] *Ibid.*, December 6, 1982, p. 29, col. 2.

[31] *Ibid.*, November 22, 1982, p. 27, col. 3.

[32] *Xin hua ci dian*, p. 467, col. 1.

soldiers." It graduated close to 300,000 within eight years
. In 1951-1953, the appellation of university was applied
lliteracy classes. There were millions upon millions of
tiny hamlet could have a couple of dozen universities.
The next years saw a drastic decline in number until 1957 when one
million were reported. However, they again mushroomed during the
commune orgy.[33] In 1958-1959, every adult was a university student.
Most of these universities were called by their subject matters, e.g.,
university of ditch-digging, of manure-mixing, etc. After the commune
fever subsided, the term university returned to its conventional usage.
Yet, there are still many universities of printing and dyeing, of river-
boating, of crocheting, of umbrella-making, etc.

Nursery

During the Cultural Revolution, it is written, nursery schools placed
emphasis on political instruction. They required "children to behave
like adults."[34] In those days, target-shooting exercises in these and
the grade schools were a daily routine. The little ones were imbued
with hatred of American imperialists who must be killed off. It was
only in late 1976 that this practice came to phase out. Since then the
way a nursery is run seems to be no different, if at all, from other
countries. October 1981 saw the Education Ministry promulgate "the
regulations for nursery school education." There are eight points in
it: living and health habits, physical activity, ethical values, language,
general knowledge, mathematics, music, art. Lower, middle and
higher classes are to have slightly modified subjects.[35] In view of the
fact that children at this stage are growing up rapidly, first priority
is given to physical education and they spend three hours a day
outdoors. Moreover, they are taught the five loves of motherland,
people, labor, science and public property.[36] Love of Mao Zedong
is dropped now.

To illustrate how a kindergarten is operated, let us take a concrete
example. In the kindergarten of Beijing's no. 2 cotton mill which has
8,200 employees, the kids are organized into ten classes of three
grades of ages 3-4, 4-5 and 6-7. Lessons are in mathematics, music,
physical exercise, Chinese, and fine art. The annual fees are as
follows:

a) board	10.5 yuan
b) childcare	2.0
c) miscellaneous	0.5
d) medical	1/2 of actual cost

[33] George P. Jan, "Mass education in the Chinese commune," *Government of communist China*, edited
by the author, San Francisco: Chandler pub. co., 1966, pp. 499-513 at 505-506.

[34] *Beijing review*, January 24, 1983, p. 23, col. 1.

[35] *Ibid.*

[36] *Ibid.*, January 7, 1980, pp. 17-29.

Items b) and d) are exempted from one-child parents.[37] In the mill, the average monthly wage is 53.1 yuan. Each worker, besides, gets a non-staple food subsidy of 5 yuan and a bonus of from 10 to 20 yuan for overtime. This makes the kindergarten fee quite low. The school enrolled 263, of whom 189 stayed there round the clock and 74 during the day only. It is up to the parents to decide the shift they prefer. The essential idea is to free them to work and certainly there is the desire to rear the youth in the communist mores of collective living. The source from which our information came does not say whether the school takes in all the workers' children of that age bracket. All the four items of expenses, it is to be noted, are limited to one child per family, a manifestation of a policy of penalizing big families (see also Chapter XIII).

The number of nursery schools has increased from 164,000 in 1978 to 170,000 in 1981. Twenty-seven thousand of them are in urban and 143,000 in rural areas. The total enrollment in 1982 was 10,560,000, representing 15 percent of the pre-schoolers.[38] It is significant to observe that nursery children were 17,130,000 in 1965, 13,955,000 in 1976 and 8,792,000 in 1979.[39] This is a sharp decline. The 1982 figure is still 3 million less than the 1976 one. In this department, were things not better during the Gang of Four days?

Primary school

In 1980 the Central Committee of the party and the State Council issued the "decision on problems of making elementary education universal," which decrees that universality be achieved as far as possible by a diversity of ways before 1990.[40] To implement this decision, the Sixth Five-Year Plan seeks "to make primary education universal or almost so by 1985 in most counties and to make junior high universal in the cities."[41] It is claimed that already some 600 of the more than 2,100 counties have reached the goal of universal primary education.[42] Today China has 140,000,000 grade schoolers. Although 93 percent of school-agers enter the school, a mere 65 percent finish it. The dropout rate is greater in the countryside than in the cities.[43] Like the kindergarten, grade school system has witnessed a shrinking registration:

[37] Ibid.

[38] Ibid., January 24, 1983, p. 22, col. 2.

[39] Zhong gu bai ke nian jian, Beijing: Zhong guo da bei ke quan shu chu ban she, 1980, p. 536.

[40] Beijing review, January 24, 1983, p. 24, col. 1; November 22, 1982, p. 28, col. 1.

[41] Ibid., December 20, 1982, p. 16, col. 1.

[42] Ibid., January 24, 1983, p. 26, col. 1, October 5, 1982, p. 3, col. 3.

[43] Ibid., p. 24, col. 1

1975-7	150,000,000a
1979	146,929,000b
1980	146,240,000c
1982	140,000,000d

a *Europa*, 1979, vol. 2, p. 124. James Townsend, *Politics in China*, 2nd ed., Boston: Little, Brown, 1980, p. 194. *Zhong guo bai ke nian jian*, p. 536 mentions the 1979 figure to be 146,620,000.

b *Zhong guo bai ke nian jian*, p. 536. However, *Europa*, 1982, vol. 2, p. 120 mentions 146,630,000.

c *Beijing review*, January 7, 1980, col. 17.

d *Ibid.*, January 24, 1983, p. 25, col. 1.

Getting back to the dropout, it is explained that many families have difficulties in making ends meet, that schools are often far from the homes and that children find it hard "to keep up with the classes."[44] With reference to the last-named cause, the media says, those who do not have a good foundation in the first couple of years feel it increasingly hard to stay in school. As a result, they lose confidence in their ability to learn, and return home. An equally serious problem arises from changed economic activity in the villages. During the reign of the Gang of Four, maintained the Chinese press, children could not help out, because sideline occupations were forbidden to the peasants. And this fact accounts for the higher school enrollment. Now the situation has changed. When the ecnonomic policy was relaxed, more older children went to work to help their parents on many production lines.[45] Another reason for dropping out is that parents often withdraw their daughters from school, because they simply do not wish to spend money for them.[46] This problem has caused great concern to authorities in one coastal province. Also contributing to the dropout rate is the way the teachers are compensated. Let us look at this in greater detail.

From 60 to 70 percent of the rural grade school teachers are hired by local communities, while 30 to 40 percent are hired by the state. The communities enjoy an enormous amount of autonomy in education, for there are no guidelines from the administration except the requirement that teachers be paid somewhat higher than the average workers in the brigade or commune. Prior to the present job-responsibility system, most neighborhoods used the workpoints plus allowance under which the teachers were assigned quotas equal to those of an ordinary worker. At the year's end, they shared the commune's profits according to the accummulated points. Besides, each received an annual pay of 250 yuan from the state. Today the scheme of calculating one's wage by workpoints is no longer feasible. Although state subsidy continues, teachers are given production responsibility for a plot of land just like any other member on the farm. After offering a portion of the harvest to the brigade as specified in the contract, the teacher keeps the remainder. He receives no further

[44] *Ibid.*, p. 25, col. 1.

[45] *Ibid.*, col. 2.

[46] *Renmin ribao*, September 3, 1981, p. 4.

income from the community. In this way, many teachers tend to pay less attention to teaching and concentrate instead their efforts on developing their fields.[47] The state has not yet taken measures to remedy this situation and it prefers to let the local communities find the solution.

A county, called Quanjiao, in Anhui province, instituted in 1980 a remuneration of rural teachers different from the preceding method. Each brigade decides a monthly pay of 30 to 40 yuan, in accordance with the production level and the ability of the teacher. That part of the wage which comes from the state goes to him directly, and the rest is paid at the end of the year when the profit of the brigade is distributed. The significant change is that the teacher is given no production responsibility for the plot of land. Quanjiao county also set up spare-time primary schools. Moreover, it adjusts the school schedule to the agricultural season so that children can return home to work during busy months. As a result the county achieved in 1980 a 96 percent rate for school-age children entering primary grades and a graduation rate of 74.3 percent.[48]

There were in 1979 more than 7,000 key grade schools.[49] These were exemplars for all others to look up to. Because they are more generously financed, they have better facilities and can hire more qualified teachers. High schools and colleges, as related later, all have models.

In the CPR as a whole, elementary teachers receive 44 yuan a month. This is, however, 15-25 yuan less than that of factory workers; worse yet, unlike them, the teachers have no bonus system and welfare subvention. Of six years in duration prior to the Cultural Revolution, a grade school lasts five years presently. It takes a child at the age of 7. An indication of the new rulers' cherishing of legalism and moralism from 1981 onwards is that children must be taught (1) the basics of law,[50] and (2) course in ethical values.[51] Nine and a half months constitute a school year, but pupils of grades 4 and 5 must do some manual labor for two weeks.

High school

Secondary education consists of four subsystems. There are, first, the "agricultural and cognate concentrated vocational schools." These are neighborhood establishments. Situated exclusively in rural China, they are intimately geared to local needs. In 1982, the enrollment was 480,000.[52] Needless to say, the students are all

---

[47] *Beijing review*, January 24, 1983, p. 25, col. 2.

[48] *Ibid.*, p. 26.

[49] *Zhong guo bai ke nian jian*, p. 541, p. 3.

[50] *Renmin ribao*, August 8, 1981, p. 4.

[51] *Beijing review*, January 24, 1983, p. 24, col. 1.

[52] *Ibid.*, October 18, 1982, p. 25, col. 1.

offsprings of farmers and the teaching is narrowly focussed. The schools teach rudimentary skills in agricultural chore, while, in a few cases, they offer senior high courses. One such school sets up four majors: accounting, tractor, starch, cement works.[53] Back in 1965, these institutions matriculated 4,433,000.[54] They totally vanished shortly afterwards until they "shot up" again in 1982.[55] The training lasts from a few months to three years. Second, there are the "industrial and apprentice schools," shifted in early 1978 from under the Education Ministry to the Labor Bureau.[56] Students are learning to be craftsmen such as carpenters or welders. These schools recruit senior high graduates for a two years' stay. At the end of 1978, there were 2,923 such institutions attended by 640,000. In the same year, the graduates numbered 97,443. Third, there are the "specialized schools." These are divided into a) technical and b) teacher training categories. As of 1979, the former had 714,000 students and the latter 484,000.[57] The technicums, to use the Russian terminology, turn out middle-level professionals like accountants and nurses. Some schools admit junior high students and require four years, but others take senior high graduates for either two or three years' study.[58] Teacher training schools are attended by junior high graduates with a flexible period from 2 to 3 years to complete the course. In 1979, there were 1,052 such schools.[59] On the average, every two counties share one school (2,136 county level units).

Fourth come the conventional high schools whose senior section used to require two years and junior section three, but from 1982, the former also demanded three years.[60] In 1979, junior high enrolled 46,130,000 and senior high 12,930,000.[61] They are aimed at imparting broad education and are by no means vocation-anchored. Witness the following courses:[62]

politics	foreign language
Chinese	history
mathematics	geography
chemistry (no physics yet)	basic farming skill
biology	hygiene
physical education	music and drawing

[53] Ibid., p. 26, col. 1.

[54] Zhong guo bai ke nian jian, p. 536.

[55] Beijing review, October 18, 1982, p. 25, col. 1.

[56] Zhong guo bai ke nian jian, p. 544, col. 2.

[57] Ibid., p. 536.

[58] Beijing review, October 18, 1982, p. 24, col. 3.

[59] Zhong guo bai ke nian jian, p. 548, col. 3.

[60] Guangming ribao, August 11, 1981, p. 1.

[61] Zhong guo bai ke nian jian, p. 536.

[62] Beijing review, January 11, 1980, p. 22.

From August 1981, a "knowledge of law" course has been added.[63] Just like grade schools, there are the so-called key high schools which number 5,200 with a registration of 510,000.[64] The conventional high schools are tailored for college education. It is criticized that they have overworked the students. In order to attain a good rate of college entrance, some teachers mercilessly swamped the youngsters with huge quantities of facts and assigned an excessive amount of homestudy.[65] The idea prevails among the authorities that the excellence of a school is measured by the number of its students successfully passing the entrance exams. In 1982, the education ministry instructed the schools to abandon this unwholesome outlook.[66]

There is a glaring imbalance between college capacity and senior high graduates. The latter numbered 72,605,000 (mostly those who flunked in the entrance exams, but tried again), while only 310,000 could be taken into institutions of higher learning. Those who failed to get in were bound to work, but they lacked the technical skill. They therefore could not readily be absorbed into the labor force. In the light of this difficulty, Beijing is determined to cut back on the regular high schools. Premier Zhao Ziyang promised to the NPC on November 30, 1982 that they are to be restructured and that vocational institutions created.[67] In addition, said he, some technical subjects are to be taught in high schools. The drastic elimination can be seen in the case of Fuxin county of Liaoning province which reduced the number of such schools from 125 to 24, because they "weren't teaching anything."[68] Clearly vocational, instead of liberal-arts, education has become the center of gravity of the reform. To endorse such a new measure, one media editorializes that "this changes for the better."[69]

There are state- and people-run high schools. The aforesaid key schools belong to the first kind and they all are in the cities, while the second kind are scattered all over the countryside. To rural schools, however, the government hands out sizeable aid. A teacher there normally receives 27 yuan a month, of which 18 come from the state.[70] Being a member of the production team, he gets a tiny plot like anybody else to grow vegetables on. The sideline income accrues to him. In comparison, his city colleague does not have such a plot,

[63] *Renmin ribao*, August 8, 1981, p. 4.

[64] *Zhong guo bai ke nian jian*, p. 541, col. 3.

[65] *Beijing review*, January 24, 1983, p. 27, col. 3.

[66] *Ibid.*, p. 28, col. 2.

[67] *Ibid.*, December 20, 1982, p. 16, col. 1.

[68] *Ibid.*, October 18, 1982, p. 25, col. 1.

[69] *Ibid.*

[70] *Guangming ribao*, January 23, 1981, p. 1; September 12, 1981, p. 1.

but instead he draws higher stipends. An urban teacher earns on the average 49 yuan a month, in addition to fringe benefits such as medical expenses, which are to be paid in villages.

Post-secondary system

Universities and colleges began to open in 1970 after a four years' closure. Their number was 434 in 1965, but it went down to 392 in 1976.[71] Since then it increased rapidly:

1979a	633
1980b	675
1981c	704
1982d	729

a *Zhong guo bai ke nian jian*, p. 535.
b *Beijing review*, December 20, 1982, p. 22, col. 1.
c *Ibid.*, January 24, 1983, p. 28, col. 2.
d *Ibid.*, December 20, 1982, p. 22, col. 1. A new university of Law and Politics was set up, *ibid.*, May 8, 1983, p. 4.

No less than 26 colleges were ordained in August, 1981. There are 93 key universities or colleges which serve as models for hundreds of others because of their alleged superior quality.[72] Like the US or the USSR, the CPR has most institutions named after places, e.g., Xiantan University (Xiantan is the county where Mao Zedong was born). However, unlike the US but like the USSR, it has subject universities, not just colleges, such as normal university, university of science and technology, medical university, agricultural university, university of military medicine, agricultural and plowing university (one each in Xinjiang and Heilongjiang), laboring university (in Anhui province), coal/chemical industrial university (in Shanxi province), industrial university, and communications university. There are 38 of these. In 1982, attending all the 729 institutions were 1,280,000 full-time students. Besides, 1,035,000 adults took one or more courses.[73] By 1985, the former group will be 1,500,000, in accordance with the Sixth Five-Year Plan.[74] This plan calls for a rise in the number of new students from 280,000 in 1980 to 400,000 in 1985, an increase of 42.2 percent. The graduates from these schools will be 1,500,000 for the years covered by the plan. "In 1985, 20,000 postgraduates are to be recruited, 5.5 times the number in 1980; and 45,000 are to complete their postgraduate studies in the five years under review."[75] Universities and colleges are providing over 800 specialities, more than 500 being related to science and engineering.[76]

[71] *Zhong guo bai ke nian jian*, p. 535.

[72] *Ibid.*, pp. 557-559.

[73] *Beijing review*, January 24, 1983, p. 28, col. 3.

[74] *Ibid.*, December 20, 1982, p. 15, col. 2.

[75] *Ibid.*

[76] *Ibid.*, January 7, 1980, p. 18.

It was not until 1981 that the CPR instituted bachelor's, master's and doctoral degrees in 10 areas of study: philosophy, law, literature, history, economics, education, science, engineering, agriculture, medicine.[77] Qinghua University and the Academy of Social Sciences have added archaeology and minority races' history, religion and languages.[78] The Academic Degree Committee of the State Council has authorized the institutions and relevant research organizations to establish degree evaluation committees, to set up thesis or dissertation defense committees and to implement the actual work of conferring the degrees. In 1979, 8,231 graduates were recruited by 300 universities or colleges and 281 research offices. Of the students, 7,088 studied in universities or colleges, 261 in Academy of Sciences, 157 in Academy of Social Sciences, 558 in departments or ministries of the central government and 167 in bureaucracies of the provinces, municipalities and autonomous regions.[79] The disciplines conferring doctoral and M.A. degrees number 805 and 2,957 respectively. All counted, 145 academic units in the universities and colleges can confer doctorates and 471 can confer M.A.'s. It is also reported that there are 1,145 directors qualified to guide doctoral candidates. Finally the government has fixed the faculty rankings as a) professor, b) deputy-professor (also translated associate professor), c) lecturer and d) assistant teacher.[80] As of 1981, the CPR had 5,078 professors, 22,251 deputy-professors, 128,386 lecturers and 37,324 assistant teachers.[81] The maximum age of graduate students is set at 35, but in extraordinary situations it may be advanced to 38.[82] At Qinghua University, the average age is 34.[83] As for salary, a professor can make at least 70 yuan a month, and a deputy-professor between 60 and 70 yuan. Lower faculty members make less than 60 yuan.

A voice is now raised in advocacy of the independence of colleges and universities from the thumb of party and administration in re a) faculty, b) finance, c) curriculum, d) facilities in general, e) sale of research products, f) public relations, and g) business management.[84] Some schools are said to proceed to exercise their autonomy. The Energy Institute of the Academy of Sciences has laid down a rule that if a member fails to write something during a year, he would be advised to quit.[85] In that establishment, there were 35 research

[77] *Ibid.*, January 24, 1983, p. 29, col. 2.

[78] *Guangming ribao,* January 18, 1981, p. 1; *Keesing's,* September 8, 1978, p. 29194, col. 1.

[79] *Zhong guo bai ke nian jian,* p. 539.

[80] *Renmin ribao,* January 13, 1981, p. 1.

[81] *Ibid.*, December 26, 1981, p. 1.

[82] *Zhong guo bai ke nian jian,* p. 539, col. 2.

[83] *Guangming ribao,* January 18, 1981, p. 1.

[84] *Ibid.*

[85] *Ibid.*

378   GOVERNMENT OF SOCIALIST CHINA

staffers; in 1980, 32 were alleged to produce one or more pieces of work. Hence only three were fired.

The hysteria of the Beijing rulers in importing technology propelled them to embark upon cultural exchanges. Many leftist foreign governments and educational hierarchies, although fully aware that they benefit nothing from such exchanges, respond with enthusiasm. They waxed so excited as to design all sorts of ties with the Chinese communists. For instance, a university in Canada arranged with Shandong University's history department a joint seminar on what the Maoists classify as slave-owning society of Confucius's time. In 1979, 79 countries sent 1,278 students to the CPR, of whom 789 were undergraduates and 489 graduates.[86] More than 100 foreign universities have connections with the CPR; and foreign teachers there numbered 383. A few such teachers, known for their admiration for the Reds, are bestowed the title of Honorific Professorship of the People's Republic of China. Eleven thousand Chinese are studying in 54 different nations or regions.[87] Upwards of 3,500 are said to have returned after completing their term of stay. Among them one hundred earned doctorates. However, the Chinese press is silent about the refusal to return and the begging for political asylum in the host countries of more than eleven hundred. So far only about 10 percent are accepted, the rest being forced to go back.

During the period from 1970 to 1976, there were no entrance exams for post-secondary systems; the recruitment was based on recommendation by the masses. An aspirant first filed the application with the leaders of the unit he was in, be it a factory, or a production team, or an office or an army platoon. It was then submitted to a general meeting for deliberation. Upon its approval, his name was forwarded to the higher authority for review. Thereupon the college admitted him. In reality, the deliberation by the masses was pro forma. Whoever had the nodding of the powerful individual in the unit would surely have the chance.[88] This was a "back door deal." The scheme was revised in 1977 with the restoration of entrance exams. However, the political checkup was still retained. It was indeed the toughest part of the evaluation ordeal a college-bound youth had to undergo. Once endorsed by an organization (no longer the mass approval as before), the application was sent to the county or city authority for further scrutiny. Having proven himself worthy, he proceeded to the written exams. The next stage was the physical.[89]

Passing the physical, he remained a candidate and ought to wait to be picked by the college. More appraisal of moral, bodily and mental virtues was performed by the enrollment board of the province, or municipality or autonomous region. Now each college was given a

[86] *Zhong guo bai ke nian jian*, p. 540 for this and the following figures.

[87] *Beijing review*, December 6, 1982, p. 25, col. 1.

[88] *Ibid.*, July 28, 1978, p. 19, col. 1.

[89] *Ibid.*, April 21, 1978, p. 12

list of the successful candidates, paying regard to their preference of choices. As for subjects, a science major was to write tests in mathematics, politics, Chinese, physics and chemistry, a liberal arts major in mathematics, politics, Chinese, history and geography. If one wishes to study a foreign language, he must taken an additional exam in that. The maximum points of an applicant were 100. It is claimed that most students had scored 70 and above in the 1978 entrance exams.[90] No later information on this is available, however.

Regarding students' background, the following somewhat outdated reports are citable; probably the present situation is the same. A spokesman of the Education Ministry stated that of the students enrolled in 1977, party members and Young Communist Leaguers made up 71.9 percent, but the rest were politically safe.[91] The executive officials of the University of Science and Technology disclosed that of the 738 freshmen for the academic year 1977-1978, over 99 percent were from families of working people. Similarly, the authority of Jiaotong University in Shanghai said that of the 1,058 intakes only 0.6 percent belonged to the exploiters' class. In the nation as a whole, the exams and selection set in motion during November-December 1977 and ending in February 1978, netted 278,000 new students.[92] More than 10 million applications were filed. Only 5.7 million got to the written stage.[93] More than 5 million were sifted out by the political checkup.[94] Approximately one half of the successful candidates were that year's high-school products and the other half were chosen from among workers, the self-prepared, the armymen, teachers, barefoot doctors and government employees. A small portion was made up of high schoolers who had not graduated, but were certified by their instructors as really outstanding and able to compete. The flunked 9 million plus were said to be able to enter teachers training courses or other types of institutions. For them the government set up 42 schools in 1978.[95] These schools, however, can only admit ca. 100,000. The remainder swarmed to the labor market and they came to boost the size of the number of unemployed.

Of the 278,000 recruits, 97.4 percent were the scions of workers, poor and lower-middle peasants and other laboring people like revolutionary soldiers, cadres and intellectuals. A further breakdown of the 97.4 percent shows that the number of those from intellectual backgrounds (professors, writers, scientists, artists and school teachers and administrators) was greater in proportion than in the previous year. This situation met with sharp criticism. An answer was

[90] Ibid.

[91] Ibid., July 28, 1978, p. 19.

[92] Keesing's, September 8, 1978, p. 29194, col. 1.

[93] Ibid.

[94] Beijing review, August 4, 1978, p. 5.

[95] Keesing's, September 8, 1978, p. 29194, col. 1.

offered that these people's children were prejudiced under the Gang of Four. Therefore, they had to study very hard. It is also said that in general they enjoyed a better environment of learning. Consequently, they scored high in the exams.[96] However, it is avowed, if one man from intellectual and another from workers' background have an identical mark, the latter would be favored.

To further explain away the increase of bourgeois elements, *Beijing review* asserted that "one cannot choose one's parents, but one can choose the road one takes."[97] On the assessment of a student, the authorities go by his world view. If he allies with the working class, he is regarded as attached to it. Mao Zedong allegedly instructed that "we take class origin into account, but we do not rely solely on it. The emphasis should be on the individual's political attitude."[98] Henceforth, intellectuals serving socialism are part of the working people; they are not the "stinking ninth category," a stigma applied to them by the Gang of Four. Family members of the bourgeois ought to be treated as equal to those of workers and peasants. Cases are however reported about under-the-counter action which is a legacy from the Gang's day. One man holding a high post in a district of Henan province took advantage of it to get his daughter registered in a college. Upon the exposure by the press on July 28, 1978, he was promptly demoted, and she was sent back by the college to where she came from.[99] Exam papers in Uygur, Kazakh and Mongolian are acceptable in order to accommodate minorities in Tibet, Neimeng, Xinjiang and other border regions.[100] It appears that minorities living inside China proper do not enjoy the privilege.

The following concrete case reveals a great deal about the class background and other aspects of student life. The Beijing Polytechnical Institute recruited its students after the downfall of the Gang of Four. The 36 members of the computer-science class were "admitted according to the principle of selecting the best after an all-round review of their academic achievement, moral qualities and physical fitness."[101] Their status is like this:

1 exploitative family
19 workers
8 peasants
8 high-school graduates (working families)

There were 24 men and 12 women. Eight were party members and the rest belonged to the communist youth league. This made up 100 percent as compared to 71.9 percent of party people among the

[96] *Beijing review*, July 28, 1978, p. 18, col. 2.

[97] *Ibid.*, April 21, 1978, p. 12.

[98] *Ibid.*

[99] *Ibid.*, August 4, 1978, p. 5.

[100] *Ibid.*

[101] *Ibid.*, January 7, 1980, p. 24, col. 1.

freshmen in the nation's universities (see above). This school is tuition-free. There are several ways of financing:

9 monthly wage (by work collectives)
16 state subsidy (6.5-22 yuan a month)
11 textbook-free or given cash to buy winter clothes

All students lived in the dormitory and paid no rent. Neither had they to disburse medical costs. The study lasted four years but after 1979, five. The class took 23 courses, including seven on computer-hardware engineering, six on computer-software engineering, five on computer systems. Others were political theory, foreign language, physical education and basic studies. Each student must do experimental work in a factory and spend ten weeks in a unit connected with a particular subject.

The best-known of all universities is Beijing University which was established by the Qing dynasty in 1898. As of 1982, it had a student body of 10,700. Faculty is 2,800 strong, of whom 136 are full professors, 516 associate professors, 1,473 lecturers, and 675 assistant teachers. The university authorities said that "one of the main problems with the faculty of our university is the fact that the core of our faculty is rather old in age. Our full professors have an average age of nearly 70," and only a handful are middle-aged or younger.[102] Another problem is the uneven composition of the faculty. In some disciplines there is no single member, while in others there are too many members. Presently there are 15 colleges, one being college of library science. In the past four years the teaching corps are said to have completed almost 100 research projects and presented more than 1,000 papers at scholarly conferences or in periodicals. The students allegedly are of very high standing. Of the 1,500 graduates of the 1978 freshmen, one third passed the examination for master's candidates. Of the 1,100 graduates of the 1977 freshmen, nearly all received bachelor degrees.[103] The cost to the state per student from admittance to graduation is 8,000 to 10,000 yuan, while a tuition-paying student costs the state 400 to 800 yuan, and a correspondence student a mere 150 yuan. Finally, the student subsidy is 19.5 yuan, plus free lodging. But one has to pay for his meals.

There are now emerging fee-paying colleges which do not provide residence.[104] As reported in the Chinese press, the eight Democratic Parties and groups (all supporters of the Reds) have been active in setting up spare-time institutions.[105] One of these is an evening law-school in Beijing. Students, although charged, pay on a reduced scale, because the parties and groups have donated significant amounts

[102] *Ibid.*, January 24, 1983, p. 29, col. 1.

[103] *Ibid.*, col. 3.

[104] *Guangming ribao*, January 18, 1981, p. 1.

[105] *Ibid.*, January 25, 1981, p. 1. The eight are listed in *Zhong guo shou ce*, Hong Kong: Da gong bao, 1980, pp. 141-142.

of money to these colleges. Besides, the parties established secondary schools devoted to tutorial education for prospective college students. The reason for this latter activity is that for each of the four years (1978-1981), there were only about 280,000 places for freshman class;[106] and since upwards of 10 million took the exams, the competition was extremely acute. One has to be really prepared in order to succeed. Moreover, beyond the age of 25, according to the legislation, a person may not be allowed to take the exams.[107] Remedial or tutorial education is vital to one's future.

Education Minister He Dongchang and Premier Zhao Ziyang have most recently laid down important guidelines for college authorities. The latter official ordered a revision of course concentrations and an improvement of teaching methods. "Over the years," we quote him, "specialities have been too finely divided."[108] This has resulted in graduates acquiring "only a limited scope of knowledge." They are unable to satisfy the needs of practical work. Neither can they pursue advanced studies. There is the difficulty for them to acquire suitable employment or to switch jobs. Along with this, the premier insisted on the intensification of the instruction of Marxism-Leninism and Mao Zedong Thought. Again we quote him: "Ideological and political work among them [students] should be done regularly, purposely and effectively." The State Council, he said, would see to it that students are taught to be workers imbued with socialist consciousness and professional knowledge. In this statement, the premier obliquely conceded to the apathy and irregularity in the learning about communism by the young people. How is the government to reverse this trend by making ideology more meaningful or more attractive? Will a course on dialectical materialism be made mandatory as it is in the secondary schools?

The Education Minister contemplated a great number of reforms.[109] In the first place, there will be a diversified post-secondary education. Heretofore, said he, the CPR has only four- or five-year colleges which are copied from the West. He thought it befitting China to establish two- or three-year colleges, since "different specialists require different amounts of schooling." In the second place, lessons can be given over the radio or television or by correspondence. These are particularly germane to mature students or adults. In the third place, there should be a rigorous and coordinated test system. Whoever passes the exams in given subjects would be offered credits, and if a person accummulates sufficient credits, he will receive a college diploma. In the fourth place, the proportion between liberal-arts and science/engineering and between students trained in higher,

[106] Main documents of the third session of the fifth National People's Congress of the CPR, 1st ed., Beijing: Foreign languages press, 1980, p. 26.

[107] Guangming ribao, March 16, 1981, p. 1.

[108] Beijing review, December 20, 1982, p. 15, col. 2.

[109] Ibid., October 4, 1982, p. 9.

CHAPTER XII

intermediate and junior cadres should slowly be balanced. Wh..
stressed vocational and technical education, he also stated that "the
number of college graduates needed by departments of finance,
economy, law, management, agriculture and light industry is far
greater than the number the state can provide." In the next place,
schools of agriculture and forestry as well as those of medicine and
education, which train specialists for the rural, pastoral and forest
areas should enroll people from these areas. He asserted that these
people "are willing to return to their home areas after graduation."
In the sixth and final place, the CPR must continue to learn from
foreign countries, including those of the third world. Just as his boss
Premier Zhao Ziyang, the minister maintained that "China's education
is aimed at training students with a socialist outlook who are willing
to serve the people." However unlike him, He Dongchang did not
utter a single word on ideological indoctrination and political guidance
on the college campuses. The fact that this individual was majoring
in aeronautics in a pre-CPR school, to be more specific, B.S. from
the fairly well-known Southwest Associated University in 1945, may
have inclined him to think little of that sort of impractical education.

Science and art

To understand the current policy in this area, we found it necessary
to envision how the Gang of Four were supposed to misread Mao
Zedong's mind and how grave a situation they had created. It is, we
think, with the farthest-fetched imagination to say that Mao was indeed
misread, because his mind was as clear as noonday. Mao instructed
the Chinese to carry out three struggles: a) for scientific experiment,
b) against class enemy and c) to increase production.[110] The
Gangsters are said to have substituted the second for the first and
totally ignored the third. One can hardly believe this rhetoric if he
recalls that it was Mao Zedong, the no. 1 Red Guard, who drove out
the teenagers to learn revolutionary lessons and to stage insurrection
against the establishment. However, what is described in the
contemporary Chinese press about the sorry state of affairs in science
and art during the Cultural Revolution is certainly true. Following but
not distorting Mao Zedong, the Gang of Four considered study of
books not appropriate for socialist revolutionary, because in the first
place, it was unproductive and in the second, it diverged from
ideology.

During the Cultural Revolution, laboratory research was replaced
by manual labor. Scientific institutes were labeled "stubborn
stronghold of capitalism" and must, therefore, be pulled down.[111]
Zhou Enlai is supposed to have advised in 1972 that apart from
workers, peasants and soldiers, the universities should recruit from

[110] Cited in *Keesing's*, December 16, 1977, p. 28725. The three are written in the Preamble of the 1978
Constitution, but only implied in that of the 1982 Constitution.

[111] *Keesing's*, December 16, 1977, p. 28725.

the graduates of high schools,[112] and he was viciously attacked by the Gang of Four as a patron of the right deviants. A Shanghai paper wrote that many important research projects were dropped, most of the staffers were disbanded and those who stayed functioned in name only. A circular issued by the Central Committee of September 18, 1977 said that the Gangsters traduced the modernization plan as reinstitution of bourgeois economy and advocated the displacement of the plan with philosophy.[113] Although the circular does not state what the latter philosophy was, it cannot be otherwise than Marxism-Leninism and Mao Zedong Thought.

The current science boss of the CPR is Fang Yi. Not unexpectedly, he fired more shots at the Gang of Four. In an address to the Standing Committee of the Chinese People's Political Consultative Conference on December 27, 1977 he called their attention to the serious sabotage by them in education and science. The gap between the CPR's attainment in these fields and that of the West has widened steadily. The research work in China virtually vanished. He saw in the country corrupted teenagers and young adults and pointed to the outmoded agriculture, industry, national defense and science and technology. All this casts a shadow on the nation's future. He concluded: "The repeated struggle around scientific and educational work between us and the Gang of Four has been a struggle between the building of a powerful and socialist country and a reversion to the primitive life of cave society."[114]

On March 30, 1978, Beijing radio accused that the Gang "deliberately confused academic with political problems," saying that in the suppression of free discussion in scholarly works, the Gang has retarded the progress of science. Theory of relativity and research hypotheses were outlawed and their proponents imprisoned. After being criticized, the All-China Geography Society was called a "hodgepodge of monsters and demons," and the members of Fudan University's Genetics Institute were sent to the countryside to engage in manual tasks. Other radio broadcasts told that the police jailed several hundreds of scientists as the secret agents of class enemies. In Jilin province, 166 members of Changchun Institute of Optics and Precision Instruments were either beaten to death or forced to commit suicide.[115]

Similar acts of the Gang were revealed in other fields. A Beijing broadcast of April 20, 1977 spoke of their "fascist rule over literature and art." Dissenting writers, artists and actors were incarcerated or deprived of the chance of creative work.[116] Another broadcast of August 11, 1977 related the Gang's "clean sweep" of all traditional Chinese and foreign art which adversely affected the people's

[112] *Ibid.*, col. 1.

[113] *Ibid.*

[114] *Ibid.*, September 8, 1978, p. 29195, col. 1.

[115] *Ibid.*, col. 2.

[116] *Ibid.*, December 16, 1977, p. 28725, col. 1; February 25, 1977, p. 28209, col. 1.

thought.[117] An official paper said that the Culture Ministry, a reserve of the Gang, was a "disaster area."[118] More than one thousand of its employees were branded spies or counterrevolutionaries. Torture was employed to exact confessions and this resulted in mayhem, madness or death. Stereotyped journalism was still another count of crime of the Gang. The *Jie fang jun bao* of September 24, 1977 deplored that such journalism, or its "ghost," still hangs on. The paper calls for the wiping out of the sham reportage.[119] Falsehood in the press had given birth to all sorts of rumors. It castigates those who knowingly "embellish the facts and depict everything as perfect." The Gang had vitiated the nation's media by forcing it to use fabrication and to spread deceptive information. The Gang's "clean sweep," adds the paper, became an all-out campaign of obscurantism.

Have the present leaders come to realize the role of science? and what has been done to improve it? Deng Xiaoping in a major policy speech to the National Conference on Education which met from April 22 to May 16, 1978 and was attended by 6,000 experts and administrators, declared that the "crux of the four modernizations is the mastery of modern science and technology."[120] In effect, Deng was saying that science and technology is the key to modernization because agriculture, industry and national defense depend on the successes in this sector. In particular he pointed to the use of science to enhance productivity of grain and iron and steel; he was very frank conceding that the CPR's efficiency in the making of iron and steel was only a "small percentage of advanced levels abroad," and its record of grain was even worse. For example, the average annual output per farmer is 1,000 kg in China, whereas in the US it is 50,000 kg. This, he said, represents a disparity of several dozens of times. In reality, one Chinese farmer produces not 1,000, but 450 kg if we take the 1980 statistics of 317 million tons of grain produced by 700,000,000 farm workers into account (see Chapter IX).

After deploring the CPR's sluggish production, Deng proclaimed an open-door policy. He urged that one should get out and learn from advanced countries. "Science and technology is a kind of wealth created in common by all mankind," stressed he. It behoves China to absorb the fortes of others. To this end, he pledged his government's readiness to help academic exchanges and to step up contacts with scientific circles of the rest of the world. Fang Yi echoed his superior by declaring that in making an evaluation of science, one should avoid negating others' strength just because of their reactionary system and idealistic outlook. China cannot afford to reject the imperialists' positive side.[121]

[117] *Ibid.*, December 16, 1977, p. 28725, col. 1.

[118] *Renmin ribao*, May 14, 1978, pp. 1, 3.

[119] *Keesing's*, December 16, 1977, p. 28725, col. 2.

[120] *Ibid.*, September 8, 1978, p. 29194, col. 1.

[121] *Ibid.*, p. 29195, col. 1.

In view of the Gang's harassment of the men of science, Deng assured them that they can from now on have more time to study and test. A guarantee was tendered by him that they get at least five-sixths of their worktime for their specialized work. That is meant to be the minimum.[122] He said he would not object to some people devoting seven days and seven nights a week to their research but the main thing is that the government should not ask them, or at any rate an overwhelming majority of them, to devour a lot of political and theoretical books, take part in numerous social activities or attend many meetings irrelevant to their line. In effect, Deng substituted job efficiency for scholastic communism. High credentials to career or reward in the People's Republic, he emphasized, will be based on the excellent achievement in practical work. "Comrades of different trades and professions are not divorced from politics when they do their best at their posts." Their research is regarded by Deng as a demonstration of their service to the proletarian cause and of their socialist consciousness. One is given to understand that if a scientist does not express anti-communist ideas, for example, by putting up posters to criticize the regime or high officials,[123] he would not only be left alone in the laboratory or study, but would fair well.

The five-sixths assurance, stated above, was already decreed by a circular of the CC of September 18, 1977,[124] but according to Renmin ribao, the decree was not put into effect.[125] Its editorial says that the essential responsibility of all Chinese during this period of socialist buildup was to consolidate the dictatorship of the proletariat and that an important step toward this goal was the strengthening of the material base. The paper considers scientific work as the impetus of progress and it voices criticism of some institutions which still wasted the time of the scientists in political meetings.[126]

Getting back to Deng's speech, scientific institutions must have powers and competence commensurate with their task. They ought not to be dictated or supplanted by the party, since their job is to produce results and train people, but not to make everybody a communist. When the government comes to evaluate these institutions, the only criterion is whether they have succeeded in fulfilling that job. It should not ask how much they mastered the Marxist philosophy. Deng dismissed the slogan of putting politics in command as "mere empty talk" if the practical job is neglected. It is incumbent upon the party branch in a scientific organization to create propitious conditions for the administrators and specialists there to go about their research. Even though Deng was not declaring political non-interference, he came very nearly to it. He promised that

---

[122] Ibid., p. 29294, col. 1.

[123] Beijing Review, January 4, 1980, p. 7, col. 1.

[124] Keesing's, December 16, 1977, p. 28725, col. 1.

[125] Ibid.

[126] Ibid., September 8, 1978, p. 29195, col. 2.

the slogan "let 100 schools of thought contend" would be honored to safeguard the right of untrammeled debates and that the government would "listen closely to experts' opinions and enable them to play their full role so that we can do better at scientific and technical work and reduce our errors as much as possible."[127]

It is true that at times during the oration, Deng still spoke of "red" in addition to "expert,"[128] however, his general position tells that the kind of red is not much of a red. In tune with this new policy, *Beijing Review* writes that loving one's motherland, laboring consciously for socialism and serving the people is red and that anyone who holds onto Marxist ideal, does a good job, continually improves himself, and makes contributions to society is to be considered red and expert. Ideology is unmistakably soft-pedalled in China. Because red and expert cannot be blended easily, the Beijing leadership have preferred the latter, paying as much homage to the former as is required by the socialist legitimacy.

Fang Yi outlined an eight-year plan of science and technology for 1978-1985 which envisaged 27 areas of research and under them 108 key projects.[129] The most essential areas are: a) agriculture, b) energy, c) material, d) electronic computer, e) laser science and technology, f) space research, g) high energy physics, h) genetic engineering. It is not necessary to enumerate all the projects subsumed in each area, but we may take the first three areas for examples. The projects under a) agriculture are soil improvement, drainage and irrigation, fertilization, new seed strains, insecticides, and plant diseases; under b) energy are oil and gas, drilling and processing technique, mechanization and automation of colliery, hydroelectric and thermal stations, atomic power and wind energy; and under c) are metallurgical technique, plastics and rubber and fibers. In 1982, the 108 projects were slashed to 40 by Premier Zhao Ziyang. He proposed "100 major problems in 38 scientific and technological research projects vital to production and construction."[130]

Fang Yi reiterated the position of freedom of scientific experiment which Deng Xiaoping has stressed so much, adding that "imposing one particular school and banning another by administrative fiat can only hamper the development of science." Even though in his speech he kept on talking of politics, he cautioned that to guide the researchers with Marxist tenets does not mean the substitution of philosophy for concrete work. In order to advance in science, the Beijing elite set forth the idea of key institutions, including not only colleges but high schools and grade schools (see also preceding

127 *Ibid.*, col. 1.

128 *Ibid.*, col. 2.

129 *Ibid.*, col. 1.

130 *Beijing review*, December 20, 1982, p. 16, col. 1.

section).[131] Due to the dearth of resources in faculty, staff, library and laboratory facilities and funds, a smaller number of institutions are set up all over the country. They serve as standards for thousands or hundreds of others. Their students are of higher quality. It is known that because these schools receive more finance, they can hire better instructors and acquire expensive equipment. More importantly, their students are selected from among a larger number of candidates.[132] All this makes such institutions elitist, and the government has to make an official denial of their being so.[133]

The People's Republic is said to have 5,714,000 scientific and technical employees, of whom 330,000 are doing research alone. Besides the science faculties of the 729 universities, there is the Academy of Sciences, the nation's center of natural studies. It is composed of more than 110 institutes. In addition, 4,300 research bureaus are established in all the ministries under the State Council and in provincial and regional governments, not counting the key enterprises' agencies of applied science. Some notable successes include the testing of atom and hydrogen bombs, the launching of carrier rockets from land and underwater, and the making of bovine insulin and yeast alanine T-RNA. But in vast areas the achievements are marginal. A recent article in *Beijing review* summarized the scientific strategy as a) drafting of a long-term scheme for a balanced growth of the economy on one hand, and of science and technology on the other.[134] China's policy of modernization aims at tangible results to be attained by the application of techniques. There will be a reform in management structure, prudent deployment of productive forces, the change of consumption pattern and the intelligent use of facilities. b) Researchers are to grapple with cardinal issues. These involve agronomy, consumer commodities, energy, transport and communication means, new materials, large-scale integrated circuits and computer technology. To be carried out are only projects which prove to be fruitful and have impact on scientific progress. The government will implement technical transformation with stress on energy conservation, a comprehensive utilization of coal, geophysical oil prospecting, high-speed oil drilling and the exploration of additional energy sources.

c) Applied techniques are to be given priority. It is written that the concern with putting the knowledge to use has always been behind the interest in basic investigation. This is because many institutes and individual scholars used to be engrossed with the theoretical side to the neglect of the practical aspect of their study. Research has to be linked with end-result. d) Science cadres are advised to select rational technological alternatives. Preferable are the techniques

[131] *Renmin ribao,* January 13, 1981, p. 3.

[132] *Beijing review,* January 7, 1980, p. 26.

[133] *Ibid.*

[134] *Ibid.,* February 14, 1983, pp. 14-18.

which can save money, fuel and raw materials and which require intensive labor-input but yield good results. e) Publicizing the outcome of scientific research and f) importing and absorbing overseas techniques are essential in modernizing the CPR's economy. After the adoption of an open-door policy in 1978 by the State Council, the accent has moved from taking in large complete sets of equipment to single items. Likewise there is a shift from stress on building of fresh enterprises to the renovation of existing ones. In the total volume of imported techniques, the share of individual articles rose from 1.2 percent in 1979 to 28.6 percent in 1981. Of the funds for technical import, the percentage of those items used for technical improvement of plants in operation rose from 0.7 percent in 1979 to 36.7 in 1981. The Chinese do not seem to consider the sending of tens of thousands of students abroad as one of the most reliable means of modernization. Is it because of the risk of defection which may take a big toll of them?

The shockwave of modernization has impacted on liberal arts. It was announced in April 1977 that a number of classical Chinese poetry banned in recent years would be republished. In May the works of William Shakespeare, Heinrich Heine and other Western authors appeared, and in October out came the works of Nikolai Vasilievich Gogol, Honoré de Balzac and Victor Marie Hugo, as well as the drawings of Van Rejn Rembrandt. Replaying of occidental music was also initiated. A concert of Ludwig von Beethoven was broadcast on March 28, 1977 to mark the 150th anniversary of his death, and recital by a Norwegian pianist in Beijing on May 19 featuring Frédéric François Chopin, Wolfgang Mozart, Beethoven and George Frederick Handel was attended by high mandarins and it was lauded in the press.[135] On October 16, 1977, an announcement was made on the publication of the piano compositions by Johann Christian Bach, Handel and Beethoven. In 1978, reprints of the preceding and other authors became available in bookstores in big cities. However, Western works of philosophy, history, politics, economics, law, and sociology were not to appear until 1981 when the Commerce Press in Beijing advertized the publishing of the Chinese translation of St. Augustine, Benedict Spinoza, Charles Darwin, Bertrand Russell, Ludwig Hegel, William James (pragmatist), Aristotle, John Locke, Jean Jacques Rousseau, the Napolean Code, Adam Smith, David Ricardo, John Keynes, Thomas Malthus, Lewis Henry Morgan, Publius Cornelius Tacitus, etc.[136] In 1983, the same publishing house put out the 69-volume *Chinese translation of world-famous academic works* which includes the books of the above authors and many more.[137] Few of these writers, we should note, appear in the Soviet Union, but the Chinese are not afraid of any of them.

[135] *Keesing's*, December 16, 1977, p. 28725, col. 1.

[136] *Renmin ribao*, January 12, 1981, p. 5. Baron Montesquieu's *The spirit of the laws* is available in bookstores, *Guangming ribao*, September 15, 1981, p. 1.

[137] *Beijing review*, November 22, 1982, p. 29.

Traditional Chinese operas and more than 100 films made before the Cultural Revolution were reissued. A display of new landscape, bird and flower paintings, the first of its kind in a decade, took place in Beijing; and pieces of classical composers of the West were set as part of the entrance exams of the Central Conservatory again for the first time since the ending of the Cultural Revolution. A number of eminent writers who were tortured by the Red Guards were rehabilitated. Lao She, who died in 1966, was given a state funeral on June 3, 1978 (there are now an increasing number of such delayed funerals). Another famous novelist, Ba Jing (elected president of the National Association of Chinese Writers in December 1981) said in an interview in February 1978 that he worked from 1966 to 1970 as a janitor in the Shanghai Writers' Association buildings and that from 1970 to 1972 he was sent to a cadres' school for reeducation. After release in the latter year, he was allowed to do some translation, but remained under surveillance.[138] All these just mentioned and numerous others were at liberty to write satires during the GMD period on the mainland. Their books were sold by the millions of copies. The GMD did not move to retaliate or silence them. Their reputation was soaring and all leftists orchestrated to laud them. When the Red regime persecuted these authors after 1949, didn't they say in private: "We did enjoy freedom before?"

The National Association of Chinese Writers, inactive during the Cultural Revolution, was resuscitated and it met on December 28-31, 1977 (first time again in a decade). There reappeared the associations of dramatists, musicians, film artists and dancers. The Guangzhou chapter of the Chinese Writers' Association was convened in April 1978 to discuss the love theme in literature, a taboo for many a year. In June 1978, five of the fourteen journals of the Academy of Social Sciences resumed publication, as were some 30 newspapers and magazines.[139] An interesting consequence of the liberation was the partial "parole" of Confucius. He was attacked during the Cultural Revolution and again in 1973-1974 for his reactionary philosophy. However, the present leaders do not want to get involved in the evaluation of him any longer. Such evaluation still goes on quite vigorously. Some communist authors do not have much love for the sage, but all seem to have a better understanding of him in light of his time which they classify as the slave period of history.[140]

Spiritual culture

Beginning in early 1981, there has been an unusual flurry of news items and editorials about the school situation, all zeroing in on student behavior. The communists openly admit that the problem

---

[138] *Keesing's*, September 8, 1978, p. 29195, col. 2.

[139] *Ibid.*

[140] *Guangming ribao*, January 22, 1981, p. 4.

comes to plague the whole nation and they view it as reflecting a deep-rooted attitude in the social body, an attitude hard to explain at the present stage of development in China. Material betterment, they are surprised, is not coupled with the heightening of public morals. "To cure the wounds in spirit is much harder than to cure the wounds in economy."[141] Deng Xiaoping spoke to a delegation of the Japanese diet that "without spiritual culture China, although rich and strong, cannot become an ideal state."[142] The vibrant rhetoric of the communists about material determinism, class struggle and proletarian internationalism have definitely come in for review, even repudiation. As a matter of fact, recent years witness the same sort of trend in the Soviet Union. Marx and Engels, as scholars of both countries come to note, have indeed assigned a high role to idealism. These scholars found it convenient to quote them in order to point up the equipollence of spiritual and material values.[143] Before the purge of the Gang of Four and the death of Stalin, the statements of Marx and Engels which compromise or outrightly negate materialism, were totally ignored. Russian and Chinese ideologues paid sole attention to those writings of Marx and Engels which placed exclusive emphasis on material force. Now, both communist forefathers are brought into full view.

A commentator of *Guangming ribao* alleges that the capitalist class "once rumored that Marxism gives only recognition to matter [but not to mind]."[144] We think the commentator should have said that it was the communists, Chinese as well as Russian, who "rumored." The Chinese have adduced from Marx and Engels a few of the most devastating sayings on materialism. They add even more devastating statements of their own. "The vulgarists," Engels is quoted, "equates materialism to gluttony, alcoholism, amusement, carnal hedonism, vainglory, love of property, stinginess, avarice, profiteering, speculation, in short, every obnoxious thing they craved for in private."[145] It is only in the final analysis, says Engels, that material and economic factor determines; one cannot deny spiritual power at all.[146] Marx, noted the Chinese, stated that it is man who changes the environment.[147]

Which of the two, mind or matter, is more decisive? Assuming that man's existing molds his consciousness, the communists cling to

[141] *Ibid.*, January 20, 1981, p. 1.

[142] *Ibid.*, February 22, 1981, p. 1.

[143] This author's "Recent trend in the Soviet dialectical materialism," part I, *Issues & Studies*, no. 10 (September 1974), pp. 81-99; part II, no. 10 (December 1974), pp. 59-82.

[144] *Guangming ribao*, February 22, 1981, p. 1.

[145] Quoting Marx and Engels, *Collected Works*, vol. 4, p. 226. The imprint is incomplete, see *Guangming ribao*, February 22, 1981, p. 1.

[146] The expression "letzer instanz" (in the final analysis) appears in Engels, "Engels an W. Borgius Dresden," Karl Marx and F. Engels, *Werke*, Berlin: Dietz Verlag, 1962-1969, vol. 39 (1968), pp. 205-207 at 206.

[147] *Guangming ribao*, January 22, 1981, p. 4.

materialism. Yet, in the light of man's active role in the shaping of his life-style, they came to doubt that premise. They hold that the "interrelation of material culture and spiritual culture is not which conditions which. That is simplistic. The relation is dialectic in character."[148] The two cultures are inseparable.[149] This amounts to saying that one should not commit himself to either materialism or idealism. In a symposium from which the preceding quotation is drawn, some expressed that material culture of socialism is fundamental to spiritual culture, but the latter is a mighty power which moves the material world ahead. The view is expressed that either inaction or wrong action on the part of man can impede the progress of society.[150] Engels, in fact, already pointed out the latter idea,[151] but the Chinese symposiants did not cite him.

Marxism teaches that social reality governs man's thought and action and that spiritual culture has a close linkage with the material culture. This, the Chinese say, must not be mechanically construed.[152] According to their "dynamic" interpretation, the two cultures are both connected and disconnected. At the present time, the Chinese press has placed emphasis on the "disconnected" side. In re the "connected" view, it is held that "without certain economic conditions, spiritual culture cannot develop, and that this culture should have a corresponding material base."[153] In social relations, this view ascribes man's bad behavior to material privation. Lenin, for one, regarded crimes to be the result of miserable life under the capitalist yoke.[154] If a man is hungry and cold, he is driven to wrongdoings.

Come to the "disconnected" side, the Chinese cite Engels that "an economically stagnant system may play the first violin in philosophy."[155] From this, they infer that a comfortable life does not necessarily lead to spiritual virtue or is conducive to a harmonious community. It may beget wickedness. Experience shows that disorder has obtained among the well-fed and -clad peoples in the world. The Chinese point critical fingers at Western countries which, they see, are vexed by arson, murder and robbery. Freedom from want does not lift up mankind, but heads for decadence.[156] Henceforth to thank

---

[148] *Ibid.*, February 20, 1981, p. 1.

[149] *Renmin ribao*, December 2, 1981, p. 1.

[150] *Guangming ribao*, February 22, 1981, p. 1.

[151] Marx and Engels, *Sochineniya*, vol. 37, p. 417; cited in A. Denisov, *Sovetskoe gosudarstvo*, Moskva: Izd-vo Moskovskogo Universiteta, 1967, pp. 216-217. Other supportive comments can be found in *ibid.*, pp. 139, 192. See also A. Denisov, "Burzhuaznoe gosudarstvo i pravo," *Teoriya gosudarstva i prava, pod redaktsiei* A. Denisov, Moskva: Izd-vo Moskovskogo Universiteta, 1967, pp. 112-137 at 120.

[152] *Guangming ribao*, February 18, 1981, p. 1.

[153] *Ibid.*, February 20, 1981, p. 1.

[154] Lenin, "Gosudarstvo i revoliutsiya," August-September 1917, *Polnoe sobranie sochinenii*, 5th ed., Moskva: Gosudarstvennoe izdatel' stvo politicheskoi literatury, 1962, vol. 33, pp. 3-119 at 91.

[155] *Guangming ribao*, February 18, 1981, p. 1.

[156] *Ibid.*, February 22, 1981, p. 1.

good society to economic affluence cannot stand to reason. There is no basis then to assert that if the daily needs are taken care of, man would naturally improve his spiritual value, nor that man's consciousness and morals follow *ipso facto* material betterment.[157] The "disconnected" stand virtually refutes the holding that social relations mirror the objective world, or that man is conditioned by the outside reality. It contains, we believe, a powerful hortatory note. In effect, the ruling clique of Beijing confesses to the difficult life of the masses, but orders them to behave well regardless. Despite the adverse environment, in other words, the communist spirit can still be made to prevail.[158] The unstated slogan is: "Let material determine nothing, but let mind determine everything." Or, "one should not be awed by the power of poverty." Otherwise, how can China break the chain of poverty and misery to reach the communist nirvana?

Moral exertion can compensate for what is lacking in economic well-being. *Guangming ribao* admonishes that "after all man must have a modicum of morals."[159] Underlying this statement is the defiance of the supposed power of the environment. The Beijing media bewails the spiritual degradation of the society at large and among the youth in particular. This, we think, is an extraordinary candor and it shows the intrepidity with which the media is washing dirty linen in public. We are wondering if this is not based on an undisclosed decision of the hierarchs, a decision to denigrate the Cultural Revolution. The aim of the Revolution was alleged by its protagonists to be the purification of the rising young souls. Instead, the present government says it is counterproductive. The denunciation of low spirit is purported to reinforce the charge of economic drawback and to justify the contemporary anti-Gang campaign. The ten disastrous years have played havoc with both mind and matter. The successors to the Chinese revolution which were the avowed objective of the Cultural Revolution, turn out to be degenerate and miscreant. They are not much of a successor. *Guangming ribao* minced no words pitying the social pandemonium in today's Cathay with blame thrown upon the past leaders and the West. "Thanks to the decade of Lin Biao, Jiang Qing and other counterrevolutionaries, the public get confused and their integrity compromised. Inevitably, modernization brings in capitalist putrescence from abroad."[160] A low moral standard is seen menacing the task of nation-building. "There obtain in Chinese society depravity, strife for privilege, obdurant bureaucratism, selfishness, money-grabbing and regnant anarchism."[161] All this is bound to lead to solipsism and to the collapse of the morale of the people. Severely

[157] *Ibid.*, February 18, 1981, p. 1.

[158] *Ibid.*, February 22 and 18, 1981, both on p. 1.

[159] *Ibid.*, February 28, 1981, p. 2.

[160] *Ibid.*, February 18, 1981, p. 1.

[161] *Ibid.*, February 22, 1981, p. 1.

impugned are the ancient, the myopic, the sordid, the ignorant, the uncouth and the numskulled amongst the Chinese.[162] *Renmin ribao* writes of the "rampant evil of society, the unrighted mind of the party, and the disgruntlement of the public," which it says, "would doom the four modernizations."[163] This is the bitterest self-criticism ever to appear in the Chinese press.

In the public is descried a widely held view that since under socialism the policy is the division of reward according to labor, individualism has to be the basic tenet.[164] Altruism should have no pride of place. It is only under communism that it would prevail. Many even go so far as to yell that "heaven condemns those who disavow their own interests."[165] This outlook is deplored by the press as befitting egoistic virtue and as deleterious to a socialist system.[166]

Unruly demeanor in colleges and high schools is commonplace and gives cause of anxiety for the government. Newspapers printed many readers' comments on it. A graduate student of Fudan University in Shanghai, for example, wrote the school administration a letter which is reproduced in *Guangming ribao*.[167] According to this man, the phenomenon he described has spread far and wide in China. What struck him the most during his first year at Fudan was the lack of sense of righteousness on the part of everyone. He saw uncivilized activity everywhere and found it particularly revolting that the administration treated it nonchalantly. Nothing was done about it. Whether it was in the dining hall, or the library, or bathing rooms, in short, wherever there was a crowd, rudeness reigned supreme. There was the shouting and pushing, there was the foul language, there was the tossing out of bread and rice all over the place. Physical struggle occurred all over the campus. Victory went to three species of men: the long-armed, the sturdy-muscled, and the brazen-faced. Look at the open stacks of the library and you will see it is literally ransacked. Not only pictures and pages were lifted, but journals were walked off with. The entire university was choked in chaos. Self-interest was at the uppermost of everyone's heart.

Another alarming phenomenon is teacher-beating by students, or cadres or parents. In six counties of Hunan province, there were 154 such incidents from 1978 to 1980.[168] In one case, the teacher was tied to a tree overnight. In another, the teacher was shot. Of the 154 incidents, 117 were settled and among these 30 were disputed acrimoniously among the public regarding the propriety of the

[162] *Ibid.*, February 18, 1981, p. 1.

[163] *Renmin ribao*, September 8, 1981, p. 2.

[164] *Guangming ribao*, February 18, 1981, p. 1.

[165] *Ibid.*, February 3, 1981, p. 1.

[166] *Ibid.*, February 22, 1981, p. 1.

[167] *Ibid.*, January 24, 1981, p. 3.

[168] *Ibid.*, January 22, 1981, p. 1.

solution. In seven cities and counties (among them Nanchong and Neijiang) of Sichuan province, there were 1,027 cases of beating from September 1979 to September 1982, of which 220 remained unsolved at the time of report (February 1983).[169] There were also such incidents in Xinjiang region.[170]

The authorities are devising ways and means to cope with the "luan" (bedlam). First and foremost there is the counseling service, termed "political work on thought." Pick up any issue of *Guangming ribao,* say from mid-1980 onward, and you would find there has been no single issue which does not report on the political work of one sort or another done by party members, administrators, teachers and young communists. The method used is persuasion rather than compulsion. Conspicuously absent are the denunciatory and mad sessions which figured so large during the Cultural Revolution. Held high presently are the traditional morals (see first section of this chapter). The youngsters are to be trained as useful elements of society. This is a far cry from drilling them as stout class-warriors. To cater to the needs of the students, school authorities are urged by the press to provide lively activities, recreation and other interesting undertakings.[171] The fact that these have to be urged indicates a lack of them in the schools.

The laxity in ideological work and the widespread apathy of school administrators and teachers toward politics can be a source of trouble for them. If in the future a different leadership should reinvigorate Marxism-Leninism and Mao Zedong Thought, they may be brought to task for being too moderate. Who can be sure that the radical wind will not outblow the pragmatical wind? *Guangming ribao* complains of too many political movements in the past.[172] They have implanted fear in the mind of the public that today's orthodoxy may be tomorrow's paganism. The leftists are chastized for their malevolence when the rightists sit at the helm, and vice versa. "The masses are taken aback by the mere talk of change, and they have lost faith in the government." The paper quotes a saw that "once bitten by a reptile, one may even be scared by the sight of a rope in a decade." We can easily understand the reluctance of the thought-workers to execute, with much ardor, the policy of the current leaders.

Each and every school is pushing for cultivating good manners and courteous expressions among the students. This is code-named "beautification."[173] Greeting words are to be used and abusives abandoned. In this campaign, the government revives many of the Confucian sayings once spitted on as feudalistic and unproletarian.

[169] *Ibid.,* February 18, 1983, p. 2.

[170] *Renmin ribao,* July 9, 1981, p. 1.

[171] *Ibid.,* February 20, 1981, p. 1.

[172] *Ibid.,* January 22, 1981, p. 1.

[173] *Ibid.,* January 20, 1981, p. 1.

Another heritage now reclaimed is the triadic unison of moral-knowledge-constitution. A well-rounded personality consists of the finest development in each of these.[174] The aim of teaching is not so much at imparting subject-matter as improving the living man.[175] Today, an affable and polished individual but not the frenzied Red Guard is the paragon of Homo sapiens.

To effectively combat the degeneracy of the youth, the government has restored the parental power which the communists have done so much to torpedo. The easiness with which the Red Guards were mobilized is imputable to the lapse of the role of the family. The contemporary rulers have come to realize the past mistakes. They earnestly call for "coordination of family and educational institutions."[176] It is conceded that the youth still spend more time at home than in other places and that the influence of the oldsters has a decisive bearing on the "beautification." In some schools, there is formulated, after wide discussion, a set of ethical rules binding upon all in the system.[177] Another means looking toward the regulation of demeanor is the assignment of a teacher to be the headmaster of a class.[178] He is empowered to follow up on his students wherever he thinks necessary, for example, by going to their bedrooms and imposing summary chastisement.[179] Such kind of hot pursuit has given rise to conflict. Some of the incidents of teacher-beatings mentioned above stemmed from it. These regulatory measures indicate the gravity of discipline problems in the schools of China.

The Education Ministry has recently ordered a number of political courses to be taught. The first year of junior high has to offer "cultivation of adolescence," the second, "basic knowledge of law," and the third, "history of social development." The first and second years of senior high have to teach "fundamentals of political economy," and "dialectical materialism" respectively.[180] This decision went into effect in the fall of 1981. Apparently, it purports to combat the ideological apathy in the schools.

Renmin ribao reported that many students have lost respect for the communist party. They no longer give credence to the superiority claim of communism. Instead, they came to cling onto extreme individualism.[181] Some doubt that socialism can save China.[182] There

[174] *Ibid.*, February 13, 1981, p. 1.

[175] *Ibid.*, February 16, 1981, p. 1. *Renmin ribao*, February 24, 1981, p. 1.

[176] *Guangming ribao*, February 16, 1981, p. 1.

[177] *Ibid.*, February 14, 1981, p. 1.

[178] *Ibid.*, February 3 and 17, 1981, both on p. 1.

[179] *Ibid.*, January 18, 1981.

[180] *Ibid.*, January 29, 1981, p. 1.

[181] *Renmin ribao*, January 22, 1981, p. 1. *Guangming ribao*, February 3 and 24, 1981, both on p. 1.

[182] *Renmin ribao*, March 19, 1981, p. 5.

are mounting complaints by students of the waste of time in learning political lessons. The thought of these students is problematical, it is written.[183] In a symposium conducted by the World History Department of the Academy of Social Sciences, one participant raised the eye-opening question as to whether class struggle or class cooperation is the impetus of social change.[184] He does not directly refute Marxism, but attempts to beat around the bush by saying that one must look at Marxism as a whole and that the system is not a dogmatic complex but the guide to action. In his view, it is only through an objective inquiry and comprehensive study that one may free himself from "lopsided metaphysics." This is as far as an intellectual can go in a still avowed communist polity. The CPR, although a nation conceived in proletarian dictatorship and dedicated to the proposition that Marxism-Leninism and Mao Zedong Thought is the official credo (see Preamble of the 1982 Constitution), has gone a long way toward some measure of liberalism. There is, of course, no freedom of speech in the conventional sense as witnessed by the sentencing to 15 years' imprisonment of Wei Jingsheng, the valiant champion of human rights. Yet there is now a great deal of "loose talk," and most important, Wei Jingshen and other defiants are not summarily shot, as they would have been in the past. We may ask: "Will the current oligarchy allow this situation to continue so as to eventually unleash a flood which they wouldn't be able to control and which could drown them?"[185]

[183] *Guangming ribao*, January 23, 1981, p. 1.

[184] *Ibid.*

[185] *Khrushchev remembers, the last testament*, Boston: Little, Brown, 1974, p. 86. This question was asked by Khrushchev in regard to the situation of his country.

CHAPTER XIII
Health and Human Services

Introduction

The People's Republic seems to have passed from a regime of death, execution and warfare to one of health, education and welfare. According to the Constitution, citizens shall be left alone in their private and home life, can enjoy rest, may have a job, be granted superannuation and assured of disability payments, and are provided with hospital care including co-op clinic services and with social assistance of diverse sorts.[1] The truth, however, is that the CPR's leaders, enamored as they were with power and especially the battle for it, just had not much energy left to bother about such written commitments. These remained perforce declaratory rather than functional. Among the rights, the most conspicuous by its absence was the right of rest promised in Article 42, paragraph 2 of the Constitution. Following the inauguration of the Beijing aristocracy in 1949, "there have been more than seventy campaigns at the national level."[2] On the average, every year witnesses two drives involving hundreds of millions whose waken time was utterly agitated.[3] Whenever a drive was on, they dared not stand by with folded arms. All were whipped up by the frenzied cadres who led them around like animals. Then there were the commissars who harangued them hours on end until their lips became blue and listeners fainted.

In the campaigns, the masses were taught to hate and assault class enemies said to be represented by some individuals. Communist credoes were rammed down the people's throats during both workhours and leisure. After the ouster of the Gang of Four, mass movements are less frequent and political agitation has slackened, but social control abides. Add to this tension the struggle for survival represented by queuing up to buy daily needs, you can imagine how little the masses know of rest. Crazed with mobilization, the Reds give the people few moments for repose. Even though Beijing has endeavored to do something to better the lot of the masses, this activity is not accorded priority. True, all communist countries have ignored the well-being of the public in favor of military muscle, but the uniqueness of the CPR is that the huge size of the population requires enormous resources to feed and clothe, resources which are beyond the capacity of the communistic economy. The problem is aggravated by the leaders' enchantment with political infighting which is bound to relegate the concern with the fate of the masses, the real proletarians, to the "lower-most" of their heart.

Chinese officials have been wont to bandy out statistics to

---

[1] The 1978 Constitution, Articles 47-50; the 1982 Constitution, Articles 32-47.

[2] James Wang, *Contemporary Chinese Politics*, Englewood Cliffs, New Jewsey: Prentice-Hall, 1980, p. 179.

[3] James Townsend, "Politics in China," *Comparative Politics Today, a World View*, 2nd, ed., Boston: Little, Brown, 1980, pp. 381-432 at 430.

demonstrate their achievement in public health, and these statistcs are higher and sometimes much higher than Western sources come up with. For example, Beijing alleges that "to date, the average life span in our country is 68.2 as against 32 in 1949." For males it is 66.9 and for females, 69.5. In the capital, it is even longer: 69.51 and 72.26 for the respective genders. Longer yet is the life expectancy in Shanghai: 70.64 against 75.48.[4] However, one occidental book gives 55-60 for both men and women,[5] while another 60.7 for males and 64.4 for females,[6] and a third 68 for both.[7] On the death rate, the Chinese media says it "has dropped from 28 per thousand in the early 50's to 6.29 per thousand today," but the 2nd and 3rd Western references mention 9.4 and 10.3 respectively.[8] In regard to the number of hospital beds, the Chinese put them in 1980 at 1,932,000.[9] With a population of 953 million,[10] it amounts to ca. 500 to a bed. However, the *World Almanac* writes of 100,000 to a bed.[11] Again, the Chinese say they provide one physician for every 2,000[12] but a Western reference indicates that there are 33 physicians for 100,000.[13] That is, 3,333 to one. Which side's information is to be believed? We would rather give the disinterested foreign estimates more credence, because the communists have been well known to use inflated figures to impress people.

The Beijing elite have developed a fine art of equating their "New China" with the old in everything and pointed, with pride, to their scoreboard. For example, the life span, as said a moment ago, is alleged to extend from 32 in 1949 to 68.2 in 1978. "The whole country," it is stated, "now boasts of 65,000 hospitals, 25 times as many as in 1949.[14] In this analogy game, the Chinese have inherited from their erstwhile brothers, the Soviets. The latter, we shall recall, are fond of comparing this or that to what it was in 1913. Neither czarist Russia nor the Chinese Republic was in fact as "terrible" as it is painted by the Reds.[15] We are wondering if everything of the ancien regime was so unworthy, why the Chinese communists should

[4] *Beijing review*, June 23, 1980, p. 21, col. 1.

[5] *Countries of the World*, Toronto: Coles Pub. Co., Chinese section p. 1.

[6] *World Almanac*, 1982, p. 526, col. 2

[7] *Hammond*, 1982, p. 547, col. s

[8] *World Almanac*, and *Hammond*, both *loc. cit.*

[9] *Beijing Review, loc. cit.*

[10] *Hammond, loc. cit.*

[11] *World Almanac, loc. cit.*

[12] *Beijing Review, loc. cit.*

[13] *World Almanac, loc. cit.*

[14] *Beijing Review*, June 23, 1980, p. 20, col. 1

[15] Michael Roskin, *Countries and concepts, an introduction to comparative politics*, Englewood Cliffs, New Jersey: Prentice-Hall, 1982, p. 221 mentions the Russian situation.

give so much trust to the pre-1949 figures, upon which their computation is based. Our remark would hardly be necessary save for the almost universal reticence of scholars on this comparison mania of the Reds.

However, when the Maoists are not playing with the equation mahjong, the data they produced seem to be less dubious, and for this reason, there is no ground to object to using them as reference. In the following pages, we would avoid the analogical statistics delivered by the Chinese communists, which are little better than *ipse dixit*. If the numbers are non-comparative in nature, there seems to be less temptation on their part to resort to exaggeration. For example, Beijing's media say that each of the 55,000 communes has a clinic.[16] In this case, it is hard to deny the assertion, since clinics can range from a full-fledged establishment to almost barren dispensary. Another example is the statement that "there is at least one general hospital in each of the nation's 2,000-odd counties.[17] This is certainly correct, because as far back as 1948, that is, before the setting up of the CPR, there was no county which did not have one.

Medical cadres

The communists aim at universal medicare, building as they are on the equality principle. Apart from the all important problem of standard of facility, the Beijing regime is moderately successful in making sanitation services accessible to all. Each of the 710,000 brigades is provided with a health unit.[18] A brigade, we shall note, consists of a cluster of hamlets. The unit is conveniently situated, not too distant from any of them. There are also portable dispensaries, mobile paramedics, and barefoot physcians (see below). The training of health cadres is on a grand scale. From 1949 to 1970, for example, medical colleges graduated some 388,000 personnel. On the average, every year turned out 17,000. They are M.D.'s, although no formal degree was conferred until 1982. The CPR also maintains schools which turn out hospital employees of junior status. During 1949-1970, some 800,000 of these were reported. In the entire country, doctors, pharmacists, nurses and kindred helpers numbered 2,642,000 in 1980.[19] The *Statesman's Yearbook* estimates the "less qualified workers" to be 700,000, a figure lower by 100,000 than the just cited junior trainees.[20] The same source writes of 350,000 physicians, 4 million health workers and midwives. As seen above, each county has one or more hospitals. There are "1,000 urban hospitals" which are said to have fine facilities. One can presume all the large cities

[16]*Beijing review*, June 23, 1980, p. 20, col. 1.

[17] *Ibid.*

[18] *Ibid., Zhong guo jian kuang*, Beijing: Wai wen chu ban she, 1983, p. 2.

[19] *Beijing reivew*, June 23, 1980, p. 20, col. 2.

[20] *Stateman's Yearbook*, 1979-1980, p. 343.

with more than 1 million inhabitants (29 cities in this category),[21] should have each several such hospitals. However, except in an emergency, only the urbanites can be treated there. According to the official statistics, the proportion of hospital beds in urban and rural areas was 38.3 percent to 61.7 percent in 1979,[22] but one must not forget that rural China has 79.4 percent of the whole population.[23] Therefore, a city resident enjoys a great deal more medical rights than his village cousin. This is particularly true with regard to hospitalization. The rural folks nevertheless are not totally neglected, even though they are served rather poorly.

Three groups are serving in the countryside. They are a) health workers numbering 2,819,000, b) midwives 709,000, and c) barefoot doctors.[24] The last are the most trumpeted about by Beijing's mouthpiece. They count 1,575,000, one-third being female.[25] The *Statesman's Yearbook* records 1,800,000 such doctors; this figure probably includes some of the other two groups. Since there are 5,660,000 production teams,[26] one doctor would have to serve at least 3 of them. In numbers of people, he takes care of 440. The ratio is big enough. In the mid-sixties, there were only 90,000 of these doctors,[27] and their popularity appears to be proved by the rapid increase in size. As one would expect, this doctor is a plain peasant looking after the sick on a part-time basis. He must possess some knowledge of old medicine. Indeed, there are plenty of these people in rural China. The system originates in the south where the epithet "barefoot" applies to men who labor in the paddyfields without any footgear.

The doctor receives only rough professional instructions prior to practicing. He is concurrently a medical man and farmhand. In addition to ministering a kind of first aid in nearly all types of cases, he does a little preventive and curative work.[28] He treats animals as well. His is one of catering to the elemental medical needs in rural CPR. *Beijing Review,* from which we draw all this information, describes at some length the function of this doctor in the Chuansha and Nanhui counties at the outskirts of Shanghai. He is said to strike deep roots among the people and his treatment of human and bestial patients is prompt and cheap. In 1958, the media asserts, when people's communes were instituted, the government set out to train

---

[21] *Beijing review,* February 11, 1980, p. 16, col. 2.

[22] *Ibid.,* June 23, 1980, p. 20, col. 1.

[23] *Ibid.,* November 8, 1982, p. 21, col. 1.

[24] *Ibid.,* June 23, 1980, p. 20, col. 1.

[25] *Ibid.,* however, *Renmin ribao,* March 5, 1981., p. 3 mentions a round figure of 1,500,000.

[26] *Zhong guo jian kuang,* loc. cit.

[27] *Beijing review,* January 14, 1980, p. 7, col. 3.

[28] *Ibid.,* June 23, 1980, p. 25, col. 2

health employees from among the peasants. The course lasted three months. Upon graduation, he was given a medical kit and started working.

The CPR has 3047 vaccinal stations, 2559 maternal wards, 219 medical graduate institutes, 107 schools of high medical learning, 543 secondary medical schools.[29] One of the medical universities is named after a Canadian leftist revolutionary physician, Norman Bethune, situated in Changchun of Liaoning province. There are 4 colleges of pharmacology (1 in the Academy of Sciences) and 2 veterinary schools.

Collective health services

As alluded to above, the barefoot doctors are not individual practitioners. They are just employees of a brigade. Being the most active of the health corps, they are the frontline soldiers in the fight against disease for 79.4% of the populace. The communist regime is instrumental in establishing the village medical service because there was little of it before 1949. Rudimentary clinic operation came into being soon after the Reds took over political power. All health units were co-ops. On the surface, membership was voluntary, but the communists actually decreed the system as they decreed anything else in that country. A certain sum of dues had to be paid by the peasants, dues which were levied as a form of tax. A number of paramedics and obstetricians were hastily coached to run the clinics. When the communes were set up, the clinics were expanded. It was at this time (1958) that the co-op medicare was introduced.[30] It was not, however, until 1969 that the system was made universal.[31] Still another decade had to elapse before regulations on rural medical work were promulgated by the Health Ministry and cognate authorities. Their orders of December 1979 are the current guidelines for the co-ops.[32] That the entire setup has taken so long to develop is indicative of divided opinion on it; during these years, the standards of service have varied a great deal from place to place.

One report says the system of barefoot doctors was denounced by the Gang of Four as reactionary[33] The Four are alleged to castigate Deng Xiaoping in 1975 when "he remarked graphically that the barefoot doctors should eventually wear shoes." In making this statement, Deng is said not only to hail the contribution of these people, but also express the hope that they should increase their knowledge and efficiency. The report regrets that the Gang of Four should have interpreted Deng's position "as an attempt to put barefoot doctors on a level with bourgeois intellectuals politically and therefore

[29] *Zhong guo bai ke nian jian*, Beijing: Zhong guo da bai ke quan shu chu ban she, 1980, p. 559, col. 1.

[30] *Beijing review*, June 23, 1980, p. 27, col. 2; January 14, 1980, p. 7, col. 3.

[31] *Ibid.*, June 23, 1980, p. 27, col. 2

[32] *Ibid.*, June 14, 1980, p. 7.

[33] *Ibid.*, June 23, 1980, p. 25, cols. 2-3.

in essence as a puff of right deviationism".[34] If we believe the government mouthpiece, the Gangsters had blocked the growth of the medical co-ops which centered on these doctors.

The co-ops are housed in the administrative quarters of the various brigades and are responsible for all the residents' health. The authorities of the brigades advance them a small amount out of the welfare fund in addition to the membership dues (one yuan a year). There is also a subvention from the state. The aforesaid decreess (of December 1979) stipulate that the clinics are to take measures to improve personal hygiene and environment. It is their duty not only to treat patients, but also to distribute preventive drugs. Much attention is directed to the old medicine involving the use of minerals, extracts from animals, insects and plants. Of these China has abundance, but their effect and the way they are utilized, in our view, are questionable and even shocking. Most "medicaments" are unsanitary, barbaric and superstitious. They give rise to disease, instead of curing it. The clinics are ordered to teach the peasants to gather plants, make and apply traditional drugs. They also train and supervise the several million strong health cadres. These are classed as assistants to the barefoot doctors. Last but not least, the clinics have the responsibility of conducting family advisory, of protecting women and children and of spreading the technique of basic hygiene among the masses.[35] Most of the above tasks are performed personally by barefoot doctors, the mainstay of China's rural medicare.

Beijing Review writes of the health system of suburban Shanghai in some detail.[36] There everyone pays from one to two yuan per annum to the clinic. The contribution of the brigade is at the same rate, that is to say, it matches the individual money. Members have only to come up with a registration fee for a visit and, if needed, a nominal injection cost of five cents. All other expenses are included in the clinic budget. However, the clinic is unable to handle serious cases. They are turned over to the commune, county or city hospital, but the clinic disburses part of the bill. A four-month old boy was said to suffer from toxemic pneumonia. He was hospitalized 20 days in Shanghai and incurred his parents 133.63 yuan for his stay. This sum, including the cost for blood tests and for emergency oxygen, was defrayed by the clinic.

We can say without difficulty that the government organ *(Beijing Review)* only describes the presentable part of the system. True enough, the vicinity of great metropolises like Shanghai do enjoy "fringe" benefits because there is no transportation question. Patients with serious problems may be sent to the municipal establishment quickly. In remote areas, however, the situation can be desperate.

34 *Ibid.*, col. 3.

35 *Ibid.*, January 234, 1980, pp. 7,8.

36 *Ibid.*, June 23, 1980, p. 27.

In accordance with the regulations on labor insurance, the factory pays one's medical expenses in full as well as his wages during sickness. We come across some compromising information, however, In the 1980 edition of the *Comparative Study of Politics*, Roth and Wilson mention the 1951 Labor Insurance Act,[37] which "covers more than 20 million productive workers, cadres and government employees." They say that "workers are protected from income loss due to injury; and some medical costs are paid as well." But there are no indications that the Act has been revised to extend the coverage to all employees and to take care of all types of cases.

It is written that workers and their dependents other than college-agers, are entitled to receive half of their medical cost from the factory. It is added, however, that if they still cannot meet the other half, a petition may be filed for supplmentary aid. Should we take the media seriously, the expense is not prohibitively high.[38] There is reported a factory workers' grandmother suffering from cholelithiasis. Every year her treatment required 20 yuan. His second boy sustained a fractured femur in an accident. His bill was between 30 and 40 yuan. This worker's salary was about 550 yuan. The entire expense comes to 10 percent of his total annual income. Again, this case is probably atypical since it appears in an official press which we may well say tend to report good news only.

Let us take a look at the mental diseases. It is counted that in Shanghai, the hospital beds increased from 400 in 1949 to 5833 in 1980[39]. During the same space of time, the number of psychiatrists was up from 12 to 528. Indeed, more and more people were driven crazy by the Reds! *Renmin ribao* says that the Gang of Four used torture to exact confessions and that many had lost their senses[40]. To cure that city's insane, attention was drawn to the group technique. There was developed a network to counter mental disease. Employees in health service, civic circles and municipal departments voluntarily organized themselves into teams to detect or treat cases. They coordinate their work with what is undertaken by city or district government. In order to ensure optimal cooperation between medical cadres and the units where the patients were formerly hired, they set up joint sessions and informal exchanges of views. The support of the patient's family and other social forces is also actively sought. To cope with recurrent aberration, special means are devised. Teams, for example, are formed by neighborhoods to take care of patients whose condition has been somewhat stabilized. The man was required to do some manual chore with little remuneration. He is provided with psychiatric diagnosis and is given "ideological

[37] David F. Roth and Frank L. Wilson, *The Comparative Study of Politics*, 2nd ed., Englewood Cliffs, New Jersey: Prentice-Hall, 1980, p. 422.

[38] *Beijing review*, June 23, 1980. p. 24.

[39] *Ibid.*, p. 27

[40] *Renmin ribao*, May 13, 1978, pp. 1,3; also *Keesing's*, September 8, 1978, p. 29195, col. 2.

406 GOVERNMENT OF SOCIALIST CHINA

education." We are highly skeptical of such education. Probably it would aggravate rather than mitigate the mental disorder.

During the period of surveillance, the patient may read, view TV, go on outings or attend sports. In 1980, there are said to be 105 groups of concerned citizens responsible for 2300 patients. Nursing societies were formed out of the patients' families, neighbors or retired workers living nearby. Their work was to make sure that the patients observed the medical order, to watch their activity and to send periodical reports to the health authority. By proffering them advisement and by solving their problems, the societies seek to eradicate the basic causes of their trouble. There were, altogether, 10,000 volunteers doing this kind of social work. Out-patients were treated once or twice a week and cadres visited them at their homes to give instruction on how to look after themselves. Besides Shanghai proper, the ten outlying counties each have mental homes equipped with about 100 hospital beds. In brigade clinics, doctors also treat the mentally sick, in addition to the other kinds of indisposition.

There are a number of specific medical policies of the government designed to improve people's health. In the first place, it is decided that ancient medicine be put to use. This idea is motivated not by the elite's persuasion, modernistic as they are, as by the sheer necessity. Without resort to the "old customs," which they detest, they simply have no way to take care of the diseased. Many methods, such as acupuncture, are of dubious value, and many others, like the qigong (breath-cure) are little short of ridiculous. The famous Yunnan bai yao, [41] said to be functioning, is without scientific basis. In the second place, research work as well as the curing of patients has claimed more and more attention. Beijing Review describes the two as being "carried out hand in hand."[42] Clinical instruction has begun to be in evidence. Many specialized areas like dermatology and neurology have become subjects of study. In the past, research work was nil as it was held that prescription was the only thing which counted. The new direction is, needless to say, a sound one, because more than other disciplines, medical study depends on laboratory tests. We may also call the reader's attention to the fact that 107 of the country's 729 fullfledged colleges are medical.

In the third place, there is presently less political interference, although it is still emphasized that health personnel should be "both red and expert," and that they "must strive for unity between ideological progress and higher professional competence."[43] During the Cultural Revolution, we shall remember, specialists and directors were ordered to the countryside to do heavy labor because the Gang of Four despised specialization and division of function. They considered this inimical to permanent revolution. As a result, health

[41] Beijing review, January 7, 1980, p. 29, col. 1.

[42] Ibid., June 23, 1980, p. 22. col. 3.

[43] Ibid.

administration was disrupted and chaos obtained. It was not until following the arrest of the Gang of Four that normal operation of the medical apparatus was restored.

In the fourth and final place, the government has begun to direct its attention to rural problems, not the least of which is medical. Up to the present, health work is poorer in the village than in the city, but the work there is done vigorously now. As one Western reference notices, "after the Cultural Revolution, some 330,000 medical workers settled in the countryside and an additional 400,000 doctors and nurses were recruited into mobile teams to tour the villages."[44] This infusion of cadres would undoubtedly improve the situation there, but the enormous increment of rural population will outpace the provision of service severalfold. The problem continues to be critical.

The Chinese communists, in order to redeem their country's name of *people's* republic, have done something, of course inadequately, in the fields of health. Besides, they have tried to find jobs for able-bodied citizens. What sort of problems are confronting them here? Let us examine the situation presently.

Unemployment

1) Urban

One of the many curses the communists poured onto the bourgeois is that their system begets unemployment. Unfortunately, however, this capitalist spectre has come to haunt the Soviet Union and the Chinese People's Republic. How does this happen? The instant section seeks to answer this query and the next section will look at the ways and means the communists have used to tackle the job problem. Prior to 1978, no one even dared to speak of unemployment in the CPR, because the authorities would have everybody believe that they had finally exorcised that spectre, provided as they were with the catholicon of planning and public ownership of the means of production. However, the severity of the situation can no longer be hidden by the glittering verbiage. Indeed, the whitest of all lies is that the body economic is robust. The classic subterfuge today is: the Gang of Four had caused the malaise.[45] In 1979, Li Xiannian, the then vice premier, declared for the first time that there were 20 million jobless and 100 million underfed.[46] These figures, are outdated by now and they were then very conservative. Clearly the ruling circles have cause to worry as the magic Marxist economy proved to be a flunk. In all honesty, they owe so many jobs to their subjects. Otherwise, how can they claim the right to rule them? Formerly the communists committed many wrongdoings (they conceded to some of them a couple of years ago).[47] However, should they stop kidding

44 *Europa*, 1979, vol. 2, p. 115.

45 John Fraser, *The Chinese, portrait of a people*, Toronto: Collins, 1980, pp. 112, 114.

46 *Britannica Book of the Year*, 1980, p. 248, col. 1.

47 *Renmin ribao*, July 1, 1981, pp. 1-5.

themselves in this problem, it may stand them in good stead from now on. When the regime, in other words, commences to identify the true problem, instead of imprisoning themselves in ideology, it can have a ray of hope in holding the reign of power. The director of the bureau of labor of the CPR mentions some of the job-seekers. He categorizes them into four groups.[48] The first group consists of the more than 20 million young people in the countryside and the more than 3 million in the cities who finish high school each year. (Among them only a fraction go on to college or join the army. They number 285,000 and 300,000 respectively.) Because they lack the skill and experience, there is great difficulty in placing them. The second group is made up of those "unable to work before because of illness or family responsibility," but now make themselves available. The third group involves "educated youths back to the cities from the countryside." These are the victims of the *Xiafang* designed to get the youngsters out of the over-crowded metropolises to the countryside as laborers. Although the third plenum of the 11th CC held in December 1978 "cancelled the policy of sending middle-school graduates to the countryside," the practice has continued and in 1980 there were 10 million *xiafanged*.[49] And the final and fourth group is comprised of school dropouts.

What is the total number of the four groups? How many are luckily placed? Except for the first batch of 23 million, the Chinese official did not state any statistic for the other three classifications. The recruitment by the army, it must be noted, does not lessen the number of unemployed by that many (300,000), because it also discharges the same number in a year. Probably the college bound are offset by the remaining groups, that is, those who are now able to work after incapacity for sometime and the dropouts. This leaves the unemployed to number 23 million. Now let us look at the employing capability of the government or public bodies. The annual records (in million) are as follows:[50]

year	total	hired by state	hired by collective or oneself
1977	5	2	3
1978	6	2	4
1979	9.02	1.95	7.07
1980	9	2.48	6.51
1981	8	1.99	6.03

Thus each year between eight and nine million jobs are created, but there are 15.5 million youths unemployed. The catch is that while the employing capacity is virtually stationary, job-seekers are incremental or rather cumulative. Let's start with 1980, by 1983 the total jobless

[48] *Beijing review*, February 11, 1980, pp. 13ff.

[49] *Ibid.*, March 28, 1983, p. 20, col. 1. *Globe and mail*, August 26, 1980, p. 11 mentioned the number.

[50] *Beijing review*, March 28, 1983, p. 21.

would have to be close to 62 million. In Shanghai alone, according to a foreign source, "150,000 young people are without jobs."[51] This is typical of other cities, the journal adds. How strange it is that the Chinese propagandized that at the end of 1981, the total number of urban youths still unemployed was merely 3.05 million![52] Where are the other tens of millions gone? So far we have been concerned with the young people. What about the adults? Since the Chinese spoke of full employment in 28 cities only,[53] one may assume that the jobless adults in all other cities and in all counties run into another tens of millions. Even those who are working cannot be said to have full jobs. The press has frankly stated that it is common that three men are doing two men's work.[54] We just cannot imagine the total number of umemployed urbanites. The word "staggering" seems appropriate to describe it.

2) Rural

There are no figures on rural unemployment. Perhaps the only reason is the impossibility of classifying them. While it is all simple to subsume a man with no work in the jobless column, the countryside presents a difficulty. A commune may have some chores for everybody. But the chores can be trivial and be done in a few hours. The problem is under-rather than outright un-employment. Then there is the seasonal character of farming. During the winters all the peasants are immobilized. Having regard to this consideration, rural China is facing serious problems of employment. According to a survey of Tiantong People's Commune of Zhejiang province, "about one-third of the laborforce was not *properly* utilized."[55] This is the same situation as in the urban areas. Recent years, it is to be acknowledged, saw the government pay some attention to the village job pattern. The agricultural manpower of the entire country is estimated to be 320 million and each year adds 20 million more.[56] If the Tiantong circumstance is representative of all parts of rural China,[57] at least 100 million peasants are not put to work properly. It is no coincidence that that many are said to have been shifted from straight farming to other lines of activity.[58] More of this anon. But the problem is not managed, let alone solved, and it is compounded by the fast multiplication of the rustics.

[51] New York Times, January 7, 1982, p. 2, col. 3.

[52] Beijing review, March 28, 1983, p. 21; January 3, 1983, p. 9; September 27, 1982, p. 20.

[53] Ibid., January 3, 1983, p. 9.

[54] Ibid., September 27, 1982, p. 20, col. 3.

[55] Ibid., March 28, 1983, p. 22, col. 2.

[56] Ibid., col. 1.

[57] Actually Tiantong is atypical, because it is situated in the topmost province, Zhejiang.

[58] Beijing review, March 28, 1983, p. 22.

3) Reasons for unemployment
According to the director of labor, there are four explanations for
unemployment.[59] The first explanation involves the legacy of the
ancien regime. In 1949, urban jobless were "about 4 million."[60] His
"People's Republic" had to engage them in production or
construction work. Such a number of unemployed in the whole country
at that inter-regnum, we feel, was not alarming, given the just-ended
civil war. If anything, the four million cannot be held to discredit the
GMD. Although historically correct, the figure is totally irrelevant to
the present situation because the "four million were assigned jobs,"
to use the director's words.

During the period of economic rehabilitation (1950-1952) and the
first Five-Year Plan (1953-1957), Beijing "basically eliminated
unemployment." This unemployment is most certainly not imputable
to the GMD legacy. Then he maintained "there was essentially no
unemployment" between 1957 and 1966. We are struck by the words
"basically" and "essentially." The director utilized them to allude to
the existence of the problem even prior to 1966, the year from which
the CPR media unanimously date the wrecking of the economy by
the Gang of Four. In this wrecking, the director finds the second cause
for the difficulty of creating sufficient employment. It is noteworthy
that he considered it the "major" reason for such difficulty. The ten
years' chaos allegedly had brought the "national economy to the brink
of collapse."[61] This quoted sentence is already seen in Hua Guofeng's
indictment of the Gang of Four at the second session of the fifth NPC
on February 26, 1978.[62] Mouthing the same words, the director added
that "many avenues of employment were blocked" by the Gang.[63].

The next reason for the unemployment was the uneven
development at the several economic fronts. This cause was also
described by him as "major". He argued that commerce and services
in the cities did not progress as expected. "Though the urban
population increased sharply in the last 20 years, the proportion of
workers and staff in light industries and trades in relation to all the
workers and staff decreased by approximately one-third". Not precise
with figures he put the reduction of jobs at several millions. The fourth
explanation to which the director did not apply the adjective major
is the "too rapid growth of the population." He attributed the growth
to the insufficient concern with family counseling, but not to the Gang
of Four who otherwise are held accountable for all the mishaps the
country has suffered, knowing that four individuals, one woman and
three men, cannot multiply the Chinese. We believe he is truthful by
not parroting the stereotypical accusation of these ousted leaders.

[59] Ibid., February 11, 1980, p. 13.

[60] Ibid., this figure also in ibid., March 28, 1983, p. 19, col. 2.

[61] Ibid., February 11, 1980, p. 14, col. 2.

[62] Keesing's, September 8, 1978, p. 29183, col. 2.

[63] Beijing review, February 11, 1980, o. 13, col. 1.

Yet, on the other hand, he is far from truthful, because he did not rank the population avalanche first among the four reasons.

Job creation

As the table of the preceding secton indicates, most jobs are in the collective and individual sector. This sector is considered to be the principal employer. The prospect of developing it, Beijing felt, is immensely greater in light of its lower productivity at the present time than the state sector. Owing to the generous financing, the goverment enterprises are slowly but surely mechanized and consequently, they have only marginal need for additional hiring. The co-ops, by contrast, can increase their output quickly because a) they require less capital and yet yield early returns,[64] they operate through independent accounting and take up profit and loss themselves, b) since they may engage in a variety of activities, they are in a position to take a larger labor force, and c) they are experimenting with new ideas in response to the market demands.

In the past, the co-ops were not encouraged, or, in the words of the above-mentioned director, "unfairly treated." Even though he did not amplify the point, he must have in mind a) that the leaders looked down upon them because they were out to enrich the individuals but not to further the interest of the whole people, and b) that national resources were mostly earmarked for heavy industry and weaponry. Thus, there were not enough materials supplied them. They had no choice except to pay meager wages to the employees. Some co-ops were reported to be barely able to carry on.[65]

In the eye of the general public, the status of the collective enterprises was inferior to the state counterpart. The new official stand is however that both are variations of socialist concern, and therefore they should coexist.[66] The government now provides more help to stimulate the collective sector which not only generates jobs for people, but offers services to satisfy the needs not met by state industries. As of 1978, the proportion of the two kinds of socialist ownership and employment are something like this.[67]

	total output	fixed assets of enterprises	number of employees
owned by whole people	80.7%	91.8%	30,410,000 71.5%
owned by collectives	19.3	8.2	12,150,000 28.5%

[64] *Renmin ribao*, August 5, 1981, p. 1.

[65] *Ibid.*, August 9, 1981, p. 4.

[66] *Ibid.*, March 28, 1981, p. 2.

[67] *Beijing review*, February 11, 1980, p. 15.

The state enterprises, as the table indicates, have four times the output of the collective ones, but use only two and half times the workers of the latter. We also see that with one-tenth of fixed assets, the collectives can employ more than one-third the workforce of the state enterprises. Prior to 1977, according to *Beijing Review,* most people were found in the state plants, but in the following two years, the collectives began to recruit more men. In 1980, nearly one-half of the newly hired were in the collectives.[68] Here is "one of the methods to solve the unemployment problem." It provides work or training for the youngsters during the waiting period. The co-ops assign them such chores as roofing, fixing broken houses, moving goods, making furniture, repairing boilers and whatnot.[69]. Again before 1977, tourists to the People's Republic were unable to obtain help in carrying luggage because the ideological behest said that the proletarians must not be exploited by the capitalists. Now this thinking is discarded and a big door for employment opens itself.[70]

To brighten the job structure, the government explores many possibilities. With apparent determination, it comes to develop trade, food industry and daily supplies. These areas "were neglected for a long time," areas which have generated large number of positions.[71] It is calculated that light enterprises are hiring 10,580,000 workers, as against heavy industry's 23,487,000.[72] The director of labor particularly points to the lightest of all enterprises, textiles.[73] This industry, by the way, was the most advanced in pre-1949 China (exclusively along the east coast). The Japanese, not the Chinese themselves, however were to be given the credit for it. In order to promote textiles, the communists have had a solid foundation in artistical skill, management, material sources and plants. Among all light industries, textiles require the least capital outlay and the trade is the easiest to learn. The two objectives of expanding textiles, like other things, are a) exporting them to gain foreign exchange and b) generation of jobs. We have already noted in the chapter on foreign trade that textile mills in the CPR are operated around the clock and that until the beginning of 1983 it had a prosperous sale to the US. "Textiles account for 25 percent of China's total retail sales of consumer goods," says the Chinese press.[74]. Although statistics are lacking, the employees in this industry may well be in the neighborhood of 5 million. We should remark that textiles are a state monopoly. It is a realm no co-ops are allowed to enter.

[68] *Ibid.,* July 21, 1980, pp. 5-6.

[69] *Ibid.,* p. 6, col. 1.

[70] *Renmin ribao,* July 18, 1979, quoted in Xue Muqiuao, *Dang qian wo guo jing ji ruo gan wen ti,* Beijing: Renmin chu ban she, 1980, p. 143.

[71] *Beijing review,* March 28, 1983, p. 21, col. 1.

[72] *Ibid.,* April 18, 1983, p. 24.

[73] *Ibid.,* February 11, 1980, p. 16, col. 2.

[74] *Ibid.,* January 31, 1983, p. 6, col. 2.

A plan has been said to be underway to organize high school graduates to set up enterprises in city suburbs engaging in agriculture, industry and commerce. They are to furnish the cities with non-staple foods, to make things for export and to supply big industrial combines with semi-finished items.[75] The government has taken steps to integrate this line of activity into the economic mechanism. As an incentive the enterprises are exempted from taxation.[76] And their profit can be used to improve the members' well-being and for reinvestment. It is undeniable that some elements of free trade have crept in. One prominent communist scholar, Xue Muqiao, however feels that a "morsel of capitalism does not hurt us, and that the socialist economy should by no means be frightened by it."[77] The state retains the authority to assign production quotas to the co-ops, but this will not take effect until the end of 1985. The enterprises, that is to say, are relieved of obligations to the state in the first quinquennium. A review of the current policy at that time may terminate the privileges the co-ops are enjoying presently. If they are doing extremely well, these privileges can be taken away by the envying government or just taxed out of existence, lest nabobs should emerge in a socialist China.

The Beijing regime has planned to build up medium and small-sized cities and towns.[78] It is hoped that more jobs can be created this way. Much, of course, depends on the capital the government is willing to provide; the investment can be astronomical if the intended cities deserve the name "city", but not the shabby agrogorod, the Soviet agricultural settlement. The Chinese project, however, has not gone beyond the talking stage.

In order to get the masses to work, the leadership has tried the conventional method of shortening laboring hours and of granting long leave to some types of employees by instituting a rotation scheme. Chemical factories, for example, are often found harmful to man because of poisonous or odious materials used there. The men can take from one to three months off yearly for recuperation or study, and their places are offered to others. "This not only helps protect the workers' physical and mental health, but enables more people to hold jobs."[79] The scheme, however, does not seem to involve great numbers, and it is of marginal value in solving the employment problem. Still another way to tackle the problem is to set up more universities and technicums to enroll students. In 1981, a batch of 26 new colleges were decreed.[80] However, if the modernization ambition of

[75] Ibid., p. 15, col. 3.

[76] Ibid., p. 16, col. 3.

[77] In a speech on March 24, 1979, Dang qian wo guo jing ji ruo gan wen ti, p. 125.

[78] Beijing review, February 11, 1980, p. 16, col. 2.

[79] Ibid., col. 3.

[80] Ibid., col. 2.

the CPR is not materialized fast enough, the degree-grandees who in 1982 numbered 310,000[81] and who may reach one and a half million a year before long (suppose each of the 729 schools turns out 2000 annually)[82], could have difficulty in obtaining suitable posts. In that case, they have to stay either unemployed or come to swarm the US colleges as the Taiwanese students are doing.

Job diversification proves to be fairly effective in tackling rural unemployment. Outright farming does not require many hands. A couple of years ago, the administration hit upon the idea of varying the activities in agriculture, including fish and poultry breeding, processing of materials for industry, transportation of communal products or sideline goods, trades, and services of many kinds. The Chinese media describes the situation of Liuzhuang brigade of Xinyang County in Henan province, where men were working in restaurants, flour and paper mills, machinery, orchards, brick kilns, trucking, sewing and tailoring, animal husbandry, dairy, cannery and woodworking. These were performed by 293 of the 580 people in the brigade. Only 265 were assigned to the farming sector. There were, in addition, 22 employed as teachers, barbers and the like.[83]

The various activities can be assumed by households as well as production teams, presently more by the former. When the households are permitted to do the work, the system is called bao chan dao hu (see also chapter on agriculture), or "production responsibility of homestead." It prescribes that farmers may sign contracts with the team management for a fixed amount of output to be delivered to it at an official price. Anything over the stipulated quantity may be sold privately on the free market and the farmers keep the profit.[84] Benefiting by this regime, peasants who just a few years ago regarded such things like watches as luxuries are even buying trucks today. A truck sales department in Nanjing sold 346 trucks to individual peasant households between January 6 and February 20, 1983.[85]. Early in 1983, the Nanjing automotive corporation dispatched representatives to Jiangsu, Anhui, Fujian, Hubei and Henan provinces to explore the potential truck sales to the villagers. It is estimated that China's rural areas will need 50,000 to 60,000 trucks annually during the last three years of the Sixth Five-Year Plan (1981-1985).[86]

Bao chan dao hu has shifted the farming activity from the rice-paddy to the hilly and reclaimable areas. It holds immense promise for rural laborforce.[87] These areas constitute 69 percent of the nation's

[81] *Ibid.*, col. 3.

[82] Beijing University graduated 3000 in 1982, *ibid.*, January 24, 1983, p. 28, col. 3.

[83] *Ibid.*, February 11, 1980, pp. 13-23.

[84] *Time*, April 4, 1983, p. 45, col. 1.

[85] *Beijing review*, April 4, 1983, p. 7. col. 1.

[86] *Ibid.*, col. 2.

[87] *Ibid.*, March 28, 1983, p. 22, col. 1.

territory and are 6 times the size of the farmland. There the rich resources are waiting to be tapped. In the aforesaid Tiantong Commune, functions have spread to forestry and other enterprises.[88] In Jiangxi province, 68 percent of its wooded surface are contracted out to peasants who plant trees, do lumbering and congnate vocations.[89] These created occupations for 2,755,000 families, with a total population of near 14 million, that is one quarter of Jiangxi's 60,521,114.[90] Bodies of water can also be rented and they prove to be highly lucrative. One peasant in Hebei province "earned $54,000 from a fresh-water farm."[91] Although Article 9 of the Constitution grants proprietorship of the land to the state or collectives, households have the right to manage the property and to reap the fruit of labor. There is no doubt of the system's contravention of the communist philosophy; the truth is, however, that ideological consistency is not to deter the ruling clique of Beijing in these days.

No less deviate from that philosophy is the policy of what amounts to free hiring and free firing, a right lodged with the management. The policy may possibly cause hardship in individual cases. But in the long run it can be a successful answer to the unemployment question. The scheme adopted goes under the name of "contract system". It envisages an agreement between the job-seekers and the enterprise, specifying the assignment, term of obligation, probation, compensation, insurance and well-being, protection, conditions for revoking or altering the detailed provisions, responsibility for breaking the stipulations, in short, all duties and rights of both parties.[92] In order to appreciate this reform which is far-reaching, we must point out that according to the current system workers are arbitrarily assigned to a unit by the labor department. Neither the enterprises nor the men have any choice in the matter. Consequently, those wishing to join a plant cannot enter, while the ones who are there do not intend to stay.

Worse yet, employees may not be sacked. Once landed in a position, one has a life tenure.[93] This is dictated by the communist view that because there are no more exploiters, it is the workers themselves who have come to own the means of production. They labor for themselves, but not for others. Such secure tenure entitles the men to an iron rice bowl; they draw fixed wages every month regardless of how poor their job-performance. Coupled with the egalitarian canon of income distribution, the contemporary practice has dampened people's enthusiasm and fettered the productive force.

[88] *Ibid.*, col. 2.

[89] *Ibid.*, April 8, 1983, p. 2.

[90] *Ibid.*, January 3, 1983, p. 3.

[91] *Time*, April 4, 1983, p. 45, col. 2.

[92] *Beijing review*, April 4, 1983, p. 5, col.1.

[93] *The economist*, April 19, 1983, p. 38, col. 3, under the new system, he can be fired.

A survey was recently conducted of 160,000 contract workers throughout the contry. It is alleged to show that the regime functions to the satisfaction of both enterprises and individual job-holders. On its side, the management can hire men in accordance with needs at the time, and can dismiss those who are not up to the expectation. This arrangement has resulted in enhancement of economic effects. The workers, on their side, do not develop the mentality of the iron rice bowl. So long as they make the utmost effort, their positions are virtually assured and at the same time, those who work harder will be better rewarded. The wages of contract workers can be higher or lower than those of the non-contract category. The Chinese paper says the new policy is in keeping with the socialist principles of distribution, namely, from each according to his ability and to each according to his work.

The contract deal was started with a circular issued by the Ministry of Labor and Personnel in February 1983.[94] It is intended to apply to the whole country before very long. During the transition period, only new employees are covered by it, while the ones already employed remain under the old arrangement. Although the new system was ordered early in 1983, it had been acted on since 1981. The director of labor said in February of that year that the centralized employment structure was undergoing a change. A jobless man must apply in the flesh at the personnel office of a plant and the latter is within its authority to decide whether to take him. Later in the year (November 1981), Premier Zhao Ziyang ordered that people ought to find employment themselves.[95] The autonomy of the enterprises in hiring and in other decisions is subsequently written into Article 16 of the 1982 Constitution. The above methods of job-creation seem to have some appreciable results, but the most striking and most promising method involves the takeover of small business by individuals.

Small business

Although a far cry from socialist collectivism, individual enterprise has been flourishing in the People's Republic. A triad of state-coop-private ownership was originally endorsed by the National Convention on Job Opportunity in August 1980.[96] It is now vested with the constitutional legitimacy in Article 11 of the basic law which reads that the "individual economy of urban and rural working people operated within the limits prescribed by law is a complement to the socialist public economy." The government, instead of prosecuting them as it did in the past, comes to protect their rights and interests. In view of the fact that any type of business needs a fair amount of capital and that individuals do not have big enough savings, encouragement is given to collective action. A number of men may

94 *Beijing review*, April 4, 1983, p. 5, col. 3.

95 *Globe and mail*, December 1, 1981, p. 13, col. 1.

96 *Ibid.*, August 26, 1980, p. 11.

pool their money together to operate some undertakings; to these collectives, the Constitution devotes no less than seven articles (8-11, 14, 17, 19). In 1980 and 1981, the self-employed individuals numbered 400,000 and 320,000 respectively, and the collectives hired 2,790,000 and 2,960,000[97]. These figures concern the situation in cities and towns only. In fact, laissez-faire has prevailed in rural communities as well, but there are no statistics on the people involved.

To illustrate what the situation looks like, we take Beijing as an example. As far back as 1980, there were 1355 collectively owned factories, stores and other services; they employed 140,000 youngsters.[98] The list gives one a general idea about the kind of activities: factories 636, building-restoration teams 95, retail stores and snack-bars 134, repairers' co-ops 352, moving-van units 36, cultural and entertaining troupes 47, and others 35.[99] Run by the respective partners, they are placed under the jurisdiction of the Beijing General Co-op for Urban Producton and Services. People in the capital used to stand in long line to get a piece of furniture, to wait a vacant table in a restaurant, or to have a haircut, and visitors there could not obtain a porter. Nowhere could one take the laundry to.[100] The picture has now differed. There are no longer shortages of these facilities or services. There appear 268 doctors and dentists in the capital engaging in private practices.[101]

As reported in the press, "foreign friends revisiting China are impressed by the vast changes taking place in the streets of cities and towns where once deserted sidewalks are now lined with small vendors' booths, all bubbling with activity.[102]" The scope of business has expanded after the adoption of the responsibility system by the 12th Congress of the CCP in September 1982 and the 5th NPC in the following December. Here we have a strange development. Each public service is assigned a quota by the government. The quota is a minimum of output for which the workers and staff are held responsible. Since it is not too high, they find it rather easy to fulfil. After delivering the agreed-upon money or goods to the state, they are free to do what they want with the tools, machines or materials of the establishment. They can put out above-quota supplies and sell them and divide the profits. However, tax must be paid. It is in their right to reinvest the money earned by making use of the state means of production.[103] Not all enterprises are currently shifted to this system. By 1985, according to the plan, 72,000 hotels, restaurants,

[97] *Beijing review*, September 27, 1982, p. 21.

[98] *Ibid.*, February 11, 1980, pp. 13-23.

[99] *Ibid.*

[100] *Renmin ribao*, January 1, 1980, p. 2.

[101] *Time*, April 4, 1983, p. 45, col. 2.

[102] *Beijing review*, March 28, 1983, p. 21, col. 2.

[103] *Time*, April 4, 1983, p. 45, col. 2.

bathhouses and barbershops will be switched over. In the desperate and confused effort to further production and improve service, the regime is embarking upon a course which would blur the line marking the public from private pockets. Some cases have been reported (*Renmin ribao,* April 16, p. 1; April 26, p. 4, both 1983.) The consquence of this development can be frightening. Professionals or entrepreneurs, operating entirely of their own, are legion in the People's Republic. There are bakers, accountants, typists, tailors, tutors, lawyers, beauticians, drivers' schools, florists, printers, tourist guides, family counselors, musicians, domestics, house-cleaners, fortune tellers, match-makers, translators, food-caterers, manicurists, cigar-stores, stationeries, book-stalls, newstands, letter-writers (for illiterates who want to correspond), painters, magicians, earwax excavators, studios, vegetable and meat vendors, etc. Some of them are organized into co-ops. They all depend on officialdom for supply of instruments, building materials, provisions, energy and credit. If managed well, they become rich. Some earn 150 yuan, but on the average, 100 yuan a month for each partner. Even if it is the latter amount, he earns more than a factory worker who draws about 44 yuan, and a grade-school teacher whose salary is also 44 yuan. On the other hand, if the co-op fails to offer commendable service or workmanship, it cannot have a good return for the labor and investment. It withers away fast. Since members do not have guaranteed income and regular employment, they just bid farewell to each other and move on to hunt for jobs in factories or government bureaus. If unsuccessful there, they may run into each other again in the municipal labor office to which they chanced to troop and which may assign them to some short courses on technical skills of various sorts.

Following the ousting of the Gang of Four, the heretofore frozen economy has been loosened a lot. As has been said previously, what amounts to the Soviet Union's New Economic Policy of 1921-1928 allows trade to be undertaken by assoicates, neighborhoods, close relatives, individuals and even ephemeral groups. Street hawkers abound. They are out for making a quick buck by profiteering. Small-time speculators dash from Beijing to Guangdong to buy imported goods there and resold in the capital at a fabulous price.[104] One man took such a trip in 12 days and he earned a sum of 400 yuan; for such an amount a university professor of the highest rank has to howl half a year (annual salary 840 yuan).

In order to encourage private business, the media seems to make a concerted effort to urge the people, *Enrichissez vous* (to get rich), by narrating many success stories. One of them involves a family trade.[105] It is alleged that the family has inherited the rare expertise of making glass grapes in more than 100 years. The skill is of

---

104 *Ibid.,* col. 1.

105 *Beijing review,* February 11, 1980, p. 17, col. 3.

Mongolian origins. In June 1979, the production of this artifact was licensed by the Beijing municipal administation and a co-op was organized to operate the business headed by the only surviving member of the family. The government declared one Liu Changshun, a self-employed restauranteur of Haerbin (Heilongjiang province), as a "model worker for his good service and reasonable prices."[106] It is alleged in a daily that one Zhang Junan of Hejin county of Shanxi province netted 10,000 yuan in 1982 by producing superb watermelons and cabbages;[107] another man in Gaomi county of Shandong province earned 17,000 yuan by producing cotton, wheat and vegetables on a 1.4-hectare of land he rented from the production team.[108] All the above activities come within the category of self-employment. They have the redeeming virtue that no exploitation of fellowman is perpetrated. However, capitalist practice in the CPR is completed in 1981 by the regime allowing co-ops to hire others as straight laborers, instead of admitting them as partners.[109]

At the uppermost in the hearts of the contemporary ruling elite is that the people's basic needs be met, and that jobs be found in one way or another for those who otherwise "had nothing to do but wander on the streets. Gradually they picked up the bad habits and, worse still, they made trouble everywhere."[110] The communists finally realize that work, but not Mao Zedong Thought, can "help them to become better men or women."[111]

Wages

The CPR's wage policy is governed by the twin saws of "one who does not work shall not eat" and "from each according to his ability and to each according to his labor." These are placed in both the 1975 and 1978 Constitutions. (Articles 9 and 10 respectively), but not in the 1954 predecessor. The 1982 successor (Article 6), however, drops the first but keeps the second saw, perhaps it is for the sake of communist humanism that one may still eat, even though he does not work. The principle of reward according to labor suffered a drawback during the Great leap of 1958-1959 and, to some extent, during the Cultural Revolution of 1966-1968 when egalitarianism was loudly proclaimed. This ism is in keeping with the goal of the communists to free man from want regardless of what he does or whether he labors at all. Being both idealist and pragmatist, the

[106] *Ibid.*, March 28, 1983, p. 20.

[107] *Renmin ribao*, April 6, 1983, p. 2.

[108] *Ibid.*, January 10, 1983, p. 6.

[109] *Ibid.*, June 20, 1981, p. 1. It was reported in *Globe and Mail*, August 26, 1980, p. 11 that the number of licenced traders, peddlers, handicraftsmen and other individual laborers inceased from 250,000 in 1979 to 400,000 in 1980. A few small businesses sprang up from 1978 to 1980. On the eve of the Cultural Revolution, about two million Chinese worked for themselves. Some were hiring helpers. The present policy links inself to the pre-1966 situation.

[110] *Beijing review*, February 11, 1980, p. 18, col. 3.

[111] *Ibid.*

Chinese Reds are vacillating on the wage issue. While they wish the leveling off of wage differentials, they are willing to come to terms with man's tendency to look after oneself. This ambivalence is expressed in Hua Guofeng's oration to the NPC on February 26, 1978: "Although we should avoid a wide wage spread, we must also oppose egalitarianism."[112]

To spur productivity, the Reds render lip service to subliminal equality. It is polemicized that they are at present practicing socialism, but not communism. The Central Committee and the State Council are said to have decided in 1974 to increase the wages of some workers and staffers, but the policy was stymied by the Gang of Four.[113] The latter were charged with vetoing a decision to call a national wage convention and branding the adjustment of compensation as "material incentive in contravention of Marxist-Leninist tenet."[114] We have no way to verify this sort of statement. That convention took place in August 1980 which did not, however, give everyone a pay boost.

There was decreed in October 1977 a wage hike for only 56 percent of industrial workers and 46 percent of the entire workers and staffers. It was said to be the first of this kind in 14 years.[115]. The scale was based on the amount already drawn. "Those who receive fairly low pay" were granted more, while the highest 10 percent were offered less. As late as 1975, it is to be noted, the top bracket of engineers received 10 times as much as factory workers at the bottom. Even among the workers themselves, the highest wages were several times the lowest.[116] Now this has changed, and because piece-rate tends to widen the differentials, the equality-minded Reds have sought to reduce the number of jobs remunerated that way.

Recognition of work performance by publicity is used by the government in a massive scale, cheap as it is. This type of reward entails no loss at all to the state. Medals or certificates, or trips to Beijing or audiences with super mandarins are used widely as incentive. In March 1978, only a few months after the pay increase, Hua Guofeng in an attempt to cultivate his charisma ordered another increase, but it proved a barmecide because he coupled the hike with the fulfilment of the production quota. The official media, in defense of the then strong man, militated for linking the "economic efficiency of a business with the interest of its workers, employees and especially the men who actually run it."[117] It remonstated them to come up with the quota.

[112] *Keesing's*, September 8, 1978, p. 29182, col. 2.

[113] *Ibid.*, December 16, 1977, p. 28727, col. 2.

[114] *Ibid.*

[115] *Facts on file*, October 28, 1977, p. 823, A2.

[116] Dwight H. Perkins, "China: economy," *Americana*, international ed., Chicago: Americana corp., 1975, vol. 6, pp. 520-521.

[117] *Renmin ribao*, September 12, 1978, cited in *Manchester guardian*, September 24, 1978, p. 4.

Beginning in 1979, China's most populous province, Sichuan, permitted certain factories to keep part of their profit as bonus if they surpassed the fixed quantity. The new deal was set in motion at once in 100 plants and in another 100 the following year. The official propaganda averred that "output of the 100 experiment enterprises had increased 14.7 percent in 1979 and profit went up 33 percent."[118] In the Soviet Union, incidentally, such an arrangement was instituted in September 1965. The Chinese government, according to its mouthpiece, would have adopted it earlier save for the opposition of the Gang of Four. We may at this juncture have a look at cost of living as it vitally affects wage earnings.

On this question, little information is available. The CPR is all but missing in the Yearbook of labor statistics. This ILO publication prints only a few insignificant trade figures and a couple on mineral production, and it does this only occasionally. A Western study reveals the 1976-1980 cost of living index to be:[119]

1975	1976	1977	1978	1979	1980
100	100.3	103	103.7	105.7	113.6

This fairly stable pattern has definitely changed due to the soaring prices after 1980, but there are as yet no research statistics on it. The same media from which the table is derived describes the family food bill (in yuan) for 1977-1978 like this:[120]

rice	25.60	poultry	6.00
other cereals	26.60	fish	4.95
pulses	3.15	eggs	7.45
potatoes	13.00	fats & oils	5.60
soya product	5.40	total	156.40
sugar	6.40	x 4.5	703.80a
vegetables	22.40	tea	7.20
fruit	7.00		711.00b
milk	2.60	wage, 1 person	720,00
meat	20.25	x 1.7	1224.00c

a Average family size, 4.5
b Per Family
c Average workers per family 1.7

Again the information is dated and later publications of the source no longer provide similar data. In all possibilities the family income cannot be more than meeting the bare necessities. The food cost, it is particularly noteworthy, constitutes 59 percent of the total earnings. In comparison, it is much higher than a Soviet family which spends from 35 to 45 percent of its income for food in recent years.[121]

[118] Facts on file, February 22, 1980, p. 132, C3.

[119] Europa, 1982, vol. 2., p. 119.

[120] Ibid., 1979, vol. 2, p. 120.

[121] P. Simush, The Soviet Collective Farm, Moscow: Progress Publishers, 1971, p. 104; Soviet Panorama, July 1975, p. 20; Moscow News, December 17, 1977, p.2.

China's semi-free economy has given rise to a wreckless spending by citizens. It is a regime of galloping prices, diminishing real income and running on inflation. These are the evils which Marx dumped on the laps of the capitalists, but he never dreamt that someday it would come to eat into the communist body politic. For many a year now, *Renmin ribao* has ceased glorifying the Chinese economy to be one of abundance as behoves a socialist polity. Since 1980 there has been virtually no issue of that daily which does not provide some space for an editorial, an opinion, a comment or just a report on the price irregularities. In the meantime, it speaks of the government's efforts in coping with the problem on various fronts, with uneven successes however.

As regards income, *Renmin ribao* has printed figures on some rural inhabitants.[122] The State Bureau of Statistics, according to the daily, made a study of 10,282 communal families scattered over 23 provinces, cities and regions. The results are as follows:

	1978	1979	Increase in a) yuan	b) percent
per capita income	133.6 yuan	160.2	26.6	19.3
consumption	116.0	134.5	18.5	15.9

breakdown of the comsumption			incr.	% in 1978	% in 1979
food	78.6	86.0	7.4	67.7	63.9 dcr.
clothes	14.7	17.6	2.9	12.7	13.1 incr.
shelter	3.7	7.7	4.0	3.2	5.7 incr.
energy	8.3	8.4	0.1	7.1	6.2 dcr.
expenses	7.6	11.1	3.5	6.6	8.3 incr.
cultural	3.2	3.2	0.5	2.7	2.8 incr.

In 1979, every 10 families had 3.6 motorcycles, 2.3 sewing machines, 2.6 radios and 5.5 watches. Regarding shelter, the study says that "most of the dwelling quarters are thatch-roofed and have ready-to-collapse earthern walls." The figures in the tables, it is noted, are not reached in four provinces: Gansu, Henan, Yunnan, Guizhou.

No such detailed analysis for later years is available but the per capita income in some areas seems to be better. As of 1980, says *Renmim ribao,* in 343 counties it is above 150 yuan[123] By comparison, in 1979 half as many counties reached that level. Among the 343 counties, 143 have per capita income above 200 yuan, 22 above 300, and 5 above 400. The highest is recorded in the Tibetan region whose Ritu county has scored 488.47 yuan. In the nation as a whole according to Zhao Ziyang, the income of a peasant is 191 yuan in 1980, but it will be 255 in 1985.[124] Data on the city dwellers are very

122 *Renmin ribao,* January 3, 1980, p. 4.

123 *Ibid.,* September 8, 1981, p. 1.

124 *Ibid.,* December 1, 1982, p. 2; also in *Beijing review,* December 20, 1982, p. 18, col.1.

scarce. The officials, it seems, do not want to talk much about it. It is from almost casual revelations in the Chinese press or from reports of Western tourists that we know something about how much the cadres are making and how well they live. Workers and staff members in state enterprises and establishments, says Yao Yilin, earned 644 yuan in 1978 but 705 in 1979[125] Premier Zhao Ziyang said the total sum of wages and salaries paid to these people was 77.3 billion in 1980 but will be 98.3 billion in 1985[126] Unlike the peasant income, he does not mention per capita earnings. We can calculate by dividing the sum by 115 million (72,440,000 staff members and 42,560,000 industrial workers) and get the per capita salary in round figures of 700 yuan for 1980 and 800 for 1984.[127] There is practically no literature on the spending pattern of these people, but reports are plentiful in the party organs depicting their luxurious housing (built with public fund, though),[128] or sumptuous meals (eating at the public fat again).[129]

Urbanites, making up 19.4% of the population, receive the solicitous attention of the Beijing oligarchy. This partiality cannot be explained easily by the rural origins of the Red regime. Many essential purchases made by the townspeople are subsidized. The following table presents the extent of government subvention during 1979-1981.[130]

items	amount
grain, 0.2 yuan per kilogram; & cooking oil, 1.6 yuan per kilogram	28.8 billion yuan
other food & vegetables	8.0
clothing & other living necessities	4.8
housing, 0.28 yuan per sq meter	3.5
medical care	11.7
recreation & sports	6.0
	total 62.8

"The annual state revenue," it is noted, "is just over 100,000 million yuan. These subsidies reflect the concern of the government for urban dwellers," each of whom benefited in 1982 on the average by 164 yuan. However, it is apologetically stated, in view of the difficult task of modernizing the country, large sums of funds are needed for construction and therefore the state cannot afford to earmark every

125 *Main documents of the third session of the fifth National People's Congress of the CPR*, lst ed., Beijing: Foreign languages press, 1980, p. 17.

126 *Renmin ribao*, December 1, 1982, p. 2; *Beijing review*, December 20, 1982, p. 18, col. 1.

127 The number 42,560,000 appears in *Beijing review*, February 11, 1980, p. 15, but a different number 34,067,000 appears in *ibid.*, April 18, 1983, p. 24. There are 320 million peasants, *ibid.*, March 28, 1983, p. 22, col. 1. The total workforce is 435 million; *Hammond* of 1982, p. 547, col. 2 says that the "working age population is about 476 million, with 75% in agriculture."

128 *Renmin ribao*, March 21, 1981, p. 3; March 29, 1982, p. 4; April 14, 1983, p. 4; April 15, 1983, p. 3; April 20, 1983, p. 4; April 24, 1983, p. 3.

129 *Guangming ribao*, October 28, 1981, p. 1.

130 *Beijing review*, October 25, 1982, p. 7. provides the following information.

cent on improving people's livelihood in the cities and towns. As for the vast rural areas, there is no such generosity at all. Peasants are inferior citizens of the People's Republic. How ungrateful the Reds Are! Let us take a close look at the workers' life. The following is derived from Beverly Carl's article concerning her Shanghai visit in late 1978.[131] All factories have an eight-grade wage scale. The Shanghai shipyard's scale ranged from 42 yuan to 124 yuan a month, with operators of huge cranes falling in the middle. Most people in the ironwork factory were in the lower grades and the average was 55 yuan a month. Those in difficult jobs got extra pay, as did the ones who labored on Sundays and holidays. Nocturnal shiftwork was not compensated with more wages, but the authorities did compensate it with some perquisites. Above-quota bonuses averaged 6.25 yuan a month. It could be as high as 21 yuan.

In regard to living style, two-room apartments are made available for five or six persons. A kitchen and a rest-room are provided for two families. There are public bathing facilities in the neighborhood. Medical expenses are minimal. Beverly Carl saw the home of a shop foreman and his wife who is a supply clerk. They have three small children. The husband and wife earn together 150 yuan a month. Living quarters cost them 5 yuan monthly. It includes hydro, rent and other utilities. Food costs 80 yuan and the remainder goes to clothes and savings. They can save 10 yuan a month and the bank pays from two to three percent interest. Carl was invited to the home of a retired worker. This woman had a family income of 190 yuan a month, including that of her husband and of her children. About 10 yuan were for rent and hydro, 100 for food, some for clothing, and the rest going to the bank.

Like all socialist countries, the CPR has the so-called social consumption fund in the manner of schooling, medicine, and cultural facilities. The per capita of this fund is reported to be 224 yuan a year. It is supposed to have increased by 99 percent since 1952.[132].

A pretty messy market

Following the partial de-control of resources by government in 1978, there has been a fierce struggle for scarce goods, which in the CPR means everything, between the many collective and state bodies. *Renmin ribao* says this inevitably drives prices up.[133] Aggravating the economic malaise is the bonus system adopted in each and every enterprise. The size of the perquisite depends on the sales of merchandise. The Commerce Ministry has at times decreed prices, but these are just too unrealistic. Enterprises find it absolutely

[131] Beverly Carl, "Contemporary law in the People's Republic of China," *Southwestern law Journal*, no. 5, February 1979, pp. 1255-1279 at 1266.

[132] *Guangming ribao*, August 13, 1981, p. 1.

[133] *Renmin ribao*, January 12, 1981, p. 4.

essential to grant bonuses to their employees in order to sustain their morale. This immediately affects the consumers, since the tags of commodities are bound to be marked up. It is mentioned in *Renmin ribao,* by way of criticism, that the executive boards of plants have always clung to the adages.[134]

> For the sake of the collective
> It is not wrong to be deceptive
>
> *   *   *
>
> To run government enterprise
> One can do anything in disguise

The only taboo, the executives think, is stealth or holdup. As a matter of principle, declares one commentator, only a few yamens have the right to appraise and approve the charges but, instead, numerous officials fix them and do it arbitrarily. They argue implausibly that their practice has the merit of fostering an "active economy" and that its outlawry would incur disasters. The commentator calls for a swift abolishment of the hydra price-command.[135]

In addition to the direct price-hiking there is the devious means of reducing the quantity or debasing the quality of wares, and there is adultering, falsifying, underweighing and short-changing.[136] Many rapacious cadres are using public transport to ship goods around from one city to another for a bonanza and they defended this activity by asking jocularly: When you add labor to a commodity, isn't its value bound to go up according to *Das Kapital?*[137] In contributing to the anarchy is the widespread speculation with daily necessities. *Renmin ribao* has reported that such items like bread, soaps, toothpaste, socks and small appliances are purchased by individuals and disposed at a 140 percent profit. The buyers, in turn, resell them at still higher charges. All such transactions are done openly in the streets. This is because in the first place, there is no anti-profiteering law on the statute-book; in the second place, goods are just too scarce; and, in the (most important) third place, speculators are self-supporting folks. The government is more than pleased to see them make a living, although not by the sweat of the brow.[138]

On January 12, 1981, *Renmin ribao* editorialized an unusually poignant criticism of the market. Although, it says, the economy has forged ahead toward prosperity through diversification, many problems are engendered in the process. Some parts of the nation are bedeviled by rampant speculation which perturbs the unity of the society and defeats the goal of the communist party. The daily indicts

134 *Ibid.*

135 *Ibid.,* January 5, 1981, p. 2.

136 *Ibid.,* December 10, 1980, p. 2.

137 *Ibid.,* December 20, 1980, p. 2.

138 *Ibid.,* December 21, 1980, p. 1; January 1, 1981, p.2.

the undesirables for "out-buying the government, disrupting the state purchase-plan, engaging in under-the-counter dealings, struggling for cash, stockpiling articles for better return, writing up labels, evading tax, manipulation of imports, selling bogus stuffs and hoodwinking the public." Having portrayed the license, *Renmin ribao* proceeds with sharp barbs. The authority, it writes, can do a lot to neutralize the crisis situation, a situation which should have been nipped in the bud in the first place. "To cope energetically with the speculation, sound laws need to be enacted. At present, our country hasn't had a comprehensive economic legislation." The State Council and various departments, true enough, grind out many "acts, regulations, decrees, rules, guidelines and whatnot. Alas, all have proved incapable of confronting the difficulties." In this circumstance, legitimate enterprises are not safeguarded but illicit operations go scot-free. "Here lies the main cause for the flowering of the speculation," deplores the media. The editorial admonishes earnestly that economic legislation is a must but before it is developed, interim measures ought to be undertaken to arrest the deterioration of the situation. However, this is not done, says it.

"What are the explanations for the price-hiking?" A correspondent of *Renmim ribao* interviewed the Commerce Minister Wang Lei (replaced by Liu Yi in May 1982) and posed him such a query. The newsman got four explanations.[139] First, there is an imbalance between financial credit and material supply; this leads eventually to a deficit in the state budget. "This reason is basic," he says. Second, the government raised the charges on "rice, cotton, oil, pork and 18 cognate products." Such action has affected many other things which, however, the government cannot subsidize. Third, the cost of producing timber, coal, steel, pig iron, bamboo material, has gone up steeply. A chain reaction is triggered, with the result that an array of items from the giant blast furnaces to babies' toys are charged more dearly. Fourth, the administration was lax in the control of some commodities and has let many trade and industrial agencies to unilaterally fix the rates. No one, we think, can dispute the four reasons. However, the Minister may well add this as the fifth: the increase of disposable income of the people which empowers them to strive for goods. Let us pause a little here to have a look at this.

According to the Chinese press, the per capita rural income (distinct from income of each peasant) in 1979 was 179.8 yuan, 29.2 yuan more than the previous year.[140] It is estimated that the spending of the entire populace on purchases in 1980 was 200 billion yuan above the 1979 level.[141] Zhao Ziyang declared to the NPC on November 30, 1982 that with the growth of industrial and agricultural production and that of the income of urban and rural residents, their consumption

[139] *Ibid.*, December 31, 1980, p. 2.

[140] *Ibid.*, January 3, 1981, p. 1.

[141] *Ibid.*, January 9, 1981, p. 1.

level rises substantially.[142] By 1985, the per capita consumption will be 22 percent more than 1980; it averages a 4.1 percent annual growth as against the 2.6 percent for the 28 years between 1953 and 1980. Of this, city dwellers get an average rise of 3.2 percent and villagers 4.2 percent. Statistics of the Commerce Ministry say that the total retail sales in 1981 registered a sum of 235,000 million yuan, that is 50 percent more than in 1978.[143] After deducting the rise in prices, the increase amounts to 36.7 percent. "The increase of retail sales in rural China was 63 percent which was faster than in the cities and towns." The total retail sales in the first six months of 1982 recorded a 9.5 percent over the same period of 1981. Now people have more money at hand but there is a dearth of practically everything; given this situation even exorbitant charges are not a deterrent to them.

What practical actions have been taken to regulate the market? The State Council has promulgated an "instruction on the strict price control,"[144] and the Commerce Ministry laid down rules for its implementation.[145] The urgency of the problem is evidenced by the adoption of all conceivable methods to halt the inflationary spiral. Early in 1981, the central organizations such as the State Council, Ministries of Forestry, Foreign Trade, Metallurgy, Textiles, Commerce and Agriculture; Supply and Sales Co-op, Marine Produce Bureau, Tourist Service, sent 14 itinerant groups to 12 provinces, whose job is to report on irregularities and to enforce the State Council's instruction.[146] To the same end, each province and city is to enact its town laws, and to send its monitoring groups to oversee their execution.[147] Many volunteers' teams are organized to help police the market and members of the Young Communist League are particularly active.[148] In Beijing there are more than 1,600 part- and full-time market patrollers.[149] Neighborhood circles are also playing an important role in the campaign.[150] In many places, citizens are armed with the government-issued full-power to look into the accounting, pricing, weighing and measuring of goods.[151] In Nanjing,

[142] His report is in *Beijing review*, December 20, 1982, p. 18, col. 1.

[143] *Ibid.*, September 6, 1982, p. 8, col. 1, for this and the following data.

[144] *Renmin ribao*, December 10, 1980, p. 1.

[145] *Ibid.*, pp. 1, 2.

[146] *Ibid.*, January 9, 1981, p. 1.

[147] *Ibid.*, January 12, 1981, p. 1; January 9, 1981, p. 1; January 10, 1981, p. 1; January 20, 1981, p. 1; December 11, 1980, p. 1; January 4, 1981, p. 1.

[148] *Ibid.*, December 10, 1980, p. 1.

[149] *Ibid.*, January 4, 1981, p. 2.

[150] *Ibid.*, December 17, 1980, p. 1; December 18, 1980, p. 2.

[151] *Ibid.*, December 17, 1980, p. 1.

428   GOVERNMENT OF SOCIALIST CHINA

even the pensioned were reactivated to monitor the sales pattern.[152] The capital city of Sichuan province, Chengdu, has set up 210 price contingents consisting of 1449 activists. In the first few months 400 cases were uncovered.[153]

Some shops were ordered to return the overcharges to the buyers, to make up the shortfalls, or to tender apologies for what they had done.[154] A certain school was told to refund the tuition found to be in excess of the authorized limit.[155] In one case, a five-year imprisonment term was meted out to a Shanghai man for fleecing the public of 11,419 yuan.[156] However, it is reported that as soon as the patrollers left, the store managers placed back the original tags.[157] In spite of all the restrictions, prices continue to climb. It is after all the masses who are suffering, not the elite, provisioned as they are from special depots, in addition to their regular stipends.[158] To the elite communism has indeed arrived.

Retirement, housing, care for the handicapped

There lacks a universal retirement plan in the CPR. Instead, each city, province and region enacts its own legislation. The retirement pay in Shanghai is 70 percent of one's last wage,[159] but in some other places, it is 90 percent. In Beijing, the trade unions in 70 percent of the factories organized committees to take care of the oldsters. Among other things, these committees "hand out pensions, distribute relief funds to those who have difficulties and make funeral arrangements."[160] They are chaired by one or two cadres from the unions or from the factory administration. Any interested pensioner may serve on a committee. The Beijing railway workers' union was said to have 8100 retirees, among whom 188 had financial problems. As a result, they were given 2290 yuan.

The retirement age for males is 60 and for females 50. Those who work underground, high above ground or in extreme temperatures may leave their jobs five years earlier. The regime encourages retirement in order to give their places to young laborers. When a father or mother in a plant retires, his or her position is filled by one of their offspring.[161] This rule creates the problem of decreasing

[152] Ibid., January 14, 1981, pp. 1,2.

[153] Ibid., April 13, 1983, p. 2.

[154] Ibid., December 17, 1980, p. 1.

[155] Ibid., December 21, 1980, p. 1.

[156] Ibid., January 14, 1981, p. 4.

[157] Ibid., December 10, 1980, p. 1; January 4, 1981, p. 2.

[158] Michael Roskin, op. cit., p. 302.

[159] Beverly Carl, loc. cit.

[160] Beijing review, July 21, 1980, p. 25, col. 3.

[161] John Fraser, op. cit., p. 93.

productivity because the young replacement does not have the experience of the outgoing parent. Although the retirement pay is not enough, the pensioners does not foot the medical bills and most of them live with their families. In Beijing, the government offers every worker 150 yuan as a gift on the day he leaves the plant; this is equivalent to three months' wage; in 1979, 20,000 retirees wanted to go back to the countryside and each got 300 yuan to cover the settlement in a new locale.[162] This generosity helps ease congestion in Beijing.

Come to rural areas, it is sheerly impossible to provide for the retired close to 40 million (age 60 above). As the press frankly put it, "until quite recently few peasants were supported by public funds after becoming too old to work."[163] Only 11 provinces and cities grant retirement benefits to upwards of 426,000 individuals. The reason why peasants are included in cities is because these cities always extend their jurisdiction to cover the surrounding hinterland (counties). Rural pensions are something of a luxury, for it is the well-situated communes which can afford to institute it. The retirement age is 65 for men and 60 for women, provided they have worked there more than 10 years. The monthly allowance is between 10 and 15 yuan, a few places give 20 yuan. The funds are drawn from the profits of the collective enterprises or from the communal treasury. That such small payment is sufficient is because "rent, water, vegetables, eggs, poultry and meat cost little or no money." As to the number of pensioners, it is incredibly small. In the country as a whole, retired workers and staff members of cities numbered 1,090,000 in 1982.[164] Beijing is said to have 116,000 such people in 1979,[165] and Shanghai between 120,000 and 140,000 in 1982.[166] The second-named city has, as of 1983, 250,000 retired peasants.[167] We would call the reader's attention to the fact that on July 1, 1982, Beijing had a population of 9,230,687 and Shanghai 11,859,748[168].

What about help to the handicapped? Included in this group are the blind, deaf and mute, and the mentally retarded. The total number are not known, but approximately 100,000 are alleged to be working for the government agencies at various levels.[169] Factories and workshops which run specifically for the handicapped are tax exempt. They manufacture about 1000 products in the electronics and

[162] *Beijing review*, July 21, 1980, p. 26, col. 3.

[163] *Ibid.*, October 4, 1982, p. 8, col. 1 provides the following information.

[164] *Ibid.*, November 8, 1982, p. 24, col. 2.

[165] *Ibid.*, July 21, 1980, p. 25, col. 3.

[166] Former figure in *ibid.*, October 4, 1982, p. 8, col. 2; latter figure in *ibid.*, November 8, 1982, p. 24, col. 2.

[167] *Renmin ribao*, April 19, 1983, p. 2.

[168] *Beijing review*, November 8, 1981, p. 21, col. 1.

[169] *Ibid.*, January 31, 1983, p. 8, col. 3.

chemical industries, machine parts, instruments and meters, light and textile output, hardware, handicrafts and sundries. Around 1300 blind are engaged in medical jobs. Those in the rural areas also have the opportunity to work, mainly in sideline production or other small outfits. As regards education, the country has 302 blind-and-deafmute schools enrolling 33,200.[170] These schools cover the primary grades and junior high only.[171].

Rural housing, as said previously, is mostly the thatch-roofed and ready-to-collapse variety. During the five years from 1980 to 1985, 2.5 billion square meters of housing are to be erected by the peasants for themselves, aside from the 300 million suqare meters of public amentities and facilities to be constructed in hamlets.[172] Urban housing is said to be on the increase continually. Residential housing of 310 million square meters will be completed by state-owned units. This averages out at 62 million square meters a year which is 2.6 times the mean annual figure for the 28 years between 1953 and 1980. The five-year plan says that urban utilities are to be installed with increasing quickness, environmental pollution is to be resolutely checked and the environment in key areas improved.

Infanticide and sterilization

The enhancement of people's welfare is related by the leadership to the size of the populace which leaped from 548 million in 1949 to 1,031 million in 1982.[173] This is an increase of 483 million.[174] From now on, under the Sixth Five-Year Plan, the annual natural rise will be kept under 13 per thousand. This compares to 14.5 per thousand in 1981 and 11.7 per thousand in 1979.[175] The decision is expressed by Premier Zhao Ziyang: "We must take effective measures and encourage late marriage (see next chapter), advocate one child for each couple, strictly control second births and resolutely prevent additional births so as to control population growth."[176] This single pregnancy goal, as it is popularly called in the CPR, has been enforced vigorously and it had led to tragedy. Local governments are given a free hand in carrying the policy into execution. Indeed a frenzied war has been declared on the mankind to be. Disciplinary infliction can be taken against disobedient cadres. A worker was expelled from Communist Party after giving birth to the 4th child.[177]

[170] Ibid., p. 9, col. 2.

[171] Zhong guo bai ke nian jian, p. 345, col. 1.

[172] Beijing review, December 20, 1982, p. 18, col. 2.

[173] Ibid., November 8, 1982, p. 20, col. 1.

[174] Ibid., March 28, 1983, p. 17, col. 2.

[175] Ibid., p. 19 (table)

[176] Ibid., December 20, 1982, p. 19. col. 2.

[177] New York times, November 3. 1982, p. 6, col. 4.

In Tianjin, the third largest city, parents who give second births pay a fine of 42 yuan to the administration as "social supply fee;" in Shanxi province, the recalcitrant parents' wages are cut by 20 percent, with the woman deprived of her vocational right and medical and cognate benefits.[178]

At the Chou Qao commune in Sichuan province, "families that have more than one child must pay a 1000-yuan fine and a fee to 'educate' the woman to have an abortion the next time."[179] That province also maintains the rule that "if a pregnant woman tries to elude the watchdog by travelling to another province, she must pay the travel expenses of officials who track her down." The authorities of Sichuan are wary of the danger a population explosion may represent, and their measures do not seem to be typical of other provinces. The fact that the province has 100 million inhabitants has given its authorities great cause for worry. Besides the draconian measures just mentioned, they decreed male sterilization. The victims have numbered some 10 million. Supposedly thankful to these steps, the population of Sichuan has risen by fewer than 10 per thousand during the past several years and was nine per thousand in 1982, rates matching the urban districts of Beijing, Tianjin and Shanghai.

How successful is the one-child per couple policy? This policy was officially enunciated in December 1982, but the plan on birth control (including this policy) has been in effect for three years.[180] Recently the State Committees of Family Planning published a study on the pregnancy rate.[181] On the average, each married woman gave birth to:

5.44 children in	1940s
5.87	1950s
5.68	1960s
4.01	1970s
2.41	1980
2.63	1981

The Committee is very gingerly about the resurgence of the rate from 2.41 to 2.63. Certainly this pours cold water, so to say, on the proponents of one pregnancy. However, the study also indicates the increase of voluntary birth curb. Throughout the country there are 170 million potentially child-bearing married women; of them 118 million have resorted to various forms of contraception. This is 69.46 percent. Furthermore, the law imposes upon the one-child parents the duty of reporting to the authorities of that fact. Certificates will be issued to them. It goes without saying that people are very afraid of facing the consequences such as paying the fine if they cannot keep the promise which the certificates signify. The reluctance of

[178] Sing tao newspapers (Canada), February 24, 1983, p. 9.

[179] The economist, April 9, 1983, p. 38 provides the following information.

[180] Globe and Mail, September 3, 1980, p. 2.

[181] Renmin ribao, April 10, 1983, p. 3.

registration, according to the study, is diminishing. Of the 30 million married couples who have one child, 14 million applied for the certificates. It means that 42.3 percent are determined to have no second births. Now turn to what we referred to as the tragedy. One of the deep-seated traditions of the Chinese is the slighting of girls and treasuring of boys. This is now reinforced by the one-child mandate and the policy of penalizing big families. Female infanticide, as a result, has reached alarming proportions. Recently the Women's Federation of Anhui Province disclosed, in a survey, that in a certain production brigade of Huiyuan county more than 40 girl babies were drowned during 1980-1981, and in Meizhuang production brigade in the first season of 1982, eight babies were born of whom three boys were reared up, but five girls were eliminated, three by drowning and two by abandonment.[182] Such drownings, death by negligence or outright murderings were taking place in other places of China.[183] A man drew a 13-year term for slaying his infant daughter,[184] a woman got a 4-year term for tossing hers into the toilet and drowning it there.[185] A local branch of the party is said to take the responsibility of bringing up an abandoned girl baby.[186] These cruelties are widespread.[187] On top of that, the babies' mothers are subject to terrible abuses. One angry husband threw her out of the house and divorced her. And the court even gave her a one year prison term.[188] Many frustrated men tormented their wives for committing the offense of not bearing boys.[189]

Given this situation, the imbalance of infant boys and girls is a foregone conclusion. According to the director of state statistics bureau, the ratio is 107.92 to 100 for the one-year bracket.[190] The difference is greater in some places. It "is a bit high [and] deserves attention," he declared. In Anhui province, he moved on, the ratio for newborn babies is 112.2 to 100; for children under three, 110.53 to 100; and for those under five, 109.84 to 100. The above mentioned Women Federation's survey of the Anhui situation summarizes the imbalance of infant boys and girls in some rural units. We reproduce the two tables it came up with.[191] The reader's attention should be

[182] Renmin ribao, April 7, 1983, p. 4.

[183] Ibid., January 31, 1983, p. 4; April 17, 1983, p. 3.

[184] Beijing review, January 31, 1983, p. 4.

[185] Renmin ribao, April 7, 1983, p. 7.

[186] Ibid., April 6, 1983, p. 8.

[187] Ibid., April 7, p. 4; April 12, p. 4; April 13, pp.1 and 4; April 17, p. 3, all of 1983.

[188] Ibid., April 9, 1983, p. 4.

[189] Beijing review, January 31, 1983, p. 4.

[190] Ibid., May 2, 1983, p. 9; also in Renmin ribao, April 19, 1983, p. 4.

[191] Renmin ribao, April 7, 1983, p. 4.

directed to the fact that girls are those who were not killed at birth.

Table I Suixi and Huiyuan counties.

Suixi	year of birth	total	boys	%	girls	%	boys over girls%
	1979	11,522	5950	51.6	5572	48.4	3.2
	1980	11,554	6115	52.9	5438	47.1	5.8
Huiyuan	1980	13,487	7593	56.3	5894	43.7	12.5
	1981	10,768	6266	58.2	4502	41.8	16.4

Table II: Huiyuan county

	total number	boys	%	girls	%	boys over girls %
Shuanggou commune	133	83	62.4	50	37.6	24.8
Lanqiao commune	104	66	63.5	38	36..5	27.0
Longkeng commune	231	145	62.8	86	37.2	25.5
Heiliu commune	285	164	57.5	121	42.5	15.0
Shaowang brigade	9	7	77.8	2	22.2	55.6
Nantai brigade	8	7	87.5	1	12.5	75.0
Qiaokou brigade	10	9	90.0	1	10.0	80.0

The situation has come to move the hierarchy. Premier Zhao Ziyang felt constrained to plead for equal treatment of boys and girls.[192] He states emphatically: "We must, in particular, protect infant girls and their mothers." Seeking to reverse the tradition, he proceeds to hold that "a couple that has only one daughter and brings her up well deserves greater commendation, support and reward than a couple that has only one son." He says in great indignation that the whole society should absolutely denounce the barbaric infanticide and mistreatment of mothers. The premier promises to set in motion the judicial machinery to take the culprits to trial.

One kind-hearted reader of *Beijing review* in Switzerland wrote to that journal with the suggestion that the state give a sum of money to families when their daughters are married and that women be given preference over men in jobs, especially intellectual professions.[193] Will the Beijing big shots heed this piece of advice?

In view of the tragedy to which the Chinese one-child policy has led, isn't it a scandal that the United Nations should present a population award to the People's Republic?[194]

[192] *Beijing review*, December 20, 1982, p. 18, col. 2.

[193] *Ibid.*, April 11, 1983, p. 1.

[194] *Ibid.*, March 28, 1983, p. 9.

CHAPTER XIV
Civil Law

Outlook on law

The Chinese ideologues have inherited their views on the nature of law from the Russian communists. They bifurcate all models of society into super- and base-parts.[1] Into the former part, they place culture, morals, thought-form, legal and ruling apparatus; and into the latter, they place the production forces and production relations. There is the cosmic rule that these forces and relations are decisive and that culture, et cetera are derivative.[2] Mankind, insist they, is moving toward a state- and class-less land where judicial and cognate mechanisms would disappear as instruments of dominance of one class by another. In the historical long run, law and government is transient. There can be neither eternal nor objective justice. In keeping with the type of class structure, the concept of legality in a community is undergoing an incessant change. Thanks to this rationale, the Maoists do not put much premium on the virtue of security and stability inherent in jurisprudence. In their mind, law is contrary to the nature of human progress and it is harmful too. There cannot and should not be immutable law or timeless equity in history.

Among the CCP oligarchs, however, some are more inclined to making trash out of lawbooks than others,[3] even though they all hold onto the utopian vision of a self-governing communist society maintained by social accord.[4] Thus depending on the faction of the CCP in control at a given period, peace and order are better in some years than in others. It is true that political combat, always waged out of the legal norm, does not make any dent on the daily round of life of the multitude because the removal of a few leaders is made known to the people through newspapers. However, there is always the tension among the elite and uneasiness in the public as to whither the political wind would shift.

To learn about the Chinese law, as about anything else of that country, one must not lose sight of the traits of Mao Zedong which have largely scarred it. During his youth, he defied the behest of his father by forming a united front with his mother and family servants; one time he threatened to drown himself by jumping into a pond, in order to bring his father to his knees.[5] This recalcitrance transferred

---

[1] Peng Zhen, "Explanation on seven laws," *Beijing Review*, July 16, 1979, p. 16, p. 1.

[2] "Wei wu zhu yi," *Xin hua ci dian*, Beijing: Shang wu yin shu guan, 1980, p. 872, col. 1.

[3] Among the leaders, Liu Shaoqi and Peng Zhen may well be called legalists, for they advocated the codification of law from the very inception of the CPR, Lung-sheng Tao, "Politics and law enforcement in China, 1949-1970," *The American Journal of Comparative Law*, no. 4, Fall 1974, pp. 725, 738.

[4] Martin Garbus, "Justice under China's new legal system," *New York Bar Journal*, no. 7, November 1978, pp. 577-584 at 584, col. 2. Karel Hulicka and Irene M. Hulicka, *Soviet Institutions, the Individual and Society*, Boston: Christopher Pub. House, 1967, pp. 279-280.

[5] Lucian W. Pye, *China*, Boston: Little, Brown, 1972, p. 219.

easily from the home to state politics. Mao's embarkation on insurrection is thus not a matter of surprise. He felt that formal rules might be needed, but that they should not be allowed to draw back the chariot of revolution. On the morrow of his revolutionary career (1926), he held that "proper limits have to be exceeded in order to right a wrong. Otherwise it cannot be righted."[6] What is meant by limits is the existing legislation or customary rule of behavior. Mao Zedong's famous saying that revolution is violence and that "it is not like entertaining a guest or making an embroidery, or painting a picture" attests to such an espousal of excesses.[7] The Chinese communists are all tarred by this mental brush. Zhou Enlai, known as a moderate, reiterated the just-quoted statement during the Cultural Revolution.[8] According to Wang Zhen (Politburo man after 1982), when in July 1930 his insurrectional unit was refused supplies by the monks of the temple where it headquartered, he just had them shot.[9] Such contempt of law on the part of the Chinese Reds has its Leninist legacy. The former Russian leader taught that the Soviet authority is based upon force and unrestricted by legalism. We quote him: "The revolutionary dictatorship of the proletariat is power won and held by the violence of the proletariat against the bourgeois, power that is not bound by any law."[10] This ethos, we think, lies at the heart of communist jurisprudence.

Posterior to the takeover of the whole of China in 1949, Mao Zedong was faced with the dilemma of either governing it without law, or decreeing some rules for both the elite and the masses to go by. The choice was not hard to make. With a view to consolidating the insurgent gain by lending it a semblance of legitimacy, a vast array of enactments were indeed ground out. An editorial of *Renmin ribao* says that 4,072 edicts and orders were promulgated during the first eight years of the communist state.[11] Among them are the awe-striking trio: Act for the Punishment of Counterrevolutionaries (February 21, 1951), Act for the Punishment of Crimes in Danger of State Currency (February 28, 1951), and Act for the Punishment of Corruption (April 21, 1952).[12] These and many others are called revolutionary

[6] Shao-chuan Leng, "The role of law in the People's Republic of China as reflecting Mao Zedong's influence," *The Journal of Criminal Law and Criminology*, no. 3, 1977, pp. 356-373 at 357, note 9.

[7] Mao Zedong, "Report of an investigation into the peasant movement in Hunan" (1927), *Government of Communist China*, edited by George P. Jan, San Francisco: Chandler Pub. Co., 1966, pp. 38-61 at 43.

[8] Cited in Claudie Broyelle, Jacques Broyelle et Evelyne Tschirhart, *Deuxieme retour de Chine*, Paris: Editions du Seuil, 1977, p. 307.

[9] Helen Foster Snow (Nym Wales), *Zhong guo lao yi bei ge min jia* (zi zhuan), Hong Kong: Wen yuan tu shu gong si, 1978, p. 97. This is a translation of *The Chinese Communists, Sketches and Autobiographies of Old Guards*, Wesport, Connecticut: Greenwood Press, 1972.

[10] Lenin, "Proletarskaya revoliutsiya i renegat' Kautskii," October-November 1918, *Polnoe sobranie sochinenii*, 5th ed., Moskva: Gosudarstvennoe izdatel'stvo politicheskoi literatury, 1963, vol. 37, pp. 237-338 at 245.

[11] Cited in Shao-chuan Leng, *op. cit.*, p. 366, note 82 where he cited the daily of October 9, 1957, p. 1.

[12] Chiu Hungdah, "Criminal punishment in mainland China: a study of some Yunnan province documents," *The Journal of Criminal Law and Criminology*, no. 3, 1977, pp. 374-398 at 377, note 21.

legislation; they are extraordinary and subject to no con'
process. The regime used them as an instrument to
maximum effect of pacification. During the immedia'
seizure period, the effort of the communists was avov._
at squelching the suspects thought to be ready to act in revenge. Fium
1954 to 1957, a Soviet style of legal system began to develop.[13] This
is followed by a period in which there was not even a semblance of
law. The regime simply went berserk in suppressing the rightists.[14]
The hurricane of this campaign blew over the Hundred Flowers,
it will be remembered. Mao Zedong assumed, rather naively, that the
communist system was safely anchored in China within an octonnium
(1949-1956). He invited the public to speak their minds without
reservation, even to the point of refuting it. After three months'
hesitancy (February-May 1957), they were pouring out heartfelt dislike
of the system. In particular, they were resentful of the lack of rule
of law.[15] Such bona fide opinion angered Mao Zedong, however. It
was considered baneful to the proletarian cause. Forthwith he ordered
the criticism to cease and desist. The free-speakers were prosecuted
as counterrevolutionary. Throughout China there prevailed a police
crackdown verging on hysteria. The judicial machinery, theretofore
functioning, came to a halt. Renmin ribao sang "in praise of
lawlessness." It equated legislation to bourgeois restraint on the
working masses.[16] For six years (1957-1962), legalism was in eclipse.

In the early sixties there was a slow veering toward normalcy,
thankful to such law-minded leaders like Liu Shaoqi and Deng
Xiaoping.[17] Unfortunately, their influence was shortlived. Beginning
in 1966, bureaucratic regularity and routine was declared inimical to
the goal of uninterrupted revolution. Imagining himself seized by the
capitalist-roaders, Mao called upon the youngsters to smash them.
In the unleashing of such ruffianism, the Justice Ministry,[18] and
procuracy were unceremoniously dismantled,[19] while the kangaroo
process eliminated countless opponents of Mao under the slogan of
the "right to rebel" (zao fan you li).[20] Nothing expresses more
graphically than this slogan the lack of sense of order in Mao Zedong.
The Gang of Four, as presently trumpeted, are the principal culprits
of counterrevolution, a term used by the Gang during the Cultural

[13] Thomas Bernstein, "The government of communist China," Government and Politics, 2nd ed., New York: Random House, 1971, pp. 227-260 at 248.

[14] Shao-chuan Leng, op. cit., p. 358, col. 2.

[15] Claudie Broyelle, et alii, op. cit., p. 151. Lung-sheng Tao, op. cit., 738.

[16] Jerome Cohen, "Will China have a Formal Legal System?" American Bar Association Journal, vol. 64, October 1978, pp. 1510-1515 at 1511; Shao-chuan Leng, op. cit., p. 359, note 26.

[17] Shao-chuan Leng, op. cit., p. 358, col. 2.

[18] Far Eastern Economic Review, October 5, 1979, p. 57, col. 2.

[19] Renmin ribao, July 13, 1981, p. 5.

[20] Claudie Broyelle, et alii, op. cit., pp. 26, 178.

GOVERNMENT OF SOCIALIST CHINA

revolution to label their victims. In reality, the Four are made to shoulder the responsibility of Mao Zedong. The restitution of law came in the wake of the modernization drive.[21] It is reasoned that "socialist revolution and socialist construction" must have universal regulatory instruments. If the instrument is either missing or abused, the communist system cannot count on the respect and cooperation of the masses. Starting from this premise, the current leaders "have taken pains to emphasize the need to restore law and order,"[22] and to improve adjudication and prosecution. Writing in *Newsweek,* Aric Press has stated that "China's economic development depends on predictable law."[23] If you want people to participate in the modernization, you ought to assure them the protection against caprice of officials. "New ideas aren't to come forth if it pays to keep mouths shut," Jerome Cohen wrote.[24] The rule of law is also the prerequisite of foreign aid. The CPR cannot lift herself up industrially by her own bootstrap, a fact which Beijing has openly stressed. It ought to import technology and investment.[25] Should the Chinese law remain chaotic or anarchic, these things surely will not be arriving. To keep her legal structure, civil no less than criminal, abreast of world standard, is the desideratum to the acquirement of expertise and finance from outside. Whether the Chinese regime is really prepared to abandon once and for all the revolutionary goal, it has no choice but to embrace the mercantile values of the bourgeois with its emphasis on articulate terms regulating business relations.[26]

Some scholars have suggested that Beijing's attempt at law-reform is motivated by the retaliation of current statesmen against their erstwhile enemy. "A great number of men who were very badly treated in the Cultural Revolution," said one writer, "are back in power and they are determined that that sort of thing will not happen again."[27] Doubtless the dominant coterie of China has decided to bring order to the people after so many years of topsy-turvydom. Yet whether the sense of revenge is the real explanation cannot be substantiated. No matter what specific causes for modernizing China's legislation, the attempt is, indubitably, a wholesome one. The former CCP chairman, Hua Guofeng, attached great importance to law. On August 18, 1977, he declared to the 11th National Congress

[21] Ronald Keith, "Transcript of discussions with Wu Daying and Zhang Zhonglin concerning legal change and civil rights," *The China Quarterly,* no. 81, March 1980, pp. 111-121 at 112.

[22] Jerome Cohen, "Criminal law, reflection on the criminal process in China," *The Journal of Criminal Law and Criminology,* no. 3, 1977, pp. 323-355 at 351, col. 2.

[23] Aric Press, "China, back to the law," *Newsweek,* October 22, 1979, p. 110.

[24] *Ibid.;* Jerome Cohen, *op. cit.,* p. 1515, col. 2.

[25] Aric Press, *op. cit.,* p. 113, col. 1.

[26] Simon Luk, "China's new legal system," *World Press Review,* May 1980, p. 59.

[27] Aric Press, *loc. cit.* The opinion is expressed by Victor Li who may be called legal Sinologist.

of the Party that "we must strengthen our public security work and the socialist legal system,"[28] and on February 26, 1978, he repeated the same point before the fifth National People's Congress.[29] Ye Jianying, former Chairman of the NPC Standing Committee, emphasized that the sine qua non of the CPR's future as a socialist system is the firm commitment to justice for all and the full blossoming of communist legality.[30] Han Yudong, deputy director of the Institute of Jurisprudence in the Academy of Social Sciences has quoted to foreign visitors one of Mao Zedong's rare utterances, made in 1962, on the role of law: "We cannot do without law. We certainly need to promote criminal and civil laws. We need not only the enacted laws, but legal precedents."[31] After setting forth the outlook on law, we propose to study the two great branches of law: civil and criminal. The instant chapter is mainly directed to the first, and the next to the second.

Underdeveloped civil law

A Sinologist, Hungdah Chiu, writes that "there is a lack of sufficient information or research materials concerning legal development in the People's Republic of China."[32] This view, we think, applies rightfully to civil, but not to criminal jurisprudence. There is indeed a plethora of works on almost every aspect of crime and punishment, but preciously few authors study civil problems. How to account for it? One reason is that writers tend to do research in fairly explored fields for whatever considerations. Another is that up to the present there is no unified civil code in the CPR. On several occasions, attempts were made to produce such a code, namely, on the eve of the Great Leap (1957),[33] at the inception of the social education move (1962),[34] and immediately before the Cultural Revolution (1966).[35] All were aborted. Not until the 4th session of the fifth NPC were some general principles for a civil code formulated.[36] But this does not prevent the adoption in March and putting into effect "on a trial basis" on October 1, 1982, the Civil-Procedure Law.[37]

---

[28] Keesing's, December 16, 1977, p. 28721, col. 2.

[29] Ibid., September 8, 1978, p. 29182, col. 1.

[30] Facts on File, March 10, 1978, p. 153, G3.

[31] Renmin ribao, March 16, 1978, cited in Donald Paragon, "Some firsthand observations on China's legal system," Judicature, no. 10, 1980, pp. 477-484 at 479, col. 1.

[32] Chiu Hungdah, op. cit., p. 374, col. 1.

[33] Shao-chuan Leng, op. cit., p. 358, col. 1.

[34] Jerome Cohen, "Will China have a formal legal system?" p. 1513, col. 1; Simon Luk, op. cit., p. 59, col. 1.

[35] David Bonavia, "Hua spells out Deng's brave new world," Far Eastern Economic Review, July 6, 1979, p. 11, col. 3; Simon Luk, p. 59, col. 2.

[36] Renmin ribao, December 9, 1981, p. 4; December 12, 1981, p. 1.

[37] Beijing review, August 16, 1982, pp. 20-24.

During the Hundred Flowers, Zhou Enlai opined that China could not have a civil as well as a criminal code until after the complete transformation of the means of production to state property.[38] His view betrays an ignorance of the role of civil law, a law which he took to be governing the state ownership of immovable goods, but not aimed at adjudicating contracts between individuals. True, socialization of the means of production may lead to the shrinkage of the scope of the civil code, but there still remains a kaleidoscope of social life to be regulated. Marriage and divorce are only the most salient aspects of it. The basis for the underdevelopment of civil enactment, therefore, may not be explicated by the view of Zhou Enlai. It was to be sought in other factors.

Among the Chinese there is the ingrained aversion to formal litigation. Runs an ancient maxim: "It is better to enter a tiger's mouth than a court of law."[39] This reflects the mixed feeling of awe and disdain of the common folks for the yamen. A quiet settlement of an issue is preferred to a confrontation before mandarins with the attendant display of paraphernalia of state power.[40] According to one estimate, ninety-five percent of all disputes are settled without the use of the court,[41] and another estimate put it at eighty-five percent.[42] The second was made by none other than the vice-president of the CPR Supreme Court. Thus, only 5 to 15 percent of the cases ever reach the court. Such readiness to accept a compromise and eschew an open collision prevades the Chinese society. For those who are disposed toward "fighting it out," there is the inconvenience and cost in hiring a lawyer and in journeying by foot to the distant town where a court was maintained. All this deters potential litigants who must think twice before plunging into the judicial morass. In their mind, the casus belli is just not worth the candle. Let's analyze at this point the conciliation process.

The immense network of mediation committees was authorized by a law of March 22, 1954.[43] They are set up wherever there is a fairly permanent collection of people, be it an apartment building, a lonely street, a mountain village, a semi-urban settlement, a campsite, a construction project or an institution. Invariably each flat of the first-named is served by a committee which has under its charge ten or so families. It deals with children and adults on accusations of petty theft, quarrels about the use of common facilities, battery and assault, verbal abuses. Most frequent, however, is marital discord.[44] In the

[38] Cited in Claudie Broyelle, et alii, op. cit., p. 151.

[39] Martin Garbus, "Justice under China's new legal system," New York State Bar Journal, no. 7, 1978, pp. 577-584 at 478.

[40] Aric Press, op. cit., p. 110, col. 2.

[41] Martin Garbus, op. cit., p. 579.

[42] Ruth Ginsburg, op. cit., p. 1521, col. 1.

[43] Jerome Cohen, op. cit., p. 349, note 152.

[44] Shao-chuan Leng, op. cit., p. 362, col. 2.

resolving of all these issues, the committeemen donate their afterwork-time.[45] Usually numbering 10, they are elected by the constituents and stay on duty until resignation. The committee is placed under the local court and, in rural areas, under the brigade as well. Should a committee fail to arrive at a solution acceptable to the disputants, they are free to go to court. Since the proposed solution is not legally binding, they do not require the committee's consent for doing that. Although the procedure used by a committee is regulated by the 1954 law,[46] it is always characterized by improvization and expedience. The committee does not pretend to set up precedents, neither does it have precedents to follow. Evidential law, if any, is of the crudest kind, and witness interrogation is informal and uncouth.

To describe this process as even quasi-judicial is euphemistic. Inordinate pressure and arm-twisting are employed at every turn by the committeemen who are, on this account, often not liked by the parties. Very active or officious are the communist party secretaries in the patching up of controversies, and the disputants' working units are equally intrusive. They interfere at all stages of the process. The final judgment of the committeemen takes the form of pecuniary compensation, or verbal denunciation by the committee, or the ordering of public apology by one party. If the apple of discord turns on the use of a communal kitchen, or bathroom, the committee can decree some rules governing their future use. Sometimes, the committee may look into the infraction of social etiquette or minor faux pas. On ideological grounds, this hodgepodge is enclothed in the "mass line;" it is taken to mean that people themselves set aright their own houses. A national conference on conciliar work was held in August 1981 in Beijing.[47] It was revealed that there were 81,000 mediation committees in China served by 5,750,000 people. In 1980, they solved 6,120,000 cases. This is said to be 10.8 times the civil cases.[48] Incidentally the latter cases would have to be 566,666.

The committee method has the merit of trial by one's peers. Besides, it proves effective because the peers have intimate knowledge of the disputants which is the basis for the judgment. They already know who are inveterate wrongdoers and who are good-natured individuals. They can declare better rulings than an impersonal court which is bound to ground its opinion on official documents or on debate in front of it. Martin Garbus sees a group therapy in the Chinese conflict-solution.[49] Neighborhood squabbles always involve misbehavior of adults and youngsters, and

---

[45] Donald Paragon, "Some firsthand observations on China's legal system," op. cit., p. 481, col. 1.

[46] Renmin ribao, August 27, 1981, p. 1.

[47] Renmin ribao, August 28, 1981, p. 1.

[48] For appellate and original cases see section on courts in the next chapter.

[49] Martin Garbus, op. cit., p. 583, col. 2.

442   GOVERNMENT OF SOCIALIST CHINA

identification of such persons is quite easy by men living or working in the same place. The committee seems to fulfil a useful purpose. Little wonder the 1982 Constitution (Article 113, par. 2) orders the organization of mediation committees in local communities,[50] and the 1982 Civil-Procedure Law devotes a whole chapter to them.[51] The operation of such unofficial bodies interdicts the resort to the juridical mechanism.

The subdued role of the ordinary court can also be explained by the socialist economy. A high portion of legal work in a capitalist nation has to do with the intricacies of commercialism which cannot happen in the CPR. That country does not have the complex income or estate tax laws as exist in Japan, for example. Wills and succession are meaningless in the CPR where nobody is allowed to amass huge wealth. The absence of private cars precludes much controversy of torts. China has no comprehensive workers' compensation which gives rise to numerous litigations in a free enterprise system. Thus, the substantive matters that make up the bulk of the task of courts and lawyers under that system simply disappear in the People's Republic.[52]

Gradually, though, the situation has begun to change. Tiny businesses based on individual or partner ownership are mushrooming both in cities and villages (see preceding chapter). Besides, production teams can from now on engage in a great variety of activities involving the entry into contracts with individual peasants. All this necessitates the development of law governing damages and claims. The modernization policy of the communists has forced them to lay down guidelines in dealing with foreigners whose succor they actively seek. The Japanese, for example, before signing anything with the Beijing authorities would ask themselves such a question: "Can agreements be taken seriously if there is no contract law?" They would be hesitant to establish a business in China due to the non-existence of a company act.[53] Specific regulations on labor relations, employment, unionization, patent protection for concerns operating in the CPR should also be made. While suits between private citizens can be, as have been, disposed of by administrative decrees or conciliation, disputes with alien firms may not be dealt with in the same way.

Presently, many civil cases involving state agencies are settled by government bodies.[54] The Ministry of Metallurgical Industry may straighten out an argument between one plant and another under its jurisdiction. However, this mode of solution is no longer regarded as

50 *Beijing review*, November 23, 1981, pp. 23-27.

51 *Ibid.*, August 16, 1982, p. 22.

52 Beverly Carl, *op. cit.*, p. 1257.

53 Aric Press, *loc. cit.*

54 *Beijing review*, November 9, 1981, p. 6; Beverly Carl, *op. cit.*, p. 1267.

appropriate. A juridical organ which is neutral and which is able to interpret the intendment of contractual provisions is all the more important as the government has been willing to assume monetary responsibility toward injured parties. In the summer of 1978, steps were taken to compensate rural units for losses caused by the government through improper transfer of labor and materials. One commune was reported to be paid the large sum of $1,000,000 for an unlawful deprivation of personnel and supply.[55]

The call for a comprehensive civil statute, as already stated, has been made several times by the regime,[56] but it met with criticism.[57] The government view is that only a unified code can satisfy the modernization needs and that legislation on property (both private and public) as well as non-property relations may be appropriately placed in it. Critiques, however, argue that at present there are difficulties to come up with an integrated enactment. The rules on civil relations and those on the economic activities of the state, they say, must be treated as pertaining to different legal categories. Further, economic enactment is an "essential leverage of the government in promoting the industrialization." It envisages three dimensions: a) relations between the government and economic bodies, b) relations between the latter bodies themselves, and c) relations between subunits of an economic body. Economic regulation has to do with:[58]

1) protection of ownership of the whole people and collectives
2) principles of planning
3) regulation of basic construction
4) production responsibility
5) cooperative organization
6) energy distribution
7) quality and standard enforcement
8) banking and trust legislation
9) income
10) profit and dividend
11) joint venture

Laws on these problems, the critics insist, cannot be put together with civil laws on engagements between individuals or tortious procedures.[59] Up to the present time, the resistance to a unified civil code has prevailed, even though some efforts are made toward achieving it.[60]

With the still simple life pattern, even in the teeming cities, there

55 Beverly Carl, loc. cit.

56 Ruth Ginsburg, op. cit., p. 1520, col. 2.

57 Beijing review, April 6, 1981, p. 16; Renmin ribao, January 27, 1981, p. 5.

58 Guangming ribao, July 18, 1981, p. 4.

59 Beverly Carl, op. cit., p. 1274.

60 Renmin ribao, December 9, 1981, p. 4; December 12, 1981, p. 1.

is no ground for fairly complex civil legislation. Gradually the regime finds it essential to produce one enactment after another, in rapid succession, to take care of the evolving modernization problems. But the judges and administrators do not seem to be prepared for the task. Most of them just do not take the trouble to become acquainted with the statutes and regulations. Two judges of Fushun county of Liaoning province, it is noteworthy, addressed a letter to *Renmin ribao* in lamentation of the economic laws and of the officials who enforce them. The letter hinted at the contradictory terms of these laws but it openly charges that the bureaucrats do not know what the contractual rights and obligations are.[61] But we ought to point out that the government is in a great hurry making laws which are poorly drafted and contain inconsistencies. In May 1981, a batch of 17 lengthy and complicated pieces of legislation were issued.[62] Most are put in effect right away. It takes all-wise administrative and judicial cadres to correctly put them into effect.

The seizure of the court, as seen above, is made unnecessary because of the enormous mediation system. What comes to the dockets of the judges are criminal and divorce cases.[63] In Hubei province, the superior court has two divisions dealing with the former, but five divisions, with the latter matters.[64] Even divorce cases are not all handled in accordance with the regular civil process, for an overwhelming number of them are disposed by judges sitting as mediators (see below).

In summation, there are seven reasons for the retarded growth of civil law in the People's Republic: 1) the universal antipathy of the Chinese society in making use of the court, 2) the unavailability of juridical organs, 3) legal expenses, 4) mediation network discharging the duties of adjudication, 5) the reluctance of making a global civil-law code, 6) inadequate training of law men, such as judges, lawyers and bureaucrats in the application of the rules of law, and 7) these rules are often hastily written and in large numbers. They are hard to digest by juridical cadres. Finally, as a footnote, let us note that *Guangming ribao* says that from the fall of 1981 there has been a course on "knowledge of law" taught in each school from primary grade to university. The three components are 1) general conception of law, 2) class content of law and 3) criminal law.[65] Where is civil law?

Law on domestic relations
Marriage

A marriage law was issued on May 1, 1950 only a few months after the forming of the communist government at Beijing.[66] This fact shows

[61] *Ibid.*, July 12, 1981, p. 5.

[62] *Beijing review,* November 9, 1981, p. 6.

[63] Shao-chuan Leng, *op. cit.,* p. 367, col. 2. *Renmin ribao,* August 1, 1981, p. 3.

[64] Shao-chaun Leng, *loc. cit.*

[65] *Guangming ribao,* August 5, 1981, p. 1.

[66] *Beijing Review,* March 16, 1981, p. 27, col. 2.

the latter's grave concern with the domestic relations of the Chinese people. However, those who are slightly familiar with the Six Codes of the preceding regime cannot escape concluding that the Reds just wanted to re-do things, with propaganda objectives in the uppermost of their mind. Actually there is very little new in the 1950 law. Such universal canons as spousal equality were provided in the family-relation part of the Six Codes. The communists were attempting to create an impression that it was they, not the previous legislators, who wrote these progressive principles into the statute. One may suppose that Beijing has implemented the law, but the old government did not. This is not true either. An official media stated candidly that "many young people did not even know there was a marriage law in [communist] China" published in 1950.[67] Indeed, the reissuance of the Marriage Law in 1980 has the plain purpose of making it more widely known.

In the section on general principles of the Marriage Law are placed such provisions as free choice of partners, monogamy, equal rights for women and family planning.[68] The last-named (family planning) often involves social harassment and administrative penalty (see preceding chapter). The neighborhood organizations, as mentioned in Chapter VI, are vested with the power to decide who should have babies and when.[69] With respect to the freedom of selecting partners, it is widely known that Chinese are forbidden to marry foreigners and even Taiwanese. In October 1982, the grandson of Lu Xun, Zhou Lingfei (a CCP technical cadre from the mainland) fell in love with a girl from Taiwan while both were in Japan. He was warned by CCP officials not to marry her. But he decided to defect. They flew to Taiwan to complete their plan. Inside China, circumstances are not progressive enough for freedom of acquaintance between sexes. Enforced betrothals are frequently reported in papers.[70] *Beijing review* writes of the rigid mode of life on the farm which militates against contacts between people.[71] As a result, there develops the "introduction system" or matchmaking. No less an authority than the National Women's Federation stated that the system is commonplace in the countryside where the opportunity of finding someone to your liking is very rare.[72] It is only too patent that the Reds cannot substantiate the claim th t that they have given marital freedom to their subjects. (When our book went to press, the alien-marriage ban was lifted. *Guowuyuan gongbao,* September 20, 1983, pp. 831-832.)

The refutation of plural marriage is in effect mentioned twice

[67] *Ibid.,* January 19, 1981, p. 7, col. 3; the State Council ordered propaganda of the 1980 Marriage Law, *Renmin ribao,* December 27, 1981, p. 1.

[68] *Beijing review,* March 16, 1981, pp. 24-27 reprints the full text of the Law.

[69] Claude Broyelle, *et alii, op. cit.,* p. 48; James Wang, *Contemporary Chinese Politics, an introduction,* Englewood Cliffs, New Jersey: Prentice-Hall, 1980, p. 140.

[70] *Renmin ribao,* January 19, 1981, p. 7, col. 4; May 14, 1983, p. 1.

[71] *Beijing review,* May 4, 1981, p. 21.

[72] *Ibid.*

because in addition to the approval of monogamy in Article 2, there is the disapproval of bigamy in Article 3 of the Marriage Law. Like sex equality, this principle is stipulated in the old Six Codes. Within the Han area, the Nationalist Government and the several warlords had forbidden polygamy. However, some ethnic minorities, particularly those in the periphery of the country, had different usages. This, as any other phase of their life, was not interfered with. It was only after 1949 that the totalitarian mold descended upon them, but the communists find it imperative to reconcile with the reality in some instances. Article 36 of the Marriage Law lets the "people's congresses and their standing committees in national autonomous areas enact certain modifications or supplementary articles in keeping with the principles of this law by taking into consideration local conditions." Such enactments, significantly enough, are not subject to the veto of the central authorities, but they must be filed with the NPC Standing Committee "just for the record of it." In late 1981, the people's congress of Tibet produced the "Modification Rules to the Marriage Law."[73] Apart from fixing the minimum age of marriage as 20 and 18 for male and female (lower by two years than the parental law),[74] they provide that "polyandry and polygyny are abrogated. However, if they existed before the coming into force of the Modification Rules (not the parental law), they would be continuously recognized until and unless their dissolution is actively sought by the parties concerned." We must point out that plural marriage is done away with in autonomous prefectures and autonomous counties within China proper. If minorities are outside these units, their polyandry or polygyny remained valid until the new law. Further, since the Marriage Law was put into execution on January 1, 1980 and since the Modification Rules of Tibet went into effect some time in November 1981, plural unions between these two dates were still contractable.[75] Only after the second date was new polyandry or polygyny proscribed.

Marriage age is fixed at 22 for a man and 20 for a woman (Article 4). There is no stipulation that parental sanction must be obtained for exceptions. Compared with the 1950 law, there is an increase of 2 years for each sex in tune with the policy of deferred marriage of the government;[76] a policy of family planning is embodied in Article 53, clause 3 of the 1978 Constitution and Article 23 of the 1982 one. Even before the promulgation of the present marriage legislation, the Communist Party had, rather illegally (because only the NPC can do it), revised the law by limiting the marital age to 30 and 25

---

[73] *Renmin ribao,* November 7, 1981, p. 4.

[74] *Beijing review,* May 18, 1981, p. 6.

[75] The exact day of the entry into the Tibetan Modification Rules is not mentioned in *Renmin ribao,* November 7, 1981, p. 4.

[76] *Beijing review,* January 19, 1981, p. 7, col. 2.

respectively.[77] The present 22-20 requirement, needless to say, can be exceeded and has indeed been exceeded. Deferment for most young people becomes an unwritten rule.[78] *Renmin ribao* says that in reality marriage nearly always occurs after 24 years of age because men and women at that time would normally graduate from college and acquire a job.[79] It is to be noted that the erstwhile 20-18 limitation was reported to have been violated in many locales. For example, the authority in Zhuge village of Hebei province decreed in 1979 that marriage licenses would not be given to men below 25 and women below 23.[80] The decision met with resistance from parents and had to be rescinded. The current 22-20 rule seems to be a happy compromise. In the past, the government enforced the late-marriage policy leniently in rural areas, as there was less control there. It is sheerly impossible for the authority to set up offices in the tens of millions of hamlets. As a result the birth-certificate requirement (Article 7) was implemented in the cities only.

Minority (of whatever age) is not the only disqualification. Forbidden are also the unions of a) lineal relatives by blood, and b) lepers. The former kind of marriage happens in scattered places and it leads to congenital malformation in infants.[81] *Shaanxi ribao* states that Lin Yu Shan district of Shaanxi province, on account of communication difficulties and of backward culture, has practiced close-kin marriage. The outcome is alarming: in an entire community, no single male is fit for military service.[82] The refusal to register leprocal marriage, in accordance with Article 6, clause (b), has to be substantiated by medical proof. For the sake of comparison, we may note that the Soviet marriage legislation disqualifies the mentally ill or imbecile.[83] Query: Can these marry in China?

In respect of equal status of spouses (Article 9), the continued use of his or her family name (Article 10), the right to work after marriage (Article 11) and the co-ownership of commonly acquired means (Article 13) are solemnized. Also provided is the responsibility of helping each other when one party is in distress (Article 14). The fact, however, is that women are definitely inferior. They are subject to various abuses. *Beijing review's* and *Renmin ribao's* report of these and appeal for their amelioration is very common (better, monotonous).[84] Family planning and birth control is proclaimed as

[77] Shao-chuan Leng, *op. cit.*, p. 368, col. 1.

[78] Beverly Carl, *op. cit.*, p. 1275.

[79] *Renmin ribao*, March 20, 1981, p. 3.

[80] *Beijing review*, May 4, 1981, p. 22, col. 2.

[81] *Ibid.*, January 19, 1981, p. 8.

[82] *Shaanxi ribao*, December 10, 1980, p. 3.

[83] Marriage Law of the USSR, Article 10. This can be found in David Lane, *Politics and Society in the USSR*, 2nd ed., London: Martin Robertson, 1978, p. 598.

[84] *Renmin ribao*, April 11, 1983, p. 4; April 12, 1983, p. 4; April 13, 1983, p. 1. Beijing review, May 2, 1983, p. 4.

a duty (Article 12). In difference from other duties envisioned in the marriage act, this one is also placed in the Constitution (Article 49, par. 2). For the breach of it, however, the criminal law stipulates no punishment. But local penalties are severe, even inhuman (see preceding chapter).

In order to consolidate the domestic relations, the law forbids maltreatment of family members and desertion (Article 3). It also accords the parents the authority to discipline the children (Article 17) and the right of husband or wife to inherit one another's property (Article 18). Similarly, children and parents are enjoined to support each other (Article 15). If either party fails to fulfill this responsibility, suits can be instituted.[85] Elder brothers or sisters who have the ability to pay the costs have the obligation to rear their younger brothers or sisters whose parents are dead or unable to bring them up (Article 23). An identical obligation is devolved on grandparents and grandchildren in their relations (Article 22). The preceding three articles (15, 22, 23) do not exist in the family law of the Republic of China, but they were a matter of custom. Both the 1950 and 1980 marriage legislations, in regulating reciprocal care and respect of family members, must be viewed against the communist value of state over private life. During the early years of the CPR, the authorities abetted the youths to inform about their bourgeois, feudal or otherwise despicable parents. Up until the death of Mao Zedong, school children were taught to love him more than their fathers and mothers. We think the Red Guards, who upheld the "right to rebel" and smashed the four olds (custom, habit, culture and thought), are the brilliant product of Maoist philosophy. Currently, the pragmatists have turned their back on that sort of quixotism. They wanted to retrieve the family virtue of yore.

Most provisions of the law under consideration are not unlike those of other countries. Yet one stipulation in the Criminal Law of the CPR bearing on domestic relations deserves special notice. According to Article 180, if a man engages in sexual intercourse with the wife of an ordinary citizen, he may be punished by two years' imprisonment. However, if she is the wife of a military man, the term is three years.[86] The Criminal Law, it is to be noted, went into effect on January 1, 1980. However, the just mentioned special protection of military people had been in practice for at least ten years.[87] That privilege was even accorded to a military man's fiancée in some cases.[88] Why is this provision furnished? The communist power is acquired by armed conquest and is maintained by the existence of the military. It is only fitting and proper that the leadership grant the uniformed personnel an extraordinary safeguard of their better halves.

[85] *Renmin ribao*, December 10, 1980, p. 2.

[86] Criminal Law of the CPR, Article 181.

[87] Chiu Hungdah, *op. cit.*, p. 378, col. 1.

[88] *Ibid.*

Divorce

On this there have been two schools of thought.[89] The one holds onto the "reason" theory that divorce may not be granted unless there are sound grounds. This view is said to be taken by the left-wingers under the Gang of Four. Against it there is the "love" theory which says that once friendship disappears, there goes the marriage. The two theories are not as far apart as it may seem, although the former makes divorce a little more difficult. It is generally maintained that a frivolous attitude toward marriage is to be prohibited,[90] but an utter alienation of mutual affection cannot be repaired by compulsory rule of law.[91] Hence the sanction of divorce (Article 24, 25). If a divorce is effected by an agreement, a simple registration with the marriage bureau is all that is called for. If, however, disputes should arise, the parties must seize the court. In handling such a dispute, the judge is instructed to try to arrange a reconciliation (Article 25, clause 2). Only after the situation proves hopeless can divorce be approved. Then there is the provision that debts incurred by both during the union must be defrayed out of the joint property (Article 32). Had the amount of the latter been insufficient to retire the debts, they are ordered to develop a solution. Failing this, the court is to make a judgment for them. If, after divorce, one party has the custody of a child, the other party is responsible for a portion or all of the necessary means for his well-being (Article 30). As a matter of principle, the mother is granted custody of a breast-fed infant. If a controversy arises on the guardianship following weaning, the court has to decide it (Article 29). The law anticipates the possibility that one party may be in financial trouble. Article 33 says in that event, the other party is duty bound to render an appropriate aid. The details are to be worked out in writing. If not, the court can interfere by making a ruling.

Divorce is always handled by mediation first. If a couple decide to see lawyers after the failure of conciliation by neighborhood groups or work units, there is no filing of divorce papers right away. Instead, the lawyers would try their hands at another mediation. Chinese media have printed many such out-of-court solutions by lawyers. Three family cases may be summarized here.[92] First, a certain Shu often beat up his wife Sheng, because he was annoyed by many daily chores. She sued for a divorce. The lawyer investigated the domestic relations and came to learn that the two were a devoted couple from the very inception of the marriage. The trouble was that Shu still harbored a feudalistic idea of the sovereignty of man and meanwhile he was abetted by someone to be rude. Basically, it was found, the marital relation was not impaired, although on the surface there was a contradiction. The lawyer, therefore, moved on to "work on that man's

[89] *Guangming ribao*, July 7, 1981, p. 3.

[90] Shao-chuan Leng, *op. cit.*, p. 367, note 91.

[91] *Beijing review*, January 19, 1981, p. 8, col. 1.

[92] *Guangming ribao*, August 1, 1981, p. 3.

thought," and he succeeded in bringing him to his senses. Consequently Shu offered an apology to Sheng. After obtaining the latter's understanding, the lawyer did not go ahead with the suit. The second case is a dispute between offsprings of an intestate Gu. Lawyers were engaged by them to seize the court. A study of the case was made by them; they proposed to grant each of the three the amount of property which consists of Gu's wages, shares of dividends and a dwelling house, in accordance with the obligations rendered by the offspring to the father during his lifetime. The problem was thus solved, due to the "working on the thought" of the contestants. The third case involves a man who has left a will which bequeathed all his property to the second wife and the children borne to her. After he died, the former wife's children claimed the legacy. To this end, they contracted lawyers to take legal action. At first, the second wife insisted on the legality of the will and refused to concede to the demands of others. Lawyers of both parties worked together to develop a compromise in the light of concrete circumstances; they persuaded all concerned to accept the proposal by appealing to their moral conscience. This effort resulted in the restoration of their friendship.

Visitors to the People's Republic are sometimes invited to witness divorce trials during recent years. Ruth Ginsburg described such a trial attended by the delegates (including her) of the American Bar Association in Shanghai.[93] The couple were employed in different plants. She alleged he had an affair with a worker in his unit, besides charging him with cruelly striking her for years. First, the conciliation committee endeavored to arrive at a solution but did not succeed. Both then went to court. One judge and two assessors heard the case. However, they did not act as a tribunal, but simply as another panel of conciliation in accordance with Article 25 of the law in question. By complying with the mass line, the court summoned the representatives of the work units before it. The couple were talked to by the judge and assessors to make up their differences for the sake of their two small children. Unable to change their minds, the trio ordered the husband and wife to retire from the courtroom. In their absence, they canvassed the opinion of the audience, that is, the co-workers of the parties. One work unit, the man's, suggested further persuasion in order to save the marriage, but the other work unit, the wife's, came forward in favor of a divorce. Due to the complete alienation of the couple, the court followed the latter recommendation. In re children, it awarded the younger one to her, but the older one to him. He was to pay, as alimony, a sum of six yuan (US $3) per month. Meanwhile, she kept the living quarters and gave some furnishings to him. This decision, let it be emphasized, is an out-of-court settlement, even though effected in it.

Two or three points should be mentioned before leaving the topic. First, the Chinese law stipulates no separation preceding divorce.

93 Ruth Ginsburg, op. cit., pp. 1521-1523.

Second, to protect military man, his wife has a harder time getting a divorce than the wife of, say, a worker. Article 26 states that if the wife of that man desires a divorce, she must obtain his consent. It means that the marriage is undissolvable unless he approves, and this in spite of the provision of Article 25, par. 2 that "complete alienation of mutual affection" constitutes a ground of divorce. Third, there is the 21 months moratorium of divorce as provided in Article 27. It reads: "The husband is not allowed to apply for a divorce when his wife is pregnant, or within one year after the birth of a child," a provision copied from the Marriage Law of the USSR.[94]

Law on Joint Ventures

Another piece of legislation of a civil character is the Law on Joint Ventures adopted on July 1, 1979 at the second session of the fifth National People's Congress and became effective on July 8.[95] Among the seven laws enacted by the same Congress, only this one took effect so soon.[96] To summarize and comment on the law, the Chinese Government may enfranchise an alien company to function within its domain in conjunction with Chinese enterprises. The venture can apply to the Foreign Investment Commission for a permit to enter into a contract with a Chinese counterpart and registration has to be done in the General Administration for Industry and Commerce (Article 3). Assuming the juridical form of a limited corporation, a venture must have at least 25 percent foreign investment (Article 4). Any profit, risk or loss shall be shared by the parties in proportion to their contribution. In order to avoid cheating of the technically immature Chinese, the law says that the technology or equipment made by the alien firm shall be "truly advanced and appropriate for China's needs" (Article 5). In case of damages caused by deliberate provision of outdated materials, there must be compensations. What constitutes outdated materials, we think, may well be a thorny issue. The joint venture is an outright technical aid that China must acquire in order to modernize her economy. One can easily imagine that the investment would take the form of financial help or physical plants provided by foreigners; but it is, for the most part, the "use of the site" that is provided by the Chinese. This is indeed stipulated in Article 7. There is also the clause that if China makes other types of contributions, she should be compensated (Article 5).

The venture has a board of directors with one or two vice-chairmen and a Chinese chairman. Of this chairmanship, Peng Zhen, the former Director of the Legal Affairs Bureau of the NPC, spoke with an air of pride to the NPC on June 26, 1979.[97] Each plant is headed by a

94 Marriage Law of the USSR, Article 14, clause 5, in Robert Lane, *op. cit.*, p. 601.

95 Both English and Chinese texts are in *Zhong guo shou ce*, Hong Kong: Da gong bao, 1979, pp. 339-348.

96 *Ibid.* mentions the different dates on which the laws took effect. For the seven laws, see Chapter VI.

97 *Beijing review*, July 13, 1979, p. 14, col. 1.

president and vice-presidents, also called general and assistant managers, who shall be chosen from the various parties to the joint venture (Article 6). In this case, there is no nationality restriction, however. These posts are highly technical and China has few qualified candidates for them. Henceforth, Beijing is not small-minded about it. Important problems are to be decided by the board through consultation of the participants on the principle of equality and mutual benefit. Interestingly enough, democratic centralism, the gimcrackery of the communists for any situation of decision-making, is not talked about here; they know well that foreigners cannot be impressed by it. Falling within the purview of the board are such basic issues as project expansion, production, business program, budget, distribution of dividends, manpower, remuneration, the termination of an undertaking, the appointment of the president and vice-presidents, chief engineer, the treasurer and the auditors as well as their functions and powers.

In re net earnings, the law envisions distribution between the parties according to their registered capital after paying the income tax for the venture (Artice 7). Foreign partners who re-invest a portion of such earnings within the CPR may get back part of the tax already paid.[98] To facilitate Beijing's financial control, the venture shall open an account with the Bank of China (Article 8). In its purchase of raw materials, fuels and auxiliary equipment, the venture should give first preference to Chinese sources (Article 9). It may also acquire them directly from the world market. Besides, the venture can sell its products outside China by distributing them through direct channels or its associated agencies or China's foreign trade establishments. The products may be put on sale inside China as well. In accordance with the foreign exchange regulations, a foreign participant may remit abroad through the Bank of China the net profit from the venture the funds he receives at the time when the venture terminates its operation, and other funds of his (Article 10). Also remittable are wages, salaries or other legitimate income earned by a foreign worker or staffer in the venture after deduction of income tax (Article 11). There is no provision in the act on juridical decision of disputes arising from this matter. Instead, it is said that any controversy between parties of a venture, which the board of directors cannot settle by way of consultation, may be referred to concilation or arbitration of government body or an agency agreed on between the parties (Article 14). It appears that foreign ventures have no trust in the Chinese courts. However later in 1982, the Chinese government subjected the venture to the jurisdiction of the latter. Let's look at this situation below.

The Civil-Procedure Law, as mentioned before, was promulgated on October 1, 1982.[99] Its fifth (final) part pertains to foreign

---

[98] A detailed taxation law was published in *Renmin ribao,* December 18, 1980, p. 2; and November 27, 1981, p. 1.

[99] *Beijing review,* August 16, 1982, p. 22.

involvement in the Chinese economy. Covered in the act are not only foreign enterprises or organizations, but foreign individuals and stateless persons. In bringing a suit to court or in being sued, they enjoy litigation rights and are obliged to abide by the court rulings according to the stipulations of this law. If Chinese citizens or enterprises are restricted of their litigation rights in civil actions in a foreign country, the Chinese government will impose parallel limitation on its citizens and enterprises in Chinese court. As to civil complaints filed against foreign persons or enterprises enjoying juridical immunity, the court will deal with the cases according to the law of the CPR or treaties the CPR has concluded with other nations or international agreements and conventions which the CPR has participated in. Finally, foreigners or organizations may engage only Chinese lawyers in the People's Republic to file suit or to defend them against a complaint in a Chinese court.

Since 1979, foreign governments and international financial bodies have agreed or already signed contracts to provide China with $5,700 million in loans. The Bank of China has buyer-credit agreements for $13,000 million with commercial banks in various countries.[100] Up to March 1983, 390 joint venture projects, 590 medium-sized or small compensatory trade projects and 4 joint offshore oil exploration and exploitation projects have been approved. However, only about 30 are in actual operation.[101] Chinese enterprises also have absorbed foreign capital in the form of equipment through such means as leasing and processing of materials provided by foreign firms. In all, the CPR has absorbed $3,000 million in foreign investments in these type of joint ventures.[102] The CPR has set up 16 construction corporations that undertake projects abroad. In 1981, these firms signed more than 300 contracts with a total value of about $500 million for engineering projects or labor services in more than 30 nations and regions. In fulfilling these contracts, the CPR has sent 25,000 technicians and workers abroad.[103]

Most of the venture enterprises in China are involved in the making of textiles, foods, beverages, electrical appliances and tourist products. The recognized merits of the enterprises are a) fast planning, b) quick implementation, c) swift experiment, d) unhesitant investment and e) immediate results, in vivid contrast to the procrastination, indecisiveness and poor productivity of Chinese factories.[104] For example, the Tianjin Sino-French Winery was signed in May 1981, began to work in June, and turned out production in

[100] *Ibid.*, March 14, 1983, p. 16, col. 2.

[101] *Ibid.*

[102] *Ibid.*

[103] *Ibid.*, p. 17, col. 1. State councillor Gu Mu said that the CPR has more than 80 joint venture enterprises, *ibid.*, April 4, 1983, p. 9, col. 2.

[104] *Guangming ribao*, October 26, 1981, p. 1.

October.[105] If it were a Chinese plant, not three months but three years would have to lapse before a drop of wine was put out. Satisfactory ventures are reported in airline food-supply with the participation of Hong Kong merchants, and petroleum drilling on the marginal sea by Sino-Japanese and Sino-French ventures. *Guangming ribao* of October 26, 1981 (p. 1) concludes that "although the venture is still in the trial stage, it holds great future as our economy expands."

Lawyers

The hatred of law on the part of the communists has inclined them to look down upon lawyers for whom they have nothing but the same hatred,[106] and from them, they said, they expect no contributions whatsoever to the people's well-being.[107] Indeed, there has been a "deep distrust of lawyers in the Chinese culture."[108] The view is widely held that attorneys are wont to complicate cases and to impede their early resolution. By all means the pettifoggers just prey upon the clients. In civil cases, the repute of lawyers is bad enough, but in criminal ones, it is much worse, because they come forward to stand by a man whom the state itself is determined to convict. The act of defending him is abominable and makes the job of advocacy beneath dignity.[109] It is interesting to note that one of the anti-Gang of Four charges runs that they clung to the view that lawyers were to be rebuked because they were "tricksters who serve the interests of criminals rather than the interest of the society."[110] This accusation leveled at the Gang of Four, we believe, can be answered by them by saying that it is not only they but practically all the communists who think that way. In an attempt to restore the virtue of law, the current rulers find it expedient to attribute all dastardly things to their fallen colleagues. The irrepute of the legal profession, we venture to say, will remain in the CPR for the foreseeable future, the present effort to rectify it notwithstanding.[111] One Western observer says that formerly "nobody dared to become a lawyer,"[112] but in reality he should add that nobody wants to become one even now. A visiting jurist in China remarked that if he was to represent a company there, he would have a business card identifying him as a "trade specialist" rather than an "attorney at law."[113]

[105] *Ibid.*

[106] Donald Paragon, "The administration of justice and law in new China," *New York State Bar Journal,* no .7, November 1977, pp. 577-584 at 579, col. 2.

[107] Beverly Carl, *op. cit.,* p. 1258.

[108] *Ibid.*

[109] Donald Keith, *op. cit.,* p. 116.

[110] *Ibid.*

[111] *Guangming ribao,* September 1, 1981, p. 3. It defends the role of lawyers.

[112] Donald Keith, *loc. cit.*

[113] Beverly Carl, *loc. cit.*

In criminal litigation, the lawyer, no less than the man standing in the dock, is put on trial. Will he perform his duties undaunted or seek to please the regime? If the latter, he would be a "mere actor in a pre-arranged morality play."[114] If the former, he can live up to the professional expectation. Observers of the Chinese trial unanimously attest to the bad luck of the accused. It was not uncommon, Jerome Cohen said, for the defense counsel to argue with ardor not for an acquittal, but for a conviction of his client.[115] A *Guangming ribao* article says that sometimes the defense lawyers are asking for heavier penalties for the accused than what the procurator demanded.[116] Recently this happened during the trial of ten. One of them, Yao Wenyuan, pleaded not guilty. He said he committed a mistake, but not a crime. Yet his lawyers Han Xuezhang and Zhang Zhong concurred to the prosecution that he indeed committed the counterrevolutionary crime.

Coming to the *Guangming ribao* article cited a moment ago, the authors urge in earnest the use of professional advocates, because according to them, laymen do not have the knowledge of law, nor the required technique in the discussion of cases and in the preparation of defense. Laymen, they move on to say, are often afraid of speaking out since they do not know the provisions of an act, but lawyers do not have this worry encumbering them. Article 29 of the Criminal-Procedure Law is adduced by them to fortify their argument. It says that lawyers are provided with the right to examine the files in the procurator's office. However, this right is not accorded non-lawyers who have only the right of communication with the accused.[117]

The lawyers, in fact, were not brave enough to make use of whatever rights they have. This is shown during the trial of ten. Five of them had two defense counsel each, but Jiang Qing, Qiu Huizuo, Zhang Chunqiao, Wang Hongwen and Huang Yongsheng "did not entrust their defense to any lawyer, nor did they request the Special Court to assign advocates for them."[118] Interestingly enough, three of the five have received the highest penalty (two death and one life imprisonment). Is it because no lawyers defended them? The answer must be in the negative. In fact, the ten lawyers provided did not function. Through the month long trial, they spoke only twice (see next chapter). They just begged for lighter penalties.[119] This situation holds true also for ordinary offenses. As reported by Simon Luk, a twenty-two year old man was prosecuted for violent robbery.[120] Under

[114] *Far Eastern Economic Review*, October 5, 1979, p. 56, col. 1.

[115] Jerome Cohen, "Will China have a formal legal system?" *op. cit.*, p. 1513, col. 1.

[116] *Guangming ribao*, August 11, 1981, p. 3.

[117] *Ibid.*

[118] *Beijing review*, February 2, 1981, p. 14, col. 1.

[119] *Renmin ribao*, December 23, 1980, p. 4.

[120] Simon Luk, *op. cit.*, p. 59, col. 3.

the stern interrogation of the judge, he admitted to hitting the government fee collector and to taking money from him. The court-appointed attorney took an onlooker's demeanor. Making no rebuttal except cross-examining the victim, he saw his role to be in furthering the state interest, but not in arguing for the accused. Given this situation, the right of defense of citizens cannot be a real one. There is a low visibility of lawyers in the CPR, and there is scarcely a need for them. In fact, lawyers are not the only ones who can prepare a case and make court appearances as is true in many countries. Besides lawyers, Article 8 of the Organic Law of the People's Courts allows the following to "practice law" in a trial: the accused himself, any citizen nominated by a social body or a work unit, the defendant's close relative or ward. At the insistence of the accused, the court has the right to commission a person (not necessarily a lawyer) to defend him. "If the defendant were deaf and dumb, the judge would appoint someone who knows sign language" to be his advocate.[121] As observers tell us, in the Chinese court, lay counsel is the rule.[122] Only between foreigners are lawyers employed.[123] This practice can hardly be conducive to a thriving profession of law.

The Chinese communists, as seen above, harbor a deep suspicion of lawyers. On the other side of the coin is the belief that law need not be studied. It is not the debate or analysis of the provisions of law, but the commonsense which is the sure guide to justice and to truth. Perchance it is on account of such a pattern of thinking that Chinese enterprises do not hire legal specialists to represent them in the negotiation of business or settling problems. This thinking was expressly stated to Beverly Carl by the spokesman of the China Council for the Promotion of International Trade.[124] There must be, we believe, a sense of discomfort on the part of government officials in having a group of sophisticated lawmen in the society. It is conceivable that in the courthouse these men can chop the communist "legislation" into pieces and beat the procurators to the wall. Can the Reds have much stomach for this situation if it were to develop?

In keeping with the need for modernization, lawyers are gradually appearing. In 1978, a Shanghai judge said to Martin Garbus that "there are no lawyers in China."[125] In late 1978 and early 1979 there were said to be "few" of them.[126] However, in 1980 lawyers were described as "availing, particularly in the larger cities."[127] The fact

---

[121] Beverly Carl, op. cit., p. 1271.

[122] Ibid., Martin Garbus, op. cit., p. 582, col. 1; David Bonavia, op. cit., p. 11, col. 2; Donald Keith, op. cit., p. 112.

[123] Martin Garbus, loc. cit.

[124] Beverly Carl, loc. cit.

[125] Martin Garbus, loc. cit.

[126] Beverly Carl, op. cit., p. 1257.

[127] Ronald Keith, loc. cit.

is that it was not until August 1980 that the Standing Committee of the National People's Congress approved the Provisional Regulations Concerning the Work of Lawyers of the People's Republic of China.[128] Its 21 Articles regulate various aspects of the legal profession. As regards the tasks of the lawyers, they are empowered to a) act as legal advisers to government bodies, enterprises and other state institutions, public organizations and rural communes, b) function on behalf of litigants in civil suits, c) defend the accused in criminal cases on application of the defendant or upon the commission of the court, d) take part in litigation on request of the party which initiates a private prosecution, e) furnish legal advice to parties who are not involved in litigation or act on their behalf in mediation or arbitration, f) answer legal inquiries from the general public and draft legal documents and other related instruments upon demand, and g) popularize the socialist legal system in the course of their duties.

There is a short bill of rights for the lawyers. They are entitled to be protected by the state law while performing a service according to law without interference from any quarters, collective or individual. They can read the files of cases with which they are dealing and investigate the concerned units and individuals while taking part in litigation. Conferred upon lawyers is also the right to meet and correspond with the defendants under detention. Finally they have the right to refuse to take up a case, being convinced that the defendant is lying.

Who can become a lawyer? A citizen who is willing to serve the socialist cause and who has the right to vote and stand for election is qualified to be a lawyer after he or she is ajudged professionally competent by way of examinations. To enumerate, the following are candidates: a) university graduates specializing in law who are engaged in judicial work or legal research or have taught jurisprudence for more than two years, b) those with professional legal training who have worked as judges or as procurators, and c) competent individuals who have done economic and scientific and technical work for more than three years, are familiar with laws and regulations in their own fields, and show their competence after receiving professional legal education. People serving in court, procuracy or public security are barred from working as lawyers concurrently.

Legal advisory offices are set up by the state, with local branches in counties, towns and districts directly under the authority of big and medium-sized city governments. Enterprises, institutions and public bodies can also organize their own specialized legal advisory offices, subject to the sanction of the Justice Ministry. These offices are organizationally led and vocationally supervised by the state judicial organs which train, examine, assign and transfer lawyers. They establish lawyers' organizations which perform various administrative

---

[128] These regulations are summarized in *Beijing review*, June 7, 1982, pp. 15-17.

functions such as the management of funds and buying of materials and equipment.

Lawyers' association are organized by lawyers themselves at the provincial, municipal and autonomous regional levels. Their job is to protect the members' democratic rights and their legitimate professional rights, assist them to exchange experiences, facilitate the performance of their functions and increase contacts between Chinese and foreign lawyers. Within the purview of the association is the rendering of help to the judicial administrative organs and to the legal advisory offices.

Fees charged for answering legal questions not involving disputes over property is between 0.5 and 3 yuan. An answer to legal inquiry involving commercial property entails a charge of from 3 to 10 yuan; in criminal cases, the rate is 10-30 yuan covering such work as legal advice, drafting papers and courtroom appearances. In exceptionally difficult cases, the highest amount is not to be more than double the above figures. If the fees were exceeded, the state will arrogate them.[129] Fees can be reduced or exempted for citizens who are unable to pay. The fact of the inability must be verified by his or her work unit, neighborhood committee or commune leaders. Also in this reduction or exemption category are 1) those who are appealing for compensation for losses or injuries incurred at work, except accidents for which the injured is held responsible, 2) requesting alimony or financial support for parents or children who have verifiable financial hardship, 3) requesting labor insurance premiums, pensions or relief funds, 4) asking for simple legal advice in which no dispute over property are involved, and 5) involved in other special cases which required that fees be reduced or waived.

Let us have a look at the legal profession of the three centrally ruled cities. Shanghai lawyers established two advisory groups in 1981.[130] They handled more than 220 civil cases that year. However, in 1982 only 59 cases were dealt with, but they investigated 6,528 contracts, answered 517 inquiries and received audience of 3,000 individuals.[131] Moreover thankful to the two groups, 413,000 yuan were said to have been recovered for the claimant units. Seventy enterprises of Shanghai are reported to hire legal consultants. In the capital, legal advisory groups were set up in 19 districts and surrounding counties; altogether there were 309 lawyers serving nine million people.[132] During 1979-1981, they offered advice to 23,000 persons, and defended 2,600 criminal cases. Besides, they wrote 2,500 complaintive papers for their clients, acted on behalf of 140 civil litigants, handled 8,000 letters and co-ordinated with related departments to settle 30 financial

129 Simon Luk, loc. cit.

130 Guangming ribao, August 1, 1981, p. 3 for this and the next information.

131 Renmin ribao, April 6, 1983, p. 4 for this and the next information.

132 Beijing review, June 7, 1982, p. 16 for this and the next information about Beijing.

disputes. On the average, 100 persons consult with the advisory groups each day.

The same kind of data about lawyers in Beijing and Shanghai are not available with regard to Tianjin. However, there is an interesting report on lawyer examinations in *Guangming ribao* of July 13, 1981 (p. 1). Although, as seen above, the 1980 Regulations authorize the legal advisory offices to examine prospective lawyers, it is the municipal government in Tianjin which does it and issues license to them. The 1981 examination had more than 400 registered applicants, but preliminary screening rejected 92. Further written and oral tests and political and medical checkups netted 63. Of these 43 were allowed to practice on full-time basis, and the remainder were part-timers. Twenty-eight percent of the recruits came from law and political-science departments of universities, 20 percent from other majors, and 40 percent were employees of legal or administrative organizations. Communists and young communist league members constituted 43 percent. This leaves 12 percent as ordinary citizens. In the selection, morals and expertise were set down as the criteria. Family background and personal record did not figure as a major factor. Yet it is conceded that without good political characteristics, a person has no chance. By this it means not only that non-communists are not going to succeed but that leftists, that is, those who are suspect of being the supporters of the Gang of Four, would be hopeless.

Reports about the legal profession outside the three cities just discussed is hard to get. Scanty information, indirect at that, seems to indicate that such a profession almost does not exist. *Renmin ribao* of April 6, 1983 (p. 4) prints a short commentary that besides Shanghai there are only 80 enterprises engaging lawyers. The commentary says that the idea of using the lawyers to settle disputes is yet a novelty to many in the country. In 1980, according to the vice-minister of justice, there were only 3,000 lawyers throughout China; it is a ratio of one for every 300,000 people. Suppose Shanghai, Beijing and Tianjin had 1,000 lawyers, that ratio would be one for every 440,000. More of this anon.

To enforce the rule of law, the government has adopted four measures. (A) An earnest and grand campaign is underway to acquaint the public with the various enactments, teaching them of the significance of and the respect for them.[133] They are told to appreciate the re-assured "personal, democratic and other rights." There have been staged discussion and study sessions in all organizations; and the law booklets are handed out in the manner Jehovah's Witnesses in the US thrust *Watch Tower* onto the passers-by. Banners of "equality before the law" are seen everywhere.[134] Party members and young communist leaguers are thrown into action

[133] *Far Eastern Economic Review*, October 5, 1979, p. 57, col. 2.

[134] Simon Luk, *op. cit., p.* 59, col. 2.

to carry the leaders' message to every individual. A "law week" or "law day" was decreed by each province or city in the first half of 1983 to familiarize the masses with the 1982 Constitution, the mediation system, legal counsel and notary scheme.[135] Frequently the drive assumes the form not of the homily on the observance of law but denunciation of the Gang of Four who they say were yelling "no law, no lawyer." We believe this all-out effort to be otiose. The public have known only too well of the tricks, brutality and caprice of the regime in the past. Didn't it drop the four freedoms from the 1978 Constitution after they were promised just a year before.?[136]

(B) Some stopgap programs are tried in the training of judges. These and the procurators and attorneys meet after working hours to study enactments of the NPC which are of current importance. On some occasions, foreign specialists are invited to give talks or to lead seminars on professional development.[137] One of these was held in March 1979 in Haerbin the foremost city of Heilongjiang province. Jerome Cohen took part in it. (C) There is the training of legal researchers. The Institute of Jurisprudence (variously translated) was set up in 1958.[138] It ceased to function shortly afterwards due to the "sabotage of Lin Biao and the Gang of Four." However, Han Yudong (deputy director) made rather an honest revelation that prior to the sabotage "there was a dearth of well-trained legal cadres in the CPR. Now the situation is worse because of the 1966-1967 turbulence." In effect, Han was saying that the Cultural Revolution did not create the shortage problem. It only aggravated it. The Institute has over 100 employees, including a number of administrators and librarians.[139] In 1981, there was one director (Wang Zhongfan), one consultant (Zhang Youyu) and two deputy directors (the aforesaid Han, and Xie Tieguang).[140] It is said to have 500,000 volumes of books at the time of its founding. There is no information about the current holdings of the library. Engaging the study of the members are such fields as theory of law and the state, constitutional law, maritime law, and public international law.[141] In mid-1979, the government published seven laws which are said to have been prepared with the assistance of the Institute in question.[142] Besides helping with the drafting of laws, it "reviews and criticizes existing laws [and] publishes reports."[143]

[135] *Renmin ribao*, April 22, 1983, p. 1. Shanghai held its "law days" in early April, see *ibid.*, April 3, 1983, p. 4.

[136] *Ibid.*, July 1, 1981, p. 4.

[137] Aric Press, *op. cit.*, p. 113, col. 2. provides this information and the next two quotations.

[138] *Ruth Ginsburg*, op. cit., p. 1518.

[139] Beverly Carl, *op. cit.*, p. 1277.

[140] *Zhong guo shou ce*, loc. cit.

[141] Beverly Carl, *op. cit.*, p. 1278.

[142] Ruth Ginsburg, *op. cit.*, p. 1519, col. 1.

[143] Simon Luk, *op. cit.*, p. 59, col. 3.

This organization does research and consultative work only. The schooling of judges and lawyers is, however, devolved onto the universities.

(D) Mao Zedong shut down all law schools during the Cultural Revolution. Only about 1000 graduated from the law faculty of Beijing University after the advent of the communists to power in 1949, and all these were pre-Cultural Revolution products.[144] On the eve of that tumult there were four university departments and an equal number of institutes enrolling law students.[145] They were out of function, as just said, and were not in full operation until 1979. The total enrollment now is about 2,000.[146] Shanghai Law School has one fifth of these.[147] This school, incidentally, has 60 teachers and 18 graduate instructors. Faculties of law are found in the following institutions: Beijing University, China People's University (both in Beijing); the Institute of Political Science and Law situated in the capital as well as Shanghai, Xian and Chongqing; Xinjiang University whose law department was opened in the fall of 1981;[148] Shantao University whose law department was opened in the fall of 1983.[149] How many lawyers does the CPR need? According to Qian Duansheng, dean of the Beijing Institute of Political Science and Law," the CPR has to have at least 10,000 lawyers if the right of defense is to be guaranteed."[150] The vice minister of justice stated that there were about 3,000 lawyers in 1980, saying the government has planned to increase the number from one lawyer per 300,000 to one per 10,000 in the cities and 50,000 in rural districts.[151] To achieve this goal, the current law trainees must be increased 800-fold.

Very difficult exams are reported given to the aspirants, that is, workers of the state bodies or judicial organs, as well as high school graduates. Students spend from twenty to twenty-five hours each week in attending classes.[152] The courses include "the theory of state and law, constitutional law, civil law, criminal procedure, history of the Chinese legal system, history of Chinese political and legal thought, and international and maritime laws."[153] These are also the research topics at the abovesaid Institute of Jurisprudence. Whether at the Institute or at the universities, Marxist-Leninist philosophy of law is a mandatory area of study.[154] After winding up the four years' work, students are conferred, beginning in 1982, a degree of bachelor of jurisprudence and assigned to the government bodies, people's courts, procuracy or legal advisory offices.

[144] Keesing's, October 3, 1980, p. 30494, col. 1.
[145] Ronald Keith, loc. cit.
[146] Keesing's, loc. cit.; Simon Luk, op. cit., p. 59, col. 3.
[147] Beverly Carl, loc. cit.
[148] Keesing's, October 3, 1981, p. 29494, col. 1.
[149] Renmin ribao, April 15, 1983, p. 3, col. 1.
[150] Ronald Keith, loc. cit.
[151] Beijing review, December 8, 1980, p. 3.
[152] Beverly Carl, loc. cit.
[153] Donald Paragon, "Some firsthand observations on China's legal system",op. cit., p. 479, col. 1.
[154] Simon Luk, loc. cit.

CHAPTER XV
Criminal Law

Bases of criminal justice

According to Peng Zhen, former Director of the Legal Affairs Bureau of the NPC Standing Committee, the CPR's criminal law put into execution on January 1, 1980 was the 34th draft and the 33rd was written in 1963.[1] The 22nd draft was done way back in 1957 by the fourth session of the First NPC. We are wondering why so many drafts are needed and why all but the last displeased the leaders. It would be extremely curious to assemble the whole collection and compare them to see just what differences there are in the texts. Before 1980, the CPR was applying the three penal statutes mentioned in the first section of the preceding chapter. The widest used is the Act for the Punishment of Counterrevolutionaries promulgated on February 21, 1951. Now all three are superseded by the new code. We propose to examine presently its basic principles.

The righting of past wrongs

The criminal legislation purports to rectify what has been officially dumped on the laps of Lin Biao and the Gang of Four during the "ten disastrous years." Explicitly, it provides that the "right of personal, democratic and other rights of citizens shall be protected against unlawful infringement by any person or institution."[2] It also says extortion of confessions through torture is strictly banned,[3] as is the gathering of crowds to beat, smash and loot.[4] Illicit incarceration and frame-ups on false charges are proscribed. Whoever fabricates evidence to accuse another person, even a convict, shall be held accountable in the light of the nature, seriousness and consequences of the act.[5] During the Cultural Revolution, it will be recalled, such malefactions were widespread. The Red Guards had a Roman holiday in tormenting, intimidating, pillaging and killing. The trial of ten from November 20, 1980 to January 25, 1981 disclosed that they and the deceased Lin Biao *et alii* masterminded all these crimes.[6] The contemporary Beijing rulers have gone on record affirming that whoever treats people with violence or puts out large- or small-character posters to libel people shall be jailed up to three years.[7]

---

[1] Peng Zhen, "Explanation on seven laws," *Beijing Review*, July 13, 1979, pp. 8-16 at 8, col. 2. The 34th is printed in *Renmin shou ce*, Beijing: Renmin ribao chu ban she, 1980, pp. 408-417.

[2] Peng Zhen, *op. cit.*, p. 11, col. 2. Criminal Law, Article 131; *Renmin ribao*, July 7, 1979.

[3] Criminal Law, Article 136.

[4] *Ibid.*, Articles 137, 159, 160.

[5] *Ibid.*, Article 138.

[6] "Written judgment of the Special Court" (January 23 [should be 25], 1981), *Beijing Review*, February 2, 1981, pp. 13-28 at 13ff.

[7] Peng Zhen, *loc. cit.* Criminal Law, Article 145.

They set forth three don'ts: don't pick on, don't paste labels, don't wield big sticks.[8] Peng Zheng said his government was to guarantee the right to criticize, to refute other's view or to express doubts and raise questions about the leadership and their work. Advisements are to be strictly distinguished from insults.[9] By unleashing the people's initiative, Beijing hoped to beget a "lively political situation of stability and unity and ensure the smooth advance of socialist modernization."[10] The 1978 Constitution (Preamble) stressed the value of "unity of will and personal ease of mind and liveliness," a phrase, however, deleted from the 1982 Constitution.

The problem posed here by the communists is as old as mankind, one of freedom versus authority. So far there has been no solution for it. In the midst of the trial of ten, *Renmin ribao* printed a special commentator's article which tries to provide an answer on how to demarcate the right of criticism from the abuse of it. The article does nothing but beat around the bush and it barely finds a way out of the entanglement by using "ifs" and "buts."[11] Just what is a crime and what is a mistake? or what is counterrevolution and what is a good-intended policy alternative? The commentator does not state.

There has set in a period of rectification after the elimination of the Gang of Four and Lin Biao. The Supreme Court is said to have reversed more than 300 cases illegally decided during the Cultural Revolution.[12] *Renmin ribao* informs that 1,130,000 such cases were examined *de novo.*[13] Of the 270,000 individuals labeled counterrevolutionary, 18,000 were cleared from 1978 to early 1979. Nearly 10 percent of the 868,000 persons convicted between 1966 and 1976 were found to be "unjustly, falsely or wrongly charged."[14] According to Peng Zhen, "about 40 percent of the verdicts condemning people as counterrevolutionaries during this period [Cultural Revolution] has been proved to be unfounded. In some areas, the figure is as high as 70 percent."[15] The communists are aware that wrongs, at times, cannot be righted meaningfully. Mao Zedong has a revealing statement: "Once a head is chopped off, history shows it can't be restored, nor can it grow again as chives do after being cut off. If you cut off a head by mistake, there is no way to rectify the mistake, even if you want to."[16] The present autocrats appear to share this view.

[8] Peng Zhen, *loc. cit.*

[9] *Ibid.*

[10] *Ibid.*, p. 11, col. 1.

[11] Reprinted in "Distinguishing crimes from mistakes," *Beijing Review*, January 5, 1981, pp. 21-23.

[12] Peng Zhen, *loc. cit.*

[13] *Renmin ribao*, December 7, 1978, p. 1.

[14] Cited in John Fraser, "Chinese jurists seek enactment of criminal law," *Globe and Mail*, December 8, 1978, p. 2, col. 2.

[15] Peng Zhen, "Strengthen legal system and democracy," *Beijing Review*, July 6, 1979, pp. 32-36 at 36.

[16] Mao Zedong, "On the ten major relations," *Beijing Review*, January 1, 1977, pp. 10-25 at 21, col. 1.

Counterrevolutionary criminality

The fact that the criminal law devotes a wh. chapter at that) to this is indicative of the importanc taches to it. One of the many charges against counterrevolution. The law delimits it as aiming at "underm.. People's Republic of China and overthrowing the political powe. the proletarian dictatorship and the socialist system."[17] Under this cover provision are listed 20 specific actions (Articles 91-102).

conspire with foreign powers
plot to topple the government
instigate officials to rebel
desert to the enemy
organize a mutiny
stage armed insurrection with many people (how many?)
break jails
spy for the enemy
steal information for the enemy
deliver arms to the enemy
lead counterrevolution
form feudal or superstitious bodies to stage counterrevolution
highjack common carriers
signal targets for the enemy
manufacture, rob or steal ammunition
blow up dikes, set fire to factories or military depots
seize state archives by force
poison people to achieve counterrevolutionary aims
abet crowds to resist officials
"use counterrevolutionary slogans or circulars or other means to spread words around with an intent to overthrow the proletarian dictatorship and socialist system" (Article 102, section 2)

The majority of the activities seem to present little problem, for they are indeed punishable, whether connected with counterrevolution or not. But the last quoted item poses a serious question. Can slogans have so much power as to endanger the state?

The traditional term treason, it is very interesting to note, does not appear in the criminal law. This may be explained by the subsumption of it in counterrevolution. Witness Article 28 of the Constitution referring to "treason and other counterrevolutionary activities." On the essence of counterrevolution, Ling Yun (minister of State Security) maintained that whether a crime is to be classified as one is based on what has been done and not on anything else.[18] A person with reactionary ideas, further pointed out he, but performing no counterrevolutionary deeds aimed at overthrowing the proletarian dictatorship and the socialist system must not be convicted of

[17] Criminal Law, Article 90.

[18] *Beijing Review*, July 13, 1979, p. 16, col. 1.

unterrevolution. The government of the CPR is "firmly against resolving ideological questions and the problem of dissidence by judicial or administrative means," except during the Gang of Four days. In a similar vein, a commentator asserted that "our criminal law absolutely refuses ideological crime and that the intent of crime and the action of carrying it out are two necessary conditions for an indictable offense."[19] This stand of the Chinese officials is a universal one. There can hardly be argument against it. But what constitutes an act? Does it have to take the form of, let us say, an armed insurrection? In the CPR, the answer is definitely no. Article 102, section 2, as quoted previously in the list, makes it crystal clear that when you speak out or paste wallpapers attacking the regime, you have acted. Militated minister Ling Yun that "it is wrong to describe them[counterrevolutionaries] as dissidents."[20] Logically one's thoughts, if unsavory to the power that be, may remain uninhibited insofar as they are kept in his bosom. Once they are given vent to, a counterrevolution is completed. This is what the just-cited *Renmin ribao* insisted on. On account of this stifling situation, one Western author criticizes the "sweeping definition of counterrevolutionary offences," for there is no objective standard to judge one's act.[21] Likewise, Claudie Broyelle *et alii* remark that in China one does not have to stage a coup d'état in order to be landed in a jail on charges of state crime.[22] Does not the proverbial sword of Damocles hang on everybody's head?

Up to the present, it appears, no one was actually convicted by the counterrevolutionary provision alone of the criminal code. The sentences handed down to the dissidents were always a hodgepodge of accusations. Even the Gang of Four and their co-defendants were charged with murder as well as counterrevolution. Wei Jingsheng (age 29) was very close to being punished under one count of counter-revolution. Yet he was also said to be guilty of committing slander against Mao Zedong and sentenced to 15 years by the high court of Beijing on November 6, 1979.[23] Another cause célèbre, the Fu Yuehua (age 34) case, was decided on December 24, 1979 by the middle court of Beijing. She was described as organizing an anti-hunger, anti-suppression, for-human-right and for-democracy group. She bravely declared communism as the author of starvation of the masses. But the procurator did not lay counterrevolution against her. Instead, she was given two years for theft and the framing up of a man who she said had raped her.[24] Why no charge of

---

[19] *Renmin ribao*, May 2, 1983, p. 5.

[20] *Beijing Review*, July 13, 1979, p. 16, col. 2.

[21] Aric Press, "China, back to the law," *Newsweek*, October 22, 1979, p. 113, col. 1.

[22] Claudie Broyelle, Jacques Broyelle et Evelyne Tschihart, *Deuxième retour de Chine*, Paris: Editions du Seuil, 1977, p. 171.

[23] *Zhong guo bai ke nian jian*, Beijing: Zhong guo da bai ke quan shu chu ban she, 1980, p. 278, p. 1.

[24] *Ibid.*, col. 2.

counterrevolution in the case? Probably hers does not meet one of the two tests of that crime: the intention. In other words, the procurator finds it hard to prove that she was contemplating the overthrow of the regime.

How many counterrevolutionaries or traitors (to use the superfluous term) are there in the CPR? Sporadic pieces of information on this come from foreign visitors. In a Shanghai prison, of a total of 2,753 inmates, 20 percent were said to be counterrevolutionaries.[25] Another prison contained 10 percent of that category.[26] What about in the nation as a whole? According to the report of the outgoing president of the Supreme Court, Jiang Hua, to the NPC on June 9, 1983, during the judicial year of 1982-1983, the counterrevolutionary offenses "accounted for a mere 0.5 percent of the crimes" (*Globe and mail,* June 10, 1983, p. 3, col. 4). Given the annual criminal convictions of three quarters of a million (see section on crime and punishment below), counterrevolutionaries would probably number 4,000. All these were actually sentenced by the courts, but there were many who have not been processed. They were taken prisoner after the Reds ran over the country in 1949. A few of them have been released amidst a fanfare of propaganda of the socialist humanity of a regime which confined them for several decades.

Ex post facto law

With an explicit resolve to stamp out all suspected opponents, the Beijing dictatorship issued three criminal decrees (see first section of preceding chapter). These contain many ex post facto clauses. For example, Article 18 of the Law for the Punishment of Counter-revolutionaries says: "The provisions of this Act also apply to those who were counterrevolutionary criminals before this Act was put into effect."[27] These were invoked to penalize past activities considered by the new "conquerors" as offenses committed by the propertied class against the proletarians or committed by officials of the overthrown government to put down the communist rebels. Besides being ex post facto, the laws in question are retaliatory and intimidating. It is openly declared that the killing of chickens is to scare monkeys.[28] Ex post facto legislation serves political rather than strictly judicial ends. During the trial of ten, the question was indeed raised that what the Lin Biao and Jiang Qing cliques did were done many years ago, but the Criminal Law came into effect on January 1, 1980.

[25] George Crocket and Morris Gleicher, "Inside China's prisons, *Judicature,* no. 9, 1978, pp. 409-415 at 414, col. 1.

[26] Beverly Carl, "Contemporary law in the People's Republic of China," *Southwestern Law Journal,* no. 5, February 1979, pp. 1255-1279 at 1273.

[27] Related in Hungdah Chiu, "Criminal punishment in mainland China: a study of some Yunnan province documents," *The Journal of Criminal Law and Criminology,* no. 3, 1977, pp. 374-398 at 379, col. 1.

[28] Shao-chuan Leng, "The role of law in the People's Republic of China as reflecting Mao Zedong's influence," *ibid.,* pp. 356-373 at 365, note 69.

"Can the bygone offenses be judged according to the present law?"[29] The answer which is little more than *ipse dixit* is provided by Wang Hanbin, vice-director of the Legal Affairs Bureau of the NPC Standing Committee as follows.

He started out by citing Article 9 of the Criminal Law that a) if an act done after the founding of the People's Republic and prior to the enforcement of the present law was not deemed an offense under the laws, decrees and policies then in force, these latter shall be the standard. b) If an act was regarded as an offense under the same laws, decrees and policies and is also subject to prosecution under the current law, the standard of criminal liability shall also be the said laws, decrees and policies. c) However, if the act is not considered an offense or the penalty for the offense is lighter under the contemporary code, this code shall apply. It is alleged by Wang Hanbin that the 1952 (should be 1951) regulations on the punishment of counterrevolutionary activities are harsher than those in the 1980 legislation. We quote him: "The [former laws] provide heavier sentences for counterrevolutionaries than the present criminal law."[30] Hence, he concludes, the present code is to be used. Let us ask this man: In view of the penalties handed down to the ten defendants ranging from death with two years' suspension for Jiang Qing and Zhang Chunqiao, life imprisonment for Wang Hongwen, to 20 years for Yao Wenyuan, 18 for Huang Yongsheng, Chen Boda and Jiang Tengjiao, 17 for Wu Faxian and Li Zuopeng, and 16 for Qiu Huizuo,[31] how can one expect more severe terms under the former "laws, decrees and policies," at least as regards the death verdict? Indeed, Peng Zhen who was none other than director of the same Legal Affairs Bureau held a contrary stand to Wang Hanbin's. He declared to the second session of the fifth NPC on June 26, 1979 that the new criminal law "stipulated heavier sentences for major active counterrevolutionary offenses and offenses that cause serious harm to society and that incur mass indignation."[32] It is significant to note at this point, too, that in the CPR, not only laws, but decrees and policies can be the bases of criminal punishment.

Presumption of innocence

Such a time-honored and nearly universal doctrine which was even adopted in the 1977 USSR Constitution (Article 160) has no roots in China,[33] and it has perhaps less to commend itself to the Chinese communists. Their general supposition runs that if one is prosecuted

---

[29] Interview reported in *Beijing Review*, January 12, 1981, pp. 20-22 at 20, col. 1.

[30] *Ibid.*, p. 21, col. 1.

[31] "Written judgment of the Special Court," p. 28.

[32] *Ibid.*, July 6, 1979, p. 33, col. 1.

[33] Jerome Cohen, "Criminal law, reflections on the criminal process in China," *The Journal of Criminal Law and Criminology*, no. 3, 1977, pp. 323-355 at 324, col. 1, and 349, col 1.

or simply interrogated by the authority, there must be a good chance that the man has done something wrong.[34] This prejudice can affect the mind of a trial judge, and since the CPR has no jural system, the belief of the judge is decisive. In this circumstance, the presumption of innocence is at the mercy of the bench. A conscionable judge would respect it, but a partisan one would not.

The doctrine is all the more important as an angry public, officially incited, want to have someone convicted. The trial of ten serves a good propaganda purpose and cannot be fair. Had they not already been dubbed counterrevolutionaries before the opening of the Special Court on November 20, 1980? Who in the whole country dared to stand out and shout that they were innocent? Even the defense counsel did not plead innocence. They only begged the Court to "reconsider the punishment" as demanded by the procurators. Five of the ten defendants did not care less to name advocates or request the Court to appoint them, knowing only too well that their day in the court is farcical *ab ovo usque ad mala.*

Two legal researchers of China declare forthright that the principle of presumption of innocence is "rubbish both in content and in form."[35] It has, they concede, played a certain progressive role in the bourgeois struggle against feudalism, but there is no room for it in the socialist judicature. Nearly thirty years ago, there was a guarded discussion in China on the principle but it was cut short by the interference of the leftists.[36] In the current discussion, two viewpoints are crystallized. a) One suggests that the bourgeois presumption of innocence and the feudal presumption of guilt differ somewhat on the stand of the judges, but both are expressions of idealism and metaphysics. Moreover, the presumption of innocence is incongruous with the task of "seeking truth from facts"[37] and is out of joint with the practice and procedure of investigation, arrest and indictment in the CPR's criminal jurisprudence. b) The other viewpoint assumes that the presumption of innocence refers to the status of the defendant before the trial starts, but it neither contradicts nor replaces the principle of "seeking truth from facts." Both schools of thought emphasize the importance of the outcome of the trial. While the first school is hostile to the principle in question, the second regards it irrelevant to criminal jurisprudence.

Most, if not all, of the judges and procurators in the trial of ten were themselves victims of theirs, and according to Article 23, clause 2 of the Criminal-Procedure Law, they must disqualify themselves in

[34] *Ibid.,* p. 324, col. 1.

[35] The two authors are Xie Cichang and Xu Chengqing, whose article on the "trends in Chinese jurisprudence" is summarized here, *Beijing Review,* April 6, 1981, pp. 14-16.

[36] Luo Yun, "Che di pi pian 'you li bei gao' de miu lun" (To criticize thoroughly the wrong theory of benefiting the defendant), *Fa xue,* no. 3 (1958), pp. 22-25.

[37] This magic phrase is spread far and wide, the 1978 Constitution, Preamble; Organic Law of the People's Procurators, Article 7; Criminal-Procedure Law, Article 4; the 1982 Constitution, Article 41, paragraph 2; the 1982 Party Statute, general program.

the case. However, Wang Hanbin thinks they do not need to do so, because they were appointed by the NPC Standing Committee. A more plausible opinion he expresses is that there is an extraordinary case at issue. Therefore, the conventional practice of withdrawal of potentially prejudicial judges and procurators does not apply. "Should there be a withdrawal, everyone would have to do so," he says.[38] Furthermore, Wang Hanbin argues, with a strong sense of self-righteousness, that the judges are trustworthy and truthful and they cannot do otherwise than base their verdict on evidence. There is no ground for one to suspect their integrity.[39] Doesn't this view collide head-on with the view of potential and unavoidable stand? Wang Hanbin must have in mind Stalin's famous saying that contradiction is a way of life under Marxism.[40]

Judicial independence

This is provided in Article 78 of the 1954 Constitution, but disappears from both the 1975 and 1978 successors. We think it should be dropped because judicial personnel are determined by and dependent on the political departments.[41] More specifically, judges are elected by the people's congresses at the corresponding levels of the system.[42] It is rather to be expected that the electees are responsible to the electors. However, judicial independence was revived in the 1979 organic law of courts,[43] and reappears in Article 128 of the 1982 Constitution. No doubt the contemporary leaders wish to impart a modicum of credence to their protestation of the rule of law. By no means, we suppose, is the real state of affairs going to differ. Indeed, the immunity of judges from political influence is not presumed. It is even outright dissonant with the spirit of the communist system "where Marxism serves as the theoretical basis, guiding our thinking."[44]

In the judgment on Lin Biao and Jiang Qing and their followers, Beijing conceded that it would not abide by such "things like eternal justice, ultimate morality or indignation, but strictly according to the principles of socialist democracy and the legal system which speaks for the will of the people."[45] It takes an unconscionable man, we would

[38] Beijing Review, January 12, 1981, p. 21, col. 1.

[39] Ibid., p. 20, col. 2.

[40] I.V. Stalin, "Politicheskii otchet tsentral'nogo komiteta XVI s'ezdu VKP (b), 27 iiunya 1930 g.," Sochineniya, Moskva: Gosudarstvennoe izdatel'stvo politicheskoi literatury, 1949, vol. 12, pp. 235-386 at 369-370. English version, his Works, Moscow: Foreign Languages Publishing House, 1955, vol. 12, pp. 242-399 at 381.

[41] Lung-sheng Tao, "Politics and law enforcement in China, 1949-1970," The American Journal of Comparative Law, no. 4, Fall 1974, pp. 713-756 at 715.

[42] Constitution, Article 60, clause 6; Article 65, clause 11; Article 104, paragraph 2. Organic Law of the People's Procurators, Articles 21, 22, 23. See also Peng Zhen loc. cit.

[43] Organic Law of the People's Courts, Article 4; Organic Law of the People's Procurators, Article 9.

[44] "Distinguishing crimes from mistakes," p. 23, col. 2.

[45] Ibid.

argue, to say that that will is represented by the contemporary leaders. A Shanghai judge told visiting US attorneys that the courts operate under the guidance of the CCP.[46] He described law as an instrument of proletarian politics to be used in class struggle, purported to promote dictatorship of the people under the party.[47] A *Guangming ribao* article repeats the same stand.[48] One writer reveals that the provincial or national party body can impose its resolution on the courts in significant cases. The entire judicial process, declares a Chinese jurist, is led by the communist party.[49] Even though the party hierarchs do not at times have the last word, they are the weightiest factor in the machine of justice. Throughout the history of the CPR, courts are an appendage of the government. The latter may either enhance or lower their influence as it sees it. The present elite do the former, but the Gang of Four did the latter.

Most judges have no or little knowledge of law.[50] Rightfully so, we suppose, because legalists may be so stubborn and so persistent on the rudimentary probity and fairness that politicians may find them a nuisance. The antipathy toward lawmen manifests itself in the prevalence of extra-judicial organizations which have "played a greater role than the courts."[51] These organizations are more amenable to outside maneuver, staffed as they are by bureaucrats known to be subservient and to be lacking an independent outlook. In the CPR, party apparatchiks are duty bound to check on the judicature to make sure that the party line is unswervingly toed. Perhaps the most salient impact of the CCP on the bench stems from the fact that all jurists are partisans and as such they must implement the CCP directives in accordance with Article 3, clause 3 and Article 10, clause 1 of the 1982 Party Statute. The respective provisions read that party members shall actively fulfil the tasks assigned them by the party, and the individual is subordinate to the organization.

In each court, there is a party committee.[52] It exercises control over the judges and other workers; and the higher party apparatus wields, in turn, authority over the committee. In respect of the judicial work, a reference book writes: "Is the fact of a case clear? Is the evidence authentic? Should a sentence be imposed? These must all be decided

[46] Donald Paragon, "The administration of justice and law in new China," *New York State Bar Association Journal*, no. 7, November 1977, pp. 577-584 at 578, col. 1. Ruth Ginsburg, "American lawyers have been observers of a turning point in the legal system of the People's Republic of China," *American Bar Association Journal*, October 1978, pp. 1517-1525, at 1519.

[47] Martin Garbus, "Justice under China's new legal system," *New York State Bar Association Journal*, no. 7, November 1978, pp. 577-585 at 580, col. 1.

[48] *Guangming ribao*, July 17, 1981, p. 3.

[49] Martin Garbus, *op. cit.*, p. 583, col. 1.

[50] Jerome Cohen, "Will China have a formal legal system?" *American Bar Association Journal*, October 1978, pp. 1510-1515 at 1511, col. 2.

[51] *Ibid.*

[52] *Renmin ribao*, April 8, 1983, p. 4, col. 1.

by the zheng-fa secretary of the local party office."[53] This secretary
is an extramural watchdog authority. But *Renmin ribao* has advocated
the abolishment of such a system of secretarial sanction.[54] It believes
that intramural supervision of juridical function by party committee
in the courthouse should be sufficient.

Mass line

The 1978 Constitution enjoins that in major counterrevolutionary
or criminal cases, the masses should be drawn in for "discussion
and suggestion."[55] Although this is for the first time written into the
basic law, the communists resorted to it almost from the very
beginning of their regime. During the land reform of 1951-1952, tens
of millions of peasants, labeled rich, were put to death in show trials
in response to the masses' outcry of "kill, kill, kill."[56] Such qualms
as cross-examination, producing of evidence, testimony of witnesses,
preferring of specific counts of charge, confrontation with victims,
rebuttal by the accused or his counsel and the like were all tossed
away as unworthy of people's justice. The 1951-1952 bloodbath is
a thing of the past, but the Reds find it impossible to abandon the
basic style. The recent trial of ten was presided over by a squadron
of judges (35);[57] two platoons (25) of procurators presented the
charges;[58] and tens of thousands of cadres were echeloned as
witnesses.[59]

In non-counterrevolutionary cases, mass line may be more realistic.
Judges actually discuss the verdict with the people inside the
courtroom. In the preceding chapter we saw the involvement of the
work units in the divorce procedure despite the silence of the 1978
Constitution on mass consultation in civil disputes. Come to criminal
law, the role of the masses is sanctioned by that Constitution as seen
above. We must point out, however, that its Article 41, clause 2 talks
of only "major counterrevolutionary or criminal cases." Presumably
insignificant ones can be spared with the requirement. Yet practice
has been that nearly all crimes, counterrevolutionary or not, have been
treated as major. And there is always mass involvement. A few
examples may be cited below.

An embezzlement trial was seen by Jerome Cohen.[60] The court
was packed with people. There was no counsel for the defendant and

[53] *Xi nan zheng fa xue bao*, no. 1, May 1979, p. 7.

[54] *Renmin ribao*, August 25, 1980, p. 1.

[55] The 1978 Constitution, Article 41, clause 2. This provision is not in the 1982 Constitution.

[56] Jerome Cohen, "Criminal law, reflections on the criminal process in China," p. 342, col. 1.

[57] "Written judgment of the Special Court," p. 28, col. 2.

[58] *Ibid.*, p. 13, col. 1.

[59] *Ibid.*, January 12, 1981, p. 22, col. 2.

[60] Jerome Cohen, "Will China have a formal legal system?" p. 1514, col. 1.

the judge played an active role by interrogating him. To the charge, the defendant confessed. Then the judge proceeded to ask for "suggestions" of the audience. Two views emerged. One argued for leniency but the other for severe punishment. The judge arrived at a compromise by putting the man to work under the supervision of the masses of his factory for three years, with the understanding that he would not have to serve a suspended two-year term if his probationary record was clean. Another trial was witnessed by Martin Garbus.[61] The defendant, (again) an embezzler, was sentenced (again) to work at his factory under the surveillance of a specific committee for two years, after the judge heard of the "suggestion" of the court audience. In still another case, the masses were divided on the prison term between two and three years, and the judge broke even by pronouncing 2.5 years for the defendant.[62] A couple of years ago, a student of the Foreign Languages School of Beijing was sentenced to die by the lower court for robbery. He made an appeal to the municipal high court. The latter sent judges to different organizations including the said school to consult the masses. No mitigating circumstance was found. He was executed on September 2, 1981.[63]

Depending on the nature of the offense, the hands of the leaders are more visible in some cases than in others. Suppose an offense is political, the party would surely come to coach the masses. The activists will distribute leaflets detailing the case long before the trial is due to open.[64] This procedure is perfectly in tune with one of the most important planks of the mass line, namely, "the communists must engage in propaganda telling the people what to do in given problems."[65] At the curtain time, everybody is well-oriented. The party-decided verdict would be suggested from the floor and approved. In other kinds of cases (non-political), there seems to be no such cue. A report by foreign tourists in Xian (Shaanxi province) told of a campaign by the public in connection with a rape incident.[66] Obviously with the connivance of some officials, the public protested to the Provincial Revolutionary Committee (now renamed Provincial Government) of Shaanxi the unfair sentencing of the young worker to twenty years, saying that the judicial body never consulted with the masses. In non-counterrevolutionary acts, as this case shows, mass participation did not take place at times.

Actually, there has been a sort of double mass line in criminal cases of the gravest nature. Apart from the "suggestion and consultation"

61 Martin Garbus, op. cit., pp. 582-583.

62 Ruth Ginsburg, op. cit., p. 1525, col. 1.

63 Renmin ribao, September 4, 1981, p. 4.

64 Shao-chuan Leng, op. cit., p. 363, note 56, and p. 361, note 49.

65 "Qun zhong lu xian," Xin hua ci dian, Beijing: Shang wu yin shu yuan, 1980, p. 694-695.

66 Shao-chuan Leng, op. cit., p. 363, note 56.

inside the trial chamber, these cases invariably call for the witnessing of executions by thousands upon thousands in big athletic grounds. Papers invariably write of it as a mass trial, but in reality the sentence has been fixed and, with very rare exceptions (see next section) approved by the Supreme Court. The execution, nevertheless, takes the form of official pronunciation of the verdict and its summary carrying out, thus according the masses the feeling of participation.[67]

The provision of mass participation in justice is being deleted from the 1982 Constitution, for whatever reasons. But the practices just described still prevail.

Equality before the law

This is stipulated in the 1954 Constitution,[68] and in that year's Organic Law of the People's Court,[69] but it was attacked for lacking a class distinction and allowing the counterrevolutionaries to claim the same protection as the revolutionaries.[70] Therefore, both the 1975 and 1978 Constitutions failed to include it.[71] Yet it reappears in the 1982 Constitution (Article 32), nay as the number one civil right in the chapter with that rubric. Before the adoption of the new Constitution, the equality principle already found its way into the 1981 Organic Law of the People's Courts,[72] and Organic Law of the People's Procurators.[73] Commenting on this principle, Peng Zhen stated that even those who are deprived of their political freedom should enjoy the right to work and to enjoy personal security.[74] Any rank or meritorious record of a person, he emphasized, would not set him above the law.[75] The purpose of the legislation is clear enough, as is the intention of the government. The crucial question, however, is what stand would the judges and the masses take toward the "disfavored classes such as the former landlords, rich peasants and bourgeois and their descendants?" May they get an identical treatment as the workers, peasants and soldiers who violate the law? In fact, the bad (also called black) elements have been in such a plight that there is hardly any chance for them to be dealt with on the same footing as the good (also called red) elements.[76]

---

[67] Renmin ribao, June 19 and 25, 1981, both on p. 4; Guangming ribao, June 25, 1981, p. 4.

[68] The 1954 Constitution, Article 85.

[69] Related in Peng Zhen, "Explanation on seven laws," p. 15, col. 1.

[70] Jerome Cohen, loc. cit.

[71] Ibid., p. 1515, col. 1.

[72] Organic Law of the People's Courts, Article 5.

[73] Organic Law of the People's Procurators, Article 8.

[74] Peng Zhen, "Explanation on seven laws," p. 15, col. 2.

[75] Ibid., p. 16, col. 2. David Bonavia, "Hua spells out Deng's brave new world," Far Eastern Economic Review, July 6, 1979, p. 11, col. 2.

[76] The five good elements are workers, peasants, soldiers, revolutionary intellectuals, and others; the five bad elements are landlords, rich peasants, bourgeois, counterrevolutionaries, and others.

Family status of a defendant used to be crucial in sentencing. Bad men were all considered potential criminals. If offenses were committed by them, they would receive heavier penalties than if the same offense were perpetrated by good people. This was particularly in evidence during frenzied political campaigns when the blacks were invariably picked up as objects of scorn and derision. In a violent argument involving some forty persons in the suburb of Guangzhou in late 1955, for example, the police singled out a man who had a counterrevolutionary history for prosecution.[77] He was given a term of five years. A man who was a factory worker and a woman whose father was formerly a Guomindang official committed an adultery in Amoy in 1971. Due to different class origins, one year was handed down to him, but two years were to her.[78] In another case, a poor peasant spreading reactionary ideas drew two years, but a former government employee drew five for an identical activity.[79] Two other cases may be cited.[80] In a 1958 incident near Guangzhou, a policeman unsuccessfully attempted to deflower a landlord's daughter and beat him up cruelly. The security agency did not wish to penalize a "good person" such as this man for what he had done to a "bad person" like the landlord. Subsequently, the frustrated rapist was handed over to rehabilitation, instead of given five to seven years as the law required. In a 1961 case happening in Enping county of Guangdong province, another policeman violated a former landlord's wife at gunpoint, but he claimed that she seduced him. Even after the facts were established beyond a doubt, the case was categorized, in Maoist doctrine, as a contradiction within the people and, therefore, no infliction should be meted out.

All the above cases are fairly old. A more recent event seems to point to a reversal of the past practice.[81] It involved a theft of some money of one worker by another. The investigation revealed that the defendant's political background was satisfactory. Yet this clean sheet was not to exonerate him. The majority of the courtroom audience recommended a harsh penalty which was forthright accepted by the judge. It is worth watching how the judicial wind is blowing. Certainly one case cannot set up a precedent. That the regime is definitely moving toward equality of law is no longer in doubt because it is the only way for it to establish some credentials with the public. Both *Renmin ribao* and *Guangming ribao* recently printed on the front page a letter written by Mao Zedong on October 10, 1937 to Lei Jintian, the chief justice of the High Court of the Shaan-Gan-Ning Border Government (a rebeldom at that time). The papers reproduced the

---

[77] Shao-chuan Leng, *op. cit.,* p. 364, note 68.

[78] *Ibid.*

[79] Hungdah Chiu, *op. cit.,* p. 389 (table)

[80] Both are cited in Shao-chuan Leng, *op. cit.,* p. 365, note 70.

[81] Martin Garbus, *op. cit.,* pp. 582-583.

facsimilae, indicating that the writing was not faked.[82] The case concerns a certain Huang Kegong. He was described as a Long Marcher and a fighter in the Jinggang Shan struggle on the side of Mao Zedong. His proposal to marry a school girl was declined by her, he then had her shot. The chief justice wrote a letter to Mao Zedong, asking instruction on the death sentence the court had decided on. At the same time, the defendant also petitioned him for clemency. In reply, Mao regretted that an exemplary revolutionary should have committed such a crime.[83] He would not interfere and the man was executed. The moral of the letter is unmistakably judicial equality. One's party card and past record make no difference in the administration of justice.

Crime and punishment

About the kinds of criminal activity and the crime rate, the Chinese press reveals a lot and it is very bitter. In mid-1981 an article in *Renmin ribao* confessed that "in recent months criminal incidences are rising."[84] Regretted the Director of the Social Security Bureau, Zhang Zhiye, that "take Shanghai for example, in 1982 public security agencies received a total of 14,000 letters and pieces of information exposing *numerous* crimes."[85] Throughout the years, this bureaucrat concluded, crimes were mounting.[86] A Western reference reported that since 1979, in cities like Shanghai and Beijing, in provinces like Anhui, Fujian, Guangdong, Hebei, Henan, Jilin, Shaanxi, and in the two regions of Xinjiang and Guangxi troops had to be called in to patrol the streets from time to time.[87] Xinxiang district (also translated as prefecture) of Henan province witnessed in one week's time more than one hundred serious cases; four hundred people were arrested.[88] This was only *one weeks'* haul, involving *serious* cases and in *one* district (Henan has 10 districts). In the nation's capital there were 2,400 such cases as murders, robberies, rapes by one or more men, arsons and thefts of more than 1,000 yuan in one month.[89] If we take the Xinxiang data as typical of all China's prefectures and equivalent units, i.e., outside the three biggest cities under the central authority, and outside the 100 cities under the jurisdiction of provinces and regions,[90] there would have to be 1,097,200 cases and 5,465,000 persons arrested in a year.

[82] *Renmin ribao*, July 11, 1981, p. 1; *Guangming ribao*, July 11, 1981, p. 1.

[83] *Renmin ribao*, July 18, 1981, p. 4 prints a detailed narration of the case.

[84] *Ibid.*, June 23, 1981, p. 1 (the article was written by three persons).

[85] *Beijing Review*, March 21, 1983, p. 17, col. 2.

[86] *Ibid.*, p. 15, col. 2.

[87] *Keesing's*, October 3, 1981, p. 30494, col. 1.

[88] *Renmin ribao*, June 23, 1981, p. 4.

[89] *Ibid.*, July 24, 1981, p. 1.

[90] *Renmin shou ce*, Beijing: Renmin ribao chu ban she, 1979, pp. 1094-1100 where the administrative divisions are listed.

Juvenile crimes are viewed as very grave. They are estimated to be 10 times more numerous than before the Cultural Revolution.[91] Most crimes, declared *Renmin ribao,* were perpetrated by youth.[92] As if confirming this information, chief procurator Huang Hoqing replaced by Yang Yichen on June 20, 1983, stated to the NPC on December 6, 1982 that "criminal offenses by adolescents constitute around 50 percent."[93]

For whatever reasons, however, the crime rate in the country is said to be on the decrease. By how much? The president of the Supreme Court Jiang Hua replaced by Zheng Tianxiang on June 20, 1983, and Huang Hoqing appeared before the NPC on December 6, 1982 with their respective report of work; while the former man said the rate was down by 24.2 percent, the latter gave 15.7 percent.[94] Elsewhere, the Director of Social Security Bureau, Zhang Zhiye, mentioned the downward rate to be 15.9.[95] The communist officials do not speak with one statistical voice. This casts a shadow on the credibility óf the figures and even the diminishing claim.

How many are convicted? Zhang Zhiye maintained that in 1979-1981 only 0.075 percent of the population were convicted annually.[96] Given the population of one billion, the number has to be 750,000 individuals. By way of contrast, he quoted the Federal Bureau of Investigation, 5.22 percent of the Americans were convicted in 1979; then he quoted the Associated Press that the reported crimes in the CPR is 1.3 percent of the US (in both he did not give the original source). In re young offenders, their crimes are also claimed to be dwindling. But here the drop is only 8.1 percent during 1981-1982.[97]

There are no statistics on the various categories of crimes other than the economic ones (next paragraph). Although all references to crimes take this sequence: murders, robberies, rapes, arsons, thefts, firebombings,[98] one may not interpret it to imply a numerical order. Declared the Chinese press that "thefts are 80 percent of China's crimes, while homicide, robbery and rape account for only 8 percent.[99] More revealing perhaps is the added statement that "even 90 percent of the murder cases involve property disputes, lovers' or marital quarrels and disputes over the right of house sites

---

[91] *Keesing's,* October 3, 1981, p. 30494, col. 1.

[92] *Renmin ribao,* November 12, 1981, p. 6.

[93] *Beijing Review,* March 21, 1983, p. 16, col. 2.

[94] *Renmin ribao,* December 17, 1982, p. 2, col. 2. Jiang Hua's report is on upper part of the page, Huang Hoqing's on the lower part, but both on the same column.

[95] *Beijing Review,* March 21, 1983, p. 15, col. 2.

[96] *Ibid.*

[97] *Ibid.,* p. 16, col. 2.

[98] *Renmin ribao,* July 24, 1981, p. 1; December 16, 1981, p. 2, cols. 1 and 2; December 17, 1982, p. 2, col. 3.

[99] *Beijing Review,* March 21, 1983, p. 15, col. 2.

or disagreements over the right to use irrigation facilities in rural areas. Only 10 percent of all murders are committed in connection with robbery or rape."[100] This clearly intimates that financial needs are pushing the Chinese to prey upon each other, hardly the Confucian model of behavior. An important caveat is that the crimes are convicted in the courts. There are "numerous" Chinese who are disciplined outside the courts after running afoul of law and are sent to be reeducated through labor camps.[101] Heaven knows how many of these un-prosecuted criminals there are!

Economic crimes are defined as financial irregularities committed by employees in state enterprises and government departments. They include smuggling or sale of smuggled goods, bribery or receiving bribes, speculation, theft of public money and illegal sale of precious relics.[102] From 1980, the Chinese began to reveal the number of cases of these crimes. In that year, it was 14,352.[103] In 1982 it shot up to more than 31,000,[104] and in 1982 it came down to 24,636.[105] Again it was up to 33,000 in 1983 (Globe and mail, June 10, 1983, p. 3, col. 4). The courts and procurators have made the fight against economic crimes their essential work.[106] The nation's press almost everyday calls for strenuous struggle with wrongdoers in this area.[107] The effort seems to have little success, as the statistics show. The juridical cadres are given the credit for having retrieved for the state treasury 38,460,000 yuan.[108] As regards the kinds of crimes of this description and the number of cases, the record during January-September 1982 is like this:[109]

10,290	stealth
5,243	embezzlement
2,278	swindling
2,011	speculation
1,138	robbery
186	smuggle
32	sale of precious relics
1,153	all others
11,331	total

[100] Ibid., p. 18, col. 1.

[101] New York times, August 12, 1982, p. 3, col. 3.

[102] Beijing Review, January 17, 1983, p. 9, col. 1; also Renmin ribao, December 17, 1982, p. 2, col. 2.

[103] Renmin ribao, March 20, 1981, p. 1.

[104] Ibid., December 16, 1981, p. 2, col. 2. The count is from January to September 1981.

[105] Ibid., December 17, 1982, p. 2, col. 2. The count is from October 1981 to September 1982.

[106] Ibid. (Jiang Hua's statement).

[107] Beijing Review, February 22, 1982, pp. 7-8; March 15, 1982, p. 3; April 10, 1982, pp. 7-8; April 26, 1982, p. 7-8.

[108] Renmin ribao, December 17, 1982, p. 2, col. 3 (Jiang Hua's statement).

[109] Ibid., col. 2 (Jiang Hua's statement).

The Chinese did not give exact definitions of these specifics. We do not know, for example, how stealth is to be differentiated from embezzlement. As for money at stake, it is stated that 250 cases involved more than 150,000 yuan each and 1,062 cases more than 10,000 yuan each.[110] Twenty-five persons received 100,000 yuan each.[111] It is further disclosed that among the convicted were 3,706 state employees including 29 working at the county level. "Nearly all of them were given the *zhong xing* (heavy penalty)," proclaimed the president of the Supreme Court.[112] The term *zhong xing* means either life imprisonment or death.[113] We suspect that the latter took a high toll of the total number of convictions. Just how big a sum of money can send one to the firing squad? The law is mute on this. The best bid is 10,000 yuan, an amount equivalent to 15 years' wage of an average state employee (see Chapter XIII). One man was shot for pocketing 190,000 yuan,[114] and another for pocketing 1,480,000 yuan which seems to be the highest figure ever revealed in the press.[115] Perhaps just to demonstrate that the law is sex-blind, a woman convicted of defalcation, was shot in Haerbin of Heilongjiang province on February 28, 1980.[116]

After analyzing the crime, let us come to the problem of penalty. The criminal law provides five principal and three accessory inflictions.[117] The five, meted out independently, are detention, control, fixed-term incarceration, life imprisonment and death; and the three, appending to these, are fine, deprivation of political right, and confiscation of property (Articles 26, 29). In duration, detention runs from fifteen days to six months (Article 33), control from three months to two years, and fixed term from six months to fifteen years (Article 40). We may note here that the 20 year sentence for Yao Wenyuan, one of the Gang of Four, imposed on January 25, 1981, seems to be in violation of this provision. His term is five years too many. All convicts are required to perform physical labor. Naturally, "death penalty applies only to the extremely vicious criminals" (Article 43). More on this sentence anon. If the defendant is an alien, the punishment may be expulsion from the country (Article 30). Several foreigners were in recent years given such a penalty, but not until they had served nearly the entire term.

[110] *Ibid.*

[111] *Beijing Review*, January 17, 1983, p. 9, col. 1.

[112] *Renmin ribao*, December 17, 1982, p. 2, col. 2.

[113] Criminal law, chapter III, sections 4, 5.

[114] *Beijing review*, December 29, 1980, p. 6.

[115] *Ibid.*, January 17, 1983, p. 8, col. 3.

[116] *Keesing's*, October 3, 1980, p. 30491, col. 1. *Zhong quo bai ke nian jian*, p. 227.

[117] Criminal Law of the People's Republic of China was published in *Renmin ribao*, July 7, 1979, taking effect on January 1, 1980.

, of criminal responsibility is 16. However, if a person 14 and 16 wounds others seriously, or commits murder, ⁄, arson, habitual theft or other grave activities in disturbance ﹍al order, may be tried as an adult (Article 14). There is the grace ⁄ision that a defendant aged 14-16 must be punished less severely. Ć⼍inese judges are given a great deal of discretion in fixing the terms. In six circumstances, they can pronounce either five, or ten years, or life imprisonment.[118] Homicide provided in Article 132 carries a penalty ranging from three years to death. In a country like the CPR where there is no jural trial, the judges seem to be accorded too much leeway in this matter. Another situation which makes the judges formidable is that if a prisoner behaves poorly, his term can be extended by them upon the recommendation of the ward. This recommendation is seldom refused.[119] The prolongation of the original sentence is in reality a new verdict. Yet there is no consultation with and suggestion by the masses as in the original sentencing; and the verdict is decided *in camera.*

Death appears to be the only sentence permitted under Article 103 which says the counterrevolutionaries, found endangering in the most serious way the state and people, *may* be put to death. The word ke yi (may) implies some choice on the part of the trial court, but the provision does not talk of life imprisonment and/or lesser terms. We are not sure of the intendment of this article. The Special Court invoked Article 103 on January 25, 1981 to sentence Jiang Qing and Zhang Chunjiao to die. There is a uniqueness in the Chinese law that the death sentence can be deferred of execution for two years (Article 43). The two convicts just mentioned were not shot right away by virtue of this stipulation. The same article also envisages that if the convict is repentant, the court may commute the term to life imprisonment. Again the two famous criminals were given such a treatment by the Supreme Court on January 25, 1983.[120] Here we must observe a) that the condition for the clemency in Jiang Qing's case is not really met, because she was described as non-repentant during her two years on death row (nothing is heard of Zhang Chunqiao) and b) that the commutation can properly be done by the re-convened Special Court. If the Supreme Court can do this, why did it take itself out of the picture in the first place?

Shooting the convict is the mandatory technique of execution (Article 45). In some cases, the criminal or his family has to pay the cost of two bullets, 0.35 yuan each (about 18¢ US) used to execute him,[121] but there is no insistence of ''no pay no execution.'' The Criminal Law in Article 155 specifies that execution, although it must be made known to the public, should not be carried out in front of

[118] Criminal Law, Articles 106, 110, 132, 139, 150 and 155.
[119] George Crocket and Morris Gleicher, ''Inside China's prisons,'' *Judicature*, April 1978, pp. 409-415 at 412, col. 2.
[120] *Beijing Review*, February 7, 1983, p. 7, cols. 2-3.
[121] Hungdah Chiu, *op. cit.*, p. 390, col. 2.

the crowds. This stipulation is frequently violated by the announcement and shooting of convicts in a big field in which tens of thousands of people are collected to watch. The events are also televised. Probably secret shootings are the rule, for reports of mass attendance of open-field execution are fairly rare, while death sentences may well run to the thousands each year. As we stated above, the president of the Supreme Court hinted at the execution of some of the 3,706 economic criminals in the first nine months of 1982. (From September 1983, announcements of executions become more numerous)

If the reprieved person repents or reforms himself, the sentence can be changed into a fixed term of between fifteen and twenty years or into life imprisonment (Article 46). Not every death sentence, however, is reprievable. Article 69 specifically declares that counterrevolutionary criminals must be killed immediately. Yet Jiang Qing and Zhang Chunqiao were given deferment of the shooting, even though they were counterrevolutionaries. The judgment against them does not explain this deviation from the law. Are there many deaths with two-year deferments? The Chinese themselves reported that in one prison of 1,900, there were 20 such inmates.[122] The death sentence, according to Article 44, does not apply to youths below 18, nor to pregnant women. Quite noteworthy is that there is a statute of limitation of criminal responsibility to twenty years (Article 76). However, the Supreme Court is vested with the authority to set this aside.

To avoid miscarriage of justice perhaps, Article 43 requires death to be sanctioned by the Supreme Court and Article 152 (1st section) of the Criminal-Procedure Law states that the president of the Supreme Court must initial the verdict.[123] One death sentence was reported in June 1981.[124] A man broke and entered an old woman's home. He robbed her of money and cigarettes (her commodity). Then he strangled her. The Shanghai middle court took cognizance of the case and gave him the death punishment. Against it he appealed to the high court, but the petition was turned down. The execution was carried out after the Supreme Court in Beijing affirmed it.[125] Is the Court's approval of death sentence mandatory? Is the approval a matter of formality? In regard to the first question, *Renmin ribao* related a case of premeditated murder.[126] The convict, sentenced to die by the middle court, was "at once shot" upon the affirmative order

[122] "Reforming criminals," *Beijing Review*, February 23, 1981, pp. 22-29. The statistics are given by Jiao Kun, deputy director of Beijing municipal bureau of public security.

[123] The Law is in *Renmin shou ce*, pp. 417-426.

[124] *Renmin ribao*, June 19, 1981, p. 4.

[125] The rules of approval were enacted by the NPC Standing Committee in its 19th session held on June 22, 1981, *ibid.*, June 23, 1981, p. 4; *Guangming ribao*, June 24, 1981, p. 4.

[126] *Renmin ribao*, April 8, 1983, p. 4, col. 3.

of the high court of Sichuan province. In regard to the second, we have so far not heard of any overruling of lower court decisions of capital punishment.

Article 15 of the Criminal Law says crime on account of insanity may not be charged against the defendant. There has been no case of such a sort yet. But a bizarre instance may be cited here. It occurred in 1967, at a time when this humanitarian rule was not in China's criminal legislation. A man committed a physical violence to a foreign diplomat in Beijing. He was prosecuted. On account of the gravity of the case, it did not go through the lower or middle court. Instead the Supreme Court assumed the original jurisdiction. Presiding the trial was the president of the court, Yang Xiufeng. It was found that the man was insane. Nevertheless, the death verdict was declared and was swiftly carried out. Yang Xiufeng attempted to commit suicide but failed.[127] Harold Hinton however asserted that he lost his post in 1967 and killed himself early in 1968.[128] In fact, though, Yang continued to serve as the president of the Supreme Court until 1975,[129] and had been very active. When he died (Nov.10, '83) he was a vice-chairman of the Standing Committee of the CPPCC.[130] Apropos of the just-mentioned case, we should remember that at that time the entire nation was soaked in xenophobia. To beat up, or even kill foreigners was something to be touted. The highest bench of the CPR, it was then deplored, had killed a good man. Amidst the excitement, the problem of executing an insane person escaped attention.

An eye-opening point of the Chinese law is the use of analogy, somewhat modified by the requirement that the approval of the Supreme Court be obtained (Article 79). The doctrine of analogy, interestingly enough, is as old as the communist regime. As early as 1934, the Reds adopted it in Article 18 of the Regulations to Put Down Counterrevolution of the Chinese Soviet Republic and in 1951 it appeared in the same kind of legislation.[131] The Chinese ideologues defended it as "one of the socialist legal categories and a necessary means to supress the enemy, to strike at the law-breakers and to protect the public."[132] However, there is a counter-argument held by many in the CPR, according to Simon Luk.[133] They felt that criminal analogy should be deleted from the code in keeping with the general

---

[127] *Facts on File*, January 19-25, 1966, p. 28, E2.

[128] Harold Hinton, *An Introduction to Chinese Politics*, 2nd ed., New York: Holt, Rinehart and Winston, 1978, pp. 236-237.

[129] Jiang Hua took over the position from him in 1975, *Europa*, 1976, vol. 2, p. 367, col. 1; *ibid.*, 1974, vol. 2, p. 351, col. 1.

[130] *Renmin ribao*, Nov. 13, 1983, p. 1, col. 1.

[131] Cheng Qingyi on analysis of analogy in criminal law, *Guangmind ribao*, August 11, 1981, p. 3.

[132] *Ibid.*

[133] Simon Luk, "China's new legal system," *World Press Review*, May 1980, p. 59, col. 1.

standard of justice. Perhaps Peng Zhen belongs to the abolitionist group. It is revealing that in his speech of June 26, 1979 to the NPC to explain the seven laws, he touched all the major principles of criminal law, but said nothing about analogy. We presume that his silence is a sign of disapproval. The only check or veto on the use of analogy is the Supreme Court. It is worth watching how often the doctrine will be resorted to by the lower courts and how often that Court will disallow it.

In vivid contrast to Western practice, the Chinese criminal justice is swift, perhaps too swift. *Renmin ribao* has clamored for the rapid elimination of bad people.[134] One case was completed within eight days from the commission of the crime to the execution of the culprit.[135] All the Chinese media were writing of the swiftness with pride.[136] The "quick and severe punishment" is unanimously seen as conducive to law and order.[137] One author alleges to have perceived in Articles 57, 132 and 150 the approval of speedy and harsh treatment of the evil-doers.[138]

In connection with the capital penalty, there is the problem of the divestment of political right. Some think that this accessory punishment is unnecessary because when a man is shot, that right is *ipso facto* extinguished. However, an article in *Guangming ribao* came to the defense of the law.[139] It gives an example that if the dead man has a manuscript, his next of kin can have it published if political right is not taken away by the state. Similarly, the deprivation of that right affects medals, titles of honor, pensions and membership of the party.

The court

The Organic Law of the People's Courts (Article 2) provides local people's courts, special people's courts and Supreme People's Court (from now on the word people's will be omitted when we mention the courts).[140] The first named consists of three layers: a) local courts serving counties, small towns and large cities' districts, b) middle courts serving prefectures, c) high courts serving provinces, regions and the cities of Shanghai, Beijing and Tianjin.[141] Embraced within special courts are military courts, railway courts, water-transport courts, forestry courts and the like. At present there are 30 high

[134] *Renmin ribao*, June 22, 1981, p. 1.

[135] *Ibid.*, p. 5.

[136] *Guangming ribao*, June 25, 1981, p. 4; *Renmin ribao*, June 5, 1981, p. 4.

[137] *Renmin ribao*, June 22, 1981, p. 1. Jiang Hua spoke of speedy and severe punishment in *ibid.*, December 17, 1982, p. 2, col. 2; Huang Hoqing spoke of that in *ibid.*, cols. 1 and 3.

[138] *Ibid.*, June 25, 1981, p. 5.

[139] *Guangming ribao*, June 26, 1981, p. 4.

[140] The Law is printed in *renmin ribao*, July 6, 1979; it became effective on January 1, 1980.

[141] Ruth Ginsburg, *op. cit.*, p. 1519, col. 2.

courts,[142] 293 middle courts and 2,570 lower courts.[143] We have little information about the special courts. It is only occasionally that newspapers refer to them. *Renmin ribao,* for example, tells that a certain Tian Jia was appointed chief justice of the military court, and a certain Chen Huan that of the railway transport court.[144] *Guangming ribao* writes that there are 20 railway middle courts and 62 railway lower courts.[145] All these courts, but not the forestry courts, remind us of the Soviet variety existing before 1958 when the USSR abolished all of them, with the exception of the military tribunals. In accordance with Article 62, clause 7 of the Constitution and Article 35 of the Organic Law of the People's Courts, the NPC elects (and removes) the president of the Supreme Court. By Article 67, clause 11 of the Constitution, the NPC Standing Committee can decide on the vice-presidents and ordinary judges. In the provinces, autonomous regions and counties, the corresponding people's congresses exercise similar power on the personnel of the courts.[146] Elsewhere in this book mention was made of the prefectures, an inviginating rung between province and county. The Han areas technically do not have these units. The prefectures have their own courts, the middle courts; but since there are no people's congresses to elect the judges there, these are appointed by the provincial people's congresses.

The minimum age of judges is 23, according to Article 34 of the Organic Law of the People's Courts. No restriction exists in respect to sex, national origin and education. Among the Shanghai judges there are a) those who were already on the bench before the revolution of 1949, b) those who are workers, peasants and soldiers having gone through short courses in law and c) those who were law-school graduates.[147] Many are party veterans certified by universities under the communist rule. In 1980, only 6 percent of the legal personnel had some education in law.[148] By way of contrast, in the Soviet Union all judges received legal training. It is back in 1936 that "only 7.6 percent of Soviet judges had a higher legal education."[149] Although

[142] *Statesman's Yearbook,* 1980-1981, p. 354. This generally reputable source wrongfully mentions 200 middle courts and 2,000 lower courts.

[143] *Guangming ribao,* December 8, 1981, p. 4 mentions the number of middle courts to be 293. The same number was given by the president of the Supreme Court, *Renmin ribao,* December 16, 1981, p. 2. The 2,570 lower courts are derived by us from the facts that each of the 2,570 local administrative units has such a court, see *Zhong guo shou ce,* Hong Kong: Da gong bao, 1979, p. 19. The number of lower courts is not mentioned by the president of the Supreme Court or the two papers just referred to.

[144] *Renmin ribao,* September 15, 1981, p.5.

[145] *Ibid.,* December 16, 1981, p. 2; *Guangming ribao, loc. cit.*

[146] Organic Law of the People's Courts, Article 35.

[147] Beverly Carl, *op. cit.,* p. 1277; Donald Paragon, "Some firsthand observations on China's legal system," *Judicature,* no. 10, 1980, pp. 477-484 at 480, col. 2.

[148] *Renmin ribao,* October 10, 1980, p. 1, this percentile is repeated in *ibid.,* December 21, 1980, p. 3.

[149] Donald D. Barry and Harold J. Berman, "The jurists," *Interest Group in Soviet Union,* edited by Gordon Skilling and Franklin Griffiths, Princeton, New Jersey: Princeton University Press, 1971, pp. 291-333 at 300.

education attainment appears to be of increasing importance, redness is by no means minimized.[150] All judges must have high political consciousness and culture and all must study Marxism-Leninism and Mao Zedong Thought.[151] Besides, they are supposed to be knowledgeable about the state policy and party line. During the dominance of the Gang of Four, the court was made up of the young, the middle-aged and the old; and each had to work at least one day per week in the field as a laborer.[152] The age formula, it is to be noted, is written into the 1978 Constitution (Preamble) as the norm for all state bodies. It is dropped by the 1982 Constitution, however.

Three judges of the Beijing High Court who hosted the American Bar Association delegates said they studied law at a two-year cadre-school but learned about the legal job by actually doing it. Two of the three judges of the Shanghai High Court were laymen. One was a former factory hand and the other an army private. They were on the bench for 20 and 30 years respectively.[153] The vice-president of the CPR's Supreme Court was a Red Armyman during the days of insurrection. He finished a politico-military course. In 1949, the CCP appointed him to that court, and he has stayed on ever since.

What is the size of the Supreme Court and of other courts? Two law professors of Beijing University told a visiting judge from the US in 1975 that they did not know the number of Supreme Court judges.[154] A Chinese reference lists one president (Jiang Hua) and four vice-presidents (Wang Weigang, He Lanjie, Zeng Hanzhou, and Zheng Shaowen).[155] No names of other members are given. One of the vice-presidents said to American lawyers that "there were over twenty judges and over twenty assistants to the judges" in his organization.[156] This number two man of the Supreme Court knew only the Court's approximate size! He also surmised that there were "about twenty judges" in the criminal division of the Beijing High Court. According to another report, Shanghai had 30 judges in 1979.[157] Since that city has one high court, one middle court and 10 local courts (one for each county), one court has to be made up of 2 or 3 judges. A comparison of Beijing and Shanghai yields an interesting point. The former's high court alone has more than 20 judges against 30 for the entire Shanghai system. Yet Shanghai has a population one third

[150] Donald Paragon, "Some firsthand observations on China's legal system," p. 481, col. 1.

[151] Idem, "The administration of justice and law in new China," p. 579, col. 1.

[152] Andrew Gayle, "Law and lawyers in China," American Bar Association Journal, March 1978, pp. 348-353 at 352, col. 2.

[153] Ibid., p. 349, col. 2.

[154] Jerome Cohen, "Criminal law, reflections on the criminal process in China," p. 343, col. 2.

[155] Zhong guo shou ce, op. cit., p. 39.

[156] Ruth Gingsburg, op. cit., p. 1520, col. 1. The Supreme Court had 44 people in Sept. 1983.

[157] Donald Paragon, "The administration of justice and law in new China," p. 578, col. 2.

larger than Beijing (ca. 12 against 9 million). Does the nation's capital have more litigations than Shanghai? Like the Russians, the Chinese use the assessors. Similar to judges, they are elected by the standing committee of the people's congress at a given level (Organic Law of the People's Courts, Article 35). They and the mass attendants at a trial may very well be intended to be a jural substitute. In the case of the attendants, their suggestion is indeed canvassed and abided by the court. The assessor lacks training in law and he learns his way by experience. Any citizen aged 23 and not deprived of political right, is eligible (Article 34). In performance of the duty (the law does not say how many days a year), an assessor gets his regular wage, that is, one without the bonus which goes with it. However, if he has no earnings, the court would compensate him (Article 39). Following the Soviet law, the Chinese code says that only in the first-instance cases are the assessors utilized. All appellate trials are conducted by professional judges (Article 10). However, in the trial of ten which is not an appellate case, there were no assessors. Unlike the Soviet law, the Chinese legislation provides deputy judges who can temporarily replace the regular ones as recommended by the president of the court and confirmed by the judicial committee thereof (Article 37).

Courts at all planes have civil and criminal panels whose number varies from place to place. By Articles 30 and 37 of the law under consideration, both Supreme Court and high courts have economic panels. These are not provided for in the local courts (Article 19). However, *Renmin ribao* reports the establishment of an economic panel in Changan county of Shaanxi province to take cognizance of contractual disputes between working teams and individuals.[158] *Beijing review* said that there were 1200-odd economic courts in the CPR.[159] We do now know if there is an enabling act for this by the NPC or its Standing Committee. Although detailed regulations are lacking, an economic panel is apparently lodged with the authority to compose inter-agency differences in financial matters. It is similar to the Soviet arbitral commission (USSR Constitution, Article 163), but while the Chinese panel is part of the regular court, the Soviet setup forms a pyramid by itself parallel to the judicature.

There seems to be no model law of organization for lower, middle or high court. In Hubei province, the high court has one president and five vice-presidents. Besides, there are five judges in the civil, and two in the criminal chambers.[160] The second chamber is divided into two sections handling respectively counterrevolution and other offenses, while the first chamber hears marriage, inheritance and property complaints. In addition, the court has bureaus of a) judicial education which trains and assigns graduates of law schools to the

---

[158] *Renmin ribao*, June 20, 1981, p. 1.

[159] *Beijing Review*, November 9, 1981, p. 7.

[160] Donald Paragon, "Some firsthand observations on China's legal system," p. 482.

various courts in the province, b) legal research and c) secretarial work.[161] The Hubei system consists of 85 local courts, 11 middle courts and one high court. It has one court for each county. Aping the Russians, the Chinese instituted the judicial committee in every court (Article 11). Not a trial panel itself, it consists of members (all judges) appointed by the standing committee of the people's congress upon the recommendation of the president of the court (Constitution, Article 67, clause 11 only mentions judicial committee of the Supreme Court). It is chaired by him and purports to summarize the court's experiences, discuss difficult problems and issues related to the trials. If the president sees fit, the chief procurator may be invited to the committee as an observer. As behoves the communist pathos, the committee operates by democratic centralism, namely the majority dominates the minority, the top controls the bottom and all obey the center. Gone is judicial independence!

Apropos of judges' stipends, information is scarce. When Andrew Gayle visited Shanghai, he was told of Judge Chu's salary to be 70 yuan a month, while Judge Chou, a much younger man, received 60 yuan.[162] For the sake of comparison, a top-notch technician of a factory earned more, and a primary-school teacher less. Taking the rate to be two yuan to one dollar, the judge sitting on the high court in Shanghai, a city of 12 million, gets an annual compensation of $400. However, he paid less than 5 percent for rent and about 20 percent for food (now around 60 percent, see Chapter XIII). Besides, medical bills are disbursed by the state. He can get along nicely with what he earns.

Turning to the jurisdiction, upper levels of courts have both original and appellate authorities but local levels have the first only. As seen above, there are four rungs in the judicial ladder. In practice, there are five if one counts the mediation committee which forestalls or interdicts 85-95% of the legal actions (see section on underdeveloped civil law of the preceding chapter). Breaking away from the pre-1949 tradition, the present regime ordains a uni- instead of duo-appellate system (Article 22). Of course, if the Supreme Court assumes the original jurisdiction, there can be no appeal. In the trial of ten, the Special Court has indeed pronounced an unappealable verdict. We can raise a legality question here. True, Article 12 of the Criminal Law authorizes the original jurisdiction of the Supreme Court, but the Special Court has no legal basis. Neither in this law nor in the Constitution can we find enabling provisions for it. Moreover, the Special Court is described as "under" the Supreme court.[163] Since it is under, there should be room for appeal. Having said all this, we still doubt as to why the Supreme Court can not hear the case itself.

[161] *Ibid.* The bureau of secretarial work is provided in Article 41 of the Organic Law of the People's Courts, but other bureaus are not.

[162] Andrew Gayle, *op. cit.,* p. 353, col. 1.

[163] "Written judgment of the Special Court," pp. 13, and 14, col. 1.

Although the law allows for one appeal, there may be two appeals both by the text of Article 14 and by actual practice. The provision says if a higher court discovers an error in the final, i.e., appellate, judgment of a lower tribunal, it has to order the latter to try the case again. If an error is detected by the higher procurator, he has the authority to launch a protest which would lead to reopening of the case. On whose petition does the higher court or procurator go over the final judgment? Suppose it is the unsuccessful litigant, the system comes back to the three-trial and two-appeal convention.

An appeal may be made by the litigant or by the procurator (Article 12), and the period in which it is to be made is ten days for both criminal and civil suits. In the Soviet Union, by way of contrast, the law specifies seven days for criminal but ten for civil cases.[164]

The statutory two-trial is actually revised in at least one recent case which took place in Heilongjiang province.[165] The defendant, a watchman, knifed a burglar to death. He was sentenced to five years in jail by the local court of Dedu county, on the basis that his self-defense action was too excessive. He appealed to the middle court which reduced the penalty to three years. Again he took the case to the high court of Heilongjiang. That tribunal handed him a not guilty judgment. A case of this nature, we must observe, does not impel the government to take a strong stand against the accused. If anything, the government is rather on his side because he got rid of a wrongdoer. However, in a counterrevolutionary case, with a hostile state against the defendant, can he appeal twice in clear contravention of Article 22?

If a sentence is found too lenient, the higher court can set it aside and a new trial would start.[166] Should a middle court mistakenly decide a case and a high tribunal overturn the ruling, it also remands the case for a new trial. Where a defendant is retried, an appeal is again permitted because the original ruling of the lower court has been declared void. However, if a middle court hands down a decision which is appealable (too harsh a sentence), the high court can lighten the penalty if the defendant appeals on that very reason and remand the case, with instruction, to the lower court.

Whether the appellate court can mete out a harsher term when the appeal is done by the defendant is not certain. Western observations on this point differ from one another. Jerome Cohen,[167] and the Amnesty International say it can and has done that,[168] but

---

[164] *Ob ugolovno-protsessual'nom zakonodatel'stve, soiuznykh respublik;* sbornik statei pod redaktsiei D.S. Kareva, Moskva: Gosudarstvennoe izdatel'stvo iuridicheskoi literatury, 1969, pp. 68, 314. See also *USSR 1977,* Moscow: Novosti Press, 1977, p. 39.

[165] *Renmin ribao,* June 24, 1981, p. 4.

[166] This paragraph derived from what Judge Li Haiqing of Shanghai High Court told Donald Paragon, "Some firsthand observations on China's legal system," p. 481.

[167] Jerome Cohen, "Criminal law, reflections on the criminal process in China," p. 344, col. 1.

[168] Cited in Ronald Keith, "Transcript of discussion with Wu Daying and Zhang Zhonglin concerning legal change and civil rights," *China Quarterly,* no. 81, March 1980, pp. 111-121 at 113.

one source says no.[169] It has been reported that when a defendant appeals a conviction to the Supreme Court in Beijing, he does not have to travel to that city. Instead the court, consisting of three judges, would come to him, e.g., journey to Shanghai to hold a hearing there.[170] We do not know if this practice is used in the provinces where the high court may be very far (several days' journey by foot) from a local court. As to be expected, an appeal must be grounded on substantive evidence or on mendacious interpretation of laws, party decrees or policy by the judges. After the trial court has entered a ruling, the high tribunal can still rectify the error in it even if the defendant fails to appeal within 10 days. That tribunal then launches an investigation of its own, for example, by sending fact-finding officials to the prison to take depositions from the convicts.

Following the arrest of the Gang of Four in October 1976, there has been a gradual increase of appellate cases. The vice-president of the CPR's Supreme Court, He Langjie, revealed to a group of visiting US jurists in late 1977 that his organization had not heard one single criminal case in the preceding eight years.[171] This piece of information was also corroborated by a Shanghai judge who stated to Donald Paragon that "there have been no appeals to the Supreme People's Court in the post-Cultural Revolution period."[172] Manifestly the Red Guards had executed summary justice to their victims. Beginning in 1978, upper-level tribunals have gone over lower-level's rulings on an impressive scale. As seen in the section on "righting of past wrongs," more than one million cases were examined and many, but not all, of them were reversed. The Shanghai High Court for example, is said to have handled 300 plus appellate cases.[173] When the American Bar Association delegates were in China on July 3-17, 1978, a vice-president of the Supreme Court described to them that his tribunal "deals with perhaps fifty to eighty appeals from the high people's courts, in any event, less than a hundred per year."[174]

In the annual report to the NPC on December 7, 1981, president Jiang Hua of the Supreme Court stated that from October 1980 to September 1981, the Court reviewed 632 criminal and 21 civil cases.[175] However in the 1982 report delivered on December 6, no similar data are offered for the period from October 1981 to September 1982.[176] Possibly no case ever came to it. Besides reviewing appeals, the Court has acted as a sort of Father Confessor in receiving personal

[169] Ibid.

[170] Donald Paragon, "Some firsthand observations on China's legal system," p. 483, col. 1.

[171] George Crocket and Morris Gleicher, op. cit., p. 410, col. 2.

[172] Donald Paragon, "Some firsthand observations on China's legal system," p. 483, col. 1; the same sort of information is obtained by Jerome Cohen, "Criminal law, reflections on the criminal process in China," p. 343, col. 2.

[173] Simon Luk, op. cit., p. 59, col. 3.

[174] Ruth Ginsburg, op. cit., p. 1520, col. 1.

[175] Renmin ribao, December 16, 1981, p. 2, cols. 1 and 2 respectively.

[176] The report is in ibid., December 17, 1982, p. 2.

audience and hearing of their grievances. On the basis of one person per visit, the following statistics are calculated.[177]

	criminal grievances	civil
Oct. 1980-Sept. 1981	15,000	15,800
Oct. 1981-Sept. 1982	17,700	12,300

The two reports made by Jiang Hua on the case work of the provincial courts at various levels yield the following figures.

	criminal settled by trial	civil	criminal by written	civil answers
Oct. 1980-Sept. 1981	250,000(a)	636,000(b)	24,000	n.a.
Oct. 1981-Sept. 1982	230,000	767,000	173,200	73,000

(a) first-instance cases 209,000 plus appellate cases 41,000
(b) first-instance cases 632,000, plus appellate cases 4,000

The reader's attention may be drawn to a) the written answers to criminal complaints ballooned from 24,000 to 173,000. This fact bespeaks of the regime's increasing concern with the rule of law and the mishandling of cases by the lower-level benches. b) Jiang Hua asserted a decline of both criminal and civil cases during 1981-1982 by 24.3 and 23.7 percent respectively. In regard to the first rate we noted in the section on crime and punishment that it was contradicted by other official information. Come to civil cases, instead of a decrease, there is an increase during the two reference years from 636,000 to 767,000. One Chinese source says that in 1980 such cases numbered 566,666 (see second section of the preceding chapter). Thus in the past three consecutive years, civil cases are steadily up. The strong possibility is that they will become more numerous on account of the diversified property ownership and the complex economic life of the people now given the green light to expand their production activity.

The procurator

The procuracy was established by a law of the first NPC in 1954,[178] destroyed in 1967 but revived in 1978.[179] During the Cultural Revolution, it was alleged that the agency had "questioned the legality of arrests and prosecutions insisted on by the police."[180] It had, therefore, to go lock, stock and barrel. Went it indeed! The field was then clear for the followers of the radicals and the public security machines to operate in. Although the 1978 Constitution (Article 43) has reinstalled the procuracy, its organization and competence were

[177] The comparative materials are drawn from the preceding two sources.

[178] Clarence McKee, "Commentary on the Chinese people's procurators," *The Journal of International Law and Economics*, no. 1, 1972, pp. 71-87 at 72, note 4. The law was enacted on September 21, 1954.

[179] *Renmin ribao*, July 13, 1981, p. 5; *Far Eastern Economic Review*, October 5, 1979, p. 57, col. 2.

[180] Jerome Cohen, "Will China have a formal legal system?" p. 1511, col. 2.

not spelled out until the middle of 1979.[181] As an instrument to maintain order, the procurator undoubtedly represents a major stride toward the rule of law. Any legislation, it is trite to say, depends for its effectiveness on the conscientious implementation. Unfortunately, the Chinese Reds have had a bad record in this respect. *Renmin ribao* acknowledged this. We quote it: "The laws we made are not faithfully executed. Even a wallposter can replace the Constitution."[182]

The Chinese procuracy is a plagiarism of the Soviet system and it has neither a counterpart in a democracy nor a predecessor in the Republic of China.[183] Article 5 of the Organic Law of the People's Procurators sets forth the following tasks: a) investigate grave offenses which involve betrayal and splitting of the country, b) study the cases discovered by itself, c) review the ones transmitted by public security bodies, d) file a protest in connection with court rulings or prosecute offenders, e) oversee the execution of criminal judgment and supervise prisons. Procurators are empowered, says Article 6, to hold officials responsible for breaching the law or encroaching on citizens' personal, democratic or other rights. On the strength of Article 9, the procuratorial authority is exercised "independently from the interference of administrative organs, groups or individuals." Legally, a valorous procurator can even take a Politburo member to court. Needless to say, this he cannot do. On the local level, too, a procurator is not known to be very "tough." The Chinese press writes, quite frequently, of local procurators' cowardice toward law-breaking relatives of party secretaries.[184] The arrest of any citizen, according to Article 12, must get his sanction or the sanction of a judge. More of this below. Said chief procurator Huang Hoqing that during the period from October 1981 to September 1982, there were 180,000 arrests by procuratorial warrants.[185] But he did not tell of the number of judicial warrants. A procurator is vested, by Articles 17 and 18, with the right to protest all errors found in the final judgment of a court to a higher tribunal. If he finds that the public security body does not have enough evidence to hand a suspect over to the court, he can order his release at once or demand that body to look into the case more thoroughly (Articles 11 and 13).

A check-and-balance mechanism is deliberately set up among the court, the public security organ and the procurator.[186] This is in reaction to the destruction of the balance in the 1975 Constitution. Article 25, section 2 of that document says the procuratorial power

---

[181] *Renmin ribao*, July 6, 1978. It took effect on January 1, 1980.

[182] *Ibid.*, December 2, 1982, p. 3.

[183] Beverly Carl, *op cit.*, p. 1272.

[184] *Guangming ribao*, August 11, 1981, p. 1.

[185] *Renmin ribao*, December 17, 1982, p. 2, col. 3. He further stated that 184,441 persons were prosecuted (including last year's concluding cases).

[186] Peng Zhen, "Explanations on seven laws," p. 12, col. 2; Beverly Carl, *loc. cit.*

is exercised by public security offices and Article 89 states therefore: "No citizen may be arrested except by decision of people's court or with the sanction of a public security organ." Although the restored procuracy wields a power of control over this organ, there are restraints on it. Mention was made a little while ago of the judicial warrants. These are sanctioned by a) Article 12 of the Organic Law of the People's Procurators, b) Article 36 of the 1982 Constitution, and c) Articles 2 and 4 of the Apprehension Regulations issued on February 25, 1979.[187] All three provisions repeat the point that the arrest of a citizen can only be done by a security agency on the order of procuracy or court. If the agency's request of a warrant is refused by the procurator, there are two options for it. It may either go to the judge or to the refusing procurator's superior (Article 14, Apprehension Regulations). The latter official must make a prompt decision (*ibid.*) As for the relation between the procurator and the judge, if the latter regards the former's prosecution as lacking in evidence or unlawful, he can return it to him for more information or tell him to make corrections.[188]

In the matter of structure, the people's procuracy (we omit below the word people's) is patterned after the judicature. What was said of the latter is applicable here. There is the Supreme Procuracy whose chief is elected or dismissed by the NPC, and his deputies are decided by the Standing Committee.[189] Likewise, at the subnational level, a people's congress appoints or removes the principal procurator but its standing committee decides the deputy procurators.[190] The procuracy is organized both according to territorial division and specific function.[191] In the former category, there are provincial, prefectural and county procuracies. The county procuracy may, with the approval of the standing committee of the people's congress, set up branch offices in mining, land-development and forestry areas. In the latter (functional) category there are military, rail- and water-transport procuracies. No matter which kind, each procuracy establishes a procuratorial committee. This body operates by democratic centralism. Different from the counterpart on the court side (the judicial committee) a procuratorial committee is less democratic but it also involves people from the outside.[192] It is stated in Article 3 of the procuratorial law that if a procurator finds himself in the minority of the said committee in decision-making, he may not obey the majority. Instead, he can take his argument to the standing

---

[187] This piece of legislation can be found in *Renmin shou ce*, p. 428. It also appears in *Renmin ribao*, February 25, 1979.

[188] An article on criminal procuracy by Jing Mesheng, *Renmin ribao*, August 4, 1981, p. 5.

[189] Constitution, Article 60, clause 7; Article 65, clause 12.

[190] *Ibid.*, Article 104, paragraph 2; Organic Law of the People's Procurators, Article 22.

[191] Organic Law of the People's Procurators, Article 2.

[192] Clarence McKee, *op. cit.*, pp. 83, 84.

committee of the people's congress and ask for a final ruling on the question at issue. The reason why such kind of provision is not mentioned in Article 11 of the court law (on judicial committee) is probably that the government wants to avoid the impression of outside interference in court decisions. Admittedly, procuracy is more political than the court and one would expect that it be controlled by the political department, i.e., the people's congress.

Within the Supreme Procuracy there are criminal, law-and-order, prison, economic bureaus; and lower procuracies are authorized to institute the same.[193] There is an indication, as seen above, on the approximate number of officials on the Supreme Court (20), but there is none on the procuratorial counterpart. We know for sure that there is one chief procurator (Zheng Tianxiang) and six deputies (Yu Ping, Zhang Su, Chen Yangshan, Wang Fu, Li Shiying, Xi Zhangyuan).[194] Are there regular procurators as there are regular judges? Interestingly enough, American legal travelers to China often inquired about the size of the Supreme Court but no one seems to have asked information on the membership of the Supreme Procuracy or on anything else about that body. According to the report of these Americans, they have entered the courts to watch trials and entered the prisons, yet they have had no access to the procuracy. We do not know if there are D.A.'s among the visiting yankees, let us use a slang. (The Supreme Procuracy had 29 people in Sept. 1983)

The legislation enjoins that the security authority conducts a preliminary hearing to ascertain the indictability of a man. Should it be satisfied that a case is established, it submits a report to the procurator. If he disapproves of it, either no arrest can be made, or, where the man is already under custody, he has to be released. On the other hand, if the procurator concurs to the report, he may still make an investigation of his own. Having determined the guilt, he would lay charges before the court.[195] As seen above, there is an intricate relation among the three agencies of public security, procuracy and court. To use one commentator's words, the new system "provides a division of labor among them, principles for their cooperation and a delicately balanced series of mutual restraints."[196] Article 137 of the 1982 Constitution stipulates that the courts, the procurators and public security bodies shall, in handling cases, divide their functions, each assuming responsibility for its own work, and that they shall coordinate with each other and restrict each other to ensure accurate and effective application of the law. Witness also Peng Zhen's declaration to the NPC on June 26, 1979 that the three authorities are "to complement and restrict each other."[197] Not

193 Organic Law of the People's Procurators, Article 20.

194 *Zhong guo bai ke nian jian, op. cit.,* p. 46, col. 2; Donald Paragon, "Some firsthand observations on China's legal system," p. 483, note 8.

195 Donald Paragon, "Some firsthand observations on China's legal system," p. 479, col. 2.

196 *Far Eastern Economic Review,* October 5, 1979, p. 5, col. 3; Ruth Ginsburg, *op. cit.,* p. 1520, col. 1.

197 Peng Zhen, "Explanation on seven laws," p. 12, col. 2.

unexpectedly, though, he hastened to add that they all follow the "leadership of the party." It is the latter body which reigns supreme in that state, he was saying in effect. The security apparatus is formidable. It directs ca. 300,000 soldiers.[198] Up to April 1983, they had no command-chain. The contingents of each province or city was directed by its own security boss. The coordination, if any, was effected through working relations of these bosses. On April 15, 1983, a National Armed Police Command was set up.[199] To use the words of CCP Secretary Chen Pixian, "it has units in every corner of the country."[200] In the top echelon, the Minister of Public Security, Liu Fuzhi, is appointed concurrently its political commissar, and Li Gang takes over the commanding post. There is a deputy-commander, two deputy-commissars and a chief of general staff. The formation is composed of voluntary and compulsory elements and is to "execute the orders of the PLA."[201] As for the status and rights of the organization under discussion, it is just like the PLA. The task, according to the afore-mentioned Chen Pixian, combines "political-thought work" with the maintenance of peace and order.[202] The importance of this new body is testified by this work. The fact that its first work-conference lasted from April 19 to 27, 1983 indicates that there is so much to discuss and so much to plan! It is unknown yet whether the *wu zhuang min bing* (armed militia) is to be abolished. Surely, the security army's 300,000 will be increased tenfold, if it is to be a thought-police as well as an action-police. A more dreadful tool is awaiting the already over-controlled Chinese.

However mighty, the public security head has some aches and pains, or to abandon the metaphor, his job is not an enviable one. He is powerful, yet vulnerable. The first security chief was Luo Ruiqing, in office from 1949 to 1959,[203] and the second chief Xie Fuzhi in office from 1960 to 1972.[204] Passing away in 1978 and 1972 respectively, Lui Ruiqing was post-humously honored,[205] but Xie Fuzhi post-humously dishonored.[206] Hua Guofeng took over from Xie upon his death. His position undoubtedly boosted his power. It may have catapulted him to the premiership and party chairmanship.[207] It was his men who arrested the Gang of Four when the mourning period for Mao Zedong was over. Yet he was so unpopular that he could

[198] *Statesman's Yearbook*, 1979-1980, p. 337.

[199] *Renmin ribao*, April 6, 1983, p. 1.

[200] *Ibid.*, April 29, 1983, p. 6.

[201] *Ibid.*, April 6, 1983, p. 1.

[202] *Ibid.*, April 29, 1983, p. 6.

[203] Bill Brugger, *Contemporary China*, London: Croom Helm, 1977, p. 416.

[204] *Renmin ribao*, December 23, 1980, p. 4.

[205] *Xin hua ci dian, op. cit.*, p. 553, col. 1.

[206] "Written judgment of the Special Court," p. 16, col. 2; "Crimes of Kang Sheng and Xie Fuzhi," *Beijing Review*, March 2, 1981, pp. 16-19.

[207] *Current Biography Yearbook*, 1977, pp. 209-213 at 210.

not make good use of the machinery. In mid-1981, the 6th plenum of the 11th CC removed him from both the party chairmanship and the chairmanship of the Military Affairs Committee.[208] One of his faults was that he made many wrongful arrests in the aftermath of the Tian-an-men demonstration in April 1976. The public-security force was not mobilized to support Hua Guofeng against Deng Xiaoping and company. In the fall of 1977, it was officially taken away from Hua, and given to a relatively unknown man, Zhao Cangbi, a Deng Xiaoping protégé [Zhao replaced on June 20, 1983 by Liu Fuzhi]. We found it noteworthy that all the previous security bosses sat in the Politburo but Zhao and Liu did not sit there. They were just ordinary members of the Central Committee.[209] This reminds us of the succession in June 1953 of Lavrenti Beria as security head by a nonentity, S.N. Kruglov. Both Moscow and Beijing obviously see eye to eye here: a potential post may not go to an already prominent figure lest he should build it handily into a juggernaut.

The remainder of this section is devoted to the power of arrest and detention. On December 20, 1954, the Apprehension Regulations were issued,[210] but they were not honored ever since, particularly during the Cultural Revolution. The normalization-bent leadership subsequently came up with a new set of rules. These were officially promulgated by the sixth session of the fifth NPC Standing Committee on December 23, 1979. Two days later, they went into effect.[211] Interestingly enough, the 1957 Control Act is left to stand (ordains Article 14 of the Regulations); this Act grants the police untrammeled discretion to deal with citizens regarded as threatening peace and order under the pretext not of criminal infliction but of "order-management and chastisement." As if to hammer home the significance of the Act, the government had it republished or rather republicized in *Renmin ribao*.[212] A comparison of the Regulations and the Act shows a) that the procuracy and court exercise no oversight on the police power under the Act and b) that detention is limited to three days under the Regulations (Article 8), but it is set at from five to fifteen days under the Act (Articles 1, 17).

There are seven situations which require summary detention by the Regulations. The sixth situation which is of some interest concerns "any curious-looking person who is suspect of having done something terribly wrong." Also sanctioned is citizens' arrest of men who are under search warrant or are being hotly pursued by the police (Article 7). Given these rules, one finds it understandable that, to quote a statement made by one Chinese to foreign visitors, "all through China,

[208] *Renmin ribao* and *Guangming ribao*, June 30, 1981, both on p. 1.

[209] *Zhong guo shou ce*, op. cit., p. 129.

[210] *Renmin shou ce*, p. 423, col. 2.

[211] *Renmin ribao*, December 23, 1979.

[212] *Ibid.*, February 23, 1979.

we have mass surveillance."[213] Any new face showing up in a community, to repeat a point previously made by us, would be tipped off at once to the authorities or grabbed to them by the masses. Upon arrest, the man's relatives must be told within 24 hours of his whereabouts (Article 3). They are also to be informed of the reason for his arrest. If the security officers carry out a summary detention, they are required to report the criminal activities and proof of these activities to the procurators within three days (Article 8). This period may be prolonged to four days. The procurators must, within three days of the report, make a decision whether to issue the warrant to legalize the detention. If their decision is negative, the detained ought to be released. It is stipulated in Article 12 that the interrogation of the detained or arrested should take place within 24 hours following the detention or arrest. Presumably the interrogation may call for three or more days for completion. Hence the 3- or 4-day provision of Article 8. Another important point to be noted is that in case of illegal arrest or detention, the officers are to be punished if it is known that they committed this act out of personal malice to frame an individual (Article 13). This provision reflects the leadership's concern with what occurred during the Cultural Revolution.

Is the 24-hour interrogation rule observed? This question was put by delegates of the Prairie Canada-China Friendship Association while visiting Beijing on May 9, 1979 to Zhang Zhongli, member of the Institute of Jurisprudence, the Academy of Social Sciences. Replied he: "Our country is so vast and transportation is difficult. For instance, in Qinghai province, if a county court wants to send a man to a commune, it takes two days. In the event of a storm, it takes longer. It is impossible, that is, to abide by the 24-hour rule."[214] The defendant, he went on, "are wrong to think that if we do not release him immediately within 24 hours, it is a violation of the law." The place of arrest, he was saying, is often without a detention facility. The nearest place which has it may be several days away by walking. Zhang is honest in front of that Sinophile group that the breach of the law is caused by nature but not by man.

The prison

A major task of the procurator is the superintendance of the prisons, according to Article 5 of the procuratorial law. It behoves us, therefore, to discuss it here. As said in Chapter VI, there are only two organizations in the Chinese government which do not bear the magic word "people." One is the State Council and the other is the jail. Zhou Enlai, we suspect, must have declined the naming of his constituency People's State Council. On the other hand, all the oligarchs seem to disdain the term "people's prison." "Let the Italian Reds have it!"

213 Michael Roskin, *Countries and conceptions, an introduction to comparative politics*, Englewood Cliffs, New Jersey: Prentice-Hall, 1982, p. 313.

214 Ronald Keith, *op. cit.*, p. 120.

they may have agreed. The purpose of punishment is allegedly one of rehabilitation, but not revenge.[215] Mao Zedong said that "prisons should be turned into schools, factories and farms.[216] They are to reeducate the law-breakers through work." Mao's idea is largely realized. Tourists' accounts tell us that there is no jail in the CPR which literally puts persons behind bars. It goes without saying that if there are solitary confinements, foreigners cannot see them. All inmates receive no pay for laboring. To the prison population, the socialist order "from each according to his ability, to each according to his work" does not apply.[217] The products of the Shanghai prison, said Beverly Carl, brought in twenty million yuan in 1978.[218] In the same year, two other Americans toured the same prison and saw a "complete printing plant [which] was producing commercial advertising literature, boxes and cartons with good quality, four-color copy about soap, perfume, auto parts and other products obviously destined for export to English-speaking countries."[219] The yearly output, they said, was upwards of $10 million. This amount jibes with the one reported by Carl, giving the exchange rate of one yuan roughly to fifty cents of US money.

Prisoners have eight hours' sleep and eight hours' work. The rest of the day is just for rest.[220] Educational materials are, not unexpectedly, the writings of Marx, Lenin and Mao Zedong, plus the constitution, newspapers and radio transcripts. Rewards go to those who reform exceptionally well. The models are said to be released earlier. Another privilege is that they can wear their own clothes. Everyone is given pocket money and provided with a job after having served his time. One's family can visit him once a month, but conjugation is absolutely prohibited. A ward was asked in 1978 by Beverly Carl about the escape problems. He replied that no such problem arose in recent years. "There was no point in escaping," he explained, "because in this highly organized economy, there would be no place for an escapee to go."[221]

Since that time (1978), the picture has changed. There are escapees now, and many of them in fact. Newspapers do not report on their going but on their coming. *Renmin ribao* revealed that within a week, 22 escapees of Shanghai prisons turned themselves in. Of them, 6 did it on their own volition and 16 were sent back by the next

[215] Zhou Zheng and Liu Bin, "Bid farewell to yesterday, a reformatory near Qinhuangdao," *Beijing Review*, January 17, 1983, pp. 19-25.

[216] Beverly Carl, *op. cit.*, p. 1272.

[217] Constitution, Article 6.

[218] Beverly Carl, *op. cit.*, p. 1273.

[219] George Crocket and Morris Gleicher, *op. cit.*, p. 414, col. 1.

[220] "Reforming criminals," *Beijing Review*, February 23, 1981, pp. 22-29 at 27, col. 2.

[221] Beverly Carl, *op. cit.*, p. 1272. Michael Roskin, loc. cit.

GOVERNMENT OF SOCIALIST CHINA

[222] In Wuhan, 106 escapees walked back to their cells according *Guangming ribao*.[223] Some inmates even made good their fleeing Hong Kong and Macao but came home from there.[224] The paper said they could not get work permits in the colonies, betraying that it is not because they were fond of prisons of the People's Republic. The seriousness of the escape problem is underscored by the fact that the NPC Standing Committee had to pass the grace ordinance that no reprisal would be taken against the escapees if they turned themselves in before July 10, 1981.[225] Although no escapee statistics are given in the paper, their number must be sizeable. Otherwise the government would not bother to take that action. The apparent increase of escapees can be explained by saying that in the past several years there was no longer a "highly organized economy" in the CPR as it was before 1978. Consequently, an inmate may find a place to hide inside China and he can even get out of it, making his way to Hong Kong or Macao.

Prisoners are either political or non-political. As stated previously the former kind of prisoners were said to be a "mere 0.5 percent." They are divided into three classes: a) historical counterrevolutionaries who were officers of the Guomindang and some of whom are said to be freed long ago, b) spies or agents of foreign governments, c) "new-born counterrevolutionaries." Article 18 of the 1978 Constitution calls this group "new-born bourgeois elements and other bad elements." They are alleged to "undermine the socialist revolution by spreading counterrevolutionary slogans or hindering production."[226] Now that the Gang of Four are gone, very few of the third group are left, it is claimed.[227] The 1982 Constitution no longer talks of new-born bourgeois elements.

Female prisoners are about 8 to 9 percent. In a Shanghai jail which two American lawyers visited there were 2,753 inmates, including 200 women.[228] In another jail, near Shanghai, out of 1,900 convicts, women numbered 125.[229] As a rule, they are not imprisoned during pregnancy or nursing. In this period, they may remain outside, but under the surveillance of the masses, i.e., neighbors or co-workers. It is only after nursing that they are brought back if their term is a long one. If it is short, the remaining time need not be served.[230]

[222] *Renmin ribao*, June 23, 1981, p. 4.

[223] *Guangming ribao*, August 4, 1981, p. 1.

[224] *Renmin ribao*, July 13, 1981, p. 4.

[225] *Ibid.*, June 23, 1981, p. 4; *Guangming ribao*, June 24, 1981, p. 4.

[226] Beverly Carl, *op. cit.*, p. 1273.

[227] *Ibid.*

[228] George Crocket and Morris Gleicher, *op. cit.*, p. 414, col. 1.

[229] Donald Paragon, "The administration of justice and law in new China," p. 583, col. 2.

[230] "Reforming criminals," p. 25, col. 1.

BIBLIOGRAPHY

"Academic discussion about Confucius," *Beijing Review*, May 30, 1983, p. 7.

Agafonov, S., "KNR-SShA: stragegiya obmana" (The CPR-US strategy of deception), *Izvestiya*, January 24, 1982, p. 4.

Agressiya pekina protiv v'etnama (The aggression of Beijing against Vietnam), Moskva: Iurid. lit., 1981.

Akimov, V.I., "Kitai, estestvennye i tekhnicheskye nauki" (China, natural and technical sciences of), *Bol'shaya sovetskaya entsiklopediya*, 3rd ed., Moskva: Izdatel'stvo "sovetskaya entsiklopediya," 1973, vol. 12, cols. 664-671.

"Kitai, narodnaya respublika, nauchnye uchrezhdeniya" (China, the CPR, scientific institutions of), *Bol'shaya sovetskaya entsiklopediya*, 3rd ed., Moskva: Izdatel'stvo "sovetskaya entsiklopediya," 1973, vol. 12, cols. 683-684.

"Kitaiskaya akademiya nauk" (The Chinese academy of sciences), *Bol'shaya sovetskaya entsiklopediya*, 3rd ed., Moskva: Izdatel'stvo "sovetskaya entsiklopediya," 1973, vol. 12, cols. 715-716.

et alii, "Result of the 'host decade' and China's economic situation," *Far Eastern Affairs* (Moscow), 2 (1979), pp. 53-70.

Aleksandrov, I., "K sovetsko-kitaiskim otnosheniyam" (On Soviet-Chinese relations), *Pravda*, May 20, 1982, pp. 4, 5.

Aleksandrov, V.A., "Imperiya tsin i russkoe gosudarstvo v xvii veke" (The Empire of Qing and the Russian state in the 17th century), *Voprosy istorii*, 5 (1982), pp. 125-128. Review of a book with that title by V.S. Myasnikov put out by Moskva: "Nauka," 1980.

Alford, William P. and David E. Birenbaum, "Ventures in the China trade, an analysis of China's emerging legal framework for the regulation of foreign investment," *Northwestern Journal of International Law and Business*, 3 (spring 1981), pp. 56-102.

Altaiskii, M.L., "Maoizm" (Maoism), *Bol'shaya sovetskaya entsiklopediya*, 3rd ed., Moskva: Izdatel'stvo "sovetskaya entsiklopediya," 1974, vol. 15, cols. 1035-1039.

"Analysis of Chinese contractual policy and practice," *Wayne Law Review*, 27 (spring 1981), pp. 1299-1358.

Andreev, M.A., "Ekonomicheskie otnosheniya kitaya s gosudarstvami ACEAN" (Economic relations of China with the ASEAN nations), *Probl. dal. vostoka*, 3 (1981), pp. 112-121.

Apalin, A., "Peking: a course towards provoking a world war," *Far Eastern Affairs* (Moscow), 3 (1979), pp. 110-126.

Ardvin, J., "Making contact," *Opera News*, 46 (March 6, 1982), pp. 28-29. S. Caldwell conducts the Central Opera.

Arnold, C.R., "With a client in China," *Commercial Law Journal*, 87 (April 1982), pp. 170-175.

Arnold, Julean and Roman H. Myers, *Commercial Handbook of China*, New York: Garland, 1981, 2 vols.

Arthur Frommer's Guide to China, 1981-1982, New York: Frommer-Pasmantier, 1981.

"An artfully vague policy, Reagan makes a China deal," *Time*, August 30, 1982, p. 19.

Azif, Herbert B., *China Trade: A Guide to Doing Business with the People's Republic of China*, Coral Spring, Florida: China research, 1981.

"Ba gao deng xue xiao ling dao ban zi jian she de geng hao"(Improve the education of the leading cadres of higher education), *Guangming ribao*, February 24, 1981, p. 1.

Bai, Dongcai, ''Zheng que dui dai shuang bao ze ren zhi'' (Treat correctly the double-responsibility system), *Renmin ribao*, June 29, 1982, p. 2.

Bao, Ruo-wang and Cheminski Rudolf, *Prisoner of Mao*, New York: Penguin Books, 1973. In French, Paqualini, Jean et Rudolf Cheminski, *Prisonnier de Mao, sept ans dans un camp de travail en China* (Prisoner of Mao, seven years in a labor camp in China), Paris: Gallimard, 1975.

Barakhta, B., ''Chto stavyat na kon? kolonka kommentatora'' (What are the stakes? a commentator's column), *Pravda*, January 4, 1982, p. 5.

''Kitai: politika otkrytykh dverei'' (China: an open-door policy), *Pravda*, June 25, 1982, p. 5, cols. 5-8.

''Pekin: reanimatsiya maoizma'' (Beijing: Maoism revived), *Pravda*, January 30, 1982, p. 5.

Barnett, A. Doak, *Cadres, Bureaucracy, and Political Power in Communist China*, New York: Columbia University Press, 1967.

China's Economy in Global Perspective, Washington: Brookings Institution, 1981.

Barthes, Roland, *Et la Chine?* (And China?), Paris: Bourgois, 1976.

Bartke, Wolfgang, ''Analyse der Politbürofunktionäre des 11. zk der KPCH, nach dem Stand von August 1979'' (An analysis of the Politburo members of the 11th plenum of the CCP after the August 1979 decision), *China aktuell*, j. 8, 1979, Juliheft, s. 836-843.

Oil in the People's Republic of China, Industry Structure, Production, Exports, Montreal: McGill-Queen's University Press, 1977.

''Das schicksal der chinesischen fuhrung aus der zeit vor der kultur-revolution'' (The fate of the Chinese leadership from the time before the cultural revolution), *China aktuell*, j. 7, 1979, Januarheft, s. 871-875.   -

''Die Verschwundung Mitglieder des 11. zk der KPCH'' (The disappearance of the members of the 11th CC), *China aktuell*, j. 8, 1979, maiheft, s. 590-592.

et alii, ''Die 4. Plenartagung des 11. Zentralkomitees der Kommunistischen Partei Chinas, 25-28/9, 1979'' (The fourth plenum of the 11th CC of the CCP, September 25-28, 1979), *China aktuell*, j. 8, 1979, Septemberheft, s. 1027-1031.

Bartlett, Magnus, ed., *All China Guide*, Chicago: Rand McNally, 1981.

Bauchau, Henry, *Mao Zedong*, Paris: Flammarion, 1982.

Bauer, Wolfgang, ''Das erwachsende einhorn, konstanten und perspektiven für das China von heute'' (A growing unicorn, stability and perspective of the present-day China), *Mercur* (Stuttgart), j. 33, 1979, no. 1, s. 19-31.

Baxter, I.F.G., ''Business with the People's Republic of China,'' *Canadian bar review*, 59 (June 1981), pp. 337-370.

Bazhanov, E.P., *Dvizhushchie sily politiki SShA v otnosnehii kitaya* (The moving force in the policy of the United States toward China), Moskva: ''Nauka'', 1982.

Beer, Patrice de, *La guerre civile en China* (Civil War in China), Paris: Casterman, 1968.

''Behind the US-China war of nerves,'' *US news and world report*, 92 (April 26, 1982), p. 6.

Bell, Olive Elizabeth, ''People's Republic of China, personal income tax,'' *Georgia journal of international and comparative law*, 11 (summer 1981), pp. 373-385.

Belov, E.A., ''Gomin'dan'' (Guomindang), *Bol'shaya sovetskaya entsiklopediya*, 3rd ed., Moskva: Izdatel'stvo ''sovetskaya entsiklopediya,'' 1972, vol. 7, cols. 143-145.

''Sin'khaiskaya revoliutsiya'' (The 1911 revolution), *Bol'shaya sovetskaya entsiklopediya*, 3rd ed., Moskva: Izdatel'stvo ''sovetskaya entsiklopediya,'' 1976, vol. 23, cols. 1312-1313.

"Tunmenkhoi" (The Tongmenghui), *Bol'shaya sovetskaya entsiklopediya,* 3rd ed., Moskva: Izdatel'stvo "sovetskaya entsiklopediya," 1977, vol. 26, cols. 929-930.

Beonio Brocchieri, Paolo, "Normalizzazione fra cina e usa" (The normalization of Sino-American relations), *Relazioni internazionali,* vol. 42, 1978, no 51-52, p. 1139.

Berger, Ya. M., "Kitai, ekonomicheskogo-geograficheskii ocherk" (China, economic geography of), *Bol'shaya soverskaya entsiklopediya,* 3rd ed., Moskva: Izdatel'stvo "sovetskaya entsiklopediya," 1973, vol. 12, cols. 648-659.

i S.I. Bruk, "Kitai, naselenie" (China, population of), *Bol'shaya sovetskaya entsiklopediya,* 3rd ed., Moskva: Izdatel'stvo "sovetskaya entsiklopediya," 1973, vol. 12, cols. 606-607.

Bergere, Marie-Claire, *Le nationalisme chinois et le mouvement du 4 mai 1919,* (Chinese nationalism and the May Fourth Movement of 1919), Paris: Publ. orientalistes France, 1978.

Bergeron, Maria, *Lettres à Yéon-Wen, mes prisons en China* (Letters to Yeou-Wen, my prisons in China), Paris: Delarge J.P., 1974.

Berman, J. Berman, Susan Cohen and Malcolm Russell, "A comparison of the Chinese and Soviet codes of criminal law and procedure," Chinese criminal code symposium, *Criminal law and criminology,* 73 (spring 1982), pp. 238-316.

Bernstein, Richard, *From the center of the earth, the search for truth about China,* Boston: Little, Brown, 1982.

Bettelheim, Charles, *Fragen über China nach Mao Tse-tungs tod* (Problems of China after the death of Mao Zedong), übers. von Walle Bengs, Dorothea Muenk, et Nina Ottomeyer, Berlin: Verlag kantstrasse Br., 1978.
Questions sur la Chine après la mort de Mao Tse-toung (Questions in China after the death of Mao Zedong), Paris: Maspero, 1978.

Biehl, Max, *Die landwirtschaft in China und Indien, vergleich zweier entwicklungswege* (Agriculture in China and India, a comparison of two ways of development), Frankfurt: Diesterweg/KNO, 1979.

Blagodatov, A.V., *Zapiski o kitaiskoi revoliutsii, 1925-1927* (Notes on the Chinese revolution of 1925-1927), Moskva: "Nauka," 1979.

Blake, C. Fred, *Ethnic Groups and Social Change in a Chinese Market-town,* Honolulu: University Press of Hawaii, 1981.

"Bliukher, Vasilii Konstantinovich," *Bol'shaya sovetskaya entsiklopediya,* 3rd ed., Moskva: Izdatel'stvo "sovetskaya entsiklopediya," 1970, vol. 3, cols. 1290-1291.

Bloodworth, Dennis, *Mao Tse-tung and the ironies of power,* Toronto: McCleland and Stewart, 1982.

Blum, Robert, *The United States and China in World Affairs,* New York: McGraw-Hill, 1966.

Bonavia, David, *The Chinese,* New York: Harper and Row, 1980.
"The fate of the 'new born things' of China's cultural revolution," *Pacific Affairs* (New York), vol. 51, 1978, no. 2, pp. 177-194.

Borisov, O., *Iz istorii sovetsko-kitaiskikh otnoshenii v 50-kh godakh, k diskussii v KNR o maotszedune* (From history of the Soviet-Chinese relation in the 1950's, a discussion in the People's Republic of China on Mao Zedong), izd. 2-e dop., Moskva: Mezhdunar. otnosheniya, 1982.
Iz istorii sovetsko-kitaiskihk otnoshenii (From the history of Sino-Soviet relations), Moskva: Mezhdunar. otnosheniya, 1981.

i B.T. Koloskov, *Sovetsko-kitaiskie otnosheniya, 1949-1979* (Sino-Soviet relations, 1949-1979), Moskva: Izd-vo "Mysl'," 1980.

502   GOVERNMENT OF SOCIALIST CHINA

Borisov, V., "Vneshnepoliticheskii kurs Pekina" (Foreign policy of Beijing), *Mirovaya ekonomika i mezhdunarodnye otnosheniya*, 8 (1978), pp. 17-25.

"Borodin, Mikail Markovich," *Bol'shaya sovetskaya entsiklopediya*, 3rd ed., Moskva: Izdatel'stvo "sovetskaya entsiklopediya," 1970, vol. 3, cols. 1720-1721.

Borontsov, V.B., *Kitai i SShA, 70-e gody* (China and the US in the 70's), Moskva: "Nauka," 1979.

Borsa, Giorgio, "La crisi cinese, un interpretazione in chive storica" (The crises of China, an interpretation of key historical events), *Relazioni internazionali*, vol. 24, 1976, no. 17, pp. 396-397.

Bouc, Alain, *La rectification, les nouveaux dirigeants chinois* (The rectification, the new directors of China), Lyon, France: Federop, 1978.

Mao Tsé-toung ou la révolution approfondis (Mao Zedong or extensive revolution), Paris: Seuil, 1975.

Brahm, Heinz, "Sowjetische intellektuelle über die chinesische Gefähr" (The Soviet intellectuals on the Chinese peril), *Osteuropa*, bd. 28, 1978, Heft 2, s. 150-166.

Braumann, Freddy, *Partizipation und betriebsorganization in China* (The participation and managerial organization in China), Bochum: Brockmeyer, Norbert, 1979.

Bressi, Giovanni, "Dopo la morte di Chou En-lai" (After the death of Zhou Enlai), *Relazioni internazionali*, vol. 40, 1976, no. 3, pp. 32-33.

"La cina un anno dopo" (China, a year after), *Relazioni internazionali*, vol. 41, 1977, no. 38, p. 878.

"L'ammodernamento della cina" (The modernization of China), *Relazioni internazionali*, vol. 42, 1978, no. 44, pp. 978-979.

"Qua cosa si muove tra cina e urss" (Thus things are moving between China and the USSR), *Relazioni internazionali*, vol. 40, 1976, no. 47, p. 112.

"Qualche novità fra cina e urss" (Something new between China and the USSR), *Relazioni internazionali*, vol. 40, 1976, no. 27, p. 652.

Breyer, Siegfried, et alii, *Die marine der volksrepublik China heute* (The navy of the CPR today), München: Bernard & Graefe, 1980.

"A brief introduction to Sun Yefang's economic theory," *Beijing Review*, June 13, 1983, pp. 16-19.

Broyelle, Claudie, Jacques Broyelle et Evelyne Tschirhart, *Deuxieme retour de Chine* (The second China tour), Paris: Seuil, 1979.

Brugger, Bill, *China: Radicalism to Revisionism, 1962-1979*, Totowa, New Jersey: Barnes and Noble Books, 1981.

ed., *China Since the Gang of Four*, New York: St. Martin, 1980.

Contemporary China, London: Croom Helm, 1977.

"Bu zhun chen gai ge zhi ji fen zhan guo jia cai wu" (Do not take advantage of the reform to take state property), *Renmin ribao*, May 3, 1983, p. 1

Buckley, W.F., "Fighters for Taiwan," *National review*, 74 (February 19, 1982), p. 193.

Burlatskii, F.M., *Mao Tszedun i ego nasledniki* (Mao Zedong and his successors), Moskva: Mezhdunar. otnosheniya, 1980.

Mao Tszedun, ideiskopsikhologicheskii portret (Mao Zedong, an ideological and psychological portrait), Moskva: Progress, 1980.

Bussac, Alain de, *La China attentive* (The attentive China), Clermont-Fer, France: Soprep, 1979.

Butterfield, Fox, *China: alive in the bitter sea*, New York: Times books, 1982.

Cadart, Claude, *et alii*, "Où va la Chine? où va-t-elle donc? l'impossible duumvirate" (Whither does China go? whither will she go then? the impossibility of the duumvirate), *Esprit, changer la culture et la politique*, 1978, no. 2, pp. 90-109.

Cai, Hesheng, *Cai Hesheng wen ji* (Collected writings of Cai Hesheng), Beijing: Ren min chu ban she, 1981.

La campagne chinoise, une grande école pour les jeunes (The Chinese countryside, a great school for the youths), trad. chinois, Beijing: n.p., 1977.

Carmichael, Peter, *China*, Würzburg: Universitatsdruckerei H. Stürtz AG, 1982. In French: *Chine*, Paris: Weber-diffusion, 1982.

"Caught in the squeeze," *Time*, 119 (May 24, 1982), p. 56.

Cerretelli, Adriana, "Luci e ombre sul commercio cino-americano" (The light and shade of Sino-American commerce), *Relazioni internazionali, j. 43, 1979, no. 6, pp. 109-110.*

"Certain measures of capitalism," *Time*, April 4, 1983, p. 45.

Chande, N., and R. Delfs, "The Taiwan question," *World press review*, 29 (January 1982), p. 29.

"Changing signals on US-China policy," *US news and world report*, 92 (January 25, 1982), p. 12. Proposed sale of warplanes to Taiwan.

Changjiang: the longest river in China, Distributor: China books & periodicals, San Francisco, 1981.

"Chen Du-siu" (Chen Duxiu), *Bol'shaya sovetskaya entsiklopediya*, 3rd ed., Moskva: Izdatel'stvo "sovetskaya entsiklopediya," 1978, vol. 27, col. 784.

Chen, Licheng and Tan Shizhong, "Developing countries' role in world economy," *Beijing Review*, March 28, 1983, pp. 13-16.

Chen, Weihang, "Xue xiao feng qi yu jiao you mu di" (The morale of a school and the objectives of education), *Guangming ribao*, February 14, 1981, p. 1.

Chen, Yi, "Chen Yi tong zhi gei di ba shi ling dao tong zhi de xin" (A letter of comrade Chen Yi to the commanding comrades of the 8th division), *Renmin ribao*, December 16, 1981, p. 3; written October 4, 1946.

Chen, Yun, "Jian she gui mo yao he guo li xiang she ying" (The construction size must be in consonance with the strength of the country), *Renmin ribao*, May 6, 1983, p. 1.

"Yao jiang zhen li, bu yao jiang mian zi" (To talk of truth, not of face-saving), *Renmin ribao*, December 31, 1981, p. 1; also in *Guangming ribao*, same date, p. 1. A reprint of a speech of May 9, 1945.

Cheng, Chu-yuan, *China's economic development; growth and structural change*, Boulder, Colorado: Westview, 1982.

Cherapanov, A.I., *Severnyi pokhov natsional'no-revoliutsionnoi armii kitaya* (Northern expedition of the national-revolutionary army of China), Moskva: "Nauka," 1968.

Zapiski voennogo sovetnika v kitae (Notes of Soviet military advisors in China), Moskva: Progress, 1981.

Chesneaux, Jan, *Sun Yat-sen,* Paris: Presses universitaires de France, 1982.

Chesneaux, Jean, *Le mouvement paysan chinois (1840-1949)* (The peasant movement in China, 1840-1949), Paris: Seuil, 1976.

et alii, Histoire de la Chine, 4. Un nouveau communisme, 1949-1976, de la libération à la mort de Mao Zedong (History of China, vol. 4, New communism, 1949-1976, from the liberation to the demise of Mao Zedong), Paris: Hatier, 1977.

"China grants tax cuts for joint ventures," *Beijing Review*, May 9, 1983, p. 7.

"China-USSR border to open," by Stanley Oziewicz, *The Globe and Mail*, June 6, 1983, p. 9.

504   GOVERNMENT OF SOCIALIST CHINA

China und seine Christen, ein neuer Weg (China and her Christians, a new way), Hrsg: Evangel. missionswerk, Hamburg: Redakt. Kürschner, Frank, Göttingen: Vandenboeck & Ruprecht, 1982.

"China's ethnic policy meets a cultural great wall," by Stanley Oziewicz, *The Globe and Mail,* June 16, 1983, p. 4.

"China's joint venture laws, first of the economic laws," *ASILs international law journal,* 4 (winter 1980), pp. 45-69.

"China's marriage law," *Beijing Review,* March 16, 1981, pp. 24-27.

"China's national minorities," *Beijing Review,* May 23, 1983, pp. 19-21.

"China's new joint venture law, analysis and economic overview," *Boston college international and comparative law review,* 4 (spring 1981), pp. 115-148.

China's socialist economy, distributor: China books and periodicals, San Francisco, 1981.

"China's wild west," by Stanley Oziewicz, *The Globe and Mail,* June 14, 1983, p. 4.

Chine, Paris: Nagel, 1978.

La Chine, Paris: Grund, 1980.

La Chine interpelle l'eglise (China questions the church), Paris: Beauchesne, 1979.

La Chine vue de sa périphérie (China viewed from the periphery), Paris: Minuit, 1976.

"Chinese ambassador to the USA on Sino-US relations," *Beijing Review,* May 16, 1983, pp. 14-15.

"Chinese bishop urges stand on subversion," *The Globe and Mail,* June 14, 1983, p. 2.

The Chinese Communist Movement, a Report of the United States War Department, July 1945, edited by Lyman P. Van Slyke, Stanford, California: Stanford University Press, 1968.

"Chinese income law is a model of brevity," translation of newly adopted foreign enterprise income tax law of the People's Republic of China, *Tax notes,* 14 (January 4, 1982), pp. 33-34.

"Chinese leaders on Sino-Japanese relations," *Beijing Review,* May 9, 1983, p. 9.

Chinois si vous saviez (The Chinese, if you knew), Paris: Bourgois, 1978.

Chistaldi, Sara, "Il raporti cina-urss" (The Sino-Soviet relations), *Relazioni internazionali,* vol. 40, 1976, no. 38, p. 864.

Chopra, Mahara K., "China nach Mao" (China after Mao), *Europäische wehrkunde* (München) j. 27, 1978, Heft 11, s. 554-563.

Choudhury, G.W., "China's policy toward south Asia," *Current History,* no. 446, vol. 76, (1979), pp. 155-158, 181-183.

Chuikov, V.I., *Missiya v kitae, zapiski voen. sovetnika* (Mission to China, notes of Soviet military advisors), Moskva: "Nauka," 1981.

"Chzhan, Siue-lyan" (Zhang Xueliang), *Bol'shaya sovetskaya entsiklopediya,* 3rd ed., Moskva: Izdatel'stvo "sovetskaya entsiklopediya," 1978, vol. 29, col. 532.

"Chzhan, Tszo-lin" (Zhang Zuolin), *Bol'shaya sovetskaya entsiklopediya,* 3rd ed., Moskva: Izdatel'stvo "sovetskaya entsiklopediya," 1979, vol. 29, col. 534.

"Chzhan, Ven'-tyan' " (Zhang Wentian), *Bol'shaya sovetskaya entsiklopediya,* 3rd ed., Moskva: Izdatel'stvo "sovetskaya entsiklopediya," 1978, vol. 29, cols. 531-532.

Clark, H.R., "Untying the knot in China (divorce)," *Time,* 119 (February 15, 1982), p. 52.

Clubb, O.E., "America's China policy," *Current* (Washington D.C.), 237 (November 1981), pp. 24-33.

The 20th Century China, 2nd ed., New York: Columbia University Press, 1972.

Cohen, Jerome, "Foreword, China's criminal code," Chinese criminal code symposium, *Criminal law and criminology*, 73 (spring 1982), pp. 135-137.

"Communiqué on fulfilment of China's 1982 national economic plan," issued on April 29, 1983 by the State Statistical Bureau, *Beijing Review*, May 9, 1983, pp. II-XII.

"Congress to name president of China," *The Globe and Mail*, June 6, 1983, p. 9.

Covell, Ralph R., "Peking magazine, the first periodical devoted exclusively to the reform in China," *Journal of Asian History* (Wiesbaden), vol. 11, 1977, no. 2, pp. 95-120.

"Crimes of Kang Sheng and Xie Fuzhi," *Beijing Review*, March 2, 1981, pp. 16-19.

Criminal law of the People's Republic of China, adopted by the second meeting of the fifth session of the National People's Congress, July 1, 1979, Chinese criminal code symposium, *Criminal law and criminology*, 73 (spring 1982), pp. 138-203.

Crisa, Danièle, *et alii*, *Chine*, Paris: Centre delta, 1980.

Croll, Elisabeth, *The Politics of Marriage in Contemporary China*, New York: Cambridge University Press, 1981.

Curtin, Katie, *Les femmes dans la revolution chinoise* (Women in the Chinese revolution), Paris: Breche, 1979.

"Da dan xuan ba shi yong nong gou da kai xin ju mian de gan bu" (Bravely select and use the cadres who are able to open a new era), *Renmin ribao*, July 6, 1982, p. 1.

"Dang zhong yang hao zhao quan guo jun min jing xing ai guo zhu yi jiao you" (The party center appeals to the armed forces and the people of the entire nation to start patriotic education), *Renmin ribao*, July 10, 1982, p. 1.

Daniel, Donald C., "Sino-Soviet relations in naval perspective," *Orbis*, 24 (winter 1981), pp. 787-803.

Dao i daoizm v kitae (Dao and daoism in China), Moskva: "Nauka", 1982.

Daubier, Jean, *Les nouveaux maitres de la Chine* (The new masters of China), Paris: Grasset, 1979.

Davydov, A.P., *Profsoiuzy kitaya: istoriya i sovremennost'* (The trade unions of China, past and present), Moskva: Profizdat, 1981.

"Defying death," *Time*, February 7, 1983, p. 32.

Deliusin, L.P., *Spor o sotsializme v kitae* (The argument on socialism in China), 2nd ed., Moskva: "Nauka", 1979.

Deng, Xiaoping, "Deng: cleaning up Mao's 'feudal mistakes,' " interview by Oriana Fallaci, *The Guardian*, September 21, 1980, pp. 17-18.

"Deng Xiaoping tong zhi tan duan zheng dang feng wen ti" (Comrade Deng Xiaoping on the rectification of the party morale), *Renmin ribao*, November 2, 1981, pp. 1, 3; also in *Hongqi*, no. 21, 1981.

"Deng on the world communist movement," *Beijing Review*, May 9, 1983, pp. 8-9. *Deng Xiaoping xuan ji*, Beijing: Renmin chu ban she, 1983.

Deng, Yingchao, "Huan qing yu hui yi" (Rejoice and recollect), *Guangming ribao*, June 29, 1981, pp. 1, 2.

"Jian deng bu yi de gao hao dang feng" (To improve unswervingly the party morale), *Renmin ribao*, March 28, 1981, pp. 1, 4.

Di san ci guo gong nei zhan da shi yue biao (Major events by months during the third GMD-CCP war), from July 1945 to October 1949, Hong Kong: Wen hua zhi liao gong ying she, 1978.

Dietrich, Kleitke, "Zu den Beziehungen der BRD, Frankreichs und Gross-britanniens mit der vr China" (Relations of West Germany, France and Great Britain with the CPR), *Deutsche aussenpolitik* (Berlin, Ost), j. 25, 1980, no. 1, s. 109-120.

Diggs, J.F., "Playing your own China card," *US news and world report*, 92 (January 25, 1982), p. 60.

"Dispute settlement in China," *ASILs international law journal, 4 (winter 1980), pp. 71-90.*

Dissemination of Scientific Information in the People's Republic of China, New York: Xerox Pub. Co., 1980.

"Distinguishing crimes from mistakes, a major issue concerning the big trial," *Beijing Review,* January 5, 1981, pp. 21-23. A translation of a *Renmin ribao* article of December 22, 1980.

Dittmer, Lowell, *Governments and Leaders, an Approach to Comparative Politics,* Boston: Houghton Mifflin, 1978, "Chou En-lai and Chinese politics," pp. 437-533.

Dittmer, P., "China ist kein Theme, eine literaturübersicht" (China is not a topic, a literature survey), *Deutschland-archiv* (Köln), j. 12, 1979, Heft 5, a. 465-466.

Dohmen, Holger, "Chinas aussenhandelsoffensive" (The foreign trade offensive of China), *China aktuell,* j. 7, 1978, Oktober Heft, s. 637-640.

"Mit Maos Tod begann Chinas Zukunft" (Mao's demise begins the future of China), *Indo-China* (Stuttgart), bd. 21, 1979, heft 1, s. 31-39.

Soziale sicherheit in China (Social security in China), Hamburg: Institut für Asienkunde, 1979.

Domenach, Jean Luc et Chen Ho-chia, *Une ténébreuse affaire, le faux record de Lushan* (The obscure affair, the false record of Lushan), Paris: Publ. orientalistes France, 1978.

Domes, Jürgen, *Politische soziologie der volksrepublik China* (Political sociology of the CPR), Stuttgart: Koch, Neft & Oetinter, 1980.

Volksrepublik China, Politik, Wirtschaft, Kultur (The People's Republic of China, policy, economy and culture), Berlin: Colloquium/KNO, 1982.

Dong, Qiwu, "You quiong bian fu, guo tai min an" (From poor to rich, peaceful nation and restful people), *Renmin ribao,* June 27, 1982, p. 2.

Donze, M.A. et Claude Sauvageot, *La Chine aujourd'hui* (China today), Paris: Jeune Afrique, 1979.

"Dose of tolerance is best for Moslems, China finds," by Stanley Oziewicz, *The Globe and Mail,* June 15, 1983, p. 3.

30 Jahre volksrepublik China, 30 Jahre lüge und betrug (30 years of the CPR, 30 years of lie and fraud), Berlin: ZK der KPD/Marxisten-Leninisten, 1979.

Dreyer, June Teufel, *China's Forty Millions,* Cambridge: Harvard University Press, 1976.

Dubarbier, Georges, *La Chine moderne* (Modern China), Paris: Presses univer-sitaires françaises, 1978.

Dubinaskii, A.M., *Sovetsko-kitaiskoe otnosheniya v period yapono-kitaiskoi voiny, 1937-1945* (Sino-Soviet relation during the Sino-Japanese war, 1937-1945), Moskva: Izd-vo "Mysl'," 1980.

"Dui jin nian de da xue bi ye sheng shuo ji ju hua" (A few words to the college graduates this year), *Renmin ribao,* May 17, 1983, p. 3.

"Dui shao er zhan kai gong chan zhu yi si xiang pin de jiao you" (Intensify the moral and character education of communism among the juveniles), *Renmin ribao,* July 8, 1982, p. 2.

Duman, L.I., *et alii,* "Kitai, istoricheskii ocherk" (China, brief history of), *Bol'shaya sovetskaya entsiklopediya,* 3rd ed., 1973, vol. 12, cols. 608-645.

Dumont, René, *Chine, la révolution,* Paris: Seuil, 1976.

Dutt, V.P., ed., *China, the Post-Mao View,* Columbia, Missouri: South Asia Books, 1981.

Edwards, R. Randle, "The gang of four trial, Chinese criminal justice in practice," includes translation of the indictment of the special procuratorate under the Supreme People's Procuratorate of the People's Republic of China, *China law reporter,* 1 (fall 1981), pp. 173-211.

Elegant, Robert, *The Centre of the World, Communism and the Mind of China,* London: Methuen, 1963.

Engelborghs-Bertels, Marthe, *La Chine rurale, des villages aux communes populaires* (Rural China, the rural people's communes), Bruxelles: Bruxelles U., 1974.

Elizarov, V.I., "Chan Kai Shi" (Jiang Jieshi), *Bol'shaya sovetskaya entsiklopediya,* 3rd ed., Moskva: Izdatel'stvo "sovetskaya entsiklopediya," 1978, vol. 29, col. 42.

"Chzhou En'-lai" (Zhou Enlai), *Bol'shaya sovetskaya entsiklopediya,* 3rd ed., Moskva: Izdatel'stvo "sovetskaya entsiklopediya," 1978, vol. 29, col. 538.

"Kitai, narodnaya respublika, pechat' " (China, the CPR, press of), *Bol'shaya sovetskaya entsiklopediya,* 3rd ed., Moskva: Izdatel'stvo "sovetskaya entsiklopediya," 1973, vol. 12, cols. 684-685.

"Kommunisticheskaya partiya Kitaya" (The Communist Party of China), *Bol'shaya sovetskaya entsiklopediya,* 3rd ed., Moskva: Izdatel'stvo "sovetskaya entsiklopediya," 1973, vol. 12, cols. 1604-1607.

"Mao Tsze-dun" (Mao Zedong), *Bol'shaya sovetskaya entsiklopediya,* 3rd ed., Moskva: Izdatel'stvo "sovetskaya entsiklopediya," 1974, vol. 15, cols. 1041-1042.

Ellis, S.L., "Decentralization of China's foreign trade structure," *Georgia journal of international and comparative law,* 11 (summer 1981), pp. 283-304.

and L. Shea, "Foreign commercial dispute settlement in the People's Republic of China," *International trade law journal,* 6 (spring-autumn 1980-1981), pp. 155-175.

Ellithorpe, H., "Now China's Deng is taking on the mandarins," *Business week,* January 25, 1982, p. 54.

"Evolution of the People's Republic of China's participation in international commercial arbitration, pragmatic prospects," *California Western international law journal,* 12 (winter 1981), pp. 128-153.

Fava, Patrice, *et alii, Chine,* Paris: Seuil, 1977.

Fejto, François, *Chine-URSS, de l'alliance au conflit* (China and the USSR, from an alliance to conflict), Paris: Seuil, 1978.

Felber, Roland, "Der Alpeiner reaktionären Tradition: chinesischer grossmachtehegemonismus und sinozentrismus in vergangenheit und gegenwart" (The nightmarish tradition of reaction, China's great-power hegemony and Sinocentralism at present and in the past), *Deutsche aussen-politik* (Berlin, Ost), j. 24, 1979, Heft 6, s. 84-97.

"Zur gegenwärtigen ausseinandersetzung um die bewertung der kulturrevolution in China" (The current argument in evaluating the cultural revolution in China), *Asien-Afrika-Lateinamerika* (Berlin, Ost), bd., 6, 1978, Heft 5, s. 824-833.

Feng, Min, "Mei guo dui su lian de liang shou ce lüe" (The double-dealing tactics of the United States with the Soviet Union), *Renmin ribao,* June 29, 1982, p. 7.

"Five-year plan for higher education," *Beijing Review,* June 6, 1983, p. 7.

Frey, K., "Science without Mao," *World press review,* 29 (March 1982), p. 58.

"Furious volley in a no-win match," *Time,* April 18, 1983, p. 30.

508   GOVERNMENT OF SOCIALIST CHINA

Ganshin, G.A., *Ocherk ekonomiki sovremennogo kitaya* (The outline of economy of contemporary China), Moskva: Ekonomika, 1982.

Gao, Shangquan, "Zheng que li jie xiu ju li fei" (Correctly understand how to restore the old and make use of the waste), *Renmin ribao*, July 13, 1982, p. 4.

Gao, Xinqing he Hu Zhiren, "Ke ai de she hui zhu yi ji ti nong min" (The likeable socialist collective farmers), *Renmin ribao*, July 13, 1982, p. 4.

Gao, Yan, "Da li fa jian gao deng zhuan ke jiao you" (Make great effort to develop professional high education), *Renmin ribao*, May 7, 1983, p. 3.

Garms, Eckard, "Wirtschaftreform in China tritt auf der Stelle" (Economic reform in China on the spot), *China aktuell*, j. 8, 1979, Oktoberheft, s. 1122-1131.

"Ge di dui fei fa jian fong fen fong ren yuan bi xu yan su chu li" (Severely punish those engaged in illegal building and sharing houses), *Renmin ribao*, May 20, 1983, p. 4.

Gegemonistskaya politika, ugroza narodam azii, afriki i latinskoi ameriki (The hegemonic policy, a threat to the people of Asia, Africa and Latin America), Moskva: Politizdat, 1981.

Gel'ras, V.G., "Sotsial'nye protivorechiya i problemy modernizatsii v KNR" (Social contradiction and the problems of modernization in the People's Republic of China), *Rabochii klass i sovremenem mir*, 4 (1981), pp. 74-82.

George, J. Mischell, D.T. Gullo and D.D. Stein, "Trade with the People's Republic of China," *Northwestern journal of international law and business*, 3 (spring 1981), pp. 21-38.

Gernet, Jacques, *Chine et christianisme, action et réaction* (China and Christianity, action and response), Paris: Gallimard, 1982.

Gerns, Willi, "In fragen der chinesischen aggression gegen Vietnam" (The question of the Chinese aggression against Vietnam), *Marxistische blätter* (Frankfurt am Main), bd. 17, 1979, Heft 3, s. 73-82.

Gigon, Ferdinand, *Et Mao prit pouvoir* (Mao took power), Paris: Flammarion, 1969.

Ginsburgh, Robert N., "China touches the tiger's bottom," *Air Force Magazine*, vol. 62, no. 6, 1979, pp. 40-45.

Goebbels, Heide M., *Volksrepublik China, atomwirtschaft und politik* (The CPR, the atomic economy and politics), Munchen: Trikout verlag, 1980.

Golfin, Jean, *La Chine et ses populations* (China and her peoples), Paris: Presses universitaires de France, 1982.

Gong, Weixin he Chen Peiyao, "Mei su zhan lüe wu qi tan pan de hui gu yu zhan wang" (The US-USSR Salt, past and future), *Renmin ribao*, July 1, 1982, p. 7.

"Gong chan dang yuan zhi you qing chun, mo you wan nian" (The Chinese communists have youth only, but no old-age), *Guangming ribao*, June 21, 1981, p. 1.

Gong ren ribao, organ of the General Trade Union, July 15, 1949-March 31, 1967, October 6, 1978-

"Gong ye sheng chan zhuo zhong ti gao jing ji xiao yi, bu yao gu pian mian zhui qiu chan zhi he su du, Zhang Jingfu zai zuo tan hui shang tan dang qian jing ji xing shi he xia ban nian ren wu" (In the industrial production, it is important to increase efficiency and profit, but one should not pursue simple output and expedition, Zhang Jingfu talked, in a discussion about the current economic situation and the tasks for the next half-year), *Renmin ribao*, July 11, 1982, p. 4.

Grieder, Jerome B., *Intellectuals and the State in Modern China, a Narrative History*, New York: Free Press, 1981.

Grobe, Karl, *Vom Western Lernen, Chinese bleiben Kader und Kommunbauern, Lamas und Studenten, Reportagen aus China* (Learning from the West, the Chinese remain to be cadres and commune peasants, Lamas and students, a report from China), Frankfurt: Fichhorn, Vito Von, 1982.

Grosier, J.B., *Les Chinois* (The Chinese), Paris: Solar, 1982.

Gruby, I.M., *Nasledie Mao Tszeduna* (The Legacy of Mao Zedong), per. s chesh., Moskva: Progress, 1981.

"Gu li nong min xiang tu di tao zi" (Encourage peasants to invest money in land), *Renmin ribao,* May 20, 1983, p. 2.

"Gu Mu qiang diao zheng que gu ji ge di zou si dao zheng xing shi, shen ru kai zhan fan zou si dao zheng yao jie jue wu ge wen ti" (Gu Mu places emphasis on the correct estimate on the smuggle situation, five problems relative to the unfolding of the anti-smuggle campaign), *Renmin ribao,* July 13, 1982, p. 1.

"Guan yu jian guo yi lai dang de ruo gan li shi wen ti de jue yi" (A resolution on several historical points since the founding of the CPR) by the sixth plenum of the 11th CC, *Guangming ribao,* July 1, 1981, pp. 1-5; also *Renmin ribao,* same date, pp. 1-5.

Guangming ribao, "directed" by the Central Committee of the CCP, June 16, 1949- *Xin hua ci dian,* p. 305, col. 1 where the Chinese words ling dao are used.

Gubaidulin, V.M., *Revoliutsionnaya vlast' v osvobozhdenykh raionakh kitaya, 1937-1945* (The revolutionary power in the liberated areas of China, 1937-1945), Moskva: "Nauka," 1981.

Gudoshnikov, L.M., "Kitai, obshchie svedeniya" (China, general information of), *Bol'shaya sovetskaya entsiklopediya,* 3rd ed., Moskva: Izdatel'stvo "sovetskaya entsiklopediya," 1973, vol. 12, cols., 598-600.

et alii, "China's third constitution," *Far Eastern Affairs* (Moscow), no. 1, 1979, pp. 54-64. Also in "Die chinesische verfassung von 1978" (The Chinese Constitution of 1978), *Sowjetwissenschaft, gesellschaftswissenschaft,* abt. j. 32, 1979, Heft 6, s. 628-636.

Guillermaz, Jacques, *Histoire du parti communist chinois, 2. De Yenan à la conquête du pouvoir, 1936-1949* (History of the CCP, vol. 2, From Yanan to the conquest of power, 1936-1949), Paris: Payot, 1975.

Le parti communist chinois au pouvoir, v. 2, du mouvement d'éducation socialiste à l'ère Hua Ko-feng 1962-1978 (The Communist Party of China in power, from the socialist education movement to the era of Hua Guofeng, 1962-1978), Paris: Payot, 1979.

Guiloineau, Jean, *La Chine, l'urss et les autres, l'Asie du sud-est et le conflit sino-soviétique* (China, the USSR and others, southeast Asia and the Sino-Soviet conflict), Paris: Plon, 1980.

Guo, Longchun, "Wei shang jian gong zuo hu xu" (Lament the commercial inspection work), *Renmin ribao,* July 9, 1981, p. 2.

"Guo jia de min zhu hua gai ge bi xu zai an deng tuan jie de tiao jian xia zu bu she xian" (Democratization of a state must be gradually realized under the condition of stability and solidarity), *Guangming ribao,* February 9, 1981, pp. 1, 3.

"Guo wu yuan gong zuo ren yuan shou ze, guo wu yuan fa bu" (The disciplinary regulations of the workers in the State Council), *Renmin ribao,* July 9, 1982, p. 1.

Halimarski, Andrzej, "Rok bez Mao Tse-tunga" (The CPR without Mao Zedong), *Nowe drogi* (Warsaw), r. 31, 1977, no. 10, pp. 152-166.

Halpin-Byrne, D., "A slash at bureaucratic fat," *McLeans,* 95 (March 22, 1982), pp. 41ff.

Hao, Huiming, "You sheng you se, zhuo you cheng xiao, Jiang Su Shanghai pu fen qi ye si ziang zheng zhi gong zhuo pian duan" (Resonant and colorful, a great achievement; some anecdotes of the political-thought work among employees in enterprises of Shanghai, Jiangsu province), *Renmin ribao,* July 13, 1982, p. 3.

Hao, Tsien Tche, *Analysè de la constitution de la république populaire de Chine, 17 janvier 1975* (An analysis of the constitution of the CPR of January 17, 1975), Paris: Editions du centre national de la recherche scientifique, 1977.

Harris, Lillian Craig, "China's relations with the PLO," *Journal of Palestine Studies,* vol. 7, 1977-1978, no. 1, pp. 123-154.

Harrison, James Pinckney, *The Long March to Power, a History of the Chinese Communist Party,* 1921-1972, New York: Praeger, 1972.

Harrison, John A., *China Since 1800,* 1st ed., New York: Harcourt, Brace and World, 1967.

Henry, W.A., "Anger over arms to Taiwan," *Time,* 119 (January 25, 1982), p. 23. Conservative criticism of decision to sell F-5E fighter jets instead of the F-5G.

Hervouet, Gérard, "Les relations internationales de la Chine: le calcul d'une continuité de la Chine: le calcul d'une continuité mesurée" (The international relations of China, a design of continuity), *Mondes Asiatique,* 1978-1979, no. 16, pp. 275-287.

Hinton, Harold, *China's Turbulent Quest; an Analysis of China's Foreign Relations Since 1949,* rev. ed., Bloomington: Indiana University Press, 1972.

An Introduction to Chinese Politics, 2nd ed., New York: Holt, Rinehart and Winston, 1978.

Hinton, William H., *Fanshen, la revolution communiste dans un village chinois* (Fanshen, the communist revolution in a Chinese village), trad. Anglais, Paris: Plon, 1971.

Hipkin, Brian, "State, law and politics," *Research in law and sociology,* 3 (autumn 1980), pp. 201-220.

Hoffman, Rainer, *Der untergang des konfuzianistischen China vom mandschureich zur volksrepublik* (The sinking of the Confucian China from the Manzhou dynasty to the CPR), Wiesbaden: Harrassowitz, 1980.

Hongqi, edited by the Central Committee of the CCP, June 1, 1958-

Honig, G., "Cina, 1977-1978," *La civilta cattolica,* a. 129, 1978, vol. 3, au. 3078, pp. 535-543.

Houa Kouo-feng, successeur de Mao Tsé-toung, souvenis biographiques (1937-1975) Hua Guofeng, successor of Mao Zedong, some biographical memories (1937-1975), Paris: Centenaire, 1979.

Howe, Christopher, *China's Economy, a Basic Guide,* New York: Basic Books, 1978.

Hsia, Tao-tai and Charlotte Hambley, "The lawyer's law: an introduction," includes translation of China's provincial regulations on lawyers, *China law reporter,* 1 (fall 1981), pp. 213-221.

Hsiung, Y.T., *Red China's Cultural Revolution,* 1st ed., New York: Vantage Press, 1968.

Hu, Ji, "Updating science and technology," *Beijing Review,* February 14, 1983, pp. 14-18.

Hu, Qiaomu, "Zuo du li zi zhu pei yang gao ji zhuan men ren cai de dao lu" (On the independent, self-determined road of educating highly qualified personnel), *Renmin ribao,* May 28, 1983, p. 1.

Hu, Sheng, "Marxism and the reality of China," *Beijing review,* April 11, 1983, pp. 14-18. Abridged translation of a *Hongqi* article, issue no. 6, 1983.

Hu, Yaobang, "Create a new situation in the fields of socialist modernization," report to the 12th National Congress of the Communist Party of China, September 1, 1982, *Beijing Review,* September 13, 1982, pp. 11-40.

"Jia qiang tuan jie nu li fen dou zheng qu xin de sheng li" (Strengthen our unity, struggle hard to achieve new victory), *Renmin ribao,* May 21, 1983, p. 1. Speech to minorities in Xinjiang.

"The radiance of the great truth of Marxism lights our way forward," report at the meeting in commemoration of the centenary of the death of Karl Marx, March 13, 1983, *Beijing Review,* March 21, 1983, pp. II-XV.

"Zai qing zhu zhong guo gong chan dang cheng li lu shi zhou nian da hui shang de jiang hua" (A speech to the mass meeting in celebration of the sixtieth anniversary of the founding of the CCP), *Renmin ribao,* July 2, 1981, pp. 1-3.

"Zai shou du ge jie ji nian xin hai ge ming qi shi zhou nian da hui shang de jiang hua" (A speech to the mass meeting in celebration of the seventieth anniversary of the 1911 revolution), *Renmin ribao,* October 10, 1981, pp. 1-2.

"Zhong luo liang dang he liang guo ren min shi huan nan zhi jiao" (China and Romania and the Chinese and Romanian parties are friends in need), *Renmin ribao,* May 11, 1983, p. 6.

Hua, Guofeng, *Poursuivons jusqu'au bout la révolution sous la dictature du prolétariat* (Let's carry to the end the revolution under the proletarian dictatorship), Beijing: Foreign Languages Press, 1977.

Huang, Huoqing, "Zui gao ren min jian cha gong zuo bao gao" (A report on the work of the Supreme Procuracy), *Renmin ribao,* December 16, 1981, p. 2. The same exercise for 1981-1982, *ibid.,* December 17, 1982, p. 2.

Huang, Jy, *et alii, Recht in China* (The rights in China), Aufsätz aus der volksrepublik China zu grundsatzfragen des rechts, ubers. von Jy Huang, Wolfgang Kessler, Jenkai Liu und Frank Munzel, Hamburg: Institut für Asienkunde, 1979.

Huang, Vivian W., "The income tax laws of the People's Republic of China," *Boston bar journal,* 25 (November 1981), p. 1319.

Huang, Wenfu, "Shi ying nong cun xin xing shi, ti gao lao dong sheng chan lu, Xinjiang fa zhan nong ye ji jie hua da you ke wei" (Adapt to the new development in rural villages, and promote productivity of labor, the great potential in the development of agricultural technology in Xinjiang), *Renmin ribao,* June 26, 1982, p. 2.

Iliushechkin, V.P., "Kitaisko-frantsuzskaya voina, 1884-1885" (The Sino-French War of 1884-1885), *Bol'shaya sovetskaya entsiklopediya,* 3rd ed., Moskva: Izdatel'stvo "sovetskaya entsiklopediya," 1973, vol. 12, col. 722.

"Investigations into Jiang Qing's crimes completed," *Beijing Review,* January 5, 1981, pp. 24-25.

Iriye, Akira, ed., *The Chinese and the Japanese, Essays in Political and Cultural Interaction,* Princeton, New York: Princeton University Press, 1980.

Isaia, Henri, *La justice en Chine* (Justice in China), Paris: Economica, 1978.

Iu'ev, M.F., *Vooruzhennye sily KPK v osvoboditel'noi bor'be kitaiskogo naroda* (20-40-e gody) (The armed forces of the Communist Party of Kampuchea in the liberation struggle of the Chinese people during the 1920-1940 period), Moskva: "Nauka", 1982.

Iur'ev, M.F., "Revoliutsiya 1925-1927 v Kitae" (The revolution in China, 1925-1927), *Bol'shaya sovetskaya entsiklopediya,* 3rd ed., Moskva: Izdatel'stvo "sovetskaya entsiklopediya," 1975, vol. 21, cols. 657-658.

Revoliutsiya 1925-1927gg v kitae (The revolution of 1925-1927 in China), Moskva: "Nauka," 1968.

"Severnyi pokhod 1926-1927" (The Northern Expedition, 1926-1927), *Bol'shaya sovetskaya entsiklopediya,* 3rd ed., Moskva: Izdatel'stvo "sovetskaya entsiklopediya," 1976, vol. 23, col. 394.

Jacob, Alain, *Un balcon à Pekin* (A balcony in Beijing), Paris: Grasset, 1982.

512   GOVERNMENT OF SOCIALIST CHINA

Jain, R.K., *Party Politics in China, Nineteen Forty-five to Nineteen eighty*, Atlantic Highlands, New Jersey: Humanities, 1980.

Jan, George P., ed., *Government of Communist China*, San Francisco: Chandler Pub. Co., 1966.

Jan, Michel, *La vie chinoise* (The Chinese life), Paris: Presses universitaires de France, 1976.

"Jasjgar bazaar is like no other," by Stanlay Oziewicz, *The Globe and Mail*, June 18, 1983, p. 11.

"Ji jie zeng chan nong cun shi xiao shang pin" (Actively produce goods salable in the rural villages), *Renmin ribao*, July 9, 1982, p. 2.

"Jia qiang jing ji he tong de tong yi guan li, gong shang xing zheng guan li zong ju ju zhang Ren Zhonglin da ji zhe wen" (Strengthen the unified control over the economic joint venture, answer of Ren Zhonglin, the general administrator of the Bureau of Industry and Commerce, to the question of newsmen), *Renmin ribao*, June 27, 1982, p. 4.

"Jia qiang si xiang jiao you ti gao ji guan dang zu zhi zhan dou li" (Strengthen the thought education, and promote the fighting capacity of the organizations and party structure), *Renmin ribao*, July 1, 1982, pp. 1, 4.

"Jia qiang si xiang zheng zhi gong zuo, jian she she hui jing shen wen ming" (To strengthen political-thought work, and build up spiritual culture of socialism), *Guangming ribao*, January 20, 1981, p. 1.

"Jian chi you ling dao you bu zhou de gai ge" (Insist on a well-led well-paced reform), *Renmin ribao*, May 16, 1983, pp. 1, 2.

"Jian deng bu yi de ji xu zhi xing san zhong quan hui de fang zhen zheng ce" (To carry out resolutely the decisions of the 3rd plenum of the 11th CC), *Guangming ribao*, January 19, 1981, p. 1. A reprint of a *Renmin ribao* editorial.

"Jian deng de zou jing ji fa zhan de xin lu zi" (Firmly follow the new path of economic development), *Renmin ribao*, December 15, 1981, p. 1.

"Jian she jing shen wen ming, dang qian yao zhua si ge feng mian de gong zuo" (To build up spiritual culture, to develop our task toward four directions at the present time), *Renmin ribao*, December 4, 1981, p. 1.

Jiang, Hua, "Zui gao ren min fa yuan gong zuo bao gao" (A report on the work of the Supreme People's Court), *Renmin ribao*, December 16, 1981, p. 2; December 17, 1982, p. 2.

"Jiao you zhe yao xian shou jiao you" (To educate others, one must himself receive education), *Renmin ribao*, May 23, 1983, p. 3.

Jie fang jun biao, organ of the Military Affairs Committee of the CCP, edited by General Political Department of the PLA, January 1, 1956-

"Jie jue nong cun neng yuan wen ti de yi ge zhong yao tu jing" (An important solution of energy problem facing the villages), *Guangming ribao*, March 16, 1981, p. 1.

"Jin yi bu ban hao zhong wai he zi qi ye" (One step further toward better management of joint ventures), *Renmin ribao*, May 14, 1983, p. 1.

"Jing ji guan xi zhong de zhong yao zhun ze" (Important guidelines of economic relations), *Renmin ribao*, December 17, 1981, p. 1.

Jones, John F., ed., *Building China: Studies in Integrated Development*, Hong Kong: Chinese University of Hong Kong, 1981.

Joyaux, François, *La Chine et le reglement du premier conflit d'Indochine* (Genève 1954) (China and the settlement of the first Indochina conflict at Geneva 1954), Paris: Sorbonne, 1979.

"Reflexions sur la puissance de la Chine populaire" (Thoughts on the strength of the CPR), *Relations internationales*, no. 17, 1979, pp. 65-78.

"Jun dui jian she de yi xiang zhan lue ren wu" (One strategical task in military construction), *Renmin ribao,* May 5, 1983, p. 1.

"K amerikano-kitaiskim otnosheniyam," *Pravda,* August 20, 1982, p. 5, cols. 7-8.

Kampaniya kritiki lin' byao i konfutsiya v kitae, 1973-1975 (The campaign of criticizing Lin Biao and criticizing Confucius in China, 1973-1975), Moskva: "Nauka," 1981.

Kang, Yao, "Yong yuan tong ren min xiu ji yu gong" (Forever share the fate with the people), *Guangming ribao,* July 7, 1981, p. 4.

Kang Yonghe, "Ti chang he tui guang xiao yi gong zi" (The promotion and spread of the system of efficiency wage), *Renmin ribao,* May 22, 1983, p. 5.

Kapralov, P.B., *Sel'skie raiony KNR v 70-e gody, tendentsii sotsial'no-ekonomicheskogo razvitiya* (Agricultural regions of the CPR in the 70's, the tendency of social-economic development), Moskva: "Nauka," 1981.

"Sotsial'no-ekonomicheskie problemy kitaiskoi derevni" (Social and economical problems of the Chinese village), *Narody azii i afriki,* 4 (1981), pp. 38-47.

Kapustin, D.T., *Taivan' i iuzhnaya koreya v kitaisko-amerikanskikh otnosheniya, 1969-1979* (Taiwan and South Korea in the Sino-American relation, 1969-1979), Moskva: "Nauka," 1980.

Kaufmann, Bernd, "Die evolution der aussenpolitik der vr China, eine historische betrachtung" (The change of China's foreign policy, an historical consideration), *Deutsche aussenpolitik* (Berlin, Ost), j. 24, 1979, no. 3, s. 92-113.

"Peking, normalisierung von beziehungen und aggression" (Beijing, normalization of relation and aggression), *Deutsche aussenpolitik* (Berlin, Ost), j. 24, 1979, no. 5, s. 119-123.

Ke, Qi, "China's space science and technology," *Beijing Review,* April 4, 1983, pp. 15-19, 24.

"Ke xue ji shu yao shi ying nong cun xin xing shi" (Science and technology must be adapted to the new situation in the villages), *Renmin ribao,* December 29, 1981, p. 1.

Keidel, A., "China: gaining efficiency through Western ways," *Business week,* May 24, 1982, pp. 172ff.

Kil, Soong-hoom, "Washington-Tokyo-Beijing relations in the post-1978 years," *Korea and world affairs,* 5 (winter 1981), pp. 537-557.

Kingman, H.K., "Dong Kingman's China exhibition," *American artist,* 46 (January 1982), pp. 70-71.

"Kitai, kitaiskaya narodnaya respublika, vooruzhennye sily" (China, the CPR, armed forces of), *Bol'shaya sovetskaya entsiklopediya,* 3rd ed., Moskva: Izdatel'stvo "sovetskaya entsiklopediya," 1973, vol. 12, cols. 659-661.

"Kitaiskaya chanchun'skaya zheleznaya doroga" (The Chinese Eastern Railway), *Bol'shaya sovetskaya entsiklopediya,* 3rd ed., Moskva: Izdatel'stvo "sovetskaya entsiklopediya," 1973, vol. 12, col. 716.

Kitaiskaya narodnaya respublika v 1979 godu, politika, ekonomika i ideologiya (The CPR in 1979, politics, economics and ideology), Moskva: "Nauka," 1981.

"Kitaiskaya narodnaya Respublika v 1980 godu, politika, ekonomika i ideologiya" (The People's Republic of China in 1980, policy, economy and ideology), *Ezhegodnik,* 1982.

Klassy i klassovaya struktura v kitaiskoi narodnoi respublike (Class and class structure in the Chinese People's Republic), Moskva: "Nauka," 1982.

Klein, Dietmer, "Zur hegemonistischen politik der Pekinger führer (The hegemonic policy of the Beijing leadership), *Einheit* (Berlin, Ost), j. 34, 1979, Heft 2, s. 194-201.

514   GOVERNMENT OF SOCIALIST CHINA

Klenner, Makiko, *Literaturkritik und politische kritik in China* (Criticism in literature and politics in China), Bochum: Brockmeyer, Norbert, 1979.

Klenner, Wolfgang, *Ordnungsprinzipien im industralizierungsprozess der vr China* (The regulatory principle in industrial process of the CPR), Hamburg: Weltarchiv, 1979.

Klerikov, V.Z., "Kitai, narodnoe obrazovanie" (China, education of), *Bol'shaya sovetskaya entsiklopediya,* 3rd ed., Moskva: Izdatel'stvo "sovetskaya entsiklopediya," 1973, vol. 12, col. 662.

Klinner, Bernhard, "Entwicklung des Aussenhandles der vr China" (The development of foreign trade of the CPR), *Wirtschaftsdienst,* j. 59, 1979, no. 11, s. 573-577.

Kneissel, Jutta, *Gesellschaftstrukturen und unternehmensformen in China, zur analyse der wirtschaftlichen entwicklung einer traditionallen gesellshaft* (The social structure and formations of enterprises, an analysis of the economic development of a traditional society), Frankfurt: Campus verlag, 1978.

KNR i razvivaiushchiesya strany (The People's Republic of China and the developing nations), Moskva: "Nauka", 1982.

Koningsburger, Hans, *Love and Hate in China,* New York: McGraw-Hill, 1966.

Köpker, Wolfgang, "Die politik Chinas in Afrika, zentrales motiv ist der konflikt mit Moskau" (The Chinese diplomacy in Africa, central objective being countering Moscow), *Beiträge zur konflikt forschung: psychopolitische aspekte* (Köln), j. 8, 1978, Heft 3, s. 81-94.

Korbash, E., "Evoliutsiya osnovnykh ekonomicheskikh kontseptsii v KNR" (Evolution of the basic economic conceptions in the People's Republic of China), *Ekonomicheskikh nauki,* 8 (1981), pp. 67-73.

Teoriya i praktika ekonomicheskogo stroitel'stva v KNR (Theory and practice of economic structure of the People's Republic of China), Moskva: "Nauka," 1981.

Kovalenko, I.I., i E.B. Zaitsev, *Neomiunkhenskaya politika v yadernyi vek* (Neo-Münich policy in the nuclear age), Moskva: Mezhdunar. otnosheniya, 1983.

Kovanda, Kuvel, "Letter from Peking," *Technology Review,* vol. 81, November 1978, no. 2, pp. 54-58.

Kristeva, Julia, *Die Chinesen, die Rolle der Frau in China* (The Chinese, the role of women in China), Berlin: Ullstein Taschenbuch-Verlag, 1982.

"Des chinoises à Manhattan" (Some Chinese at Manhattan), *Tel guel* (Paris), no. 69, 1977, pp. 11-16.

Kriukov, M.V. et al., *Drevnie kitaitsy v epokhu tsentralizovannykh emperii* (The ancient Chinese in the period of centralized empires), Moskva: "Nauka," 1982.

Kuchler, Ulla et Johannes Kuchler, *La Chine,* Paris: Bibliothèque des arts, 1979.

Kuleshov, N.I., *Pekin protiv natsional'no-osvoboditel'nogo dvizheniya* (Beijing against the national liberation), Moskva: Mezhdunar. otnosheniya, 1981.

Kunadze, G.F., *Yapono-kitaiskie otnosheniya na sovremennom etape (1971-1980) (Sino-Japanese relations in the epoch of 1971-1980), Moskva: "Nauka," 1982.*

Kuo, Heng Yu, *Die komintern und die chinesischen revolution, die einheitsfront zwischen der KP Chinas und der kuomintang 1924-1927* (The Comintern and the Chinese revolution, the United Front of the CCP and the GMD, 1924-1927), Paderborn: Schöningh Paderborn, 1979.

Kux, Ernst, "Die politischen auseinandersetzung im heutigen China um gesellschaft und zukunft" (The political debate in present China on society and future), *Universitas* (Stuttgart), j. 34, 1979, Heft 7, s. 715-719.

Kuz'min, V.V., *Pekin v amerikanskoi strategii, problemy sblizheniya i protivoborstva* (Beijing in the American strategy, the problems of rapprochement and enmity), Moskva: Mezhdunar. otnosheniya, 1978.

Larin, A., "Britain in China's foreign policy," *Far Eastern Affairs* (Moscow), 3, 1979, pp. 86-96.

La Ruth, E., and Katherine S. Kinderman, *In the Eye of the Typhoon,* New York: Harcourt, Brace, and Jonanovich, 1980.

Lauriola, Luca, "Cina paee aperto" (China opens up), *Eintesi economici,* a. 30, 1978, no. 7-10, pp. 26-36.

Leclerc du Sablon, Jean, *Mein geliebtes China* (My beloved China), ubers. von Waldemar Sonntag, Bonn: Hieronimi, 1980.

"Legal aspects of Sino-American oil exploration in the South China Sea," *Journal of international law and economics,* 14 (1980), pp. 443-484.

Lemoyne, J., "Softball diplomacy," *Newsweek,* 99 (March 8, 1982), p. 48.

Leng Shao-chuan, "Criminal justice in post-Mao China: some preliminary observations," Chinese criminal code symposium, *Criminal law and criminology,* 73 (spring 1982), pp. 204-237.

Leninskaya politika SSSR v otnoshenii kitaya (The Leninist policy of the USSR toward China), Moskva: "Nauka," 1968.

Levine, Steven I., "China und die sowjetunion, unüberbrückbare feindschaft oder ein neuer anfang?" (China and the Soviet Union, uncompromising animosity or a new beginning?), *Europa-archiv,* bd. 34, 1979, Heft 20, s. 611-622.

Lewis, J.B. and B.L. Ottlev, "Reflections on the modern Chinese legal system," *Washington University law quarterly,* 59 (winter 1982), pp. 1165-1230.

Lewis, John Wilson, *Leadership in Communist China,* Ithaca: Cornell University Press, 1963.

ed., *Major Doctrines of Communist China,* New York: W.W. Norton, 1964.

Lexique politique de la Chine contemporaine (Political lexicon of contemporary China), Paris: Centenaire, 1979.

Leys, Simon, *The Chairwoman's New Clothes, Mao and the Cultural Revolution,* New York: Schocken, 1981.

Chinese Shadows, Hammondsworth, England: Penguin Books, 1977.

Images brisées, Confucius, Lin Pao, Chou En-lai, Mao Tsé-tung et Li Yi-che (The broken images of Confucius, Lin Biao, Zhou Enlai, Mao Zedong and Li Yizhe), Paris: Laffont, 1976. *Broken Images,* New York: Schocken, 1981.

"Li, Da-chzhao" (Li Dazhao), *Bol'shaya sovetskaya entsiklopediya,* 3rd ed., Moskva: Izdatel'stvo "sovetskaya entsiklopediya," 1973, vol. 4, cols. 1284-1285.

"Li, Li-san' " (Li Lisan), *Bol'shaya sovetskaya entsiklopediya,* 3rd ed., Moskva: Izdatel'stvo "sovetskaya entsiklopediya" 1973, vol. 14, cols. 1313-1314.

Li, Xi he Liu Changzu, "Rang gen duo de gong ying pin xia dao nong cun" *(Let more commodities flow down to the villages), Renmin ribao,* June 26, 1982, p. 3.

Li, Yizhe, *Chinois si vous saviez, à propos de la démocratie et de la legalité sous le socialisme chinois* (The Chinese, if you knew, in regard to democracy and legality under Chinese socialism), Paris: Bourgois, 1976.

"Lin' byao" (Lin Biao), *Bol'shaya sovetskaya entsiklopediya,* 3rd ed., Moskva: Izdatel'stvo "sovetskaya entsiklopediya," 1973, vol. 14, col. 1417.

Ling, Yun, "Ling Yun on counterrevolutionary offences and capital punishment," *Beijing Review,* July 13, 1981, pp. 16-17.

Liu, Guisheng he Qian Sun, "Ma ke si zhu yi zai zhong guo zao qi chuan bo wen ti pian xi" (An analysis of the problem on the early study of Marxism in China), *Renmin ribao,* May 25, 1983, p. 3.

516 GOVERNMENT OF SOCIALIST CHINA

Liu, Reilong, "Lun chuan tong nong ye xiang xian dai nong ye de zhuan hua" (Discuss the change of traditional agriculture to a modernized one), *Renmin ribao,* May 13, 1983, p. 3.

Liu, Shaoqi, *Liu Shaoqi xuan ji* (The selected writings of Liu Shaoqi), *Beijing:* Renmin chu ban she, 1981 (vol. 1).

"Liu, Shao Tsi" (Liu Shaoqi), *Bol'shaya sovetskaya entsiklopediya,* 3rd ed., Moskva: Izdatel'stvo "sovetskaya entsiklopediya," 1974, vol. 15, cols. 370-371.

Loescher, Gil and Ann P. Loescher, *China Pushing Toward the Year 2000,* Harcourt, Brace, and Jonanovich, 1981.

Loh, Pa Ye, *Nach China mit liebe* (Return to China with affection), Bad Liebenzell: Liebenzeller mission, 1980.

Lok, P., "Deng keeps on coasting," *McLeans* (March 8, 1982), p. 95.

Lottman, H.R., "China's publishing operations reorganized," *Publishers weekly,* 221 (May 28, 1982), p. 16.

Lowenthal, Richard, "Zum stand der politischen entwicklung der Volksrepublik China," *Europa archiv,* 1981, pp. 597-604.

Lu, Jining, "Quan guo bian zheng wei wu zhu yi tao lun hui guan dian jian jie" (A summary of the viewpoints aired at the discussion of the All-China Material Dialectic Polemics), *Renmin ribao,* July 6, 1982, p. 5.

Lu, Wenbing, "Cong gao ying de yin qian qiu, Dong Biwu tong zhi zai er ci guo nei ge ming zhan zheng shi qi de ji ge pian duan" (Eternalization of moral uplifting, some recollections on the activities of comrade Dong Biwu during the second period of the revolutionary war), *Guangming ribao,* June 21, 1981, p. 2.

Lu, Zupin, "Liang qi ya zhi ren cai shi jian de jiao xun" (Lessons from two events in keeping down talented men), *Renmin ribao,* July 9, 1982, p. 4.

Lun she hui zhu yi jing shen wen ming (On spiritual culture of socialism) by Mao Zedong, Zhou Enlai, Liu Shaoqi and Zhu De, Beijing: Zhong guo renmin jie fang jun zhan shi chu ban she, 1981.

Lutteri, Paolo, "Consolidamento dell'autorità politica e modernizzazione dell'economie in cina" (The consolidation of political power and modernization of economy in China), *Rivista internazionale di scienze economiche e commerciali* (Padova), a. 26, 1979, no. 5, pp. 476-490.

Mabire, Jean, *L'été rouge de Pékin, la révolte des boxeurs* (The red summer in Beijing, the revolt of the boxers), Paris: Fayard, 1978.

Machetzki, Rüdiger, "Chinas wirtschaft aus sowjetischer sicht: ein vergleich sowjetischer und amerikanischer schätzung" (The economy of China from the Soviet viewpoint, an equation of the Soviet and American estimates), *China aktuell,* j. 8, 1979, Februarheft, s. 130-133.

McKnight, Briant, *The Quality of Mercy, Amnesty and Traditional Chinese Justice,* Honolulu: University Press of Hawaii, 1981.

Mäding, Klaus, *Strafrecht und massenerziehung der Volksrepublik China* (Criminal law and mass education of the CPR), Frankfurt: Suhrkamp/KNO, 1979.

Main documents of the third session of the fifth National People's Congress of the People's Republic of China, 1st ed., Beijing: Foreign Languages Press, 1980.

Malaude, Ch., "La rèconciliation sino-japonaise" (The Sino-Japanese rapprochement), *La nouvelle revue des deux mondes* (Paris), janvier 1979, pp. 107-114.

Manezhev, S.A., *Ekonomicheskie otnosheniya KNR so stranami iugo-vostochnoi azii* (The economic relations of the CPR with states of southeast Asia), Moskva: "Nauka," 1980.

Mann, P., "Reagan's F-5g decision pleases no one," *Aviation week and space technology*, 116 (January 18, 1982), pp. 16-17. Advanced fighter sales to Taiwan denied.

Mao Zedong, "Mao Zedong tong zhi zai jie fang zhan zheng shi qi wei xin hua she xie de si pian xin wen gao" (Four news items written by comrade Mao Zedong for *Xin hua* news agency during the liberation war), *Guangming ribao*, July 9, 1981, p. 1. A reprint of texts appearing from October 1948 to April 1949.

"Mao Zedong tong zhi zai kang ri zhan zheng chu qi guan yu jian chi du li zi zhu de yu jie zhan zheng de wu ge dian boa" (Five telegrams of comrade Mao Zedong [to Peng Dehuai] concerning independent and autonomous guerilla tactics during the first stage of the resisting-Japanese war), *Guangming ribao*, July 7, 1981, p. 1. A reprint of texts of September 1937.

"Qi da gong zuo feng zhen" (Guideline of the 7th Congress's work), *Guangming ribao*, July 16, 1981, p. 1. A reprint of a speech of April 21, 1945.

Quotations from Chairman Mao Zedong, Beijing: Foreign Languages Press, 1966.

Selected Works, 1st ed., Beijing: Foreign Languages Press, 1965-1977, 5 volumes.

Martin, Helmut, "Friedliche wiedervereinigung statt militärischer befreiung, Peking umwirbt taiwan mit neuen methoden" (Peaceful reunification instead of armed liberation, Beijing is wooing Taiwan with new means), *China aktuell*, j. 8, 1979, Februarheft, s. 128-129.

Martynov, A.A., "Natsional'no-osvoboditel'naya voina kitaiskogo naroda protiv yaponskikh zakhvatchikov, 1937-1945" (The national liberation war of the Chinese people against the Japanese usurpers, 1937-1945), *Bol'shaya sovetskaya entsiklopediya*, 3rd ed., Moskva: Izdatel'stvo "sovetskaya entsiklopediya," 1974, vol. 17, cols. 1079-1083.

Masi, Edvorda, *China Winter: Workers, Mandarins and the Purge of the Gang of Four*, New York: Dutton, 1982.

Mazurov, V.M., *SShA-kitai-yaponiya perestroika mezhgosudarstvennykh otnoshenii, 1969-1979* (The US, China and Japan rebuilding international relations, 1969-1979), Moskva: "Nauka," 1980.

Mehnert, Klaus, "Stichwort 'atemberaubend,' China end 1978" (The headword 'breathholding," China at the end of 1978), *Osteuropa*, 29 (1979), no. 3, s. 187-196.

"Mei guo yi xie wan gu pai yao ba zhong mei guan xi la xiang dao tui, gu chui liang ge zhong guo, jian chi xiang taiwan chu xiu wu qi" (Some American stubborns hold back the Sino-US relations, and clamor for two-China policy in support of arms sales to Taiwan), *Renmin ribao*, July 11, 1982, p. 6.

Meienberger, Norbert, "Chinas neue Ziele" (The new objectives of China), *Schweizer monatshefte für politik, wirtschaft und kultur* (Zürich), j. 58, 1978, h. 11, s. 861.

Meier-Ebert, Heinz, "Contracting in China, some aspects from practical experience, transcript," *International business law*, 9 (November 1981), pp. 438-440.

Meiner, Louis-Michel, *La Chine au present* (China today), Paris: Klincksieck, 1979.

Menzel, Ulrich, *Wirtschaft und politik im modernen China, eine sozial-und wirtschaftsgeschichte von 1842 bis nach Maos tod* (Economy and politics of modern China, a survey of social and economic development from 1842 to the post-Mao era), Wiesbaden: Westdeutscher verlag, 1979.

Michael, Franz, and George Taylor, *The Far East in the Modern World*, rev. ed., New York: Holt, Rinehart and Winston, 1964.

Millar, T.B., "The triumph of pragmatism: China's links with the West," *International Affairs* (London), vol. 55, 1979, no. 2, pp. 195-205.

"Millions put to work in 1982," *Beijing Review*, June 6, 1983, pp. 5-6.

Monnier, Claude, *Impressions de Chine* (Impression of China), Lausanne, Suisse: Eibel, 1975.

"More authority for enterprises revives the economy," *Beijing Review,* April 6, 1981, pp. 21-27.

Morton, W. Scott, *China: Its History and Culture,* New York: Harper and Row, 1980.

Moskalev, A.A., *Politika KNR v natsional'no-yazykovym voprose* (The policy of the CPR in the national-language problem), Moskva: "Nauka," 1981.

Mosyko, G.H., *Armiya kitaya, orudie avantiuristicheskoi politiki maoistvo* (The Chinese army, an instrument at the service of the adventurist policy of the Maoists), Moskva: Voenizdat, 1980.

Mu, Qing, Ge Qiaoren, Lu Fuwei, "Li shi de shen pan" (Judgment of history), *Guangming ribao,* January 27, 1981, p. 3.

Murasheva, F.G., "Agressivnye voiny kitaya protiv V'etnama" (The Chinese aggressive war against Vietnam), *Voprosy istorii,* no. 6, 1979, pp. 96-107.

Murray, D.M. "The great walls of China," *Today's education,* 71 (February-March 1982), pp. 50-53. An American's experience with cultural barriers.

Myashnikov, V., "Ideological bankruptcy of Peking's falsifiers of history," *Far Eastern Affairs* (Moscow), 1 (1979), pp. 28-38.

Nagornyi, A.A. i A.B. Parkanskii, *SShA i kitai, ekon. i nauch. tekhn. aspekty, kitaiskoi politiki vashingtona* (The United States and China, the economic and scientific-technological aspects of the China policy of Washington), Moskva: "Nauka," 1982.

Nanjing University, Dept. of Agricultural Economics, *Economic Facts,* 1980, 4 vols.

Näth, Marie-Luise, "Staatsinteresse und ideologie in der Aussenpolitik der Volksrepublik China" (State's interest and ideology in the foreign policy of the CPR), *Sozialismus in theorie und praxis,* Berlin: V. Hannelore, 1978, s. 347-372.

"National People's Congress," *Beijing Review,* June 6, 1983, pp. 16-18.

Needham, Joseph, "Report from the People's Republic of China," *Internationale Zeitschrift für Erziehungswissenschaft,* bd. 25, 1979, h. 1, s. 73-83.

"New round of Euromissile talks," *Beijing Review,* May 30, 1983, pp. 11-12.

"Ni men song lai hao lu feng, jing shen wen ming zan" (You send down a good style of traveling, praise of the spiritual culture), *Renmin ribao,* July 9, 1982, p. 1.

Nieh, Yu-hsi, "Der unbeständige Pekinger Frühling" (The brief Beijing spring), *China aktuell,* j. 8, 1979, Novemberheft, s. 1217-1222.

Nikiforov, V.N., *Kitai v gody probuzhdeniya Azii* (China in the years of the awakening of Asia), Moskva: "Nauka," 1982.

Niu, Gen, "Tan bian" (On change), *Guangming ribao,* January 22, 1981, p. 1.

"No FX for Taipei, no joy in Peking," *Newsweek,* January 25, 1982, p. 46.

"No trump," *Time,* April 5, 1982, p. 43. Moscow's attempt to reopen talks with China.

Les nouvelles institutions chinoises, la constitution de 1975 (The new institutions of China, the 1975 constitution), Paris: Documentation française, 1975.

"Nu li shi xian su du yu xiao yi de tong yi" (Strive to achieve the unity of speed and efficiency), *Renmin ribao,* May 18, 1983, p. 1.

Obshchestvo i gosudarstvo v kitae (Society and state of China), sb. statei, Moskva: "Nauka," 1981.

Ogden, Suzanne, "China's position on UN Charter review," *Pacific Affairs* (New York), vol. 52, 1979, no. 2, pp. 210-240.

On the social transformation of China minority nationalities, New York: Xerox Pub. Co., 1980.

Opasnyi Kurs kitai posle Mao Tszeduna (The dangerous course of China after Mao Zedong), Moskva: Politizdat, 1980.

Orleans, L.A., "Science, elitism and economic readjustment in China," *Science,* 215 (January 29, 1982), pp. 472-477.

"Osvobozhdennye raiony" (The liberated areas), *Bol'shaya sovetskaya entsiklopediya,* 3rd ed., Moskva: Izdatel'stvo "sovetskaya entsiklopediya," 1974, vol. 18, col. 1648.

Pang Yongjie and Li Shanquan, "Building socialist spiritual civilization," *Beijing Review,* May 2, 1983, pp. 16-19.

Parish, William L., and Martin K. Whyte, *Village and Family in Contemporary China,* Chicago: University of Chicago Press, 1980.

Paterson, Neil, *Wettfahrt nach China, die biographie miner urgrossmutter* (Motor-race to China, a biography of my great grandmother), Hamburg: Rowohlt taschenbuch verlag, 1979.

Pattison, J.E., "China's developing legal framework for foreign investment, experience and expectations," *Law and policy in international business,* 13 (1981), pp. 89-175.

Pean, Pierre, *Après Mao, les managers* (The managers after Mao), Paris: Fayolle, 1977.

Pei Monong, "China's future position in Asia," *Beijing Review,* April 18, 1983, pp. 15-19.

Pekinskaya propaganda, tseli, metody, organizatsi (Beijing's propaganda, purposes, methods and organizations), Moskva: Mysl', 1982.

Peng, Zhen, "Explanation on seven laws," *Beijing Review,* July 13, 1979, pp. 8-16.

"Strengthen legal system and democracy," *Beijing Review,* July 6, 1979, pp. 32-36.

The People's Republic of China, 1949-1979, a documentary survey, 5 volumes, edited by Harold Hinton, Wilmington, Delaware: Scholarly Resources Inc., 1980.

Perelomov, I., "Historical legacy and China's policies," *Far Eastern Affairs* (Moscow), 1 (1979), pp. 121-130.

"Kitai, narodnaya respublika, iuridicheskaya nauka" (China, the CPR, the juridical science of), *Bol'shaya sovetskaya entsiklopediya,* 3rd ed., Moskva: Izdatel'stvo "sovetskaya entsiklopediya," 1973, vol. 12, cols. 680-682.

Perry, Phillip M., *China Business Directory,* Westport, Connecticut: Technomic Pub. Co., 1980.

Peters, Helmut, "Wissenschaftlich-theoretische konferenz über die sozialökonomische problematik des gegenwärtigen China" (Conference on science and theory in regard to the social-economic problems of the present-day China), *Deutsche aussenpolitik* (Berlin, Ost), j. 25, 1980, no. 2, s. 112-116.

Peyrauhe, Alain, "La nouvelle contestation en Chine" (The new struggle in China), *Tel guel* (Paris), no. 80, été 1979, pp. 38-58.

"Poker-faced planner named new head of state of China," by Stanley Oziewicz, *The Globe and Mail,* June 20, 1983, p. 9.

Pokert, Nanfred, *Die Chinesische Medizin* (The Chinese medicine), Unter Mitarb. V. Ullmann, Christian, Düsseldorf: Econ-Verlag, 1982.

Pomp, R.O., T.A. Gelatt, S.S. Surrey, "Evolving tax system of the People's Republic of China, *Texas international law journal,* 16 (winter 1981), pp. 11-78.

Ponomareva, I.B., *Balans sil, amerikanskaya teoriya i praktika, politika, SShA v iugo-vostochnoi azii i na dal'nem vostoke* (Balance of force, American theory and practice, the policy of the United States in south-eastern Asia and in the Far East), Moskva: Mezhdunar. otnosheniya, 1982.

Poyer, Joe, *Der Chinesische Faktor* (The Chinese factor), München: Goldmann Wilhelm, 1982.

"Prove good faith by deeds, Chinese Premier tells Soviets," by Stanley Oziewicz, *The Globe and Mail,* June 7, 1983, p. 4.

"Pu fen che jun shi pian ju, yue nan dang ju jiang cong Kampuchea che chu ta de pu fen qin lue jun dui" (Partial withdrawal of troop is deception, the Vietnamese authority will take out part of the invasion armies from Kampuchea) after July 7, 1982, *Renmin ribao,* July 10, 1982, p. 6.

Qi, Wen, *Chine, apercu general* (China, a general view), 2nd ed., rev., Paris: Editions du centennaire, 1982.

"Recent legal developments in the US-China economic relations," *Business law,* 36 (July 1981), pp. 1699-1732.

"Reform of the employment system," *Beijing Review,* April 4, 1983, pp. 5-6.

Reiflur, Sam, *Yi king, le plus ancien traité divinatoire* (Yi jing, the oldest prophetic treatise), Paris: Albin Michel, 1982.

Ren Tao, "Reform holds the key to success," *Beijing Review,* May 16, 1983, pp. 15-23.

Ren Tao and Yue Bing, "Population and employment," *Beijing Review,* March 28, 1983, pp. 17-22.

Ren, Yan, "Soviet Union promotes collective-contract system," *Beijing Review,* April 4, 1983, p. 12.

"Ren zhen zuo hao gong zheng gong zuo" (To perform the notary-public work conscientiously), *Renmin ribao,* June 29, 1982, p. 4.

Reusch, Türgen, *1st China noch sozialistisch? entwicklung und perspektiven des maoismus* (Is China socialistic? the development and perspective of Maoism), Frankfurt: Verlag marxistische blätter, 1979.

"Revolutionary wrongs redressed in China," by Stanley Oziewicz, *The Globe and Mail,* June 10, 1983, p. 3.

Rich, F.R., "Joint ventures in China, the legal challenge," *International lawyer,* 15 (spring 1981), pp. 183-211.

Richer, Phileppe, "Aux origines de la politique chinoise en Afrique noire, 1949-1960" (The origins of China's diplomacy in black Africa, 1949-1960), *Modes asiatiques,* no. 15, 1978, pp. 163-181.

La Chine et le tiers monde, 1949-1970 (China and the third world, 1949-1970), Paris: Paylot, 1971.

Riklin, Alois, "Das gras der wind, eindrucke nach einer Chinareise" (The grass of the wind, an impression of a China tour), *Schweizer monatshefte für politik, wirtschaft und kultur,* j. 59, 1979, heft 8, s. 609-623.

Roby, Jerry I., "Is the China market for you?" *Harvard Business Review,* vol. 58, 1980, no. 1, pp. 150-158.

Roche, J.P., "The Moscow card," *National review,* 34 (February 5, 1982), p. 130.

Rodiere, Michèle et Roland Trotignon, *Chine,* Paris: Assinter, 1980.

"Role of brain trust brought to play," *Beijing Review,* May 30, 1983, pp. 5-6.

Rong, Jingben, "Xue xi ma ke si guan yu lao li lao dong de lun shu" (Learn from Marx's writings about mental labor), *Renmin ribao,* May 4, 1983, p. 5.

Roth, David F., and Frank L. Wilson, *The Comparative Study of Politics,* 2nd ed., Englewood Cliffs, New Jersey: Prentice-Hall, 1980; 1st ed., 1976.

Rosenfeld, Lulla, *Des Chinesisches Orakel Bergisch Gladbach* (The Chinese oracle Bergisch Gladbach), Lubbe: G. KNO, 1982.

Ruge, Gerd, *Begegnung mit China* (To meet China), Neumarkter: Goldmann, Wilhelm Verlag, 1980.

Sagen aus China (The sayings out of China), Frankfurt: Fischer taschenbuch verlag, 1980.

Saltykov, G.F., *Sotsial'no-psikhologicheskie faktory v politicheskoi zhizni rabochego klassa KNR* (Social-psychological factors in political life of the workers' class of China), Moskva: "Nauka," 1981.

Samarin, I.N., "Kitai, narodnaya respublika, ekonomicheskaya nauka" (China, the CPR, economical science), *Bol'shaya sovetskaya entsiklopediya,* 3rd ed., Moskva: Izdatel'stvo "sovetskaya entsiklopediya," 1973, vol. 12, cols. 678-680.

Samuel, Yvon, *Chine 79, une brèche dans la grande muraille* (China in 1979, a breach in the Great Wall), Paris: J.C. Simoen, 1979.

Sander, Lin, T., *Geister und Drachen der Chinesen* (The spirits and dragons of the Chinese), Hamburg: Tessloff, 1982.

Sanders, S.W., "How the Gang of Four is haunting Deng?" *Business week,* May 31, 1982, pp. 45-46.

Sarkesian, Sam C., and James H. Buck, *Comparative Politics, an Introduction,* Sherman Oaks, California: Alfred Pub. Co., 1979 (China: pp. 180-250).

Schelle, Orville, *Les Chinois,* Paris: Librairie generale française, 1980. Previous edition has the subtitle of *la vie de tous les jours en republique de Chine* (The daily life of the Chinese), Paris: Belfond, 1978.

Schier, Peter, "Uber den stand der vorbereitung bzw einberufung der volkskongresse der provinzen, autonomen gebiete und regierungsunmittelbaren stadte" (On the preparation of calling of congresses in the provinces, autonomous regions and cities directly controlled by the central government), *China aktuell,* j. 8, 1979, Septemberheft, s. 1016-1026.

Schon, Jenny, *Frauen in China, eine Studie über die gesellschaftliche Stellung der chinesischen Frau vor 1949* (Women in China, a study of social position of the Chinese woman before 1949), Bochum: Brockmeyer Bochum, 1982.

Schurmann, Franz, *Ideology and Organization in Communist China,* new enlarged ed., Berkeley: University of California Press, 1968.

Schwiedrzik, Wolfgang M., *Literatur frühling in China? gespräch mit chinesichen schriftstellern* (A literature spring? conversation with Chinese literati), ubers. von Susanne Weigelin, Köln: Prometh verlag, 1980.

Segalen, Victor, *Le fils du ciel, chronique des jours souverains* (The son of heaven, a chronicle of the days of the rulers), Paris: Flammarion, 1976.

Seuberlich, H.E., "China heute" (Today's China), *Europäische wehrkunde* (München) j. 28, 1979, Heft 10, s. 494-501.

Seymour, James D., ed., *The Fifth Modernization: China's Human Rights Movement, 1978-1979.* Pine Plains, New York: Caleman, Earl M. Enterprises, 1981.

"Sha zhu nong yong wu zi gong ying de bu zheng zhi feng" (To cut short the irregularity in the supply system in the villages), *Renmin ribao,* May 23, 1983, p. 2.

"Shan gao ren yao gao qing zhu zhong guo gong chan dang cheng li lu shi yi zhou nian" (Mountain is high but man is higher, in honor of the 61st anniversary of the Chinese Communist Party), *Renmin ribao,* July 1, 1982, p. 2.

"Shan yu kai fa he shi yong bao gui de zhi li zi yuan" (To well develop and use the valuable intellectual resources), *Renmin ribao,* May 22, 1983, p. 1.

"Shang xia zuo yu, qi xin xie li jian she hui zhu yi jing shen wen ming" (To build up socialism's spiritual culture by concerted efforts of each and every person), *Guangming ribao,* February 20, 1981, p. 1.

"Shang ye bu men bu neng si nian yi ben jing" (The departments of commerce may not go by book), *Renmin ribao,* July 10, 1982, p. 3.

Shaw, Yu-ming, "Die chinesische kulturals herausfordering des Westens" (The Chinese culture as demanded by the West), *Concilium,* j. 15, 1979, Heft 6-7, s. 347-357.

"She hui zhu yi fa zhi de zhong da sheng li" (A great triumph of socialist legal system), *Guangming ribao*, January 26, 1981, p. 1.

"She hui zhu yi guo jia yi deng yao you gao du di jing shen wen ming" (A socialist country must have a high-level spiritual culture), *Guangming ribao*, February 18, 1981, p. 1.

"She hui zhu yi jing shen wen ming de jia zhi" (The value of spiritual culture under socialism), *Guangming ribao*, February 22, 1981, p. 1.

"Shou xian xiang dao wo shi gong chan dang yuan" (First think that I am a member of the communist party), *Renmin ribao*, July 7, 1982, p. 5.

Shovinisticheskaya politika maoistskogo rukovodstva vo vnutrennei mongolii (The chauvinist policy of the Maoist leaders in Mongolia), Moskva: "Nauka," 1980.

Shulman, Alex, *Der tunnel nach China* (The tunnel to China), Köln: Kiepenheuer & Witsch, 1980.

"Sian'skie sobytiya" (The Xian event), *Bol'shaya sovetskaya entsiklopedia*, 3rd ed., Moskva: Izdatel'stvo "sovetskaya entsiklopediya," 1976, vol. 23, col. 983.

"Sin'tszyan-uigurskii avtonomnyi raion, istoricheskii ocherk" (Xinjiang Uygur Autonomous Region), *Bol'shaya sovetskaya entsiklopediya*, 3rd ed., Moskva: Izdatel'stvo "sovetskaya entsiklopediya," 1976, vol. 23, cols. 1316-1317.

"The 6th Five-Year Plan (1981-1985) of the People's Republic of China for Economic and Social Development," adopted by the fifth session of the Fifth National People's Congress, December 10, 1982, excerpts, *Beijing Review*, May 23, 1983, pp. I-XVI; May 30, 1983, pp. I-XVI.

Smedley, Agnes, *Lebenswege in China, begegnungen* (The Chinese way of life, from experience), Berlin: Oberbauverlag, 1979.

Vom sterben des alten China (From the death of old China), Berlin: Oberbauverlag, 1978.

Smith, W.E., "A decade of measured progress," *Time*, March 15, 1982, p. 27.

Snow, Edgar, *Red Star Over China*, New York: Random House, 1938.

Snow, Helen (Foster), *The Chinese Communists; Sketches and Autobiographies of the Old Guards*, Westport, Connecticut: Greenwood Press, 1972.

Social Sciences in China, 1 (March 1980) This is a quarterly journal, published by the Social Science Publishing House of China.

Solntsev, V.M., "Kitai, yazykoznanie" (China, linguistics of), *Bol'shaya sovetskaya entsiklopediya*, 3rd ed., Moskva: Izdatel'stvo "sovetskaya entsiklopediya," 1973, vol. 12, col. 682.

Sormani, Pietro, "Il ritiro della cina dal vietnam" (The withdrawal of China from Vietnam), *Relazioni internazionali*, vol. 43, 1979, no. 10, p. 203.

Sorokin, V.F., "Mao Dun'" (Mao Dun), *Bol'shaya sovetskaya entsiklopediya*, 3rd ed., Moskva: Izdatel'stvo "sovetskaya entsiklopediya," 1974, vol. 15, cols. 1034-1035.

Sotsial'nye organizatsii v kitae (Social organizations in China), sb. statei, Moskva: "Nauka," 1981.

Sovetskii soiuz i kitaiskaya narodnaya respublika, 1949-1979, sb. dokumentov (The Soviet Union and the Chinese People's Republic, 1949-1979, a collection of documents), sost. A.A. Brezhdev i S.N. Goncharenko, Moskva: Mezhdunar. otnosheniya, 1981.

"Sovetsko-kitaiskii konflikt" (The Sino-Soviet conflict), *Bol'shaya sovetskaya entsiklopediya*, 3rd ed., Moskva: Izdatel'stvo "sovetskaya entsiklopediya," 1976, vol. 24, cols. 92-93.

Spence, Jonathan D., *The Gate of Heavenly State: The Chinese and Their Revolutions, 1895-1980*, New York: Viking Press, 1981.

Spengler, Tilman, "Wenn China nicht klappt" (If China does not work well), *Kursbuch* (Berlin), no. 57, 1979, s. 9-32.

Starr, John Bryan, "China's economic outreach," *Current History*, 449, (1977) no. 79 pp. 49-52, 87-88.

Stepanov, E.D., *Kitai na morskikh rubezhakh* (China at the maritime front), Moskva: Mezhdunar otnosheniya, 1980.

Stewart-Smith, D.G., *The Defeat of Communism*, 1st ed., London: Ludgate Press, 1964.

Stoessinger, John G., *Nations in Darkness: China, Russia and America*, 3rd ed., New York: Random House, 1981.

Sulitskaya, T.I., *Kitai i frantisya 1949-1980* (China and France in 1949-1980), Moskva: "Nauka," 1982.

Sulzberger, Cyrus Léo, *Post scriptum*, Paris: Albin Michel, 1976.

Sun, Dongmin, "Wai ceng kong jian de mei su jun bei jing sai" (The US-USSR armed rivalry in the outer space), *Renmin ribao*, July 10, 1982, p. 7.

Sun, Qimeng, "Shi xing liang zhong bu tong de jian du" (To practice two different kinds of supervision), *Renmin ribao*, July 1, 1982, p. 5.

"Sun, Tsin-lin" (Song Qingling), *Bol'shaya sovetskaya entsiklopediya*, 3rd ed., Moskva: Izdatel'stvo "sovetskaya entsiklopediya," 1976, vol. 25, cols. 222-223.

"Sunchzhunkhoi" (The xingzhonghui), *Bol'shaya sovetskaya entsiklopediya*, 3rd ed., Moskva: Izdatel'stvo "sovetskaya entsiklopediya," 1976, vol. 23, col. 1309.

Suttmeier, Richard P., *Science, Technology and China's Drive for Modernization*, Palo Alto, California: Hoover Institution Press, 1980.

Tang, Peter S.H., and Joan M. Maloney, *Communist China: the Domestic Scene, 1949-1967*, South Orange, New Jersey: Seton Hall University Press, 1967.

Tao, Hua he Zhao Suying, "You guan lian chan ze ren zhi de ji ge wen ti" (Several questions in connection with the system of collective production), *Guangming ribao*, February 9, 1981, p. 2.

Tche-hao, Tsien, *Le droit chinois* (The Chinese law), Paris: Presses universitaires de France, 1982.

Terrill, Ross, *L'Avenir de la Chine* (The future of China), trad. Americain, Paris: Flammarion, 1979. Same as *The Future of China After Mao*.

800,000,000, the Real China, New York: Delta Pub. Co., 1972.

The Future of China After Mao, New York: Delta Pub. Co., 1978. Same as *L'Avenir dela Chine*.

Territorial'nye prityazaniya pekina, istoriya, sovremennost' (Territorial claims of Beijing, past and present), Moskva: Politizdat, 1979.

Thiemann, Wilhelm, *China, photographische Aufzeichnungen aus den Jahren 1926-1936* (China, a photographical scene of the years from 1926 to 1936), Munchen: Simon/Magiera, 1982.

"Threatening a second lesson," *Time*, March 2, 1983, p. 41.

Le Tibet vu par les Tibétains; un document sur la civilisation fascinate d'un pays dont l'accès est interdit aux occidentaux depuis trente ans (Tibet as seen by the Tibetans, a document on the fascinating civilization of a country the access to which was prohibited to the Westerners in thirty years), Paris: Editions du Fanal, 1982.

Tien, H. Yuan, ed., *Population Theory in China*, Armouk, New York: M.E. Sharpe, 1980.

Tikhvinskii, S.T., "Sun' Yat Sen," *Bol'shaya sovetskaya entsiklopediya*, 3rd ed., Moskva: Izdatel'stvo "sovetskaya entsiklopediya," 1976, vol. 25, cols. 223-225.

Tissier, Patrick, *Deux modèles d'avant garde dans la construction du socialisme*

524   GOVERNMENT OF SOCIALIST CHINA

en république de China, Taking pouring l'industrie, Tatchai pour l'agriculture (Two models of vanguard in the construction of socialism in the CPR, Daqing in industry, Dazhai in agriculture), Paris: Nouveau bureau d'édition, 1975.

Titarenko, M.A., Antisotsialisticheskii kurs pekina (The anti-socialist course of Beijing), Moskva: Mezhdunar, otnosheniya, 1979.

Titarenko, M.L., "Kitai, narodnaya respublika, obshchestvennye nauki" (China, the CPR, social sciences of), Bol'shaya sovetskaya entsiklopediya, 3rd ed., Moskva: Izdatel'stvo "sovetskaya entsiklopediya," 1973, vol. 12, cols. 671-675.

Toscano, Alberto, "C'era una volta l'alleanza cina-urss" (The turning round of the Sino-Soviet alliance), Relazioni internazionali, vol. 43, 1979, no. 15, p. 324.

"Il peso della cina" (The importance of China), Relazioni internazionali, vol. 44, 1980, no. 3, p. 35.

"La cina attaca il vietnam" (China attacks Vietnam), Relazioni internazionali, vol. 43, 1979, no. 8, p. 155.

"La cina dopo l'assemblea popolo" (China after the people's congress), Relazioni internazionali, vol. 43, 1979, no. 27, p. 590.

"La cina festeggia il trentennale riflettendo" (China celebrates the 30th anniversary of the revolution), Relazioni internazionali, vol. 43, 1979, no. 41, p. 889.

"Obiettivi internazionali di pechino" (The international objectives of Beijing), Relazioni internazionali, vol. 43, 1979, no. 28, pp. 616-617.

Townsend, James, Comparative Politics Today, a World View, 2nd ed., Boston: Little, Brown, 1980, "Politics in China," pp. 381-432.

Politics in China, 2nd ed., Boston: Little, Brown, 1980.

and Roland Bush, eds., The People's Republic of China, a Basic Handbook, 2nd enlarged ed., New York: Learning resources in international studies, 1981.

"Trends in Chinese jurisprudence," Beijing Review, April 6, 1981, pp. 14-16.

30 let KNR (30 years of the CPR), Moskva: Politizdat, 1980.

Underdown, Michael, "The Chinese revolution and inner Mongolia," Papers on Far Eastern History, no. 19, Canberra: The Australian National University, 1980, pp. 203-222.

"Urban senior citizens surveyed," Beijing Review, May 23, 1983, pp. 9, 21.

V neba kitaya 1937-1939; vospominaniya sovetskikh letchikov-dobrovol'tsev (In the sky of China during 1937-1939, reminiscences of Soviet volunteer-airmen), Moskva: "Nauka," 1979.

Van Geem, Isabelle, Crier avant de mourir, la tragédie du Tibet (Cry before death, the tragedy of Tibet), Paris: Laffont, 1977.

Varnan, F., Put' maoistvo (The Maoist way), per. c veng., Moskva: Progress, 1979.

Vasil'ev, L.S., Problemy genezisa kitaiskogo gosudarstva, formirovanie osnov sotsial'noi struktury i politicheskoi administratsii (The problems of genesis of the Chinese state, the formation of the basis of social structure and political administration), Moskva: "Nauka," 1982.

"The veep takes on an angry China," US news and world report, 92 (May 17, 1982), p. 16.

Vernant, Jacques, "Les orientations actuelles de la Chine" (The current orientation of the CPR), Defense nationale, a. 34, 1978, août-sept., pp. 123-130.

Vetter, Horst F., "China nach Mao, was hat sich geändert, was bleibt?" (China after Mao, what has changed and what has remained?) Herder korrespondenz, vol. 33, 1979, no. 5, s. 262-267.

"Die transformation der revolution, politische veränderungen in China nach Mao Zedong" (The transformation of the revolution, political change in China after Mao Zedong), Internationales Asienforum (München), j. 10, 1979, Heft 1-2, s. 85-102.

Vyatkin, R.V., "Kitai, narodnaya respublika, istoricheskaya nauka" (China, the CPR, historical science of), *Bol'shaya sovetskaya entsiklopediya*, 3rd ed., Moskva: Izdatel'stvo "sovetskaya entsiklopediya," 1973, vol. 12, cols. 676-678.

Wallace, James, "Between US and China, a sweet and sour relations," *US news and world report*, 92 (March 1, 1982), p. 28. Effect of US arms sales to Taiwan.

"Peking's new frontier: where China, Russia vie (Sinkiang)," *US news and world report*, 92 (March 8, 1982), pp. 62-63.

Waller, D.J., *The Government and Politics of Communist China*, London: Hutchinson University Library, 1970. 3rd ed., 1981.

Wang, Bingqian, "Guan yu 1980 nian guo jia jue suan he 1981 nian guo jia gai suan zhi xing qing kuang de bao gao" (A report on the execution of 1980 and 1981 budgets), *Renmin ribao*, December 15, 1981, pp. 3, 4. The same exercise for 1981 and 1982, *ibid.*, December 2, 1982, p. 1.

"Jiang jiu sheng cai, ju cai, yong cai, jia su she hui zhu yi jian she" (Study the principles of producing, accumulating and utilizing wealths, accelerate socialist construction), *Renmin ribao*, June 29, 1982, p. 5. Excerpt from *Yi ju ba er zhong guo jing ji nian jian* (The 1982 Annal of China Economy).

Wang, Guangyao, "Dui cheng shi lu hua gong zuo de ji dian jian yi" (Several suggestions on the work of making the city green), *Renmin ribao*, July 10, 1982, p. 5.

Wang, Gungwu, *China and the World Since 1949; the impact of independence, modernity and revolution*, London: Macmillan, 1977.

Wang, James, *Contemporary Chinese Politics, an Introduction*, Englewood Cliffs, New Jersey: Prentice-Hall, 1980.

Wang, Zheng, "Jia qiang gan bu lun xun jiao you, ti gao gan bu dui wu su zhi, wei qing zhu zhong guo gong chan dang cheng li lu shi yi zhou nian er zuo" (Strengthen the cadres' rotation training, and enhance the quality of the cadre corps, in celebration of the 61st anniversary of the Chinese Communist Party), *Renmin ribao*, July 1, 1982, p. 1.

"Warm missive," *Time*, January 10, 1982, p. 25.

Wassermann, Ursula, "Zurich conference on trade with China," *Journal of world trade law*, November-December 1981, pp. 553-557.

Wegels, Oskar, "Die neue chinesische Verfassung vom 5. märz 1978" (The new Chinese Constitution of March 5, 1978), *Jahrbuch des öffentlichen rechts der gegenwart* (N.F. Tübingen), bd. 27, 1978, s. 501-534.

Weggel, Oskar, "China und Laos, vor dem scherbenhaufen einer jahrelangen partnerschaft" (China and Laos, before the breakup of many years' friendship), *China aktuell*, j. 8, 1979, Märzheft, s. 191-218.

"Chinas erziehungsfeldzug gegen Vietnam" (China's lesson-teaching-campaign against Vietnam), *China aktuell*, j. 8, 1979, Februarheft, s. 98-127.

"Nach dem erziehungsfeldzug, nun das erziehungsgespräch, fünf verhandlungsrunden, fünf sitzungen and fünf themen" (After the lesson-teaching-campaign came the lesson-teaching conversation, five negotiations, five sessions and five topics), *China aktuell*, j. 8, 1979, Maiheft, s. 568-589.

Wei, Guoqing, "Cai quan jun zheng zhi gong zuo hui yi sheng de jiang hua" (A speech at the all-army political-work conference), *Guangming ribao*, February 4, 1981, p. 1.

"Wei shen mo qiang xing jie guan min ban qi ye?" (Why take over by force people-run enterprises?) *Renmin ribao*, May 17, 1983, p. 2.

Weiss, P., "La république populaire de Chine et la proche-orient" (The CPR and the near East), *Politique étrangére*, a. 43, 1978, no. 2, pp. 181-198.

"Wen ding jia ting cheng bao ze ren zhi" (Stabilize the family-rent responsibility system), *Renmin ribao*, May 8, 1983, p. 1.

Wen hui bao, June 21, 1949-

"Wen yi gong zuo zhe yao jia qiang li lun xue xi" (Workers in art and literature must strengthen the study and learning of theory), *Renmin ribao,* June 26, 1982, p. 1.

Whiting, Allen S., *Modern Political System: Asia,* Robert E. Ward and Roy C. Macridis, Englewood Cliffs, New Jersey: Prentice-Hall, 1963, "China," pp. 117-214.

Wickert, Erwin, *China von innen gesehen* (China, viewed from inside), Stuttgart: Deutsche Verlags-Anstalt, 1982.

Willeke, Bernward H., "China killoguium in Hofheim" im Taunus am 21-23, June 1979, *Neue zeitschrift für missionwissenschaft,* j. 35, 1979, Heft 4, s. 304.

Willey, F., "China's capitalist road (Szechwan)," *Newsweek,* 99 (April 12, 1982), p. 42.

"Sober second thoughts," *Newsweek,* 99 (May 24, 1982), pp. 46ff.

"An unhappy anniversary," *Newsweek,* 99 (March 15, 1982), pp. 47-38.

"Where is Deng Xiaoping?" *Newsweek,* 99 (February 22, 1982), pp. 42ff.

Die wirtschaft osteuropas und der volksrepublik China 1970-1980, bilanz und perspektiven (The economy of Eastern Europe and the CPR, 1970-1980, a balance sheet and perspective), Stuttgart: Kohlhammer, 1978.

Die Wirtschaft Osteuropas und der VR China zu Begin der achtziger Jahre (The economy of East Europe and the People's Republic of China at the beginning of the 1980's), Stuttgart: Kohl/Hammer, 1982.

Witke, Roxane, *Comarade Chiang Ching* (Comrade Jiang Qing), Paris: Laffont, 1978.

Wood, Frances, *Through the Year in China,* North Demfet, Vermont: David and Charles, 1981.

"Written judgment of the Special Court Under the Supreme People's Court of the People's Republic of China," *Beijing Review,* February 2, 1981, pp. 13-28.

Wu Naitao, "The pillars of tomorrow, Youth League members join modernization drive," *Beijing Review,* May 2, 1983, pp. 23-27.

"After careful thought and comparison, increased conviction in Marxism among Beijing University students," *Baijing Review,* May 2, 1983, pp. 20-23.

Wu, J.T., *Chinese transformation, a program reference table,* Hamburg: the author (privately printed), 1982.

Xia, Shuzhang, "Cong xian fa xiu gai cao an kan xing zheng li fa de ren wu" (The responsibility of the executive and legislature viewed from the stance of the new constitution), *Renmin ribao,* June 29, 1982, p. 5.

Xie, Heng, "Why the crime rate is declining," interview with Xie Heng, director of Social Security Bureau under the Ministry of Public Security, *Beijing Review,* March 21, 1983, pp. 15-18.

Xin hua she bulletins, started in April 1937 in Yanan, English releases from September 1944.

Xue, Muqiao, *Dang qian wo guo jing ji ruo gan wen ti* (Some economic problems currently facing our country), Beijing: Ren min chu ban she, 1980.

"Xue hui shi yong fa lu wu qi wei hu she hui an ding tuan jie" (To learn how to use juridical means to maintain social stability and solidarity), *Guangming ribao,* January 27, 1981, pp. 1, 3.

Yan, Jiaqi, "Lun gai ge" (On reform), *Renmin ribao,* July 6, 1982, p. 5.

Yang, Jianbai, "Lue lun su du he xiao yi wen ti" (A brief discussion of the efficiency and profit question), *Renmin ribao,* June 29, 1982, p. 5.

"Yao cai pei yang shao nian de ke xue su zhi shang xia gong fu" (Making effort to improve scientific education of the youths), *Guangming ribao,* June 20, 1981, p. 1.

Yao, Yilin, "Wai zi yao yong yu zhong dian jian she he ji shu jie fang" (Foreign investment should go to crucial construction and technical reform), *Renmin ribao,* May 21, 1983, p. 1.

"Yao zhong si tu zhuan jia" (To attach importance to the raw experts), *Renmin ribao,* May 26, 1983, p. 2.

"Yi feng yi su ying xin nian" (Change habit and welcome the new year), *Renmin ribao,* December 28, 1981, p. 1.

"Yi ju ba yi gao deng xue xiao zhao sheng gong zuo de gui deng" (Regulations on the recruitment of students to the schools of higher learning in 1981), approved by the State Council, *Guangming ribao,* March 16, 1981, p. 1.

Yin, John, *Sino-Soviet Dialogue on the Problem of War,* The Hague: Martinus Nijhoff; New York: International publication service, 1971.

Yee, Herbert S., "China's reunification offensive and Taiwan's policy options," *World today,* 38 (January 1982), pp. 33-38.

"Yong xin yan guang ren shi xin wen ti" (New problems to be viewed in new light), *Renmin ribao,* July 13, 1982, p. 1.

"Yong zi ji de xing dong shu xie guang cai de li shi" (To write glorious history by one's action), *Renmin ribao,* December 5, 1981, p. 1.

Yu Guangyuan, "Ke xue de guang hui zai yan an shan yao" (The brilliance of science emits from Yanan), *Guangming ribao,* July 8, 1981, p. 4.

Yuan, Ge, "Yao xiang qian kan, bu yao xiang qian kan" (To look forward, not look at the money), *Guangming ribao,* February 11, 1981, p. 1.

Yurkov, S., "China's shadow over south Asia and the Middle East," *Far Eastern Affairs* (Moscow), 3 (1979), pp. 64-72.

"Zai an ding tuan jie de ji chu shang, she xian guo min jing ji tiao zheng de ju da ren wu" (Implement the nine tasks of readjusting national economy on the basis of stability and solidarity), *Guangming ribao,* January 1, 1981, pp. 1, 3. A reprint of a *Renmin ribao* editorial.

"Zai tiao zheng zhong ke xue ji shu yao tong guo min jing ji xie tiao fa zhan" (During the readjustment, science and technology must be developed in conjunction with national economy), *Guangming ribao,* January 15, 1981, pp. 1, 3.

Zaichikov, V.T. i P.N. Kropotkin, "Kitai, priroda" (China, nature of), *Bol'shaya sovetskaya entsiklopediya,* 3rd ed., Moskva: Izdatel'stvo "sovetskaya entsiklopediya," 1973, vol. 12, cols. 600-606.

Zaitsev, E.M., "Sovetsko-kitaiskie soglasheniya" (Sino-Soviet agreements), *Bol'shaya sovetskaya entsiklopediya,* 3rd ed., Moskva: Izdatel'stvo "sovetskaya entsiklopediya," 1976, vol. 24, cols. 90-92.

Zhang, Dezheng, "Shu de le jian wang zheng?" (Who suffers from forgetful disease?), *Renmin ribao,* June 27, 1982, p. 6. Criticism of US Taiwan policy.

Zhang, Qihua, "Xi ban ya jia ru ou zhou gong tong ti wen ti ge jian" (The halting up of the Spanish entry into the European community), *Renmin ribao,* July 7, 1982, p. 7.

Zhang, Qingfu he Li Puyun, "Yi xiang yi yi shen yuan de gai ge" (A reform of the most profound meaning), *Renmin ribao,* July 9, 1982, p. 5. Comment on the new constitution.

Zhang, Tailei, *Zhang Tailei wen ji* (Collected writings of Zhang Tailei), Beijing: Ren min chu ban she, 1981.

Zhang, Zhiye, "How do China's lawyers work?" *Beijing review,* June 6, 1983, pp. 19-27.

Zhao, Ziyang, *Dang qian de jing ji xing shi he jing hou jing ji jian she de feng zhen* (The current economic situation and the general guideline for future economic buildup), Beijing: Renmin chu ban she, 1981, this is a full text of the "Zheng fu gong zuo bao gao," see below.

"Report on the Sixth Five-Year Plan," delivered at the fifth session of the Fifth National People's Congress on November 30, 1982, *Beijing Review*, December 20, 1982, pp. 10-35.

"Speech at Beijing south-south conference," *Beijing Review*, April 18, 1983, pp. I-VIII.

"Zai guan yu he zuo yu fa zhan de guo ji hui yi shang de fa yan" (An address to the international conference of cooperation and development), at Cancun, Mexico, October 22, 1981, *Renmin ribao*, October 24, 1981, p. 1.

"Zheng fu gong zuo bao gao" (Government report) to the 4th session of the 5th National People's Congress, *Renmin ribao*, December 1, 1981, p. 1. This is the Chinese variety of the State of the Union message.

"Zheng que dui dai zhi shi fen zi de ru dang wen ti" (To confront correctly the problem of intellectuals' joining the party), *Renmin ribao*, May 23, 1983, p. 3.

"Zheng zhi an ding shi jing ji tiao zheng de bao zheng" (Political stability is the guaranty of economic readjustment), *Guangming ribao*, January 17, 1981, p. 1. A reprint of a *Renmin ribao* editorial.

"Zhi chi min zhu dang pai kai zhan zhi li zhi bian gong zuo" (To support democratic parties and factions in their effort to dedicate to the frontier work), *Renmin ribao*, May 22, 1983, p. 1.

"Zhong chao yu hao guan xi zhong de yi jian da shi" (A great event in the Sino-Korean relationship), *Renmin ribao*, December 20, 1981, p. 1.

Zhong gong dang shi jiang yi (Lecture outline on the history of the CCP), Guangzhou: Guangdong ren min chu ban she, 1981.

"Zhong gong zhong yang, guo wu yuan guan yu da jie jing ji ling yu zhong yan zhong fan zui huo dong de jue ding" (The party center and State Council decided on the punishment of the economic crimes), *Guangming ribao*, April 14, 1982, pp. 1, 2.

Zhong guo di tu ji (Chinese atlas), cartography by Lin Chong, text by Huang Jiushun, Hong Kong: Xin yu chu ban gong si, 1980.

Zhong guo fa zhi bao (China law and institutional journal), enlarged edition, January 1982-

Zhong guo gai kuang (China handbook), Beijing: Ren min chu ban she, 1980.

Zhong guo gong chan dang da shi nian biao (Chronological events of the CCP), Beijing: Ren min chu ban she, 1981.

Zhong guo gong chan dang lu shi nian (Sixty years of the CCP), Shanghai: Shanghai ren min chu ban she, 1981.

Zhong guo jian kuang (China briefings), Beijing: Wai wen chu ban she, 1982-1983. Printed in conventional scripts aimed at overseas Chinese. They cover diverse subjects such as agriculture, shepherding, rare animals, trade, religion, physical education, historical cities, natural sciences, journalism, handicrafts, publication, social sciences, etc.

Zhong guo jing ji nian jian, 1981 (China economic almanac).

Zhong guo qing nian bao, organ of the Chinese Communist Youth League, April 27, 1951-August 19, 1966, October 7, 1978-.

Zhong guo shou ce (China handbook), Hong Kong: Da gong bao, 1979.

"Zhong gong ye yao tiao zhen feng xiang" (To reorient the development of heavy industry), *Renmin ribao*, November 16, 1981, p. 1.

Zhong hua renmin gong he guo gong zheng zan xing tiao li (Interim regulations on the notary public of the Chinese People's Republic) promulgated by the State Council on April 13, 1982, *Renmin ribao*, June 29, 1982, p. 4.

Zhong hua ren min gong he guo kai guo wen xian (Foundation documents of the Chinese People's Republic), Hong Kong: Wen hua zhi liao gong ying she, 1978.

"Zhong hua ren min gong he guo zui gao ren min fa yuan pan jue shu" (Judgment of the Special Court of the Supreme People's Court of the CPR), *Guangming ribao*, January 26, 1981, pp. 2, 3.

"Zhong shi dui dang de ji ceng zhu zhi de zheng dang gong zuo" (To stress the adjustment work at the party's basic level), *Renmin ribao*, June 27, 1982, p. 1.

"Zhong shi gao hao qi ye de jing yin" (Emphasize the management of collective enterprises), *Guangming ribao*, March 21, 1981, p. 1.

"Zhong shi ji si tui wu de jian she" (Place emphasis on the building up of anti-smuggle teams), *Renmin ribao*, July 13, 1982, p. 5.

"Zhong yu dang de shi ye, chen shi fan ying shi dai" (Be faithful to the party affairs, and take up the challenge of the era), *Guangming ribao*, March 25, 1981, p. 1.

Zhou, Enlai, *Zhou Enlai xuan ji* (Selected writings of Zhou Enlai), Beijing: Ren min chu ban she, 1981 (vol. 1).

"Zhu he fei zhou jie fang ti er shi zhou nian" (To congratulate the 20th anniversary of the liberation of Africa), *Renmin ribao*, May 25, 1983, p. 6.

Zhu, Xuefan, "Ge ming dao di, ying jie xin de sheng li" (Struggle to the end and welcome new victories), *Guangming ribao*, June 29, 1981, p. 4.

Zi, Zhongyun, "Li shi de kao nian xin zhong guo dan sheng qian hou mei guo de dui tai zheng ce" (Historical test, the US policy toward Taiwan during the time when the new China was born), *Renmin ribao*, July 13, 1982, p. 6.

"Zong jiao xin yang zi you shi yi xiang chang qi zheng ce" (The freedom to believe in religion is a long-term policy), *Renmin ribao*, May 12, 1983, p. 2.

"Zong jie jing nian, jing yi bu zuo hao ji shu zhi qing ping ding gong zuo" (Summation of experience, one step further toward evaluation of technical nomenclature), *Guangming ribao*, July 27, 1981, p. 1.

ABC (Anti-Bolshevik Corp.), 107
Academic degrees, 377, 381, 461
Academy of Sciences, 209, 377, 388, 403
Academy of Social Sciences, 306, 377, 397, 439
Act for the Punishment of corruption, 436, 467
Act for the Punishment of counterrevolutionaries, 436, 463, 467, 468
Act for the Punishment of Crime in Damage of State Security, 436, 467
Acupuncture, 406
Administration, 55, 60, 90, 129, 131, 140, 144, 145, 161, 164, 171, 172, 174, 177, 188, 280, 281, 306, 307, 315, 349, 358, 368, 372, 377, 414, 418, 426, 457, 459, 461, 465, 491
Adult education, 366, 367, 368, 370, 376, 382
Adultry, 475
Afghanistan, 1, 204, 218, 230, 231, 234, 235
Africa, 246, 247, 248
Age of criminal responsibility, 480
Agnosticism, 32
Agrarian reform, see Land reform
Agricultural Bank, 311
Agricultural producers' co-op (APC), 257, 258, 259, 260, 261, 262, 263, 269, See also Co-ops
Agricultural schools, 373, 374
Agriculture, 6, 11, 55, 68, 74, 111, 141, 190, 205, 251, 256, 257, 261, 267, 268, 269, 272, 274, 283, 285, 289, 290, 291, 293, 294, 295, 305, 321, 322, 326, 328, 357, 365, 383, 384, 385, 387, 413, 414
Agrogorod, 321, 413
Agrunachal Pradesh, 234
Aid to regional government, 16
Airforce, 191, 194, 197, 202, 203, 218
Airlines, 314, 315, 323
Aksai Chin, 190, 232
Alabama court, 220
Albania, 193, 209, 222, 232, 245, 246
Algeria, 248
Aliev, G., 92
Alimony, 450, 458
All-China Geography Soviety, 384
Amazon, 4

American Bar Association, 450, 485, 489
Amnesty International, 488
Amur, 1, 2, 3, 222, 227, 258
Analogy in criminal law, 482, 483
Anarchism, 393
Anda County (Heilongjiang), 321
Andropov, Yuri, 91, 92, 182, 231
Anfu faction, 43, 44
Angola, 193, 248
Anhui, 10, 53, 105, 179, 196, 316, 376, 414, 432, 476
Antigua and Barbuda, 248
Anti-illiteracy, 366, 367, 368, 370
Anti-Japanese University of Politics and Armed Affairs, 369, 370
Anti-rightist campaign, 261, 291, 384, 437
Aphrodisiacs, 10
Arab-Israeli war (1973), 241
Arabs, 193, 241
Arctic system (rivers), 2
Argentina, 276
Armament, 204, 205, 206, 283, 338, 339, 354, 399, 411, See also — Military modernization
Armed forces, 7
Armed insurrection, 466
Armenian Soviet Socialist Republic, 138
Army, see Armed forces
Army-party relations, 130
Arrest and detention, 495, 496
Arson, 476, 477, 480
Art and literature, 109, 149, 150
Artificial satellites, 206, 207, 390
Artillery, 194, 195, 200
ASEAN, 230
Asia, 1, 193, 212, 218, 227, 230, 232, 235, 236, 237, 241, 336, 355
Assessors (court), 450, 486
Associated Press, 477
Associations and societies, 390
Atlanta, 217
Atlantic Richfield California, 318, 347
Atomic Energy Institute, 349
Atomic Research Center, 349
Australia, 276, 340, 343, 345, 349
Austria, 349
Autarky, 6, 308
Autonomous regions, 15, 16, 153, 158, 160, 163, 165, 173, 174, 176, 177, 178, 184, 185, 189, 197, 257, 296, 300, 367, 377, 378, 380, 422, 476, 483, 484

Autumn-Spring (722-481 B.C.) 28
Aviation technology, 203
Axis Powers, 253

Ba Jing, 390
Baker, Howard, 219
Ban on secession, 16
Bandung Conference, 247
Bangladesh, 233, 234
Bank of China, 311, 350, 351, 452, 453
Bank of Communication, 311
Bank of Continental China, 305
Bao zhan dao hu, 212, 273, 414, 415
Baoding, 189
Barefoot doctors, 401, 402, 403, 404
Barnett, Doak A., 390
Basins, 6
Bawei Ansha, 1 (& fn 1)
Beidaihe, 120
Beijing, 1, 8, 13, 43, 44, 45, 46, 49, 52, 64, 66, 69, 82, 115, 116, 120, 121, 124, 130, 153, 155, 163, 165, 175, 187, 188, 194, 195, 196, 197, 209, 214, 215, 216, 220, 233, 235, 236, 241, 243, 274, 286, 321, 325, 333, 335, 336, 337, 355, 356, 365, 369, 389, 390, 399, 417, 427, 428, 429, 431, 444, 458, 459, 476, 481, 483, 485, 486
Beijing Polytechnical Institute, 380, 381
Beijing University, 64, 65, 381, 461, 485
Beijing-Guangzhou railway, 4, 313
Beijing-Haerbin railway, 313
Beijing-Shanghai railway, 4
Beijing-Tongliao railway, 312
Beilun, 1
Bergland, Bob, 336
Beria, Lavrenti, 495
Berlinguer, Enrich, 245
Bhutan, 1
Bhutto, Ali, 234
Bigamy, 446
Birobidjon Autonomous Region, 3
Birth control, 11, 12, 13, 177, 295, 404, 430, 431, 432, 447, See also family planning
Black (bad) elements, 474, 475, 483, 498
Blucher, Vasily, 48
Blumenthal, Michael, 217, 335
Bo Yibo, 93, 169, 236

Bohai, 2
Bohai Bay, 317
Bolshevik Revolution, 64
Border Government, see Shaan-Gan-Ling, Ji-Cha-Jing
Borodin, Michael, 48, 49, 51, 67
Boundary, 1,2
Bourgeois, 286, 287, 288, 306, 380, 436, 438
Bourgeois decadence, 114, 115, 117, 118, 121, 122, 148, 149, 150, 296, 297, 365, 392, 393, 448
Bouyei, 18
Brezhnev, Leonid, 182, 221, 228, 230, 231, 283
Bribery, 478
Brigades, 262, 263, 264, 267, 270, 271, 273, 274, 300, 372, 373, 401, 403, 404
British, 36, 43
Brown, Harold, 204, 217
Broyelle, Claude, 486
Bruce, David, 215
Buddhism, 45
Budgets, 158, 161, 171, 175, 288, 305, 308, 310, 358, 366, 426
Bukharin, Nikolai, 256
Bulganin, Nikolai, 223
Bureaucracy, see administration
Bureaucratic capitalism, 103, 132, 146
Bureaucratism, 148, 297, 393
Bureaucrats, 292, 295, 299, 361, 365, 379, 385, 395, 405, 444, 460, 461, 471, 473, 478, 479, See also cadres
Burlingame Mission (1867), 212
Burma, 1, 23, 60, 189, 192, 193, 230, 232, 240
Bush, George, 219
Businesses, 456
Businessmen, 287, 416, 454
Butcher, Willard, 336
Cabinet, 41, 42, 91, 170
Cadres, 139, 140, 148, 149, 160, 176, 179, 181, 186, 205, 255, 264, 272, 276, 280, 281, 292, 295, 296, 306, 322, 338, 349, 359, 360, 364, 365, 367 (educational), 379, 383, 388, 394, 399, 401, 405, 420, 423, 425, 428, 429, 430, 438, 444 (judicial), 456, 460, 461, 465, 470 (judicial), 472, 473, 478, 479, 484. See also bureaucrats
Cai O, 42

Cai Shufan, 249
Caidam basic (Qinghai), 5, 317
Califano, 336
California, 2
Canada, 1, 276, 333, 340, 343, 345, 346, 349, 357
Cao Kun, 44
Cape Breton Island, 2
Capital investment, 290, 291, 294, 301, 302, 303, 304, 305, 309, 320, 325, 339, 344, 352, 354, 358, 360
Capitalism, 71, 102, 116, 121, 139, 142, 146, 225, 277, 358, 383, 384, 413
Capitalists, 132, 327, 391, 412, 422
Carl, Beverly, 424, 456, 497
Carsten, Karl, 243
Carter, J., 90, 215, 216, 217 (& fn 41), 218, 221, 222, 334, 335, 336
Cash crops, 282, 327
Cash reserves, See foreign exchange
Castro, Fidel, 246
Catholicism, 144
CCP, 7, 40, 54, 65, 66, 67, 68, 69, 70, 71, 74, 75, 81, 99, 101, 102, 103, 104, 106, 107, 109, 110, 111, 112, 115, 117, 122, 125, 126, 129, 130, 131, 133, 136, 138, 149, 153, 154, 156, 160, 164, 171, 172, 178, 181, 182, 183, 184, 185, 194, 196, 212, 221, 224, 227, 235, 245, 246, 251, 252, 254, 261, 263, 264, 280, 286, 290, 291, 296, 297, 358, 364, 365, 377, 386, 394, 396, 424, 430, 445, 446, 471, 494
  Chairman, 130, 145, 166, 172, 184, 494, 495
  Discipline, 76, 78, 79, 80, 81, 85, 96, 97, 99
  Membership, 75, 76, 80, 81, 86, 483 (post-humous deprivation)
  Membership dues, 81
  Rights and duties of card carriers, 77, 78, 99
  Withdrawal of party cards, 77
CCP Statutes
  1945 Statute - 83
  1956 Statute - 83, 95
  1969 Statute - 83, 119
  1977 Statute - 73, 83, 185
    Art. 2, clause 1 - 73
    Art. 19, clause 2 - 73

General program - 117
1982 Statute - 83, 186
  Art. 1 - 75
  Art. 2, paragraphs 2,3 - 78
  Art. 3 - 73, 78, 81, clause 1 - 73,78, clause 3 - 471, clause 4 - 101
  Art. 4 - 77, 78
  Art. 5, paragraphs 1,6 - 85
  Art. 8 - 73
  Art. 10 - 74, clause 1 - 471, clause 4 - 75, clause 5 - 73, 75, clause 6 - 74, clause 10 - 13, 75, clause 11 - 75
  Art. 11 - 87
  Art. 14 - 75
  Art. 15, paragraphs 1,2 - 75
  Art. 16, paragraph 3 - 73
  Art. 18 - 81, 82, 87, paragraph 1 - 93, paragraph 2 - 83
  Art. 19 - 82, clause 5 - 84, clause 6 - 93
  Art. 20, paragraph 1 - 84, 85, 89, paragraph 2 - 85
  Art. 21, paragraph 1 - 90, 91, 93, paragraph 2 - 90, paragraph 4 - 185, paragraph 5 - 91
  Art. 22 - 98, paragraph 2 - 91, 93, 94, paragraph 3 - 85, 94
  Art. 24 - 87
  Art. 26, paragraph 1 - 97
  Art. 28, 29, 30 paragraph 2 - 98
  Art. 32, clause 2 - 73
  Art. 33, paragraph 2 - 99
  Art. 34, paragraph 1 - 78, 87
  Art. 35 - 79, 81
  Art. 37, paragraphs 1, 2, Art. 38, paragraph 2, Art. 39, paragraph 2 - 79
  Art. 40, paragraph 2 - 85, paragraph 3 - 84, 85, 90
  Art. 43, paragraph 3 - 91, 95, paragraph 6 - 95
  Art. 44, paragraph 1, 4, Art. 45, paragraph 2 - 96
  General program - 21, 72, 73, 148
  Chapter I - 95
  Chapter VI - 78
  Chapter VII - 79, 95

Ceausescu, Nicolas, 214
Census, 7, 8, 10, 14, 18, 19, 20, 21, 23, 25, 26, 138 (& fn 33), 276, 367
Central Advisory Commission, 17, 19, 20, 23, 26, 82, 85, 86, 91, 93, 94, 95, 96,

Central Asia, 14
Central Bank, 311
Central China, 44, 116, 200
Central China Bureau, 110
Central Commission for Discipline
   Inspection, 17, 18, 19, 20, 24,
   26, 82, 86, 91, 95, 96, 97, 113
Central Committee (CC)
   Admission of new party
   members, 76
 \ Advocates presidential setup,
   166
   Agricultural policy, 10th plenum
   (1962), 268
   Approval of National Congress
   resolution, 82
   Authorities, 85, 88, 90, 93, 98
   Cancellation of xiafang
   (Dec. 1978), 408
   Central Advisory Commission,
   relation with, 93, 94
   Central Commission for
   Discipline Inspection, relation
   with, 96
   Central Military Commission
   appointed, 12th plenum (1982),
   185
   Convocation of National
   Congress, 81, 82
   Daqing praised (1981), 322
   Decree of census-taking (1981),
   7
   Deletes freedom provisions from
   constitution (Dec. 1978), 143
   Deng Xiaoping reseated in
   Politburo (10th plenum), 123
   Denounces Cultural Revolution,
   117
   Disciplining of committeemen,
   80, 85, 96
   Election of its members, 82, 84
   Expulsion of Gao Gong & Ruo
   Shushi, 111
   Factions in, 104
   Five-sixths assurance, 386
   Frequency of meetings, 85, 86
   Gang of Four denounced (1977),
   384
   Great Leap Forward, 259
   Hearing of complaints, 78
   Hua Guofeng phased out, 6th
   plenum (June 1981), 127, 135,
   495
   Increases state purchase prices
   (1978), 280

Lin Biao approved heir to Mao,
   118
Liu Shaoqi removed, 8th
   plenum (1970), 166
Lushan plenum (August 1959),
   112
Mao Zedong denounced
   (1981), 74
Membership profile, 84, 86, 87,
   89, 96, 103, 104
Militarists in, 196
Minority members in, 17, 19,
   20, 23, 24, 26
National Congress, relation
   with, 81, 82
Nomination of premiership,
   130, 157, 182, 183
NPC, relation with, 155
Open door policy (1978), 344
Politburo, relation with 88, 89,
   90
Qualification of committeemen,
   87, 94
Report to National Congress,
   82
Resolution on rotation of office
   (Dec. 1978), 144
Role in Cultural Revolution, 89,
   121
Song Qingling offered party
   card, 77
Standing Committee, relation
   with, 17, 90, 91, 92
Universal education, resolution
   on (1980), 371
Zungyi conference (Jan. 1936),
   106

Central Executive Committee
   (GMD), 50, 67, 105
Central Front Committee, 107
Central Institute of Nationality
   Studies, 22
Central Military Commission, 151,
   153, 157, 162, 163, 183, 184,
   185, 194
Central People's Government, 111,
   132, 134 (& fn 22), 138, 159,
   168, 178, 181, 185, 212, 253,
   360, See also Government,
   State Council
Central Working Conference, 149
Centralism, 74, 75
Centralization (economy), 307
Chahaer, 20, 54
Chaling Soviet, 252

Changan (Shaanxi), 14, 486
Changbeishan, 18
Changchun (Liaoning), 292, 403
Changjiang, 314, 316, 354
Changsha (Hunan), 64, 103
Chaosen, 18
Chartered Bank, 351
Chen Boda, 86, 115, 166, 468
Chen Cheng, 56
Chen Duxiu, 63, 64, 65, 102, 106
Chen Eugene, 51
Chen Huan, 484
Chen Junming, 44, 47
Chen Liyun, 120
Chen Mingren, 200
Chen Muhua, 89, 169, 300, 339,
    345, 354, 357, 360
Chen Pixian, 93, 494
Chen Shaoyu (Wang Ming), 104,
    105, 108
Chen Xilian, 86, 94
Chen Yangshan, 493
Chen Yi, 110, 117, 153
Chen Yonggui, 274
Chen Yun, 89, 91, 96
Cheng Qian, 200
Cheng Zihua, 179
Chengdu, 194, 195, 196, 259, 428
Chengdu Plain, 6
Chengdu-Chongqing railway, 4
Chengdu-Kunming railway, 4
Chernenko, K., 92
Cheysson, Claude, 243
Chief Procurator, 79, 158, 163,
    175, 493
Child-parent relations, 148
Chile, 329
China & South China Bank, 311
China Association for Promoting
    Democracy, 178 (& fn 53)
China Democratic League, 178,
    (& fn 53)
China Democratic National
    Construction Association, 178
    (& fn 53)
China International Trust &
    Investment Bank, 311
China Investment Bank, 355
China State Bank, 311
Chinese Eastern railway, 48, 64,
    324
Chinese in Malaysia, 247
Chinese in Vietnam, 238
Chinese Peasants & Workers
    Democratic Party, 178
    (& fn 53)
Chinese People's Institute of

Foreign Affairs, 243
Chinese Republic, 54, 70, 142,
    214, 218, 350, 400, 448, 491
Chinese Russians, 14, 24, 25
Chinese students abroad, 349, 378,
    389, See also overseas Chinese
Chinese Turkestan, See Xinjiang
Chirac, Jacques, 242
Chiu Hungdah, 439
Chongqing (Sichuan), 58, 59, 60,
    129, 253, 303, 314, 461
Chongqing-Guiyang railway, 4
Chou Quo commune (Sichuan),
    431
Chumlongma, 5
CIA, 204, 276, 330 (& fn 51)
Circulation funds, 312
Cities, 97, 98, 122, 137, 154, 158,
    160, 173, 174, 188, 198, 251,
    261, 278, 281, 295, 300, 354,
    371, 375, 377, 395, 401, 402,
    407, 408, 409, 413, 417, 422,
    424, 429, 442, 443, 447, 456,
    461
City districts, 483
City government, 378, 427, 428,
    457
Civil cases, 441, 444, 452, 453,
    454, 457, 458, 475, 486, 488
Civil law, 439, 444, 487
Civil-procedure law, 439, 440, 442,
    452, 455
Civil rights, 131, 134, 141, 143,
    144, 397, 463, 474, 491
Civil war (China), 117, 129, 136,
    181, 188, 212, 252, 285, 312,
    410
Civilian supremacy, 151
Claims settlement (with US, 1979),
    335
Class background in crime, 475
Class struggle, 48, 55, 66, 71, 72,
    112, 122, 135, 136, 139, 252,
    383, 397, 399, 471
Clinics, 400, 401, 403, 404, 406
Clubb, O, Edmund, 101
Coal, 263, 264, 298, 300, 301, 302,
    303, 312, 313, 315, 316, 317,
    319, 341, 348, 353, 387, 388
Coastal State Corporation, 337
Coca-Cola Company, 337
Co-determination, 149
Coexistence, 210, 223, 232
Cohen, Jerome, 438, 455, 472, 488
Cohongs, 361
Collective leadership, 73, 145, 257,
    358

Collectivization, 30, 55, 146, 165, 254, 255, 256, 257, 258, 260, 261, 267, 271, 286, 289, 291, 371, 416

Colonialism, 132, 211, 249, 352

Comintern, 48, 49, 51, 64, 68, 102, 103, 222, 251

Commander-in-chief, 166, 167, 172, 182, 194

Commerce, 322, 354, 410, 413

Commerce Ministry, 424, 427

Commission of Nationalities Affairs, 17

Commune, 111, 114, 118, 122, 140, 145, 189, 191, 258, 259, 260, 261, 262, 263, 264, 265, 267, 268, 269, 270, 271, 272, 292, 309, 322, 370, 372, 373, 402, 409, 443, 457

Communications, 6, 7, 190, 311, 313, 354, 388

Communism, 63, 64, 65, 67, 71, 76, 108, 114, 122, 127, 130, 131, 136, 137, 144, 189, 222, 259, 285, 291, 294, 296, 297, 385 394, 396, 420, 466

Communist humanism, 419

Communist manifesto, 72, 368

Communist Party of France, 243

Communist Party of Italy, 245

Commutation of sentence, 480, 481

Conciliar cases, 441

Conciliation and mediation, 440, 441, 443, 444, 449, 450, 452, 457, 487

Conference of the Toilers of the East, 105

Confucius and Confucianism, 9, 27, 28, 29, 30, 31, 32, 33, 35, 63, 101, 166, 378, 390, 395, 478

Congo, 164, 248

Conscription, 189, 200

Constitution (in general), 42, 71, 131, 399, 491

Constitution of Jiangxi Soviet, 55

Constitutional amendment - 159, interpretation - 163

Constitutional Pact, 41

Constitutions of the CPR
1949 pre-constitution
Common Program
Art. 1 - 132, 134 (& fn 22), 252, 253
Organic Law of the Central People's Government - 132, 134

Art. 5 - 168
Arts. 26-30 - 134
Organic Law of the CPPCC
Art. 3 - 132, 134
1954 Constitution - 71, 134, 143, 156, 182, 183, 253
Preamble - 212, 221
Art. 1 - 136
Art. 23 - 154
Art. 24 - 156 (& fn 11)
Art. 25 - 156
Art. 27 - 183
Art. 40 - 167, 183
Art. 42 - 166, 167, 182, 183
Art. 43 - 166, 167
Art. 47 - 168
Art. 73-84 - 134
Art. 78 - 470
Art. 85 - 474
Art. 90, paragraph 2 - 143
1978 Constitution — 15, 134, 139, 143, 147, 150, 154, 166, 167, 182, 183, 210, 211
Preamble - 130 (& fn 4), 138, 139, 210, 249, 464, 485
Art. 1 - 136
Art. 2 - 14, 16, 133
Art. 5, paragraph 6 - 146
Art. 6 - 136
Art. 7 - 270, 277, paragraph 1 - 137, paragraph 2 - 139
Art. 11 - 268, paragraph 2 - 141
Art. 15, paragraph 2 - 139
Art. 16 - 148, 156
Art. 18 - 498
Art. 19 - 172, 182 (& fn 11), 197, 198, 199, paragraph 1 - 182, 184, paragraph 2 - 181, 184 paragraph 3 - 185
Art. 20 - 156
Art. 21 - 156 (& fn 11)
Art. 22, clause 4 - 182, clauses 8, 9 - 158, clause 10 - 156
Art. 24 - 160
Art. 25, clause 13 - 174
Art. 37 - 174
Art. 41, clause 2 - 472 (& fn 55)
Arts. 41-43 - 134, 490
Art. 45 - 143, 460
Art. 47 - 143
Arts. 47 - 50 - 399 (& fn 1)
Art. 53, clause 2 - 446, clause 3 - 446, 492
Chapter 3 - 143
1982 Constitution 15, 16, 20,

71, 72, 119, 130, 134, 137,
138, 140, 141, 143, 144, 145,
146, 148, 150, 167, 171, 184,
185, 193 (& fn 64), 197, 210,
211, 460
Preamble - 71, 72, 131, 133,
135, 136, 137, 138, 139
(& fn 37), 141, 147, 148, 150,
151, 156, 308, 349, 352, 397
Art. 1, paragraph 1 - 136,
paragraph 2 - 146
Art. 2 - 134, 141, paragraph
1-278, paragraph 2 - 148
Art. 3 - 141, paragraph 4 - 137
Art. 4, paragraph 1 - 148,
paragraph 3 - 137
Art. 5 - 131
Art. 6 - 12, 137, 145, 419
Art. 7 - 12, 134, 145
Art. 8 - 12, 134, 145,
paragraph 1 - 145, 269, 270,
417, paragraphs 2, 3 - 145
Art. 9 - 12, 145, 146, 415,   417,
paragraph 1 - 306
Art. 10 - 12, 145, 417,
paragraph 1 - 137, paragraphs
2, 4 - 146
Art. 11 - 13, 145, 416, 417
Art. 13 - 147, paragraph 2 -
146
Art. 14 - 149, 417
Art. 16 - 146, 149, 416,
paragraph 1 - 307, paragraph
2 - 140
Art. 17 - 148, 417, paragraph 2
- 140, 149
Art. 18 - 147
Art. 19 - 149, 417
Art. 20 - 149
Art. 21 - 138, 139 (& fn 37),
149
Art. 22 - 149, 150
Art. 23 - 446
Art. 24 - 130, 137, 148,
paragraph 2 - 148
Art. 27 - 148
Art. 28 - 131, 144, 465
Art. 29, paragraph 1 - 184,
198, paragraph 2 - 198, 199
Art. 30, paragraph 2 - 173
Art. 31 - 141
Art. 32 - 77, 399, 474
Art. 33 - 77, 399, paragraph 2 -
178
Art. 34 - 77
Art. 35 - 77, 143, 399,
paragraph 4 - 144

Art. 36 - 77, 399, 492,
paragraph 4 - 144
Art. 38 - 77, 143, 148, 399
Arts. 39, 40 - 399
Art. 41 - 141, 147, 399
Art. 42 - 399, paragraph 1 -
143, paragraph 2 - 398,
paragraph 3 - 149
Arts. 43, 44 - 77, 399
Art. 45 - 77, paragraph 1 -
143, 399
Art. 46 - 77, 369, 399
Art. 47 - 77, 150, 399
Art. 48 - 77
Art. 49 - 77, 148, paragraph 2
- 448
Art. 50 - 77, 142
Art. 51 - 77, 144
Art. 52 - 77, paragraph 2 - 165
Art. 53 - 77, 81
Art. 54, 55 - 77
Art. 56 - 77
Art. 58 - 156 (& fn 11)
Art. 59 - 159
Art. 60, paragraph 1 - 156,
paragraph 2 - 158
Art. 61, paragraphs 1, 2 - 158
Art. 62 - 156, 157, clauses 1,3
- 157, clause 5 - 157, clause 6
- 184, clauses 9, 10, 13, 14 -
158, clause 15 - 156
Art. 63 - 157, clause 10 - 184
Art. 64, paragraph 1 - 157,
159, paragraph 2 - 159
Art. 65, paragraphs 1,2 - 160
Art. 66 - 151, paragraph 1 -
79, 160, paragraph 2 - 79
Art. 67, clause 8 - 137, clause
11 - 184, 484, 487, clause 12 -
184, clause 14 - 151, 170
Art. 69 - 157, clause 9 - 184
Art. 70, paragraphs 1, 2,
Art. 71, paragraphs 1, 2 - 159
Art. 72 - 159, paragraph 1 -
167
Art. 73 - 159
Art. 74 - 160
Art. 75 - 160, paragraph 2 -
160
Art. 79, paragraph 1 - 184,
paragraph 3 - 79, 168, 184
Art. 80 - 168
Art. 81 - 151, 167
Art. 84, paragraphs 2, 3 - 168
Art. 85 - 168
Art. 86, paragraph 1 - 168,
184, paragraph 2 - 170,

paragraph 3 - 168
Art. 87, paragraph 2 - 79, 158,
    170
Art. 88, paragraph 2 - 170
Art. 89 - 151, 170, clause 7 -
    183, clause 8 - 159, clause 9 -
    170, clause 10 - 151, 184,
    clause 12 - 141, clause 14 -
    137, clause 15, 137, 158
Art. 90, paragraph 1 - 170
Art. 91 - 170
Art. 93 - 151, paragraph 1 -
    183, paragraph 3 - 184
Art. 95, paragraph 1 - 270, 271
Art. 96 - 137
Art. 97, paragraph 1 - 154
Art. 99, paragraph 2 - 175
Art. 100 - 307
Art. 101, paragraph 2 - 175,
    184
Art. 103, paragraph 1 - 175
Arts. 104, 107, 109 - 176
Art. 110, paragraph 2 - 137
Art. 111, paragraph 1 - 177,
    184
Art. 113, paragraph 1 - 176,
    paragraph 2 - 442
Arts. 114, 116, 117 - 176
Art. 118, paragraph 1 - 177
Art. 119 - 177
Arts. 120, 121, Art. 122,
    paragraph 2 - 177
Art. 124, paragraph 2 - 79, 158
Art. 126 - 175
Art. 128 - 157, 470
Art. 130, paragraph 2 - 79, 158
Art. 133 - 157
Art. 137 - 493
Chapter 2 - 141, 143
Chapter 3, sections 1, 4 - 184,
    section 5-173
Chapter 6, section 3 - 176, 184
Preliminary draft of 1982
    Constitution, 165
Art. 19, paragraph 4 - 177
Art. 73 - 193 (& fn 64)
Art. 76 - 184
Art. 86 - 168
Art. 90, clause 4 - 157
Consumer goods, 258, 268, 280,
    288, 289, 292, 304, 305, 325,
    339, 345, 388, 412, 425
Consumption, 302, 388, 422, 427
Continental shelf, 202, 211, 352
Contract system, 415, 416
Contradictions, 71, 72, 150, 475
Co-ops, 145, 146, 148, 257, 258,

271, 272, 306, 311, 403, 404,
    408, 411, 412, 413, 415, 416,
    417, 418, 419, 424, 442, 443
Coordinate Committee on Export
    Controls (NATO), 340
Copyrights, 147
Corruption, 31, 147, 436
Cossiga, Francisco, 245
Cote, Rene, 36
Council of National Defense, 166,
    167, 183
Counterrevolution, 114, 124, 131,
    144, 148, 165, 385, 393, 437,
    455, 464, 465, 466, 467, 469,
    472, 474, 475, 480, 481, 486,
    488, 498
Counties, 20, 21, 24, 25, 26, 97,
    98, 137, 140, 153, 158, 173, 174,
    175, 176, 178, 274, 292, 371,
    374, 394, 395, 401, 406, 409,
    422, 429, 446, 457, 458, 483,
    484
County Government, 368, 378, 484
CPPCC, 20, 23, 27, 132, 133 (& fn
    19), 134 (& fn 22), 183, 384, 482
Crime by insanity, 482
Crime rate, 476, 477, 490
Crimes, 30, 281, 292, 439, 463,
    464, 466, 476, 477, 478, 479,
    480, 481, 482, 483, See also
    specific offenses such as arson,
    bribery, counterrevolution,
    economic crimes, murder, rob-
    bery, slander, smuggling, theft,
    treason
Criminal cases, 444, 454, 455, 457,
    458, 464, 466, 473, 474, 481,
    482, 489
Criminal law, 80, 85, 90, 165, 439,
    440, 444, 448 (& fn 86), 463,
    465, 467, 468, 469, 472, 475,
    476, 478, 479 (& fn 117), 480,
    483, 486, 489
Criminal procedure law, 165, 461,
    481
Criminals, 454, 455, 477, 480, 481,
    497 (& fn 220), 498 (& fn 230)
Cuba, 209, 246, 247
Cui, Naifu, 179
Cultural Revolution, 33, 74, 82, 83,
    86, 89, 92, 96, 101, 108, 113,
    114, 115, 116, 117, 118, 119,
    121, 125, 126, 134, 139, 147,
    149, 163, 171, 182, 185, 186,
    188, 190, 191, 195, 198, 200,
    203, 213, 226, 232, 234, 241,
    268, 269, 280, 282, 288, 296,

297, 306, 325, 328, 330, 339,
359, 364, 365, 367, 370, 373,
383, 393, 395, 406, 407, 419,
436, 437, 438, 439, 460, 461,
463, 477, 489, 490, 495, 496
Culture, 115, 149, 150, 158, 176,
177, 295, 302, 308, 309, 322,
336, 366, 392, 435.
Culture Ministry, 385
Customs revenues, 43
Czechoslovakia, 213, 226, 244, 326
Dai, 18
Dairen (Liaoning), 324
Dalai Lama, 20, 21, 22, 23, 45, 189
Damansky incident, 119, 213, 226,
280
Dao de jing, 31
Daoism, 31, 32
Daqing, 320, 321, 322
Dauer, 20, 24
Dazhai, 270, 273, 274, 321
Death sentence, 473, 474, 476,
479, 480, 481, 482, See also
execution by shooting
Decision-making, 140, 155, 297,
307, 358
Dedu County (Heilongjiang), 488
Defense Ministry, 182, 183, 189,
200
De Gaulle, Charles, 36
Dehli, 232, 233
Democracy, 35, 37, 43, 63, 74, 75,
131, 140, 141, 149, 174, 257,
363, 470
Democratic centralism, 67, 74, 75,
115, 141, 452, 487, 492
Democratic parties and groups, 74,
178 (& fn 53), 381, 382
Deng Liqun, 93
Deng Xiaoping
Activity during civil war, 89
Balanced economy, 360
Central Advisory Commission,
Chairman of, 91, 93
Consolidation of power, 80, 127
CPPCC honorable chairman
(1978-1983), 133
Criticism of, (1982) 127, (1966)
92, 114, 116
Downfall (1967, 1976), 124
During Cultural Revolution, 113,
114, 116, 117, 118
Elbowing out Hua Guofeng, 80,
124, 127, 173, 495
Five-sixths assurance, 386
Foreign investment law, 353
France, relation with CPR, 243

Gang of Four, 403
General Chief of Staff, 86, 172
Japan, relation with CPR, 236
"Let 100 schools of thought
contend," 386, 387
Linkage system of economy, 146
Military Commission, chairman
of, 86, 91, 185
North Korea, relation with CPR,
247
On education, 365, 366, 385,
386, 387
Open door policy, 385
Pakistan, relation with CPR, 234
Personal control of China denied,
358
Policy accord among leaders,
358
Politburo man 89, Standing
Committeeman, 91
"Politics in command"
criticized, 386
Pragmatical policy, 113, 124,
294, 347
Praise of barefoot doctors, 403
Problem of school exams, 366
Receiving Mitterrand in Beijing
(1983), 243
Red and expert reinterpreted,
366, 387
Salary of, 311
Sojourn in France (1920's),
153
Spiritual culture of China, 391
Suppression of workers in
Zhejiang (1975), 188
Taiwan question, 215, 216
Teachings of, 74
Thailand, visit of, 239
US, relation with CPR, 121,
215, 217, 219, 336
USSR, relation with CPR, 221,
228, 231
Work collective elects its
leaders, 149
Deng Yingchao, 89, 90, 96, 133
Deng Zihui, 260
Denmark, 341, 349
Dentists, 417
Denver, 39
Deputies, 154, 155, 156, 157, 159,
160, 169, 175, 176, 178, 179
Deputy Chief Procurator, 184
d'Estaing, Valery Giscard, 242
Deutsche Bank (Frankfurt), 351
Dialectics, 71, 296, 382, 391, 392,
393, 396

540   GOVERNMENT OF SOCIALIST CHINA

Dissenters, 384, 466
District government, 405
Districts, 457
Dittmar, Lowell, 266
Divorce, 440, 444, 449, 450, 451, 472
Dogmatism, 105, 131
Dong, 26
Dong Biwu, 166, 172
Dongbei Plain, 6
Dongga Luosangchilie, 22
Donghai, 1, 2
Dongxiang, 24
Double contract system, 12
Du Juns, 40, 53
Duan Qirui, 42, 43, 44, 45
Dudus, 42, 43, 53
Due process, 437
Dushanzi, 314

East Asiatic Company, 361
East China, 110, 116, 117, 282, 317
East China Sea (Donghai), 1
East Sea Fleet, 201
Eastern Europe, 112, 244, 291, 293, 325, 338
Economic aid to China, 323, 324, 325
Economic courts, 486
Economic crimes, 477, 478, 481
Economic laws, 443
Economic relation with Japan, 236
Economic responsibility system, 355
Economic Study Center (State Council), 300
Economy, 113, 116, 122, 125, 134, 145, 161, 165, 170, 176, 204, 256, 264, 268, 269, 282, 286, 288, 289, 291, 294, 295, 296, 298, 299, 302, 306, 308, 327, 328, 357, 360, 383, 388, 389, 391, 399, 407, 410, 413, 416, 418, 422, 442, 451, 454, 497, 498
Education, 7, 11, 53, 114, 148, 158, 165, 176, 177, 190, 295, 302, 309, 322, 363, 364, 365, 366, 369, 372, 383, 384
Education Ministry, 370, 374, 375, 379, 382, 396
Egalitarianism, 113, 122, 263, 264, 267, 273, 401, 415, 419, 420
Egypt, 213, 241, 248, 332
Eighth Route Army, 59, 117
El Salvador, 248

Election law, 82, 153 (& fn 1), 154, 155, 160, 175 (& fn 49), 178, 179
Elections, 131, 140, 148, 149, 153, 155, 158, 162, 168, 169, 170, 175, 176, 178, 179, 457
Electric power, 290, 301, 302, 303, 315, 316, 319, 336, 349, 387
Embezzlement, 472, 473, 478, 479
Employment, 11, 12, 143, 145, 281, 382, 408, 410, 411, 412, 413
Empress Cixi, 18
Enactments, 436, 440, 443, 444, 445, 446, 456, 457, 459, 460, 483, 489
Energy resources, 5, 205, 312, 315, 318, 319, 320, 348, 387, 388, 389
Engels, Friedrich, 72, 368, 391, 392
Enping County (Guangdong), 475
Eren basin (Neimeng), 317
Ethiopia, 247
Equality before the law, 143, 178, 474
Equatorial Guinea, 247
Estonian Soviet Socialist Republic, 138
Europe, 64, 209, 227, 242, 243, 244, 333, 340, 349
European Economic Community, 242, 244, 349, 357
Ex post facto law, 467, 468
Examinations, 365, 366, 369, 375, 378, 379, 380, 381, 382, 390
Execution by shooting, 474, 480, 481, 482, 483
Exploiting class, 135
Export, 303, 331, 332, 337, 342, 343, 344, 345, 346, 352, 353, 354, 360, 413
to Canada - 346, European Economic Community - 357, Hong Kong - 329, 345, Japan - 328, 329, 345, Non-socialist countries - 331, Romania - 345, Socialist countries - 331, USSR - 325, 326, 345. Of farm product, 261, 290
Export-Import Bank (US), 217
Extremism, 28, 30, 149
Ewenki, 20

Factionalism, 101, 104, 105, 107, 108, 110, 111, 112, 113, 114, 115, 116, 117, 118, 139, 264, 302, 358, 399, 435, 438

Factories, 118, 296, 297, 299, 300, 306, 315, 325, 354, 418, 421, 424, 428, 429, 497
Faculty ranks, 377, 381
Family, 396, 440
Family planning, 410, 445, 446, 447, See also birth control
Family Planning Commission, 8, 169
Fanshi faction, 127, 139, 271, 302
Far East, 64, 235, 242
Far East Autonomous Region, 3, 10
Far Eastern Military District, 226
Farm laborers, 254
Farm output, 258, 260, 264, 265, 268, 280, 282, 289, 290, 295, 300, 301, 302, 304, 307, 310, 329, 330, 346, 353, 426
Fauna, 5
FBI, 477
Feng Guozhang, 42, 43, 44
Feng Yi, 89, 169, 384, 385, 387
Feng Yuxiang, 44, 45, 49, 50, 52, 53
Fertilization, 278, 279, 290, 329, 334, 387
Feudalism, 132, 140, 148, 469
Field army, 185, 197
Finance, 53, 55, 161, 162, 176, 177, 307, 308, 383, 426, 438
Finance Ministry, 311, 353
Finland, 349
Firebombing, 477
Five-anti campaign, 286, 287
Five good and five bad elements, 474 (& fn 76)
Five guarantees, 13
Five-Year Plans, 205, 311
    1st (1952-1957), 258, 259, 260, 289, 290, 291, 293, 298, 326, 410
    2nd (1957-1962), 293, 294, 296, 298, 326
    3rd (1966-1970), 296, 297, 298
    4th (1971-1975), 297, 298, 300
    5th (1975-1980), 300, 301, 302, 366
    6th (1981-1985), 300, 302, 304, 312, 314, 315, 316, 317, 318, 320, 344, 353, 366, 371, 376, 414, 430
    7th (1985-1990), 316, 353
Five-Year Plans (USSR), 260, 262, 289
Flora, 5
Food production, 114, 282, 289,

290, 295, 300, 301, 302, 304, 307, 310, 330, 339, 346
Food program (USSR), 283 (& fn 198)
Ford, Gerald, 215, 334
Four Books, 28
Four olds, 448
Foreign Affairs Association, 215
Foreign aid rendered by CPR, 237, 238, 240, 245, 247, 332, 346
Foreign banks in CPR, 351, 453
Foreign exchange, 261, 282, 290, 311, 318, 327, 330, 331, 334, 345, 350, 412, 452, See also hard currency
Foreign investment, 147, 165, 217, 236, 244, 310, 328, 340, 341, 347, 348, 353, 354, 357, 358, 438, 451, 452, 453
Foreign Investment Commission, 451
Foreign loans, 147, 309, 337, 344, 348, 352, 359, 438, 453
Foreign policy, 158, 159, 162, 171, 209, 210, 211, 212, 248, 323, 327, 328
Foreign trade, 14, 147, 304, 308, 311, 325, 326, 328, 329, 330, 335, 340, 341, 342, 344, 345, 347, 349, 350, 353, 355, 356, 357, 358, 359, 360, 412, 438, See also trade with specific countries
Foreigners in China, 452, 453, 456, 479, 482, 495, 497, 498 (spies)
Foreigners in the CPPCC, 133
Forestry, 5, 283, 290, 415
Forestry courts, 483, 484
Foshan (Guangdong), 367
France, 44, 153, 158, 207, 242, 244, 317, 332, 340, 341, 343, 345, 347, 349, 351, 352
Fraser, John, 21 (& fn 115)
Freedoms, 129, 143
French bankers' loans, 328, 335, 336, 341, 357
From each according to his ability, 136
Front organization, 154
Fu Yuehua, 466
Fu Zuoyi, 130, 187, 200
Fudan University, 384, 394
Fujian, 2, 7, 14, 44, 53, 145, 195, 196, 197, 354, 414
Fulbright, William, 215
Futian insurgency, 107, 108

Fuxian County (Liaoning), 375
Fuzhou (Fujian), 2, 194, 195

Gabon, 248
Gagarin, Yuri, 77
Ganbu, 78, 79
Gang of Four, 22, 80, 83, 85, 86,
    97, 115, 119, 120, 121, 122, 123,
    124, 125, 127, 138, 139, 145,
    165, 174, 189, 198, 199, 228,
    269, 271, 273, 277, 298, 299,
    300, 357, 358, 359, 364, 367,
    371, 372, 380, 383, 384, 385,
    386, 391, 393, 399, 403, 404,
    405, 406, 407, 410, 418, 420,
    421, 431, 449, 454, 460, 463,
    464, 466, 471, 479, 485, 489,
    494, 498
Gansu, 5, 19, 21, 22, 45, 173,
    195, 422
Gao Gong, 106, 110, 111, 113, 282
Gaoshan, 14
Garbus, Martin, 441, 456, 473
Garden plot, 268, 269, 272, 277,
    278, 279, 282
Gayle, Andrew, 487
General auditor, 157, 158, 161,
    163, 167, 168, 170, 184
General Chief of Staff, 172, 194,
    197, 198
General Galen, See Blucher
General logistics command, 194
General Political Department, 127,
    186, 194, 299
General program, 71, 75, 76, 117,
    131, 148
General Secretary (CCP), 183
General Secretary (State Council),
    160, 161, 167, 168, 169, 170
Geneva, 213, 333, 338
Geng Biao, 89, 169, 172, 204, 218
Germany, 27, 43, 63
    East Germany, 244, 326, 332,
        343
    Nazi Germany, 181, 245
    West Germany, 168, 242, 243,
        244, 316, 319, 326, 332, 340,
        341, 343, 345, 349, 352
Ghana, 164
Ginsburg, Ruth, 450
GNP, 190, 249, 295, 300, 307, 318,
    353
Gobi, 2
Gold reserves, 311
Gong zuo ze ren zhi, 9, 10, 148,
    272, 273, 372, 386, 417
Gorbachev, M.S., 92

Government, 130, 132, 145, 170,
    174, 175, 176, 177, 179, 191,
    249, 265, 268, 269, 277, 278,
    280, 281, 282, 283, 286, 287,
    302, 303, 309, 315, 316, 318,
    335, 351, 353, 355, 358, 360,
    363, 367, 369, 375, 377, 379,
    382, 385, 386, 387, 388, 393,
    394, 395, 396, 402, 406, 407,
    408, 409, 411, 412, 413, 416,
    417, 420, 421, 422, 424, 425,
    426, 428, 443, 444, 447, 452,
    453, 459, 460, 461, 465, 466,
    474, 488, 493, 495, 496, 498,
    See also Central People's
    Government
Government Administration
    Council, 168
Government control of courts, 470,
    471
Governors (provinces), 158
Grade schools, 8, 19, 21, 25, 26,
    27
Graduate students, 376, 377, 378
    (foreigners)
Grain production, 12, 265, 267,
    268, 274, 275, 279, 282, 292,
    293, 302, 304, 330, 333, 385
Grain purchases, 215, 216, 275,
    295, 329, 330, 334, 337, 340,
    342
Grand Canal, 4
Great Leap Forward, 88, 112, 113,
    116, 158, 188, 191, 205, 225,
    259, 261, 273, 277, 282, 291,
    294, 295, 296, 419, 439
Great Proletarian Cultural
    Revolution, See Cultural
    Revolution
Great Wall, 54
Grishin, V.V., 82
Ground force, 194, 197, 199, 200
Gu Mu, 93, 169, 453 (& fn 103)
Guandong Army, 60, 110
Guangdong, 2, 4, 10, 15, 26, 38,
    43, 44, 45, 53, 142, 189, 196,
    316, 348, 354, 418, 476
Guangdong Provincial Bank, 311
Guangdong-Hankou railway, 220
Guangxi, 4, 5, 15, 26, 27, 36, 42,
    43, 45, 46, 47, 53, 196, 476
Guangzhou, 2, 46, 47, 48, 49, 50,
    53, 59, 64, 65, 102, 120, 126,
    188, 194, 196, 286, 335, 361,
    475
Guangzhou government (GMD), 46,
    48, 49, 50, 67

Guerilla warfare, 56, 57, 117, 189, 198, 239, 248, 267, 285
Guinea, 248
Guizhou, 4, 5, 26, 43, 45, 195, 316, 422
Guomin ge ming jun, 53
Guomindang, 35, 36, 37, 40, 41, 42, 45, 46, 47, 49, 51, 65, 66, 67, 68, 69, 101, 102, 104, 106, 107, 112, 115, 117, 129, 142, 154, 183, 218, 222, 223, 235, 237, 252, 264, 285, 286, 323, 324, 390, 410, 475, 498
Guomindang Revolutionary Committee, 107

Haerbin (Heilongjiang), 460, 479
Hai Rui ba guan, 121
Hai wai guan xi, 142, 297
Haig, Alexander, 218
Hainan, 2, 187, 192, 347
Han, 6, 13, 14, 15, 16, 18, 19, 20, 23, 24, 25, 26, 27, 36, 37, 78, 148, 160, 169, 173, 176, 177, 189, 196
Han dynasty (206 B.C.-222 A.D.), 13, 14
Han Guang, 96
Han Hao, 121
Han Xuezhang, 455
Han Yudong, 439, 460
Handicapped, 429, 430
Hangjiahu Plain, 6
Hangzhou, 120, 243
Hankou, 36, 37
Hanoi, 230, 237, 238, 239, 240
Hanyang, 36
Hanyang arsenal, 51
Hao Jianxiu, 93
Harbors, 2, 314
Hard currency, 337, 345
Harrison, John H., 182 (& fn 8)
Havana, 246
Hawaii, 37
Hay, John, 212
He Dongchang, 367, 382, 383
He Lanjie, 485, 489
He Yingqin, 56
Heze (Shandong), 15
He who does not work shall not eat, 136, 137
Health cadres, 401, 402, 404, 405, 406, 407
Heath, Edward, 242
Heavy industries, 258, 268, 288, 290, 294, 302, 310, 326, 338, 346, 352, 411, 412
Hebei, 5, 19, 42, 54, 173, 179, 189, 199, 317, 341, 365, 476
Hehao (river loop), 3, 6
Heilongjiang, 1, 10, 14, 15, 19, 20, 195, 228, 376, 488
Henan, 10, 50, 60, 105, 195, 316, 365, 414, 422, 476
Heng Samrin, 237, 238
Hengduan, 2
High courts, 20, 23, 25, 26, 27
Beijing, 466, 485
Hubei, 487
Shaan-Gan-Ning border government, 473, 475
Shanghai, 481, 485, 488, 489
Sichuan, 482
High schools, 7, 8, 19, 21, 25, 26, 27, See also junior high, senior high, vocational training and agricultural schools
Hinton, Harold, 211, 482
Hiroshima, 60
Historical materialism, 71
Hitler, Adolf, 221
Hong Kong, 1, 7, 38, 41, 50, 74, 114, 133, 189, 202, 218, 243, 326, 327, 329, 332, 337, 343, 345, 349, 350, 352, 360, 498
Hong Kong & Shanghai Banking Corporation, 351
Hong Xuezhi, 184, 194
Hongshui, 316
Hongxian, 41, 42
Honolulu, 38
Hospitals, 400, 401, 402, 406
Housing, 11, 292, 303, 321, 322, 340
Houston, 1, 217
How to be a good communist, 115
Hoxha, Enver, 245, 246
Hu Hanmin, 42, 49, 50
Hu Na, 221
Hu Ping, 120
Hu Qiaomu, 89
Hu Qili, 93
Hu Yaobang
As General Secretary, 96
Feudal decadence blasted, 148, 150
In Politburo - 89, Standing Committee - 91
Independent foreign policy, 151
Large population, but little arable land, 277
Mao Zedong denounced, 125
On grain output, 274 (& fn 144)

Party members' low morale
deplored, 79
Self-reliance emphasized, 308
Sideline production urged, 278,
306
Sino-Soviet detente, possibility
of, 230
Third world, unite, 210
Hua Guofeng
Attack on socialist imperialism,
211
Berlinguer, Enrich, visit with, 245
Capital investment, 351
Chairman of Military Commission
(1976-1981), 185
Criticism of Gang of Four, 269
Cultural Revolution praised, 117
Daqing extolled, 321, 322
Dazhai extolled, 274
Deploring effects of Cultural
Revolution, 296, 299, 410
Divestment of premiership
(1981), 92
Economic plan, 301, 302, 304, 351
Edged out, 126, 127, 139, 173,
358, 495
England, journey to, 244
Fanshi faction, 139, 302
First use of atomic bomb
disavowed, 192
France, journey to, 144
Germany (w), journey to, 244
Giving size of Chinese
peasantry, 276, 277
Iran, journey to, 241, 246
Italy, journey to, 245
Minister of Public Security, 123,
494, 495
Modernization, 281
Named CC Chairman (1977), 86
On education, 365
Personality cult, 42
Politburo member, 89
Premiership (1976), 124, 172
"Principles laid down" denied,
124, 125
Publicly criticized, 127
Regionalism, 281
Rejuvenation of commune, 271, 272
Relation with Gang of Four, 124,
125, 269, 296, 410
Romania, journey to, 244
Rule of law, 438, 439
Salary of, 85
Security work, 439
Support of sideline production, 278

Supporters of Hua removed, 94
Ten year plan, 279 (& fn 176)
Thailand, relation with CPR, 239,
410
Third world, relation with CPR,
210
US, relation with CPR, 215, 216,
336
USSR, relation with CPR, 222,
224, 225
Versus Deng Xiaoping, 80, 124,
126, 127, 173, 174 (& fn 48)
"With you in command, I am at
ease," 126
Yugoslavia, journey to, 244, 246
Huabei, 316
Huabei Plain, 6, 10
Huainan, 316
Huang Hoqing, 477, 491
Huang Hua, 169, 222, 230, 231,
233, 239
Huang Kecheng, 96, 112, 172
Huang Kegong, 476
Huang Yongsheng, 120, 121, 172,
455, 468
Huang Zhen, 213, 219, 241
Huanghai, 2
Huanghe, 3, 4, 316
Huangpu, 201
Huangpu Academy, 49, 67, 68, 117
Huangtu, 5
Hubei, 5, 10, 105, 195, 414, 444,
486
Hui, 14, 18, 20, 24, 25, 26, 169
Hulan, 228
Humanism, 137
Hunan, 5, 15, 24, 42, 43, 53, 55,
65, 117, 189, 211, 394
Hunan harvesting revolt, 102
Hundred-flowers campaign, 261
Hungary, 140
Huolinhe, 316
Hutchinson Whampoa, 361

Idealism, 391, 392, 419, 420, 469
Ideology, 97, 125, 127, 134, 138,
139, 140, 147, 186, 209, 212,
230, 245, 251, 262, 303, 366,
382, 383, 408, 412, 415, 441,
466, 482
Illiterate, 8
Ilyichev, Leonid, 229
Immigration & naturalization
service, 221
Imperialism & imperialists, 48, 211,
221, 224, 232, 241, 245, 246,
267, 323, 327, 370, 385

Import, from
Argentina, Australia, Canada (all grain) 333, Chile 329, E. Germany, Egypt, Morocco, Netherlands, Pakistan, Singapore, Sri Lanka, Sudan, W. Germany 332, France 332, 340, Hong Kong 329, 332, 345, Italy 329, 330, Japan 328, 329, 332, 345, 347, 357, Non-socialist and Socialist countries 331, US 333, 334, 335, 337, 338, 340, 345, USSR 325, 326, 332, 339, 345, Western Europe 339
Imprisonment, 475, 479, 480
Income tax, 310, 452
Incomes, 415, 421, 422, 442, 443, See also wages
Cadres, 420, 423, 479
Co-op members, 411, 418
Family, 421, 422, 424
Foreigners in CPR, 452
Judges, 487
Peasants, 274, 280, 282, 422, 426
Pensioners, 428
Per capita, 301, 422
Professors, 377, 418
Rural residents, 426, 427
Teachers, 373, 375, 418, 487
Technical personnel, 487
Urban residents, 426, 427
Workers, 373, 418, 420, 423, 424, 428
India, 1, 14, 20, 22, 51, 112, 192, 209, 210, 225, 230, 232, 233, 234, 290, 328
Indian Ocean system (rivers), 3
Individual economy, See private economy
Individualism, 30, 31, 32, 394, 396, 411
Indo-China, 39
Indojiang, 3
Indonesia, 193, 209, 240, 247, 326
Industrial output, 299, 300, 301, 302, 305, 307, 329, 353, 426
Industrialization, 10, 11, 17, 46, 68, 74, 253, 261, 281, 290, 292, 294, 312, 315, 322, 443
Industries, 114, 141, 205, 236, 281, 289, 290, 291, 292, 294, 297, 321, 324, 365, 384, 385, 413, See also light industries, heavy industries
Infanticide, 430, 431, 432, 433
Inflation, 310, 359, 422, 427

Inland navigation, 4, 314
Institute of Atomic Energy, 205
Institute of Economics, 306
Institute of Jurisprudence, 439, 460, 461, 496
Institute of Tibet, 22
Intelligentsia, 63, 74, 75, 153, 179, 280, 379, 397, 403
International Atomic-Energy Conference, 207
International law, 151, 221 (& fn 61), 460, 461
International Monetary Fund, 310, 359
Internationalism, See proletarian internationalism
Ioffe, Adolf, 48, 66, 222
Iran, 241, 246
Iron rice bowl, 416
Irrigation, 4, 290, 292, 293, 387
Islamabad, 234
Israel, 241
Italy, 245, 329, 332, 343, 345
Ivory Coast, 248

Jackson, Henry, 215, 230
Jalinda, 1
Jamaica, 2
James Bay, 2
Japan, 1, 2, 13, 27, 39, 40, 41, 42, 43, 44, 46, 47, 48, 49, 52, 53, 54, 55, 57, 58, 59, 63, 68, 69, 70, 87, 104, 110, 117, 140, 187, 210, 211, 212, 218, 223, 235, 236, 237, 240, 285, 313, 318, 319, 324, 332, 334, 337, 339, 341, 345, 347, 352, 355, 357, 359, 442
Jardines, 361
Jefferson, Thomas, 264
Ji-Cha-Jing border government, 59, 114, 252
Ji Denggui, 86
Ji Pengfei, 169, 242
Jian (Jiangxi), 103
Jiang Hua, 172, 467, 477, 479, 481, 485, 489, 490
Jiang Jieshi, 6, 27, 35, 40, 48, 50, 51, 53, 54, 55, 56, 57, 58, 59, 61, 67, 68, 69, 70, 106, 117, 182, 212, 223
Jiang Jingguo, 218
Jiang Nanxian, 364
Jiang Qing, 115, 119, 121, 123, 124, 393, 455, 467, 468, 470, 480, 481
Jiang Tengjiao, 120, 468

Jiangsu, 10, 53, 60, 196, 316, 319, 414
Jiangxi, 53, 55, 57, 195, 196, 251, 415
Jiangxi Provincial Action Committee, 107
Jiangxi Soviet, 6, 55, 56, 57, 58, 59, 68, 70, 84, 98, 104, 105, 107, 110, 114, 129, 198, 222, 252
Jiaotong University, 379
Jilin, 19, 195, 292, 384, 476
Jinan, 194, 196
Jincheng Banking Corporation, 311
Jing, 26
Jing ji te cu, 142, 158
Jinggang Shan, 476
Jinmen, 2, 7, 205
Job responsibility, See gong zuo zen ren zhi
Joint companies, 323, 349, 352
Joint Economic Committee (US Congress), 298
Joint fleet, 120
Joint ventures, 165, 316, 344, 346, 348, 349, 352, 353, 442, 443, 451, 452, 453, 454
Journalism, 385
Ju Qiubai, 102, 103, 106
Ju San Society, 178 (& fn 53)
Judges, 444, 450, 456, 457, 460, 461, 469, 470, 471, 472, 473, 474, 475, 480, 484, 485, 486 (deputy judges), 487, 489, 491, 492
Judicial independence, 470, 471, 472, 487
Judiciary, 53, 55, 131, 143, 153, 161, 165, 171, 175, 176, 179, 435, 437, 440, 441, 443, 444, 449, 452, 453, 456, 457, 461, 466, 469, 471, 478, 480, 483, 484 (& fn 143), 485, 486, 487, 488, 489, 490, 491, 492, 493, See also high courts, middle courts, Supreme Court
Jungar (Xinjiang), 316, 317
Junior high schools, 363, 364, 365, 369, 371, 374, 375, 382, 394, 396, 430 (for blind)
Junzi, 28
Jurisprudence, 444, 457, 460, 461
Justice, 134, 435, 456, 470, 472, 481, 483, 489
Justice Ministry, 437, 457
Juvenile crimes, 477, 480

Kachin (Burma), 192
Kamenev, G., 256
Kampuchea, 193, 227, 231, 235, 237, 238, 246, 332
Kang Sheng, 115
Kang Shien, 169
Karakhan declaration, 64
Karmal Babrak, 234
Kashmir, 190
Kazakstan, 1, 24, 25, 232, 380
Kenya, 248
Key high schools, 373, 375, 387
Key primary schools, 373, 387
Key universities, 321, 373, 376, 387
KGB, 169
Khabarovsk, 228
Khamba, 20, 23, 192
Khan Sahabzada Yagub, 234
Khrushchev, Nikita, 88, 112, 116, 205, 221, 223, 224, 225, 260, 293, 296, 397 (& fn 185)
Khutukhtu, 20, 45
Kim, Il Sung, 247
Kindergarten, 370, 371, 379
Kirgiz, 1, 24, 25
Kissinger, Henry, 214, 215
Korea, 2
Korean War (1950-1953), 191, 192, 194, 198, 200, 202, 212, 213, 254, 255, 288, 289, 324, 325, 333
Korla, 314
Kountche, Seyni, 247
Kreps, Juanita, 217, 334, 335, 353, 358
Kriangsack Chumanan, 239, 240
Kunaev, D.A., 92
Kunlun, 2, 5
Kunming, 195
Kuqa, 314

Labor Bureau, 408
Labor force, 375, 379, 409 (rural), 411
Labor unrest, 188, 189
Ladakh region, 232
Lakes, 5
Lamaism, 20
Land commissions, 255
Land ownership, 146, 147, 252, 253, 256, 257, 258, 271
Land reform, 55, 171, 251, 252, 253, 254, 255, 256, 262, 472
Landlordism, 102, 104, 135, 253, 254, 255, 286, 474, 475

Language rights, 16, 177
Lanzhou, 194, 195
Lanzhou-Baotao and Lanzhou-
  Urumqi railways, 313
Lao She, 390
Lao Zi, 31, 32
Laos, 1, 190, 191, 193, 237
Latin America, 246
Law, 435, 436, 437, 438, 439, 450,
  454, 456, 457, 460, 461, 467,
  471
Law enforcement, 491
Law of the Sea Conference, 249
Law on Joint Ventures, 353
Lawyers, 144, 442, 449, 453, 454,
  455, 456, 457, 458, 459, 460,
  461, 469
League of Nations, 69
Leagues, 20
Learn from Daqing, 321
Learn from Dazhai, 274
Learn from the army, 118, 190
Lebanon, 241
Leftists, 395, 449, 469
Legal counsel, 455, 456, 457, 460,
  461, 469, 472, 473
Legalism, 29, 30, 134, 141, 253,
  373, 436, 439, 459, 471, See
  also rule of law
Legislation, 158, 159, 160, 162,
  165, 176, 278, 307, 311, 353,
  426, 436, 437, 438, 443, 449,
  491
Lei Jintian, 475
Lenin, 48, 64, 66, 67, 70, 101, 105,
  223, 256, 296, 392, 436, 497
Leninist Young Communist
  League, 76
Lesotho, 248
"Let 100 schools of thought
  contend," 387, 437, 440
Lhasa, 21, 23
Li (courteous), 29, 32
Li (tribe), 18
Li Chang, 96
Li Dazhao, 64, 65, 105, 106
Li Desheng, 196
Li Er, See Lao Zi
Li Gang, 494
Li Hongzhang, 38
Li Jing, 40
Li Jingchuan, 116
Li Liejun, 42
Li Lisan, 103, 104, 197
Li Peng, 169
Li Qiang, 217, 334, 338
Li Tesheng, 89

Li Shiying, 493
Li Weihan, 93
Li Xiannian, 89, 91, 127, 166, 172,
  243, 281, 321, 407
Li Yizhe, 141
Li Yuanhong, 39, 43, 44
Li Zhengshan, 45
Li Zongren, 45, 53
Li Zuopeng, 121, 468
Liang Qichao, 42
Liao (river), 3
Liao Chengzhi, 89
Liaodong Peninsula, 2, 187
Liaoning, 19, 20, 172, 195, 316,
  369, 403
Liberal arts, 328, 389, 390
Liberalism, 397
Liberation, 36, 122, 141, 193, 216,
  218, 296, 332
Lienqin, 1, 2
Life imprisonment, 479, 480, 481
Life span, 406
Light industries, 288, 290, 294,
  304, 326, 346, 383, 410, 412
Lin Biao, 33, 67, 83, 113, 117, 118,
  119, 120, 121, 122, 155, 166,
  167, 172, 187, 192, 198, 298,
  393, 460, 463, 464, 467, 470
Lin Liguo, 120, 121
Lin Yu Shan (Shaanxi), 447
Ling Yun, 465, 466
Link system (USSR), 470
Linzhi (Tibet), 21
Literature and art, 383, 384, 389,
  390
Litigation, 440, 442, 444, 448, 452,
  453, 455, 457, 458, 486, 487,
  488
Liu Bocheng, 89
Liu De, 107, 108
Liu Fuzhi, 494, 495
Liu Lantao, 116
Liu Shaoqi, 92, 108, 110, 113, 114,
  115, 116, 117, 118, 122, 126,
  156, 166, 172, 182, 206, 256,
  294, 298, 299, 435 (& fn 3),
  437
Liu T.C., 290
Liu Teqiao, 107
Liu Xiang, 45
Liu Yi, 426
Liu Zhidan, 106, 110
Liu Zunhou, 45
Living Buddha, 22
Living standard, 285, 291, 293,
  295, 296, 421, 422, 424, 426,
  427, 487

Loba, 14, 20, 23
Local government, 131, 137, 140,
    145, 153, 154, 158, 163, 173,
    174, 175, 176, 177, 178, 179,
    308, 373, 430
Local party government, 82, 83,
    85, 95, 96, 97, 98
Local people's courts, 483, 485,
    486, 487, 488, 489
Local people's procurators, 492
London, 245, 350
Long March, 55, 57, 58, 68, 84, 94,
    105, 110, 114, 117
Long Shuqing, 189
Lord Shang Yang, 29
Los Angeles, 1
Lu Dingyi, 115
Lu Hongdao, 45
Lu Shun, 201
Lu Yongting, 45, 46, 47
Lu Yongxiang, 44
Lu Zhongling, 45
Luk Simon, 455, 482
Luo Ruiqing, 113, 172, 198, 494
Lushan conference, 86, 112, 113,
    264, 266

Ma Guorui, 96
Macao, 7, 38, 74, 189, 350, 352, 498
McArthur, Douglas, 192
McMahon line, 232, 234
Mahmond Tayeb Abdul Rahim, 241
Majority-minority (race) relations,
    115, 116
Malaysia, 193, 239, 240, 247, 326,
    343, 345
Malenkov, Georgi, 139
Manchuria, 3, 18, 19, 44, 48, 52,
    53, 54, 57, 58, 60, 61, 64, 70,
    110, 111, 116, 117, 140, 187,
    200, 223, 285, 312, 323, 324,
    350, 352
Manzhou, 14, 15, 18, 19, 20, 36
Manzhou dynasty, see Qing
Manzhouli-Suifenhe railway, 313,
    324
Manzhouguo, 324
Mao Zedong
    Agrarian reform, 61
    APC, 259, 260
    Appeal to CC, 88
    Art and literature, 109
    Attempt at his life, 120, 121, 165
    Authoritarianism, 75
    Bulganin's visit with, 223
    Central Executive Committeeman
        (GMD), 67

Challenge of CPSU leadership,
    291
Characteristics of, 435
Children coached to love of,
    370, 448
Class background of cadres, 380
Co-determination, 149
Collectivization of agriculture,
    256
Commune, 259, 260
CPPCC honorable chairman, 133
Cultural Revolution, 114, 115,
    118, 121, 190, 297
Death of, 209, 448, 494
Debate with Peng Dehuai, 86,
    111, 112
Dispute with CPSU, 224, 225,
    260, 293
Downgrading of, 73, 125, 135
Economic self-reliance, 359
Education of prisoners, 497
Entraps GMD, 70
Fanshi faction, 127, 139
Five-Year Plan (2nd), 294
Ford's visit with, 215
Fu Zuoyi, 187
Futian incident, 107, 108
Gang of Four, 438
Heading Military Commission, 185
Hua Guofeng, 127
Jiangxi Soviet, 55, 251
Khrushchev's visit with, 223
Kissinger's visits with, 214, 215
Korean War, 324
Land reform legislation, 253
Law schools ordered closed, 461
Lei Jintian's letter to, 475
Lin Biao, 118, 119, 120, 155
Linkage economy, 146
Long March, 110
Luan appreciated, 264
Massacre of peasantry, 262
Material well-being deplored,
    117, 296
Militia, 199
Nixon's visit with, 215
Opposed by Chen Shaoyu, 104
Organic Law decreed, 130
Packs CC sessions with
    supporters, 89
Party & state zhuxi, 92, 113,
    166, 172, 173
Pompidou's visit with, 242
Proclamation of the founding of
    CPR, 232
Proletarian message to the
    masses, 363

Red Guards, 119, 122, 383
Refuses to commute death
   sentence, 476
Revolutionary Committee, 174
Revolutionary psyche, 327
Right to rebel, 365 *
Righting of wrongs, 464 *
Rule of law, 121, 436, 439
Semi-retirement, 123 *
Slander of, 466
Socialization of CPR, 289
State zhuxi, 113, 167
Taking of Changsha, 103
Ten major relations, 464
   (& fn 16)
Thoughts attributed to him, 71,
   72, 74, 77, 99, 138, 139, 140,
   144, 397, 419, 437, 485
Three banners, 320
Tito's visit with, 243
Turns China upside down, 70
University librarian, 65
Western technology, 156
Whole people's ownership, 271
Xiafang, 280, 281
Xiantan, 376
Zhang Guotao, 69, 105, 113
Zhenfeng, 108, 109, 113
Zungyi conference (Jan. 1936),
   106, 113
Maoergai conference, 69, 106
Maonan, 26
Marchais, George, 243
Marco Polo, 245
Marco Polo bridge, 70
Marginal sea, 211
Maring (Sneevliet), 65, 102 *
Market control, 425, 426, 427, 428
Marriage, 11, 440, 444, 445, 446,
   447, 448, 449, 486
Marriage Law, 12, 444, 445, 446,
   447, 449, 450, 451
Marriage Law (USSR), 447
   (& fn 83), 451 (& fn 94)
Marshall, George, 60, 61, 212
Martial law, 163, 167, 188
Marx, Karl, 64, 72, 115, 153, 368,
   391, 422, 497
Marxism-Leninism, 73, 74, 77, 79,
   99, 108, 114, 118, 134, 138, 139,
   144, 150, 164, 177, 185, 190,
   222, 231, 246, 251, 262, 267,
   363, 369, 382, 384, 386, 387,
   391, 392, 395, 397, 420, 461,
   470, 485
Mass line, 148, 160, 249, 441,
   450, 472, 473, 474, 480

Mass of people, 42, 48, 78, 99,
   104, 116, 118, 124, 129, 135,
   139, 140, 143, 148, 149, 174,
   181, 190, 248, 251, 256, 268,
   280, 285, 286, 378, 393, 395,
   399, 404, 413, 436, 437, 438,
   441, 472, 473, 474, 480, 496,
   498
Materialism, 391
Matheson & Company, 361
May 4th Movement, 63, 65
Mazu, 2, 7, 205
Mechanization, 278, 279
Medical co-ops, 403, 404
Medical institutions, 403, 406
Medical services, 12, 149, 158, 176,
   177, 302, 309, 366, 369, 376,
   381, 399, 401, 402, 403, 404,
   405, 406, 407, 424, 429, 487
Medicine, 404, 406
Mediterranian, 2
Medvedev, Roy, 147
Meng (league), 174
Menggu, 14, 18, 19, 20, 106
Menggu Plateau, 6
Mengzang Commission, 27
Mengzi, 9, 30
Mental diseases, 405, 406
Mermax, Louis, 243
Miao, 14, 15, 18, 26
Middle courts, 466, 481, 482, 483,
   484, 486, 487, 488
Middle East, 241
Middle schools, See junior high,
   senior high, high schools,
   secondary education
Midland Bank, 351
Militarism, 182
Military Affairs Committee, 127,
   182, 184, 185, 186, 194, 495
Military aid to Palestinians, 241, to
   Thai communists, 239
Military commission, 17, 85, 86, 91
Military courts, 483, 484
Military districts, 195, 196, 197
Military modernization, 188
   (& fn 33), 193 (& fn 63), 199 (&
   fn 88), See also armament
Military Police, 201
Military regions, 196, 197, 200
Military scientific council, 349
Military training, 322
Militia, 131, 144, 185, 188, 197,
   198, 199, 201, 207
Min chuan (rights of citizens), 38
Min Sheng (public welfare), 38

Min zu (national independence), 38, 69

Minerals, 5, 146, 323, 324, 341, 352, 354, 421

Ming dynasty (1368-1644), 36, 121

Ministers, 157, 158, 161, 162, 167, 168, 169, 170

Ministry of Foreign Economic Relations and Trade, 339, 350

Ministry of Labor and Personnel, 416

Ministry of Metallurgical Industry, 442

Ministry of Public Security, 494

Ministry of State Security, 169, 465

Minority races, 13, 14, 15, 16, 17, 19, 145, 150, 160, 173, 176, 177, 189, 196, 380, 381, (& fn 105), 446

Missile forces, 195, 201

Mitsui Mining Concern, 317

Mitterrand, Francois, 243

Mo Ti, 32, 33

Moderates, 124, 126, 146, 150, 173, 222, 259, 327, 395, 436

Modernization, 10, 11, 46, 63, 71, 74, 86, 87, 112, 123, 141, 156, 175, 198, 199, 200, 201, 209, 217, 245, 268, 269, 281, 291, 297, 298, 308, 312, 313, 315, 318, 320, 326, 339, 341, 342, 345, 347, 349, 351, 352, 354, 358, 360, 364, 365, 366, 368, 384, 385, 388, 389, 393, 394, 399, 413, 423, 438, 442, 443, 444, 451, 456, 484

Moganshan, 5

Mohe, 1

Monarchism and monarchists, 41, 43, 44

Monba, 23

Mondale, Walter, 217, 336

Mongolia, 1, 120, 230, 325

Monogamy, 446

Moral, 30, 31, 373, 393, 395, 396, 426, 459, 470

Morocco, 248, 332

Moscow, 2, 45, 48, 101, 103, 116, 142, 205, 223, 225, 229, 231, 236, 323

Moscow University, 36

Most-favored-nation privilege, 335, 336, 357

Motorways, 314

Mountains, 5, 6

Mozambique, 193, 248

Mudanjiang, 3

Mulao, 26

Multi-class revolution, 67, 68, 286

Munich, 244

Murder, 476, 477, 478, 480, 481

Mutual aid teams, 236, 257, 260

Nagasaki, 60

Nanchang, 68, 103

Nanhai, 2

Nanjing, 1, 59, 120, 187, 194, 427

Nanjing Treaty (1842), 2, 243, 360

Nantong, 354, 395

Nation-Protection Army (Hu guo jun), 42

National Armed Police Command, 494

National Assembly (France), 153

National Association of Chinese Writers, 390

National bourgeois, 132, 286, 287, 288

National Commerce Bank, 311

National Congress
1st (1921), 81, 105
2nd (1922), 3rd (1923), 4th (1925), 81
5th (1927), 81, 103
6th (1928), 81, 102
7th (1945), 81
8th (1956), 81, 85, 259
9th (1969), 81, 86
10th (1973), 81, 86, 245
11th (1977), 81, 86, 210, 222, 249 (& fn 244), 274, 298, 301, 304, 438, 439
12th (1982), 17, 25 (& fn 145), 26 (& fn 156), 79, 80, 81, 86, 89, 93, 127, 150, 185 (& fn 12), 274, 277, 278, 306, 417
Convocation, 82
Deputies elected to, 82
In relation to CC, 83, 84, 85, 95
Party Statute approved, 83
Size of membership, 84, 85, 86, 150

National Conference on Education, 365, 385

National Conference on Teacher Recruitment, 365

National defense, 74, 141, 151, 162, 190, 192, 196, 202, 268, 309, 384, 385

National Government, 6, 27, 51, 52, 53, 54, 56, 58, 59, 60, 61, 66, 69, 70, 90, 104, 105, 108, 129, 181, 183, 187, 194, 196,

197, 198, 199, 202, 212, 213,
219, 220, 221, 235, 251, 253,
285, 324, 356, 446
National income, 294, 319
National People's Congress (NPC)
1st Congress, 1954-1958 - 259,
463, 490
2nd Congress, 1958-1964 - 294,
295
3rd Congress, 1964-1975 - 298,
301
4th Congress, 1975-1978 - 123,
155, 274, 276, 277, 298, 410,
420, 439
5th Congress, 1978-1983 - 73,
125, 127, 132, 148, 193, 211,
249 (& fn 245), 267, 268, 277,
300, 301, 302, 304, 306, 309,
313, 353, 360, 361, 366, 375,
417, 423 (& fn 125), 426, 451,
477
6th Congress, 1983- - 13, 16,
17, 18, 19, 20, 23, 25, 26
Agricultural policy (1962, 1963),
268
Amendment to Constitution, 174
As highest organ of state power,
153
Authorities, 151, 156, 157, 159,
164, 253
Chairmen, 79, 160, 161, 166,
168, 218, 439
Chief Procurator chosen, 492
Constitution adopted, 132, 156
Control power, 163
Convocation, 165, 169
CPR vice-president elected
(1983),
Criminal code rubber-stamped
(1954), 463
Deng Xiaoping named vice-
premier, 123
Economic courts set up, 486
Election to, 140, 153, 154
Enactment of special economic
law, 142
In relation to CC 155, to State
Council 170, to NPC Standing
Committee 151, 160, 161, 165
Law on Joint Ventures approved
(1979), 353
Legislative power, 460
Marriage law revised, 446
Members of State Council in, 169
Minority nationalities in, 17, 18,
19, 20, 23, 25, 26
Organization, 158, 159, 160

Overseas Chinese deputies, 153,
154
Patent law enacted, 147
Principles of civil code laid down,
439
Procuratorate established, 490
Recruitment of officials, 157,
158, 162, 182, 183, 184
Regional law registered in, 16
Sessions, 156
Seven points declared, 294, 295
Sixth Five-Year Plan sanctioned,
267, 300
Sounding board for Jiang Hua
(1982), 477, Hu Yaobang (1979),
211, Hua Guofeng (1978), 125,
249 (& fn 244), 274, 298, 299,
410, 420, (1960) 301, 302,
Huang Hoqing (1982), 477,
Peng Zhen (1979), 193, 451,
468, 483, 493, Wang Bingqian
(1982), 309, Zhao Ziyang (1981),
277, 360, (1982) 304, 306, 313,
360, 366, 367, 375, 426, (1983)
13, Zhou Enlai (1956) 259
Supreme Court President named,
484
Taxation law developed, 310
Ten tasks (1962) proclaimed,
294, 295
Tenure, 155
Vice-chairmen, 79, 160, 161
Zhao Ziyang appointed premier,
127
NPC Standing Committee
Amendment of budget law, 161
Appointed by NPC, 157
Appointment and removal of high
officials, 161, 163, 164, 184,
484, 486
Authorities, 160, 161, 162, 163,
164, 165, 166, 167, 168
Call of election to NPC, 162
Chairmen, 79, 160, 161, 166,
167, 168, 218, 439
Compared to Supreme Soviet's
Presidium, 183
Control over Supreme Court &
Procuratorate, 162
Declaration of state of war, 151,
162
Diplomatic authorities, 163, 167,
231
Enactment of Apprehension
Regulations (1979), 495
Endorsement of the 1982
Constitution, 132

Fixing quota of NPC deputies, 154
Frequency of meetings, 164, 165
Hearing report of economic planning agencies, 280, 298, 301, of Zhao Ziyang on government spending, 360
In relation to party leadership, 161, to State Council, 162, 163, 170
In Sino-Soviet diplomacy, 231
Instituting Special Court & Special Procuracy (1980), 165
Interpretation of law & decree, 163
Law of foregiveness on returned escapees, 498
Minority deputies in, 22
On military service, 200
Organization, 160, 463, 468
Promulgation of law on lawyers 457, of martial law 163
Proposal to amend the constitution, 162
Ratification & cancellation of treaties, 163, 167, 171
Registration of regional marriage legislation, 446
Restructuring of State Council, 165
Revision of social & economic plan, 161
Setting up of titles & ranks, 163
Supervised by the NPC, 157
Supervision over bureaucracy 164, local elections 179
Taking cognizance of regional laws, 16, 176
Veto power, 137, 163
Vice-chairmen, 79, 160, 161
National Revolutionaries, 45, 48, 49, 50, 52, 53, 68
National Women's Federation, 445
Nationalism, 231
Nationality policy, 15, 20
Nationalization plan, 48
Natural gas, 315, 317, 347, 387
Natural law, 31
Naxi, 25
Navy, 194, 195, 197, 200, 201, 202, 324
Ne Win, 240 (& fn 184)
Negue Francisco Nacie Nguema, 247
Nehru Jawaharlal, 209, 232
Neijiang, 395
Neimenggu, 5, 10, 14, 19, 20, 25, 27, 45, 54, 68, 173, 195, 196, 312, 313, 316, 380
NEP (New Economic Policy, USSR), 48, 146, 256, 268, 286, 418
Nepal, 1, 5, 21, 23, 190, 191, 192, 230, 332
Netherlands, 244, 332
New Army (Qing), 36, 39
"New democracy," 132
New enemy class, 135, 136
New Fourth Army, 69
Ngapoi Ngawang Jigme, 22
Ni Zhifu, 89
Nians, 36
Nie Rongzheng, 89, 185
Niger, 247
Nikoruskii, 65
Nile, 4
Nine-point proposal, 22, 142, 218
Nineteen-eleven Revolution, 36, 37, 38, 39, 40, 118, 142
Nineteenth Route Army, 53, 56
Ningbo (Zhejiang), 2
Ningxia, 5, 10, 25, 27, 138, 173, 195, 313
Nixon, Richard, 213, 214, 215, 226, 230, 235, 333, 356
North America, 2
North China, 3, 44, 46, 52, 53, 54, 59, 60, 65, 69, 110, 283, 285
North Korea, 1, 247, 324
North Sea Fleet, 201
North Vietnam, 193, 213, 237, 238, 332
Northeast Bureau (CCP), 110, 111, 282, 316, 317
Northeast China, 207
Northeast Frontier Area (India), 232
Northern Expedition, 47, 48, 49, 50, 51, 52, 53, 54, 55, 56, 66, 68
Northwest China, 44, 53, 252
Nuclear energy, 315, 348, 349, 387
Nujiang, 3
Nurseries, 321, 370

Ob River, 3
Offshore oil exploration, 337, 347, 348, 352, 453
Ogarkov, Nikolai, 231
Ohira Masayoshi, 240
Oil, 236, 241, 300, 317, 318, 319 321, 322, 323, 325, 334, 346, 347, 348, 352, 353, 357, 387
Okuma, 47
"Open door notes" (1899), 212

Open door policy, 147, 151, 308, 333, 344, 355, 385, 389
Opium War (1839-1842), 36
Organic Laws on the People's Courts 456, 470 (& fn 43), 474, 483, 484, 486, on the People's Procurators, 190, 470 (& fn 43), 474, 491, 492 (& fn 190), 493, 496
Organic Laws (pre-constitution), 130, 132, 133, 134, 168
Organizational Department (CCP), 111
Original and appellate jurisdiction, 486, 487, 488
Orogen, 14, 20
Overseas Chinese, 7, 38, 74, 133, 142, 153, 158, 179, 247, 311, 326, 346, 453, See also Chinese students abroad
Overseas Chinese Banking Corporation, 351
Ownership patterns, 146, 147, 490
Oyuwan, 105

Pacific region, 4, 227, 236
Pacific system (rivers), 3
Pakistan, 1, 190, 193, 230, 232, 233, 234, 247, 332, 345
Palestine, 193, 241
Pamirs, 2
Pan-American Airways, 216, 336, 355
Paracels, 192
Paragon, Donald, 29 (& fn 176), 30 (& fn 179), 489
Pardon, 162, 163, 167
Parental authority, 448
Paris, 242, 244
Parliamentarism and parliaments, 40, 41, 42, 43, 44, 46, 131, 153, 157, 170, 223
Parties, 42, 43
Party apparatus, 471, 472
Party-army relations, See army-party relations
Party secretaries, 258, 262, 321, 377, 441, 471, 472, 491
Party-state relations, 99, 129, 144, 145, 157, 184, 186
Passivism, 31
Peace (ho-ping), 28, 29, 206
Peaceful coexistence, 150
Pearl Harbor attack, 253
Peasants, 12, 74, 75, 104, 111, 132, 178, 179, 189, 190, 211, 251, 253, 254, 256, 264, 266,

268, 269, 272, 273, 277, 278, 279, 280, 287, 291, 293, 311, 328, 367, 368, 369, 370, 372, 379, 380, 383, 402, 403, 409, 414, 415, 424, 429, 430, 442, 472, 474, 475, 484
Pel'she, A., 92
Penalty, See punishment
Peng Dehuai, 86, 111, 112, 113, 121, 172, 198, 264
Peng Zhen, 89, 116, 134, 135, 155, 161 (& fn 14), 165, 166, 167 (& fn 29), 193, 435 (& fn 1), 451, 463 (& fn 1), 464 (& fn 8), 468, 474, 483, 491 (& fn 186), 493 (& fn 197)
Peng Zhong, 89
Pension, 428, 429, 483 (posthumous deprivation)
People and non-people, 135
People's Bank, 285, 311
People's Broadcasting System, 18
People's Construction Bank, 311
People's democratic dictatorship, 74
People's Revolutionary Military Council, 183
People's war, 196, 198, 199
Perkins, Dwight, 328
Perry Mission (1853), 63
Persian Gulf, 193, 241
Petroleum, 290, 317, 346
Petty bourgeois, 132, 286, 287, 288
Philippines, 42, 193, 239, 240
Phillips, Christopher H., 337
Phnom Penh, 230
Physical education, 366, 370, 381
Physicians, 400, 401, 406, 407, 417
Pingpong diplomacy, 214, 226
Pingshuo, 316
Ping-xing Pass, 117
Pipelines, 315
Plains, 6
PLA, 23, 70, 90, 110, 112, 117, 118, 119, 120, 127, 129, 130, 131, 145, 153, 154, 166, 167, 171, 172, 181, 182, 183, 184, 185, 186, 187, 188, 189, 190, 191, 192, 193, 194, 195, 197, 198, 199, 200, 201, 204, 207, 212, 232, 365, 408, 494
PLO, 332
Plural marriage, 445, 446
Pol Pot, 237, 238
Poland, 214, 244, 326

Police, 144, 188, 198, 281, 437, 490, 495
Politburo, 17, 18, 20, 26, 80, 85, 88, 89, 90, 91, 92, 93, 94, 95, 103, 115, 122, 124, 127, 166, 193, 196, 274, 299, 358, 360, 491, 495
Politburo Standing Committee, 17, 85, 90, 91, 94, 95, 123, 127
Political commissars, 186, 189, 194
Politics in command, 109, 118, 122, 125, 139, 150, 296, 386
Polyandry, polygamy, 446
Pompidou, Georges, 242
Population, 7, 8, 9, 10, 11, 14, 199, 274, 275, 276, 277, 291, 295, 311, 407, 410, 430, 431
Population policy, 7, 9, 11, 12, 13, 295, 430, 431, 432, 433
Port Arthur, 223, 324
Postal service, 43, 55
Pragmatism and pragmatists, 32, 83, 114, 122, 126, 146, 150, 173, 209, 225, 268, 289, 296, 302, 303, 306, 308, 352, 358, 365, 419, 420, 448
Prairie Canada-China Friendship Association, 496
Precedent, 475
Precipitation, 4
Prefectures, 15, 21, 24, 25, 26, 97, 98, 137, 140, 173 (& fn 46), 174, 175, 176, 178, 446, 476, 483, 484
Presidents (CPR), 42, 79, 116, 136, 145, 153, 157, 160, 161, 167, 168, 182, 183, 206, 294, 484
Presidium (USSR), 159
Press, Frank, 216
Presumption of innocence, 468, 469, 470
Prices, 285, 286, 290, 310, 419, 422, 424, 425, 426, 427, 428
Primary party organizations, 98, 99, 185
Primary schools, 363, 364, 369, 371, 373, 375, 430 (for blind), 444
Prime ministers, 42, 79, 157, 158, 161, 167, 168, 169, 170, 172, 173, 182, 279, 494
Prisons, 168, 465, 466, 467, 473, 480, 489, 491, 493, 496, 497, 498
Private economy, 145, 147, 273, 277, 278, 286, 287, 288, 416, 417, 442

Private landsale, 147 (& fn 53)
Procuratorate, 20, 23, 25, 26, 27, 131, 153, 157, 161, 165, 175, 176, 455, 456, 457, 460, 461, 467, 470, 472, 478, 487, 488, 490, 491, 492, 493, 494, 495, 496
Production and construction corps, 197, 201
Production forces, 385, 435
Production relations, 435
Production teams, 262, 263, 264, 267, 269, 270, 271, 272, 273, 279, 281, 300, 375, 402, 405, 419, 422, 442, 486
Project 571, 120
Proletarian dictatorship, 55, 75, 81, 104, 131, 132, 134, 135, 136, 139, 164, 179, 181, 385, 397, 465
Proletarian internationalism, 114, 122, 391
Proletarian revolution, 68, 251
Propaganda, 138, 189, 192, 193, 194, 213, 228, 230, 235, 238, 239, 248, 262, 367, 445, 467, 469, 473
Provinces, 15, 16, 17, 22, 25, 40, 42, 43, 44, 46, 47, 49, 52, 53, 54, 82, 85, 97, 98, 111, 137, 140, 148, 153, 154, 158, 160, 163, 165, 173, 174, 175, 176, 187, 188, 196, 251, 257, 299, 300, 307, 319, 320, 322, 350, 354, 358, 365, 367, 377, 422, 427, 428, 429, 476, 483, 484, 489
Provincial government, 365, 377, 378, 388, 427, 428, 473, 484, 487
Provisional Regulations on Lawyers, 457
Public health, See medical services
Public security force, 131, 176, 177, 185, 188, 189, 198, 201, 490, 491, 492, 493, 494, 495
Punishment, 439, 448, 455, 468, 472, 475, 480, 481, 482, 483, 497
Putonghua, 177
Puyang district (Henan), 317
Pu Yi, Henry, 37, 39, 44

Qi, 97, 173, 174
Qian Duansheng, 461
Qian Xinzhong, 8, 11

Qiao Guanghua, 247
Qiao Shi, 93
Qin dynasty (221-207 B.C.), 13, 28, 29, 35
Qin Jiwei, 89, 196
Qing dynasty (1644-1911), 18, 35, 36, 37, 38, 39, 40, 43, 44, 45, 118, 196, 197, 220, 381
Qingdao (Shandong), 201
Qinghai, 5, 10, 19, 21, 173, 195, 314, 496
Qinghua University, 377
Qingzang, 5
Qiu Huizuo, 120, 455, 468
Quanjiao County (Anhui), 373

Racial equality, 148
Radicalism and radicals, 123, 124, 182, 199, 218, 222, 252, 277, 283, 299, 490
Railway courts, 483, 484
Railway lines, 4, 46, 296, 303, 312, 313, 325
Rangoon, 119, 192
Rao Shushi, 110, 111, 113, 282
Rape, 466, 475, 476, 477, 478
Reagan, Ronald, 204, 218, 219, 220, 221
Rebellion, 36, 189, 252, 365, 448
Red Army, See PLA
Red (good) elements, 474, 475
Red Guards, 22, 113, 115, 118, 119, 122, 149, 150, 182, 186, 188, 232, 233, 280, 296, 297, 306, 365, 383, 390, 396, 448, 463, 489
Red versus expert, 366, 387, 406, 459, 485
Regional forces, 197, 198
Regional government, 15, 16, 17, 20, 22, 23, 25, 26, 137, 388, 446, 484
Regional party organization, 15, 16, 20, 22, 23, 25, 36, 98
Regionalism, 110, 111, 188, 281, 292
Rehe, 20, 54
Religion, 144, 377
Ren (humane), 29
Renaissance, 118, 139
Reorganization Loans, 40, 41
Representative assembly, 131
Republicanism, 37, 41, 42
Retail trade, 305
Retirement, 13, 399, 406, 428, 429
Retrenchment and readjustment, 303, 305, 309, 360

Revenues, 299, 303, 304, 308, 309, 423
Revisionism, 116, 118, 121, 122, 127, 139, 146, 225, 246, 296, 327
Revolt, 189, 251
Revolution, 36, 37, 39, 64, 113, 114, 115, 116, 118, 122, 125, 139, 190, 211, 296, 365, 393, 406, 436, 437, 474, 498
Revolutionary committee, 174
Rhodesia, 248
Rich peasants, 132, 135, 211, 253, 254, 255, 272, 474
Right of counsel, 456, 461
Right of criticism, 464
Right of secession, 137
Right to rebel, See zao fan you li
Rightists, 395, 404, 437
Rito County (Tibet), 422
Rivers, 2, 3, 314
Robbery, 473, 477, 480, 481
Rockefeller, David, 336, 359
Roman Empire, 10, 14
Romania, 214, 244, 246, 332, 343, 345, 383
Romanov, G.V., 92
Rotation of office, 158, 169, 170
Rousseau, Jean Jacques, 32
Roy, M.N., 51
Ruijin (Jiangxi), 55, 104
Rule of law, 29, 30, 131, 134, 143, 459, 470, 490, 491, See also legalism
Rural investment, 328
Ruyuan Yaozu, 15
Rykov, A.I., 256

Salar, 25
Salaries, 303, 311, 423, 479, 487
Sales market, 527
Salim Ahmed Salim, 211
Salt, 6, 57
San Francisco, 217
San Min Zhu Yi Friendship Society, 107
Sanding Doje Tagno, 22
Santa Fe Minerals, 347
Sato Eisaku, 235
Saudi Arabia, 341
Schlesinger, James, 336
School curriculum, 374, 375, 377 (universities), 460 (institutes)
School discipline, 365, 366, 390, 391, 393, 396
Schools, 118, 296, 321, 364, 365,

366, 369, 372, 374, 375, 379, 382, 388, 395, 444, 497, See also junior high, senior high, universities
Science and technology, 63, 74, 139, 141, 149, 150, 158, 176, 203, 205, 206, 216, 236, 243, 268, 295, 302, 307, 309, 315, 320, 339, 341, 344, 353, 354, 369, 370, 376, 378, 379, 382, 383, 384, 385, 386, 387, 388, 389, 438, 351
SEATO, 234, 239
Seattle, 217
Secondary education, 369, 373, 382, 384
Secret societies, 32
Secretariat, 85, 91, 92
Secularism, 32
Security Council (UN), 171, 249
Security forces (local), 16
Seeckt, Hans von, 57
Seko Mobuto Sese, 248
Self-criticism, 139, 185, 394
Self-employment, 417, 418, 419, See also small business
Senior high schools, 363, 364, 365, 374, 375, 380, 382, 384, 394, 408
Services industry, 410, 412, 414, 417, 418
Seven-point program, 268, 294, 295, 296, 334
Seventh Fleet, 213
Sex equality, 446, 447
Sey Fudin, 89
Shaan-Gan-Ning border government, 59, 60, 69, 108, 114, 252
Shandong, 2, 10, 52, 54, 60, 63, 173 (& fn 46), 196, 316, 317
Shanghai, 1, 2, 4,8, 13, 37, 42,46,47,50, 51, 56, 59, 64, 65, 82, 104, 110, 120, 121, 153, 163, 164, 165, 173, 175, 187, 194, 195, 196, 199, 201, 216, 286, 316, 337, 342, 354, 369, 399, 404, 405, 406, 409, 424, 428, 429, 431, 450, 458, 461, 476, 483, 485, 487, 497, 498
Shanghai Communique (Sun-Ioffe, Jan. 26, 1923), 48, 66, 222
Shanghai Communique (February 28, 1972), 214 (& fn 30), 222
Shanghai Communique (August 17, 1982), 220
Shanghai-Hongzhou railway, 313

Shanhaiguan, 120, 121
Shantou jing ji te cu, 142
Shanxi, 3, 5, 44, 50, 57, 68, 106, 108, 110, 129, 195, 274, 312, 313, 316, 317, 376, 431, 473, 476
Shanxi-Chahaer-Hebei, see Ji-Cha-Jing border government
Shcherbitskii, V.V., 92
Shen Hongying, 45
Shen Jueren, 338
Shen Junru, 172
Shenyang (Liaoning), 45, 54, 187, 194, 195, 196, 197
Shenzhen special economic zone, 142, 349
Shen Zong (Emperor), 121
Sheng Shicai, 27
Shijiushuo (Shandong), 348
Shipbuilding, 334, 341, 349
Shultz, George, 219, 220, 221
Si ge yuan ze (four principles), 138, 144
Si qing (four clearances), 118
Siberia, 235, 262
Sichuan, 4, 5, 10, 13, 21, 22, 39, 42, 43, 45, 53, 69, 105, 154, 173, 195, 279, 283, 314, 316, 395, 421, 431
Sichuan railway protest, 39
Sideline production, 268, 269, 277, 278, 282, 306, 353, 372, 375, 414
Sihanouk Prince Norodom, 237
Sikkim, 1
Singapore, 326, 332, 343, 345
Sino-French war (1884), 38
Sino-Indian clashes, 192, 225, 232
Sino-Japanese war (1894-1895) 38, (1937-1945) 49, 52, 59, 70, 87, 110, 117, 235, 236, 237, 324
Sino-US defense treaty (1954), 216
Six Codes, 445
Six power consortium, 40
Slander, 466
Small business, 306, 416, 417, 418, 419, See also self-employment
Smuggling, 478
Snow, Edgar, 115
Social consumption fund, 424
Social control, 148, 149, 150, 177, 399
Social welfare, 12, 143, 177, 373
Socialism, 71, 122, 127, 136, 138, 139, 146, 212, 223, 257, 258, 260, 277, 363, 380, 387, 392,

394, 396, 420
Socialist countries, 323, 325, 328, 329, 331, 356
Socialist education campaign, 118, 439
Socialist Party of France, 243
Socialist system, 464, 465
Society, 435, 454, 468
Soldiers, 75, 160, 179, 186, 189, 191, 264, 379, 383, 448, 451, 465, 474, 484, 485
Solzhenitzyn, Alexander, 340
Somalia, 246, 247
Song Jiaoren, 46
Song Ping, 169
Song Qingling, 37, 51, 76, 166, 172
Song Rengqiong, 89
Song Zhenming, 321
Song Zheyuan, 70
Songliao basin, 317, 320
Sorrow of China, 4
South Africa, 193, 248, 323
South Asia, 241
South China, 46, 53, 59, 60, 103, 283
South China Sea, 347
South Korea, 337
South Sea Fleet, 201
South-South cooperation, 354
South Vietnam, 192, 214, 227
Southeast Asia, 213
Southern Europe, 249
Southwest Asia, 14, 241
Southwest China, 53, 116
Sovereignty, 134, 135, 136, 153, 193, 210, 227, 230, 249, 324
Special committees (under NPC), 158, 159
Special Court (under Supreme Court), 119, 165, 199, 455, 469, 480, 487
Special courts, 483, 484, See also military courts, railway courts, water-transport courts, forestry courts, trial of ten
Special procuratorate, 165, 469
Speculation, 425, 426
Spiritual culture, 127, 390, 391, 392, 393, 394, 395, 396, 397
Spratly islands, 192
Sputnik commune (Xinyang), 259, 261
Sri Lanka, 164, 247, 332, 345
Stalin, 27, 51, 67, 68, 102, 103, 104, 125, 136, 154, 222, 223, 254, 260, 262, 291, 293, 323, 391, 470

Standard of living, 11
State, the, 32, 262, 263, 272, 273, 280, 287, 288, 369, 372, 373, 375, 381, 382, 404, 454, 460, 461, 465, 487
State and revolution, 29
State Committee of Family Planning, 431
State Council, 3, 7, 16, 17, 126, 137, 151, 153, 158, 159, 162, 163, 165, 168, 169, 170, 171, 172, 173, 177, 183, 185, 186, 195, 231, 259, 260, 300, 305, 307, 353, 360, 369, 371, 377, 388, 389, 420, 426, 427, 496, See also Central People's Government
State councillors, 79, 157, 161, 167, 168, 169, 170
State Department, 212, 218, 220, 221
State Deposits, 312
State enterprises, 288, 295, 296, 299, 300, 305, 306, 307, 309, 310, 311, 315, 319, 320, 357, 369, 389, 411, 412, 415, 416, 417, 423, 424, 425, 451, 453, 456, 457,
State expenditures, 308, 309, 366, 369
State farms, 191, 271, 272
State loans, 312
State-party relations, See party-state relations
State Planning Commission, 111, 165, 169, 170, 298, 305
State secret, 308
Statute of limitation, 481
Steel production, 263, 290, 292, 293, 299, 301, 302, 303, 338, 341, 342, 347, 385, 426
Sterilization, 13, 431
Strategic forces, 195
Strauss, Robert, 336
Stuart, Douglas, 354
Student behavior, See school discipline
Submarines, 202, 267
Sudan, 332
Suerkarno, 209
Suez canal zone, 241
Sui dynasty (589-618), 35
Suiyuan, 20
Sukovic, Mijat, 244
Sun Fo, 51
Sun Yat-sen, 37, 38, 39, 40, 45, 46, 47, 48, 49, 50, 59, 65, 66,

67, 140, 142, 182, 222
Sun Yefang, 306, 307 (& fn 139)
Sungari, 3
Superpowers, 210, 242
Supreme Court, 89, 157, 159, 162,
  464, 467, 474, 480, 481, 482,
  483, 485, 486, 487, 489, 493.
  President, 79, 158, 172, 482, 484
Supreme Procuratorate, 157, 159,
  162, 492, 493
Supreme State Conference, 166,
  167
*Surging tide of socialism in the
  Chinese rural areas,* 259 (& fn
  46)
Su Yu, 113
Swatow insurrection, 102
Swire group, 361
Taiping rebels (1850-1864), 36, 40
Taiwan, 2, 7, 22, 36, 58, 74, 112,
  122, 141, 142, 143, 154, 173,
  183, 193, 194, 196, 202, 212,
  214, 215, 216, 217, 218, 219,
  220, 224, 230, 235, 239, 243,
  310, 337, 356, 357, 449
Taiwan Democratic Self-
  government League, 178 (& fn 53)
Taiwan Relations Act, 219, 220
Tajik, 1, 24
Takasaki Tatsunosake, 329
Tan Pingshan, 106
Tan Shaoyi, 47
Tan Tianshi, 96
Tan-Zam railway, 247
Tan Zhenlin, 93
Tanaka Kakuei, 235
Tang dynasty (618-906), 196
Tang Jiyao, 42, 45, 46, 47
Tang Shenzhi, 53
Tangshan earthquake, 124, 341
Tanzania, 193, 248
Tarim basin, 5
Tatar, 14, 24
Tax (USSR), 310
Tax, 43, 47, 53, 251, 258, 285,
  309, 311, 328, 403, 413, 417
Teachers, 364, 365, 366, 372, 373,
  374, 375, 376, 378 (foreign), 379,
  388, 394, 395, 396, 414
Ten-task resolution, 268, 294, 295,
  296
Terrorism, 36, 188
Test Ban Treaty (1963), 206
Textbook issues, 337
Textiles, 337, 338, 346, 357, 412,
  453
Thailand, 193, 238, 239, 240, 247

Thatcher, Margaret, 243, 244
Theft, 466, 475, 476, 477, 480
Thermonuclear forces, 112, 171,
  192, 199, 201, 202, 204, 205,
  206, 207, 226, 249, 388
Third world, 210, 211, 246, 248,
  249, 326, 354, 383
Three popular principles, 37, 59
Three-world concept, 210
Tian-an-men demonstration, 124,
  495
Tian Han, 115
Tian Jia, 484
Tian Jiyun, 169
Tianjin, 8, 13, 45, 82, 90, 153, 163,
  164, 165, 173, 175, 194, 195,
  216, 319, 337, 354, 369, 404,
  431, 459, 476, 483
Jianjin conference of warlords, 44
Tianjin-Shanghai railway, 313
Tianshan, 219
Tiantong people's commune
  (Zhejiang), 409, 415
Tibet, 4, 5, 10, 21, 22, 27, 45, 187,
  192, 195, 196, 232, 233, 314,
  350, 380, 422, 446
Tikhonov, N.A., 92
Time zones, 1
Tinsulanoda Prem, 240
Tirana, 245, 246
Tito, 209, 243, 244, 245
To each according to his work,
  114, 136, 137, 173, 258, 269,
  272, 295, 372, 375, 393, 416,
  419
Tokyo, 38, 39, 41, 42, 54, 192,
  236, 237, 328
Tolubka V., 226
Tong Ming Hui, 38, 39, 40, 42
Topography, 6
Tourism, 216, 341, 355, 356, 453
Tow, William, 354
Town (township), 153, 154, 173,
  174, 175, 176, 417, 424, 457, 483
Trade, with
  Albania, 246
  Australia, 333, 340, 343, 345
  Canada, 340, 343, 345
  Czechoslovakia, 326
  Denmark, 341
  E. Germany, 326, 332, 333, 343
  Egypt, 332
  France, 332, 341, 343, 345
  Hong Kong, 326, 328, 329, 330,
    332, 343, 345
  Hungary, 326
  India, 232, 233

Italy, 243, 329, 332, 345
Japan, 326, 328, 329, 332, 340,
  341, 343, 345
Malaysia, 326, 343, 345
Morocco, Netherlands, 332
Non-socialist countries, 331, 332,
  342
Pakistan, 332, 345
Poland, 326
Romania, 332, 333, 343, 345
Singapore, 332, 343, 345
Sri Lanka, 332, 345
Sudan, 332
United Kingdom, 326, 332, 341, 348
US, 215, 217, 333, 334, 335,
  336, 337, 338, 343
USSR, 304, 325, 326, 327, 328,
  332, 333, 345
W. Germany, 326, 332, 341, 343,
  345
W. Europe, 340
Trade corporations, 350, 360
Trade practices, 349, 350, 351,
  352, 353, 355, 356, 360
Trade unions, 65, 105, 428
Traditionalism, 63, 130, 364
Training for respect of law, 373,
  375, 396, 444
Transport, 11, 309, 312, 313, 314,
  315, 320, 322, 348, 354, 388,
  414
Treason, 465, 467
Treaties, 151, 162, 163, 164, 167,
  171, 453
Trial courts, 489
Trial of ten (Nov. 1980-Jan. 1981),
  455, 463 (& fn 6), 464, 466, 467,
  469, 472, 487, 494 (& fn 206),
  See also Special Court
Troops, 42, 43, 98, 111, 112, 119,
  184, 188, 189, 190, 191, 192,
  193, 196, 197, 212, 213, 225,
  229, 232, 246, 272, 314, 476
Trotsky, Leon, 67, 68, 102, 256,
  280, 291
Trudeau, Pierre, 340
Truman, Harry, 60, 61, 194, 212
Truth, 116, 456, 469 (through facts)
Tujia, 15, 25
Tungal tribe, 18
Turks, 6
Twenty-one Demands, 41, 63
Ulanho, 18, 89
UN, 192, 202, 211, 214, 221, 222,
  228, 232, 233, 234, 238, 241,
  243, 247, 248, 249, 355, 433
  Charter, 171

Unemployment, 11, 122, 143, 281,
  293, 407, 408, 409, 410, 412,
  414, 415
UNESCO, 367
Unitarism, 137, 138, 159, 308
United Front Department, 18
United fronts, 58, 59, 65, 66, 67,
  68, 69, 70, 74, 101, 102, 104,
  105, 106, 123, 210, 217, 218,
  222, 251, 252
United Kingdom, 41, 44, 207, 242,
  243, 244, 245, 326, 332, 340,
  341, 345, 349, 351
Universities, 7, 8, 19, 21, 25, 26,
  27, 321, 359, 363, 364, 369, 370,
  375, 376, 377, 378, 379, 380,
  381, 382, 383, 388, 394, 408,
  413, 444, 459, 461, 484
  Village universities, 368, 369,
  370
University of Science and
  Technology, 379
Urban uprising, 251
Urbanization, 8, 10
Urga, 48
Urumqi (Xinjiang), 194, 195, 314
US
  Beijing hierarchy courted, 226,
    227, 228
  Belittled by Mao Zedong, 224
  Cease-fire proposal in Middle-
    East (1973), 241
  Cessation of cultural exchanges
    with CPR (1982), 221
  China policy, 209, 211, 212, 213,
    215, 217, 219, 220, 222, 226,
    245
  Chinese students trained in, 349
  Congress, 204, 386
  Constitution, 158
  CPR textiles in, 367
  Criticized by CPR, 119, 191, 209,
    210, 212, 213, 221, 222, 235
  Deng Xiaoping's visit, 121
  Disengagement in Southeast
    Asia, 240
  Embargo on Chinese import, 324
  Federal court ruling against
    CPR, 220-221
  Grain production, 385
  Hu Na incident, 221
  Joint Economic Committee
    (Congress), 298
  Mediation in Chinese civil war,
    60, 66
  Navy, 201, 202
  Pingpong diplomacy, 226

Policy toward insurrectional communists, 129
Presidents' visit to CPR, 214, 215, 216, 235
Recognition of CPR, 216
Relation with Japan 235, 236, Vietnam 237, 239, Thailand 239, France 243, Taiwan 142, 194, 205, 214, 216, 217, 218, 219, 220
Supply of grain to CPR, 276
Technical aid to CPR, 217, 218, 219, 340
Trade with CPR, 333, 334, 335, 336, 337, 338, 345, 360
Underground nuclear tests, 207
Withdrawal from China loans (1913), 40
Wu Peifu supported, 44
Yalta agreement, 324
USSR
Accusation of Beijing regime, 224, 229
Activities in ASEAN, 231, 235
Afghanistan in Sino-Soviet diplomacy, 230, 231
Agrogorod, 321, 413
Albania in Sino-Soviet diplomacy, 245, 246
Beijing government (1922-1924), 46
Bifurcation of society, 435
Bogus federalism charged, 138, 159
Border dispute with CPR, 227, 228, 229
Chen Shaoyu, 104
Chinese hostility charged, 119, 123, 191, 209, 217, 221, 222, 228, 231
Civil & Criminal appeals, 488
Collective farm, 421 (& fn 121)
Collectivization of agriculture, 254, 262, 291
Constitution, 77, 130, 131, 134, 136, 137, 141, 143, 144, 145, 148, 149, 151, 153, 154, 158, 159, 160, 161, 163, 165, 168, 170, 173, 178, 183, 186, 210, 249, 468, 486
Contradictions with CPR, 72
Council of Defense, 183
Council of Ministers, 130, 169, 181, 184, 231
Court jurisdiction, 486
CPR adventurism charged, 213, 225, 227

CPR's US policy attacked, 205
CPSU, 68, 71, 76, 80, 81, 84, 91, 92, 93, 101, 105, 125, 129, 136, 181, 223, 224, 271, 280, 291
CPSU Statues, 67, 73, 76, 77, 82, 85, 99, 101, 137
Cuba in Sino-Soviet diplomacy, 246
Czarist Russia, 400
Detente with CPR, 221, 222, 230, 231
Dialectical materialism, 291
Direct & indirect democracy, 140
Domination over Europe charged, 242
Economic aid to Chinese communists, 60, 64, 68, 69, 112, 202, 204, 324, 328
Europe in Sino-Soviet diplomacy, 242, 243, 244
Factional struggle, 256
Feng Yuxiang, 44, 45, 52
Food bill in Soviet families, 421
Food program (Brezhnev), 283
Gao Gong, 111
Great Leap criticized, 205
Guangzhou government, 46, 47, 48, 49, 50, 51, 52, 64, 66, 67, 68
Hua Guofeng's attack on, 244, 245
Ideological influence, 64, 67, 251
Income tax, 310
India in Sino-Soviet diplomacy, 225, 231, 232, 233, 234
Japan in Sino-Soviet diplomacy, 235, 237, 324
Kampuchea in Sino-Soviet diplomacy, 237, 238, 246
League of Nations, 69
Leaning toward, 212, 224, 323
Legal system, 437
Li Xiannian's attack on, 243
Link system in agriculture, 270
Manchuria, 60, 111
Military aid to CPR, 204, 205, 288
Missile forces, 207
Model for Chinese communists, 55, 251, 285, 289, 326
Mongolia in Sino-Soviet diplomacy, 230
Navy, 202
New Economic Policy, 146, 256, 268, 418
Paracels & Spratly islands, 193

Peng Dehuai's collusion charged, 111, 112
Presidium of the Supreme Soviet, 161, 165, 183, 231
Price structure, 291
Procuracy, 491
Prohibited marriage, 447
Red Army, 64, 197
Relation with US, 335
Revisionism, 114, 116, 118, 122, 139, 225, 260, 296
Russian Soviet Federal Socialist Republic, 1, 138
Second economy, 306
Sheng Shicai, 27
Sino-Soviet frontier areas, 1, 3, 24, 219
Sino-Soviet treaty (1955), 205
Socialist imperialism, 210, 221, 222, 228, 231, 245
Special courts, 484
State farm, 272
Supreme Soviet, 153, 159, 161, 181
Taiwan, 217
Technicum, 374
Termination of Sino-Soviet agreements, 225, 228
Trade with CPR, 325, 326, 327, 328, 331, 332, 338, 339, 343, 345
Unemployment, 407
United front, 68, 69, 235
Universities, 376
US cease-fire proposal in Middle-East opposed, 241
US in Sino-Soviet diplomacy, 218, 219, 225, 227, 230, 235
Vietnam in Sino-Soviet diplomacy, 227, 229, 231, 237, 238, 246
Violent revolution, 436
Warned by Deng Xiaoping, 217
Western classics, 389
Withdrawal of aid to CPR, 291, 293, 294
Yalta agreement, 111
Zhang Guotao, 106
Ussuri, 1, 2, 3, 226, 227, 228, 358
Ustinov, D.F., 92, 230
Utilitarianism, 33
Uzbek, 24, 25
Uygur, 14, 15, 18, 23, 24 (& fn 138), 25, 160, 380
Vagpayee, 233
Vance, Cyrus, 215
Vanuata, 248

Venezuela, 249
Versailles Treaties, 63
Veto, 162, 163, 176
Vice-governors of provinces, 184
Vice-premiers, 157, 158, 162, 167, 168, 169, 170, 173, 184, 204, 218, 243, 407
Vice-president (CPR), 79, 158, 168, 184, 223
Vice-president (Supreme Court), 184, 440, 484, 485, 489
Vientiane, 230
Vietnam, 1, 2, 158, 191, 193, 197, 209, 229, 231, 237, 238, 239, 240, 246,
Vietnam war, 192, 239
Village life, 6, 12, 153, 177, 184, 407, 408, 414, 424, 442, 445, 461
Vital statistics, 7, 8
Vladivostok, 51, 324
Vocational training, 19, 20, 25, 26, 27, 373, 374, 375, 383, 418
Voitingskii, Grigori, 64, 65
Wages and wage policy, 114, 165, 173, 259, 281, 287, 303, 310, 371, 372, 393, 405, 411, 415, 416, 419, 420, 421, 423, 424, 429, 479, See also incomes
Waimenggu, 19, 312
Waldheim, Kurt, 211
Walk-on-two-legs, 85, 225, 267, 291
Waller, A.D., 254
Wallposters, 189, 386, 463, 466, 491
Wan Li, 89, 93, 169
Wang Bingqian, 147, 169, 304 (& fn 121), 307, 309, 357
Wang Congwu, 96
Wang Dongxing, 86, 94
Wang Enmou, 116
Wang Fu, 493
Wang Hanbin, 468, 470
Wang Heshou, 96
Wang Hongwen, 121, 125, 188, 455, 468
Wang Jingwei, 49, 50, 52
Wang Lei, 426
Wang Shiwei, 108
Wang Weigang, 485
Wang Weiguo, 120
Wang Youping, 229
Wang Zhen, 89, 436
Wang Zhongfan, 460
War, 28, 30, 112, 151, 158, 162, 167, 182, 198, 206, 223, 224, 228, 252

Warlords, 6, 27, 40, 42, 43, 44, 45,
    46, 47, 49, 53, 54, 55, 58, 59,
    64, 65, 66, 68, 70, 83, 105, 129,
    196, 251, 252, 446
Warring states, 28
Warsaw, 213, 333
Warsaw Powers Pact, 213
Washington, 1, 204, 217
Water-transport courts, 483
Weapons development, see
    armament
Wei Guoqing, 18, 89, 126, 127,
    186
Wei Jingsheng, 397, 466
Weihe, 316
Weihe Plain, 6
West Hill conference, 49
Western Europe, 211, 242, 334,
    337, 339, 340, 355
Western Hemisphere, 2
Western Powers, 40, 41, 47, 48,
    52, 63, 64, 65, 122, 147, 191,
    223, 323, 327, 333, 340, 352,
    383, 392, 393
Wetzel, Georg, 57
Wheelock Marden, 361
White guards, 48
Whiting, Allen S., 35, 101
Wilson, Woodrow, 40
Women, 19, 20, 23, 25, 26, 179,
    262, 263, 361, 368, 372, 445
Woman prisoners, 481, 498
Woodcock, Leonard, 217, 336
Work collectives, 365, 368, 369,
    442, 443
Workers, 74, 75, 132, 136, 160,
    165, 179, 251, 264, 280, 281,
    296, 299, 303, 322, 369, 370,
    371, 379, 380, 382, 383, 405,
    410, 412, 415, 416, 417, 420,
    425, 429, 474, 484
Working class, 67, 135, 179, 380
World Bank, 310, 348
World communist movement, 291
World revolution, 102
World War I, 63, 153
World War II, 223, 253
Wu De, 86, 94, 166, 172
Wu Faxian, 120, 121, 468
Wu Han, 115, 121
Wu Peifu, 44, 45, 52
Wu Techeng, Wu Tingfang, 47
Wu Xueqian, 169, 221
Wuchang, 39
Wuha, 1
Wuhan, 36, 50, 59, 68, 103, 189,
    194, 195, 314, 498

Wuhan government, 50, 51, 52, 68

Xiafang, 280, 281, 408
Xiamen, 2
Xiaoren, 28
Xibe, 24, 25
Xinjiang Autonomous Region, 1, 3,
    10, 14, 19, 23, 25, 27, 45, 116,
    173, 189, 195, 219, 223, 226,
    227, 228, 229, 314, 323, 325,
    350, 352, 376, 380, 395, 476
Xikang, 69, 106
Xi Zhangyuan, 493
Xi Zhongxun, 89, 93
Xian crisis, 57, 58, 69, 461, 472
Xiang Zhongfa, 102, 103, 104
Xiangshan (Guangdong), 37, 38
Xie Fuzhi, 494
Xie Juezai, 172
Xie Tieguang, 460
Xin (faithful), 29
Xin hua ribao, 129
Xin qing pian, 63
Xing Zhong Hui, 38, 39
Xining-Lhasa railway, 313
Xinxiang district (Henan), 476
Xu Shichang, 42, 44
Xu Shiyou, 89, 172, 185
Xue Muqiao, 310, 353, 413
Xuzhou conference of warlords, 44

Yalta agreement, 60, 111, 324
Yalu, 1,3
Yan Xieshan, 44, 53
Yanan, 57, 58, 108, 109, 110, 112,
    198, 222, 369
Yancheng, 110
Yang Dezhi, 89, 172, 184, 194
Yang Hucheng, 57, 58
Yang Jingren, 18, 169
Yang Shangkun, 89, 115, 185
Yang Sheng, 45
Yang Xiufeng, 172, 482
Yang Yong, 93
Yang Zhenwu, 172
Yang Zhu, 30, 31
Yangzi, 4, 59, 314
Yangzi basin, 10, 45, 53, 58, 59,
    60, 68, 188, 283
Yao, 26
Yao Wenyuan, 121, 125, 455, 468,
    479
Yao Yilin, 89, 93, 165 (& fn 23),
    169, 423
Yao Zhongda, 367

Yarlung Zangbu Jiang, 3
Ye Jianying, 91, 92, 127, 142, 155, 165, 166, 172, 185, 188, 218, 321, 439
Ye Qun, 120, 121
Ye Ting, 69
Yi (righteous), 28
Yi (Tribe), 14, 18
Yian Ye Commercial Bank, 311
Yiminhe, 316
Yin Fatang, 23
Yinchuan Plain, 6
Young Communist League, 319, 380, 427, 459
Youths, 115, 117, 119, 121, 122, 148, 297, 364, 365, 366, 367, 371, 378, 379, 382, 384, 390, 391, 393, 395, 396, 408, 409, 412, 413, 417, 437, 441, 445, 448, 477, 481
Yu Ping, 493
Yu Qiuli, 89, 93, 165, 184, 186, 280, 298, 301
Yuan dynasty (1278-1368), 35
Yuan Shikai, 36, 37, 39, 40, 41, 42, 45, 46, 47, 118
Yuanbaoshan, 316
Yugoslavia, 122, 222, 243, 244, 246
Yungui, 5
Yunnan, 5, 10, 19, 21, 22, 26, 42, 43, 45, 46, 47, 60, 106, 189, 193, 195, 197, 239, 314, 348, 422

Zaire, 246, 248
Zambia, 247, 248
Zang (Tibetans), 14, 18, 20, 21, 22, 23, 160
Zao fan you li (right to rebel), 406, 448
Zengmu Ansha, 1 (& fn 1)
Zeng Guofan, 36
Zeng Hanzhou, 485
Zeng Zhongxuan, 47
Zhanjiagang, 354
Zhang Aiping, 169, 184
Zhang Chunqiao, 119, 121, 123, 124, 125, 299, 455, 468, 480, 481
Zhang Guotao, 65, 69, 105, 106
Zhang Jingfu, 169
Zhang Su, 493
Zhang Tingfa, 89
Zhang Wentian, 113
Zhang Xueliang, 53, 54, 57, 58

Zhang Xun, 44
Zhang Youyu, 460
Zhang Zhijiang, 45
Zhang Zhiye, 476, 477
Zhang Zhong, 455
Zhang Zhongli, 496
Zhang Zuolin, 44, 45
Zhao Cangbi, 495
Zhao Hengti, 45
Zhao Yiya, 127
Zhao Ziyang
  Afghanistan, relation with CPR, 235
  Africa, tour of (1982-1983), 247, 248, 341
  Appointed as premier, 92, 127, 169, 172, 173, 279
  Burma, relation with CPR, 240, 241
  Capital overexpansion condemned, 304, 358
  Capitalist decadence lamented, 148
  Consumption fund, 426
  Curtailment of population, 13
  Education policy, 366, 383
  Energy, 312
  Foreign trade, 360, 361
  Growth of production, 300, 319
  High schools, 375
  Illiteracy, 367
  In Central Committee, 89, 91
  Industrial organization, 306
  Infanticide deplored, 433
  Insufficient arable land, 277
  Japan, tour of (1982), 236
  Joint venture, 348
  Kampuchea, relation with CPR, 235
  Late marriage urged, 430
  Minority races in state-building, 16
  Peasant income, 422
  Philippines, tour of (1981), 240
  Prefectures, 173 (& fn 46)
  Research projects, 387
  Retrenchment of state budget, 303
  Self-employment urged, 416
  Southeast Asia, relation with CPR, 240
  State budget on culture, public health, 366
  Sun Yefang praised, 307
  Technical transformation, 320
  Ten principles of rationalized economy, 302

Transport, 312, 313
Universities, 382
US, relation with CPR, 220
USSR, relation with CPR, 235
Wages, 423
Yugoslavia, relation with CPR, 244
Zhejiang, 2, 5, 10, 44, 53, 189, 196, 316, 319, 320
Zhenfeng, 105, 108, 109, 113
Zheng Shaowen, 485
Zheng Tianxiang, 172, 477, 493
Zhengzhou, 189
Zhili faction, 43
Zhong xing (heavy penalty), 479
Zhongshan, 37
Zhou dynasty (1122-221 B.C.), 28, 31
Zhou Enlai
  Advocacy of violence, 436
  Canada, relation with CPR, 340
  Coexistence, 232
  Commune system, 256, 260
  Congo, aid to, 164
  CPR's oil needs, 318
  Death of, 123, 124, 126, 271
  Deng Xiaoping, relation with, 122
  Disapproval of the name *People's* State Council, 168, 496
  During Cultural Revolution, 203, 297
  Europe, relation with CPR, 242
  Five-Year Plans, 301
  France, relation with CPR, 242
  Ghana, aid to, 164
  Grain purchase from Canada, 340
  Great Leap opposed, 259, 260
  Hua Guofeng, relation with, 124
  Huangpu Academy, 67
  Lin Biao's coup (1971), 120, 121
  Mao Zedong, relation with, 123
  Modernizations, 156, 298
  No civil code until complete state ownership, 440
  Nuclear weaponry urged, 205, 206
  Oil production, 317, (& fn f)
  Orchestration with Nehru, 209, 232
  Pingpong diplomacy, 214
  Popularity of, 122
  Pragmatism, 114, 122, 171, 203, 256, 294, 436
  Premiership, 171, 172
  Red Guards urged moderation, 203, 297
  Role in Xian crisis (1036), 58
  Sojourn in France (1920's), 153
  Soviet revisionism castigated, 221
  Sri Lanka, aid to, 164
  University admission policy, 383
  US, relation with CPR, 119, 214
  USSR, relation with CPR, 119, 221
  Views different from Mao Zedong, 104
  War-preparation, call for, 227
Zhou Jiangping, 120
Zhou Yinren, 44
Zhou Yuchi, 120
Zhu De, 117, 155, 166, 223
Zhuang, 14, 15, 18, 26, 27, 36, 160
Zhuge, (Hebei), 447
Zhuhai, 142
Zhujiang, 4, 6
Zi Gong Dang, 178 (& fn 53)
Zia ul-Haq, 234, 235
Ziaozuo-Zhicheng railway, 4
Zinoviev, Grigori, 256
Zongli Memorials, 37
Zunda, 196
Zungarian basin, 5
Zungyi conference (Jan. 1936), 105, 106, 113

Past